Songs of Zion

Songs of Zion

THE AFRICAN METHODIST
EPISCOPAL CHURCH IN THE
UNITED STATES AND SOUTH AFRICA

James T. Campbell

To John,

with whom I share a common
history — The African Methodist
Episcopal Church — and a
cherished friendship.

faithfully,

Rae

New York   Oxford
OXFORD UNIVERSITY PRESS
1995

October 2006

Oxford University Press

Oxford   New York
Athens   Auckland   Bangkok   Bombay
Calcutta   Cape Town   Dar es Salaam   Delhi
Florence   Hong Kong   Istanbul   Karachi
Kuala Lumpur   Madras   Madrid   Melbourne
Mexico City   Nairobi   Paris   Singapore
Taipei   Tokyo   Toronto

and associated companies in
Berlin   Ibadan

Published by Oxford University Press, Inc.,
198 Madison Avenue, New York, New York 10016

Oxford is a registered trademark of Oxford University Press

Library of Congress Cataloging-in-Publication Data
Campbell, James T.
Songs of Zion : the African Methodist Episcopal Church
in the United States and South Africa / James T. Campbell.
p. cm.   Includes bibliographical references and index.
ISBN 0–19–507892–6
1. African Methodist Episcopal Church—United States—History.
2. Methodist Church—United States—History.
3. African Methodist Episcopal Church—South Africa—History.
4. Methodist Church—South Africa—History.
5. Missions—South Africa—History—19th Century.
6. South Africa—Church history.   I. Title.
BX8443.C36   1995
287′.83—dc20   94–19872

1 3 5 7 9 8 6 4 2

Printed in the United States of America
on acid-free paper

For Andrea

PREFACE

The wilderness and the solitary place shall be glad for them; and the desert shall rejoice, and blossom as the rose.

It shall blossom abundantly, and rejoice even with joy and singing: the glory of Lebanon shall be given unto it, the excellency of Carmel and Sharon, they shall see the glory of the LORD, and the excellency of our God.

Strengthen ye the weak hand, and confirm the feeble knees.

Say to them that are of a fearful heart, Be strong, fear not: behold your God will come with vengeance, even God with a recompence; he will come and save you.

Then the eyes of the blind shall be opened, and the ears of the deaf shall be unstopped.

Then shall the lame man leap as an hart, and the tongue of the dumb thing sing: for in the wilderness shall waters break out, and streams in the desert . . .

And the ransomed of the LORD shall return, and come to Zion with songs and everlasting joy upon their heads: they shall obtain joy and gladness, and sorrow and sighing shall flee away.

ISA. 35:1–6,10

In 1892 a group of black Christians in Pretoria, South Africa, withdrew from the Wesleyan Methodist Missionary Society. Led by an ordained Methodist minister named Mangena Mokone, the group began holding services in Marabastad, the burgeoning African location on Pretoria's western edge. They called themselves "Ethiopians," after the prophecy of African redemption in Psalms 68: *"Princes shall come out of Egypt; Ethiopia shall soon stretch out her hand unto God."* Three years later, after a seemingly providential set of contingencies, the founders of this fast-growing movement came into contact with the leaders of the African Methodist Episcopal (AME) Church, the oldest and largest church in black America. In 1896, the Ethiopian Church was formally incorporated as the South African arm of the AME Church.

Thus began one of the most remarkable episodes in the intertwined history of Africa and black America. Over the next fifteen years—a period encompassing the Anglo-Boer War, imperial reconstruction, and the consolidation of the

Union of South Africa—African Methodism exploded across the subcontinent. By 1910 congregations had sprouted from the docks of Cape Town to Barotse-land, north of the Zambesi. Close to forty thousand Africans—urban workers, peasants, clerks, teachers, even disaffected chiefs—had joined the AME Church. Tens of thousands of others had been touched by its message. For a brief historical moment, this venerable African American institution stood at the center of one of the most dynamic popular movements in Africa.

The book which follows traces this historical convergence from both sides of the Atlantic. In simplest terms, it is a study of transplantation, showing how a creed devised by and for African Americans was appropriated and transformed in a variety of South African contexts. More broadly, it is a study of the complex human and imaginative traffic that binds African and African American experience, a traffic that began in the days of the transatlantic slave trade and continues into our own time. The book's central premise, to resort to the kind of jargon I have tried to eschew in the text, is that African and African American identities are and have always been mutually constituted. Focusing on a transatlantic institution such as the AME Church throws this reciprocal process into sharp relief, while casting new light on two radically different yet tragically similar societies.

It is customary at this point to recount some portentous episode to explain how one's book came to be. Alas, I have nothing to offer, just a chance encounter in a card catalog during my first year in graduate school. I was seeking references for a paper on African "survivals" in the New World, a hoary historical problem well suited to a student who was already frustrating supervisors by refusing to declare himself unequivocally an "American" or an "African" historian. En route to "African Religions," I came across several references to "African Methodism." At the time I knew more or less what most American historians know about the AME Church: that it began in Phila-delphia, sometime after the Revolution; that its founder was a freed slave named Richard Allen; that it rose in the nineteenth century to become, in W. E. B. Du Bois's words, "the greatest Negro organization in the world." I even knew vaguely that the Church had established missions in Africa, though I assumed that meant Liberia. In any event, I checked out a few books, hoping to find something for my paper.[1]

My initial reaction was one of disappointment. Despite the claims of innu-merable historians, there is little evidence that African Methodism's founders intended to express any special identification with Africa when they named their movement. *African* was the standard term of reference for black people in late-eighteenth-century America; free people of color in particular preferred it to *Negro,* which carried a connotation of enslavement. Virtually every black church, school, and fraternal society was denominated African, a practice that continued until the 1820s and '30s, when the rising threat of African coloniza-tion prompted the first in a series of collective changes of address. At the level

of religious worship as well, the imputation of some kind of "African" character to African Methodism seemed problematic at best. While recognizably
African religious practices occasionally surfaced in AME services, they were
generally disdained, if not actively suppressed, by church leaders. Bishop
Daniel Alexander Payne, for example, devoted much of his life to stamping out
"fugue" singing, "Fist and Heel worship," "Voudoo" dancing, and other
"strange delusions"—precisely the practices that scholars today identify as the
most important survivals of Africa in the New World.[2]

And yet Africa suffused the sources I was reading. From the moment of its
inception, the AME Church was consumed by African issues—by debates on
emigration, on missions, on the meaning of enslavement itself. Even colonizationism, which most church leaders adamantly opposed, forced African Methodists to reflect on their relationship with their ancestral continent, on the
strange providence that had carried them from Africa and that now threatened
to return them there. It struck me that historians, in their relentless search for
evidence of Africa in the realm of culture, had paid insufficient attention to
Africa's pervasiveness in African American intellectual and imaginative life,
particularly in the imagination of black Christians.

At first glance, I found this puzzling. Like most historians, I was disposed to
see the adoption of Christianity as a step toward black "acculturation" in
America, and thus a movement away from Africa. In retrospect, however, it all
seems perfectly plain. Wherever one stands in the great debate over the origins
and character of African American worship, there is no denying that slaves
found solace in the creed of their captors. In the Old Testament particularly,
they encountered a God who was immanent in the world, who loved justice
and cherished the lowly. Yet even as Christianity answered some of the existential questions of African American experience, it posed others. How could a
just and loving God—a God, in slave narrator Olaudah Equiano's words,
"without whose permission a sparrow cannot fall"—subject millions of people
to the agony and humiliation of captivity? How could black Christians reconcile the joy they felt in their new faith with their horror at the means of its
acquisition? If African Americans were indeed akin to the Israelites of the
Exodus, were they too destined to return to Canaan, across the sea? What is
striking about all these questions is the way they revolved, implicitly or
explicitly, around Africa. In a sense, black Christians could not establish their
own identity until they had defined their relationship with their ancestral
continent.[3]

Somewhere along the line I learned about the AME Church's career in South
Africa, yet when I tried to pursue the matter I found myself frustrated. To be
sure, there were a dozen books and articles that treated the South African AME
Church, yet all seemed to be written by American historians with little sense of
South Africa or by South Africanists with little sense of where African Method-
ism came from or what it represented. The questions that concerned me

seemed invariably to fall through the middle. Who specifically joined the church in South Africa? What did Africans see when they looked to black America, and how did that vision shape their sense of their own predicament? How did an established institution, already nearly a century old, adapt itself to such radically new circumstances? What happened when Africans and African Americans actually encountered one another, not as imaginative foils, but as coworkers within a single institution? Eventually I determined to pursue these questions myself. The result, several revolutions later, is this book.[4]

Given the study's unusual shape and scope, a brief road map may be helpful. Book One focuses on the AME Church in the United States. Chapter 1 examines the origins and politics of African Methodism in postrevolutionary America, placing the church in the context of the broader struggles of free people of color in an era of intensifying racism. Chapter 2 ranges across the nineteenth century, exploring the sometimes bitter conflicts that attended the AME Church's evolution from a small sect to a half-million-member institution. Chapter 3 examines African American images of Africa, focusing on debates within the church over emigration, colonization, and missions. Together, these chapters establish a kind of institutional baseline to help the reader understand how the AME Church came to South Africa and what happened to it after it arrived. The chapters can also be read as a study in the contextual nature of ideas, showing how a religious and political impulse forged in the egalitarian fires of revolution could, over the course of a century, evolve into something quite different.

Book Two proceeds from the other side of the Atlantic. Chapter 4 examines the origins of black independent churches in South Africa and retraces the course that led the leaders of one such church into the harbor of African Methodism. Chapters 5 and 6 are close social history, examining the AME Church's entrance and evolution in a series of specific South African locales. Together, the chapters seek to repopulate the history of independent Christianity, to give flesh and historical specificity to a movement that is too often treated as a kind of generic African phenomenon. At the same time, the chapters examine some of the different meanings that black America evoked among Africans.

Book Three focuses on "middle passages," on men and women who moved between American and South African worlds. The climax of the book—the anticlimax, really—comes in Chapter 7, which recounts the careers of the African American bishops and missionaries sent out in the early twentieth century to supervise the AME Church's newest mission field. Chapter 8 pursues a similar tack, examining the social origins, American experiences, and subsequent careers of South African students educated in the United States under AME auspices. The final chapter charts the increasingly complex cross-traffic between the United States and South Africa in the decade between 1919 and 1929, a period that saw the emergence of new rivals to the AME Church's long-time dominance of the transatlantic trade. A brief epilogue carries the story down to the present.

A study of this nature inevitably intersects with dozens of historiographical debates. In general, I have been content to address such issues implicitly, as they arise in the narrative. Several years ago, however, I took an oath to include in my preface a few paragraphs briefly stating the book's major contentions, in deference to all the suffering graduate students who will not have time to read further. There are many things I would like to say: about the perils of "nationalist" teleologies; about the surprising forms of consciousness one finds working the margin of "social" and "intellectual" history; about the difficulties of conveying a language and a vision of history rooted in the Old Testament to modern readers, many of whom have difficulty taking religious experience and consciousness seriously. For the moment, however, let me highlight just three issues.

At the most grandiose level, this book represents an attempt to reintegrate—I use the term for want of a better one—African American and American history. In an intellectual climate that questions the capacity of language to communicate meaning and, by implication, the ability of people to fathom any experience other than their own, there is a growing tendency to portray black life—and "the black church" in particular—as unfolding in a separate realm, a realm simultaneously organic to those within and opaque to those without. Within this framework, the AME Church is often held up as the preeminent "separatist" institution—"the cultural womb of the black community," the crucible of "a visionary collective consciousness," the wellspring of "incipient Black consciousness and anti-colonialism," to quote a few recent studies. That African Methodism represented a haven from a hostile white world is unquestionably true, but there is a danger here of distorting both the context and the content of religious independence. The founders of African Methodism had no intention of "turning their backs" on white America, especially not at a time when 90 percent of African Americans remained enslaved. Quite the contrary, the establishment of independent churches opened new avenues for engaging with the dominant society, both politically and culturally. Evidence of this engagement surfaces all through the pages that follow—in African Methodists' vigorous participation in revolutionary-era debates over slavery, race, and human equality; in church leaders' preoccupation with finding "appropriate" outlets for female religiosity; in the AME campaign to "uplift" the freedmen in the wake of the Civil War; even, paradoxically, in the church's outreach to Africa. In this sense, the whole book can be read as a vindication of Ralph Ellison's wonderful admonition in *Shadow and Act:*

[To] fashion a theory of American Negro culture while ignoring the intricate network of connections which binds Negroes to the larger society . . . is to

attempt a delicate brain surgery with a switch-blade. And it is possible that any
viable theory of Negro American culture obligates us to fashion a more adequate
theory of American culture as a whole.[5]

This study also represents an exploration of the possibilities of comparative
history. Some of the most important recent contributions to this growing field
have come in the form of comparisons of the United States and South Africa.
What follows both does and does not fit within that corpus. While various
comparative lines of inquiry are pursued, I am ultimately less interested in
comparing and contrasting two discrete settings than in examining a single
institution that bridged them. The distinction is more than a semantic one.
For the period under study, the AME Church represented the most important
point of contact between black America and South Africa, a conduit through
which flowed people, performance genres, political ideas, even dress and hair
styles. Focusing on this interchange, on the process by which ideas and idioms
were appropriated and recast, yields a host of comparative questions, but ones
more closely grained than those generated by more conventional comparisons.
Why, for example, did "industrial education" decline in popularity in South
Africa at the very time it was emerging as a racial panacea in the United States?
Why were South African officials receptive to African American political and
pedagogical influences in certain contexts and terrified of them in others?
What happened when a protest tradition conceived amid a bourgeois revolution was transplanted to another society where bourgeois liberalism was attenuated and in retreat? How did black church leaders in different contexts
respond when their congregants began pushing the logic of religious independence in unexpected directions?[6]

There is still another dimension to the problem. The AME Church was more
than a conduit; it also served as a kind of looking glass in which Africans and
African Americans examined one another and, in the process, reexamined
themselves. Put differently, the historical actors themselves were engaged in a
comparative exercise, each group using the other as a reference point around
which to reinterpret its own identity, history, and destiny. Not surprisingly,
such comparisons tended to be profoundly self-referential, but they are all the
more revealing for that. Again, this has implications for the practice of comparative history. By setting aside for a moment our own ideas about what is
significant or worth comparing and instead taking seriously the comparisons
that Africans and African Americans themselves drew between their situations,
we can begin to move beyond structures and formal movements to consciousness, to the actual fashioning of individual and collective identities. This is a
terrain that comparative historians have generally been ill prepared to enter.

Finally, this book represents an intervention in a set of debates clustered
around the question of "Afrocentrism." As I proceeded with this study, it
became more and more apparent that transatlantic "bridges" like the AME

Church were not that unusual, that the borders that define historical inquiry were not the borders of lived experience for the historical actors themselves. Long after the decline of the transatlantic slave trade, black life continued to be shaped by a constant traffic between Africa and the New World, evidence of which surfaces again and again in this book. The first black students to enroll in an American college were Africans, sailors from the Gold Coast. The AME Church's first African-born bishop, F. H. Gow, was the son of a West Indian father and a Pennsylvania-born mother who had settled in Cape Town in the late 1880s. One of the South African church's earliest supporters was a Gold Coast–born newspaper editor who had settled in the Cape after several years in New York. The list could be extended, but the point is clear: the "African Diaspora" is not just an academic way of acknowledging that people of African descent live in many different places; it is an important historical site in its own right. Part of the goal of this book is to bring that site into clearer focus.[7]

Having stated that proposition, however, I dissent from what many take to be its corollary: the idea that blacks across the diaspora are united by some kind of essential racial consciousness, transcending manifest gulfs in history and culture. To say that black people moved across national borders is not to say that they were unaffected by the cultures in which they lived. However deeply felt their affinity for Africa, however ambivalent their feelings about the United States, the African American men and women who sailed to South Africa under the auspices of the AME Church could not simply jettison nearly three centuries in America in mid-Atlantic. The very fact that they traveled as missionaries, determined to "emancipate" their brethren from the "bondage" of ignorance and sin, suggests just how qualified and self-referential their identification with Africa remained. Similarly, South Africans approached African Americans with a variety of beliefs and assumptions that inevitably had more to do with their own experiences and aspirations than with any African American realities. To put the matter in the parlance of postcolonial anthropology, Africans and African Americans confronted one another as "Others," but in a context where the trope of race served not to distinguish but to render lines of similarity and difference immensely problematic. To put the matter more simply, people exist inside rather than outside history. If there is a single moral to be drawn from the sometimes wrenching tale that follows, it is this.

Finally, a note on language. Whatever else they may or may not have in common, the United States and South Africa unquestionably share an extraordinary fecundity in racist language. The pages that follow are crammed with terms that many will find offensive or distasteful. In the main, these words are confined to quoted material, though I have occasionally resorted to them to evoke the spirit or tone of a contemporary source. Obviously such usage implies no endorsement of that tone or spirit.

Any scholarly work is a collective enterprise, this one more than most. Careful reading of the footnotes will reveal many of my debts, but here let me say an additional thank you to several people whose generosity and support went far beyond the call of duty.

My greatest debts are to George Fredrickson, David Kennedy, and Richard Roberts, who constituted my dissertation committee at Stanford University when this study was first taking shape. Bruce Schulman, David Wills, Bill Worger, Nancy Clark, Tom Jackson, Daryl Scott, and Steve Mufson all read portions of the dissertation-in-progress and offered cogent suggestions. Lorraine Sinclair steered me from harm's way in innumerable ways. Special thanks also to the members of the Core Colloquiam *Kaffeeklatsch,* who provided a model of collegiality that I still cherish.

At Northwestern I have been blessed with wonderful colleagues and students, whom I would like to thank collectively. An additional thank you, however, is due Jim Oakes, Nancy Maclean, Robert Wiebe, and Clarence Ver Steeg, who slogged through the entire dissertation, uncovering layers of significance that I had completely overlooked, and to Dayo Gore, Wallace Best, Darcy Scott Martin, Keith Breckenridge, and Catherine Burns, who all lent their aid at pivotal moments.

My debts to colleagues on the other side of the Atlantic are even greater, if only because of my considerable ignorance when I first arrived in South Africa. Thanks to Russell Ally, William Beinart, Belinda Bozzoli, Philip Bonner, Colin Bundy, Matthew Chaskalson, Stephen Clingman, Tim Clynick, Richard Cope, Tim Couzens, Peter Delius, Veit Erlmann, Michelle Friedman, Tim Keegan, Jeremy Krikler, Paul la Hausse, Lis Lange, Shula Marks, the late Thomas Matsitela, Santu Mofokeng, the late Mos Molepo, Thomas Nkadimeng, Mahlomola Ntoane, Sue Parnell, Patrick Pearson, Debbie Posel, Karin Shapiro, and the late David Webster. I am completely at a loss to express my gratitude to Bruce Murray and Charles van Onselen, except to say that I have never had truer (or more irascible) friends.

Several ministers and members of the South African A.M.E. Church consented to be interviewed or otherwise gave of their time and wisdom. Acknowledgement is made to most in the footnotes; here, a special thanks to Bishop Harold B. Senatle, the Reverend Daniel Modisapodi, and the Reverend G. Z. Lethoba.

Staffs of two dozen libraries and archives have been unfailingly helpful and efficient. Particular thanks are due Jacqueline Brown of the Wilberforce University Archives, Anna Cunningham of the University of the Witwatersrand Historical Papers Library, and Russell Maylone, curator of Special Collections, Northwestern University.

Generous financial support was received in the form of a postgraduate fellowship from the Rotary Foundation of Rotary International, a Charlotte Newcombe doctoral dissertation grant, a Summer Stipend from the National

Endowment for the Humanities, and a Fulbright African Regional Research Grant. In this context, I should probably also acknowledge my parents and my siblings, Jodi, Jack, Chris, Andy and Tony, all of whom must at times have felt like granting agencies. Any of them would have been justified demanding progress reports before accepting my phone calls; I am thankful that none of them ever did.

A host of other people provided essential moral and material support. Thank you, Jefferson Morley, Stephen Davis, Hon. and Mrs. Philip R. Mancini, Phil and Nancy Mancini, Ebenaezar and Maria van Niekerk, Ruth Edgecombe, Lester Weinstine, Bob Edgar, Rosemary Zagari, Steve Vandermyde, Molly and Connie Anderson, Sandy Prosalendis, Maureen Swan, Jim Blakemore, Glen Adler, Dorothy Wheeler, Mary Barton, Sid and Heidi Nestler, and Mike Foreman. If I have one regret, it is that my friend Martin Griffin did not live to see me finally finish something. Somehow I think he would have appreciated the irony.

Andrea van Niekerk made this study possible in more ways than I can say. Our children, Thomas, Daniel, and Leah, made finishing it almost impossible. I love them all.

Evanston, Ill.   J. T. C.
August 1994

CONTENTS

BOOK ONE

1. Vindicating the Race, 3

2. Harnessing the Spirit, 32

3. Through the Looking Glass, 64

BOOK TWO

4. Stretch Forth Thy Hands, 103

5. African Methodism as a Social Movement, I, 139

6. African Methodism as a Social Movement, II, 180

BOOK THREE

7. The Making of a Religious Institution, 215

8. "The Seed You Sow in Africa," 249

9. Middle Passages, 295

Epilogue, 328

Notes, 337

Index, 397

BOOK ONE

And Jacob went out from Beersheba, and went toward Haran.

And he lighted upon a certain place, and tarried there all night, because the sun was set; and he took of the stones of that place, and put them for his pillows, and lay down in that place to sleep.

And he dreamed, and behold a ladder set up on the earth, and the top of it reached to heaven: and behold the angels of God ascending and descending on it.

And, behold, the LORD stood above it, and said, I am the LORD God of Abraham thy father, and the God of Isaac: the land whereon thou liest, to thee will I give it, and to thy seed;

And thy seed shall be as the dust of the earth, and thou shalt spread abroad to the west, and to the east, and to the north, and to the south: and in thee and in thy seed shall all the families of the earth be blessed.

And, behold, I am with thee, and will keep thee in all places whither thou goest, and will bring thee again into this land; for I will not leave thee, until I have done that which I have spoken to thee of.

And Jacob awaked out of his sleep, and he said, Surely the LORD is in this place; and I knew it not.

And he was afraid, and said, How dreadful is this place! this is none other but the house of God, and this is the gate of heaven.

And Jacob rose up early in the morning, and took the stone that he had put for his pillows, and set it up for a pillar, and poured oil upon the top of it.

And he called the name of that place Beth-el . . .

GEN. 28:10–19

1

Vindicating the Race

The history of African American Christianity is bound up with the history of American slavery. African Americans encountered Christianity in the context of enslavement, and it was as captives that they began the long process of making the gospel their own. The process varied across time and space and defies generalization or easy description. Sometimes conversion came quickly, in explosive moments of "awakening"; more often, it unfolded over generations, as Christian beliefs and practices insinuated themselves into slaves' daily rounds. In some settings, the new creed seems almost completely to have displaced older religions, which survived only in a handful of disembodied beliefs and rituals. In other places, Christian usages were grafted onto still vital African religious traditions, producing dynamic, richly syncretic creeds. Yet whatever the pace or pathway, slaves across the Americas were drawn into the dialectic of conversion, transforming the religion of their captors even as it transformed them.[1]

In Latin America, slave conversion was at least nominally encouraged by church and state. Ships arriving in New Spain were often met by Catholic priests, who baptized their human cargoes and occasionally undertook their religious instruction. Conversion was equally common in Brazil; indeed, by the end of the seventeenth century Portuguese shippers were required to certify slaves as Christian before embarking for the New World, a requirement usually met by perfunctory mass baptisms. In North America, on the other hand, slaves' initial encounter with Christianity took place almost entirely outside whites' purview. Dispersed population, shortages of ministers, and uncertainty about the legal basis of slavery all militated against any systematic efforts to baptize or instruct slaves. Bills passed by the Virginia legislature in 1667 and in Maryland a few years later alleviated the legal uncertainty, establishing captivity as a condition of birth unaltered by religious conversion. Even then, most slaveholders remained indifferent or actively hostile to the idea of instructing their bondsmen, largely out of "fears that slaves would not grasp the distinction between spiritual and temporal equality." Missionaries of the Society for the Propagation of the Gospel, which undertook work among North American slaves in the early eighteenth century, complained constantly of masters who denied them access to their bondsmen, on the grounds that religion made them "proud and saucy" and "not so good servants."[2]

African Americans responded to Christianity in a variety of ways. Some rejected it. An S.P.G. missionary in Virginia, for example, complained that his first baptismal candidates' progress was hampered by the fact that "all other slaves do laugh at them." Others hearkened to Christianity's call, though the paucity of documentation makes it difficult to say precisely who or why. Most black Christians in seventeenth-century records were free people of color, though this probably says more about the character of the evidence than about any relative proportions. Among the enslaved, the largest number of converts appear to have been baptized in the West Indies prior to transhipment to the mainland. At least some of these early converts saw conversion as a means to freedom; the Virginia law of 1667, in fact, may have been prompted by petitions brought by Christian slaves. For others, Christianity's appeal was less instrumental than existential. In the Old Testament story of the Exodus in particular, African Americans found a parallel for their own travails, as well as the promise of a future when captives would go free and the righteous would be rewarded. Whatever their individual motives, black Christians were soon sprinkled all through the mainland colonies, from Puritan Massachusetts to the South Carolina frontier. Some apparently commenced holding services independently, prompting legislatures in at least two colonies to ban the practice.[3]

The pace of conversion accelerated in the eighteenth century, especially after the Great Awakening, a surge of evangelical revivals that cascaded across the North American colonies in the middle third of the eighteenth century. Itinerant evangelists, led by the redoubtable George Whitefield, plied the backroads of the colonies, preaching an unadorned, enthusiastic Christianity that appealed to the lowly and ill educated. In light of the exaggerated claims of some historians, it is worth noting that few awakeners were what we would call racial equalitarians. While many condemned masters for cruelty and for neglecting their slaves' spiritual needs, few questioned the institution of slavery per se; a few owned slaves themselves. Even so, their message posed a profound challenge to slavery, and indeed to all worldly hierarchy. Thousands of awakened slaveowners manumitted their bondsmen or undertook to provide them with religious instruction. African Americans, in turn, rallied to the evangelical message. Dozens of contemporary accounts attest to the prevalence of people of color, slave and free, at revivals, and even to the existence of occasional black evangelists. Indeed, one of the primary charges laid against the

Awakening by disgruntled "Old Lights" was that it elevated the lowly to positions of religious authority. "They are chiefly indeed young Persons," complained Boston's Charles Chauncey, "sometimes Lads, or rather Boys; Nay, Women and Girls; yea Negroes, have taken upon them to do the Business of Preachers."[4]

Aftershocks of the Awakening continued to rumble through the last half of the eighteenth century, propelling ever more African Americans into the burgeoning evangelical churches. In several southern cities, black Methodists and Baptists established independent congregations under the leadership of black evangelists. More surprising, in retrospect, whites and blacks often came together in worship, participating jointly in Methodist classes and love feasts and in the ubiquitous revivals. Evangelical churches enjoyed a particularly rich harvest in the Chesapeake—in Maryland, Delaware, and parts of northern Virginia, where the political uncertainties of revolution were exacerbated by plummeting tobacco prices and chronic debt. Included in the evangelical harvest was a young Delaware slave named Richard, future founder of the AME Church.[5]

The broad contours of Richard Allen's life are familiar to historians, thanks largely to a spiritual autobiography that Allen dictated to his son shortly before his death. Born a slave, Allen was awakened in his youth by an itinerant Methodist evangelist, an event that set him on a course to freedom and the Christian ministry. By the time of his death in 1831, he had risen to become one of the most revered leaders in black America, as well as bishop of America's first independent black church. Yet as familiar as we are with Allen's history, it is worth rehearsing again, if only because of the significance he himself attached to it. Like Olaudah Equiano, Frederick Douglass, and the other classic slave narrators, Allen viewed his life paradigmatically, as a parable of racial elevation for black and white alike. For those still enslaved, Allen's passage from ignorance and slavery to enlightened freedom blazed a trail to be followed; for skeptical whites, it provided proof of blacks' innate moral and intellectual capacity; for all, it offered a vivid illustration of the workings of Providence in human affairs. All these themes would be woven into the very fabric of the church that Allen founded. In this sense, Allen's "Life Experiences and Gospel Labors" functions as African Methodism's creation story.[6]

Like most spiritual narrators, Allen began his account not with his birth but with conversion, sometime before his eighteenth birthday. Fortunately, we know something of his early years, thanks to recent archival discoveries by Gary Nash. He was born in 1760 in Philadelphia, the slave of a prominent lawyer and planter. At the age of eight, he was sold, along with his mother and siblings, to Stokely Sturgis, a threadbare Delaware planter. In his memoir Allen remembered Sturgis as a "tender, humane man," more "like a father to his slaves than anything else." Like so many "good masters," however, Sturgis regarded his creditors more highly than his slaves. In the early 1770s he settled his debts by selling off Richard's mother and several of his siblings. While Allen expressed no bitterness in his account, the experience must have been devastating and probably helped prepare the young slave for the evangelicals' message.[7]

Some time later, Richard and his brother were awakened by an itinerant Methodist preacher. The conversion itself appears to have followed the standard morphology, with the preaching of the Word provoking an agonizing self-appraisal. "I was awakened and brought to see myself, poor, wretched and undone," Allen recalled. The ensuing weeks brought moments of elation followed by days of crushing doubt, culminating in a convulsive salvific moment—a moment rendered in the language of liberation:

> One night I thought hell would be my portion. I cried unto Him who delighteth to hear the prayers of a poor sinner, and all of a sudden my dungeon shook, my chains flew off, and, glory to God, I cried. My soul was filled.

Such imagery, it should be noted, was not uncommon. The reference to dungeons and chains, for example, came directly from a popular Charles Wesley hymn. Such words, however, doubtless had special significance for a slave. Forever after, Allen would continue to link salvation and freedom, investing that familiar Pauline equation with specific and literal meaning.[8]

The ensuing weeks brought a dramatic change in the two brothers' outward aspect. Secure in their newfound spiritual freedom and determined to refute the common charge that "religion made us worse servants," they attacked their work around the plantation with a will, even skipping their cherished weekly class meetings "if we were likely to be backward with our crops." Such conduct made a powerful impression on their master. Though an "unconverted man" himself, Sturgis became "convinced that religion made slaves better and not worse, and often boasted of his slaves for their honesty and industry." At Richard's behest, he opened his home to itinerant preachers, including the peripatetic Francis Asbury, founding father of the Methodist Episcopal Church in the United States. Shortly after Asbury's visit, he welcomed Freeborn Garrettson, a charismatic Methodist preacher who was himself a former slaveholder. Garrettson's sermon, based on the text *"Thou art weighed in the balance, and art found wanting,"* pierced Sturgis's heart. From that moment forward, he "could not be satisfied to hold slaves, believing it to be wrong. And after that he proposed to me and my brother buying our times . . ."[9]

Richard at least grasped the opportunity. (The fate of Allen's brother remains unclear.) Over the next few years, he labored in a variety of ventures, exhibiting the industry and entrepreneurial imagination that were to become two of his most celebrated qualities. He chopped wood, mended shoes, manufactured bricks, and hauled salt, eventually accumulating the price stipulated by Sturgis. In 1783 the twenty-three-year-old slave purchased his freedom, sealing his independence by adopting a surname: Allen.[10]

Several aspects of the account are worth remarking. The first is Allen's almost sublime faith in the leveling power of Christianity. Just as darkness depends on a shuttering of light, so, Allen believed, did slavery depend on the exclusion of Christian enlightenment. Once that gloom had been pierced, once slaves had felt "the favour and love of God dwelling in their hearts," the whole edifice would crumble. Degraded slaves would exhibit a new dignity, a devotion to Christian service, to melt the hearts of all but the most unfeeling masters. Manumissions would multiply. The sheer force of Christian example, exhibited by bondsmen redeemed from the slavery of sin, would help redeem America from the sin of slavery. This simple faith, born of personal experience, shaped Allen's antislavery convictions in distinctive ways. While pamphleteers such as David Walker, Allen's self-proclaimed disciple, urged slaves to cast off their chains by force, Allen advocated "patient waiting" and warned of the tyranny of a "wrathful disposition." "That God who knows the hearts of all men, and the propensity of a slave to hate his oppressor, hath strictly forbidden it to his chosen people," he wrote: "*thou shalt not abhor an Egyptian, because thou wast a stranger in his land.* Deut. xxiii. 7." Instead, he argued that slaves could advance their own freedom by attending faithfully to their duties and cultivating ties of Christian fellowship with their masters, as he and his brother had done. Those few slaves whose masters were immune to Christian influence would at least have the consolation of "that freedom which the sons of God enjoyed."[11]

Even more remarkable is the sense of representativeness that pervades the narrative, the sense of participating in an ongoing racial trial. Even as a slave, Allen was aware of whites' skepticism about black Christians; he and his brother heard neighbors whisper that "Stokely's negroes would soon ruin him." In the face of such scrutiny, every act became magnified; the slightest evidence of indolence or insolence confirmed white skepticism and cast another obstacle before the numberless bondsmen groping for redemption. This sense of representativeness, and the almost palpable feelings of obligation that flowed from it, would become abiding features in elite black politics in America, exhibited nowhere more dramatically than in the AME Church.[12]

Even as he strove to raise his purchase price, Allen labored for Methodism, stopping at farms and crossroads to preach the gospel. Once free, he redoubled his efforts, establishing himself as one of the movement's most effective evangelists. A testimonial written in the 1780s by three prominent white Methodists hailed Allen's extraordinary energy and commitment.

> After the War he Believed it to be his Duty to Travel abroad as a Preacher of Righteousness, and for the first six Months Traveled at his own Cost, and the Remainder of his Religious Journeys his expences was for the most Part defrayed

by the Religious Society of which he was a Member; he Traveled into various parts of New York, New Jersey, Pensilva., Delaware, Virginia, Maryland, North and South Carolina; and also spent about two Months in visiting the Indian Natives.

Word of this powerful new preacher soon reached Bishop Asbury, who invited Allen to accompany him on a planned tour of the South. While doubtless flattering, the offer came with conditions that gave the perceptive young freedman pause. "He told me that in the slave countries, Carolina and other places, I must not intermix with the slaves, and I would frequently have to sleep in his carriage, and he would allow me my victuals and clothes," Allen remembered. "I told him I would not travel with him on these conditions . . . that I thought people ought to lay up something while they were able to support themselves in times of sickness or old age." When Asbury noted that he himself made no such provisions, Allen's reply was fearlessly direct. "I told him he would be taken care of, let his afflictions be as they were . . . but I doubted whether it would be the case with myself." In the end, he continued to preach independently, working when necessary "so that no man could say I was chargeable to the connection." "My hands," he concluded in an oft-quoted passage, "administered to my necessities.[13]

Early in 1786 Allen's itineracy took him back to Philadelphia for what he thought would be "a week or two" of preaching. Long the center of American philanthropy, the City of Brotherly Love was fast becoming the hub of black life in the new republic. Thousands of freedmen and women poured into the city in the decades after the Revolution, beneficiaries of the ongoing transition from tobacco to cereals in the city's hinterlands. In 1780, when Pennsylvania passed the nation's first gradual abolition act, Philadelphia boasted scarcely a thousand people of color, slave and free, constituting about 3 percent of the city's population. Ten years later, African Americans accounted for almost 10 percent of Philadelphians, a proportion that remained more or less constant for the next half century. By 1830, close to 15,000 blacks lived in the city, all but a handful of them free. In contrast to the white population, only a fraction of the growth in the city's black population stemmed from natural increase. The bulk came from new arrivals, many just days removed from slavery.[14]

For the most part, black migrants to Philadelphia encountered not the promised brotherly love but poverty and indifference fast slipping into hostility. Under the terms of Pennsylvania's gradual abolition law, slaves and their children were often bound out for long and dreary indentures, a device to compensate masters and to instill the habits of industry that blacks allegedly lacked. Newly arrived freedmen were consigned to similar fates, often through the good offices of philanthropic groups like the Pennsylvania Abolition Society. The more fortunate found jobs at the port, working as mariners, dockworkers, caulkers, and the like, positions that afforded a measure of autonomy but that left them vulnerable to the era's frequent commercial slumps. In the

end, most freedmen and women settled into the same niches they had occupied
as slaves, especially domestic labor. (According to the 1790 census, more than
half of black Philadelphians resided in white homes.) Educational facilities
were virtually nonexistent; well into the 1780s the only school for children of
color was a small academy run by Quaker abolitionist Anthony Benezet. The
local Anglican Church, blessed with a series of liberal rectors, welcomed black
congregants, but other white denominations, including the Methodists, made
little or no effort to convert or minister to people of color. Even the vaunted
Quakers declined to accept African Americans at regular meetings, preferring
to entertain the inner light in segregated services. [15]

Stigmatized as idle and vicious, bereft of spiritual leadership, blacks in
Philadelphia were ripe for Allen's evangelical message. "My labor was much
blessed," he recalled in his memoir. "I soon saw a large field open seeking and
instructing my African brethren, who had been a long forgotten people, and
few of them had attended public worship." The elder at St. George's Methodist
Church gave Allen access to the pulpit at 5:00 A.M. each day, and he began to
gather a small following. He also preached on the city commons, sometimes a
half dozen times in a day. While the fruits of this early labor went to St.
George's, Allen appears already to have concluded that black Methodists
needed a church of their own to address their distinctive problems and needs.
His proposals in that direction, however, found little support among established leaders of the black community, most of whom inclined toward
Anglicanism or Quakerism. [16]

His first initiative blocked, Allen set out to promote the methodical virtues
by other means. In 1787 he and another community leader, Absalom Jones,
established the Free African Society, black America's first mutual aid society.
Organized on a nondenominational basis, the society welcomed all black men
and women who led "orderly and sober" lives. As that proviso suggests, the
basic insurance functions of the organization were laced with a strong dose of
moral reformism. Indeed, a special "Committee of Monitors" was appointed to
visit society members in their homes to ensure that they lived frugal, upright
lives. Such institutions, Allen and Jones wrote in the society's preamble,
would help lift African Americans out of "their irreligious and uncivilised
state" and into the full light of Christian independence. [17]

The Free African Society proved a great success, spawning sister institutions
in New York, Boston, and Newport, as well as a handful of benevolent and
fraternal organizations in Philadelphia itself. From the outset, however, the
society was riven by denominational tensions. Still convinced that blacks
needed a church of their own, Allen strove to impose Methodist usages on the
society, antagonizing most of his colleagues in the process. In November 1788
a special F.A.S. committee proposed commencing each meeting with fifteen
minutes of silence, largely in deference to the Quaker owners of the building in
which they met but also as an antidote to the "previous predilections of a large

number of the members composing this Society in favor of an unconstrained outburst of feeling in religious worship." By early 1789 things had reached such a pass that Allen was formally read out of the organization on charges of convening irregular meetings, "attempting to sow division among us," and generally engaging in "refractory" behavior.[18]

Allen was soon back in harness. In late 1790 he joined other leaders of Philadelphia's black community in a campaign to raise money for an independent "African Church." The object, according to physician Benjamin Rush, one of the group's white patrons, was to establish a nondenominational "union," gathering together blacks from various churches, as well as the mass of black people "ignorant and unknown to any religious society." Such a scheme, while doubtless more ecumenical than Allen would have liked, represented a major step toward achieving his vision of a separate black church. In its solicitation for funds, the group defended itself against charges of schism, stressing the "necessity and propriety of separate and exclusive means" to raise a proscribed and ignorant people. The merits of the argument were underscored in 1792 by the famous episode in St. George's Methodist Church, when Allen, Absalom Jones, and the church's growing black contingent were ordered to seats at the back of a newly constructed gallery. When white trustees tried forcibly to remove Jones during prayers, the entire group "went out of the church in a body." The episode produced a wave of sympathy for the seceders, enabling them to raise the necessary funds and to commence building a church of their own. Allen, as "the first proposer of the African church," was selected to turn the first spade. "Here," he concluded, "was the beginning and rise of the first African Church in America."[19]

Initially, Allen's plans reached no further than erecting a separate church for Philadelphia's people of color; he certainly did not foresee severing ties with organized Methodism, the connection under which he "was born and awakened." When Anglican leaders approached him with an offer of ordination, Allen declined, declaring that he "could not be anything else but a Methodist." When Absalom Jones accepted the Anglicans' offer, taking the newly erected African Church and most of its membership with him, Allen remained steadfast. With a small group of Methodist loyalists, he commenced holding services in a blacksmith's shop, while slowly raising funds to build another church. When the new church opened in 1794, Allen invited Bishop Asbury to preach the dedicatory sermon, clear evidence of his desire to remain within the Methodist fold. Asbury complied, but it was one of his subordinates who gave the place its name, when he offered a prayer that the new church would become "a bethel to the gathering in of thousands of souls." Forever after, the church was Bethel, the House of God.[20]

There was more to Allen's fidelity to Methodism than mere parochialism. "Notwithstanding we had been so violently persecuted," he later recalled, "we were in favor of being attached to the methodist connection; for I was confident that there was no religious sect or denomination would suit the capacity of colored people as well as the Methodist." Allen valued Methodism's openness to religious feeling, its simple doctrine, its reliance on "spiritual or extempore preaching," which suited an "unlearned" people better than dry scriptural exegesis. Methodism also emphasized discipline, vital to a people assailed by poverty and vice. To Allen, frugality, temperance, industry, and the other classic Methodist virtues represented more than a means to eventual salvation; they provided a formula by which blacks could lift themselves up from their impoverished, degraded state, a possibility his own life exemplified. This formula was reinforced by concrete structures—regular preaching, weekly classes, quarterly love feasts, cathartic revivals—that helped keep individuals on the narrow path, while providing a desperately needed sense of community and belonging.[21]

Allen may have been certain of Methodism, but Methodist authorities were deeply suspicious of him. Asbury was at best ambivalent about the Bethel enterprise. While he admired Allen's evangelical talents, he also put great stock in Methodism's institutional integrity and fretted about schism. His ambivalence was perhaps best expressed in 1799, when he ordained Allen a Methodist deacon, an unprecedented promotion for a man of color, but one that came without full sacerdotal powers. The local Methodist establishment was forthrightly hostile. Embarrassed by the episode in St. George's, Philadelphia Methodists tried first to compel the seceders' return, threatening to read them out of connection. When challenged to cite any specific violation of Methodist descipline, they relented and resorted instead to professions of friendship and concern. It was in this latter guise that a prominent white Methodist offered to draw up articles of incorporation for Bethel Church—articles that, Allen and his followers later discovered, bound them to the Methodist Conference, lock, stock, and barrel. One elder, citing the articles, ordered the church closed and locked, prompting the Bethelites to adopt an "African Supplement" reasserting control of the church they had built.[22]

The Bethelites retained formal links with the Methodist Episcopal Church for more than two decades, despite constant skirmishing over property, membership, and ministerial authority. Methodist authorities were endlessly ingenious in their efforts to recapture the seceders: one elder encouraged a dismissed trustee to pursue a suit against Bethel; another challenged the congregation's control over membership by providing a quarterly ticket to a woman whom the congregation had read out of meeting; still another opened a rival black church on Bethel's doorstep, in an effort to siphon off membership. Methodist leaders also tried various legal devices to regain title to Bethel Church, once nearly forcing it onto the auction block. Perhaps most cynical of all, Methodist authorities refused to bestow communion on the seceders or charged extortionate fees to do so. Such efforts caused endless rancor, but they did nothing to stem the growth of Bethel's membership, which had risen to almost thirteen hundred by 1813.[23]

By 1815 the relationship between the Bethelites and Methodist authorities had deteriorated to the point that a white elder seeking to take the pulpit for Sunday morning service was forcibly impeded by members of the congregation. The elder immediately filed for a writ of mandamus, pursuing his claim all the way to the Pennsylvania Supreme Court. The dispute snapped the last fraying cord of loyalty binding the Bethelites to the Methodist Episcopal Church. Early in 1816 the court found for the congregation, effectively establishing Bethel Church as free and independent.[24]

Even before the court handed down its decision, Allen had begun corresponding with black Methodists in other cities, many of whom had endured similar outrages at the hands of Methodist authorities. The most significant response came from Baltimore, where rivalries between white and black local preachers and another row over seating had prompted black Methodists to establish their own Bethel Church. The leader of the Baltimore congregation was Daniel Coker, a man whose life reminds us just how peculiar America's "Peculiar Institution" really was. Coker was born on a Maryland plantation, apparently of a union between a black slave and a white servant woman; his given name was Isaac. To conceal the circumstances of the birth, the infant was registered as the son of a mulatto slave woman in the neighborhood, sparing community sensibilities at the cost of consigning a freeborn child to a lifetime of slavery. For a slave Isaac received a good early education, thanks to the "perverseness of his young master," who refused to go to school without his playmate. Sometime in the late 1790s he escaped to New York, where, in an effort to throw off pursuers, he adopted the name of his white half-brother, Daniel Coker. He completed his education and began preaching in the Methodist Church before accepting an offer to return to Maryland to open a school. With the help of several white patrons, he purchased his freedom and settled in Baltimore, where he quickly earned distinction as a preacher, teacher, and antislavery spokesman.[25]

Perhaps because of the strange turnings in his own experience, Coker remained preternaturally alert to the workings of Providence in human affairs. Surveying the struggles of black Christians along the eastern seaboard, he discerned clear evidence of an unfolding divine plan. His first antislavery pamphlet, published in 1810, included a list of more than a dozen "African Ministers . . . of the Author's Acquaintance," as well as lists of churches and local preachers, all to "show what God is doing for Ethiopia's sons in the United States of America." The Bethelites' legal triumph supplied yet another piece of the puzzle. On hearing of the Pennsylvania Court's decision, Coker convened a thanksgiving service in Baltimore, where he delivered a rousing sermon comparing African Americans to the Israelites and the Supreme Court victory to the end of the Babylonian captivity. Just three years later, Coker would take that parallel to its logical conclusion and embark for Africa as a missionary.[26]

In the wake of the court decision, a dozen black churchmen from Pennsylva-

nia, Maryland, Delaware, and New Jersey gathered together in Philadelphia's
Bethel Church and formally incorporated themselves as the African Methodist
Episcopal Church. (Protracted negotiations with Methodist separatists in New
York City proved unavailing; six years later the New Yorkers launched their
own independent denomination, the AME Zion Church.) In the best Protestant fashion, the delegates portrayed themselves not as schismatics but as
keepers of the true faith, struggling to stem Methodism's declension. "It is to
be awfully feared that the simplicity of the Gospel that was among them" had
disappeared, Allen charged. "We would ask for the good old way, and desire to
walk therein." To underscore their claim, the founders adopted Methodist
doctrine virtually intact. What innovations were contained in the *Doctrines and
Discipline of the African Methodist Episcopal Church*, first published in 1817, all
aimed at purifying Methodism of un-Wesleyan innovations. AME ministers,
for example, were not permitted to wear robes, restoring a prohibition that had
lapsed in the Methodist Episcopal Church. The office of presiding elder, an
intermediate position between bishop and elder, was abolished on the grounds
that it smacked of Catholicism. (Robes and presiding elders both reappeared
later in the century.) Most important, the delegates reasserted John Wesley's
prohibition against membership by slaveholders, a ban that white Methodists
had found it politic to ignore.[27]

The only apparent contention in the first AME conferences concerned the
selection of a bishop. Delegates initially elected Daniel Coker, but several
Philadelphians protested. Their objections no doubt reflected loyalty to Allen,
but their main concern, according to a participant in the meetings, was Coker's
color: "He being nearly white, the people said they could not have an *African
Connection* with a man as light as Daniel Coker at its head." A proposal to elect
two bishops was rejected by Allen, lest skeptical whites dismiss the whole
enterprise as a product of personal ambition. After another ballot, Allen was
elected and consecrated through the laying on of hands by the assembled
ministers. The episode apparently wounded Coker, and relations between him
and his fellows remained strained ever after. Ultimately, however, it was he,
with his acute sense of Providence, who best captured what the moment meant
to participants, in a passage from I Peter, which he appended to one of his early
pamphlets:

> But ye are a chosen generation, a royal priesthood, and an holy nation, a peculiar
> people; that ye should shew forth the praise of him who hath called you out of darkness
> into his marvellous light: which in time past were not a people, but are now the people of
> God: which had not obtained mercy, but now have obtained mercy, . . .[28]

The revolution of the Bethelites was encompassed within a second, larger
revolution. As several recent historians have shown, the forty years after independence were a time of profound upheaval in American society, as the forces
unleashed by political revolution reverberated through the structure of the new

nation. Prevailing conceptions of citizenship and community, gender and family, authority and obligation were all subject to renegotiation in light of the new nation's professed republican creed. In the realm of religion alone, the two generations after the American Revolution produced a profusion of new sects and movements, posing a host of questions about ministerial authority, the scope of individual autonomy, and the value of inherited dogma.[29]

A mere recital of dates suggests the complex linkages binding African Methodism to these broader transformations. Richard Allen's passage from slavery to freedom coincided almost exactly with the colonies' passage to independence; his purchase price was denominated in revolutionary scrip. The Free African Society, cornerstone of northern black institutional life, was founded in Philadelphia in 1787, even as the framers of the American Constitution gathered in nearby Independence Hall. More ominous, the Bethelites' long struggle with Methodist authorities coincided with a mounting assault on the position and prerogatives of free people of color, who fit but uneasily into the new nation's social taxonomy. Indeed, the formal incorporation of the AME Church in 1816 preceded by less than a year the founding of the American Colonization Society, an organization devoted to removing this anomalous and "troublesome" population from U.S. shores.

There is more here than chronological coincidence. The creation of an American nation entailed complex processes of boundary drawing, which touched the emerging AME Church in myriad ways. What did terms like freedom and equality mean in practice? Did they apply to African Americans? Did black people possess the requisites of republican citizenship, or were they somehow, by nature or experience, disqualified? There is simply no way to understand African Methodism, or the culture and politics of antebellum black America in general, without taking cognizance of this context, without recognizing the perils and possibilities that Allen and his comrades themselves recognized in America's revolutionary transformation. In a less obvious sense, the reverse may also be true—that is, we cannot fully appreciate the meaning of the American Revolution without focusing on institutions like the AME Church and on the broader struggles of the nation's free people of color; for it was this embattled population, itself largely a by-product of revolution, that posed the first and most fundamental test of the revolutionaries' "self evident" creed.

Before proceeding, however, it is necessary to take issue with some of the analytical categories that prevail in the study of African American Christianity, and African American history generally. With several conspicuous exceptions, scholars remain mired in a set of overlapping dichotomies in which movements and ideologies are cast as militant or accommodationist, separatist or integrationist, "nationalist" or assimilationist, and so forth. While such categories have some basis in debates within the African American community, they have acquired a scholarly life of their own, producing all manner of simplification and reification. At their crudest, they reduce all black politics, indeed all black life, to a stark choice: reject the dominant order or succumb to it, resist or submit. The problem, of course, is that historical actors rarely perceive their actions or alternatives in such simple terms. Subaltern people in particular routinely operate in the terrain between resistance and accommodation, deflecting the initiatives of the powerful, carving out small spaces for self-assertion, appropriating elements from different belief systems and orders of knowledge to create novel, eclectic forms of consciousness. The measure of these beliefs and practices lies not in consistency or theoretical rigor but in their capacity to sustain life, to speak to the needs and experience of people in specific historical circumstances. [30]

Inevitably, this same complexity and historical particularity is built into the institutions that oppressed people fashion, nowhere more obviously than in the first black independent churches. Bulwarks of racial solidarity, these institutions became vehicles of class differentiation; progenitors of an enduring nationalist tradition, they were simultaneously arenas of assimilation, within which tens of thousands of African Americans imbibed the manners and mores of the dominant society. Most paradoxical of all, these separatist institutions, conceived as refuges from a hostile white world, became the seedbed of a liberal, inclusive political tradition that championed racial equality and the right of African Americans to share fully in the fruits of American democracy.

The solution to these apparent paradoxes lay, as always, in history, specifically in the complex intersection of slavery, race, and the American Revolution. As scholars have noted, independence left African Americans an ambiguous legacy. At the most obvious level, the Revolution spawned a "contagion of liberty" which appeared for a time to threaten the whole edifice of American slavery. At a time when colonists proclaimed their commitments to "freedom" and denounced British plots to "enslave" them, it was almost inevitable that chattel slavery would attract increased scrutiny and opprobrium. Slavery seemed the epitome of hypocrisy, a practice so contrary to American professions that it vitiated the entire republican experiment. By happy coincidence, such sentiments emerged during a period of profound crisis in the slave economy, redoubling their impact. In northern seaports such as Philadelphia and New York, a series of sharp commercial contractions and the growing availability of free labor combined to render slavery increasingly uneconomical. Analogous processes were afoot in the Upper South, as thousands of planters, ground between mounting debt, soil exhaustion, and plummeting tobacco prices, shifted to cereal production. The result, North and South, was a dramatic increase in private manumissions, commencing in the 1760s and accelerating through the war and early national period. [31]

Ideological and economic pressures converged to produce a series of antislavery victories. Virginia led a clutch of southern states in liberalizing manumission laws, helping to produce a more than fivefold increase in the population of free people of color in the nation's first three decades. In 1780 three of every four African Americans in Delaware were slaves; thirty years later, three in four were free. State after state closed its ports to the African slave trade, a process that, according to the conventional wisdom of the time, ensured slavery's eventual extinction. Most important, the decades after 1776 produced the nation's first abolition acts, beginning, appropriately, in Pennsylvania. In retrospect, Pennsylvania's Gradual Abolition Act of 1780 was a cautious affair: technically, it freed no one, while the imposition of long indentures effectively passed the costs of abolition onto slaves themselves. Nonetheless, it provided a valuable model for other states, five of which proceeded, through legislative enactment, court decision, or constitutional provision, to draw the curtain on slavery.[32]

Unfortunately, the era spawned countervailing processes as well, which would eventually outstrip the libertarian impetus of the Revolution, with disastrous consequences for all blacks, slave and free. As Winthrop Jordan has shown, the last decades of the eighteenth century witnessed a remarkable crystallization of racial thought. It is difficult to unravel this process, because the discussion of "race" took place in many registers and was often embedded in larger debates about hierarchy, national identity, and the endowments of nature. Jordan, characteristically, frames his explanation in terms of revolutionary "self-scrutiny," suggesting that the very act of declaring themselves free and independent forced white Americans to account for those in their midst who were neither. At a deeper level, the concept of race, like the concept of revolution, was rooted in a series of intellectual transformations associated with the European Enlightenment: in the development of natural science, with its zeal for classification; in debates about human variety and plasticity generated by European expansion; in a "gradual secularization of thought" in the western world as a whole. Whatever the precise sources, the result was an explosion of speculation about African Americans, much of it couched in the deceptively transparent language of natural science. By the early nineteenth century, the invidious but diffuse sense of "otherness" that had long attached to African Americans was fast congealing into a distinctly modern conception of race, complete with the imputation of innate, ineradicable inferiority to those classified as Negro.[33]

Just as ideas of liberty and equality were fueled by broader social and economic transformations so too did the developing conception of race feed on the world around it. The opening of upland cotton cultivation in the 1790s provided slaveowners with a new lease on life and more or less put paid to the embryonic southern antislavery movement. At the same time, social and economic turmoil at home, combined with the perceived excesses of the French Revolution abroad, produced a sharp domestic reaction, a pervasive sense that the Revolution had gone too far. The racial dimension of such fears, always smoldering below the surface, burst aflame with the revolution in Haiti.

Thousands of refugee slaveholders washed up in the United States, bearing lurid tales of slaves drunk on liberty and equality. The Gabriel Prosser rebellion of 1800 brought the point still closer to home. In this broad climate of reaction, racial ideas gained rapidly in popularity, until they acquired an almost self-evident quality. With each passing year it became easier to argue that slavery was not only appropriate but necessary; that all African Americans, slave or free, were slavish; that nature had so distinguished certain groups of people that the premises of the Declaration of Independence simply did not apply.[34]

Perhaps the most remarkable thing about this development is that it flew in the face of the other great intellectual current of the age: environmentalism. Even before the American Revolution, natural scientists had begun to formulate a conception of adaptation, raising the possibility that differences within and between species were not fixed by nature but were rather products of sustained exposure to different physical environments. Such speculations found support in the sensationalist epistemology of John Locke, with its idea of the human tabula rasa. How many Americans actually read Locke's *Essay Concerning Human Understanding* is an open question, but its premises suffused eighteenth-century parenting manuals, pedagogical tracts, and popular fiction, as Jay Fliegelman has shown. The implication, again, was that character was not fixed but malleable, and hence susceptible to cultivation. In a sense, the Revolution itself was an expression of Americans' environmentalist faith. For all their talk of the "rights of Englishmen," the crux of the colonists' position was that they were no longer British, that long exposure to the New World had made them a people in their own right, ready to bear the responsibilities of self-government.[35]

This environmentalist ethos obviously ran counter to the emerging concept of race, and for a time provided a bulwark against it. Pioneer abolitionists such as Anthony Benezet, Benjamin Rush, and Samuel Stanhope Smith used environmentalist assumptions to attack slavery, arguing that blacks' degradation betokened no inferior endowment but was rather "the genuine offspring of slavery." For many early abolitionists, in fact, this represented the institution's chief iniquity: not only did slavery violate man's natural right to liberty, it blunted the mental, moral, and spiritual faculties of otherwise competent human beings. In the long run, however, environmentalism proved a weak reed before the surging racist tide. For all their egalitarianism, environmentalist writers rarely contested the "fact" of black inferiority, arguing rather about the sources of that deficiency and the prospects for amelioration. Moreover, most partook of the era's naturalistic temper, blithely assuming that the effects of environment could be read where it mattered: in the body. Thus, Smith not only argued that African Americans' mental and moral faculties were improving through exposure to the American environment but insisted that this improvement was registered physically, in both sharpening of countenance and lightening of skin. Similar premises underlay Rush's notorious suggestion that blackness was a tropical disease akin to leprosy that would, when cured, leave blacks white. Such concessions fatally weakened environmentalism's antislavery thrust. Indeed, it was only a matter of time before proponents of black inferiority began appropriating environmentalist language, arguing, for example, that exposure to luxuriant tropical climes had rendered blacks indolent and intellectually torpid. More perverse still, slavery's defenders could argue that the very experience of captivity had so dulled slaves' wits that manumission would be folly—akin, in the words of one commentator, to "refusing aid to infants in their cradles."[36]

Among Americans, no man more clearly articulated the emerging racial paradigm than that great doyen of revolutionary liberalism, Thomas Jefferson. In *Notes on the State of Virginia,* written at the behest of French correspondents and published in 1785, Jefferson set out to catalog the faculties of his state's diverse inhabitants, producing in the process a virtual primer on postrevolutionary racism. Blacks were tolerant of heat but susceptible to cold. They emitted a pungent odor. They required little sleep, often following a day of labor with "amusements" late into the night. While whites exhibited a pleasing openness of aspect, African Americans' emotions were hidden behind a "veil" of monotonous blackness. Above all, blacks were deficient in the "endowments of the head." They lacked forethought. While most possessed a gift for music, they showed little ability in higher arts like poetry and sculpture. Imitative and capable of feats of memory, they were markedly inferior in imagination and reason. In contrast to Native Americans, whose "sublime oratory" proved "their reason and sentiment strong, their imagination glowing and elevated," no black had ever "uttered a thought above the level of plain narration." Anticipating the environmentalist rebuttal, Jefferson insisted that these deficiencies were "not the effect merely of their condition of life." Roman slavery, after all, had produced great artists and poets, even though "the condition of their slaves was much more deplorable than that of the blacks on the continent of America." "It is not their condition then, but nature, which has produced the distinction," he concluded.[37]

Perhaps aware of the challenge such a conclusion represented to his own most cherished convictions, Jefferson did enter a caveat—a caveat that itself revealed how deeply the naturalistic assumptions of the era had penetrated his thought. "To justify a general conclusion," he warned, "requires many observations, even where the subject may be submitted to the Anatomical knife, to Optical glasses, to analysis by fire, or by solvents. How much more then where it is a faculty, not a substance, we are examining. . . ." Further research was doubly imperative, he added, in a case "where our conclusion would degrade a whole race of men from the rank in the scale of beings which their Creator may perhaps have given them." In effect, Jefferson invited others to rebut his hypothesis, an offer that, to his growing dismay, scores of men and women accepted. For all his noncommittal tone, however, Jefferson's own convictions were patent: blacks were slaves; they could never be freemen.[38]

Few people were as "advanced" in their racial thinking as Thomas Jefferson. Nonetheless, racist ideas were clearly becoming more pervasive as the nineteenth century dawned. One can chart their progress in any number of ways: in popular responses to the Prosser Rebellion; in the increasingly confident defense of slavery by southerners; in subtle but significant shifts in political thought. When conservatives in Virginia amended George Mason's 1776 Declaration of Rights so as to exclude slaves, for example, they did so on classically Lockean grounds: having never entered the "state of society," slaves were not privy to the social contract or to the rights which flowed from it. By the early nineteenth century, this delimitation of revolutionary principles was routinely acknowledged, by liberals and conservatives alike, in nakedly racial terms. "You may ask perhaps Why the Negroes were born Slaves," wrote Thomas Rodney, brother of the antislavery founding father Caesar Rodney, in one of the era's most appalling racist diatribes. "And may you not as well ask why the Buzzards are obliged to eat nothing but Carrion, and the Tumble bugs to work continually among Excrements? Nature answers by saying It was Necessary and therefore she has fitted them for it and made it their delight."[39]

Obviously, racist ideas helped legitimize slavery, as Rodney's comment suggests, and it was in the guise of proslavery ideology that racism would make its most dramatic mark in antebellum America. In practice, however, racist conceptions bore as hard, if not harder, on free people of color. If all African Americans were slavish, if black inferiority was inward and ineradicable, then free blacks could not, must not, exist. The result, North and South, was a virtual assault on free people of color. Everywhere, free blacks were denounced as ignorant and vicious, as the most "loathsome" and "degraded" population in the world. Writers accused them of idleness and impertinence, of fencing stolen goods, of fomenting unrest among slaves. In 1802 Virginia, the state that had led the liberalization of manumission laws a quarter of a century earlier, passed a bill restricting private manumissions. Other states went further, requiring that owners arrange transport out of state for any slave they proposed to free or even obtain a legislative act before proceeding. In many northern states, free blacks were required to take out certificates of citizenship, to post bonds of good conduct, and to demonstrate employment or be bound out as apprentices. Miscegenation laws tightened. An ominous pattern of segregation began to emerge, marked by separate schools, penitentiaries, even cemeteries. Several states passed laws preventing free blacks from taking up residence; the legislature of liberal Pennsylvania, the bellwether of American benevolence, entertained five separate bills to do the same. The culmination, of course, came in 1817 with the founding of the American Colonization Society, just a few months after the launch of the AME Church. In a slave republic, free people of color had no place.[40]

This was the world within which Richard Allen and his comrades operated, a world of revolution and reaction, of expansive liberalism and intensifying racism. Negotiating this terrain was a difficult task, one that pushed African American leaders in different directions. At the most obvious level, racial proscription produced a proliferation of autonomous black institutions within which African Americans could develop their own spiritual, social, and economic resources free from the provocations and petty humiliations they endured in white institutions. This quest for autonomy, however, did not imply that Allen and other black independent churchmen had turned their backs on the broader society. On the contrary, the rising racist tide propelled them into an ever more intimate engagement with white America, both politically and culturally. Faced with an ideology that derided blacks as base and inherently slavish, leaders like Allen and Absalom Jones were compelled to defend their fitness, their right to and capacity for republican citizenship. In effect, it fell to African Americans, not for the last time, to keep America's revolutionary promise alive.

Of these intertwined impulses—toward separation and toward inclusion—the first is more easily grasped, if only because the early African Methodists were forced to articulate it most clearly. Denounced as schismatics by white rivals, Allen and his comrades defended the "necessity and propriety" of a separate black church. In the broadside for the original African church, they stressed the "attraction and relationship" between black people, grounded in their lack of education, their "humble attainments in religion," and their shared experience of discrimination. In short, African Americans shared a basic empathy that provided a foundation for collective uplift. This belief surfaced in virtually everything independent church leaders wrote: in the Bethelites' pledge to "build each other up"; in Absalom Jones's exhortations to African Americans to "arise from the dust" and "become a people"; in Daniel Coker's eloquent defense of blacks' right "to sit down under our own vine to worship, and none to make us afraid."[41]

It is important, of course, to see these sentiments in their own time, to avoid telescoping them into later black nationalist ideology. The racial affinity claimed by Allen and others was predicated on shared experience and condition; the idea that blacks shared an essential, distinctive racial genius, elaborated by later writers like Edward Blyden and W. E. B. Du Bois, was at best latent in their thought. Nonetheless, the rise of black independent churches did mark a crucial juncture in the history of black nationalism. These humble institutions both reflected and fostered an emerging sense of peoplehood, of membership in an "imagined community" of black people, transcending the barriers of time, space, and condition.[42]

This imagined community clearly embraced southern slaves. Most of the early AME Church leaders had tasted slavery's "bitter pill," and they expressed their identification with southern slaves eloquently and often. "We who know how bitter the cup is of which the slave hath to drink, oh, how we ought to feel for those who yet remain in bondage," Allen and Absalom Jones wrote in their aptly entitled epistle "To the People of Color." A host of daily events conspired to keep these feelings of affinity alive, to remind free blacks of the realities of the Peculiar Institution and of their own anomalous position in a slave republic. Philadelphia welcomed more than ten thousand newly freed slaves in the three decades after 1787, as well as untold thousands of fugitives, many of whom found shelter in Allen's home or in the basement of Bethel Church. Slavecatchers came hard on the fugitives' heels, emboldened by federal laws that increasingly placed the onus on blacks to prove their claim to freedom. Reenslavement through cases of mistaken identity or outright kidnapping remained an ever present threat. (One slavecatcher made the mistake of detaining Allen, landing in jail for his troubles.) Less dramatic but equally important, black Philadelphians experienced daily the opprobrium that came with membership in a despised race. Such people well understood that the chains binding southern slaves shackled them as well.[43]

This assertion of shared identity was accompanied by a jealous defense of African American autonomy. While leaders such as Allen and Jones gratefully acknowledged the support of white allies, their long battle with the elders of St. George's Church had left them determined never again to be subject to white authority, either economically or ecclesiastically. This determination was registered in every facet of African Methodism: in church leaders' emphasis on property ownership; in their concern with keeping church buildings free of attachments; in their endless sermons against debt and indolence. AME ministers stressed the virtues of self-employment, of using one's own hands to provide one's "necessities." Of those original African Church trustees whose occupations can be traced, fully three-quarters were self-employed. Allen alone launched a dozen different business enterprises, eventually accumulating an estate valued at more than eighty thousand dollars. Such conduct obviously accorded well with Methodist doctrine, but in the hands of African Methodists it took on a distinctly racial edge. Debt, after all, almost invariably meant debt to whites, and that meant dependence. Much of the middle-class tone of African Methodism, which later generations of black nationalists would deride as bourgeois and elitist, flowed directly from this determination never again to be subject to whites.[44]

This commitment to autonomy, however, did not imply that the early African Methodists had abandoned America. Even as they stressed the distinctiveness of African Americans' plight and the necessity of separate institutions, AME leaders continued to see blacks' future in terms of the broader society. Allen in particular possessed an abiding faith in the beneficence of American institutions and looked optimistically to the day when people of color would enjoy all the rights and privileges of republican citizenship. Similarly, AME leaders never renounced the values and mores of the dominant culture or doubted their applicability to black people. On the contrary, they conspicuously embraced them, the better to rebut racist stereotypes about black inferiority. If there is a key to the politics of African Methodism, and to antebellum black politics generally, it lies here, in the belief that blacks could, through the force of their own example, "vindicate" their capacity and thus speed the coming of freedom. The AME Church itself became a central exhibit in the campaign, a concrete refutation of the allegation that blacks were incapable of self-government.[45]

No one better exemplified these paradoxes than pamphleteer David Walker, whose epochal *Appeal to the Coloured Citizens of the World* is rightly hailed as a watershed in the history of black nationalism. An ardent admirer of Richard Allen, Walker was firmly convinced of the value and necessity of separate African American institutions. He also went as far as anyone in antebellum America in asserting the existence of a distinctive black racial genius, suggesting, for example, that blacks exceeded whites in qualities such as piety and compassion. Nonetheless, Walker refused to turn away from white America, labeling such a course both impolitic and irresponsible. With so many of their brethren in chains, he argued, free people of color had an obligation to engage white society, to confront and refute the allegations made against them. Such a task, as Walker well knew, often implied accepting the dominant society's frame of reference and terms of debate. Walker's 1829 *Appeal,* for example, was deliberately framed as a reply to Jefferson's *Notes on the State of Virginia.* "Do you believe that the assertions of such a man, will pass away into oblivion unobserved by this people and the world?" he asked. "If you do you are very much mistaken. . . . I say, that unless we try to refute Mr. Jefferson's arguments respecting us, we will only establish them." Walker followed his own admonition in the pages that followed, marshaling evidence of blacks' religious elevation, their love of liberty, and their educability (a capacity unwittingly conceded in statutes prohibiting teaching slaves to read and write), all of which he juxtaposed with examples of white hypocrisy and cruelty. The very existence of the pamphlet challenged the most sinister charge of all—the allegation that blacks were incapable of reasoning or employing language beyond the level of "plain narration."[46]

In replying to racist calumnies, antebellum black writers almost invariably took Christianity as their starting point, the idea, in the words of the Bethel Church charter, that "all are one in Christ Jesus." Blacks and whites were fashioned from the "same clay"; they shared "one universal Father," who "made of one blood all the nations of the earth." This common humanity in turn implied a shared endowment of sensations, sentiments, and faculties, which a lifetime of bondage could dim but never extinguish. Black people were "fellow rationals"; they cherished families, valued justice, hoped and grieved. "We can tell you, from a degree of experience," Richard Allen and Absalom Jones declared, "that a black man, although reduced to the most abject state human nature is capable of, short of real madness, can think, reflect, and feel injuries. . . ." What passed for innate inferiority was in fact a product of stultifying environment, a reflection of "the contrary effects of liberty and slavery upon the mind of men."[47]

Independent Methodist minister John Marrant pushed the argument even further, blending Christianity and environmentalism in a manner designed to turn racist ideology on its head. It was not blacks who were deficient in moral sensibility, he suggested, but whites—whites whose hearts had become so hardened by generations of slaveholding that they unflinchingly indulged in hypocrisies and cruelties unimagined by any other race of men. "Man is a wonderful creature," Marrant argued in a 1789 sermon, "and not undeservedly said to be a little world, a world within himself, and containing whatever is found in the Creator." Yet if all this were true, he continued,

> then what can these God-provoking wretches think, who despise their fellow men, as tho' they were not of the same species with themselves, and would if in their power deprive them of the blessings and comforts of this life, which God in his bountiful goodness, hath freely given to all his creatures to improve and enjoy? Surely such monsters never came out of the hand of God. . . .

Such logic not only highlighted the essential sinfulness of slavery but presented whites as well as blacks as its victims. More important, it threw open the question of who might legitimately claim the mantle of Christianity, kicking out in the process one of the central intellectual props of white supremacy.[48]

This strategy of reversal—of appropriating Christian ideals and turning them back against their professors—received its most elaborate exposition in Daniel Coker's "Dialogue Between a Virginian and an African Minister," published in 1810. In Coker's brilliantly mordant set piece, an earnest, rather plodding Virginian trots out a succession of proslavery arguments, each of which is demolished by a quicker-witted black cleric. In the pamphlet's pivotal moment, the minister literally and figuratively seizes the Bible from the white man's hands. "I have something to offer in favour of slavery," the Virginian begins.

> *Virginian.* . . . I shall draw my argument from the scriptures, and I suppose you will not call them into question, or rail against what they tolerate. Pray, have you ever studied divinity?
> *Minister.* No sir, I have never studied it in the way I expect you mean . . . but, let this be as it may, God can teach me by his spirit to understand his word. Pray let me hear, or rather let me see the scripture that tolerates this worst of evils.
> *Virginian.* By all means. Have you a bible?
> *Minister.* Yes sir, I should be sorry if I had not, for I live on *"the sincere milk of the word."* 1 PET. ii 2. Here is the bible sir.
> *Virginian.* Well sir, will you please find it? for I seldom read the bible, but I think I have heard our minister quote a passage of scripture to prove that slavery was just. . . .

Bible in hand, the minister produces a long exegesis of slavery in the Old and New Testaments, establishing God himself as an advocate of those in bondage. "But does it not now appear," he concludes, "that these mighty pieces of artillery may be fairly wrested from your minister, and turned upon the hosts of the mammonites, with very good effect?" The hapless Virginian concedes the point.[49]

Obviously, Marrant and Coker were not the first people to grasp Christianity's vision of spiritual equality and direct it back against an unjust social order. Since the dawn of Christianity rulers and ruled have struggled to contain or to loose the gospel's egalitarian implications. Such arguments, however, had a particularly strong purchase in the decades after the American Revolution. This was an era, recall, of intense national self-scrutiny, when white Americans routinely invoked Providence and anxiously scrutinized events for any diminution of divine favor. In such a context, worries that slavery jeopardized the nation's providential standing and even invited divine retribution were never far below the surface. African American pamphleteers were not above exploiting such fears, especially in the aftermath of the Haitian Revolution. "If you love your children," Richard Allen and Absalom Jones wrote in 1794,

> if you love your country, if you love the God of love, clear your hands from slaves, burden not your children or country with them. Our hearts have been sorrowful for the late bloodshed of the oppressors, as well as the oppressed, both appear guilty of each other's blood, in the sight of him who said, he that sheddeth man's blood, by man shall his blood be shed.[50]

Assertions of blacks' humanity, grounded in common origin and shared endowment, also immediately begged the question of rights. The central premise of the Declaration of Independence, after all, was that rights inhered in people by virtue of their humanity; they were not concessions from power but endowments from nature's God. Rights, moreover, were universal. As one revolutionary leader put it: "*{R}ights* imply *equality* in the instances to which they belong and must be treated without respect to the dignity of the persons concerned. . . ." Thus in asserting their standing as members of the human community, black petitioners and pamphleteers implicitly and sometimes explicitly laid claim to the entire catalog of rights and privileges enumerated by American revolutionaries. In so doing, they broadened their critique from slavery alone to all forms of racial proscription in America, including the barriers erected against free people of color.[51]

Among early churchmen, it was Absalom Jones who worked the seam of Christianity and revolutionary liberalism most assiduously. In 1797 Jones authored what appears to be the first African American petition ever submitted to the United States Congress, written on behalf of four black men who had been kidnapped back into slavery. "If notwithstanding all that has been publicly avowed as essential principles respecting the extent of human right to freedom," he wrote, "we cannot claim the privilege of representation in your councils, yet we trust we may address you as fellow-men." He proceeded to describe the history of each petitioner, to show that they were indeed fellow men, possessed of "natural affections, social and domestic attachments and sensibilities." As such, their enslavement was wrong not only in the particular case but as a matter of general principle; it represented "a Governmental defect, if not a direct violation of the declared fundamental principles of the Constitution." Jones concluded by broadening his plea to include the plight of all people of color, slaves and freemen alike, who were treated with "a degrading partiality" and deprived of "that public justice and protection which is the great object of government."[52]

Two years later Jones submitted a second petition, this one addressed to the President and Congress and signed (or, more frequently, marked) by seventy black Philadelphians, including Richard Allen. In it, Jones sharpened his attack on American hypocrisy, highlighting not only kidnappings but discrimination in law, the barbarous interstate slave trade, and restrictions on private manumissions that prevented even liberally inclined masters from obeying the dictates of conscience. As in his first petition, Jones strove to be both proper and conciliatory: he conceded that some masters had been burdened with slaves by inheritance and, like many black leaders of his generation, stopped short of demanding immediate, unconditional abolition. On the fundamental question, however, he was unstinting. America's treatment of black people, slave and free, contradicted national principles; it transgressed the golden rule; it shocked "the feelings of Man." The conclusion was inescapable: "[I]f the Bill of Rights, or the declaration of Congress are of any validity, we beseech that as we are *men,* we may be admitted to partake of the Liberties and unalienable Rights therein held forth. . . ."[53]

In the petitions and pamphlets of independent church leaders such as Jones, Richard Allen, and Daniel Coker, one can see the emergence of a distinctive and enduring African American political tradition that fused environmentalism, Christian universalism, and revolutionary liberalism into a compelling critique of all forms of racial discrimination. When Martin Luther King, Jr., vouchsafed to America his dream during the 1963 March on Washington, he was employing a rhetorical form that was almost as old as the United States itself. Ultimately, however, rhetoric was not enough. White people's assessments of African Americans, as Richard Allen well knew, were shaped not only by abstract beliefs but by a thousand daily interactions—interactions that, in Allen's opinion, all too often confirmed white prejudices. The battle thus had to be joined not only at the level of argument but on the field of daily conduct, with African Americans bearing the responsibility of proving their fitness for freedom.

Inevitably, the onus fell on free people of color, who had access to education and religious instruction and thus the wherewithal to elevate themselves. In effect, free blacks provided a test case in the ongoing debate between racists and environmentalists. By leading unimpeachable lives, by exhibiting industry, intellect, and character, they could vindicate the race's potential and advance the cause of abolition. On the other hand, idleness, criminality, even a slovenly appearance confirmed white biases and undermined the entire race's struggle for justice and equality. Allen and Jones incessantly reminded their fellow freedmen and women of this responsibility, most notably in their address "To the People of Color." "[M]uch depends on us for the help of our colour more than many are aware," they wrote:

> [I]f we are lazy and idle, the enemies of freedom plead it as a cause why we ought not to be free, and say we are better in a state of servitude, and that giving us our liberty would be an injury to us, and by such conduct we strengthen the bands of oppression, and keep many in bondage who are more worthy than ourselves. . . .

"We intreat you," they concluded, "to consider the obligations we lay under, to help forward the cause of freedom."[54]

The myriad institutions that flourished in the shadow of Bethel Church reflected this analysis. Allen himself participated in at least a dozen benevolent and moral reform societies, from Philadelphia's first black Masonic temple to a Magdalene Society for wayward girls. Education was the most obvious vehicle of racial "elevation," and Bethel Church became a kind of community schoolhouse, hosting weekly classes and Sunday school, an "African Evening Free School" for adults, and a common school for "Children of African Descent." The logic behind such initiatives was perhaps best articulated by the founders of the Pennsylvania Augustine Society, who gathered in Bethel Church in 1818 to launch a campaign to build a local high school for blacks. "[Let us] use the best energies of our minds and of our hearts to procure for our children a more extensive and useful education," they resolved, for "upon their intellectual, moral and religious improvements depend the future elevation of their standing in the social, civil and ecclesiastical community." Put baldly, blacks could never expect to be accorded full equality until they proved they merited it.[55]

At their best, such initiatives and institutions fostered feelings of personal responsibility and mutual obligation, which would themselves become crucial resources in African Americans' ongoing struggle for justice. Yet there were hazards here. Most obvious, the politics of racial vindication placed enormous pressure on free people of color. In effect, Allen asked free blacks to bear the burden not only of race but of racism, to scrutinize their own actions through the eyes of an omnipresent and unforgiving white audience. Every act became magnified; every lapse confirmed white prejudice and betrayed the hopes of millions. If there are historical origins to what W. E. B. Du Bois called the "second sight" of the American Negro, that "sense of always looking at one's self through the eyes of others, of measuring one's soul by the tape of a world that looks on in amused contempt and pity," they are here.[56]

There were other problems. Even as it placed enormous pressure on free people of color, the strategy of racial vindication invested the ultimate power of judgment in whites. The whole notion was predicated on the belief that prejudice would wilt before reason, that whites would modify their views when presented with compelling counterevidence. Yet people, as Allen learned, can be "wilfully blind and extremely partial" in their perceptions, especially on questions of race. The lesson was brutally underlined in the fall of 1793, when an outbreak of yellow fever attacked Philadelphia, reducing the city to a charnel house. With medical facilities hopelessly overburdened, physician Benjamin Rush approached Allen and other black leaders and suggested that they take over the tasks of nursing the sick and burying the mounting piles of corpses. (Reports of previous yellow fever outbreaks in the West Indies had convinced Rush—incorrectly, in the event—that blacks were immune to the disease.) Sensing an opportunity to win white gratitude and respect, Allen quickly organized medical and burial details, even securing the release of dozens of convicts to assist in the campaign. Through the months of the fever, black men and women dispensed water, succored the sick, and buried the dead, usually without remuneration. Allen himself expended over four hundred pounds to buy caskets and hire gravediggers, less than half of which he ever recovered. As the city's physicians died or fled, Rush showed blacks how to mix and dispense medicines; "knowing we could both bleed"—the Shakespearean echo was apt, though apparently inadvertent—he instructed Allen on drawing blood from the stricken, which remained the standard treatment against the fever.[57]

Alas, any hopes that such selfless service would win white gratitude or provoke a reassessment of racial assumptions were quickly dashed. The first history of the epidemic, rushed into publication by Matthew Carey, a leader of Philadelphia's Irish community, scarcely mentioned African Americans, except to condemn them for "profiteering" and "plundering the dead." The pamphlet quickly went through three editions. Stunned, Allen and Absalom Jones replied with a narrative of their own, accompanied by a series of addresses and testimonials. In the narrative, they recounted the coming of the fever and the hasty flight of white citizens (including the eminent Mr. Carey); they offered detailed financial statements; they contrasted the courage and devotion of black men and women with the "atrocious cruelty" of poor whites, some of whom turned out members of their own families in a desperate effort to save themselves. Finally, they saluted the three hundred African Americans who, in the ultimate assertion of their common humanity, died in the plague. "Thus were our services extorted from us, *at the peril of our lives,* yet you accuse us of extorting *a little money from you,*" they railed, in a passage which came as close to genuine rage as anything either man ever wrote. The accompanying addresses, while more temperate, likewise betrayed the authors' anger and frustration at the sheer intransigence of white prejudice. Having "reduced us to the unhappy condition our colour is in," they asked, "[will you now] plead our incapacity for freedom?" The very question, however, acknowledged whites' power to do precisely that.[58]

Finally, racial vindication, with its assumptions about respectability and collective destiny, could all too easily slip into paternalism, with elite, "elevated" blacks setting themselves up as guardians of the manners and morals of the lower classes. This possibility was already evident in 1787 in the establishment of the Free African Society's Committee of Monitors; it was even more blatant in the yellow fever pamphlet, in which Allen and Jones invited whites to bring "any complaint about our colour" to their attention so they could "warn, rebuke, and exhort" the offenders. The class implications of all this were exhibited in particularly dramatic fashion in 1808, in the aftermath of a celebrated murder of an elderly white woman by a drunken black man. In the wake of the episode, Allen hastened to jail to take the condemned murderer's confession, which he published along with an "Address to the Public and People of Color." "See the tendency of dishonesty and lust, of drunkenness and stealing," he thundered. "See the tendency of midnight dances and frolics. While the lustful dance is delighting thee, forget not, that 'for all these things God will bring thee into judgment'." A few months later, he chartered a Committee for the Suppression of Vice and Immorality, aimed explicitly at curbing the perceived excesses of Philadelphia's black lower classes. Of all the institutions and initiatives with which Allen was involved, none more starkly revealed the bourgeois presuppositions of racial vindication, or the thin line that separated a strategy of collective liberation from a formula for class-based social control. Allen's assault on dancing was particularly poignant, for these "midnight revels" represented not only a rare and precious space for autonomous recreation among Philadelphia blacks but one of the most dramatic examples of African cultural persistence in early-nineteenth-century North America.[59]

We shall have occasion, in the chapters that follow, to revisit all these themes. Before we do so, it is worth entertaining one final question. Did racial vindication work? Obviously, black petitions and pamphlets did not produce immediate abolition, but did they move their intended audience? Did the conspicuous virtue and respectability of men such as Absalom Jones and Richard Allen induce white Americans to revise their conclusions about black character and capacity?

On the surface, the answer to all these questions is no. For people so patently reasonable, it must have been marvelous to see the sheer illogic of racial prejudice—to observe the various devices by which white Americans resisted the implications of their principles and the evidence of their eyes. Examples of

African American humanity and character were discounted or ignored, while isolated instances of black perfidy were seized and elaborated. The transparent distinction of a man like Daniel Coker was dismissed as the exception that proved the rule or, worse, as proof of the ameliorative influence of white blood. When petitions and pamphlets cut too close to the bone, racists denied black authorship. Thus, a conservative congressman assured his colleagues that the petitions from Philadelphia were actually the work of white abolitionists who, frustrated in their own campaign, had placed the documents "into the hands of these black *gentlemen*." (One South Carolina congressman, in a comment wonderfully revealing of postrevolutionary reaction, blamed the whole flap on "this new-fangled French philosophy of liberty and equality. . . .") Fortified by such reassurances, a majority of congressmen endorsed James Madison's conclusion that the petitions of black Philadelphians had "no claim on their attention."[60]

When such devices failed, racists found refuge in the concept of imitation, arguing that African Americans' ostensible achievements did not evince any innate capacity but were merely the product of a well-developed imitative faculty. Here was the cruelest turn of the screw. All the qualities that early church leaders strove to instill—the dignified dress, the sober demeanor, the careful language—ceased at a stroke to be emblems of blacks' capacity and common humanity and became instead badges of their permanent minority. Thomas Jefferson, who once invited readers to submit evidence of black distinction, became a past master of the tactic. Phillis Wheatley's poetry, he concluded, was devoid of originality and inspiration. Benjamin Banneker's celebrated almanac (even assuming he had written it) was derivative, while his accompanying letter revealed a mind "of very common stature." Eventually, Jefferson grew irritated with the whole business, accusing abolitionists of "puffing" every mediocre black person they could find.[61]

Once achievement had been confined within the concept of imitation, elite African Americans' self-conscious respectability became mere pretense, ripe for satire. It is no coincidence that so many of the pioneers of minstrelsy, the classic racist genre of the nineteenth century, hailed from Philadelphia or that they directed their spleen at middle-class, urban blacks. The oafish figures lampooned by Philadelphia artists such as Edward Clay and David Claypool Johnson were Christians, often Masons. They dressed in elaborate costumes and sported every imaginable affectation. Their dialogue, when not utterly nonsensical, was absurdly highfaluting. The very manner in which black physiognomy was rendered—the flattened noses, the prognathous jaws—reminded the audience that the whole enterprise was a charade, that these were not men but apes disporting themselves as gentlefolk. As these equations settled into place, the righteous appeals of black church leaders ceased to chafe white consciences and became mere insolence, if not outright provocations.

Institutions built as refuges from racism were denounced as wellsprings of discontent, even as the source of deteriorating race relations. "In the olden time," a nostalgic Philadelphia historian wrote in 1830,

> dressy blacks and dandy coloured beaux and belles, as we now see them issuing from their proper churches, were quite unknown. Their aspirings and little vanities have been growing since they got those separate churches. Once they submitted to the appelation of servants, blacks, or negroes, but now they require to be called coloured people, and among themselves, their common call of salutation is—gentlemen and ladies.

Thirty to forty years ago," the author concluded, "they were much humbler, more esteemed in their places, and more useful to themselves and others."[62]

From here it was but a short step to violence. In cities throughout Jacksonian America, white mobs periodically rampaged through black neighborhoods, targeting churches, schools, businesses, elite homes—all signs of black independence and prosperity. Black Philadelphians alone endured five such attacks in the twenty years between 1829 and 1849. In the 1834 riot, two black churches, one Methodist and one Presbyterian, were razed. A few years later, a white mob torched Pennsylvania Hall, headquarters of the local abolitionist movement. Bethel Church itself was visited in 1825 by a group of young ruffians who poured red pepper into the stove in the midst of a service. A stampede ensued, as worshippers struggled to escape the acrid, choking smoke. Four church members died in the melee.[63]

In light of all this, it is tempting to dismiss the whole political project of early African Methodism as flawed, to see Allen's and his comrades' determined campaign to vindicate themselves in white eyes as futile, even counterproductive. This conclusion, however, ought not be ventured too hastily. Even ignoring the problems of hindsight, it quickly leads us back to the same tired dichotomies in which anything short of a complete rejection of all things American appears hopelessly naive and tantamount to surrender. More concretely, such an analysis ignores the genuine achievements of the political tradition that the early independent church leaders did so much to build. Elite blacks played a vital (and still underappreciated) role in the history of American abolitionism, sustaining antislavery sentiment through the decades of postrevolutionary reaction. On five separate occasions between 1802 and 1814, the Pennsylvania legislature rejected bills that would have closed the state's borders to freedmen and women fleeing the South, thanks largely to the protests of Philadelphia's free black community. Black agitation also lay behind the enactment of personal liberty laws in half a dozen northern states, including Pennsylvania—laws that provided at least some refuge from the regime of the slavecatchers. Finally, as we shall see in a subsequent chapter, black Philadelphians played a pivotal role in the battle against the American

Colonization Society, exposing colonizationism for the proslavery vehicle that it was.[64]

Even that litany does not fully capture the significance of the political tradition embodied in the first African American independent churches. Ultimately, church leaders' protests were animated not just by opposition to slavery but by a profound belief in human equality, a belief they saw explictly endorsed in both the charters of American government and the Bible which Americans professed to honor. In pushing the logic of this position, in insisting that all forms of racial discrimination were both un-Christian and un-American, free people of color helped push American abolitionism beyond mere antislavery to the broader question of black citizenship. If, as Eric Foner has suggested, the signal feature of American Reconstruction was the direct participation of the former slaves themselves in the political struggle to determine their future, at least part of the credit belongs to independent churchmen like Richard Allen, Daniel Coker, and Absalom Jones, who sustained a vision of black equality and citizenship in the prison house of American slavery.[65]

2

Harnessing the Spirit

Over the course of the nineteenth century, the small seed of religious independence sown by Richard Allen and his comrades in Philadelphia blossomed into a great institution. By the time of Allen's death in 1831, the AME Church boasted congregations in every northern state and several southern ones, with a total membership of more than ten thousand. By the beginning of the Civil War, membership exceeded fifty thousand. In 1896, when the South African AME Church was established, African Methodists numbered nearly half a million, thanks to a vast infusion of southern freedpeople after the Civil War. As the twentieth century dawned, few disputed the assessment of the young W. E. B. Du Bois, whose epochal *The Souls of Black Folk* characterized the AME Church as "the greatest Negro organization in the world."[1]

Success, however, carried costs. The dramatic increase in scale wrought profound changes in African Methodism. Inevitably, the church became more structured and hierarchical, as leaders struggled to accommodate tens of thousands of new members. These changes, in turn, posed fundamental questions about the church's character and mission—questions that pitted leaders against laity, the learned against the "ignorant," the free-born against the freed. If we are to understand how the AME Church came to be in South Africa, and what happened to it after it arrived, we need first to understand these transformations and struggles.

From the outset, African Methodism was an expansive creed. Fired by prophecy, the leaders of the new church dispatched emissaries across the northern states, inviting other African American Christians to join them in their Bethel. Thousands heeded the call. In its first five years, the church absorbed congregations in New York state, New Jersey, eastern and central Pennsylvania, and all along the Maryland shore. Although adherents came from a variety of denominational traditions, the lion's share appear to have been defectors from the Methodist Episcopal Church, whose congregations hung, in the words of one AME founder, "like ripe fruit, only waiting to be plucked." In 1823 Allen sent an elder across the Alleghenies to begin organizing African American settlers in the Ohio Valley. By the early 1830s, when the Pittsburgh, or Western, Annual Conference was inaugurated, African Methodist elders plied a dozen circuits across western Pennsylvania and Ohio. The church also boasted a handful of congregations in Canada's growing black expatriate community.[2]

Just as the church plucked Methodist congregations, so did it rely on Methodist techniques. Itinerant ministers such as William Paul Quinn, David Smith, Jordan Early, and the felicitously named Moses Freeman traveled the countryside, preaching at camp meetings and revivals, organizing congregations and circuits, and moving on. Surely the most extraordinary of these early itinerants was Paul Quinn, the AME Church's celebrated "missionary to the West" and later its fourth bishop. Although there are several versions of Quinn's origins, he seems to have been an Indian (of the South Asian rather than Native American variety). The son of a Calcutta mahogany merchant, Quinn first encountered Christianity in the late eighteenth century, probably through some British Quaker merchants or sailors. Disowned by his Hindu parents, he embarked for Britain in the early nineteenth century, carrying letters of introduction to several prominent Quakers. With their help, he proceeded on to America, eventually ending up in Bucks County, Pennsylvania, working at a sawmill. In the arbitrary racial taxonomy of his new home, this upper-caste Indian was now a Negro.[3]

Soon after his arrival in the United States, Quinn converted to Methodism. He had already begun to preach when the AME Church was founded in 1816, and he quickly rallied to its banner. He attended the first AME-sponsored camp meeting in 1818, preaching alongside Richard Allen. A year later, he was ordained an AME deacon. Over the next quarter century, Quinn established himself as the church's most effective evangelist, organizing scores of congregations across Pennsylvania, Ohio, Indiana, and Illinois. In 1844 he was elevated to the bishopric.[4]

Evangelist David Smith, less renowned in church annals, was scarcely less remarkable. An illiterate former slave, Smith began preaching in his native Maryland at the age of twelve. He was one of the first men to join the AME connection and attended the inaugural General Conference in 1816. He remained a minister for the next sixty years. In contrast to Quinn, who prided himself on being the AME Church's first minister on horseback, Smith traveled on foot, sowing congregations from Connecticut in the north to New Orleans in the south. Like Quinn, he enjoyed his greatest success in Ohio—in cities like Cincinnati, as well as in smaller towns like Chillicothe, Yellow Springs, and Xenia, where communities of African Americans huddled in the shadow of the state's notorious Black Codes. Excluded from schools, poor houses, and even cemeteries, black Ohioans found in African Methodism a vital spiritual resource, as well as a firm foundation for collective organizing. Smith, the self-proclaimed "father of Benevolent Societies in the West," established not only churches but schools, burial societies, masonic temples, and all manner of mutual aid schemes. Long after he had gone to his reward, the state of Ohio remained an AME stronghold.[5]

Evangelization was not without its ambiguities, or its hazards. The "low class of whites," Smith later recalled, "were very much opposed to the prosperity of the colored people" and resented an independent, self-respecting institution like the AME Church. Paul Quinn survived a stab wound sustained when an Ohio camp meeting he had organized was attacked by a white mob. Opponents disrupted churches and schools, and AME itinerants endured harassment and arrest. To circumvent such hostility, many ministers became adept at cultivating the "better class" of whites. When entering a new town, Quinn presented authorities with letters from prominent Quakers in Britain and America, attesting to his good sense and moderation. Smith, who also traveled with a satchel full of testimonials from whites, capitalized on his status as a freemason, preaching in masonic halls when debarred from local churches. The masonic connection was even more critical to J. W. Early, another pioneering AME preacher. Arrested in Illinois and charged as a runaway, Early escaped almost certain reenslavement by flashing a masonic signal to the magistrate, who promptly ordered his release.[6]

The hazards of evangelization were even greater in the South, where a series of uprisings led by Christian slaves had left southern whites deeply suspicious of black independent churches. A few AME itinerants did cross the Mason-Dixon line, but for the most part the church's growth was confined to border regions like the Maryland shore and the western counties of Virginia, where the plantation system was not well developed and restrictions on black movement were unevenly enforced. The church also established a foothold in several southern and border cities, where there was relative social fluidity and considerable overlap between slave and free populations. Survival in such circumstances obviously entailed accommodation, and ministers labored unceasingly to reassure whites of their honorable intentions. David Smith, who organized the first AME congregations in Washington, D.C., took great pride in the trust reposed in him by whites: "The white people thought a great deal of me, because I did not say anything to their slaves about becoming free from their earthly masters, but impressed upon them the necessity of becoming free from the devil." Church leaders in New Orleans were sufficiently persuasive to receive a special exemption from the state legislature, though with the proviso that they confine their work to free blacks and meet only in the daytime. Authorities in St. Louis were so impressed with the moderation of local AME leaders—including future U.S. Senator Hiram Revels—that they contributed money for a new church building. Even the most skillful accommodation, however, could not obviate the deeper contradictions of an independent black church in a slave society. St. Louis authorities, for example, periodically closed the church they had endorsed, and routinely arrested AME ministers crossing into Missouri from free Illinois. Southern congregations also remained vulnerable to the ebb and flow of the southern economy, particularly with the spread of cotton cultivation into Mississippi and Alabama. In Baltimore alone, more than three hundred members fell from AME rolls in the 1820s when they were sold futher south.[7]

The contradictions of southern expansion were graphically illustrated by the church's meteoric rise and fall in Charleston, South Carolina. The roots of the Charleston church reached back to 1817, when several hundred black men and women, slave and free, withdrew from the local Methodist congregation. Having somehow heard of the AME Church, the seceders sent a request for affiliation to Bishop Allen. A year later, their leader, Morris Brown, traveled to Philadelphia to meet with Allen. In 1820 the AME General Conference formally welcomed the Charlestonians into connection. Despite constant white harassment and the periodic arrest of Brown and other leaders, the church grew. At the moment of connection, it counted fifteen hundred members, establishing South Carolina as the AME Church's second largest conference; over the next two years, membership reportedly doubled to nearly three thousand.[8]

At that very moment, however, Charleston was convulsed by the Denmark Vesey conspiracy. Whether the uprising conceived by Vesey was as massive as panicky whites believed, and whether the AME Church played as pivotal a role in the plot as critics charged, are matters of considerable debate. What is clear is that the church bore the brunt of white reaction. Whites alleged that Vesey, who undoubtedly was a member of the church, had preached sedition from the pulpit and used weekly class meetings to plan his bloody insurrection. Morris Brown was cast as his counselor. The official commission that looked into the conspiracy, while somewhat more temperate, accepted the analysis: "On investigation, it appeared that all concerned in that transaction, except one, had seceded from the regular Methodist Church in 1817, and formed a separate establishment in connection with the African Methodist Society in Philadelphia. . . ." In the days that followed, the church was banned and dozens of alleged conspirators were hanged. Morris Brown, secreted out of the state by a sympathetic white politician, survived to become the AME Church's second bishop, but it was another forty years before African Methodism returned to Charleston.[9]

Even with the collapse of the South Carolina conference, the AME Church's early expansion was little short of staggering. North of the Mason-Dixon line at least, the AME Church was well on its way to becoming the preeminent

black institution in America. Yet therein lay the rub. Institutions are different
from movements, with different dynamics and needs. As African Methodism
grew in size, it became more bureaucratic. Offices and boards multiplied to
oversee everything from publications to support for "worn-out" ministers.
Financial resources, such as they were, were consolidated in the hands of the
General Conference, control of which increasingly rested in the hands of an
educated, professional ministry. New ordinances appeared, specifying procedures for everything from laying a cornerstone to deposing a bishop. In
short, what had begun as a religious rebellion was evolving into an established
church. [10]

This process was obviously not unique to African Methodism. On the
contrary, the movement from "sect" to "church" constitutes one of the central
themes of Protestant history, as H. Richard Niebuhr long ago observed.
Virtually all the great Protestant churches began with small knots of saints,
rebelling against religious establishments they regarded as worldly, ritualistic,
and corrupt. Taking root in society's lower orders, most tended toward anti-
authoritarianism, eschewing theological training and other conventional trap-
pings of religious authority in favor of insight, enthusiasm, and an openness to
spirit. Such movements, however, had a way of becoming victims of their own
success, as Niebuhr argued. Insofar as they spoke to popular aspirations and
needs, they attracted large followings, necessitating new structures and hierarchies. The sharp critiques of social injustice became muffled as devotees
percolated up into the respectable classes. Enthusiasm waned, leaving liturgy
and ritual to provide what spontaneity and spirit no longer could. Sects became
churches. [11]

No movement better illustrates Niebuhr's model than Methodism, which
always possessed something of a divided institutional soul. On one hand, the
early Wesleyan movement was an extraordinarily decentralized affair, that
invested authority in an army of itinerant ministers and lay preachers, many
with little formal religious training. On the other hand, Methodism retained a
strong episcopal center that reigned supreme on questions of doctrine and
discipline, finance, and ministerial appointments. The stresses implicit in this
situation first became apparent in English Wesleyanism, which was wracked in
the early nineteenth century by a seemingly endless series of schisms and
disputes arraying ministers against congregations, the poor and the working
class against the "better classes," defenders of enthusiastic "low" Methodism
against those developing a taste for more cerebral fare. By mid-century, mainstream English Methodism had lost more than a million adherents and most of
its political edge. The process unfolded more slowly in the United States,
where the persistence of revivalism and the exigencies of western expansion
kept Methodists closer to their evangelical roots. Yet even in America, Methodism was becoming respectable, a process registered in the tone of it services,

in the rising educational standards of its clergy, and, most ominously, in the church's growing reticence on the subject of slavery.[12]

African Methodism was immune to some of these developments. Poverty alone ensured that the church's center remained relatively weak. Ministerial salaries, for example, came not from central church coffers but from local donations, a situation that ensured that ministers remained responsive to the concerns of their congregants. The problem of upwardly mobile members losing touch with their humble roots was obviously much reduced in an African American church, especially in the racial climate of the early nineteenth century. The very fact of being an independent organization of black people ensured that the church could never fully accommodate itself to the dominant order, which rested on the assumption that blacks were slavish and incapable of self-government. Paradoxically, however, AME leaders' very preoccupation with rebutting those stereotypes helped push the church down the road toward respectability. Eager to demonstrate African Americans' capacity to skeptical whites, a new generation of church leaders, coming to power after Richard Allen's death, launched a series of reforms to "improve" AME worship. In the process, they touched off a struggle for the very soul of African Methodism.

In the great mid-century battles between "liberty and order," the forces of order were invariably marshaled by Daniel Alexander Payne, the AME Church's sixth bishop. A tiny, puritanical man of mixed African, European, and Native American descent, Payne was born in 1811 in Charleston into a free and devoutly Methodist family. Following the death of his parents, he was apprenticed to his brother-in-law, a carpenter and leader of the city's free brown elite, a group conspicuous by its absence during the Vesey conspiracy. Called in his youth to become an "educator to thy people," Payne taught himself mathematics, physical science, and classical languages, mostly in the hours before sunrise, when he went to work. At eighteen he opened his first school, a small academy for black children that flourished until 1835, when an act of the South Carolina legislature forced it to close. Fleeing north, Payne made contact with leaders of the Methodist Episcopal Church, who offered him the education he coveted, but only on condition that he commit himself to the Liberian mission field. Declining, he enrolled instead at a Lutheran seminary in Gettysburg, Pennsylvania, where he pursued a degree in theology, a degree he ultimately failed to complete, having destroyed his eyesight in the pursuit.[13]

Payne settled in Philadelphia in about 1840, where he again opened a school. Not surprisingly, he encountered many leaders of the local AME Church, who urged him to join their connection. Initially, he demurred, out of disdain for the church's low educational standards. Like Richard Allen before him, however, he soon concluded that a viable black independent church represented one of the most powerful blows that people of color could strike against white racism, and thus against slavery. He joined the church in 1841 and was accepted into full ministerial connection two years later. For the next fifty years, he devoted himself to African Methodism, laboring as minister, first denominational historiographer, founder and president of the first AME college, and, from 1852 onward, bishop. No single individual, with the possible exception of Richard Allen himself, did more to shape the trajectory and tone of African Methodism.[14]

Payne's first target was education, which he believed his predecessors had shamefully neglected. African Methodism's founders, he declared in his pioneering denominational history, "gave no concern to founding schools of learning." The charge was patently unfair. Almost from the moment of their exit from Philadelphia's St. George's Church, AME leaders launched educational initiatives, including common schools, night schools for adults, and Sunday Bible-reading schools. By the time Payne joined the church, reports and resolutions on education were regular features of annual conferences. It was true, however, that these early efforts had accomplished little. Black schools everywhere were hamstrung by poverty and the paucity of trained teachers, as well as by the common practice of binding black children out as apprentices. Payne was also correct when he complained that many ministers were no better educated than their charges. While men like Allen and Daniel Coker possessed some schooling, the bulk of African Methodism's founders had no formal education. In Baltimore, ministers were forced to hire Allen's son to keep early conference minutes, since none of them could write. Conditions had improved somewhat since those days, but the majority of AME itinerants in the early 1840s remained illiterate. Some apparently made a virtue of their lack of education, beginning sermons with boasts of "never having rubbed their heads against college walls." For Payne there was simply no way such men could meet the spiritual needs of an advancing people.[15]

Payne's approach was straightforward: the first task was "to improve the ministry; the second to improve the people." In 1842, while still an unordained local preacher, he introduced resolutions at the Philadelphia and Baltimore annual conferences prescribing to all "deacons and elders, licensed preachers and exhorters, the diligent and indefatigable study of . . . English Grammar, Geography, Arithmetic, Rollin's Ancient History, Modern History, Ecclesiastical History, [and] Natural and Revealed Theology." A year later he made the case for an "intelligent ministry" in a series of "Epistles on the Education of the Ministry," published in the short-lived *AME Church Magazine*. At the 1844 AME General Conference, he outraged many of his elders by offering a resolution proposing a regular course of study for prospective ordinees. Educated ministers, he contended, would lift the tone of AME services, as well as "the mass of general ignorance" that weighted the black community. Equally important, they would demonstrate African American capacity, forcing the race's enemies "to acknowledge the doctrine of the unity of the human race, and our downtrodden people as an integral part of it." With characteristic bluntness, he challenged African Methodists to choose "between darkness and light, between ignorance and knowledge," between "baptized superstition" and Christian enlightenment.[16]

Payne's proposals landed, in his words, "as when a firebrand is cast into a magazine of powder." "Reckless slander," railed one critic; "infidels could do no more," said another. If the proposed theological curriculum were adopted, an opponent predicted, "discord and dissolution will necessary take place in the Church between the ignorant and intelligent portions of it." Gradually, however, Payne turned other church leaders to his point of view. His most important supporter was Bishop Morris Brown, who, despite his own lack of formal schooling, regarded education as vital to the progress of the race. As the 1840s progressed, prospective ordinees were subjected to increasingly rigorous examinations. (Payne proudly recalled sitting on the first ordination committee to turn candidates away.) Lay exhorters, who had always operated on the margins of the institutional church, were examined and licensed. In 1845 Payne established a short-lived AME seminary; a decade later, he helped found Wilberforce University, America's first black college. These grand initiatives were accompanied by a raft of smaller reforms aimed at creating a more settled and enlightened ministry. Reports on ministerial education became a regular feature of General Conferences. Magazines, book concerns, and literary and historical associations were organized. The Baltimore conference passed a resolution prohibiting ministers from keeping barbershops or oyster houses, a homely but important step on the road to a professional clergy.[17]

Even as he struggled to raise the educational qualifications of the ministry, Payne endeavored to lift the tone of AME services, which he found, to say the least, distasteful. In "those days," he recalled, "men and women who made the most and greatest noise, and the most extravagant gesticulations, were regarded as the greatest Christians." Ministers, dependent on congregations for support, perpetuated the "fanaticism," "stamping, beating the Bible, cutting odd capers" to get the poeple "shouting, jumping, and dancing." Again, Payne offered no quarter. In each of his ministerial posts, he set out "to modify the extravagances in worship" he encountered, including swaying, jumping, and other such "bad habits." "Singing and praying bands"—small cells of worshippers, often women, renowned for their late-night ecstatic services—came in for withering attack. These "midnight religionists" were "ignorant and deluded," Payne declared; their all-night sessions served only to sap their intellects, while rendering them utterly "unfit for labor."[18]

Rehearsing these struggles late in life, Payne obviously had incentive to exaggerate the degree of emotionalism in early AME services. Even so, there is reason to accept the substance of his characterization. The accounts we have from the early days of Bethel Church echo Payne's description. John Watson, a leader of Philadelphia's white Methodist establishment, offered a catalog of AME excesses in an 1819 pamphlet titled "Methodist Error," including "extravagant emotions," "bodily exercises," and a kind of incessant murmuring that threatened to drown out the preacher's words. Pavel Svin'in, a Russian traveler and artist who visited Philadelphia in 1814, left an even more vivid account of an AME service in which the preacher's description of damnation "loosed such a howl" that "the vaulted ceiling trembled." The congregants, Svin'in continued, "leapt and swayed in every direction and dashed themselves to the ground, pounding with hands and feet, gnashing their teeth, all to show that the evil spirit was departing from them."[19]

Lest such accounts be dismissed as mere products of white racism—which to a considerable extent they were—there is corroborating evidence from Richard Allen himself. For all his preoccupation with respectability and self-control, Allen remained a child of the revival, where spontaneity and emotional outburst were the order of the day; indeed, his expulsion from the Free African Society in 1789 flowed at least in part from his devotion to such practices. Allen explicitly addressed the issue in a "Spiritual Song," which he published in the early nineteenth century. The song was cast as a conversation between two Methodists, one of them deeply troubled by the emotionalism he had witnessed at that morning's service. "I fear such religion is only a dream," the skeptic begins. "The preachers were stamping, the people were jumping, / And screaming so loud that I neither could hear, / Either praying or preaching, such horrible screeching, / 'Twas truly offensive to all that were there. . . ." His companion, clearly speaking for Allen himself, defends the practices, adducing various scriptural warrants to show that such behaviors were enacted "by Christians of old." "When Peter was preaching, and boldly was teaching, / The way of salvation in Jesus' name, / The spirit descended and some were offended, / And said that the men they were fill'd with new wine. / I never yet doubted that some of them shouted, / While others lay prostrate by power struck down. . . ." He proceeds to warn his doubting friend of the snares of public opinion, even of reason itself. The verse ends with the two companions praying together, hearts glowing, love flowing. Whatever its poetical merits, the song lends credence to contemporary descriptions of Bethel Church as a place where the Spirit held sway.[20]

In fairness to Payne, he was not strictly averse to religious emotion. Like all good Methodists, he believed that conversion began with the conviction of the sinner, a process that required the preacher to "re-echo the thunders of Sinai." He himself once "spoke so long and so loud" that he ruptured his vocal chords, leaving him speechless for almost a year. For Payne, however, conviction was only the first step in a longer morphology of conversion. Having indicted sinners, the preacher needed to cultivate them, to discipline their faith and illuminate their understanding. To short-circuit that process, to reduce religion to an endless round of emotional releases, accomplished nothing. It brought the sinner no nearer redemption, while leaving African Americans fit objects of white ridicule.[21]

The issue of emotionalism intersected with the question of religious music. Like the Psalmist, Payne saw music, both vocal and instrumental, as man's most precious medium for venerating God. Characteristically, however, he insisted that music engage both "the spirit and the understanding." African Americans' beloved "corn-field ditties" might produce "the wildest excitement amongst the thoughtless masses," he wrote, but they had no place in the repertoire of enlightened Christians. The same was true of congregations' "self-made fugue tunes," which, according to Payne, were invariably "transcripts of low thoughts, ignorance, and superstition." One of his first priorities as a minister was to replace the music congregations loved with more edifying fare.[22]

For historians, Payne's assault on music is particularly significant, for it struck directly at one of the most distinctive and vital features of early African American Christianity. Significantly, it was Richard Allen who produced black America's first hymnal, *A Collection of Hymns and Spiritual Songs from Various Authors,* which he published in 1801 for use in Bethel Church. Like most contemporary compilations, Allen's collection relied heavily on the work of composers such as Charles Wesley and Isaac Watt, whose hymns were standard fare for Methodists in England and the United States. The balance of the collection, however, came not from mainstream churches but from the evangelical revivals and camp meetings that Allen frequented and had never before been published. Often spontaneously created and passed down by word of mouth, these "spiritual songs" were ideally suited to the lowly and illiterate. The images were vivid, the sentiments straightforward; many were cast in the first person, providing a basis for intense subjective experience. Most of the songs circulated without music—Allen's hymnal included no musical notation—enabling congregations to adapt them to different tunes and to mix and match choruses and verses. One white observer at a camp meeting was surprised to hear black revivalists singing religious songs in the "husking-frolic method" of southern slaves; another, visiting Bethel Church, was appalled to hear a hymn sung to "Fol de Rol," a popular tune of the day.[23]

If Bethel Church is anything to judge by, early AME congregations brought the performance of these spiritual songs to a high art. Singing often began with a deacon or assistant "lining out" verses, a familiar enough practice in evangelical churches but one that articulated uncannily well with African practices of call and response. Lining out often overlapped with the so-called "old way," in which a line from a psalm or hymn was repeated by the congregation in a kind of semichant and then gradually embroidered. This practice too had a distinguished Protestant pedigree in the custom of the responsorial psalm, while resonating with African traditions of polyphony. "At the end of every psalm," Pavel Svin'in reported, the entire congregation, men and women alike, sang verses in a loud, shrill monotone. This lasted about half an hour. When the preacher ceased reading, all turned toward the door, fell on their knees, bowed their heads to the ground and set up an agonizing, heart-rending moaning. Afterwards, the minister resumed the reading of the psalter and when he had finished sat down on a chair; then all rose and began chanting psalms in chorus, the men and women alternating, a procedure which lasted some twenty minutes.

Despite its patronizing tone, Svin'in's account conveys both the majesty and the unmistakeable Africanity of early African Methodist music. [24]

Even before Payne's ordination, African Methodist church leaders had begun to move toward a more orthodox hymnody. In 1818 Richard Allen and Daniel Coker published an official church hymnal, befitting African Methodists' new standing as "a distinct and separate body of people." Compared to the pocket-sized 1801 collection, the new hymnal was a substantial affair, with more than 300 selections, almost 250 of which were drawn from standard Methodist hymnals. Only fifteen of the spiritual songs that had distinguished Allen's first collection remained. By the publication of the next edition, in 1837, the AME hymnal was virtually indistinguishable from those used in white denominations. Two years later a black Methodist church in New York City hosted a performance of Handel's *Messiah,* under the direction of Morris Brown, Jr., an event that Payne later hailed as a landmark in the development of African American sacred music. [25]

With Payne's entrance, the battle over music was joined in earnest. As a lay preacher and later minister at Bethel, he helped organize the church's first "scientifically trained" choir, beginning a trend that soon spread to other AME congregations. A few years later he successfully introduced instrumental music into his Baltimore congregation, rebutting critics with a raft of references from Scripture. (The only biblical passage quoted in full in Payne's autobiography is Psalms 150, the last of David's hymns of praise: *"Praise ye the Lord . . . Praise him with the sound of the trumpet: / Praise him with psaltery and harp. / Praise him with the timbrel and dance: / Praise him with stringed instruments and organs... Let everything that hath breath praise the Lord."* Ever vigilant, Payne added a footnote, explaining that the word *dance* referred not to "our vulgar dance" but to an instrument of biblical times.) To ensure a supply of refined fare, Payne organized sacred concerts and hymn-writing competitions. He himself composed several hymns, all a universe removed from the rude and simple spiritual songs that had once distinguished AME worship. [26]

African Methodist lay people did not simply acquiesce to these attempts to reform their religious lives. On the contrary, antebellum reformers' efforts ignited bitter conflicts within congregations. According to Payne, many church members, especially old and ill-educated women, refused to accept "note singing," accusing him of "having brought the devil into the church." The introduction of a regular choir at Bethel in 1841 provoked a bitter schism that carried hundreds of members out of the AME connection. In many cities and towns, congregations exploited ministers' financial dependence, "starving out" those associated with the reforms. Payne himself was rejected by a Baltimore congregation in 1850. The people, he reported, found no fault with his character but alleged that he was "too proud to take tea with them," that he "kept too fine a carpet" and refused to let them sing their beloved "ditties." One "infuriated" woman, upset by the reforms as well as by Payne's role in a dispute over church title, attacked the tiny minister with a club. Payne escaped unscathed, but one of his associates was properly concussed.[27]

Despite such resistance, Payne's reforms were gradually registered on the institutional face of African Methodism. While an AME seminary remained decades in the future, literacy was enshrined as a prerequisite for ordination. Trained choirs became an accepted feature of African Methodist worship, and in time a point of great congregational pride. Most important, prevailing modes of worship, while certainly more resilient than Payne might have wished, changed markedly. Certain characteristic features of African American Christianity—*extempore* preaching, the call and response between preacher and congregation—endured, but others—dancing, trances, spirit possession—were driven to the margins and eventually out of African Methodism. Many of these battles would be rejoined after the Civil War, as the church struggled to assimilate hundreds of thousands of former slaves, but by that time AME leaders were virtually unanimous in their support of an educated ministry and in the importance they attached to "order and decorum" in worship. In short, African Methodism was well down the road from sect to church.

There is a certain aptness in Payne's being assaulted by a woman, for the reforms he championed—the campaigns to improve the ministry, music, and modes of worship—all struck directly at African Methodist women. In the nineteenth century, as in the twentieth, black women bore a distinct burden of oppression and exhibited a special affinity for enthusiastic, evangelical Christianity. Often isolated in white people's backyards and kitchens, black women found solace in the warmth and communalism of AME love feasts and revivals; assailed by poverty and sexual depredation, they found in African Methodism's ideals of dignity and self-possession a basis for organizing and revaluing themselves. While church membership statistics are not broken down by sex, there is little doubt that women represented the majority of early African Methodists, as well as the most enthusiastic purveyors of the "extravagances" and "superstitions" Payne decried. When the world they had created was threatened, women resisted.

By the lights of most male church leaders, the appropriate outlet for female religiosity lay in organizations like the "Daughters of Conference" and local "Mothers' Associations." The Daughters' origins reached back to the very first AME General Conference, when Sarah Allen, Richard Allen's wife, and other

churchwomen took it upon themselves to mend the clothes of attending ministers. By 1827 the organization had received episcopal sanction, and branches
spread throughout the church. As their name and origins suggest, the Daughters of Conference operated within prevailing assumptions about women's
nature and role, enshrined in the developing ideology of domesticity: they
provided hospitality at church conferences, raised money for needy ministers,
visited the sick, and dispensed "motherly counsel." Similar assumptions governed the Mothers' Association movement, launched by Daniel Payne shortly
after he joined the AME ministry. Organized at the congregational rather than
the conference level, Mothers concentrated on "home training," especially on
instilling virtues of purity and chastity in the race's young women. Long before
the emergence of black domesticity advocates such as Anna Julia Cooper and
Fanny Jackson Coppin, Bishop Payne portrayed women as the moral conserva-
tors of the race, and family life as the engine of racial progress. "What the
families of a race are the race will be, nothing more, nothing less," he declared. [28]

Women, however, had their own ideas about their nature and obligations,
as well as their own preferred religious outlets. In terms of the enthusiasm they
awakened among their members, institutions such as the Daughters and the
Mothers were dwarfed by the so-called "singing and praying bands." These
small cells of worshippers, ubiquitous in early African Methodism, purveyed
an enthusiastic, pentecostal Christianity, quite out of keeping with the deco-
rous and cerebral mode of worship promoted by Payne. Bands prayed and sang
late into the night, experiencing trances, the gift of tongues, and other spiritual irruptions. While open to all, bands became the special province of
women, many of whom, under spur of the Spirit, undertook the role of
preacher. [29]

Theologically, the praying bands were organized around the idea of sanctification, a doctrine with a long and problematic history in evangelical Protestantism. According to proponents, the infusion of divine grace at the moment
of awakening—what Christians called justification—was not the culmination
of conversion but rather a preparation for a more thoroughgoing transformation, called sanctification. A "second, distinct work of the Holy Ghost,"
sanctification destroyed "the very root of sin that is in the heart," enabling the
saint to live in harmony with God's will. Warrant for the doctrine was found
primarily in the New Testament, especially in the story of the first Pentecost in
Acts. When proponents did turn to the Old Testament, they looked less to
the Pentateuch, with its tales of patriarchs and chosen people, than to the
prophets, those ragged figures in the desert who pursued their callings in the
face of popular derision. Like their biblical mentors, sanctified Christians
experienced visions; they grappled with Satan; they were visited by dreams and
voices, which bade them pray, travel, preach. [30]

It takes little imagination to see the appeal of sanctification—or Holiness, as it was also known—to women, the poor, the ill-educated, and all those "weaker vessels" cut off from conventional sources of religious authority and status. It is even easier to appreciate the anxiety the doctrine awakened in Protestant establishments, which saw in adherents' unswerving devotion to their "ethereal attendant" the awful specter of antinomianism. The result, in mainstream Protestantism, was a distinct movement away from sanctification, paralleling each denomination's evolution from sect to church. John Wesley, for example, endorsed the idea of a "second blessing," but by the early nineteenth century the doctrine was primarily the property of Free Methodists and other evangelical splinter groups. Though mainstream Methodists continued to acknowledge the possibility of sanctification, they usually portrayed it as a kind of deathbed transformation, reserved for the aged or very ill.[31]

Within African Methodism, as within English Methodism before it, the debate over sanctification came to center on the activities of a small cadre of female Holiness preachers, the most famous of whom was Jarena Lee. A free born domestic servant, Lee joined Philadelphia's Bethel Church in 1804 and was awakened during a sermon by Richard Allen. Yet she found no consolation, only fleeting moments of happiness followed by long stretches of "awful apprehension." Learning of the doctrine of sanctification from a passing black evangelist, she became convinced that her conversion had been incomplete. Eventually she received the second blessing and, later, the call to preach. Despite ill health and the rebukes of her coreligionists—including her AME minister husband—she answered the call. Over the next forty years, she preached thousands of sermons all across the northern United States, awakening innumerable sinners, black and white alike.[32]

Rebecca Cox Jackson, another celebrated black Holiness preacher, also emerged from Philadelphia's Bethel Church. Born in 1795 and orphaned in her youth, Jackson grew up in the home of her older brother, Joseph Cox, one of Bethel's founders and trustees. She was already a mature women in the early 1830s, when she experienced justification and, later, sanctification. Shortly thereafter, she began convening "covenant meetings" with other professors of Holiness. Her penchant for dreams and visions, and her advocacy of various forms of bodily mortification—including celibacy—quickly brought her into conflict with AME Church leaders, including her brother, who believed she was "agoing crazy." In 1837 Jackson broke with both family and church, left Philadelphia, and entered a community of Shakers.[33]

A handful of other women within and on the margins of the AME Church followed the path blazed by these women. Julia Foote, a domestic servant and African Methodist from Schenectady, New York, was awakened in the late 1830s and sanctified a year and a half later. She spent the next sixty years preaching Holiness, sometimes traveling under AME auspices, sometimes independently, sometimes under the AME Zion Church, in which she was eventually ordained. Zilpha Elaw, a Philadelphian and sometime preaching companion of Jarena Lee, traveled even further afield, pursuing her call in the southern states, where she risked arrest and enslavement, and later in England. Amanda Smith, a generation younger than Elaw and Foote, traveled furthest of all, carrying the doctrine of Holiness from her home in Philadelphia to Britain, India, and Africa.[34]

All these women left spiritual autobiographies, providing insight into their motives and beliefs, as well as into the broader world of African American Christianity. Significantly, none of them evinced interest in organized feminism, which they regarded as one more form of worldliness. Insofar as they felt compelled to justify their actions, they did so by professing their helplessness in the face of a divine command to preach. Yet in the very act of answering the call, these female prophets challenged nineteenth-century America's most fundamental assumptions about femininity and social order. Within the prevailing ideology of domesticity, women were custodians of the home, whose public identities were subsumed by those of their husbands. These women spoke in public and scandalized contemporaries by traveling without male companions. All struggled against unsanctified husbands who feared the notoriety and ridicule that their wives' activities attracted. Jackson alone advocated celibacy, but all portrayed marriage as an obstacle to their calling. Jarena Lee and Amanda Smith both found refuge in widowhood. (Smith, convinced that her husband had become an impediment to her spiritual growth, actually prayed for him to leave.) Julia Foote justified neglecting her spouse with a passage from Isaiah: *"For thy Maker is thine husband."* Zilpha Elaw went so far as to warn her "dear unmarried sisters in Christ" of the dangers of being "yoked" to an unsanctified man. Better, she wrote, "if a millstone were hung about your necks, and you were drowned in the depths of the sea. . . ."[35]

Even more ominous was the challenge these women posed to the idea of instinctual motherhood, upon which the whole ideology of domesticity hinged. Jarena Lee left a sickly child in the hands of relatives in order to go and preach; with the help of the Spirit, she reported, "not a thought of my little son came into my mind" during the entire absence. Smith regularly placed the Spirit's demands before those of her children, once even spending her family's last pennies on biblical tracts, which she then distributed for free. Elaw left her child for more than two years to go and preach. Indeed, one of the turning points in her life came during a severe illness, as she faced the prospect of being separated from her daugher. She began to weep but then realized that such behavior "did not comport with an absolute submission to the will of God; and evinced the inordinate strength and force of those ties by which I was still bound to this earth. I then, in prayer, pledged myself afresh to God, begging that he would effectually wean me from all the excesses of nature's ties." By the lights of most nineteenth-century Americans, such a prayer was tantamount to a renunciation of womanhood itself.[36]

As much as any single challenge, Holiness forced antebellum churchmen to weigh their evangelical inheritance against the needs of a developing institution. On one hand, it was difficult to find fault with the women's doctrine. The idea of a second blessing was firmly rooted in the writings of John Wesley, not to mention the New Testament. For every biblical verse church leaders could cite, women such as Lee and Foote could advance two of their own. ("Did not Mary *first* preach the risen Saviour?" asked Lee.) Atop it all, it was difficult for AME Church leaders, having so recently rebelled against religious persecution themselves, to turn on dissenters in their own midst. Indeed, the arguments advanced by female Holiness preachers—that God was *"no respecter of persons"* [Acts 10:34], that He often chose *"the weak things of the world to confound the mighty"* [1Cor. 1:27]—were the very ones that African Methodism's founders had directed against white Methodists.[37]

On the other hand, there was no denying the danger these women posed to authority and "good order" within the church. When the dictates of the Spirit were at stake, all were utterly unamenable to discipline, whether in the shape of popular opinion, ministerial edict, or the "by-laws of church government." "Sisters," Julia Foote exhorted, "[do] not let what men may say or do, keep you from doing the will of the Lord and using the gifts you have for the good of others." All had little respect for education, which, untempered by spiritual insight, amounted to little more than "licentious intellectuality." Zilpha Elaw went so far as to argue that education impeded inspiration; the "wise and learned," she observed in her autobiography, rarely experienced "the heavenly discipline of God's Holy Spirit." Jarena Lee agreed. Just as "the blind have the sense of hearing in a manner much more acute than those who can see," so did the ill educated seem to have special insight into the "operations of the Holy Spirit."[38]

Needless to say, these women did not share AME Church leaders' growing preoccupation with "order and decorum" in worship. "Order in divine worship and in the house of God is graceful and appropriate," Elaw conceded,

> but the life and power of religion is not identified with, nor in proportion to, the polish of the minister, the respectability of the congregation, or the regularity and method of its services: the most abrupt and extraordinary vicissitudes of weather are frequently productive of more benefit than the nicest graduated scale of temperature. . . .

Amanda Smith made a similar point. While prepared to worship anywhere, with anyone, Smith harbored a special love for the AME Church, finding within it a feeling of belonging and acceptance that she found nowhere else. (Even the most enthusiastic of white evangelicals tended to look askance at black women, she noted, as if uncertain whether their outbursts bespoke real inspiration or superstition and drunkeness.) Yet for all her devotion to African Methodism, Smith was troubled by the changes she saw overtaking the church—by the rise of "formalism" and the growing preponderance of "dressed-up" people who preferred the "tinsel regalia" of "high-toned" society to the simplicity and fervor of old-time religion. She eventually took to worshipping in a plain Quaker bonnet and shawl, as a judgment against her fellows. "We colored people did not use to get up off our knees quick like white folks," she observed acidly in her autobiography; "when we went down on our knees to get something, we generally got it before we got up. But we are a very imitative people, so I find we have begun to imitate white people, even in that. Lord help us."[39]

There was more at stake here than decorum or ministerial prerogative. These women's indifference—indeed, hostility—to all marks of worldly distinction posed a fundamental challenge to the whole political project of African Methodism. Education, financial independence, all the marks of preferment and progress so assiduously cultivated by church leaders, were mere human distinctions, vanities, that were as nothing beside the election of the Spirit. While AME leaders spoke of elevating and vindicating the race, women such as Zilpha Elaw enjoined their followers to "abhor the pride of respectability, for that which is highly esteemed among men, is an abomination in the sight of God." Even literacy was a dubious value, for while it provided access to the revealed Word, it remained a human instrument, full of "double meaning . . . impurity, bombast, and other defects." Such a medium was but a pale shadow of the "pure" and "heavenly" tongue spoken by inspirited saints.[40]

AME Church leaders' changing attitude toward female preachers provides a useful index of the church's evolution from sect to church. The issue first arose in 1803, when Dorothy Ripley, an English Holiness preacher, approached Richard Allen with a request to preach at Bethel. After meeting with Bethel's trustees, Allen politely but firmly rebuffed her: female preachers, he wrote, were "diametrically opposed to the letter and spirit of the rules of [our] society in particular, and the discipline in general of the Methodist Episcopalian Church." Significantly, however, Allen never questioned the legitimacy of Ripley's call, and he later shared the pulpit with her at the first AME camp meeting. Within the church itself, however, the best he could do was offer a compromise, welcoming Ripley as an unlicensed exhorter, a position that allowed her to lead prayers and to expound whatever scriptural lesson the minister had chosen. The actual right to preach—to select and interpret a biblical text—remained a male prerogative.[41]

When Jarena Lee reported her call a few years later, Allen again had recourse to Methodist discipline, which "knew nothing at all" about women preachers. ("O how careful ought we to be, lest through our by-laws of church government and discipline, we bring into disrepute even the word of life," Lee wrote in her spiritual autobiography.) For several years Lee contented herself with occasional exhorting at the small New Jersey congregation pastored by her husband. After his death, she returned to Philadelphia and began holding prayer meetings in her home. In 1819, spurred by "an altogether supernatural impulse," she interrupted a minister at Bethel Church to announce that she, like Jonah, the subject of the lesson, had "delayed to go at the bidding of the Lord." Bishop Allen, in the audience, stood up, but instead of rebuking her he announced his conviction that Lee "was called to that work, as any of the preachers present." A short time later Lee commenced her career as an itinerant lay exhorter, with the bishop's endorsement. Even then, however, he refused to confer on her a formal license to preach.[42]

Such ambivalence never entirely evaporated. Morris Brown and Paul Quinn, Allen's episcopal successors, upheld the principle of a male ministry and refused to license women as lay preachers, but both expressed admiration for female Holiness preachers' spiritual gifts. Bishop Brown even attended one of Rebecca Cox Jackson's covenant meetings after hearing charges that she was "aholding class meetings and aleading the men." Much to the chagrin of her opponents, he declared, "If ever the Holy Ghost was in any place, it was in that meeting." Right up to the Civil War and beyond, women such as Smith and Elaw continued to encounter sympathetic AME ministers, who preached sanctification or at least welcomed them to do so. There is no mistaking, however, the turning of the tide. Even before Daniel Payne's arrival, female preachers encountered growing opposition and ridicule in the church, often orchestrated by younger, more educated ministers, many of whom "fought holiness with more zeal and vigor than they did sin." A quarterly meeting of the Philadelphia Conference in the late 1830s denounced Rebecca Cox Jackson as a heretic. Lee, returning to Philadelphia in 1839, found herself marginalized. "I remained in the city about three months," she reported, "and received appointments in our churches on Thursday nights, although in years past I always had them at any time, Sunday afternoons not excepted." Five years later, when Lee approached the AME Book Concern with plans to publish an expanded edition of her spiritual autobiography—the first edition had been published independently in 1836—she was flatly rejected. The manuscript, its reviewers reported, was theologically suspect and "written in such a manner that it is impossible to decipher much of the meaning contained in it."[43]

The conflict came to a head in a series of conference meetings in the 1840s and '50s. In 1844, a group of women calling themselves the Daughters of Zion—not, significantly, the Daughters of Conference—petitioned the General Conference for recognition of their priestly calling. The all-male body rejected the plea. The 1848 General Conference was marginally more conciliatory: while once again refusing to license women as ministers or even as lay preachers, it did make vague provision for recognizing traveling female exhorters. Even that concession was too much for some delegates. A substantial minority, led by Daniel Payne, entered a "solemn protest" against this "Anti-Scriptural, anti-domestic and revolutionary" idea, an idea calculated to "introduce *distraction* into Annual Conferences, the Quarterly Conference, and throughout the several States and circuits." While women continued to press the issue, the outcome was no longer in doubt. A motion to license women at the 1852 General Conference was so soundly defeated that proponents declined to renew the issue. When the idea was next mooted, at the 1864 Conference, delegates refused even to discuss it.[44]

Probably the most striking thing about this struggle is the ease with which women's opponents appropriated the dominant culture's domestic ideology—an ideology whose norms and prescriptions the vast majority of African Americans could not, in the circumstances of their lives, hope to uphold. Licensing women, Payne's 1848 letter of protest argued, threatened the "sacred relationships which women bear to their husbands and children, by sending them forth as itinerant preachers, wandering from place to place, to the utter neglect of their household duties and obligations. . . ." The *Christian Recorder*, a Philadelphia-based church newspaper launched in 1856, agreed, adding that women were constitutionally ill equipped for strenuous mental or physical labor; when God needed a leader, he chose a Noah, "not his wife." An article titled "Women: Her True Sphere," published in Payne's short-lived *Repository of Religion and Literature*, made a similar argument. Women, the author wrote, lacked the "sublime qualities" that entitled men to "absolute rule." While naturally religious, women would make their contributions in the home, where their "refining influence" and grace in "the art of pleasing" gave them a special role in the rearing of children. When women pushed beyond the home, "into the empire which belongs exclusively to man," they invariably "lost all the gentle and attractive grace of their sex."[45]

In these invocations of domesticity, we are once again brought face-to-face with the central paradox of African Methodism, with that strange force that drew these proud and independent separatists back to the world from which they had fled. Even as they turned away from a hostile and hypocritical white world, church leaders were forever glancing back over their shoulders, knowing all too well that the "enemies of the race" were watching, eager for any sign of deviation or declension. The problem was particularly acute on a matter like domesticity. Like all hegemonic ideologies, domesticity's genius lay in its self-effacement, its capacity to make its prescriptions appear inevitable, normal—not prescriptions at all, but mere reflections of nature. The costs of transgression were enormous, especially for African Americans. The spectacle of women traveling alone, neglecting children, and preaching and ministering to men would inevitably be seized upon by racists and offered as proof of blacks' deficiency, even in the most intimate and "natural" of human pursuits.

Lurking beneath these anxieties about black womanhood was a deeper and even more alarming problem—the problem of black manhood. Manhood, as David Leverenz has shown, emerged in the middle decades of the nineteenth century as one of the central preoccupations of American culture. As capitalist transformation eroded older notions of masculinity, grounded in leisure or republican independence, a new conception began to crystallize, defining manhood in terms of individual enterprise, competitive success, power over others. Unlike previous conceptions of manhood, this status was theoretically open to all, which only ensured that those who possessed it remained perpetually insecure and subject to those gnawing fears of humiliation that were such a hallmark of mid-century American letters. Such anxieties were by no means confined to white men, as Leverenz's close reading of Frederick Douglass's successive autobiographies shows. If anything, masculine insecurity was amplified among blacks, who bore in slavery the ultimate stigma of violated manhood. African Americans, to paraphrase Douglass's famous chiasmus, had been made slaves; the problem was to make them men.[46]

The upshot of all this was a virtual obsession with racial manhood, beginning in the 1840s and '50s and peaking in the decades after the Civil War, as African Americans negotiated the perilous transition from slavery to freedom. Nowhere was this concern more dramatically recorded than in the writings of African Methodist leaders, many of whom came to reinterpret the whole history and meaning of their movement in its light. Long portrayed as an institution to uplift and vindicate the race, the AME Church now became specifically an agency to express and develop black manhood. The AME Church, Daniel Payne declared in his denominational history, was begun to help blacks "feel and recognize our individuality and our heaven-created manhood." Bishop Wesley Gaines, himself a former slave, agreed: the primary task of the church, and of the race as a whole, was to rehabilitate "manhood"— "that individuality and aspiration of spirit, which are the first conditions of self-respecting character, either in an individual or in a race." A dozen other denominational histories and memoirs echoed the contention. Surely the most elaborate development of the theme came in Benjamin Tanner's *Apology for African Methodism*, published in 1867. Rehearsing the opposition that Allen and his fellows encountered, the editor and future bishop declared:

> The great crime committed by the Founders of the African Methodist Episcopal Church was that they dared to organize a Church of men, men to think for themselves, men to talk for themselves, men to act for themselves: A Church of men who support from their own substance, however scanty, the ministration of the Word which they receive; men who spurn to have their churches built for them . . . men who prefer to live by the sweat of their own brow and be free.

Such sentiments obviously did not bode well for female Holiness preachers. Within this framework, female preaching was more than an inappropriate use of women's natural religiosity: it represented a threat to the entire African Methodist project. Black women's struggle for equality, not for the last time, would be sacrificed on the altar of racial manhood.[47]

All this casts a different light on the establishment of new offices for African Methodist women in the late nineteenth century, offices that have been held up by scholars as evidence of women's triumphant self-assertion. The 1884 AME General Conference's decision to grant women the right to hold exhorters' licenses, for example, came forty years after the Daughters of Zion first broached the issue. Even then, the Conference passed an accompanying resolution, ensuring that women so licensed would remain subordinate to local ministers and would never hold a pastoral charge. (When maverick bishop Henry Turner ordained a woman deacon in 1885, he was reprimanded by his fellow bishops, who immediately set the appointment aside.) The handful of other institutional innovations of the late nineteenth century were likewise designed to keep women firmly in their place. In 1868, for example, the General Conference established the office of local stewardess, the first official position conceded to women. Unlike stewards, however, stewardesses exercised "no legislative or judicial discretion"; they were "merely assistants," deputed to "look after the females of the church." Power to nominate and confirm them was vested in local ministers and boards of stewards, who also held the right of dismissal.[48]

The office of deaconess, established at the very end of the century, was similarly circumscribed. The official AME Deaconess Manual, written by Bishop Abraham Grant, began by defining "woman" as "pre-eminently the helper of man" and thus "the mother of all social, educational, and religious efforts of man." The office's responsibilities flowed from these assumptions. In addition to assisting local ministers, deaconesses visited the sick and distressed. They rescued fallen women and oversaw the training of girls. Grant especially admonished deaconesses not to allow their work to compete with their wifely duties: "Women, if married, should so know how to demean themselves as not to prejudice the work in the minds of their husbands. A woman who has not the confidence of her husband can do but little good in church work." The gulf between such an office and the priestly office claimed by women such as Jarena Lee and Zilpha Elaw could scarcely have been greater.[49]

None of this is meant to deny African Methodist women's agency or reduce them to mere victims of male oppression. Nor is it to deny the significant powers that women continued to exercise within the church, especially in matters financial. African missions, for example, could not have existed without the agency of churchwomen, as we shall see in a subsequent chapter. Concepts like agency and power, however, lose all meaning when divorced from structural constraint or from the specific historical contexts in which they operate. In the case of the AME Church, as in most Christian communities, the power that mattered most was the power to preach—to speak and to expound the Word of God for the benefit of sinners. In claiming that right, and in grounding their claim in divine election, women such as Lee and Elaw posed a fundamental challenge to the structure and operation of African Methodism. By the 1860s and '70s, that challenge had been effectively contained. Like all

Protestants, AME women would continue to enjoy independent access to the Bible, and some would hear the call of the Spirit. A few would have their spiritual gifts recognized by coreligionists, male and female. But within the framework of the institution, women's right to preach was strictly limited, and always contingent on men. Women intent on pursuing a priestly calling, such as Julia Foote or the redoubtable Amanda Smith, would do so in other denominations or as independent missionaries. In time, the very existence of these "Sisters of the Spirit" would be effaced from the historical record of the church. Thus the centennial history of the AME Missionary Department, published in 1940, devoted its short discussion of "pioneer women" to Sarah Allen and other paragons of nurturing femininity: "These noble women served as missionaries in the real sense of the word. They taught the children, sewed and cooked for the needy, encouraged, inspired and guided the men as they labored to establish the African Methodist Church on a permanent basis."[50]

Yet even as church leaders conquered one challenge, a still greater one loomed before them. With the shelling of Fort Sumter in April 1861, 4 million men, women, and children stepped forward on the path from slavery to freedom. The Jubilee was at hand.

Freedom came first to the slaves of Washington, D.C. In April 1862 Abraham Lincoln signed a bill abolishing slavery in the District of Columbia. A few days later Daniel Payne, the AME Church's resident bishop in Washington, penned an address to the freedmen titled "Welcome to the Ransomed." The sermon compressed into a few pages Payne's vision of African American elevation and progress. More important, it portended the AME Church's approach to the 4 million southern slaves standing on the threshold of freedom. "Enter the great family of Holy Freedom," Payne wrote,

> not to *lounge in sinful indolence*, not to *degrade yourselves by vice*, nor to *corrupt society by licentiousness*, neither to *offend the laws by crime*, but to the *enjoyment of a well regulated liberty*, the offspring of generous laws . . . to habits of industry and thrift—to duties of religion and piety—to obligations of law, order, government. . . .

He concluded by enjoining the former slaves to build stable homes and families, to educate themselves, and, above all, to "work, work, work."[51]

This was the most portentous moment in African American religious history, the moment, in E. Franklin Frazier's felicitous phrase, that the "institutional church" of free people of color in the North met the "invisible church" of southern slaves. The AME Church stood squarely at the conjuncture. African Methodist missionaries flooded south in the wake of the Union Army, gathering up congregations, organizing circuits, dispensing sacraments. By the end of Reconstruction, AME congregations were spread across the Old Confederacy, from Florida to Texas. The encounter had a profound effect on the social and religious lives of the freedpeople, as well as on the institutional face of African Methodism. Former slaves, many of whom were accustomed to worshipping in small, secret cells, entered a structured, centralized religious world that linked them to other black communities across the nation and beyond. As much as any institution, the AME Church provided the foundation for a new, genuinely national African American community. For their part, AME leaders struggled to cope with more than a quarter million new adherents, who entered the church with their own religious traditions and practices, which often had little to do with those the church sought to inculcate. Though its political and financial centers of gravity remained northern, the AME Church was increasingly a southern institution.[52]

It is difficult to determine the number of AME missionaries working in the South in the wake of the Civil War. Clarence Walker, in an important study of the church during Reconstruction, identified more than seventy in the years between 1863 and 1870 alone. First to arrive were James Lynch and J. D. S. Hall, dispatched by Bishop Payne to Port Royal in the summer of 1863. Port Royal, in the South Carolina Sea Islands, was the site of one of the most ambitious experiments in the entire Reconstruction era. Land abandoned by whites was parceled out to freedmen in a conscious attempt to sow an independent black yeomanry. Schools were erected, local officials elected, and the foundation for a thriving black community laid, all under the sometimes paternalistic eye of the Union Army. The area offered fertile soil for Lynch and Hall, who simply assumed control of abandoned church buildings and congregations. By the end of the year the AME Church boasted a half dozen Sea Island congregations. The following year Lynch followed the Union Army into Charleston and thence to Savannah, the city where John and Charles Wesley had first disembarked 130 years before. He gathered in another half dozen congregations in the two places, including the remnants of the Charleston church scattered after the Vesey conspiracy.[53]

To some extent, the church's initial success among the freedmen was a product of circumstance. Many southern ministers had fled before the Union Army, leaving former slaves in a state of what one AME missionary termed "physical and moral interdict." With "no one to baptize their children, to perform marriages, or to bury the dead," many black Christians had nowhere else to turn but the AME Church. Yet there was more than circumstance here. After years of meeting in secret or sitting in galleries listening to white ministers intone Pauline injunctions about authority and obedience, southern blacks valued the opportunity to congregate openly, in churches of their own, led by ministers of their own color. Indeed, this separatist impulse was one of the defining features of the entire postwar period. All across the South, emancipation spawned black churches, benevolent societies, fraternal orders, fire companies. For former slaves, the right to assemble openly and without white supervision was a central dimension of freedom.[54]

Such feelings were reciprocated by AME missionaries, who almost universally agreed that the former slaves would best be served by a black church. While recognizing white missions' superior resources, church leaders insisted that consanguinity more than compensated for penury. Black ministers were blood of the freedmen's blood, flesh of their flesh; they could "feel and enter into all the sympathies of our poor down-trodden brethren" in a way white ministers never could. The sentiment was perhaps best captured by Bishop Alexander Wayman, who opened the AME Church's first church in Virginia with a sermon from Genesis 37: *"I seek my brethren."* The verse, which Wayman had selected years before in anticipation of just such a moment, became a standard inaugural text among arriving AME missionaries, so well did it express their feelings of kinship and providential reunion.[55]

Elation, however, was tempered by anxiety, almost awe, at the enormity of the task the church had undertaken. Gathering congregations, like emancipation itself, was only a first step. The real task was to prepare men and women who had known only slavery for the responsibilities of freedom, for the "independent and self active" exercise of their duties as citizens, breadwinners, parents. Unlike many of their white contemporaries, AME missionaries were confident that southern blacks could make the transition, that their degradation was a function of experience and environment rather than any innate slavishness. On the other hand, church leaders accepted the contemporary nostrum that slavery was poor preparation for freedom. They fretted about freedmen's lack of education, their apparent taste for vice, and their deficient "home life," symbolized in a sea of "irregular" unions and "illegitimate" children. Above all, they worried that the freedmen, despite years of working dusk to dawn, had never known self-directed labor or the discipline of the market and might revert to idleness once compulsion was removed.[56]

There was more here than Victorian fastidiousness or bourgeois moralism. As always within the AME Church, the preoccupation with propriety and racial uplift was tied to a broader political project. Since the days of Richard Allen, church leaders had accepted that securing the right to participate fully in American society depended in large measure on African Americans themselves, on their ability to rebut racial stereotypes and to earn white respect. Emancipation presented a golden opportunity. By raising up the freedmen, by shaping them into an industrious and intelligent citizenry, African Methodists could shatter racist myths once and for all. Failure, on the other hand, would provide ammunition to those who had maintained all along that slavery was blacks' natural condition. In effect, the racial trial continued in a new venue.

Such concerns were paramount in the aftermath of Appomattox, as Bishop Payne and a handful of AME elders sailed into Charleston harbor to inaugurate formally the church's southern work. It was a voyage full of portent, especially for Payne, who was returning to the city from which he had been exiled thirty years before, almost to the day. That evening, the group held services in

Charleston's Old Bethel Church. At the end of the service, R. H. Cain, one of Payne's lieutenants and a future U.S. congressman, dispensed the Lord's Supper, to the wonderment of the assembled.[57]

Payne organized the South Carolina Annual Conference, established the offices and committees prescribed by the AME *Discipline,* and, with a final benediction, dispatched his ministers to the countryside. The results were nothing short of spectacular. By the time the 1866 South Carolina Conference assembled, African Methodism had swept through Virginia, the Carolinas, and Georgia and had begun to spread into Alabama and Florida. Conference rolls counted almost fifty thousand members, equaling the membership of the entire antebellum AME Church. AME ministers established churches in hundreds of cities and towns, engorging entire congregations of the discredited Methodist Episcopal Church, South. To accommodate the flood of converts and accessions, Payne ordained more than forty deacons and elders, many of them former slaves. A year later, with the torrent continuing, he ordained an additional ninety-eight men.[58]

The church enjoyed its most spectacular growth in Georgia, thanks largely to the indefatigable Henry Turner. Like Payne, Turner was a freeborn South Carolinian who had fled north in the 1830s. While destined to make his historical mark in the cause of African emigration, he labored through the Civil War and Reconstruction to secure African Americans' place in the United States, serving as an army chaplain, a Freedmen's Bureau agent, a state legislator, and an AME missionary. Deputed by Payne to "plant and train mission churches" in Georgia, Turner crisscrossed the state, holding revivals and camp meetings. In the space of three months, more than ten thousand souls were added to AME rolls. The greatest harvest came in provincial cities like Macon, Marion, and Augusta, which had experienced huge influxes of blacks from the countryside in the aftermath of war. (In this as in innumerable other respects, the AME Church's southern mission prefigured its later career in South Africa.) The work eventually grew so large that the church was forced to establish a separate Georgia Conference, with its own bishop; in the decade that followed, the Georgia Conference was subdivided twice more. By the early 1880s the AME Church boasted sixty-three circuits and more than a hundred thousand members in Georgia alone.[59]

While a dozen memoirs describe expansion from the perspective of church leaders, we know little about how the process looked to those who were its objects. Probably the closest approximation of the experience comes from the autobiography of Levi J. Coppin, the man destined to serve as the AME Church's first resident bishop in South Africa. Coppin was born in 1848 in tiny Cecilton, Maryland, a freeman in a mixed community of free people and slaves. He was seventeen when African Methodism arrived in Cecilton, in the person of Bishop Alexander Wayman. Writing half a century later, Coppin still recalled the people's astonishment at Wayman's "intelligence" and "princely appearance," as well as their resolution to join the AME connection. More important, he remembered what it meant to the people of Cecilton, many of them long-time Methodists, finally to have a church of their own.

> We would now have our own class leaders, who in addressing us would say brother and sister . . . and, in times of sorrow, give words of comfort. We would now have our children baptized, and give them names. Call them "John Wesley," and "Richard Allen," and "Abraham Lincoln" if we wished. Give our daughters and sons in marriage. Recognize the relation of parent and child, and grand child, and brother and sister.

Never again would blacks be consigned to the gallery or reduced to meeting in secret "behind the wood."[60]

Affiliation with the AME Church brought dramatic changes in the structure and scale of religious experience in Cecilton. New hierarchies emerged as the congregation "affected an internal organization, with trustees, stewards, and the whole machinery of a well-ordered church." A Sunday school was established, with young Coppin, one of the few literate people in the community, serving as superintendent. Coppin also served as choirmaster, endeavoring to teach the people to sing "scientifically and correctly," in keeping with AME policy. The community's horizons were further broadened by the arrival of black celebrities, introduced by the local minister "that we should from time to time get to see a fair sample of what the race and church had produced, and thereby strengthen our confidence in the race, and increase our love for the church." T. G. Steward, Henry Highland Garnet, and Frederick Douglass all found their way to tiny Cecilton, connecting its citizens with the race's ongoing struggles across America and the world.[61]

In addition to illuminating the AME Church's appeal, Coppin's account records some of the conflicts and tensions generated by southern expansion. Not surprisingly, many whites reviled the new church. Dozens of AME ministers in the South had brushes with mobs and "Ku Kluxes." The Cecilton church was once attacked, after local whites heard that a Yankee minister—one of two or three white men ordained by the AME Church in the nineteenth century—was preaching there, "calling the 'niggers' brother and sister." Less dramatic but more pervasive was opposition from white Methodist competitors. Methodists in Cecilton, for example, filed suit to reclaim their old building, failing only when they could not produce a deed. Struggles over church affiliation and title were even more complex in the states under military reconstruction, due to the suspension of civil law. Often disputes became three-sided, with the Methodist Episcopal Church, South, holding deeds to buildings, the Methodist Episcopal Church, North, claiming them by order from the Secretary of the Army, and the AME Church claiming them by dint of occupation. In several cases, AME leaders fell into alliances of convenience with southern Methodists, who preferred to hand their congregations over to

blacks rather than to their Yankee rivals. (Speculation that the Methodist
Episcopal Church, South, would cede all its black congregations to the AME
Church was rife in the late 1860s, subsiding only in 1870, when the south-
erners launched their own Colored Methodist Episcopal Church.)[62]

Even as church leaders battled white opponents and rivals, familiar tensions
began bubbling up within the church itself. Conflict erupted first on the issue
of ordination. By the 1860s Daniel Payne's campaign for an educated ministry
had been won; almost to a man, AME leaders agreed that "the pulpit must be
in advance of the pew." Former slaves, however, had their own traditions of
religious leadership, embodied in the figure of the slave exhorter. Many of
these charismatic and uneducated preachers had been ordained in the church's
initial surge south, but their rise was abruptly cut off in 1866, when the AME
House of Bishops passed a resolution reasserting literacy as a prerequisite for
ordination. While it is not clear how strictly the standard was enforced, at least
some ministers were dismissed or placed under the supervision of northern
missionaries. In such instances, the freedmen were quick to register their
dissent. AME members in Little Rock, for example, denounced the whole
principle of an educated ministry in a petition demanding the reinstatement of
their old minister. Significantly, they included a complaint against carpetbagger churchmen who came south "seeking offices, and assuming the most
prominent positions," a charge later repeated, almost verbatim, by South
Africans.[63]

Regional tensions, implicit in the Little Rock petition and in the whole
debate over an educated ministry, burst into the open at the 1868 General
Conference. According to existing church policy, conference seats were reserved for constituencies with at least eight hundred lay members at the start of
the quadrennium, a criterion that obviously excluded southern delegates.
Rather than amending the requirement, northern ministers insisted on enforcing it, arguing that men just three years removed from slavery lacked the
experience and maturity to vote on important church affairs. Eventually the
southern delegates were seated, but only after a divisive debate. With each
passing year, the breach widened, southerners complaining of northern arrogance and neglect, while northerners expressed dismay at southern ministers'
ignorance and indifference to church procedures. Not surprisingly, the leader
of the northern opposition was Daniel Payne, who found southern leaders
contentious and unwilling to defer to superior age, experience, or wisdom.
"Such men seem to think that because they are free they are qualified to govern
the planetary system," he complained in his memoirs. Regional resentments
reached a climax at the 1880 General Conference, when southerners elected
two favorite sons, Henry Turner and R. H. Cain, to the House of Bishops, over
Payne's strenuous opposition.[64]

Much of the dispute between northern and southern church leaders revolved
around questions of politics, particularly the question of whether ordained

ministers should accept elective office. All across the South, the AME Church served as a staging area for political mobilization. Ministers and class leaders acted as community spokesmen, often riding their religious affiliation to political office. Hiram Revels, the first African American to sit in the U.S. Senate, was an AME minister. R. H. Cain represented Charleston in the U.S. Congress for two terms in the 1870s. Henry Turner was one of eleven AME ministers to serve in the South Carolina state legislature and played a key role in drafting the state's first postwar constitution. Nine delegates to the 1867 Georgia constitutional convention were African Methodist clergymen, as were seven members of the Florida state legislature.[65]

Even this catalog does not capture the church's political centrality. Many of the crucial struggles of the Reconstruction era unfolded at the local level, with black justices of the peace, Bureau agents, sheriffs, and voters' registrars all able to influence the way state and federal enactments were felt on the ground. The years of Radical Reconstruction witnessed the emergence of several local black political machines, many of them centered in the AME Church. T. W. Stringer, an AME minister in Vicksburg, Mississippi, used his position to become perhaps the most influential black man in the state. He organized a host of lodges and schools and played a leading role in the 1868 constitutional convention. In Georgia, T. G. Steward was drafted as Macon's first black voters' registrar, primarily because he was the only literate black man in the vicinity. Later he worked with Henry Turner in the local Freedmen's Bank, a crucial institution in the effort to seed an African American middle class. Most remarkable of all was Tunis Campbell, a carpetbagger and sometime AME preacher on the Georgia Sea Islands. Born an Episcopalian and trained for the Liberian mission field, Campbell joined the AME Church prior to the Civil War, an affiliation that helped him gain an appointment as Freedmen's Bureau agent for St. Catherine's Island. Using the church as a political base, he won election as a state senator and later as local justice of the peace. For five years he ran the island as a virtual autocrat: he wrote a local constitution, established churches, schools, and a host of black-run businesses and even succeeded temporarily in banning whites from the island. His power was broken only in 1871, when the "redeemed" Georgia legislature made justices of the peace legislative appointees rather than elected officials.[66]

Clearly, southern ministers and congregations saw no disjunction between religious and political callings. Their northern coreligionists, however, were less comfortable with the mix. While ministers such as Richard Allen and Daniel Coker had commented freely on the issues of the day, most of their successors conceived their callings in more narrowly professional ways. Daniel Payne, in particular, worried that political involvement, which was inherently worldly and corrupt, would compromise ministers' devotion to their work. In his youth, he had turned down a job as an antislavery lecturer to pursue the ministry, a decision he came to regard as one of the turning points of his life.

While Payne acknowledged that many southern office holders had been con-
scripted by their constituents, he expressed nothing but contempt for those
"rabid politicians" who chased after office, neglecting their duties and endan-
gering the church's good reputation with inflammatory statements. At the
1872 General Conference, he supported a motion to bar ministers from holding elective office, a motion that southern delegates succeeded in having
tabled.[67]

Parallel struggles unfolded at the congregational level as AME ministers,
many of them new to the South, confronted tightly knit communities of
former slaves. Even the most ardent missionaries approached their charges with
a certain ambivalence, their feelings of kinship and racial affinity counter-
balanced by a profound sense of cultural distance. The very language of mission
work—the talk of "uplifting" and "elevating" the "long neglected children" of
slavery—was steeped in paternalism. In such a context, the goal of empower-
ing freedmen was ever in tension with the idea of reforming them, of defining
for them the parameters of what Bishop Payne called "well regulated liberty."[68]

This tension was most obvious in church leaders' preoccupation with instilling "habits of industry" among the freedmen. Like most whites, AME leaders
accepted that slavery stifled individual responsibility and bred indolence and
shiftlessness. They also tended, again like white observers, to take the dramatic withdrawal of plantation labor in the immediate aftermath of the war as
proof of the adage. Fearful that such behavior would confirm white biases,
church leaders supported the Freedmen's Bureau campaign to get blacks working and hailed the growing number of freedmen signing labor contracts. In
weekly classes and Sunday sermons, they preached the virtues of industry and
"accumulation," that "motive for the creation of individual wealth which at
last is the capital of a nation." Such advice, of course, was time-honored
Methodist doctrine, but it also had a distinctly republican ring, in the sense
that personal application was assumed to lead eventually to proprietorship, and
proprietorship to respect.[69]

Church leaders were equally concerned with former slaves' manners and
morals, which one minister described as "lamentably inadequate to meet the
requirements of their new responsibilities." Boisterousness, use of alcohol or
tobacco, and inappropriate dress, whether shabby or overly ostentatious, were
all condemned from the AME pulpit. In best bourgeois fashion, many ministers emphasized "home life." Homes should be full of bric-a-brac, declared
Wesley Gaines, a minister and future bishop. They should ring with music,
played, of course, on the "better instruments," like mandolin and piano,
rather than "the Jewsharp and the banjo." In the kitchen, women should lay
"aside the skillet and the ash-bed for the cooking-stove and the range."
("Nothing of a material nature is more civilizing than proper diet, properly

served," Gaines wrote.) Church leaders also stressed hygiene, in one instance even accepting the sponsorship of a southern soap manufacturer. In a quid pro quo that spoke volumes about the emerging New South, the AME Church received sixteen hundred dollars to help build Morris Brown College in Atlanta, a center for training ministers and teachers; in return, ministers were enjoined to remind their congregants that "cleanliness was next to godliness," especially when one washed with "Big Real" soap.[70]

The most persistent and debilitating stereotypes that attached to the former slaves were sexual. A century before the Moynihan Report, black and white intellectuals argued that slavery had shattered the black family and eroded slaves' sense of sexual propriety. Slaves had lived "as the cattle did, with no moral code or restraint except that which was given by nature." Women bore children out of wedlock, while men, barred for centuries from assuming the responsibilities of fatherhood, neglected the children they sired. Most AME leaders, to their credit, put the onus of responsibility on whites, particularly on salacious white masters, who, in the words of the *Christian Recorder*, "made prostitutes of a majority of the best women of a whole nation of people, against their will." Yet whatever the diagnosis, the prescription remained the same: blacks needed to reform their familial and sexual lives. An entire generation of AME ministers bent themselves to the task, declaring "the beauty of modesty and the sanctity of the marriage relation" from "pulpit and school house." Thousands of slave marriages were sanctified. Young women were lectured on the importance of virginity, men on the "duties of social life and family responsibilities." The church, in Levi Coppin's words, became an "Ecclesiastical Court House" for correcting those who were "irregular in their connubial relations." Men and women were brought before the bar of the community and read out for cohabitation, infidelity, or neglect of children. Such sins, within the framework of racial vindication, not only degraded individuals; they undermined the whole race's struggle for respect and equality.[71]

Inevitably, this concern with respectability led AME leaders to seek to "improve" the freedmen's standards of religious worship. Missionaries arriving from the North were decidedly uncomfortable with the religious practices they found among the bondsmen, with their "weird singing" and "hand clapping." Most were particularly bemused by the ring shout, that ecstatic, counterclockwise shuffle that represented perhaps the most dramatic African survival in North America. Almost instinctively, they attempted to stamp such practices out. As in the North, church leaders organized choirs and introduced the edifying fare of the AME hymnal. While revivalists themselves, they endeavored to restrain the freedmen's "natural enthusiasm," lest adherents "mistake mere physical excitement for divine unction." Even the popular Henry Turner, whom Bishop Payne chided for his "florid . . . not to say bombastic" preaching style, worried about the erosion of religious standards, to the point that he actually introduced a motion urging the adoption of "ritualism and the use of clerical vestments." Such innovations, he argued, would help "create an atmosphere of formality and dignity in worship services."[72]

Predictably, the individual most preoccupied with religious improvement was Daniel Payne. In his travels through the South, the aging bishop denounced "Fist and Heel" worship, drumming, "Voudoo" dancing, and all the other "strange delusions" he witnessed among the freedmen. In one remarkable passage in his autobiography, Payne described an encounter with a ring shout during a visit to an outstation in 1878:

> About this time I attended a "bush meeting," where I went to please the pastor whose circuit I was visiting. After the sermon they formed a ring, and with coats off sung, clapped their hands and stamped their feet in a most ridiculous and heathenish way. I requested the pastor to go and stop their dancing. At his request they stopped their dancing and clapping of hands, but remained singing and rocking their bodies to and fro. . . . I then went, and taking the leader by the arm requested him to desist and to sit down and sing in a rational manner. I told him also that it was a heathenish way to worship and disgraceful to themselves, the race, and the Christian name.

The crowd, he recalled, "walked sullenly away." The leader later approached him and explained, "Sinners won't get converted unless there is a ring."[73]

The encounter reminds us that freedmen did not simply acquiesce to AME missionaries' efforts to reform their religious lives. The very fact that ring shouting surfaced in an 1878 service suggests that the church had been at best partially successful in its campaign to "elevate" the freedmen. Payne himself acknowledged the problem. "I have remonstrated with a number of pastors for permitting these practices, . . ." he wrote, "but have been invariably met with the response that he could not succeed in restraining them, and an attempt to compel them to cease would simply drive them away from our Church." Freedmen exhibited this same independence on other issues as well, unwittingly recapitulating decades of struggle in the northern church. They defended their own notions of religious authority, deriding ministers they deemed cold or condescending. (The people of Cecilton, Levi Coppin recalled, dismissed the erudite T. G. Steward as a "Presbyterian.") They resisted "note singing" and other "radical innovations" in services. Many doubtless continued to sing and dance as the spirit moved them.[74]

Insofar as church leaders did impose consistent standards of ordination and conduct, they did so at the cost of potential membership. As they learned more about the AME Church, many former slave exhorters elected not to affiliate, lest they lose their standing. African Methodists also found themselves increasingly on the losing end of competition with Baptist churches, which typically allowed greater scope for emotion and a range of syncretic practices. While the Baptists' decentralized institutional structure handicapped them in the early race for southern accessions, by the end of the century they had far outstripped

Methodists in membership. Ironically, the AME Church's fidelity to the dominant culture's religious standards also left it vulnerable to counterattack by white churches. In the early 1870s the Methodist Episcopal Church, North, ordained several dozen black ministers, the bulk of whom were allegedly less educated, more enthusiastic, and more tolerant of popular "superstitions" than their AME counterparts. The Methodist Episcopal Church, South, attempted a similar gambit, imposing lenient ordination standards in its Colored Methodist Episcopal Church. Over time, many adherents picked up by the AME Church in the wake of the war drifted into other churches.[75]

Ultimately, few of the expectations unleashed by the opening of the AME Church's southern mission came to pass. The idea of gathering all the former slaves beneath the banner of African Methodism proved chimerical, as did the goal of raising up a prosperous black yeomanry. Nonetheless, the two decades after the Civil War represented the most dynamic period in nineteenth-century African Methodism's tumultuous history. Like the proverbial mustard seed, the tiny movement sown by Richard Allen and his comrades in Philadelphia had grown into a stately church of almost half a million adherents. Equally important, the AME Church had grown into a genuinely national institution—the one institution that bridged, however imperfectly, the chasms of class, color, and prior condition in African American life. As such, the church became one of the central arenas within which African Americans addressed the fundamental questions of their identity, history and destiny. Those questions led inexorably back to Africa.

3

Through the Looking Glass

After reading the first two chapters of this book, one might be forgiven for asking what was "African" about African Methodism. Notwithstanding its name, the AME Church was clearly the most respectable and "orthodox" of black American independent churches. While some recognizably African elements surfaced in services, AME leaders tended to disdain if not actively to suppress those beliefs and practices that scholars today celebrate as signs of Africa's persistence in the New World. The whole point of "racial vindication" was to demonstrate blacks' capacity to uphold "recognized standards" in their personal and collective lives and thereby to hasten abolition and full inclusion in American society. Surely people interested in connections between black America and Africa should look elsewhere than the AME Church.

Better yet, they should rephrase the question. With a few notable exceptions, historians of black America have been so preoccupied with finding evidence of Africa in the realm of culture that they have overlooked the continent's pervasiveness in black intellectual and imaginative life. In a nation ruled by the descendants of Europe, Africa is and has always been the touchstone of black distinctiveness, the literal and figurative point of departure for the construction of African American identity, whatever one conceives it to be. And nowhere was the question of African Americans' relationship with Africa more explicitly confronted than in the AME Church. From the moment of its inception, the church was consumed by African issues—by debates on the merits of emigration and colonization, the value of African missions, the meaning of slavery itself. Long before the establishment of the South African AME Church in 1896, black Christians had gazed through the looking glass, searching for identity and explanation in the dim reflections of a distant continent.

The year 1816 was a significant one in the developing relationship between black America and Africa. While Richard Allen and his associates established the African Methodist Episcopal Church, Robert Finley, a white Presbyterian from New Jersey, laid the groundwork of the American Colonization Society. Appalled by the "degraded" and "vicious" condition of the former slaves who poured into his district in the two generations after the Revolution, Finley advocated resettlement of freed blacks in a government-purchased territory on the west coast of Africa. Like so many segregationist projects, "colonization" was cast in liberal, humanitarian terms. Despite his personal distaste for black people, Finley was convinced that they were "improvable" and would blossom into full maturity once removed from the shadow of captivity. Removing freed slaves would also undercut the primary argument against abolition and thus hasten the extinction of American slavery. A variety of other arguments were grafted onto these basic contentions: colonization offered a providential means to extend the gospel to Africa and thereby to atone for slavery; it promised to remove an unassimilable underclass from the young nation's midst; it opened new commercial possibilities. To a temperament as buoyantly optimistic as Finley's, the apparent alignment of so many interests was proof that the whole enterprise was born of God. [1]

Finley's scheme was actually the culmination of more than forty years of debate among black and white intellectuals. As early as 1773 Samuel Hopkins, a Presbyterian minister in Newport, Rhode Island, proposed sending educated Christian Africans back to Africa as missionaries. Hopkins's plan revolved initially around two Gold Coast sailors, Bristol Yamma and John Quamine, who worshipped in his congregation, but after corresponding with Ezra Stiles, another prominent New England divine, he was persuaded that African Americans, "well instructed" and "inspired with the Spirit of Martyrdom," would suffice equally for the task. Both men hoped the scheme would stimulate a large-scale voluntary emigration of blacks back to Africa, while speeding the end of the slave trade. Hopkins's main object, however, was to remove a moral albatross from the neck of American society. A disciple of Jonathan Edwards, he worshipped a stern, wrathful God who could not be expected forever to tolerate the injustices visible daily on the wharves of Newport. In the climate of revolutionary America, with colonists casting compulsively for some sign of providential favor, such ideas cut a wide swath. Leaders such as Thomas Jefferson, while unable to believe that blacks could ever be assimilated into American life, took it for granted that the republican experiment was doomed unless something was done about slavery. The most famous passage in Jefferson's *Notes on the State of Virginia*—"Indeed I tremble for my country when I reflect that God is just: that his justice cannot sleep for ever"—follows a discussion of the merits of colonization. [2]

What evidence there is suggests that African Americans were exploring many of the same questions, in much the same terms. At the very time

Hopkins conceived his plan, the Massachusetts Assembly entertained a petition from four slaves, requesting facilities for self-purchase. Once free, the four
pledged to return to Africa, where they proposed to establish a colony. Africa
also surfaced frequently in the poetry of the celebrated Phillis Wheatley, which
dwelt on the providential hand that had lifted blacks from the darkness of a
"Pagan land" into the light of Christian civilization. Wheatley, in fact, was
one of the first people Hopkins informed of his scheme, and she heartily
endorsed it, adding an allusion to the prophecy of Ethiopian redemption in
Psalms 68. (So heartfelt was Wheatley's support that one of Hopkins's colleagues wrote back, suggesting that she marry Yamma or Quamine and move
to Africa herself; she politely declined the offer.) Even independent church
leader Absalom Jones, a man who devoted his life to securing full equality for
blacks in America, speculated that some individuals might be destined to
return to Africa. In an 1808 sermon commemorating the abolition of the slave
trade, Jones observed:

> It has always been a mystery why the impartial Father of the human race should
> have permitted the transportation of so many millions of our fellow creatures to
> the country, to endure the miseries of slavery. . . . Perhaps his design was that
> a knowledge of the gospel might be acquired by some of their description, in
> order that they might become qualified to be the messengers of it, to the land of
> their fathers.

"Who knows," he concluded, "but that a Joseph may rise up among them,
who shall be the instrument of feeding the African nations with the bread of
life. . . ."[3]

Olaudah Equiano, the slave mariner whose narrative established many of the
conventions of African American autobiography, also grappled with the meaning of enslavement and the possibility of a return to Africa. Even as he vividly
described the trauma of capture and transportation, Equiano continued to
regard the whole experience as divinely ordained. "By all the horrors of that
trade was I first torn from all the tender connections that were naturally dear to
my heart," he wrote in his dedication, "but these, through the mysterious
ways of Providence, I ought to regard as infinitely more than compensated by
the introduction I have thence obtained to the knowledge of the Christian
religion. . . ." Throughout his account, Equiano explored the parallel between African Americans and the Jews of the Exodus, arguing in one passage
that blacks were descendants of the Israelites who had been darkened by
overexposure to the sun. Implicit in that parallel, of course, was the suggestion
that African Americans too might someday be destined to carry what they had
learned back to the land of their ancestors. Equiano himself later endeavored to
travel to Africa as a missionary.[4]

African American interest in Africa received an enormous spur with the
founding of the Sierra Leone colony in 1787. Initially established as a dumping

ground for "the Black Poor of London," Sierra Leone became a homeland for thousands of former slaves, mostly from Britain, Canada, and the West Indies, as well as for an untold number of Africans "recaptured" by the Royal Navy in its campaign against the slave trade. Word of the West African colony raced through the black community in the United States. In Boston, Prince Hall, founder of the first black Masonic lodge and a correspondent of Richard Allen's, led a group of petitioners in requesting transportation to the colony. In Newport, emigration was endorsed by the Free African Society, which presented its decision in a memorial to its parent body in Philadelphia. The Philadelphia chapter's carefully couched reply revealed how involved the African issue was already becoming. "If any apprehend a divine injunction is laid upon them to undertake such a long and perilous journey in order to promote piety and virtue," the Philadelphians wished them godspeed. At the same time, they committed themselves to remaining in America and working toward the full abolition of slavery. Significantly, even the qualified support they gave emigration was cast in terms not of racial affinity but of Christian universalism: "[E]very pious man is a citizen of the world."[5]

The most influential of the early emigration advocates was a black ship's captain named Paul Cuffe. Cuffe was a man of many parts—of mixed African and Native American descent, he was a devout Quaker, a skilled sailor, and an ambitious entrepreneur who rose from poverty to become one of the wealthiest black men in the United States. Converted to the emigrationist banner in the first decade of the nineteenth century, he embarked in 1811 on a joint civilizing and commercial venture to the Windward Coast of Africa, an area he had often plied on whaling voyages. He visited Sierra Leone, returning via London, where he obtained a preferential trading agreement from the colony's sponsors in exchange for recruiting and transporting skilled colonists. In a circular published in 1812, Cuffe argued that emigration would remove the "yoke of oppression" from African Americans, enabling them to "rise to be a people." At the same time, emigration promised to "regenerate" Africa through the balm of Christianity, civilization, and, not coincidentally, commerce.[6]

Cuffe's voluntary emigration plan appealed to at least a segment of America's free black population. In Baltimore, a pro-emigration group was formed under the leadership of future AME Church founder Daniel Coker. In Philadelphia, Cuffe met with several community leaders, including wealthy sailmaker James Forten, a confidante of Richard Allen's and a distinguished abolitionist in his own right. Cuffe easily recruited passengers for a voyage, but his plans were upset by the outbreak of war between Britain and the United States in 1812. The U.S. Congress refused to grant him a waiver to trade with an enemy colony, while the subsequent peace treaty explicitly excluded American merchants from British-controlled ports. Cuffe did succeed in transporting one company of thirty-eight settlers to Freetown in 1816, but the group received a frosty reception from local authorities. After some debate the settlers were allowed to land, but Cuffe was refused permission to offload the goods he had brought to trade. In the end, he lost about eight thousand dollars on the venture, the first of many commercial setbacks in the history of the African emigration movement. Cuffe died before he was able to muster the resources for a second voyage, allegedly leaving behind a waiting list of more than two thousand would-be emigrants.[7]

Even before Cuffe's death, the torch of African repatriation had passed into the hands of Robert Finley's American Colonization Society. Appreciating at least some of the lessons of Cuffe's failure, Finley decided to headquarter the A.C.S. in Washington. What the swampy environs of the tiny capital lacked in comfort was more than compensated for by the easy access he enjoyed to America's most prominent politicians. Speaker of the House Henry Clay, General Andrew Jackson, and Bushrod Washington, George Washington's nephew and heir, were all quickly recruited to the colonizationist cause. One plays politics at one's cost, however. The first casualty was Finley's facile linkage of emigration and abolition. Even in 1817 few politicians outside New England were prepared to sponsor an idea that seemed even indirectly to menace slavery. Henry Clay, in a widely publicized speech at the Society's inaugural meeting, enjoined Finley to avoid the "delicate question" of emancipation altogether and to focus instead on the problem of free people of color:

> Can there be a nobler cause than that which, whilst it proposes to rid our country of a useless and pernicious, if not dangerous portion of its population, contemplates the spreading of the arts of civilized life, and the possible redemption from ignorance and barbarism of a benighted quarter of the globe?

With that one speech, any hope that colonization would facilitate abolition went aglimmering.[8]

The rise of the A.C.S. generated enormous controversy within black America—controversy that inevitably played itself out within the AME Church. On one hand, the church represented the primary vehicle through which African Americans sought to demonstrate their fitness for American citizenship. This project colonization clearly menaced. On the other hand, the idea that they had been ordained to carry Christianity and civilization back to the land of their foreparents struck a chord with many black Christians. Men and women even remotely conversant with the Bible could find a dozen passages confirming the mandate, not only in Exodus, but in Kings, Isaiah, and Nehemiah. The entire Old Testament was a story of dispersal and reunion, captivity and return. If the Lord could fit slavery itself to His purposes, surely the same might be true of a tawdry little organization like the A.C.S.

The range of responses to colonization was graphically illustrated by events in Philadelphia and Baltimore. Enraged by the "unmerited stigma" that Clay had cast upon free people of color, Richard Allen joined James Forten and Absalom Jones in convening a protest meeting at Bethel Church. "Three thousand at least attended," Forten reported to Paul Cuffe, "and there was not one sole that was in favour of going to Africa. They think that the slave holders want to get rid of them so as to make their property more secure." Forten himself felt some ambivalence on the issue. He was convinced, he told Cuffe, that blacks "would never become a people until they com out from amongst the white people"; at the same time, however, he recognized that "the majority is decidedly against me" and had "determined to remain silent." The Bethel meeting concluded by passing a set of resolutions that established the terms of a generation of anticolonization activity. First, the delegates asserted their right to remain in America, the "land of their nativity," a land "manured" by "their blood and sweat." They also reiterated their commitment to those still in bondage: "We never will separate ourselves voluntarily from the slave population of the country; they are our brethren by ties of consanguinity, of suffering, and of wrong." An additional resolution, which bore the unmistakable stamp of Richard Allen, stressed the importance of elevating the race in America before contemplating any return to Africa. Sending untutored blacks back to Africa, the resolution argued, would only hasten their reversion to barbarism and (in a revealing parallelism) to slavery: "Without arts, without science, without a proper knowledge of government, to cast into the savage wilds of Africa the free people of color, seems to us a circuitous route through which they must return to perpetual bondage."[9]

By all accounts, the response from Philadelphia startled the sponsors of the A.C.S., who had taken Paul Cuffe's popularity as evidence of black support. Clearly they failed to grasp the distinction African Americans drew between emigration and colonization, between the right of an individual voluntarily to remove to Africa and what appeared to be a state-sponsored mass deportation. Belatedly appreciating the point, Finley hastened to Philadelphia, where he assured black community leaders that colonization would remain strictly voluntary. Any hopes that he had converted the Philadelphians, however, were dashed a few months later, after another mass meeting at Bethel. The second meeting, again chaired by Allen, sharpened the attack on the A.C.S., arguing that colonization would remove the only population genuinely committed to uplifting the slaves. "Let no purpose be assisted which will stay the cause of the entire abolition of slavery," the meeting resolved. Even the wavering Forten was now firmly in harness. Indeed, his condemnation of colonization as a slaveholders' plot played a pivotal role in steering abolitionist William Lloyd Garrison down the road toward immediatism.[10]

Yet even as Allen rallied opposition to the A.C.S., his counterpart in Baltimore, Daniel Coker, packed his bags for Africa. In February 1820 Coker and his wife and son, along with ninety other men and women, boarded the schooner *Elizabeth* and embarked for Sherbro Island, off the coast of what would become Liberia, to plant the first A.C.S. colony. Coker was undoubtedly aware of his coreligionists' skepticism, but such doubts counted little against what seemed to him a divinely ordained plan for African redemption. In his shipboard journal, which the A.C.S. rushed into publication, he went so far as to argue that the whole question of the Society's motives was irrelevant, since it was merely a providential instrument. "Oh my God, what is God about to do for Africa?" he wrote. "Surely something great." Late into the evening, he pored over the plans for the community, ruminating on the prophecy in Isaiah 18, in which a people from *"the land shadowing with wings, which is beyond the rivers of Ethiopia,"* a people *"scattered and peeled . . . meted out and trodden under foot,"* would be gathered by God at the foot of Mount Zion.[11]

Such enthusiasm proved difficult to sustain once the colonists actually reached Africa. The Sherbro king, to Coker's dismay, was ravaged by alcohol and distinctly unreceptive to the idea of an African American colony, especially when he grasped the settlers' desire to extinguish the lucrative trade in slaves. Internally, the community was riven by a series of disputes between the settlers and the two white agents of the A.C.S., with Coker often caught in the crossfire. Most serious, the group was decimated by disease, proving, for neither the first nor the last time, the limits of blacks' supposed immunity to "tropical fevers." Within a matter of months, most of the expedition's leaders were dead. The remnant of the colony, led by Coker, abandoned Sherbro Island and took refuge in Freetown. Coker eventually became the headman of a "recaptive" village, where he succeeded in planting a small, nondenominational church, as well as a Sunday school for "the little naked sons of Africa." He died after a few years, fulfilling his pledge to give his life to "bleeding, groaning, dark, benighted Africa."[12]

Richard Allen viewed Coker's enterprise with decidedly mixed emotions. Obviously, he opposed any trafficking with the A.C.S. He also believed throughout his life that the missionary energies of his young church were most efficiently spent at home. On the other hand, he was a committed evangelist, who could scarcely condemn efforts to expand Christ's kingdom. In the end, Allen agreed to pronounce a benediction on the *Elizabeth,* though he apparently offered no other support. There is no evidence on how he viewed Coker's travails in Africa, if indeed he was aware of them. Yet for all his ambivalence, Allen was unable to suppress a certain pride in the presence of an AME minister in Africa, proof in itself of how deeply the romance of the continent had seeped into the black church. In the second edition of the AME *Discipline,* he boasted that "God has spread the word through our instrumentality on the barren shores of Africa," a claim that not only overlooked his own lack of support but that betrayed Coker's plea not to introduce the spirit of denominationalism into African missions. In time AME leaders would forget entirely their opposition to Coker, who, with the aid of the publicists of the A.C.S., joined Baptist missionary Lott Carey as black America's first martyr to Africa.[13]

Despite their overwhelming opposition to the A.C.S. and to anything smacking of forced expatriation, black leaders continued to wonder whether their destiny might lie elsewhere than in the United States. Such speculations were fueled by intensifying discrimination against free people of color all across America. New York, for example, restricted black access to the ballot in 1821, even as it extended universal suffrage to white males. Several western states passed "Black Codes," restricting settlement by African Americans, slave or free. In the South, manumissions, which had surged in the generation after the Revolution, slowed to a trickle, and free people of color faced a battery of new restrictions. In such a context, emigrationist sentiment continued to swell. The 1820s alone saw the emergence of black-led schemes centered on the Caribbean, Texas and Mexico, Canada, and even, on occasion, Africa (though proponents of these schemes were invariably at pains to distinguish themselves from the A.C.S.).[14]

Early in the decade, emigration activity focused on Haiti. In 1823 Jean Pierre Boyer, president of the black republic, extended an invitation to African American colonists. Boyer hoped that an influx of skilled settlers would revive Haiti's moribund economy, while strengthening commercial linkages between the island and the mainland. He dispatched an emigration agent to the United States and pledged forty dollars to defray the cost of each settler's passage. He also launched an extensive publicity campaign, capitalizing on black frustrations and on the enormous prestige that Haiti had commanded among African Americans since the days of Toussaint L'Ouverture. In Haiti, Boyer promised, black settlers would have land, opportunity, dignity. The island was a "sacred asylum" where the wounds of slavery would be "healed by the balm of equality."[15]

Boyer's offer generated enormous enthusiasm among free people of color, often in precisely those communities most adamantly opposed to colonization. Unlike the leaders of the A.C.S., Boyer was a black man. Moreover, his invitation carried no implication that African Americans were unassimilable, still less that they were "useless" or "dangerous." On the contrary, he offered blacks an opportunity to help build a nation, to improve their own lot while demonstrating their race's capacity for self-government. Boyer's offer had a particular appeal within the AME Church, which had itself been conceived for just such ends. By mid-1824, a "Haytien Emigration Society" had been founded in Philadelphia, based in Bethel Church and chaired by none other than Richard Allen. Of the two thousand African Americans who emigrated to Haiti in the next few years, a substantial portion were members of Bethel. (Among the émigrés was Allen's own son, John.) In 1827, in response to a plea from the settlers, the church dispatched a missionary, Scipio Beanes, to Haiti.[16]

Few of the expectations unleashed by Haitian emigration came to pass. Most of the money advanced by Boyer found its way into the pockets of U.S.

emigration agents, prompting the President to withdraw the subsidy. On the island itself, a range of disputes erupted between African American settlers and Haitian citizens and officials, disputes exacerbated by differences of culture, language, and religion. Two hundred disillusioned settlers returned to the United States in 1825, and a steady trickle followed in succeeding years. The AME mission, despite some early successes, was caught in the downward spiral. Many of the church's adherents returned home. Scipio Beanes was dogged by ill health and spent most of his time in the United States. Calls for ministers from several struggling AME congregations on the island went unheeded. When African Methodist missionaries returned to the island a half century later, they found virtually no trace of the original mission. Like Daniel Coker's African venture, however, the Haitian expedition left its mark on the institutional memory of the church. However unsuccessful on their own terms, both initiatives helped to legitimize mission activity, to foster the idea that the AME Church possessed an obligation toward blacks beyond the borders of the United States. [17]

By the end of the 1820s the focus of emigration activity had shifted north to Canada. Many of the African American slaves who flocked to British lines during the Revolutionary War had ended up in Canada, where they lived as free people. Over the years they were joined by a steady stream of fugitive slaves and disillusioned free people of color. The stream swelled to a flood in 1829, after the implementation of the notorious Ohio Black Codes. Enacted in 1804 though rarely enforced, the codes required all black Ohioans to carry papers certifying their freedom and to post bonds of five hundred dollars as guarantees of good behavior. In 1829 city officials in Cincinnati, confronted with a dramatic expansion in the local Afro-American population, announced their intention to begin enforcing the requirements. Even before they had the opportunity, a mob rampaged through the city's black ward, beating residents and burning their homes. In the wake of the episode, about two thousand black Ohioans, a substantial portion of them African Methodists, trekked to Canada. [18]

A few emigrationists continued to advocate Africa as a destination, but they confronted almost universal suspicion and scorn. In the late 1820s, for example, a small meeting was held at Bethel Church at the behest of one of Allen's subordinates. The memorial from the meeting lamented the restrictions that made African Americans "strangers" in the land of their birth and proposed Africa as a field where blacks might escape the "stain and evil of slavery" and underwrite "the extension of civilization and the gospel." Immediately, however, the group found itself tarred as colonizationist. Rumors swirled that Allen had joined hands with the A.C.S., prompting an eloquent disavowal from the old bishop. Such experiences convinced most black leaders that it was best to ignore the continent altogether. [19]

African Americans' uncertainty about their future was glaringly apparent in the National Negro Convention Movement, which held its first meeting in Philadelphia in 1830. Inevitably, the inaugural gathering convened in Bethel Church, with Richard Allen, only months from death, in the chair. The title that the delegates adopted for themselves—"The American Society of Free Persons of Color, for Improving their Condition in the United States; for Purchasing Lands; and for the Establishing of a Settlement in Upper Canada"—eloquently expressed their continuing ambivalence about the United States. On one hand, the convention endorsed the Ohio exodus, recounting the oppression the emigrants had endured and praising them for their determination to live "in a land where the laws and prejudices of society will have no effect in retarding their advancement to the summit of civil and religious improvement." On the other hand, most delegates remained convinced that blacks could improve their lot in the United States, a conviction underscored with yet another broadside against colonization: "This is our country. Beneath its sod lie the bones of our fathers. . . . Here we were born, and here we will die." Several delegates advocated strategies of economic self-help, arguing, in the timeworn logic of racial vindication, that blacks would never earn white respect so long as they were impoverished and confined to vice-ridden urban slums. Among the solutions broached at the meeting were cooperative land purchase and the encouragement of agricultural and mechanical arts—in effect, the cultivation of an independent black yeomanry. In the process, delegates revealed again that paradoxical process that drew African Americans back to the values and operating myths of the society from which they were excluded.[20]

Whatever their attitudes toward emigration, leaders of the Convention movement shared a hatred of the A.C.S., as well as a distinct aversion to Africa, which remained burdened with ideas of blacks' inferiority and unfitness for American citizenship. The Convention's preference for the term *Negro*, previously disdained for its connotations of enslavement, was itself an attempt to distance African Americans from their ancestral continent. The fifth National Negro Convention, in 1835, went so far as to urge blacks "to remove the title of African from their institutions, the marbles of churches, and etc." After some debate, African Methodists kept their corporate name, but the word *African* was effaced from thousands of black schools, churches, and benevolent societies all across America.[21]

Thus the 1830s, a critical period in the development of black nationalist ideology, were marked by a recession of interest in and discussion about Africa. The A.C.S., which never claimed much of a constituency among white northerners, was declining in the South, especially after the defection of Andrew Jackson. (The panic engendered by the Nat Turner uprising provided a brief fillip for colonizationism but ultimately did not stop its downward spiral.) Blacks were virtually united in their opposition to colonization, and most were chary of anything to do with Africa. Within the AME Church, a residuum of romance about Africa survived, expressed in occasional resolutions about re-deeming souls "enshrouded in midnight darkness," but nothing came of them. The 1844 AME General Conference did establish a Home and Foreign Mission Society, but "foreign" at the time essentially meant Canadian. Richard Allen's episcopal successors—Morris Brown, Paul Quinn, and, later, Daniel Payne—all stressed the priority of "home missions" and showed little inclination to revive the West African work begun by Daniel Coker.[22]

In the late 1840s, however, the cords tying African Americans to their ancestral home tautened once again. In 1847 Liberia became an independent republic. While primarily a product of the A.C.S.'s mounting debt, indepen-dence prompted many black Americans to reassess their position. Between 1847 and 1848 migration to Liberia grew tenfold. It contined to swell in the years that followed, as a series of devastating political defeats cast doubt on blacks' future in America. The so-called Compromise of 1850, for example, included an exacting fugitive slave law that vacated state personal liberty laws and required northerners to assist in the capture and repatriation of escaped slaves. So strict were the bill's provisions that free people of color misidentified as fugitives had almost no legal recourse to prevent their enslavement. The Kansas-Nebraska Compromise four years later reopened to slaveholders territo-ries that had previously been closed, undermining hopes that slavery would wither on its own. Most ominous, the Supreme Court's decision in the 1857 Dred Scott case virtually effaced any legal distinction between slaves and free people: All blacks, by Justice Taney's logic, were aliens under the Constitu-tion, possessing no rights that whites "were bound to respect." With each new setback, Liberian emigration accelerated. Thousands of other African Ameri-cans embarked for Canada or the West Indies.[23]

Among those who embarked for West Africa in the 1850s were Alexander Crummell and Edward Blyden, two of the towering figures of black history, whose ideas about Africa and its relationship to African American life shaped debate for the next half century. Crummell, a freeborn New Yorker and an Episcopal minister, had been a prominent critic of colonization in the early 1840s. By the end of the decade, however, he had suffered enough indignities at the hands of white Americans, and of his Episcopalian colleagues in particu-lar, to wash his hands of the United States. In England on a fund-raising trip, he enrolled at Queen's College, Cambridge. On his graduation in 1853, he made his peace with the A.C.S. and embarked for Liberia. From that moment until 1872, when his disenchantment with Liberia's mulatto ruling class drove him back to America, he remained one of colonization's most eloquent spokes-men.[24]

Like so many nineteenth-century black Christians, Crummell does not easily lend himself to the dichotomies conventionally used to characterize African American politics. At the core of his thought lay what Wilson Moses has called "civilizationism"—a belief in a unitary civilization to which all people were, at varying paces, progressing. This belief did not, however, imply that Crummell was indifferent to race pride or that he subscribed to the dominant society's vision of African history as an uninterrupted tale of barbarism. On the contrary, he maintained that Africa had been the true cradle of civilization, providing Europe with many of the values and conceptions that the world would later accept as "Western." Unfortunately, the continent had then lapsed into isolation, depriving it of the intercultural contact that was the motor of civilized development. What Africa needed was external stimulus, which would ignite the process of "regeneration" and enable Africans to rejoin the universe of civilization. Crummell maintained that African Americans possessed a peculiar fitness and a special obligation to accomplish the task.[25]

Edward Blyden advanced a broadly similar argument. Born in the Danish West Indies, he came to the United States in 1850 to study for the ministry. Denied any opportunity, he embarked for Liberia, where he served as a Presbyterian missionary and agent for the A.C.S. Ultimately, however, it was as an intellectual and pan-Africanist that Blyden was to make his historical mark. In *Liberia's Offering,* published in 1862, and in books and articles published over the next forty years, Blyden explored the providential hand in African American history. Blending his own historical research with the work of other black intellectuals, and with a healthy dose of colonizationist ideology, he argued that slavery had been ordained by Providence to prepare African Americans for the task of redeeming their ancestral continent.[26]

As that formulation suggests, Blyden shared many of Crummell's presuppositions about Christianity, civilization, and the proper direction of African development. At the same time, however, he was much more inclined to discern in blacks a distinctive racial genius that deserved to be preserved and cultivated. Indeed, one of his chief arguments for emigration was that blacks could never fully develop their distinctive faculties—what Du Bois would later call their "gift to the world"—while remaining in America; like the Jews in Babylon, they could not sing the songs of Zion in a foreign land. In time such convictions would grow into a genuine reverence for indigenous African culture and agency, variously exhibited in Blyden's defense of native dress, his sympathetic investigations of Islam, and his withering critique of the Americo-Liberian mulatto elite. By the end of his life, he had even come to wonder whether the redemption of Africa might best be left to Africans themselves, though by that time his earlier formulations had been deeply sown in African American thought.[27]

Antebellum America's most famous emigrationist, however, was neither Crummell nor Blyden but Martin Delany. Born in western Virginia of a free mother and a slave father, Delany grew up in Pennsylvania, where he converted to the AME Church. In the late 1840s he settled in New York state, joining Frederick Douglass on the staff of *The North Star.* Like Douglass, he opposed colonization, insisting on African Americans' right to live in the land of their nativity. Unlike Douglass, however, his faith waned after the Fugitive Slave Act. In 1852 Delany published *The Condition, Elevation, Emigration, and Destiny of the Colored People of the United States,* in which he advocated emigration to Central and South America. The dispute with Douglass broke into the open the following year at a meeting of the National Negro Convention. When Douglass pushed through a resolution opposing emigration, Delany and a handful of dissidents withdrew and began organizing the National Emigration Convention, an institution devoted to finding a refuge outside the United States for black people.[28]

Even after his conversion, Delany continued to give Africa a wide berth. The inaugural Emigration Convention in 1854 apparently discussed the continent in a "Secret Session," but its published proceedings stressed the advantages of emigration to Central America, the West Indies, or Canada. (Delany himself moved to Ontario.) Gradually, however, Delany's attitude shifted. While he continued to disdain the A.C.S. and Liberia—a "miserable . . .burlesque on a government," he called it—he began to wonder whether black Americans were indeed destined to return to Africa. Ironically, his interest seems to have been spurred by two white missionary texts, Thomas Bowen's *Central Africa: Adventures and Missionary Labours in the Interior of Africa* and David Livingstone's *Seventeen Years' Explorations and Adventures in the Wilds of Africa,* both published in 1857. In 1859 Delany set out for West Africa, to Yorubaland, one of the areas described by Bowen, to locate land for an African American homeland.[29]

Delany landed first in Liberia, where he met Blyden and Crummell, before proceeding on to Lagos. In December 1859 he and his companion, Jamaican-born Robert Campbell, signed a treaty with an Egba king ceding part of Yorubaland for an Afro-American colony. Both travelers published short accounts of their journey in order to boost interest in the new settlement, scheduled to open in 1862. Campbell's book was cast as a descriptive and "scientific" account: as in most contemporary European and American travel writing, Africa was presented as a problem in natural history. Delany's account was both more polemical and more interpretive, delving into a range of questions on the meaning of black history and the future of civilization in Africa. As polemic, the message was straightforward: "our plan must be . . . Africa for the African race and black men to rule them." As interpretation, however, the account grew more problematic, crystallizing many of the tensions and ambiguities that underlay black Americans' interest in Africa. Delany maintained, for example, that African Americans shared a special racial affinity with Africans. White missionaries might labor in the field, he wrote, but ultimately African redemption could be brought about only by "descendants of Africa," by people *"homogeneous* in all the *natural* characteristics, claims, sentiments and sympathies" of Africans. At the same time, however, Delany evinced little regard for indigenous culture; when he spoke of African redemption, he foresaw the same thoroughgoing transformation of social life envisioned by white missionaries. Indeed, he accused existing missions of being too tolerant of indigenous culture, of placing religious over "temporal" development—a failing that African Americans, with their excessive religiosity, were all too likely to repeat. Africans would never acquire "civilization," he argued, until their whole social life, their "habits, manners, and customs," even what they ate and how they ate it, had been uprooted.[30]

There was an obvious tension here, between Delany's professed affinity for African "sympathies and sentiments" and his apparent disdain for African culture. In retrospect, that tension was probably unavoidable. Delany had gone as far down the path toward pan-Africanism as one could while still maintaining the antebellum black elite's convictions about Christianity, civilization, and racial progress, convictions forged in the struggle against American slavery. The tension would return to plague a later generation of African Americans, but Delany was relieved of the problem. In the spring of 1861, a year before the scheduled departure of the first Niger colonists, Providence again took a hand.

It is by now a truism that the American Civil War began not as a war to free the slaves but as a war to preserve the Union. Abraham Lincoln, while no friend to the Peculiar Institution, was forthright about the distinction. In a famous letter to editor Horace Greeley, written in August 1862, Lincoln declared: "If I could save the Union without freeing *any* slave I would do it, and if I could save it by freeing *all* the slaves I would do it; and if I could save it by freeing some and leaving others alone I would also do that. What I do about slavery, and the colored race, I do because I believe it helps to save the Union. . . ." Yet even as he wrote, Lincoln had begun to realize the impossibility of waging a war against the Slave Power without waging war against slavery. A few months before, he had signed a bill abolishing slavery in the District of Columbia, removing an excruciating embarrassment to the federal government. In September he issued the Emancipation Proclamation, to take effect in all states still in rebellion on January 1. By the time of the decisive battles of mid-1863, abolition had been firmly established as a Union war aim.[31]

As emancipation loomed, white and black attitudes toward emigration and colonization diverged sharply. Among white Americans, the prospect of 4 million slaves suddenly acquiring freedom kindled a revival of colonizationism. Lincoln himself dabbled with various colonization proposals, coupling freedom with mass removal to Central America or Haiti. Such talk was at least partly designed to preempt white opposition to emancipation, but Lincoln also seems to have entertained doubts about the possibility of assimilating blacks into American society. Whatever their innate capacity—an issue on which he was much more open-minded than Thomas Jefferson—he feared that blacks would never be accepted as equal citizens by whites, especially in the aftermath

of a bitter war. Among African Americans, on the other hand, interest in
colonization and emigration dwindled as the war progressed. Through 1861
and '62, many continued to see wholesale removal from America as blacks' only
viable option. Alexander Crummell and Edward Blyden both published their
first books in 1862 and made successful American tours. With the prospect of
complete emancipation, however, most African Americans turned decisively
back toward the goal of American citizenship. Daniel Payne, who had flirted
briefly with the A.C.S., denounced colonization and led a deputation to the
White House to lobby against the various Central American schemes. Martin
Delany canceled the passage of the first Niger colonists and went to work as an
army recruiter. In 1864 he was commissioned a major in the Union Army and
marched south at the head of a black regiment. After the war he went to work
for the Bureau of Refugees, Freedmen and Abandoned Lands, a federal agency
designed, at least in theory, to prepare freed slaves for the responsibilities of
citizenship. With the passage of the Fourteenth and Fifteenth Amendments,
interest in Africa evaporated almost completely as African Americans strode
confidently toward full participation in American life.[32]

Needless to say, such expectations proved unavailing. With the Compromise of 1876 and the overturning of the Civil Rights Act six years later, the
federal government essentially washed its hands of the freedmen. Blacks,
consigned to the mercies of southern "Redeemers," were hounded from political office and shackled by laws designed to restore their economic subservience.
The two decades that followed brought Jim Crow, lynch law, and the beginning of systematic disfranchisement. Tumbling cotton prices and a seemingly
endless economic depression did the rest, locking hundreds of thousands into
virtual debt peonage. Everywhere, the dreams of citizenship and equality that
had grown so luxuriantly in the seedtime of Reconstruction lay parched and
stunted.

Amid this climate of despair, a diffuse but widespread African emigration
movement sprouted across the cotton belt. Many who enlisted were tenants
and sharecroppers, the "mudsills" of southern society, whose interest in Africa
waxed as cotton prices waned. Others were at least relatively well off, owning
farms or working in cities as artisans, preachers, and teachers. All along the
economic spectrum, southern blacks turned their eyes back across the Atlantic.
The time had come, the minister of Atlanta's Bethel AME Church announced
after the Democratic victory in 1892, for blacks "to leave Georgia and go to
their own country, Africa, where they would have equal rights and help govern
and have street cars of their own."[33]

The late-nineteenth-century back-to-Africa movement differed from its antebellum predecessor in several important respects. While a wizened American
Colonization Society continued to promote African American removal, control
of the idea had long since passed out of its hands and into the hands of black
ministers and politicians, most of whom had directly experienced the realities

of the redeemed South. While some emigrationists maintained formal linkages with the A.C.S.—Henry Turner, a man whose name would become synonymous with the postwar back-to-Africa movement, was a vice president of the Society—they insisted that emigration remain strictly voluntary and vigorously rejected any imputation of black incapacity for citizenship. Equally important, the geographical basis of emigrationism had shifted decisively. Debates over colonization and emigration in the prewar years had been centered, almost inevitably, in the North: the question, after all, was what to do with free people of color, the majority of whom lived in the free states. Postwar emigrationism, in contrast, was a distinctly southern affair. In South Carolina and in parts of Arkansas and Oklahoma, entire communities sold their belongings and embarked for the coast to meet ships—sometimes real, often imaginary—bound for the "promised land" of Liberia.[34]

In other respects, however, the antebellum and postbellum back-to-Africa movements converged. Both traced the same skein of questions about identity and history, and posed the same cruel dilemmas. Both generated far more enthusiasm and opposition than actual emigration. Finally, debates over emigration in both periods were played out largely within the black church, nowhere more vociferously than within the AME Church. As in the antebellum period, the AME Church became an arena for debating the meaning of Africa, for organizing emigrationist schemes, and, simultaneously, for rallying emigrationist opposition.

Back-to-Africa sentiment first welled over in South Carolina. In the winter of 1877–1878, a group of black leaders in Charleston, including the aging Martin Delany, chartered the Liberian Exodus Joint Stock Steamship Company. As word of the company's formation spread, thousands of people flooded into the city from the surrounding countryside. Startled company directors scraped together a few thousand dollars to purchase a ship and hurriedly arranged a voyage. In the spring of 1878, a crowd of ten thousand gathered at Charleston harbor to bid farewell to the bark *Azor* and its complement of 206 emigrants.[35]

African Methodists played a central role in the *Azor* expedition. The creation of a joint stock company was first proposed by the pastor of the local AME Church, B. F. Porter, who went on to serve as the company's first and only president. Porter's efforts were seconded by R. H. Cain, a future AME bishop and secretary of the church's Missionary Department. Cain, who came south to minister to the freedmen in 1865, was the state's most prominent black politician, having served as a delegate to the state constitutional convention, as a state senator, and, from 1872 to 1876, as a member of the U.S. House of Representatives. Following Redemption, he returned to Charleston, where he promoted African emigration in his own newspaper, *The Missionary Record*. J. M. Brown, the AME Church's resident bishop, also encouraged the *Azor* venture and consecrated the ship prior to its departure. At least thirty of the emigrants, including the group's leader, a young minister named Samuel Flegler, were African Methodists.[36]

As the *Azor* made ready, the old linkage between African American emigration and African redemption remained intact. Porter, who addressed the throng seeing off the ship, characterized the migrants as Christian soldiers whose very presence would speed "the evangelization of the millions of their people who now sat in darkness." Henry Turner also spoke, reminding the crowd that the humble bark bore not just "a load of humanity" but the future of both Christianity and the race. Returning to Africa with "the culture, education, and religion acquired here," the settlers would ignite the process of redemption, "until the blaze of gospel truth should glitter over the whole broad African continent." Standing on the very spot where untold thousands of African slaves had first disembarked in America, looking across the harbor where the first shots of the Civil War had been fired, it was easy to believe that another providential moment was at hand.[37]

As buoyant as such beliefs were, they could not keep the Liberian Exodus Joint Stock Steamship Company afloat. Like Paul Cuffe's Sierra Leone venture before and Marcus Garvey's Black Star Line after, the Liberian line was scuttled by debt; the *Azor* went to the auction block after a single voyage. Thousands who had come to Charleston in hopes of gaining a passage to the promised land found menial jobs in the city or drifted back to the countryside. Those fortunate enough to secure a place on the *Azor* fared scarcely better. Twenty-three of the ill-provisioned emigrants died en route to Liberia; disease claimed dozens more after their arrival. The emigrants did succeed in planting a small Liberian Mission Church, but the expected flood of African converts never materialized. Over the next few years, many disillusioned emigrants returned home to America. By the end of the century, only a handful remained at the small settlement the settlers had planted on the St. Paul River.[38]

In retrospect, the chief significance of the *Azor* episode lay in the emergence of Henry Turner as the guiding spirit of the back-to-Africa movement. Throughout the 1860s and early '70s, Turner had vacillated on emigration. He first publicly committed himself to the idea in 1862, after hearing a speech by Alexander Crummell. As the war dragged on, however, he glimpsed in the carnage a kind of ritual expiation that would wash away the stain of slavery and enable Americans of all races to live together in harmony. Even before Lincoln issued the call for black volunteers, Turner began mustering troops in his Washington churchyard. He served as a chaplain in the Union Army and after the war went to work with the Freedmen's Bureau. The restoration of the Slave Power in 1865–1866 left him casting for a passage to Africa, but with the onset of Radical Reconstruction he tacked back toward incorporation. He served in the Georgia constitutional convention and won election to the state legislature, but when white legislators refused to seat him and his black colleagues, he took his leave with a scathing address in which he virtually foreswore allegiance to the United States. He was somewhat mollified by the reseating of black legislators in 1869, but the final collapse of Reconstruction in 1876 removed any lingering doubt. From that moment on, Turner pursued the goal of African emigration with unquenchable energy and zeal. His vitriolic attacks on the United States, and on any black leaders who questioned his prescriptions, made him one of America's most visible political leaders.[39]

Turner's thought was a curious amalgam of racial chauvinism, evangelical Protestantism, and Social Darwinism. Taken in isolation, few of his ideas were original. His beliefs in "providential destiny" and blacks' psychological and constitutional "fitness" for African work were common currency among antebellum emigrationists, including Alexander Crummell, Edward Blyden, and Henry Highland Garnet. Turner's myriad steamship ventures, and his more general linking of civilization and commerce, had precedents all the way back to Paul Cuffe. The emphasis on race pride was pure Martin Delany. Even Turner's vision of a great Christian empire emerging in Africa was not wholly original. Throughout the nineteenth century American disciples of Swedish philosopher Emmanuel Swedenborg had looked to Africa for the rise of a new, spiritually purified Christianity to supplant the exhausted and materialistic Christianity of the West. Swedenborg's ideas were picked up by several African American churchmen, including Theophilus G. Steward and AME Zion bishop James Theodore Holly, both of whom linked the prophecy to African Americans' outreach to Africa. Steward and Holly were both friends of Turner's.[40]

Ultimately, Turner's distinction lay less in his originality than in his talents as a popularizer, his capacity to synthesize different ideas and communicate them to a mass audience. Few African American leaders have possessed such a rapport with plain, uneducated folk, such an intuitive understanding of popular aspirations and resentments. While other leaders made a cult of circumlocution, Turner was blunt and fearless. He responded to the Supreme Court's "Barbarous Decision" on the Civil Rights Act, for example, by denouncing the American flag as a "rag of contempt" and the Constitution as a "dirty rag, a cheat, a libel, [which] ought to be spit upon by every negro in the land." Southern sharecroppers and tenants who felt estranged from their ostensible leaders delighted in Turner's denunciations of the "fungus class" of black leadership, which clung to life in the shadow of white power. With his genius for invective, Turner happily consigned these "miserable timberheads," "Negro dirt-eaters," and "spittoon-lickers" to the extermination that awaited them in America.[41]

In the AME Church Turner possessed an ideal forum for broadcasting his views. A succession of church offices—secretary of the Book Concern, presiding elder, acting head of the Missionary Department, and, beginning in 1880, bishop—enabled him to move about the South, spreading the back-to-Africa gospel. Using episcopal patronage unabashedly, he accumulated dozens of emigrationist protegés. He also founded two church-related newspapers, *The Voice of Missions* and *Voice of the People,* which functioned as his personal broadsheets. Both papers pressed the emigration issue, juxtaposing articles on American racial atrocities with stories of Africa's vast, untapped wealth. The masthead of *Voice of the People,* for example, included a map of the world, counterposed between America and Africa. Sketches of the Supreme Court building and a hanging black man filled a map of the United States, along with words like "Oppression," "Disenfranchisement," and "Degradation." At the other end of the Atlantic lay a half-illuminated Africa, "The Great Future of the Race," characterized by "Liberty," "Self Reliance," "Christianity," and "Manhood." A ship floated in mid-ocean above the legend "Emigration or Extermination Awaits the Black Man."[42]

Turner's militancy and mass appeal have made him a favorite of contemporary historians, who have elevated him alongside Delany, Blyden, and Marcus Garvey in the pantheon of black nationalism. The characterization has considerable merit. Others, notably Blyden, had emphasized "nationality" and the importance of maintaining an independent Liberia, but it was Turner who raised the idea into a central pillar of black nationalist thought. Throughout his life he maintained that blacks would earn white respect, and recover their own self-respect, only when they demonstrated their capacity to maintain a nation of their own. Programs of racial elevation and "self-help" that stopped short of that goal were foredoomed. "[Booker T.] Washington's policy is not worth a cent," Turner wrote, in one of his more temperate denunciations of a rival leader. "Nothing less than a nation owned and controlled by the Negro will amount to a hill of beans." He went so far as to compose a national anthem, "Africa," sung to the tune of "America"—sung, that is, to the tune of "God Save the Queen": "My native country thee / Land of the black and free / Of thee we sing."[43]

Turner also grasped modern black nationalism's core psychological premise: the belief that oppression represented an individual as well as a political phenomenon, which needed to be addressed internally as well as externally. In characteristically unstinting fashion, he argued that slavery had stripped African Americans of their "manhood," leaving them content to play the role of "scullion." So persuaded were blacks of their own inferiority that they tried to efface themselves, applying potions to lighten their skin and strip the kink from their hair. (No selection in the AME hymnal more enraged Turner than "Whiter than Snow," a song Daniel Payne regarded as a personal favorite.) Worst of all, African Americans had embraced the white man's disdain for Africa. Like Edward Blyden, Turner believed that black people would never come to terms with themselves until they learned to take pride in the continent that had given them both life and color. At every opportunity he argued that Africa was "the cradle of civilization," a place with a "glorious history" and a radiant future. He spoke with pride of his own African heritage, which he traced to an African "prince" brought to the Carolinas in the eighteenth century.[44]

As always, however, labels such as nationalism must be used with care and with a keen awareness of the dangers of reading contemporary values and assumptions into the past. For all his emphasis on race pride and "consanguinity," Turner never articulated a vision of black racial genius, which would become a hallmark of twentieth-century black nationalist ideology. And for all his expostulations on the wonders of African civilization, he continued to see Africa through a distinctly American lens. Concepts such as "providential destiny" and "African redemption" presupposed that black Americans were different from Africans, that they had attained a status to which their "benighted" and "barbarous" brethren still aspired. One searches Turner's writing in vain for any suggestion that African culture was legitimate or worthy of preservation in its own right. Even the terms in which he sketched Africa's "Great Future" betrayed a western, indeed, a distinctly Gilded Age, sensibility. Africa was to be conquered for Christ; "darkness" and "paganism" were to be banished; the silence of a "slumbering" continent was to be broken by the hum of the railroad and the music of the spindle.[45]

These tensions—between racial affinity and cultural distinctiveness, between a reverence for Africa's past and a commitment to western-style progress—were not new, nor were they unique to Turner. Insofar as black nationalism first emerged among literate, Christian African Americans, it was plagued by a basic conundrum. How could one reconcile respect for Africa with Christian evangelicalism? How could one subscribe to the dominant society's conceptions of progress, education, and civilization without endorsing the implication of white superiority? The solution for Turner, and for many other supporters of the African American outreach to Africa, lay in a kind of modified evolutionism in which Christianity and "civilization" appeared not as white inventions but as universal principles toward which all peoples gravitated. Spreading the gospel and western civilization to Africa thus implied no violence toward African civilization but merely speeded Africa along the path it was preordained to follow. The argument borrowed liberally from Alexander Crummell, but Turner added his own distinctive Social Darwinist gloss, arguing that centuries of isolation had allowed the once precocious black race to fall behind more materially minded whites. Both variations denied whites a monopoly on Christian civilization, enabling Turner and thinkers like him to reconcile race pride with equally firm commitments to Christianity and Western-style progress.

Traveling to Africa often laid bare the tensions and ambiguities in African American perceptions of Africa. Turner made the passage four times, visiting Liberia and Sierra Leone in 1891, 1893 and 1895 and South Africa in 1898. His long letters home invariably emphasized Africans' "manliness"—their erect bearing, courage, integrity, and so forth. In one of his 1891 letters,

Turner went so far as to argue that Africans were superior to African Americans, offering as evidence various personal phrenological observations, as well as the testimony of a 108-year-old African man who told him that "during the times of the slave trade there were no 'big blood' first-class Africans sold to the white man, unless they were war prisoners." The idea that "we poor Negroes were the tail-end of the African races" struck a chord with the bishop, especially insofar as it helped explain his compatriots' maddening passivity. (His own ancestor-prince, needless to say, had been one of the war captives.) Turner predicted that leadership of the race would in time gravitate away from Afro-Americans and back toward native Africans, whose perpendicular foreheads, prominent chins, and narrow lips evinced race pride and "the highest type of intellectuality."[46]

Remarkably, however, such statements prompted no reassessment of the broader premises of African "redemption." However much Turner loved tweaking the "Africa-haters" with arguments about African superiority, he continued to see Africans as "heathens" to be "awakened." His initial response on putting into Freetown for the first time was horror at the naked boatman who met his ship. "Things are gloomy here," he remarked to a companion. Such "Dark Continent" preconceptions lent an occasional note of unintended irony to Turner's commentaries. In one letter, for example, he defended Africans against the charge of paganism—the African, he argued perceptively, was more attuned to the "invisible forces" of the universe than the materialistic European—yet in the next breath he blithely predicted that this sensitivity would make it "an easy matter for him to transfer his faith from superstition to Christ Jesus the Lord." Even more striking was Turner's ambivalence about European imperialism. On one hand, imperialism came in for scathing attack, especially in regard to the liquor traffic. The Europeans—Germans especially—were pouring "rum and death" into the continent, in a seemingly deliberate campaign of extermination. At the same time, however, Turner saw imperialism, particularly the British variety, as a boon. Europeans were "opening up" Africa, stimulating enterprise, uncovering the limitless wealth that had lain for centuries beneath a "slumbering" people. In one extraordinary letter, he praised British efforts to suppress the internal slave trade, under which rubric he included polygamy. "God save old England, is my prayer!" he declared.[47]

Similar tensions suffused the writings of Turner's disciples. Edward Ridgel, a young AME minister from Arkansas, was probably the Bishop's most loyal follower. In 1893 he and his wife, together with another young volunteer, accompanied Turner on his second trip to Liberia, intent on remaining as missionaries. Ridgel died in a boating accident after a few years in the country, but not before completing a revealing little book titled *Africa and African Methodism*. In tone and argument, the book closely followed Turner. The "fearful catastrophe" of southern Redemption, Ridgel wrote, was "a divine visitation" to persuade blacks "to leave the haunts of American slavery and pitch their tents on the free and sacred soil of Africa, and assist in the establishment of a mighty Negro empire." Ridgel also warned of the "powerful tendencies toward white men absorbtion [*sic*], in principle, habit, etc." that existed in America. The African American "must return home and become re-negroized, if you please, before he can fully appreciate himself and his people." Yet when confronted with Africans in the flesh, Ridgel exhibited the same Victorian sensibility that his mentor had. African Americans would be "astonished to see how degraded these poor heathens are," he wrote in a letter to the Indianapolis *Freeman.* "You can see grown men naked, and women nearly the same way. Awful, awful, awful! The gospel is needed here." Obviously, such a lament was partly calculated: insofar as mission work depended on voluntary subscriptions from concerned Christians, all nineteenth-century missionaries had a vested interest in portraying Africa as sunk in depravity. Nonetheless, the letter betrays that ambivalence that dogged even the most ardent emigrationists.[48]

Nowhere was such ambivalence better exhibited than in *Glimpses of Africa,* a travel account written by Charles Spencer Smith, an AME minister who would later spend eighteen tumultuous months as the church's resident bishop in South Africa. Born in Canada, Smith went south after the Civil War, serving briefly in the Arkansas state legislature. Like Turner, he embraced the cause of emigration in the wake of Redemption, quickly establishing himself as one of the church's experts on African history and culture. Inevitably, however, the books Smith had at his disposal were written by white travelers and missionaries, most of whom operated well within the "Dark Continent" conventions of African reportage. The hazards of all this first became obvious in 1894, when Smith embarked for West Africa. While his goal was to identify opportunities for returning African Americans, he fashioned himself as a kind of jungle explorer, cramming his kit with the complete works of H. M. Stanley and a wardrobe of flannel suits, parasols, and pith helmets, all white. Smith was also careful to include "scientific instruments"—a barometer, thermometer, and compass—which he used to record the temperature, atmospheric pressure, and precise location of various well-trod West African ports.[49]

Inevitably, Smith's primary interlocuters were white officials, under whose tutelage he was transformed from militant emigrationist to ardent colonial apologist. Aside from a supportive preface by Bishop Turner, obviously written without benefit of having read the manuscript, Smith's *Glimpses of Africa* was indistinguishable from a hundred other nineteenth-century African travel accounts. Africans were childlike and decorated themselves in exotic, sometimes offensive ways. European imperialism (save the decadent Portuguese variety) was a blessing, exposing "savages" who had known only "indolence" and "immediate gratification" to the virtues of sustained labor. African American emigration was unnecessary, since Europeans were already doing all that was necessary "to lift the long-benighted masses into the light of civilization and progress." Ultimately, all that remained of the race pride that Smith had espoused prior to his departure was the familiar colonial cant about the integrity and "tractability" of the "raw" native, compared to his roguish civilized cousin. Having emerged in the AME hierarchy as a Turner lieutenant, Smith transformed himself into the bishop's most determined critic, stumping the country to expose the distortions that he believed underlay the back-to-Africa movement.[50]

Smith's was anything but a lonely campaign. The vast majority of African American leaders, including virtually the entire AME House of Bishops, regarded emigration as folly. "A rolling stone gathers no moss," warned Bishop Wesley Gaines, one of Turner's most implacable foes. Like his friend and associate Booker T. Washington, Gaines had begun life in slavery, rising to become one of black America's leading apostles of the New South creed. (Gaines and Washington were the only black representatives on the organizing committee for the 1895 Atlanta Cotton States and International Exposition, the festival of southern boosterism at which Washington delivered his famous "Atlanta Compromise" speech.) Like the Tuskegeean, Gaines believed that blacks should "cast down their buckets" where they were, capitalizing on the growing opportunities afforded by southern "commercial and industrial" development. The money squandered on emigrationist fantasies alone, he argued, could immeasurably increase black property holdings, which, in a materialistic nation like the United States, was certain to enhance the race's prestige.[51]

Not all AME leaders subscribed to Gaines's happy prognosis for southern life, but most shared his opposition to emigration. Even after the southern victories in the General Conferences of the 1880s, the balance of African Methodist leadership remained in the hands of northerners, the descendants of the antebellum free black elite. With little direct experience of the redeemed South, such leaders were inclined to dismiss Turner's tirades as exaggerated and impolitic. At a deeper level, emigrationism challenged their most deep-seated political convictions. Since the days of Richard Allen, the thrust of African Methodism, and of elite African American politics in general, had been to emphasize black progress. If whites could only be induced to discard their stereotypes and to look honestly at the strides made by black Americans, the chief impediment to full citizenship would fall away. Even in the dark days of the 1880s and '90s, elite leaders continued to sound the theme of progress, with paeans to blacks' "unprecedented advance" and "remarkable achievements" in the few decades since emancipation. Into the fray stepped Bishop Turner, braying about "scullions," dismissing racial progress as illusory, imperiling everything for which "responsible" race leaders labored. The fact that Turner publicly excoriated his rivals as "coons" and "dirt-eaters" doubtless contributed to their dislike.[52]

The northern attack on Turner was led by Benjamin Tanner, a future AME bishop and editor of the church's flagship newspaper, the *Christian Recorder*. In background and temperament, the Philadelphia-born Tanner was everything Turner was not—educated, wealthy, and more than a little condescending. (Prior to joining the ministry, Tanner had been a barber, the archetypal occupation of the presegregation black elite.) In an 1883 editorial Tanner called emigration folly and dismissed Turner as just one more in a line of black demagogues come to stir up the mob. "What one thoughtful man among us writes outweighs in value the whole Niagara of eloquence common to our people," he declared. In a later article he compared leaving America in search of opportunity to "running from the sun for both heat and light." Other critics took up the attack, warning that emigration smacked of disloyalty and thus undercut black efforts to prove themselves worthy of republican citizenship. (One *Christian Recorder* correspondent, writing even before Turner's notorious screed against the Constitution, advocated putting the bishop on trial for treason.) Opponents enjoyed a field day in 1891–1892 when a group of AME Church members from Oklahoma, seduced by an emigrationist charlatan, sold their farms at a loss and arrived in New York to meet a nonexistent Liberia-bound ship. The Oklahomans' fate became a national cause célèbre, and half a dozen New York papers joined the *Christian Recorder* in calling for Turner's head.[53]

If the objection to emigration was simply that it loosed African Americans from their moorings and discouraged property accumulation, then Turner's opponents should have spoken out against all migrations, whether to Kansas, California, or Liberia. A few, including Bishop Gaines, did. In most cases, however, there was a distinct edge to criticisms of African emigration, which bespoke black elites' continuing uneasiness with the continent. Since the birth of the American Colonization Society, African repatriation had carried the implication that African Americans lacked the capacity to participate equally in national life. Moreover, the racist stereotypes that attached to Africans— that they were indolent, brutish, and oversexed—were precisely the ones that African Americans struggled against at home. In such a context, many black leaders went to great lengths to distance themselves from Africa. One AME minister, writing in the *Church Review,* maintained that two centuries in America had divested black Americans of any allegiance to or affinity for Africa:

> The American Negro is no more African today than descendants of the Pilgrim fathers are Europeans; not as much, for . . . the Negro brought no civilization, [and] hence took that which he found. He lost his heathenism and accepted Christianity, and in many cases became so intermingled until he has lost his color.

Another minister, writing in the same journal, even revived the idea of dropping "African" from the AME Church's name. With the Fifteenth Amendment, he wrote, "the mission of the word 'African' was ended." The task now facing black Americans was to "erase race and nationality" in order to align themselves more closely with "the land of our birth and adoption."[54]

This second attempt to elide Africa from African Methodism succeeded no better than had the first, half a century before. Neither, however, did Bishop Turner succeed in convincing his coreligionists to embrace the identity implicit in their name. Indeed, in the short term his efforts seem to have had precisely the opposite effect, impelling many influential black leaders to renounce any association with Africa. As for actual emigration, not much occurred. For all the sound and fury, the postbellum back-to-Africa movement carried scarcely a thousand African Americans back to the promised land of Africa. By any measure, that migration was far less significant than the continuing westward and northward drift of America's black population or the accelerating movement to urban centers, North and South.

In the longer term, however, the movement that Turner led had a profound effect on the AME Church and on the developing relationship between black American and Africa. Like Garveyism a generation later, the late-nineteenth-century back-to-Africa movement reinjected the issue of Africa into African American political and intellectual life. Black Americans were forced, sometimes reluctantly, to examine their relationship to Africa and to ask what, if any, obligation they owed to the continent. A growing number in the 1880s and '90s found the answer in Christian missions. Saving Africa for Christ, long treated as a kind of ancillary benefit of emigration, slowly emerged as a project in its own right.

The first permanent AME mission in Africa was planted in Liberia in 1878 by the *Azor* settlers. Established as a by-product of emigration, the mission was something less than a ringing success. Many of the original colonists were claimed by fever; others returned home to America. Samuel Flegler, head of the AME contingent, remained in Liberia less than two years. His successor, an aging émigré named Clement Irons, made no effort to open work among the indigenous population, devoting himself instead to a steamboat concession on the St. Paul River. S. J. Campbell, who assumed control of the mission in the late 1880s, lavished his energy on a coffee plantation ceded to him by the Liberian government. The only "heathens" with whom he had contact were the young Africans who labored on his plantation, which Campbell dignified with the title of "industrial school." Taking the argument about slavery as a providential school to its logical conclusion, Campbell and other Americo-Liberian settlers argued that plantation labor benefited Africans by exposing them to the blessings of "civilization" and sustained industry.[55]

The dozen or so other AME missionaries who came to Liberia in the late nineteenth century left a scarcely more edifying legacy. William H. Heard, a Henry Turner protégé appointed U.S. consul to Liberia in the 1890s, made nary a pretense of preaching to Africans, whom he regarded as "annoyances," "savages," and impediments to interior trade. Heard eventually rode his African experience all the way to the AME bishopric, yet in 1898 he was able to write an entire book about Liberia without mentioning the problem of evangelization. Ultimately, it is difficult to find any evidence of genuine missionary activity by the AME Church in Liberia. One disenchanted churchman, reflecting back on the history of the mission in 1916, dismissed the whole enterprise as a sham, perpetuated by "adventurers" and "parasites" who were more interested in their sinecures or in securing back-door admission to the General Conference than in expanding Christ's kingdom.[56]

Membership rolls seem to bear out that bleak assessment. On the arrival of the *Azor,* the church immediately attracted several hundred adherents, virtually all African American settlers, including many who had been AME members before emigrating to Liberia. Thereafter the church languished. When Bishop Turner arrived to organize the Liberian Annual Conference in 1891, church rolls counted just four hundred souls, concentrated almost exclusively in the settler enclaves. As late as 1915, AME membership in Liberia totaled just 436. The gulf between expectation and reality could scarcely have been greater. In his speech at the launch of the *Azor,* Turner had boldly predicted that Africans would flock to a church of their kith and kin, until "the blaze of gospel truth should glitter over the whole broad African continent." In fact, AME missionaries had far less impact among Liberia's indigenous people than their much maligned white counterparts, who as outsiders were at least immune to the corrosive insularity of Americo-Liberian society.[57]

The AME Church enjoyed marginally more success in neighboring Sierra Leone. The historical origins of the church reached back to the late eighteenth century, when thousands of black Canadians, many of them refugees from the American Revolution, embarked for the new colony on the Windward Coast. Included in the exodus were several hundred adherents of the Countess of Huntingdon Connexion, a London-based evangelical sect with a large black contingent. Through the first half of the nineteenth century, the Huntingdon church grew slowly in Sierra Leone, attracting new emigrants from Canada, as well as scores of African "recaptives." By the 1880s, however, the church was in decline; it possessed no supervisor and had long since lost contact with the parent body in London. Somehow, members of the Freetown congregation heard of the AME Church, and in 1885 they issued a "call" requesting connection. If later South African experience is any guide, they probably saw affiliation with a black American church as a way to secure the material benefits of missionary sponsorship without surrendering ecclesiastical control to whites.[58]

AME leaders responded to the call by dispatching a young missionary, J. R. Frederick, to Sierra Leone, with instructions to assume control of the congregation and to install African Methodist discipline and usages. A West Indian by birth, Frederick was almost unique among early AME missionaries in his sensitivity to Africans and African culture. While he too concentrated his efforts in the settler enclaves, he welcomed native converts into his church and stressed the importance of learning Africans' languages and customs. With fellow West Indian Edward Blyden, he launched a "Dress Reform Society" to encourage the wearing of traditional clothing, a radical departure from standard missionary practice, which regarded adoption of western dress as an essential step toward civilization. Frederick also shared Blyden's relative tolerance of Islam, which he saw as erroneous but productive of self-reliance, sobriety, and piety. A second AME missionary, Sarah Gorham, arrived three years behind Frederick and opened up a small mission station at Magbele, seventy-five miles in the interior. By the time of Bishop Turner's visit in 1891, the Sierra Leone church boasted more than five hundred adherents and a half dozen ministers, including two defectors from the Wesleyan mission and one grandson of the pioneer AME missionary Daniel Coker.[59]

Despite its promising beginning, the Sierra Leone church soon languished, primarily due to chronic shortages of funds. Even as its U.S. membership neared half a million, the AME Church remained an impecunious institution, especially relative to white mission churches. Most years, the church's Missionary Department was unable even to pay missionaries' passages to Africa, forcing would-be volunteers to undertake speaking tours to raise their fares. Sarah Gorham appears to have reached Sierra Leone by accepting an appointment to Liberia from the American Colonization Society and then deserting. Her mission at Magbele constantly suffered for want of money and closed completely after her death in 1894. Three years later, a "disheartened" Frederick led his entire congregation out of the AME Church. By the turn of the century, AME membership in Sierra Leone had dwindled to a few hundred, where it hovered for the next several decades.[60]

While the lack of support for the Sierra Leone mission was primarily a function of the church's poverty, it also bespoke church leaders' continuing uneasiness about Africa. Northern ministers, who still controlled the bulk of AME resources, tended to view African mission work as a component of Turner's emigration madness, and many declined to support it. In 1884 the House of Bishops did establish an annual Easter Day mission collection, at Turner's urging, but with the proviso that at least half the money raised be dispensed on "home" missions. Young Edward Ridgel, touring AME congregations in 1892 to raise money for a passage to Liberia, was startled by northerners' lack of "evangelical fire." "Ridgel, you are foolish," he was told by Bishop Tanner. "I would not think of going to Africa. If I had my way I would abandon our African mission field at once. We have no business in Africa." While Tanner was an extreme example, other church leaders shared his skepticism. Through the 1880s, returns from the annual Easter Day mission collection averaged less than three thousand dollars.[61]

Senior Bishop Daniel Payne, still a formidable force in church politics, shared some of the doubts about African missions but took a more balanced position. Throughout his life Payne warned against frittering away the church's "small purse" on African missions, especially in view of the pressing priorities in the United States. In an 1885 article titled "The Past, Present and Future of the A.M.E. Church," written for the inaugural volume of the AME *Church Review,* he reminded his coreligionists of the work yet to be done on the home front, pointing particularly to the baleful state of the church's schools. In a backhanded criticism of Turner, he cautioned against the "Don Quixotic idea of 'Ecclesiastical Imperialism' . . . of bringing every negro on earth under our Discipline." Such a path, he warned, could lead to "our disintegration." Implicit in that admonition was not only Payne's preoccupation with institutional solidity but his abiding concern with the race's reputation. To launch African missions that the church could not sustain—"paper missions," he called them—invited white ridicule and undermined black Americans' ongoing struggle to prove their fitness for republican citizenship. Unlike Tanner, however, Payne did not completely discountenance mission work. He accepted that African Americans, as Christians, possessed an obligation to spread the gospel and in 1884 proposed sending two missionaries to Central Africa on a trial basis. When the call came from Sierra Leone two years later, it was Payne who dispatched Frederick. From that moment until his death in 1893, the old bishop almost singlehandedly kept the Sierra Leone mission afloat, raising more money in his Ohio district each year than the rest of the church combined. Much to Bishop Turner's chagrin, however, Payne insisted on paying Frederick directly, rather than through the Missionary Department, lest the Department rush into commitments the church could not match.[62]

Northern skepticism and crippling shortages of funds would remain abiding features of the AME Church's African outreach. By the early 1890s, however, a growing number of church leaders had begun to follow Payne's lead, laying the foundations of a new mission consensus. To be sure, leaders such as Bishop Tanner continued to resist all things African, while Bishop Turner continued to weave emigration and evangelization into a single cloth. Between those extremes, however, many churchmen were prepared to separate the two issues, accepting the obligation of missions without endorsing African repatriation. A few discerned that success in the African mission field, far from undermining blacks' status in America, might actually enhance it.

The emerging consensus on missions reflected a series of developments within American Protestantism in general, and African Methodism in particular. Despite centuries of interaction, it was only in the last third of the nineteenth century that white Americans really awakened to Africa's existence as a distinct historical and philosophical problem. Stanley's pursuit of Livingstone on behalf of the New York *Herald* captivated millions of readers and helped establish the African travel account as one of the century's most popular literary genres. The imperial "Scramble for Africa" contributed to the growing interest, touching off a worldwide debate on the fate of the continent. The

1893 Columbian Exposition in Chicago included a special "Congress on Africa," bringing together scholars, missionaries, and politicians from around the globe in a week-long symposium on the future of the "Dark Continent." This explosion of interest had an especially dramatic effect on American evangelical churches, which had always lagged behind their European counterparts, at least as far as Africa was concerned. By the end of the century, it was almost de rigueur for a denomination to possess at least one African mission.[63]

In contrast to the AME Church, most white denominations were able to sustain African missions financially. Their problem, rather, was finding people to staff them. Among white Americans, the continent's appeal remained largely voyeuristic: while many were prepared to open their hearts to Africa's poor, benighted people, few were prepared to venture to the continent themselves, especially given its reputation as a "white man's graveyard." African American missionaries offered ideal surrogates. According to the racial assumptions of the day, they possessed a peculiar "affinity" for Africans, as well as a special "fitness" for the rigors of the African climate. They were also taken to be more accustomed to privation than whites, always an asset in a missionary. Inspired by such beliefs, the main American evangelical churches launched systematic campaigns to encourage missionary vocations among African Americans.[64]

There was, of course, nothing new about using blacks in African missions. Northern Methodists had tried to recruit Daniel Payne for the Liberian field in the late 1830s; the Presbyterians set up an entire school, Lincoln University, to train Africans and African Americans for mission work. The campaigns of the late 1880s and early '90s, however, were of a whole different order. Representatives of white churches toured black churches and colleges all across the South, searching for new recruits; they sponsored essay- and hymn-writing contests focusing on African Americans' distinct duty to Africa. Northern Methodists were particularly active. In 1890 they instituted "Friends of Africa" clubs in all their Freedmen's Aid schools across the South. Four years later, they established the Stewart Missionary Foundation in Atlanta for the express purpose of training southern blacks for the African field. During the 1895 Cotton States Exposition, where Booker T. Washington catapulted himself to fame, the Stewart Foundation hosted an international conference aimed at explicating black Americans' relationship and obligation to Africa.[65]

The campaign proved short-lived. By the beginning of World War I, most white churches had retreated from the idea of using black mission workers, after protests from colonial governments in Africa and a few celebrated conflicts with black missionaries in the field. By that time, however, the seeds of evangelism were well sown. In a sense, white churches succeeded in doing what Bishop Turner's polemics could not: they legitimized interest in Africa, erasing that taint of inferiority and unassimilability that the continent had carried since the rise of the A.C.S. Perenially preoccupied with managing their institution along "recognized lines," AME leaders realized that their church would never be fully accepted until it too had joined the scramble for Africa.[66]

Support for African missions also reflected the influence of new women's organizations within the AME Church, organizations that were themselves rooted in broader changes within American Protestantism in the years after the Civil War. Between 1868 and 1872, Congregationalists, Methodists, Presbyterians, Baptists, and Episcopalians all established separate women's missionary societies, with an eye not only to freedmen's work but to the growing Chinese mission field. African Methodists were characteristically quick to follow suit. In 1874 the *Christian Recorder* issued a challenge to "representative" women of the race to take the lead in mission work. The summons was answered by a group of bishops' wives, who inaugurated the Woman's Mite Missionary Society. Over the next two decades, the W.M.M.S. became the church's chief fund-raiser for mission activity; the very name of the organization referred to the process by which members consolidated their small "mites" into substantial sums. Most of the organization's energies were initially devoted to the church's struggling mission in Haiti, but in the late 1880s and early '90s Bishop Payne enlisted it in the Sierra Leone work. In one of his last official acts, Payne joined with a remarkable collection of Ohio churchwomen to organize the first national convention of the W.M.M.S. in July 1893. Over the next few years, the society spread from its Ohio base, sprouting local branches all across the northern states. At the same time, a kindred organization, the Women's Home and Foreign Missionary Society, was launched in the South under the sponsorship of Henry Turner. Both organizations grew so rapidly that the 1900 AME General Conference set aside an entire "Women's Day" to discuss women's missionary work.[67]

Between them, the W.M.M.S. and the W.H.F.M.S. developed a distinctly feminine interpretation of African redemption, demonstrating yet again the continent's extraordinary conceptual elasticity. Historically, churchmen like Henry Turner had conceived of Africa as a "fatherland" that African Americans would "conquer for Christ," thereby reclaiming their lost "manhood." African Methodist women, on the other hand, typically portrayed the continent as a "motherland," impoverished and defiled, in need of women's healing touch. Monthly periodicals such as the *Missionary Searchlight,* the organ of the W.H.F.M.S., and the Mite Society's evocatively titled *Women's Light and Love for Heathen Africa* reminded women of their special responsibility to Africa, providing a feminine counterpoint to the sometimes militaristic imagery of Turner's *Voice of Missions.* In the most elaborate instances, Africa became a synecdoche for black womanhood, a kind of collective mother, struggling to protect and nurture her children in the face of ignorance and outrage.[68]

Several "representative women" of the race, including such figures as Hallie Quinn Brown, Sara J. Duncan and Fanny Jackson Coppin, rose from the ranks of the W.M.M.S. and the W.H.F.M.S. to positions of genuine eminence within the AME Church, and indeed within black America as a whole. In light of our previous discussion, however, it is important to emphasize that the women's mission movement represented something less than the triumph of female "collective power" over entrenched male interests. Much of the initial impetus for the movement came from male church leaders, who defined the parameters of women's participation and exercised ecclesiastical authority over their activities. In terms of religious leadership, the movement represented less a challenge to the existing male church hierarchy than a ratification of it. Unlike antebellum female Holiness preachers such as Jarena Lee and Zilpha Elaw, who claimed religious authority on the basis of direct inspiration, the women who presided over AME mission societies generally held office by virtue of marriage. The first president of the W.M.M.S., Mary A. Campbell, was the wife of an AME bishop, as were six of her first seven successors. Ministers' wives presided over local chapters. The southern W.H.F.M.S. seems to have offered somewhat greater scope for women to achieve office in their own right, yet it too remained under the supervision of ministers and resident bishops, who were customarily addressed as "fathers."[69]

At the level of ideology, both the W.M.M.S. and the W.H.F.M.S. operated within prevailing canons of domesticity, with all the attendant ambiguities and paradoxes. On one hand, domestic ideology defined women as society's primary agents of acculturation, thus conferring on them a vital social role, especially among a group like African Americans, who were still widely perceived as not yet fully cultured. Women represented the "fundamental agency under God in the regeneration . . . of the race, as well as the groundwork and starting point of the progress upward," wrote Anna Julia Cooper in her classic *A Voice from the South,* a book dedicated to AME Bishop Benjamin Arnett. Such a perspective could be and was used to justify black women's right to higher education, as well as to an enhanced role in political affairs. As always with domesticity, however, elevation was purchased at the cost of self-effacement. In its black as in its white incarnation, domestic ideology enshrined notions of female selflessness and service that themselves posed a barrier to women's equal participation in church and society. Significantly, the women of the W.M.M.S. chose as their charter 1 Corinthians 13, Paul's disquisition on the distinctly feminine virtue of charity.[70]

The tasks undertaken by women's mission societies reflected these gendered assumptions. For all their alleged affinity for the "children" of Africa, women were not presumed to be equipped for the rigors of mission work themselves, except as missionary wives. The two obvious exceptions, Sarah Gorham and Amanda Smith, were both forced to travel to West Africa under the auspices of white organizations, rather than as representatives of the AME Church. Within both the W.M.M.S. and the W.H.F.M.S., women continued to be defined as "helpmeets," with responsibility for encouraging missionary vocations, offering prayers for mission work, and raising funds through teas and bazaars, as well as year-round "self-denial." Control over mission pursestrings was certainly significant: in at least one case, leaders of the W.M.M.S. refused to hand over money they had raised for the Haitian mission because they disapproved of the man assigned to the field. The basic division of labor, however, remained intact. While mission work offered African Methodist men a field for distinction, it offered African Methodist women an opportunity to serve and thereby to express their intrinsic nature.[71]

Yet even granting these limitations, there is no questioning the importance of organizations like the W.M.M.S. and the W.H.F.M.S. in the developing African American mission movement. In transposing mission work into an expression of female nature, these organizations helped bridge some of the breaches that Africa had torn within the church. Bishops Benjamin Tanner and Henry Turner, bitter rivals on most issues, could agree on the value of women's missionary work, as could their wives, both of whom served as society presidents. More concretely, women's missionary societies came to represent a substantial vested interest within the AME Church, unequivocally committed to the cause of African "redemption." For the next half century and beyond, much of the enthusiasm for African missions and most of the money were generated by women.

Finally, the emerging consensus on African missions reflected a changing of the guard in AME Church leadership. Advocates such as Henry Turner and R. H. Cain always maintained that "Africa spirit" would blossom only after the generation of church leaders raised in the shadow of slavery had passed away, and in a certain sense they were right. Eight AME bishops died between 1887 and 1894, completely transforming the ten-member House of Bishops. With the exception of Cain himself, all of the deceased were northerners; most had been born before 1820 and had come of age during the 1830s and '40s, as free people of color struggled to establish their right to remain in the United States. Not surprisingly, most were leery of Africa, which carried the odor of colonization. The bishops who replaced them, in contrast, came of age in the 1860s and '70s, long after colonization had been discredited, and most were at least open to the possibility of AME missions in Africa.[72]

Equally important, the 1880s and '90s saw the emergence of a stratum of ambitious young ministers, many of whom became ardent supporters of African mission work. Born too young to have participated in the epochal events of slavery and Reconstruction, men such as Levi Coppin and H. B. Parks embraced Africa as their generation's field for heroism. Coppin, born in Maryland in 1848, was the pastor of Mother Bethel Church in Philadelphia and the editor of the AME *Church Review*. An avid collector of books about Africa, he promoted missions in the pages of his journal and led all AME ministers in annual Easter Day collections. Elected to the episcopacy in 1900, he served as the church's first resident bishop in South Africa. H. B. Parks, also a future bishop, was cut from much the same cloth. Born in Georgia in 1856, he was just forty years old—young by AME standards—when he became secretary of the church's Missionary Department. Even Benjamin Tanner's son Carleton hearkened to Africa's "Macedonian Cry." In 1902 he volunteered for the South African mission field, where he spent two controversy-filled years. Among his proudest achievements was the establishment of the South African *Christian Recorder,* a short-lived periodical modeled on the paper his father had edited two decades before.[73]

In remarkably short order, support for African missions had crystallized into a distinct ideology, portraying African evangelization as the next step in the progressive emancipation of the black race. At the core of this ideology lay the "providential hand" theory of African American history, first articulated by antebellum emigrationists. Leaders like Coppin and Park characterized slavery as "a school of hard experiences"—an "industrial" school, in the parlance of the time—ordained by God to prepare African Americans for the task of African redemption. Beliefs about epidemiology and "natural sympathy" were grafted onto the argument until African Americans alone appeared capable of carrying Christianity and civilization into Africa. The African "will hearken to your message where the white messengers have failed," boasted Parks. "You can understand his nature and he can understand you. It is not the spiritual love of the white missionary, but the sympathy of blood. . . ." M. C. B. Mason, a black Methodist minister, elaborated the argument in a speech at the Stewart Foundation's 1895 conference on Africa. While Mason evinced no interest in emigration—the United States is "our country," he assured delegates—he insisted that African Americans had a special "obligation" to save Africa. The task is ours, he declared, "by racial affinity, by providential preparation, by special adaptation, by divine command. . . ."[74]

While Mason's argument borrowed liberally from emigrationism's store of ideas, its central thrust was precisely the opposite. Despite Bishop Turner's assurances that some blacks would always remain in the United States, emigration clearly implied a renunciation of American identity. The black missionary movement implied nothing of the kind. On the contrary, its advocates conceived missions not only as a way to redeem Africa but as a way to enhance black status within America. Lifting Africa from "barbarism" to the light of "civilization" promised to alleviate a major source of the stigma that attached to black people everywhere, while providing a compelling demonstration of African American progress and prowess. "In all your thirty years of freedom, you have never had such an opportunity to prove your strength," Mission Secretary Parks enthused. Levi Coppin agreed. The time had come, he argued, for the AME Church to take its place among the "agencies for the redemption of the world," and what better place to begin than Africa, where "the natural love of race" and "ties of affinity" lent the church a comparative advantage?[75]

Such arguments, in essence, recast the African interest in the timeworn idiom of "vindicating the race." Like the mission to the freedmen after the

Civil War, African missions provided African Methodists, and African Americans generally, with a stage on which to demonstrate their capacity. As such, they represented a logical next step in a process begun when Richard Allen and his comrades tramped out of Philadelphia's St. George's Church. "We believe that as God prepared Moses to lead Israel out of Egypt," an AME minister wrote in the *Church Review*,

> so he also prepared Richard Allen, and established the A.M.E. Church. First—to demonstrate to the world the capacity of the Negro race variety for self-government and intellectual development. Second—to carry the Gospel to the emancipated Freedmen of the South. Third—to redeem Africa, our fatherland.

"Bleeding Africa is plaintively calling to the A.M.E. Church, 'Send us light and civilization,'" he concluded.[76]

It was a compelling argument, one that offered African Americans explanation and purpose, those most precious of religious consolations. Yet there were problems. No matter how sincere AME leaders were in their devotion to Africa, their interest remained profoundly self-referential: Africa represented a field for African American heroism, a vindication of centuries of suffering, a solution to the riddle of black American experience. Africans, if they entered the picture at all, existed primarily as abstractions, imaginative foils around which African Americans could define their own identity and destiny. Depending on the demands of the situation, they could be parents or children, brethren or barbarians. The African "is your kith and kin," H. B. Parks reminded readers in one mission solicitation, "savage though he be." The same ambivalence surfaced in black hymnody, which, in a population that was still largely illiterate, remained a crucial vehicle for disseminating ideas. "Stretch forth thy hand to kindred o'er the sea," wrote Levi Coppin, an accomplished composer. "Our cause is one, and brothers still are we." On the other hand, "Come Over Here and Help Us," the most popular AME mission hymn of the period, projected Africa as a stereotypical "Dark Continent," against which African American progress could be measured: "Shall we, whose souls are lighted / With wisdom from on high, / Shall we to men benighted / The lamp of life deny?" Images of illumination also suffused Alexander Camphor's classic "Hymn of Sympathy and Prayer for Africa," which won the Stewart Missionary Foundation's 1894 hymn-writing contest. Camphor showed unusual sensitivity to African culture during his later career as a Presbyterian missionary in the Congo, but in 1894 his vision of Africa remained parochial at best. "How can we remain contented in illuminated homes, / While our brother gropes in darkness, and in heathenism roams? / Should not his complete salvation be our earnest, prayerful plea / Till that long-neglected country shall be free, yes, wholly free."[77]

The final couplet was especially allusive. In linking salvation and emancipation, Camphor completed an extraordinary act of appropriation, which cast

African work as an extension of African Americans' own tortuous journey from slavery to freedom. African Methodists elaborated the theme in endless sermons, essays, and articles. It was the duty of black Americans to "knock off" Africans' "fetters"; to "break the bands of superstition" and "chains of ignorance" that bound them; to answer "the calling of captives and slaves for deliverance"; to "emancipate" their brethren "from the long night of ignorance." Surely the most elaborate development of the metaphor came in AME Bishop Benjamin Arnett's speech to the Columbian Exposition's "Congress on Africa." In the course of one byzantine sentence, Arnett managed to allude to emancipation six times, all to show African Americans' primacy in the redemption of Africa.

> But the hand that holds the banner of liberty and truth must be a free hand, a trained hand, a hand without manacle or chain, that the people who sit under the shadow and region of death may see through the light of opportunity, the chainless hand of their brother bidding them break the bonds of superstition, ignorance and sin, and arise to the stature of freemen.[78]

From the standpoint of propaganda alone, the equation of heathenism with slavery and of missions with emancipation represented a stroke of genius. What better way to inspire feelings of affinity and obligation among people who were themselves only a few decades removed from bondage? There was more here than propaganda, however. Embedded in the parallel lay an apparent solution to that tension that had dogged the black outreach to Africa since the days of Daniel Coker. In labeling Africans slaves, groping for freedom, African Americans at once marked them as profoundly similar to yet fundamentally different from themselves. Like degraded southern slaves a generation before, Africans were fully competent human beings who would blossom once exposed to the light of Christian civilization. Like the slaves, however, they remained enchained by ignorance and darkness and required some external agency to lift them to the light. And who better to provide that assistance than African Americans, who had themselves traveled the road from barbarism to civilization, from slavery to freedom? The whole formulation put African Americans in the enviable position of being able to identify simultaneously with Africans and with the "civilizing" agencies that presumed to save them, to indulge the romance of racial affinity from the security of cultural distance.

The implications of all this would become apparent once the AME Church began working in South Africa. In the short term, however, late-nineteenth-century mission ideology helped bridge the divisions that Africa had carved within African Methodism, while answering the deepest existential yearnings of a dispossessed and despised people. Impoverished southern tenants who dreamed of an African promised land and elite northern leaders clinging to the goal of assimilation in America could unite on the necessity of liberating Africa for Christ. Above all, the dream of emancipating Africa offered invaluable assurance. Amid the darkening days of racial reaction, the opening of African missions provided proof that history was progressive, that the ordeal of slavery had indeed meant something, that black Americans were yet a chosen people, destined to play a special role in the unfolding design of Providence. Thus were African Americans borne back to Africa, that strange mirror of a continent, land of their ancestors and their children.

BOOK TWO

Hear, O our God; for we are despised; and turn their reproach upon their own head, and give them for a prey in the land of captivity:

And cover not their iniquity, and let not their sin be blotted out from before thee: for they have provoked thee to anger before the builders.

So built we the wall; and all the wall was joined together unto the half thereof; for the people had a mind to work.

But it came to pass, that when San-bal-lat, and Tobiah, and the Arabians, and the Ammonites, and the Ashdodites, heard that the walls of Jerusalem were made up, that the breaches began to be stopped, then they were very wroth,

And conspired all of them together to come and to fight against Jerusalem, and to hinder it.

Nevertheless we made our prayer unto our God, and set a watch against them day and night . . .

And I looked, and rose up, and said unto the nobles, and to the rulers, and to the rest of the people, Be not ye afraid of them: remember the Lord, which is great and terrible, and fight for your brethren, your sons, and your daughters, your wives, and your houses. . . .

And I said unto the nobles, and to the rulers, and to the rest of the people, The work is great and large, and we are separated upon the wall, one far from another.

In what place therefore ye hear the sound of the trumpet, resort ye thither unto us: our God shall fight for us.

So we labored in the work: and half of them held the spears from the rising of the morning until the stars appeared.

NEH. 4:4-9, 14, 19-21

4

Stretch Forth
Thy Hands

In 1892, one hundred years after Richard Allen and his comrades walked out of Philadelphia's St. George's Methodist Church, a group of black Methodists in Pretoria, South Africa, withdrew from the Wesleyan Methodist Missionary Society and established an independent African Methodist church. They called their movement the Ethiopian Church, or *Tiyopia,* after the prophecy of African redemption in Psalms 68. Through a seemingly providential series of contingencies and chance encounters, the leaders of the South African Ethiopian Church came into contact with Bishop Henry Turner and the leaders of the African Methodist Episcopal Church in the United States. In 1896 the Ethiopians were formally accepted into the AME connection.

The chapter which follows examines the history of the Ethiopian Church from its origins in nineteenth-century European missions through its amalgamation with the AME Church. In effect, the chapter charts the other side of the looking glass, exploring the origins and politics of African independent churches, as well as African Christians' complex reflections on the subject of black America. At the same time, it represents an attempt to repopulate "Ethiopianism," to give historical specificity and human faces to a movement that is too often treated as a kind of generic African phenomenon. The chapter begins with a brief and necessarily schematic examination of European missions, focusing on the changing place of African religious workers, who would provide the foot soldiers of the Ethiopian Movement. The second section offers a collective portrait of Ethiopian leadership. The final section traces the chain of events that led the leaders of this fast-growing African independent church into the arms of a black American mission church.[1]

To people prone to discerning the hand of Providence in human affairs, the hundred years separating the beginnings of the AME and Ethiopian churches seemed full of portent. The sheer symmetry of the interval suggested that the union between the churches had been foreordained, that Africans and African Americans were traveling the same historical path, with Africans trailing a century behind. While the ways of Providence remain mysterious, the interlude probably had less to do with historic paths and relative progress than with the relatively slow dissemination of Christianity in South Africa. The decades after Jan van Riebeeck's arrival at the Cape in 1652 saw only desultory missionary activity, mostly among imported slaves. The first Moravian mission to the "Hottentots" opened only in the 1730s, as the Great Awakening rolled through the North American colonies. Mission work among Bantu-speaking peoples, the bulk of the subcontinent's population, began only after the first British annexation of the Cape. In 1799, the year the members of Philadelphia's Bethel Church published their Articles of Association, the first representatives of the newly formed London Missionary Society sailed into Table Bay. The Wesleyan Methodist Missionary Society, destined to become South Africa's largest mission, was the second British society to arrive: it opened work in the Cape in 1816, the year the AME Church was formally incorporated. With the arrival of the eastern Cape settlers in the 1820s, evangelization began in earnest. By the middle of the 1830s, Wesleyan, L.M.S., Anglican, and Scottish Presbyterian mission stations were scattered throughout the Cape, as well as north and east across the Orange and Kei Rivers. American Congregationalists, German Lutherans, and French Catholics and Evangelical Protestants followed in the British missionaries' train, carrying the gospel into Zululand, the Transvaal, and Basutoland. By the 1890s more than two dozen mission societies were operating in southern Africa.[2]

While a host of factors shaped the trajectory of particular missions, all the different denominations shared certain assumptions and encountered similar problems. Missionaries everywhere promoted "conversion," a simple term for an immensely complex transformation. Conversion referred primarily to a religious reorientation in which Africans renounced their "customs" and "heathenish superstitions" and adopted Christian beliefs and values. Religious belief, however, was only one part of the package. Nineteenth-century missionaries ultimately envisioned nothing less than a total reformation of African life. At the most quotidian level, conversion implied a host of changes in Africans' daily round: converts wore Western dress, lived in square homes rather than round huts, and cultivated with ploughs. More broadly, conversion involved the transplantation of a whole "universe of signs and practices" from the West—new orders of knowledge, new styles of argumentation and demonstration, new conceptions of subjectivity itself. Implicit in missionary invocations of "progress," for example, were radically new conceptions of time, individuality, and community. Similarly, missionaries' sharp separation of "religion" and "politics"—a separation that Ethiopian churches were later accused of transgressing—rested upon a distinction between sacred and secular that must have appeared quite novel to most Africans. In ways both manifest and latent, missionaries were avatars of modernity.[3]

Missionaries, who wrote prolifically on the progress of their enterprise, developed a variety of images and metaphors to describe the process of conversion—images and metaphors that inevitably reveal as much about the missionaries themselves as about the Africans who were their presumed objects. Not surprisingly, most missionaries fell easily into the language of paternalism, casting their charges as children and themselves as stern, demanding fathers. Under their tutelage, Africans would grow in time into responsible adults. Beneath such language lay a pervasive assumption about the nature of authority in African societies. To European missionaries, traditional society was prima facie cruel and despotic; even the most sensitive mission observers tended to overlook the consensual dimensions of chiefly rule. The corollary was that Africans needed authority, needed discipline, to function, and would be nonplussed by anything less. Many missionaries deliberately emulated what they imagined to be "traditional" authoritarianism on station, adjudicating disputes and dispensing punishments (including, on some occasions, the lash) in ways they deemed to be chiefly.[4]

Less obvious but no less revealing was the language of cultivation, of planting and harvesting, that suffused nineteenth-century mission accounts. Horticultural images, of course, pervade the Bible—faith is a mustard seed; the Word falls upon stony or fertile ground; we reap what we sow—but such images operated in a distinct way in a colonial setting. In effect, they reduced Africans to part of the natural world, features of the landscape, to be cultivated by the missionary husbandman. The spread of Christianity thus represented more than the victory of one religious system over another; it marked the triumph of culture over nature, order over chaos. This equation proved extraordinarily enduring, even as South Africa was transformed from an agrarian to an industrial society. As late as the 1920s a leader of the South African Compounds and Interior Mission, an organization focused on Witwatersrand mine compounds, ruminated:

> I sometimes liken the native to a patch of his native veldt in the bush: wild, free, a natural home of bush thorn and wild things; a land neither cared nor sown. He wishes without restraint to follow his own wild native inclinations.

The missionaries' task, the author concluded, was to "reclaim" the land—to uproot, fence, and plough.[5]

Fittingly, this process of reclamation took place on a particular landscape. At the heart of evangelical enterprise lay the mission station, an enclosed community, typically encompassing a chapel, a school, perhaps a workshop, and ample lands for converts to cultivate. Stations (to extend the horticultural metaphor) were hothouses, controlled environments to protect the tender shoots of the Word from the presumed inclemency of both African and settler societies. Living on station drew individuals physically and culturally away from "tribal" society, and from what missionaries regarded as an overwhelming temptation to "revert to heathenism." At the same time, stations were built remote from cities and towns to give "impressionable" and "imitative" converts an opportunity to assimilate civilization's "virtues" before encountering its more seductive "vices." This aversion to urban life, shared by virtually every South African mission society, would be dramatically exposed during the rapid urbanization that followed the mineral discoveries.[6]

If mission societies had one other feature in common, it was their dearth of early converts. Missionaries enjoyed some success at moments of great social stress—in the aftermath of drought and war or in periods of economic and epistemological rupture, such as that occasioned by the disastrous 1856–1857 Xhosa cattle killing. They also enjoyed success among groups like the Mfengu, a reconstituted "tribe" of nineteenth-century refugees that occupied a buffer region along the eastern Cape frontier. But where African societies were more or less intact, converts were few and far between. Missionaries themselves recognized the pattern, which in time helped turn many into avid boosters of imperialism. (Christianity fared but poorly where African societies were in their "aboriginal vigour," an L.M.S. missionary conceded in the 1890s, but "where there is a measure of disorganisation . . . so there is preparation for the seed of the word.") Initially, however, subjugation of African polities proceeded slowly and unevenly in South Africa, and missionaries had to content themselves with slim pickings. What converts did trickle in were often fugitives of one sort or another. Many were women, fleeing unwelcome marriages or the demands of the levirate system. Others sought refuge from traditional justice, obligations of clientage, or traditional restrictions on accumulation. Such converts, as even the most optimistic missionaries conceded, were often drawn less by Christianity than by its material accoutrements, especially education and access to land.[7]

Between missionaries' emphasis on individualism and their control over valuable resources, stations became loci for the introduction of new patterns of stratification into African society. In the eastern Cape in particular, mission stations became centers of peasant agriculture, with converts selling surpluses on the colonial market and using the proceeds to purchase the habiliments of "civilised" life. Some became quite prosperous, using profits from agriculture to branch out into trading, transport riding, and other enterprises. Missionaries were invariably heartened by this "propensity to stratification." Notions of appropriate class structure were among the most deeply embedded of missionary assumptions, and the appearance of a "progressive" class of Africans—English-speaking, dressed in Western styles, committed to education and individual mobility—seemed an incontrovertible token of progress. Missionaries labored to bring this class into consciousness of itself, portraying converts as a racial "vanguard," a "leaven" to uplift the inert mass around them, a "bridge" between "civilisation and savagery."[8]

The final image was especially apposite, for in innumerable ways African Christians did bridge European and African worlds. Mission converts occupied a host of interstitial positions within the colonial bureaucracy, working as clerks, postal workers, court interpreters, and the like. African intermediation was even more important within the missions themselves. For missionaries entering new areas, African converts were essential linguistic, cultural, and political guides. As the work became settled, these same converts assumed a variety of positions within the mission hierarchy, working as evangelists and lay preachers, translators, teachers, and occasionally as ordained ministers. Indeed, most of the day-to-day business of evangelization was conducted by Africans, who visited outstations, convened classes, succored the sick, and buried the dead. While nineteenth-century accounts of "missionary labours" invariably stressed the heroism and intrepidity of white fathers, Christianity owes much of its success in Africa to Africans.[9]

Methodism, with its decentralized structure and tradition of lay participation, was especially well equipped to capitalize on African talent and zeal. By the 1890s the Wesleyans boasted more than a thousand black local preachers in Natal alone. Africans played an even more prominent role in spreading Methodism in the Transvaal, where Boer officials were distinctly inhospitable to British missionaries. Wesleyan officials visiting the far northern Transvaal in the 1880s were startled to find entire congregations organized by African converts, shining forth like beacons "amidst heathen darkness." Probably the most celebrated of these black pioneers was Samuel Mathabathe, who spent nine years laboring as an unpaid Methodist evangelist in the Zoutpansberg without once being visited by a white missionary. Michael Boweni, another unpaid local preacher in the area, also came in for praise from white missionaries. Boweni "ferrets around the country seeking for neglected kraals where people have never been blessed with the presence of a white missionary," a Wesleyan superintendent reported in 1887. Later, Boweni helped guide Wesleyan missionaries into Mashonaland.[10]

Initially at least, this practical devolution of authority was consistent with missionary goals. The idea that European agency was temporary constituted the bedrock of the missionary creed. Different societies, of course, subscribed to different timetables. Fired by antebellum reformers' characteristic faith in the capacity of proper institutions to mold character, the New England Congregationalists who founded the American Zulu Mission anticipated ceding authority to Africans after just one generation. British missionaries were generally more diffident, yet they too expected to surrender ecclesiastical control and instilled that expectation in their converts. Africans, in the inevitable metaphor, would husband the seeds that Europeans had sown.[11]

As the nineteenth century progressed, however, European mission societies began quietly to retreat from this commitment. To be sure, no society ever explicitly recanted the ideal of a self-sustaining church, and African mission workers labored on in expectation of their eventual majority; yet missionaries were clearly pushing back their estimated time of departure. Probably the best index of the shift comes in the declining tempo of African ordinations. Christian communities everywhere are organized around the sacraments—baptism, communion, confirmation, sometimes absolution and marriage—and dispensing sacraments is generally the province of an annointed ministry. African ordinations thus represented the touchstone of missionary expectations. By this criterion, most missionaries apparently expected to stay awhile. After a flurry of ordinations in the 1870s and '80s, the growth of the African ministry slowed in every major denomination. At the same time, those blacks who did receive ordination encountered a host of new obstacles and restrictions. It was in this gulf between missionary pronouncement and practice that Ethiopianism was born. [12]

The issue of native ordination arose first in the Free Church of Scotland, which licensed South Africa's first black minister, Tiyo Soga, in 1856. While this early ordination set a worthy standard, its value as precedent proved limited. Indeed, Soga's mastery of the theological curriculum at Edinburgh probably inhibited future ordinations by convincing church leaders that African ministerial candidates should be evaluated on the same criteria as Europeans, including their mastery of Latin, Hebrew, and Greek. It was thus not until the mid-1870s that the Free Church licensed additional Africans, a group of about half a dozen that included Elijah Makiwane and future independent churchmen Edward Tsewu and P. J. Mzimba. From the early 1880s on, the church virtually discountenanced African ordinations. The London Missionary Society, the other major British congregational mission in South Africa, followed a similar path: It appointed its first black minister in 1873 and its second, Walter Rubusana, in 1884, before more or less abandoning the project. [13]

L.M.S. and Free Church missionaries' reluctance to entrust authority to Africans stemmed at least in part from the demands of congregational polity, which placed considerable responsibility in the hands of local ministers, especially in the area of church finance. (If there was one constant in nineteenth-century South Africa, it was whites' conviction that Africans could not handle money.) Such concerns counted less in the Church of England, which was financially centralized and governed episcopally, and the Anglicans did in fact adopt a more liberal ordination policy. Yet here too one can discern a general battening down on opportunities for African mission workers. Like their peers in the Free Church, Anglican leaders insisted on maintaining the same educational standards for African and European ordinees, eventually relaxing only the classical languages requirement. The church ordained its first black deacon in 1870 and a black priest three years later. By the 1880s, however, the Anglicans seem to have adopted a tacit policy of restricting Africans to the deaconate, where they enjoyed no independent access to the sacraments. Several Africans served as deacons for more than twenty years without ever receiving Holy Orders. Under pressure from black mission workers, the church eventually instituted a less rigorous ministerial exam for deacons with ten years experience, but the practical result, as one Anglican bishop conceded, was that Africans seldom entered the priesthood without serving at least a decade-long apprenticeship. [14]

Advance and retreat was most pronounced in the Wesleyan Methodist Missionary Society, which ordained by far the largest number of African ministers. In 1866 the Wesleyans accepted four Africans, including Charles Pamla, as ministers on trial. As Methodists, W.M.M.S. leaders were less concerned with formal training than with evangelical effectiveness—even European ministerial candidates received only one year of theological education, compared to at least three in the Free Church—and Africans proved singularly effective as evangelists. The four probationers gathered in hundreds of souls in the 1866–1867 eastern Cape revivals, and all were accepted into full ministerial connection in 1870. Encouraged by the experiment, the Wesleyans established a training course for African ministerial candidates at Healdtown, the denomination's flagship school. In 1879 the Society's leaders in London dispatched an English minister, James Kilner, to South Africa to hasten the development of an indigenous ministry. During his tour of the country, Kilner accepted about seventy African ministers on trial, many of them older men with considerable evangelical experience but little formal education. (One of the candidates Kilner examined and licensed was future Ethiopian Church founder Mangena Mokone.) Yet the very fact that Kilner had to be sent from England suggests that the commitment of local Wesleyan leaders to an African ministry had begun to wane. Following Kilner's departure, the pace of black ordinations slowed markedly. In 1884 the Wesleyan synod moved to increase educational standards for African ministers. While such a move did not preclude ordinations, it dealt a severe blow to the aspirations of older, less educated evangelists, many of whom would later enter the Ethiopian ministry. [15]

Missionaries' treatment of those who did earn ordination provides further evidence of their receding commitment to "home rule." Again, the Wesleyans best illustrate the point. Beginning in about 1880, white ministers in Queenstown, the district with the largest black Christian population, began informally to segregate their district conferences, effectively disfranchising African ministers. The practice spawned a stormy debate at the Wesleyans' 1883 General Conference, but proponents ultimately carried the day, arguing that blacks possessed too much of a herd mentality to be entrusted with votes on church affairs. (The problem with integrated conferences, a missionary recalled in 1904, was that native ministers "used to sit all together like a flock of sheep and vote the same way.") Once sanctioned by the General Conference, segregation quickly spread to other conferences. By the late 1880s black ministers across South Africa had been consigned to shadow meetings outside the Wesleyans' regular district conferences. Even then, European chairmen and secretaries were appointed to monitor their deliberations. [16]

African mission workers were marginalized in other ways as well. Without exception, European mission societies paid African ministers very small stipends, usually between 10 and 20 percent of what their white counterparts received. Blacks also generally received no allowances for wives and children. Such discrimination was invariably justified in terms of the limited expense of a "native lifestyle," but that very argument betrayed something deeper— concern that well-paid Africans would somehow lose touch with who they were and where they had come from. Doubtless the most extreme example of keeping Africans "in their place" came in the Compounds Mission, which entered South Africa after the mineral discoveries. To prevent its African evangelists from developing inflated ideas of their own importance, the mission required them to devote at least three hours per day to cooking and cleaning for their European superintendents. [17]

As if such safeguards were not sufficient, most societies adopted a policy of assigning African ministers to established stations, where they would be assured of European supervision. Seasoned ministers and evangelists, often accustomed to working with considerable autonomy, found themselves subject to white superintendents, many with little experience in the actual business of spreading the gospel. Such treatment was doubtless personally galling, but even more disturbing was the way in which the new policy inhibited evangelization. Chained to existing stations, many African ministers found themselves unable to reach and convert their brethren at the very moment they held the sacraments in their hands. What candidates they did bring forward for baptism and confirmation were subjected to increasingly searching examinations by white supervisors, many of whom openly questioned Africans' standards. "Deacons and other prominent members of our church have no hesitation or shame in bringing young men and women forward as fit and proper persons to be received as full members of the church, who cannot read a verse of the New Testament, and are often otherwise utterly unworthy," an L.M.S. missionary complained in 1897. Such a statement betrayed little of the optimism and evangelical ardor that his predecessors had carried into South Africa a century before. [18]

It is difficult to account for the shift within European missions, if only because missionaries themselves evinced so little awareness of it. African mission workers, on the other hand, were keenly sensitive to the changes overtaking their world, and devised a number of explanations for them. Probably the most common—certainly the most common among those who later became Ethiopians—was to lay the blame on "new" missionaries, implicitly contrasting contemporary missionaries with the pioneers who had first brought the gospel to South Africa. While "old" missionaries such as Robert Moffat and John Philip were remembered as humble, pious, and untainted by racism, their successors were characterized as arrogant, supercilious, and racist. Frequently they were described as insincere, a perception that doubtless reflected African puzzlement at their apparent indifference to evangelization. They were also often characterized as "young," suggesting that missions, in elevating inexperienced Europeans over older African workers, violated deeply held beliefs about the appropriate relationship between age groups. At the very least, the policy laid bare the reality of racial preferment within the missions.[19]

Obviously there was a large measure of nostalgia in Africans' fond recollections of "old time" missionaries, but there was also a grain of truth. Early mission stations were by no means islands of nonracialism, but they generally were characterized by a considerable degree of racial familiarity. No matter how hard the first missionaries struggled to preserve social distance—and many were obsessed with the problem, lest the process of cultural transmission be somehow reversed—their isolation and dependence, along with the absence of an overarching colonial order to structure race relations, eroded boundaries. The consolidation of colonial rule in the mid- to late nineteenth century and the simultaneous emergence of a settler society made it possible for missionaries to introduce a more formal racial etiquette, and most apparently did so. Oral accounts are rife with reports of missionaries receiving converts only at the kitchen door, refusing to drink tea with converts, disdaining to embrace black infants during baptism—charges that uncannily echo the complaints of early African American religious separatists. Given perennial accusations that they "spoiled the native," missionaries no doubt had pragmatic reasons for observing the racial codes of settler society. At the same time, many missionaries were clearly becoming settlers themselves and found such codes congenial.[20]

Equally important, missionaries in the late nineteenth century operated in a different intellectual milieu than their predecessors. While early missionaries were rarely apostles of racial equality, they generally attributed Africans' "benighted" condition to experience and environment rather than race; with proper guidance, the African constituted an "improvable member of the human species." Emergent racist ideas, which in America were fast consigning blacks to a status of innate, ineradicable inferiority, naturally had less purchase in Britain, which contended neither with slavery nor with a large free black population. (Insofar as middle-class Britons were in the business of constructing "Others," they devoted most of their attention to the working class emerging in the "dark jungles" of Manchester and Leeds.) Most of the early British mission societies also had close links with the antislavery movement, which remained a bulwark of environmentalism. Indeed, one of the explicit goals of the early evangelical missions was to vindicate Africans' innate capacity for civilization, to prove that the African was not irremediably the slave.[21]

A host of events in the last third of the nineteenth century combined to erode this environmentalist faith. The apparent debacle of Jamaican emancipation, culminating in the Morant Bay uprising of 1865, provoked a backlash throughout the British world against what came to be called "sentimental negrophilism." American Reconstruction, the course of which was followed avidly by Britons at home and abroad, was likewise taken as evidence of the folly of entrusting blacks with responsibilities they were not yet equipped to bear. Late-century developments in formal racial ideology lent an almost self-evident quality to the increasingly pessimistic prognosis. "Scientific" racism challenged the whole notion of racial progress by proving (in its own terms) that black inferiority was intrinsic. The shibboleths of Social Darwinism, while themselves environmental, pushed in a similar direction: racial progress was at best glacially slow and conflict-ridden. For whites to encourage it in an inferior race was at best futile and at worst suicidal.[22]

Obviously there were limits to how far missionaries could take such ideas, which challenged the whole logic of mission work. Indeed, at its most extreme, racism challenged evangelical Christianity itself, which rested on the premise that all humans possessed souls and a capacity to reason and were thus susceptible to redemption. There is no question, however, that missionaries partook of the intellectual developments of the age or that these developments shaped their attitude to their converts. James Stewart, principal of Lovedale Institute and South Africa's most prominent missionary, responded to an 1884 protest from African students with a lecture that was pure Social Darwinism, though with a distinctive Christian twist:

> Starting but as yesterday in the race of nations, do you soberly believe that in the two generations of the very imperfect civilisation you have enjoyed and partially accepted, you can have overtaken those other nations who began that race two thousand years ago, and have been running hard at it for a thousand years at least?

Coming as it did from the leader of a church renowned for its faith in the transforming power of education, the remark betrayed a sea change in missionary expectations.[23]

Finally and perhaps most important, missionaries' more restrictive attitude was part and parcel of a broad reassessment of the place of educated Africans in South Africa, a reassessment propelled by the mineral discoveries. The opening of the Kimberley diamond fields in 1871, followed a decade and a half later by the discovery of gold on the Witwatersrand, unleashed in southern Africa an industrial revolution that, in its compression and ferocity, was unique in the world's history. The liberal paradigm of the mid-nineteenth century, which promised gradual economic and political incorporation to Africans as they moved up the scale of "civilisation," was among that revolution's early casualties. Cape liberalism, as Stanley Trapido has shown, was rooted in a political economy dominated by merchant capital, which conceived of Africans as both producers and consumers in an expanding commercial world. Mining capital, the engine of the new order, had a very different priority: cheap labor. The mineral revolution did open up new interstitial niches for educated Africans, notably as mine clerks, and it provided a short-term windfall for peasant producers; but in the long run, the new South Africa had little place for the stereotypical "school native," with his smattering of skills and pretensions to respectability. Africans, in short, were to be hewers and drawers, in a society cleaved not by "civilisation" but by race.[24]

All these factors—the consolidation of settler society, changes in racial ideology, the revolution in political economy wrought by the mineral discoveries—worked to transform the relationship between European missionaries and their African converts. Even in retrospect, the rapidity of the change is astonishing. As late as 1875 an ordained African minister represented the pinnacle of missionary achievement, a flesh-and-blood vindication of evangelical enterprise and of Africans' innate potential. A quarter century later, the same figure was a changeling, whose very existence menaced social order. Even more astonishing was the apparent ease with which missionaries adapted to the new circumstances. While mission spokesmen continued to defend the principle of African education well into the twentieth century, they increasingly did so in terms of enhancing native "usefulness." Many spoke openly about restricting black educational preferment, to prevent Africans from developing a taste for idleness or aspirations beyond their station. Education, an Anglican missionary told the South African Native Affairs Commission in 1904, should be "very limited," lest it "spoil the character of the Native," which was "not sufficiently morally strong to be able to carry a very wide amount of learning." A rough consensus emerged on the need to limit instruction to Standard III— the equivalent of fifth grade—a level that sufficed to make the native "a more intelligent worker" without risking spoilage.[25]

Insofar as missionaries evinced any awareness of the new dispensation, they did so through a subtle change in paternalist discourse. Where once converts were portrayed as children, in the last decades of the nineteenth century they came increasingly to be characterized as adolescents. The comments of a delegate at the first South African General Missionary Conference in 1904 were typical:

> The natives have begun to grow impatient under restraints. . . . We have perhaps been too slow in realising that they have grown, and are no more mere children, but more like young men and young women. They are not yet of age, but they are no more mere children. . . .

Oddly, however, this adolescence did not imply imminent adulthood; it was a racial category rather than a generational one. As such, it was profoundly revealing of changing missionary beliefs. The essence of adolescence lay in having achieved the appearance of adulthood without the substance, without that self-awareness and maturity that make for independence. Adolescents lack "patience and self control"; they overvalue their own capacities; they are restive and chafe against what they deem unwarranted restrictions. Precisely because they lack the capacity to discern their own shortcomings, the need for adult control is patent. In virtually every way, missionaries' treatment of their charges came to accord with the metaphor.[26]

All paternalistic discourse serves to obscure conflict, yet rarely does one see this containment function exhibited so starkly. Seen through the comforting lens of racial adolescence, disputes with aggrieved African mission workers required no compromise, no reexamination of restrictive church policies; on the contrary, they were themselves proof of missionary rectitude. Such a conception was to leave white mission societies singularly ill equipped to understand or respond creatively to the challenge of Ethiopianism. Paris Evangelical Mission superintendent Edward Jacottet, an unyielding man even by missionary standards, responded to the rise of independent churches in the tones of a wounded parent. "It was the missionaries who educated, protected and civilised you," he declared in an open letter to the Ethiopian Movement. *"We* have educated you, you owe to *us* all you know, and the first thing you do is turn against *us* the weapons *we* have provided you with."[27]

Free Church of Scotland missionaries were similarly bewildered in 1899 when their senior African minister, P. J. Mzimba, led a bitter secessionary movement at the Lovedale congregation, a movement that eventually cost the church more than ten thousand adherents. While the roots of the dispute were complex, missionaries' response was elegant in its simplicity. James Stewart, who had worked closely with Mzimba for more than twenty years, assumed the role of bereaved father, vacillating between bitterness at his protégé and frustration with himself for having entrusted Mzimba with too much responsibility. "He said he could not get on with the white man," Stewart complained in his testimony to the South African Native Affairs Commission. "But the white man made him what he was." J. D. Don, a Free Church colleague, agreed. "We cannot afford to act upon the assumption that the native is really equal to the European," Don wrote.

> There is something wanting in the best of them. . . . I have been notoriously . . . a partisan of the native ministry, but have sorrowfully modified some of my earlier ideas. . . . They are at their best as assistants, or as ministers working under the surveillance of Europeans.

If a single statement distilled the origins of Ethiopianism, it was this one.[28]

Mzimba was far from alone in his rejection of missionary tutelage. In the last decades of the nineteenth century, every major denomination in South Africa endured schisms, often led by their most trusted African ministers. The process began with fleeting separatist movements among Wesleyans in Pondoland and at a P.E.M. station in Basutoland. The first lasting independent movement was the Tile Thembu Church, established in 1884 by Nehemiah Tile, a disaffected Wesleyan minister. The L.M.S. endured a similar, though less publicized, schism a year later at its station at Taung. In the Transvaal the first stirrings of independency date to 1889 and the formation of the Lutheran Bapedi Church by black converts of the Berlin Mission Society, under the leadership of an eccentric German missionary. A year later Joseph Kanyane Napo, an Anglican lay preacher in Pretoria, established the African Church, with himself as bishop. Two independent churches were formed in 1892—the African Native Church, a kind of historical stepchild of the Tile Thembu Church, founded by a Wesleyan minister named Jonas Goduka; and, most significant for our purposes, Mangena Mokone's Ethiopian Church. In the mid-1890s the Free Church of Scotland and American Board both lost congregations in Johannesburg. The century ended with Mzimba's spectacular secession at Lovedale. [29]

Each of these movements was the product of a unique set of circumstances, yet together they testified to swelling African disaffection with European missionaries. The roots of much of twentieth-century South African politics are here, in African Christians' bitterness at a world that preached progress and incorporation while practicing restriction and exclusion. What is striking initially, however, is how narrowly African grievances were cast. Mangena Mokone, for example, laid responsibility for Africans' slow "progress" squarely on European missionaries, as if their hypocrisy were all that prevented colonial society from delivering on its promise. Missionaries, he explained in one of his first letters to AME leaders in the United States, had "made a trade of the word of God, giving false reasons that education and Christianity spoil the coloured. Consequently we have taken a disbelief on them." He concluded the letter with a prayer for education. In the very act of renouncing his faith in missionaries, Mokone reiterated his faith in their creed. [30]

Mokone's narrow focus may have been naive and in a certain sense unfair, but it was not surprising. Missions were not the only arena in late-nineteenth-century South Africa in which African aspirations were throttled, but they were certainly the most obvious. It was missionaries, after all, who had nurtured expectations of mobility and racial progress through education; thus, their efforts to restrict educational advancement, under whatever circumstances, could only be interpreted as perverse. It was missionaries who had prepared Africans for the responsibilities of the Christian ministry and then refused to bestow them. Perhaps most important, missionaries had supplied Africans with a universalist creed against which their own conduct could be measured and found wanting. In extolling education and then withholding it, in awakening in their converts a zeal for evangelization they were not themselves prepared to match, in preaching a gospel of universal brotherhood while erecting barriers of racial exclusion, European missionaries invited criticism on their own terms. And it was in precisely such terms that they received it. In the perpetual dialectic of Protestantism, they instigated their own reformation.

The career of Ethiopian Church founder Mangena Maake Mokone exhibited all the tensions embedded in the relationship between European missionaries and African mission workers. Fortunately, we know something of Mokone's early life, for he, like Richard Allen a century before him, dictated a brief autobiography to his son shortly before his death. The virtual archetype of the uprooted African convert, Mokone was born in 1851 in Sekukuniland, in the eastern Transvaal. Traversed by raiders and refugees during the *mfecane,* the series of wars and migrations ignited by the rise of the Zulu state a generation before, Mokone's birthplace remained a focus of political instability in the 1850s and '60s, as a revived Pedi paramountcy struggled to assert itself against lesser African chiefdoms and newly arrived Dutch-speaking trekkers. A Zulu *impi* passed through the area in the year of Mokone's birth; thirteen years later, Swazi raiders attacked his home village, killing most of his family. Mokone apparently survived by hiding in the bush and later found refuge on a Boer farm. It was common practice at the time for Boer farmers to hold young Africans, acquired through capture or trade, as *inboekselings,* a station somewhere between apprentice and slave. Something of the sort may have befallen Mokone; he certainly spoke fluent Dutch. By 1870, however, he was back under the authority of the Pedi paramount, joining a contingent of young men trekking from Sekukuniland to Natal for work. Like most early Pedi migrants, he probably intended to work only long enough to purchase a rifle. He labored on a sugar plantation for six months before moving to Durban, where he worked as a "kitchen boy." It was in Durban that he first attended church, initially to placate his employer's wife, who had caught him smoking cannabis. Like so many of South Africa's uprooted, Mokone proved susceptible to Christianity's message. Converted by a Wesleyan missionary, he was baptized in 1874. A short time later, he began to preach.[31]

At the time of his conversion, Mokone possessed little or no education. He began attending a Wesleyan night school, where he learned to read the Bible, and eventually completed Standard IV, the equivalent of sixth grade. He dreamed of pursuing his education at Healdtown, the premier Wesleyan training institute in the Cape, but was deterred by his missionary mentors, who apparently feared losing the services of a valuable evangelist. The refusal left its mark on Mokone, who remained forever aggrieved at the missionaries, whom he believed had held him back. In the short term, however, it only redoubled his hunger for learning. By the end of his life, he possessed a formidable education, acquired mostly through self-instruction. In addition to Sepedi and Dutch, he had a firm command of English and at least some familiarity with IsiXhosa, German, and the classical languages. Judging from an inventory of his library, included in the papers of his estate, he was also an avid reader of history, geography, and theology.[32]

Mokone spent the late 1870s working as an unpaid evangelist, supporting himself during the week as a carpenter's apprentice. By all accounts, he was a powerful preacher: a European who chanced to interrupt one of Mokone's sermons was appalled to find his auditors prostrate on the floor, weeping. When James Kilner came to Natal in 1880 in search of potential ministers, he was told of Mokone. The young preacher was summoned from his workshop, still in his carpenter's apron, and examined on the spot. Despite his lack of formal education, he was accepted as a minister on trial. Eight years later, he was ordained a full Wesleyan minister.[33]

Mokone served the first two years of his probation in Natal, but in 1882 he was transferred to Pretoria, capital of the Transvaal. His language skills may have recommended him for the post: unlike most British missionaries, he spoke both Dutch, the language of the Zuid Afrikaansche Republiek government, and Sepedi, the home language of many of the early African settlers in the capital. With the exception of a new station outside Potchefstroom, the Wesleyans were still not well established in the Transvaal, and Pretoria quickly became the focus of their efforts. In 1883 the Society purchased a farm near the city on which they established Kilnerton Institute, the Transvaal's first African teacher training institution. Mokone, working under a white superintendent, opened the church and school at Kilnerton, building the fittings for each with his own hands.[34]

In the years that followed, Mokone moved about the Transvaal, meeting many of the men who would later help him launch the Ethiopian Church. He opened Wesleyan missions in the Waterberg and at Makapanstad and also served briefly at Potchefstroom and Johannesburg, at the time a swelling mining camp. In 1892 he returned to Pretoria as minister and principal of Kilnerton Institute, though in practice he remained subordinate to at least two European missionaries. He labored briefly at Kilnerton—among his students was S. M. Makgatho, a future president of the African National Congress—but in October 1892 he resigned from the Wesleyan ministry. Determined to "serve God in my own way," he gathered a congregation and began holding services in a private hut in Marabastad, the burgeoning African location on Pretoria's western edge.[35]

Rather than any single episode, a long train of grievances prompted Mokone's decision—grievances which he compiled and attached to his letter of resignation. The list, preserved in a pamphlet written by his son, is worth reproducing in full. Not only does it enumerate the frustrations of a proud and talented African mission worker, it shows how those frustrations honed racial consciousness. As such, it functions as a kind of manifesto of the Ethiopian Movement.

1. Our district meetings have been separated from the Europeans since 1886. And yet we are compelled to have a white chairman and secretary.
2. Our district meetings were held in a more or less barbaric manner. We are just like a lot of Kaffirs before the landrost for passes. What the white man says is infallible. . . .
3. This separation shows we can't be brothers.
4. The wives and children of Native ministers have no allowance from the Society whatsoever. Only the whites have it. . . .
5. The Native ordained minister is of no use to his own people. He cannot exercise his rights as a minister or be placed in a position of trust . . . whites will be placed over the black man as superintendents.
6. Native ministers only get from £24 to £60 per annum, while the white minister gets £300 per annum.
7. In the Transvaal, no Native minister has the right to use the Mission Property . . . only the whites are supplied with ox-wagons and furniture.
8. It is a great shame to see the homes of Native teachers and ministers. A stable is preferable. At Waterberg I was obliged to build my own house and at Makapanstad I spent £3.12 on the house for reeds, skins, etc.
9. The Native minister holds class meetings, prayer meetings, visit [sic] the sick, pray for them, preach, bury and teach school, while the white ministers' work is to marry, baptize and administer communion. They will never go to visit the sick or pray for them, and when they die, your Native minister must go to bury your own people. This is not Christianity, not brotherly love, nor friendship. If this is true, then white ministers are unnecessary. . . .
10. The white ministers don't even know the members of their circuits. They always build their homes one or two miles away from the congregation.
11. No Native minister is honoured among the white brethren. The more the Native humbles himself, the more they make a fool of him.
12. We have been in the Wesleyan Ministry for twelve years and not one of us has ever received the Minutes or the Annual Report. . . . We are called 'Revs' but we are worse than the boy working for the Missionary. . . .
13. As Principal of Kilnerton Institute, I was not esteemed as one who belongs to or has any say in the school. A student may be discharged . . . and no one would tell me anything about it. . . .
14. When a student is sick, the poor nigger will be sent at once to the classroom, shivering under his blanket . . . [and] told that he is lazy, not sick. . . . The boy who speaks rather straight will be considered a bad one.

"If all this is so," Mokone concluded, "where is Justice? Where is brotherly love? Where is the Christian sympathy? God in heaven is a witness to all these wrongs."[36]

Despite the tone of the list, the seceders initially remained on reasonably amicable terms with their former church. Mokone requested and received a removal certificate, establishing that he had left the Wesleyans in good standing. Wesleyan authorities, convinced that the whole business would collapse on its own, made no attempt to compel the seceders to return, though they did send a patronizing letter to Mokone, expressing disappointment that he had not first come to them with his grievances. When the seceders finished erecting a new church building in Marabastad, Mokone, like Richard Allen a century before, invited one of his former supervisors to preach the dedicatory sermon. By significant coincidence, the visiting missionary preached from Genesis 28—*"And he called the name of that place Bethel"*—the text used to dedicate Philadelphia's Bethel Church a century before. The Pretoria church took its name, however, not from Genesis but from Psalms 68: *"Princes shall come out of Egypt; Ethiopia shall soon stretch forth her hands unto God."* The verse was emblazoned on a banner which hung above the altar at the opening service.[37]

There is sometimes a great deal in a name, and much of the essence of Mokone's movement was distilled in the name Ethiopia. Since the publication of the King James Bible in 1611, Ethiopia had served as a generic term for Africa. It thus possessed both a literal reference, to contemporary Abyssinia, the one African state not yet under colonial rule, and a metaphorical one, to an undifferentiated biblical Africa, existing outside historical time. In practice, the two references shaded into one another. In invoking Abyssinia, Mokone and his congregants laid claim to a thousand-year Christian history that belied the popular notion of a uniformly barbarous African past; indeed, the presence of a Christian kingdom in Africa at a time when Europe was sunk in paganism inverted colonial history, portraying Africa as the true cradle of civilization. At the same time, aligning their movement with a biblical Africa provided the Ethiopians with a rich set of associations: the grandeur of Solomon and Sheba; the humility of Simon of Cyrene, who helped Christ bear his cross to Calvary; the ardor of the Ethiopian charioteer who sought baptism from Philip in Acts of the Apostles. Such images again illuminated the role of Africans in the dawn of Christianity and offered another pedigree independent of the missionaries. In all its guises, "Ethiopia" offered a charter for independence.[38]

Word of the new church spread rapidly along African mission networks, first in the Transvaal, where Mokone was a familiar figure, and later in the eastern Cape, where the majority of black Christians still lived. By mid-1895, when the correspondence between Mokone and the leaders of the AME Church in the United States began, a dozen African ministers and local preachers had rallied to the Ethiopian Church, usually bringing substantial congregations with them. While none of these men left autobiographical sketches akin to Mokone's, we can glean enough details about their lives to piece together a kind of collective portrait of the first generation of Ethiopian leadership. Obviously these dozen clerics did not encompass the entire independent church movement, which by 1895 boasted well over a thousand adherents. Nonetheless, their diverse passages through late-nineteenth-century South Africa offer further insight into the origins and character of Ethiopianism.

Mokone's first recruit, and the only non-Methodist among the early Ethio-

pian leaders, was Samuel James Brander. Like Mokone, Brander was one of
South Africa's uprooted. His father, Bakhatla by birth, was one of the thousands of Transvaal Africans who entered the eastern Cape labor market in the
mid-nineteenth century. Like so many migrants, he was converted along the
way, probably after stopping over at a mission station. He married a Christian
woman who, according to Brander, was of African American descent. (Unfortunately, there is no way to corroborate this claim, though, as we shall see, it
could well be true.) Samuel, the couple's first son, was born in Colesberg in
1851 and educated at a Wesleyan mission school. With the opening of the
Kimberley diamond fields in the early 1870s, the Branders went into the
transport riding business. Staked by his father to two teams and wagons,
Samuel worked as a contractor for two years, occasionally plying the road
between Port Elizabeth and Kimberley himself, before settling permanently on
the diamond fields. He remained in Kimberley nearly a decade. During that
time, he left the Wesleyan mission, where he was a class leader, and joined the
Church of England. The switch was apparently occasioned by a dispute between his father and a Wesleyan missionary, though Brander later claimed that
he was drawn by the greater "solemnity and grandeur" of the Anglican mass.
He was elevated to the office of reader and then catechist, but not to the
ministry.[39]

In 1884 Brander accepted a salary of one pound per month to open a mission
station in the "dark district" of the Waterberg, north of Pretoria, on a farm
bequeathed to the church by an English parishioner; it was doubtless here that
he met Mokone, who was stationed in the district at the same time. He set
about preparing the mission, investing twenty pounds of his own money to
have the farm surveyed. When the Anglicans refused to reimburse him for the
survey or to pay even the paltry salary they had promised, Brander, by all
evidence a fiercely proud man, grew aggrieved. After long hesitation, he
resigned from the Anglican Church, apparently a few months prior to
Mokone's resignation from the Wesleyans. Sometime in 1893, Brander joined
the Ethiopian Church, carrying with him a congregation of about sixty souls.
He was later ordained an AME minister, though his stay in the church was to
prove brief.[40]

Mokone found his next recruits on the goldfields, thirty miles south of
Pretoria. With an African population drawn from across the subcontinent,
Johannesburg offered fertile soil for the vision of shared African identity embedded in Ethiopianism. Perhaps more important, the city had a severe shortage of white missionaries, thanks both to the hostility of the Z.A.R. government, which was preternaturally suspicious of *uitlander* churchmen, and to
missionaries' own aversion to urban life. (The logic of siting mission stations in
rural areas, after all, had been to shield converts from precisely the species of
"civilisation" they were likely to encounter in the brawling mining camps
strung east and west along the gold reef.) African converts showed no such

aversion; on the contrary, Christians were significantly overrepresented among early African settlers on the Witwatersrand. By 1895 the Wesleyans alone had sixty-five black lay preachers on the Rand, all operating with virtually no white supervision. Mokone undoubtedly knew many of these men from his tenure in Johannesburg in the early 1890s and from his periodic visits thereafter. Three of them—S. J. Mpumlwana, Jantjie Zachariah Tantsi, and Abraham Mngqibisa—joined him in the Ethiopian ministry.[41]

While Mpumlwana's origins remain obscure, some evidence remains about Tantsi and Mngqibisa. Both hailed from well-trod mission fields along the Cape frontier. Mngqibisa, the man credited with opening the first Wesleyan chapel on the Witwatersrand, was born among the Amazibi near Fort Beaufort in 1850. Tantsi, a Thembu, was born in Engcobo at about the same time. Both were probably born into Christian families; Mngqibisa was almost certainly the son of a traditional doctor by the same name whose conversion was noted by a Wesleyan missionary in the 1830s. One can only speculate about the sources of the pair's disaffection from the Wesleyans. Both may have been victimized by the church's growing preference for young, well-educated ministerial candidates over the older, experienced evangelists preferred by James Kilner. Perhaps they simply questioned the necessity of white supervision, having worked so long without it. Whatever the case, they joined Mokone. Tantsi, the better educated of the two, was immediately inducted into the probationary ranks of the Ethiopian ministry. After a year of instruction, he was formally ordained in a scrupulously correct, if highly irregular, ceremony presided over by Mokone and Joseph Kanyane Napo, self-proclaimed bishop of Pretoria's independent "African Church." Mngqibisa was apparently ordained a short time later. By early 1894 the Ethiopians had consecrated their first chapel on the Witwatersrand.[42]

Jacobus Gilead Xaba, Mokone's next recruit, was the youngest of the early Ethiopians and the holder of the most elite pedigree. The Xabas hailed initially from Basutoland but had fled their home during the *mfecane,* settling eventually in Natal, in the prosperous, ethnically diverse peasant community clustered around the Wesleyan mission station at Edendale. Thomas Xaba, Jacobus's father, was a modestly successful peasant, who managed to bequeath to his son over two hundred acres of land, including nine acres of the original Edendale farm. Jacobus's cousin, Jonathan, became a Wesleyan minister and one of South Africa's most distinguished translators of religious texts. Jacobus himself schooled at Edendale and Healdtown, where he probably trained for the ministry. He returned briefly to Natal—he received a Natal exemption from native law in 1886—before setting out for Heilbron, in the northeastern Orange Free State. At the time, he was probably a ministerial probationer.[43]

Xaba labored for a few years as a preacher and teacher at Heilbron, but, like so many African mission workers, he fell afoul of his European superintendent. Details of the conflict are obscure, but at some point Xaba was suspended. He evidently refused to relinquish his pulpit; he seems also to have neglected to report his suspension to the Free State authorities, in order to keep the pass that allowed black mission workers to travel freely. (His former superintendent, writing a decade later, charged him with lying, falsifying a testimonial, and forging a pass.) When discovered, he was arrested and dismissed from the ministry. He contacted Mokone and was formally "re-obligated" to the Ethiopian ministry in late 1894. From that date until his premature death a decade later, Xaba remained the movement's most ardent and effective evangelist. Not surprisingly in light of his own experience, he remained a critic of pass laws.[44]

If Xaba was the youngest of the original Ethiopians, Marcus Gabashane, thirty years his senior, was the oldest. Little evidence remains about Gabashane's early life, aside from the circumstances of his birth: he was born in 1831 in the small Sotho community at Thaba 'Nchu, on the border of Basutoland and the Orange Free State. Like Mangena Mokone, Gabashane entered a world in upheaval. Already by 1831, the first of more than twelve thousand Seleka Barolong refugees had arrived at Thaba 'Nchu, dislodged from their homes in the west by Mzilikazi's Ndebele. Many of these Setswana-speaking refugees, including their chief, Moroka, had converted to Christianity during their decade-long flight, and Wesleyan missionaries accompanied them to the settlement. In 1834, as Gabashane turned three, the first *Voortrekkers* arrived. Despoiled of their stock by Mzilikazi's raiders, the Boers found refuge with Moroka, who provided them with land and cattle. Gabashane remained in the village for the next several decades, long enough to see the Barolong and Boers combine against their Basotho hosts, and then to watch as the Boers reduced their erstwhile allies to vassalage.[45]

Gabashane thus spent his youth and early adulthood at the very point of the colonial project. Under the patronage of Moroka and the missionaries, Thaba 'Nchu became the most important Wesleyan station in the Free State, a showplace which "re-echoed with the hum of industry and the voice of lesson and song." A large chapel was raised, schools were opened, land was parceled out and put to the plough. (One of the final acts of Moroka's successor was to establish individual tenure, ensuring Thaba 'Nchu's future place as one of the last islands of black land ownership in apartheid South Africa.) Unlike most of the Ethiopian Church founders, Gabashane never became very accomplished in English—Wesleyan schools at Thaba 'Nchu used Setswana as their medium of instruction—but he did attend school, and he clearly imbibed that devotion to education so characteristic of African mission converts. Each of his eleven children, several of whom later joined him in the AME ministry, was equipped with the finest mission education. Salathiel, the oldest, left Lovedale in the early 1880s to open a Wesleyan school in Fauresmith, the Free State village where Marcus was working as a local preacher; Abel, destined to become one of the AME Church's most fiery ministers, studied at Bensonvale; Henry traveled to the United States under AME auspices to train as a medical doctor. How and why Gabashane eventually fell out with the Wesleyans is not clear, but his few surviving letters ring with frustration at white missionaries—at their racism, their indifference to spreading the gospel, their apparent determination to keep African mission workers in a state of perpetual tutelage.[46]

These first half dozen leaders all came from the interior, and, with the possible exception of Gabashane, all were personally acquainted with Mangena Mokone before joining his movement. Already, however, Ethiopianism had begun to spread. Sometime in late 1894 or '95, Mokone led a delegation of Ethiopians to the eastern Cape in an effort to recruit other dissident African ministers. One of the group's first calls was to Jonas Goduka, a former Wesleyan minister and the founder, in 1892, of the African Native Church, a movement that seems to have absorbed most of what was left of the original Tile Thembu Church. While determined to keep his church independent, Goduka apparently agreed to assist Mokone, and the two men issued a joint call for young men to join their ministry. Coming in a period of declining mobility for educated Christians, the call yielded another half dozen ministerial recruits, including Benjamin Kumalo, Isaiah Sishuba, J. Gqamana, and future Native National Congress founder Henry Reid Ngcayiya.[47]

Benjamin Kumalo's background was broadly representative of this second stratum of Ethiopian leadership. Like Jacobus Xaba, Kumalo came from Natal, from a prominent *amakolwa,* or Christian, family, in this case of the Anglican variety. By the time of Benjamin's birth in 1867, however, the family, or at least Benjamin's branch of it, had begun to lose its purchase on the land. In contrast to Xaba, who inherited two hundred acres of land, Kumalo inherited just forty acres. Like so many Christian peasant families, the Kumalos attempted to preserve their class position through investments in education, sending Benjamin to Edendale and briefly to Lovedale, but the effort proved unavailing. After failing the examination for a Cape Elementary Teacher's Certificate, Benjamin cast about for a job in the colonial bureaucracy, vainly offering his services for free to local magistrates in order to learn the trade of interpreter. For such an individual, scrabbling for a handhold in the ebb tide of nineteenth-century Cape liberalism, Mokone's call for ministers opened a precious avenue of mobility, and Kumalo leaped at the offer.[48]

The Ethiopians' most coveted recruit, however, was James Mata Dwane, one of the Wesleyan Church's most distinguished black ministers. Three years Mokone's senior, Dwane was born in the Transkei among the Gcaleka Xhosa, where his father was a tribal counselor. For reasons that remain obscure, the family fled their home during Mata's youth, taking refuge with the Amagqunukhwebe and their "model" chief Kama, who controlled a large location at Middledrift, awarded by the Cape administration as a reward for his collaboration during the Frontier Wars. Mata's older sister, who married a Christian, was the first in the family to convert; it was she who gave him his first shirt. A short time later, the boy set off to meet the missionaries himself, filled with a mixture of fascination and fear. (Part of his trepidation, he later recalled, stemmed from the term that missionaries had adopted for conversion—*ukugqobhoka*, literally, "to pierce with an assegai.") He was taken in by a Wesleyan missionary, who baptized him as James and raised him as his ward. Dwane studied at Healdtown and, after a brief career as a schoolteacher, pursued the ministry. He was accepted as a probationer in 1876 and into full ministerial connection five years later.[49]

Judging from surviving letters, Dwane was a proud and sensitive man, who felt keenly the sting of racial discrimination. He submitted and later withdrew a letter of resignation from the Wesleyan Church in 1884, apparently over the issue of segregated district conferences. A decade later, he resigned for good after a dispute over a proposed African college. Having himself negotiated the passage from "ignorance and darkness" to Christian enlightenment, Dwane believed passionately in education and chafed against the mounting restrictions within mission schools. Sometime around 1894 he had the opportunity to travel to England to raise money for a college. While few details about the trip or Dwane's precise plans survive, he apparently envisioned an African-run training institution, to be erected on land donated for the purpose by his chiefly patron, William Shaw Kama; this in any event was the plan he later pursued in the AME Church. (The namesake of a pioneer Wesleyan missionary, William Shaw Kama briefly studied for the ministry himself, in the same cohort as Dwane. With the death of old Kama, he abandoned the plan and acceded to the chieftainship.) Not surprisingly, the college scheme found a more receptive audience in England than in South Africa, and when Dwane returned he was ordered to turn over all the money he had raised to the church's general fund, to be dispensed by the (white) district conference. He surrendered the money, resigned from the Wesleyan Church, and joined the Ethiopians. He quickly rose to the top of the young church's hierarchy, displacing even Mokone, though his tenure too was to prove abbreviated.[50]

Confronting the defections of some of their most trusted African assistants, European missionaries lurched instinctively back to their ideas about racial adolescence. Ambitious, "restless" young Africans, impatient with the missionaries' exacting Christian "standards," were seduced by the Ethiopians' offer of offices and high-sounding titles. This interpretation, in less polemical form, has found its way into much of the historical literature. Insofar as it has any merit, it pertains to the second stratum of Ethiopian leadership, to men such as Benjamin Kumalo and H. R. Ngcayiya, who joined the church once it was a going concern. Such a characterization, however, is singularly misleading for the original leaders of the movement. These were not restless young Africans; on the contrary, they were mature, experienced evangelists. With the exception of Xaba and Gabashane, thirty-four and sixty-three, respectively, the founders of the Ethiopian Church were all in their mid-forties. These men were the product of an earlier mission generation, one that had internalized, perhaps too well, the missionary vision of individual mobility and racial progress. Their own upward path to the ministry was both proof and promise of what Africa would become. For such individuals, the new realities emerging within European missions at the end of the century—the restrictions on education, the petty authoritarianism, the apparent indifference to spreading the gospel— cut to the core of individual identity. Having abandoned whatever consolation or meaning could be found in traditional belief, these men were left with two alternatives: they could accept that the bulk of their lives had been spent in pursuit of a mirage, or they could conclude that the missions had been corrupted, that the fault lay not in the message but in its professed messengers. In this sense, their rebellions served as much to vindicate their pasts as to secure their futures.[51]

The other feature that emerges from this collective portrait is the Ethiopians' extraordinary mobility, in both cultural and geographical terms. All the church's founders had been tossed about in the maelstrom that was nineteenth-century South Africa. Their lives had been shaped by the *mfecane,* by colonial wars of conquest, by the mineral revolution, and, of course, by the spread of evangelical Christianity. In the process, all had been ripped loose from traditional or ethnic moorings. Samuel Brander, born of a Bakhatla father and, perhaps, an African American mother, grew up in the eastern Cape, traveled to Kimberley, and eventually settled in the Waterberg. Mngqibisa and Tantsi, also from the eastern Cape, settled on the Rand. Xaba came of age in the polyglot community at Edendale and pursued his first ministry among ethnically diverse town dwellers in the Orange Free State. Dwane grew up as a refugee and later the ward of a Wesleyan minister; as an adult, he traveled to Britain. In turn-of-the-century parlance, these men had all been comprehensively "de-tribalised." For them, the notion of a shared black identity embedded in the word "Ethiopian" was not some unobtainable idea but a conviction carved in experience.

In 1896, less than four years after the launching of the Ethiopian Church, James Dwane sailed to the United States to arrange the movement's amalgamation with the AME Church. We have already traced the forces that impelled African Americans toward the African mission field in the 1890s; it remains to examine the process from the other side of the Atlantic. What prompted a group of newly independent African Christians to seek affiliation with a black American church? What did black South Africans see when they looked to black America? How did the encounter shape their sense of themselves, of their history and destiny?

It is conceivable that some of the early Ethiopians had actually met African Americans in their travels. By the middle of the nineteenth century, several hundred black Americans were scattered across southern Africa, especially in port cities like Cape Town, Durban, and Port Elizabeth. Ports, as historians are only beginning to realize, were more than commercial entrepots. They were the intellectual clearinghouses of the nineteenth century, crossroads where travelers of every shade and experience mingled and exchanged ideas. Black people were deeply implicated in this cultural and intellectual commerce. Close to a third of the seamen on U.S. merchant ships and whalers in the nineteenth century were African Americans, including, in the antebellum period, many runaway slaves. By the end of the century, African Americans could be found in every port in the Atlantic world, often mingling with other people of color from around the globe.[52]

Not surprisingly, Cape Town boasted South Africa's most substantial "diaspora" community, composed of black Americans, Gold Coasters, Ethiopians, Indians, and West Indians, especially Jamaicans, who provided many of the city's stevedores. Other South African cities also attracted significant, if less visible, contingents, as the pioneering research of Keletso Atkins shows. As paradoxical as it may seem today, nineteenth-century South Africa represented a refuge for African Americans, especially in the antebellum period, when fugitive slaves had but to disembark to lay claim to freedom. Several such individuals surface in colonial records, primarily because of their ambiguous status in law. Probably the most famous black émigré was Yankee Wood, who arrived in South Africa just after the Civil War and elected to stay. He settled eventually in Kokstad, where he opened a hotel and established a newspaper. Another African American was brought up before a magistrate in Durban in 1862 for encouraging an African woman to break an indenture; slavery, he allegedly told her, was not permitted in the British Empire. Atkins has even uncovered an abortive South African emigration scheme, launched during the desperate years of the late 1850s. In 1859 a splinter group from the National Emigration Convention, disillusioned with the other prospective destinations for emigrants, sent a deputation to the Cape to locate land for a prospective colony. The plan found little support in the Cape, but, in one of the innumerable ironies arising in the wake of the transatlantic traffic, it struck a chord among the perennially labor-short planters of Natal. With war in America on the horizon, many Natal planters were looking to expand into cotton production, and they saw African Americans as ideal laborers—plentiful, skilled, and already broken to the task. For better or worse, the Civil War intervened, and nothing came of the plan. The deputation returned to America, and the plantation owners were left to make their fortunes in sugar, using indentured laborers imported from India.[53]

Migration between the United States and South Africa increased in the wake of the mineral discoveries. Hundreds of white Americans came to South Africa in the early 1900s, until more than half of the mines on the Witwatersrand were managed by Americans. (One frustrated Rhodesian mining engineer complained that it was impossible to get a job without an American accent.)

African Americans were equally prominent in the swelling transatlantic traffic. Several "Negroes" surfaced in Kimberley, working as machinists, tradesmen, and the like; at least one carved out a niche for himself in the illicit diamond trade. On the Witwatersrand, black Americans were sufficiently conspicuous for the Z.A.R. government explicitly to include them in an antiliquor ordinance. A few individuals made it even further into the interior: an African American working on the Delagoa Bay railroad won a celebrated suit in the early 1890s after he was assaulted by a white policeman; another worked as a compound manager on a Rhodesian gold mine; still another served in the British South Africa Company's Rhodesian police force. Several members of this black expatriate community would later find their way into the AME Church. West Indian–born photographer Francis Gow and his Pennsylvania-born wife, Sarah, for example, settled in Cape Town in the 1880s. Both became prominent members of Cape Town's emerging "Coloured" elite and leaders of the AME Church in the western Cape.[54]

Even if they had no personal contact with black America, the early Ethiopians were well acquainted with its history. The circumstances of America's Civil War, for example, were well known to literate Africans, and probably to nonliterate ones as well. (The Cape Town call of the Confederate battleship *Alabama* spawned one of South Africa's most enduring folksongs.) The postwar travails of America's freedmen were a staple in mission periodicals, especially Lovedale's *Kaffir Express*. The gist of such articles, and of the related books that stocked mission libraries, was that the freedmen had been unprepared for equality and should invest themselves in education and economic development rather than politics. Future independent churchman P. J. Mzimba cited Afro-American historian George Washington Williams's *History of the Negro Race in America* in an article in the late 1880s which argued (ironically, in light of Mzimba's later history) that Africans should eschew politics in favor of the "Negro" strategy of accommodation and economic uplift.[55]

Music provided a less explicit, though ultimately more important, source of information about black America, as David Coplan and Veit Erlmann have shown. American minstrel songs were published in Cape Town as early as 1828. Twenty years later, Joe Brown's Band of Brothers became, in one nineteenth-century historian's pungent phrase, the "first band of vocalists to give South Africans a taste for nigger part singing." As Erlmann has pointed out, the music South Africans were hearing was actually less an Afro-American tradition than a white genre "in which white performers with blackened faces mimicked and ridiculed blacks," but it was no less popular for its inauthenticity. Indeed, for two decades after the 1862 visit of the famous Christy Minstrels, "blackface minstrel shows became the dominant form of white musical and theatrical entertainment in South Africa," with local troupes sprouting in most cities and towns. Minstrelsy seems to have had an even more profound impact on "Coloured" workers in the Cape, many of whom were themselves descended of slaves. The annual parade begun in 1888 by Cape Town's "Coloured" minstrel troupes survives today in the greasepaint and parodic pageantry of the city's "Coon Carnival."[56]

As important as such developments were, they pale in comparison to the impact of Orpheus McAdoo's Jubilee Singers, an African American singing troupe that visited South Africa during an 1890 world tour. Between 1890 and 1989, the McAdoo Singers toured three times, performing more than a thousand concerts in literally every city in South Africa. The tours opened up a lasting cultural channel between black America and black South Africa and, through an extraordinary set of contingencies, precipitated the union of the Ethiopian and AME churches.

The roots of "Jubilee" music reach back to the late 1870s, to the celebrated Fisk University Singers, who first popularized the "sorrow songs" of American slavery. The term itself came from Leviticus and referred to the day of freedom. This orientation was reflected in the choir's repertoire, which featured African American sacred music rather than the minstrel parodies that white audiences had learned to expect of black performers. Orpheus McAdoo, a graduate of Hampton University, toured Australia and the Pacific with the Fisk Singers in the 1880s before hitting the hustings with a venture of his own. While much of the McAdoo troupe's repertoire came out of minstrelsy, the singers eschewed blackface and, initially at least, the juggling and jokes of "Bones" and "Mr. Tambo," the minstrel show's staple sidemen. Spirituals were interspersed with old minstrel standards, creating, in the words of one South African reviewer, a blend of "the pathetic and the humorous," which McAdoo could tailor to fit the tastes of his audience. Over time, the McAdoo Singers reverted to a more traditional minstrel framework, perhaps to retain their white audience, but Afro-American sacred music remained the heart of their repertoire.[57]

Public response to the Jubilee Singers, especially during their first visit, was nothing short of sensational. While a few newspaper critics, accustomed to the pace and frivolity of the minstrel show, found the Singers' emphasis on "sombre religious selections" laborious, most were frankly overwhelmed. Such music has "never before been heard in this country," a Cape Town reviewer wrote. The Singers' performance was "inspired, as if they were lifting up their voices in praise of God with hopes of liberty." On the diamond fields, the McAdoo Singers' initial two week run drew "delighted and full houses . . . of a more mixed character than have perhaps ever been gathered together in four walls in Kimberley." In Pretoria, President Paul Kruger took his entire cabinet to a lunchtime show, having been assured that the performance was more akin to a religious service than an "entertainment." The old *Dopper* claimed never to have entered a theater before and he may never have done so again, but he was moved by what he heard: according to one newspaper report, "tears could be seen streaming down the rugged features of the President" during McAdoo's rendition of "Nobody Knows the Trouble I've Seen."[58]

The McAdoo Singers' visit touched South Africans across boundaries of race and class, but it had its most galvanic effect on African Christians, including many who were later prominent in the independent church movement. Mangena Mokone was a devotee of choral music—like many members of South Africa's Christian elite, he kept an organ in the parlor of his home—and there is no question that he saw the Singers perform during their stay in Pretoria. H. R. Ngcayiya, a future Ethiopian and later a founder of the South African Native National Congress, was performing with a local jubilee troupe in Burghersdorp in 1890 even before the McAdoo Singers had finished their tour. In Kimberley the Singers made a profound impression on a number of young Africans who later played prominent roles in the founding of the South African AME Church, including Charlotte Manye, then a schoolteacher, Henry Msikinya, director of the Wesleyan Church choir, and Simon Hoffa Sinamela, Msikinya's Presbyterian counterpart. Sinamela later moved to Pretoria, where he taught in the new Ethiopian school and organized the young church's choir. Mokone himself clearly had no doubt that Jubilee music was appropriate for the new church. "Our teacher, the Rev. Simon Hoffa Sinamela, sings nearly as those Jubilee Singers of 'Virginia'," he boasted in an 1896 letter. "Our choir has much interested the people and some said that they had never heard such a choir in South Africa."[59]

Long after the curtain had fallen on the McAdoo Singers' final performance, these independent church leaders remained devoted to black American sacred music. Sinamela, who went on to become one of the AME Church's most fiery preachers, composed a number of original hymns for the young church, including "Kgoshi Sekukhuni," a Sepedi hymn that fused traditional praise poetry, mission hymnody, and the Jubilee style. In the early years of the century Sinamela itinerated across the highveld and into Basutoland, carrying an organ on the back of an oxcart, stopping at villages to perform and proselytize. Ethiopian Church founder Jacobus Xaba was in the United States translating Afro-American spirituals for the South African church's hymnal when he died in 1904; the project was later completed by his colleague, J. Z. Tantsi. In the Cape, Francis Gow and his musically gifted children, three of whom eventually joined him in the AME ministry, remained the most important purveyors of African American sacred music in South Africa for the next half century.[60]

How does one explain these independent African Christians' extraordinary receptivity to Afro-American music? To some extent, it was a matter of propitious timing. Even before the McAdoo Singers' arrival, a number of African Christians had begun to explore alternatives to European hymnody. Frustrated by the stilted rhymes and crabbed lyrics of the mission churches' vernacular hymnbooks, composers such as John Knox Bokwe consciously set out in the 1870s and '80s to develop a musical appreciation of Christianity that was distinctively African. Bokwe's hymns, as David Coplan has pointed out, preserved much of the inherited choral tradition: they were sung a capella or accompanied only by organ, using four-part harmonies and a diatonic scale. At the same time, however, the new hymns were recognizably African: they incorporated traditional melodies, utilized the idiomatic possibilities of vernacular languages, and enshrined the "overlapping call and response" pattern characteristic of Cape Nguni music, and sub-Saharan music in general. By 1890 Bokwe's hymns had been widely dispersed through African mission congregations, largely by word of mouth, and they were certainly familiar to Mokone, who doubtless recognized their significance.[61]

There was much in this new hymnody that prefigured religious independency. One of Bokwe's first projects, for example, was to transcribe the hymns of Ntsikana; he later wrote a biography of the Xhosa prophet. According to tradition, Ntsikana was awakened by divine revelation and had already begun preaching when the first missionaries arrived. He thus represented a Christian pedigree independent of whites, much as the concept of "Ethiopia" did. Bokwe himself seems never to have pushed his ideas to this conclusion: he remained loyal to the Free Church of Scotland until his death early in the twentieth century. Other pioneers of the genre, however, were closely associated with the independent church movement. Enoch Sontaga, the composer of "Nkosi Sikelel' iAfrika," the hymn destined to become the national anthem of a democratic South Africa a century later, was the son-in-law of Ethiopian founder Abraham Mngqibisa and a prominent member of P. J. Mzimba's African Presbyterian Church. "Nkosi Sikelel' iAfrika," which quickly became a standard hymn in the South African AME Church, epitomized the new hymnody. Arranged in four parts, the song revolved around an antiphony of male and female voices. The lyrics, later translated into dozens of languages, were originally written in powerfully idiomatic IsiXhosa: "God bless Africa / Raise high her horn." Such music presumed no European intermediary between Africans and a Christian God.[62]

The slave songs of the McAdoo Singers accorded uncannily well with the new hymnody. While the historical roots of African American music lay in West Africa, there was much here recognizable to a South African audience. The songs enshrined the call and response pattern; their lyrics were earthy and idiomatic and revolved around an immanent God invested in nature. At the same time, the songs, like the hymns of Bokwe, maintained internalized standards of Christian propriety: they were somber, arranged in standard four-part harmonies, and sung a capella or with keyboard accompaniment. (White religious leaders in both South Africa and North America had endeavored to suppress drumming in religious worship.) Above all, the sorrow songs, like the hymns of Bokwe and Sontaga, attested to the possibility of mature Christian expression outside a European mold. As such, they could scarcely but appeal to a group of African Christians already chafing under white missionary control.[63]

Music, however, was only one part of the McAdoo Singers' message. As the first African Americans that most South Africans had ever seen, the Singers attracted no end of scrutiny and comment. Africans discussed their history, their color (compared by one African reviewer to the high yellow of the Khoi), their dress and bearing. It is difficult to say with certainty what conclusions Africans drew, since the troupe projected a range of different images. Onstage, the Singers moved from the Sambo of "Shoo Fly" and Stephen Foster's "Massa's in the Cold Ground" to the righteous believers of "Turn Back Pharaoh's Army" and "God Delivered Daniel." Offstage, they projected another image entirely, an image that to black South Africans in 1890 must have seemed the very embodiment of sophistication. Their dress was dapper, their demeanor urbane. They spoke English fluently, a hallmark of elite status in South Africa. (A number of Africans were reportedly startled to discover that the Singers spoke no vernacular languages.) While separated from slavery by just a generation— McAdoo himself was born a slave—they moved easily through South African society as "honorary whites," packing in mixed audiences and winning the plaudits of white society. In Cape Town, the troupe performed for the governor; in Kimberley, they were feted by the mayor.[64]

In the end, the conclusion that Mangena Mokone and his colleagues drew— the conclusion that African audiences seem almost universally to have drawn— was that African Americans were more "advanced" than they. This idea was to have an abiding impact on South African black culture, as Coplan's work shows. For much of the twentieth century, black America would remain a symbol of urbanity and sophistication among black South Africans, especially in cities. A range of people, from politicians to advertisers, would seek to appropriate the American imprimatur, invoking the "Negro" model to defend political action or inaction, to promote new musical styles, and to sell everything from hair straighteners to maize meal. More striking still, Africans almost invariably attributed blacks' "progress" in the United States to one factor: education. Whatever African Americans were presumed to be, it was education that had made them that way.[65]

Orpheus McAdoo himself encouraged that conclusion. Everywhere he went, he regaled audiences with accounts of black American achievements in education and the professions, of entire colleges run by and for black people. While in Kimberley, McAdoo funded a scholarship to send a young African to Hampton Institute, his alma mater. (The student, Titus Mbongwe, was tragically killed in a British rail accident while en route to the United States.) The gist of McAdoo's remarks can be gleaned from a review of an 1890 performance in Kimberley, written by a young African. After reviewing black American history and describing the Singers' physical appearance, the writer concluded:

Hear! Today they have their own schools, primary, secondary and high schools, and also universities. They are run by them without the help of whites. They have magistrates, judges, lawyers, bishops, ministers and evangelists, and school masters. Some have learned a craft such as building etc. etc.

"When will the day come when the African people will be like the Americans?" he concluded. "When will they stop being slaves and become nations with their own government?"[66]

The final question is twice revealing. Not only does it reveal some of the ways Africans apprehended and misapprehended African American history and experience; it also suggests that the encounter with black America was helping Africans to comprehend their own experience in new ways. It may not be too fanciful to suggest, for instance, that the encounter with black America helped popularize the imagery of "slavery" and "freedom" that would become such a staple of black political rhetoric in twentieth-century South Africa. Spokesmen for the Industrial and Commerical Workers' Union, for example, routinely addressed audiences as "fellow slaves," often explicitly contrasting their condition with that of their emancipated brethren in the United States. Obviously, the idea that Africans were enslaved was not literally true, but it had a powerful imaginative truth; to borrow a phrase from Clifford Geertz, it offered Africans "a vocabulary in terms of which to grasp the nature of [their] distress and relate it to the wider world." This is not to suggest that black South Africans were oblivious to their oppression before African Americans lent them words to describe it. Nor is it to suggest that no black South Africans had ever employed slavery in this context prior to the arrival of Orpheus McAdoo; slavery was an obvious enough image, after all, especially to a group of people whose primary encounter with literacy was through the Bible. Yet at the very least, the encounter with black America gave an additional resonance to this familiar Old Testament concept. In calling themselves slaves, South Africans appropriated not just words but an entire history—the history of another group of blacks who had successfully passed through a similar trial. Slavery was thus invested with the certainty of freedom, the promise of yet another Jubilee Day. In African Americans, the Bible's abstract promise of redemption became the stuff of history. The Word became flesh.[67]

The chain of events that led to the amalgamation of the Ethiopian and the AME churches commenced in Kimberley's "Fingo Location," home to the diamond fields' small Christian elite. Fingo Location's residents were clerks, teachers, interpreters, tradesmen, the flower of nineteenth-century missions. As Brian Willan has shown, it was a cohesive community, bound together by churches, schools, debating societies, cricket clubs, and, above all, music. Here was a fertile field for African American music, and the visit of the McAdoo Singers spawned a host of imitators. Indeed, two members of McAdoo's players, including pianist Will Thompson, elected to stay in Kimberley to perform with a local troupe. The community's eclectic culture is graphically illustrated by the musical program for the 1897 debut of the local Philharmonic Society, a troupe that included Thompson, future National Congress leader Solomon Plaatje, and newly arrived AME minister H. R. Ngcayiya. The evening's program ranged from one of the hymns of Ntsikana to John Knox Bokwe's "Kaffir Wedding Song" to the minstrel standard "Pickin' on de Harp," concluding with "God Save the Queen."[68]

In late 1890 two enterprising white businessmen, impressed by the depth of local talent uncovered by the McAdoo Singers' visit, began putting together an African Jubilee Choir for a tour of Great Britain. Portraying themselves as philanthropists, the promoters touted vague plans to build an industrial school for Africans with tour profits. Probably their most original idea was to have the singers perform the first half of the program in vernacular languages, resplendent in native costume, and the second half in English, in sober Victorian dress, providing audiences with an object lesson in Africans' potential for development—potential, the *Christian Express* remarked in a supportive editorial, "long since proved in the case of the negro slaves in America." From the outset, however, the choir was dogged by recriminations and allegations of unmet promises. By the time the choir set out on a shakedown cruise to the eastern Cape, most of its original Kimberley members, including future AME minister Simon Sinamela and his brother Paul, had abandoned ship. The promoters managed to fill their complement at Lovedale and set off for Britain. In London, the choir performed for parliamentarians and at a reception for Queen Victoria before the tour was engulfed in acrimony and more allegations of unpaid salaries. It ended after two years with one of the singers under arrest for concealing the birth of a child and most of the remainder stranded in a London hotel.[69]

The singers straggled back to South Africa, to lamentations from the initially supportive *Christian Express*. When the same promoters announced plans for another tour, this time to include North America, the original choir members gave them a wide berth—all save one. She was Charlotte Manye, a twenty-one-year-old teacher at a Kimberley mission school. Blessed with an imposing physical presence and a rich contralto voice, Charlotte was one of the African Choir's featured performers. According to her younger sister Kate, a choir member who disdained the second tour, Charlotte's whole purpose in reenlisting was to get to the United States, where she hoped to pursue her education. The claim is not as farfetched as it might seem. Manye had sung at the farewell concert for Titus Mbongwe when he departed on his ill-fated journey to Hampton Institute. She had also apparently met some African Americans in London who confirmed what she had heard about American educational facilities. If this was indeed Manye's intention, the second tour, on the surface more disastrous than the first, was a great success. After a year traveling through Britain, Canada, and the United States, the singers were once again abandoned by their promoters, this time in Cleveland. They were rescued by Reverdy Ransom, a young AME minister who would later win distinction as a founder of the Niagara Movement. Like many young church leaders, Ransom was an enthusiastic supporter of the African mission movement, and he saw in the stranded singers, already adept in two worlds, ready-made missionaries. With the support of AME Senior Bishop Benjamin Arnett, Ransom arranged to enroll a half dozen of the singers, including Manye, at Wilberforce University, his Ohio alma mater. There, under the tutelage of a handful of black professors, including the young W. E. B. Du Bois, the singers began their training as AME missionaries.[70]

What followed has been preserved as a kind of oral tradition within the South African AME Church. Sometime in 1894, Charlotte Manye wrote to her sister Kate in Johannesburg, apparently on paper emblazoned with the letterhead of AME Bishop Henry Turner, a frequent visitor to the university. Kate chanced to show the letter to Mangena Mokone. (In most accounts, Mokone is cast as the girls' "uncle," but he appears rather to have been a family friend. He and the girls' father hailed from the same part of Sekukuniland.) After reading Charlotte's rapturous descriptions of Wilberforce, Mokone penned a brief letter to Bishop Turner, dated May 1895. He told Turner about his "Ethiopian Mission" (an institution "entirely managed by us blacks of South Africa") and enquired about tuition costs at Wilberforce, "as I have some youths here in my mission whom I can send to you as students, who will become teachers after completing their studies there." Turner printed the letter in the *Voice of Missions,* directed to the attention of Wilberforce; he also sent Mokone a copy of the paper, followed by the AME *Discipline.* A short courtship ensued, preserved in the columns of the paper. Early in 1896 delegates to the third annual conference of the Ethiopian Church voted to seek affiliation with the AME Church. They appointed three men, Mokone, Jacobus Xaba, and James Dwane, to travel to the United States to arrange the union.[71]

Those historians who have addressed the issue have generally concluded that the Ethiopians were drawn to the AME Church by the promise of education. The argument, as far as it goes, is accurate. Even as the Ethiopians abandoned mission churches, they continued to accept missionaries' equation of education and racial progress. Many left European churches precisely because of the limitations they encountered in mission schools. The irony, of course, was that in doing so they cut themselves off from the only available source of education in South Africa. The AME Church offered an ideal solution to the problem. Given their exaggerated notions about black American educational attainments, it was easy for the early Ethiopians to believe that they had at last found the key that would unlock the future of the race.

Ultimately, however, African Methodism offered more than material support. As Mokone and his colleagues pored over the *Voice of Missions,* they must have felt a profound sense of legitimation. Here was another group of black

Methodists, disdained by their white brethren, who had sought the sanctuary of their own church. The sense of recognition was doubtless sharpened as they read the "Historical Preface" in the AME *Discipline,* which recounted the tale of Richard Allen and the founding of the AME Church in terms eerily reminiscent of the Ethiopians' own experiences, even down to the biblical verse used to dedicate their respective churches. From its humble beginning in Philadelphia, the church of Allen had grown into a vast enterprise to redeem Africa, an enterprise that the Ethiopians were now being asked to join. It was a bracing prospect.[72]

Given the sheer number of coincidences and contingencies, it was inevitable that African churchmen would see the hand of Providence at work. "The prophecy predicted by the Psalmist, 68, approaches its perfection," Jacobus Xaba wrote in an early letter to the *Voice of Missions.* Even more revealing was the comment of a correspondent from Cape Town. "When I saw in your paper, your freedom, I could not help shedding tears for my poor native country. You are born of God (as Moses in Egypt). Brothers consider that carefully." Mangena Mokone turned not to Exodus but to Nehemiah, the prophet who rebuilt the temple in Jerusalem after the Babylonian captivity and welded the scattered Israelites back into a nation. Mokone ended one letter with a haunting reference from Nehemiah, chapter 4: *"So we laboured in the work: and half of them held the spears from the rising of the morning till the stars appeared."*[73]

As delegates to the 1896 AME General Conference assembled in New York, all waited anxiously for the arrival of the Ethiopian delegation. In the event, only Dwane arrived, and he a week after the Conference had adjourned. Both Xaba and Mokone, he explained, had been late reaching Cape Town, apparently due to difficulties in raising money for their passage, and he had been forced to leave without them. Though most conference delegates had dispersed, church leaders convened a rousing reception for Dwane at Philadelphia's Mother Bethel Church. From Philadelphia, he entrained for Atlanta, where Bishop Turner accepted the Ethiopians' application at a hastily arranged session of the North Georgia Annual Conference. Dwane was reobligated to the AME ministry and appointed general superintendent of the South African church, with authority to reobligate the remainder of the Ethiopian ministry to the AME Church.[74]

Back in South Africa, Dwane was already a controversial figure. His selection to the U.S. delegation, only months after joining the Ethiopian Church, had spawned considerable resentment among his more established colleagues—resentment redoubled when he embarked without waiting for Mokone and Xaba and returned as general superintendent. In America, however, Dwane was an ideal representative for the South Africans. Self-possessed, eloquent, by far the best educated of the Ethiopian ministers, he seemed to American audiences to synthesize native nobility and Western education, to offer a flesh-and-blood model of what the African could become. For all his polish and education, "he has never lost touch with Kaffir sympathies," the *Voice of Missions* raved. In 1896, and during a second American visit in 1899, he traveled through most of the southern states, visiting colleges, meeting politicians (including President McKinley), speaking everywhere to packed lecture halls. Adept at gauging the susceptibilities of his listeners, he held audiences spellbound with tales of his birth in a world "enveloped in ignorance and darkness," of his youthful conversion, his struggle for education, his battles with white missionaries. Everywhere he stressed the need for an institution of "higher learning" in South Africa, where Africans could be trained as ministers and teachers. African American audiences greeted him with hallelujahs; they penned poems about him and organized local "Dwane Missionary Societies." Southern whites, much to Turner's amusement, lined up to shake his hand and invited him into their homes, intimacies they could scarcely have imagined extending to their black neighbors.[75]

Dwane returned from his first visit to America in early 1897. A few weeks later, the twenty ministers of what had been the Ethiopian Church gathered together at Lesseyton, outside Queenstown, and were formally reobligated to the AME ministry. Any bitterness caused by Dwane's rapid ascent in the church hierarchy was temporarily forgotten as he regaled his fellows with tales of black America's "wonderful progress." When he announced that American church leaders had committed themselves to building a South African college, the conference exploded in a paroxysm of prayer and thanksgiving. A revival kindled at the conference carried African Methodism across the eastern Cape and into the Transkei, drawing thousands of new adherents into the church. In Pretoria and its environs, Joseph Kanyane Napo, founder of the African Church and temporarily an African Methodist, reported baptizing up to two dozen adults and children a day. Abraham Mngqibisa enjoyed equal success on the farms around Johannesburg, where he numbered among his converts one old man who had initially dismissed Ethiopianism "as another 'manic' besides that great one of Nonquase." (Nongqawuse was the Xhosa girl whose millenarian prophecies precipitated the 1856–1857 Xhosa cattle killing.) With the sanction of black America, what had been madness suddenly seemed plausible.[76]

As new congregants poured into the church, both Dwane and Mokone began to worry about the movement's lack of structure. Such fears were shared by African American church leaders, several of whom were openly skeptical about the South African venture. In answer to Dwane's summons, an aging Henry Turner, patron of the South African church, set out for Africa. Turner, who had previously organized the AME Church's work in Liberia and Sierra Leone, arrived in Cape Town in March 1898 and spent the next six weeks gathering the burgeoning Ethiopian movement into the institutional confines of African Methodism. He inaugurated annual conferences in the Transvaal and Cape, outfitting each with all the committees and offices prescribed in the

AME *Discipline.* He established circuits, appointed presiding elders, and explained church doctrine on everything from dispensing sacraments to ministerial robes. (Several of the ministers who entered the church from Anglicanism insisted on wearing surplices over their cassocks, producing a series of disputes and at least one secession.) Given the excited state of affairs, it doubtless took some time before AME customs and usages really took hold in the church, which most Africans continued to call *iTiyopia.* Indeed, the continuing struggle of African American leaders to impose their vision and methods on African congregations would constitute one of the central themes in the subsequent history of the South African church. At the very least, however, Turner's visit gave the movement some institutional ballast, which it would need to navigate the stormy seas ahead.[77]

The most immediate significance of Turner's visit lay simply in the spectacle it offered South Africans of a black bishop—a spectacle that continues, nearly a century later, to reverberate through the accounts of oral informants. Africans responded with celebration, whites with consternation, to the sight of what one AME minister called "the future of the black race of this continent." Turner naturally gloried in the visibility. In Cape Town, audiences packed the Opera House to hear him lecture on "The Unity of the Race" and "The Spiritual Crisis of the World." (By Turner's standards, the speeches were unusually temperate, but they clearly struck a chord with their audiences, holding out black American progress as a measure of what Africans could accomplish.) From the Cape, Turner ventured to Bloemfontein, where he met with Free State officials, and thence to Johannesburg, where he was greeted by a throng at the railroad station. Orpheus McAdoo's Jubilee Singers, back in the Transvaal on another tour, performed for the crowd, which filled the street outside the AME Church to hear the bishop preach. In Pretoria, Turner officiated at the first meeting of the Transvaal Annual Conference, taking time off for a formal audience with Z.A.R. President Paul Kruger. Kruger, who apparently saw the new church as a potential counterweight to the hated British missions, received the bishop cordially, even deigning to shake his hand, a courtesy he professed never before to have extended to a black man. While little came of the meeting, it did produce one of the more surreal moments in South African history: the angry African American emigrationist and the aging Boer patriarch discoursing on their shared admiration for the republican form of government.[78]

During Turner's six-week visit, the church doubled again in size. In Johannesburg alone, three more congregations joined the AME connection, most notably an independent Presbyterian congregation led by Edward Tsewu. Invitations from a dozen other congregations in the Transvaal Turner declined for want of time. By the time he left the country, the fledgling church boasted more than eleven thousand members, and Turner confidently expected membership to double yet again before the 1900 General Conference. The only apparent obstacle to the AME Church's spread was the shortage of ministers, and Turner did what he could to alleviate it. In all, he ordained sixty elders and deacons, most after only cursory examinations. Concerned that this number might not sustain the church until the next episcopal visit, Turner took the even more controversial step of annointing Dwane a "Vicar-Bishop," investing him with powers of ordination. While such an action was not exactly unprecedented in the church's history—Paul Quinn had briefly held the title of suffragen bishop in the early 1840s—it had no warrant in the AME *Discipline,* which provided for the election of bishops at quadrennial General Conferences. Turner, however, defended the move as necessary, given the South African movement's phenomenal growth and its distance from the mother church.[79]

Turner returned to the United States in mid-1898, confident that the South African church had been launched on the proper course. Yet even as he sailed away, a raft of problems was bobbing up in his wake. In South Africa, the bishop's promiscuity in dispensing ordinations provided fodder for the church's opponents, who argued that "Ethiopianism" eroded Christian "standards" and should be regulated or suppressed. Turner's many antagonists in the United States seized on the irregular promotion of Dwane to challenge the whole South African enterprise. Most important, church leaders in both Africa and America began having to confront some of the simplifications and misapprehensions that underlay their merger. For all the talk of racial affinity and providential reunion, Africans and African Americans had come together in distinctly self-referential terms. Africans' perceptions about black America, for example, said as much about their own aspirations and grievances as they did about any objective realities of African American life. Similarly, African American interest in Africa grew out of a century-long debate over black people's place in the United States, a debate in which Africans served primarily as imaginative foils. None of this is particularly surprising, nor was it particularly problematic so long as Africans and African Americans remained apart. It was quite another matter, however, to work side-by-side within a single institution.

All these problems would play themselves out in the early years of the twentieth century, as a series of African American bishops and missionaries came to South Africa to assume control of the AME Church's newest field of operations. Before examining that process, however, it is useful to probe beneath the institutional surface, to move from the level of leadership to the movement's rank-and-file. Who were the people who came, in their thousands, into the AME Church in its first decade and a half in South Africa? What did they find in African Methodism, and what did they forge from it?

Richard Allen. (Daniel A. Payne, *History of the African Methodist Episcopal Church*, Philadelphia, 1891.)

Daniel Coker. (Daniel A. Payne, *History of the African Methodist Episcopal Church*, Philadelphia, 1891.)

W. Paul Quinn, African Methodism's "missionary to the West." (Daniel A. Payne, *History of the African Methodist Episcopal Church*, Philadelphia, 1891.)

Daniel Payne, from an 1843 lithograph. The Bible is open to John 1:29: "The next day John seeth Jesus coming unto him, and saith, behold the Lamb of God, which taketh away the sin of the world." (Courtesy of the Wilberforce University Archives.)

Henry McNeal Turner. (Courtesy of Moorland-Spingarn Research Center, Howard University.)

Portrait, apparently retouched, of C. S. Smith "and his adopted family of Dwalla children," Cameroon, 1894. The uniform reflects Smith's standing as a Mason. (C. S. Smith, *Glimpses of Africa: West and Southwest Coast*, Nashville, 1895.)

Mangena Maake Mokone. (J. M. Mokone, *The Early Life of Our Founder*, Johannesburg, 1935.)

Jacobus Xaba, Ethiopian Church founder in the Orange Free State. (Sara Duncan, *Progressive Missions in the South*, Atlanta, 1906.)

The South African Choir in "traditional" garb, London, 1891. Note the Victorian-style beadwork and the tiger-skin rug in foreground. (*Review of Reviews 4:21*, London, 1891.)

Bishop Henry Turner welcomes James Dwane and the Ethiopian Church into the AME Connection, Atlanta, 1896. Witnessing the union are Missionary Secretary H. B. Parks and Joseph Flipper, pastor of Atlanta's Allen Temple. (L. L. Berry, *A Century of Missions of the African Methodist Episcopal Church*, New York, 1942.)

Bishop Henry Turner and the Transvaal Annual Conference, Pretoria, 1898. (Courtesy of
Moorland Spingarn Research Center, Howard University.)

"The American Colony" in Capetown, ca. 1903: Reverend and Mrs. A. H. Attaway, Bishop
Levi J. Coppin, Fanny Jackson Coppin, and Carleton Tanner. (L. J. Coppin, *Observations of
Persons and Things in South Africa, 1900–1904*, Philadelphia, 1905.)

South African students at Wilberforce University, ca. 1893. Charlotte Manye is seated at center. (R. R. Wright, Jr., *Encyclopedia of African Methodism*, Philadelphia, 1948.)

The AME House of Bishops, gathered at John Wesley's grave during the 1901 Ecumenical Methodist Conference in London. Seated, left to right: Charles Spencer Smith, Evans Tyree, Moses Salter, Benjamin Tanner, John Wesley Gaines, Benjamin Arnett, Benjamin Franklin Lee, and William Derrick. Cornelius Shaffer and James Handy stand third and fourth from left. John Albert Johnson, who served in South Africa from 1908 to 1916, stands at extreme right. Reverdy C. Ransom, another future bishop, stands at rear. Missing are Levi J. Coppin, who was in South Africa, Henry Turner, and Abraham Grant. (Courtesy of the Wilberforce University Archives.)

Charlotte Manye Maxeke, ca. 1930. (T. D. Mweli Skota, *The African Yearly Register*, Johannesburg, 1932.)

Bishop W. T. Vernon and his wife Emily with unidentified Africans during a visit to Basutoland, 1922. (*AME Church Review 38:4*, 1922.)

5

African Methodism as a Social Movement, I

The amalgamation of the Ethiopian and AME churches culminated a remarkable historical convergence between black Christians at opposite corners of the Atlantic. For African American Christians, the opening of the African mission field helped salve the pain of the past: slavery, for all its horror and brutality, had been progressive, a part of God's unfolding plan for the redemption of Africa. For Mangena Mokone and his comrades, the prospect was equally invigorating. Seen through the prism of black America, their humble rebellions in places like Marabastad and the Waterberg resolved themselves into the stuff of prophecy. As Jacobus Xaba put it, "The prophecy predicted by the Psalmist, 68, approaches its perfection."[1]

Ultimately, however, the handful of leaders gathered around Mokone neither encompassed African Methodism nor exhausted its meanings. If the South African church had remained the province of a handful of dissident clerics, it would scarcely have generated the enthusiasm it did or struck such fear into the hearts of colonial officials. In the decade and a half after its founding—a period that encompassed the South African War, imperial reconstruction, and the creation of the Union of South Africa—African Methodism exploded across the southern African subcontinent. By the formation of the Union of South Africa in 1910, the young church boasted upwards of forty thousand full members within the Union alone. Thousands more people had been touched by the church's message.[2]

Arriving at one of the most delicately poised moments in South African history, the AME Church naturally attracted considerable scrutiny and comment. Editors, missionaries, and magistrates traded "Ethiopian" rumors, blaming the independent church movement for everything from the fractious behavior of chiefs to an apparent epidemic of "native insolence" on highveld farms. In the eastern Transvaal, African Methodism's arrival ignited a full-blown panic, sending farmers all across the region scurrying into laager. That the rumored rising never materialized did little to dampen white anxiety. On the contrary, officials' inability to confirm reports of agitation, or even to document a single case of seditious preaching, came to be cited as evidence of the movement's sinister intent. As one native commissioner put it, AME "chaps" were "too wide awake" to preach what they allegedly practiced.[3]

Lack of evidence did not stop European observers from devising their own interpretations of the independent church phenomenon. In a novel variation of the agitator thesis, colonial officials and white missionaries assured themselves that the source of the Ethiopian "poison" was black America. The "influx of the American negro with his peculiar ideas" was giving the "wrong warp" to native aspirations, diverting Africans "from the true path of industrial improvement." Black Americans had injected "new born energy" into a sluggish race; they had added a "directing brain" to a previously disorganized black body. Most ominous of all, African Americans presented Africans with the spectacle of a black population undivided by language or ethnicity, thereby threatening one of the central props of white supremacy. Everywhere, observers reported sharpened "racial self-consciousness," as well as unwonted "cohesion" among people previously riven by tribe. Not coincidentally, the movement seemed to be strongest in cities, which teemed with "half-educated" Africans, many of whom had lost "the strong feelings of loyalty to their hereditary chiefs" that distinguished "natives" in their "raw" state. The dangers of the situation were evident not only in the spreading rebellion against European missions but in the proliferation of African political organizations, which carried the Ethiopian quest for racial equality into the secular sphere.[4]

Today, a century later, most of these conclusions remain embedded in the historical literature, albeit in less invidious form. Almost without exception, historians describe "Ethiopianism" as an urban movement, appealing to the "educated" and "de-tribalised." Politically, the movement is routinely characterized as "proto-national," as one step in a nationalist teleology that culminated in the formation of the South African Native National Congress in 1912. Historians also continue to infer the movement's character from its association with black America, to the point where African agency sometimes disappears altogether and the whole movement becomes a "reflex response" to developments in the United States. The *Oxford History of South Africa,* to take just one example, places its two-page treatment of independent Christianity in the chapter on African nationalism, in the context of a discussion of the emerging African elite. Having left behind their own "traditions," members of this educated, urban elite were susceptible to "Ethiopianism," an impulse that the authors portray as emanating from nineteenth-century black America. How the independent church movement came to be associated with black America, and what that association meant to different groups of Africans, the authors do not suggest.[5]

There are certainly elements of truth here. The Ethiopian, later the AME, Church did first take root in cities—in Marabastad, outside Pretoria, and on the Witwatersrand. Many of its adherents, and most of its leaders, were recruited from the mission elite and embraced black America as a model of racial progress and unity. There is also some merit in the association of African Methodism with African nationalism. AME ministers and lay people played prominent roles in the vigilance associations, congresses, and political unions that emerged in the aftermath of the South African War; during one period in 1907, the church was represented simultaneously on the executives of the Cape, Transvaal, and Free State Native Congresses. Nearly a dozen of the men who launched the South African Native National Congress had been touched by the AME Church and by the broader traffic with black America which the church facilitated.[6]

It does not take long, however, to reach the limits of these generalizations. The standard portrayal of African Methodism as "urban" and "proto-national" cannot explain the church's popularity in the reserves of the eastern Cape and Transkei, where the majority of people still worked the land, acknowledged the authority of chiefs, and moved within more or less ethnically bounded communities. Still less can it explain the lively traffic between the AME Church and revanchist African chiefs, several of whom adopted the church as a kind of state religion. Nor can the standard portrayal of African Methodism be easily reconciled with the movement's enduring influence among black share-croppers in the Free State and western Transvaal. Even within cities, the church's constituency and character defy convenient generalization. In Cape Town, for example, the church became the province of an emerging Coloured elite that wore its affiliation with black America as a badge of distinction. Living through a plague scare and a concerted effort to push nonwhites out of the central city, leaders of this community found in the church a means to distance themselves from the city's African working class, a portion of which met in a nearby AME Church of its own.[7]

How can one account for this diversity? For white missionaries, the answer was patent: Africans lacked the capacity to maintain institutional order and "standards." "The history of Ethiopianism," a leading missionary reported,

> has made it abundantly clear that the natives are deficient in the sense of law and order, lax in their exercise of discipline, and to a large extent incapable of directing their own affairs, and in especial, their financial affairs.

Put bluntly, the AME Church was diverse because it was black. Deprived of the discipline and structure provided by white supervision, the independent church movement had simply dissolved into its constituent elements. It had become "Cave of Adullam" open to anyone with a bit of "ambition" and an axe to grind against Europeans.[8]

Stripped of the racist husk, there is an important kernel of truth here: African Methodism was a highly decentralized affair. We have already had occasion to explore this issue in a U.S. context, to examine the efforts of African American church leaders to impose a degree of institutional order and regularity on a sometimes recalcitrant rank-and-file. In the South African case, the central church was weaker still, leaving even more room for local diversity. To be sure, African American church leaders endeavored to introduce their discipline and doctrine: they mailed catechisms and church periodicals to South Africa and dispatched Bishop Henry Turner to organize annual conferences and institute denominational usages. For the most part, however, the South African AME Church spent its formative years with little or no direct supervision from the United States. As an imaginative presence, black America remained ubiquitous within the church, but that presence was rarely mediated by face-to-face contact. Even when the first African American supervisors arrived in 1901, their influence remained quite limited, thanks to wartime travel restrictions and later to a state travel ban deliberately crafted to keep AME leaders out of the Transvaal and Orange Free State.

Financially, the church was even more decentralized. AME leaders loved to tout the value of the church's property holdings, which reached into tens of millions of dollars, but in terms of daily operations the church remained an impecunious institution, forever struggling to meet its obligations and pledges. Inevitably, pledges to mission fields were the first to be sacrificed, leaving churches in places like South Africa more or less to their own devices. The South African church, in turn, was far too poor to pay ministers' salaries or pensions or to make anything more than token investments in local AME schools. The result, in terms of ecclesiology, was a kind of de facto congregationalism beneath an episcopal veneer. African American bishops retained the power to ordain ministers and assign them to more or less promising circuits, but how much a minister actually received in salary depended on the largesse of his congregation. Such a situation left African Methodism perenially vulnerable to "capture from below." Ministers who failed to address local concerns or to accommodate local practices could quickly find themselves hungry.

Obviously, this line of analysis should not be pushed too far. While less structured than its American counterpart, the South African church boasted a published *Discipline,* an established episcopacy, and a substantial body of procedure and precedent, all of which lent it a degree of institutional solidity unmatched by other African independent churches. Compared to the myriad "Zionist" sects that emerged in South Africa in the interwar years, the AME Church appears structured and stable indeed. Taken on its own terms, however, the South African AME Church remained a diffuse, decentralized movement. In the early years in particular, it was less a single institution than a mold into which local communities could pour their own convictions and concerns.

What generalizations, then, can we make? Was African Methodism just a concatenation of local movements, or were there structures and ideas that united and defined it? Ultimately, the only way to answer these questions is by tracing the church's entrance and evolution in specific contexts. The chapters that follow attempt to do just that. This chapter examines the origins and politics of African Methodism in two settings: in the urban Transvaal, where Ethiopianism was born, and in the towns and countryside of the Orange Free State, where small, ethnically mixed communities of Africans struggled to maintain an economic foothold in a period of convulsive change. Chapter 6 examines less a place than a phenomenon: the rapid spread of African Methodism through the "reserves" of southern Africa, where chiefs and their subjects grappled with an increasingly intrusive colonial state. It ends with a brief conclusion, examining the unity in diversity that defined African Methodism.

The AME Church in the Urban Transvaal

African Methodism's entrance coincided with the most dynamic period in South African history. Gold production began on the Witwatersrand in 1886, just six years before the founding of the Ethiopian Church in nearby Pretoria. The next quarter century brought unremitting political, economic, and social upheaval, punctuated by a botched coup, civil war, a series of short, sharp depressions, and a sweeping political and economic reconstruction. These cataclysms reverberated through the subcontinent, and indeed the world, which came to depend on the Witwatersrand for 40 percent of its annual gold production. They were focused, however, in the Transvaal, which was transformed in a single generation from an isolated agrarian republic into the industrial engine of a modern nation-state. It was here, in the furnace of South Africa's industrial revolution, that Ethiopianism was forged.[9]

As we have seen, the history of the Ethiopian Church commenced in Marabastad, a rock-strewn slum on Pretoria's western edge. Founded in 1888 to house the city's growing African population, Marabastad was the Transvaal's first urban African "location." From the outset, Marabastad attracted an extraordinarily diverse population. The earliest and largest contingents in the community appear to have been Bakwena and Bakhatla, drawn from the surrounding countryside. Pedi migrants, mostly young men, came in large numbers as well, dominating the local market for domestic servants. Marabastad also attracted an unusually large proportion of Dutch-speaking *oorlams,* the deracinated descendents of African apprentices and slaves, who appear to have constituted something of an artisanal elite.[10]

With the opening of the goldfields forty miles to the south and the subsequent arrival of the Delagoa Bay railroad, more voices were added to the linguistic and cultural babel. Migrants from as far afield as Swaziland, Zulu-land, the far northern Transvaal, and the eastern and western Cape poured into Pretoria, settling in Marabastad or one of the new municipal compounds. The city was also home to a thousand Cape Coloured people—*Kaapsche Baastarde,* in administrative parlance—and to more than two thousand Africans from the Portuguese territories. Not all settled permanently—Mozambican migrants, for example, often used Pretoria as a way station before proceeding to the larger labor markets of Kimberley and the Witwatersrand—but many did. Mar-abastad in particular possessed an unusually settled African population, a circumstance reflected in its relatively equal populations of women and men. At a time when women represented less than 5 percent of the African popula-tion on the Witwatersrand, they constituted more than 40 percent of Mar-abastad residents. [11]

While difficult to document, it appears that many of those settling in Marabastad were Christians, who used skills acquired in mission schools to carve out permanent niches for themselves as clerks, tradesmen, shopkeepers, and so forth. European mission societies, however, were conspicuous by their absence. Historically, mission stations had been conceived as rural institu-tions, relying on control over land to attract converts and direct their adapta-tion to "civilisation." Through most of the nineteenth century, the only missionaries active in Pretoria were German Lutherans of the Berlin Mission Society, who opened a station on the edge of the city in 1866. Wesleyan missionaries, hindered by the Z.A.R. government's hostility to *uitlanders,* arrived eighteen years later. Even then, the Wesleyans concentrated not on Marabastad but on Kilnerton, a farm outside of town. [12]

Independent Christianity first germinated in this gap between urban Afri-cans' demand for religious facilities and the small European supply. Even before the founding of the Ethiopian Church, a group of Marabastad Anglicans, bitter at years of missionary neglect, began accepting the sacraments from their African local preacher, Joseph Kanyane Napo. Their movement culminated in the establishment of the "African Church" in 1890, with Kanyane Napo as self-proclaimed bishop. Marabastad Wesleyans were probably less aggrieved, hav-ing been regularly serviced from Kilnerton, but they too were sufficiently estranged from white missionaries to identify with Mangena Mokone in his battle with Wesleyan authorities. By 1893, Marabastad's newly opened Ethio-pian chapel boasted a congregation of more than one hundred souls. [13]

Marabastad was the seedbed of Ethiopianism, but it was in another city, forty miles to the south, that the movement sunk its first deep roots. In the years after 1886, Johannesburg exploded from nothing into a "New Babylon," a sprawling boomtown peopled by adventurers from across the globe. All the material conditions that facilitated the growth of Ethiopianism in Marabastad obtained here, and on a vastly greater scale. Accelerating urbanization brought an unprecedented mixing of peoples. As in Marabastad, a disproportionate number of the early arrivals were Christian. A one-day census taken in 1896 counted nearly forty-five hundred "Protestant" Africans within three miles of the Johannesburg market, a figure representing nearly a third of all Africans counted in the city. (While scarcely high in absolute terms, this was easily three times the proportion of Christians in South Africa as a whole.) Finally, European missionaries were even slower to begin work on the Witwatersrand than they had been in Pretoria, seeing in the slums and compounds mushrooming along the line of gold reef a confirmation of all their worst fears about urban life. A few mission societies began working on the Rand in the 1890s—the Salvation Army, with its brass bands, was the most conspicuous—but demand for churches, schools, and ministers far outstripped supply.[14]

As white missionaries debated how to respond to the rise of the Witwatersrand—several advocated a Kimberley-style closed compound system—African Christians defected to the Ethiopians. Mangena Mokone dedicated the first Ethiopian chapel in Johannesburg in 1894. During Bishop Turner's brief stopover four years later, three entire congregations joined the AME connection, including an independent Presbyterian congregation under Edward Tsewu. By the beginning of the South African War in late 1899, there were nearly a dozen AME churches on the Witwatersrand, from Boksburg and Germiston in the east to Krugersdorp and Roodepoort in the west. Johannesburg itself claimed at least three African Methodist congregations, in Newtown, Fordsburg, and Vrededorp.[15]

To some extent, the church's initial success in the Transvaal was a product of circumstance. Between accelerating urbanization and the rural proclivities of white missionaries, thousands of African Christians had escaped the orbit of the established churches, creating an unparalleled opportunity for independent churches. Yet circumstance alone is not a sufficient explanation. Amid the dust and coal smoke and corrugated iron of the industrializing Transvaal, a new urban African culture was aborning, a culture peculiarly receptive to the vision of black unity embodied in African Methodism. An individual strolling through a Johannesburg slum in 1898 would have encountered Africans of every conceivable hue, speaking an amalgam of a dozen different languages, dressed in everything from skins to frock coats and occasionally both. In music alone, one would have encountered a dizzying range of idioms and instruments: Salvation Army brass bands; migrants playing reed flutes; *oorlams* street musicians performing Afrikaans folk songs on the *tiekiedraai;* "Coloured" piano players pounding out ragtime on Saturday night and Christian hymns on Sunday morning. The whole urban Transvaal was a vast crucible, out of which came a distinctive musical and cultural style that a later generation, in an apparent reference to Marabastad, dubbed *marabi.*[16]

This is not to suggest, of course, that Africans simply checked prior identities at the gates of the city; in Johannesburg in particular, ethnic consciousness often acquired new sharpness as successive groups of immigrants competed for economic and social space. Nonetheless, the process of urbanization clearly did facilitate the development of new, more inclusive conceptions of African identity. In this sense, missionaries who accused the Ethiopians of fomenting an unnatural cohesion among Africans rather missed the point. At one level, the charge was patently true: Ethiopianism, and later African Methodism, clearly encouraged Africans to identify with one another, and indeed with black people across the diaspora. At the same time, however, the movement was as much the product of African cohesion as its cause. Just as the process of urbanization in the United States nourished racial consciousness and made possible a phenomenon like Garveyism, so did the material realities of the industrializing Transvaal nurture Ethiopianism.[17]

Identifying who precisely joined the infant church is a difficult task. What direct testimony we have comes from white observers, whose perceptions were filtered through a haze of hostility and racial presupposition. In innumerable government, missionary, and journalistic accounts, African Methodists were characterized as "ambitious," "immature," "half-educated"—in effect, the jetsam of European missions. "Restless and dissatisfied," filled with aspirations beyond their ken, these mission rejects flocked into a movement where ignorance and vice posed no obstacle to acceptance. A report in a 1904 Johannesburg newspaper neatly summarized the case.

> Each year hundreds of natives are turned out of [mission] schools, cursed with the rudiments of an education which suffices only to make them despise manual labour as degrading. Crammed as they are with a knowledge which fades like a breath on a looking glass, they drift to cities and towns in search of employment, sloughing their primitive virtues and absorbing most white vices. These boys are the readiest converts to such a propaganda as the Ethiopian.

"And so," the author concluded, "Ethiopianism is most rampant in cities, where this type of native concentrates. . . ."[18]

Once again, a kernel of truth lay inside the racist husk. While the absence of church records makes a definitive accounting impossible, the vast majority of adherents apparently did enter the AME Church as accessions from mission churches rather than as actual "converts." A few were well educated—many of Mokone's congregants in Marabastad had attended Kilnerton—and most seem to have possessed at least a smattering of education. After years at mission stations or on Boer farms, most felt little if any loyalty to traditional authorities. Ethnically, the church was a hodgepodge. A surviving subscription list from the dedication of the first Ethiopian chapel in Marabastad in 1893 includes Mokoenas and Dhlaminis, Hlatwayos and Motaungs, as well as names like Oliphant and Windvogel, indicative of *oorlams* origins. It is also likely that the church attracted a relatively youthful constituency, if only because of the disproportionate number of young people settling in Pretoria and on the Rand. As second- or third-generation Christians, such individuals may well have lacked their parents' attachments to particular denominations. They also often bore the brunt of the new racial dispensation in industrializing South Africa, making them twice susceptible to the appeal of independent church movement. The only unambiguous error in the quotation above lies in the author's characterization of Ethiopians as "boys": nearly half the people on the Marabastad church subscription list were women. Yet even that fact serves to vindicate the broader point that Ethiopianism was rooted in an emerging class of permanently urbanized Africans.[19]

In class terms, too, there is probably some merit in contemporary character-izations of the church. As a general rule, urban Christians were better off than their "heathen" counterparts, a testament to the education and skills they brought with them to the city, as well as to their longer and more whole-hearted involvement in the colonial economy. A characteristic pattern around the turn of the century was for peasant families to divert capital from agricul-ture into education and various entrepreneurial activities in order to enter the city from a position of strength. Much the same was true of *oorlams,* who used the skills they had acquired on the farms, along with their facility in Dutch, to pursue trades that were generally closed to Africans. Many such people found their way to African Methodism. One of the oldest surviving documents pertaining to the church, in fact, is an 1896 petition from church members in Marabastad, written in Mangena Mokone's hand, enquiring about the new Z.A.R. pass law. The law, the petitioners explained, was a special burden to them, since many possessed "no masters" and thus had no one to sign their passes. "Members of our congregation have coffee shops [and] eating houses," they explained; "others are carpenters, or have licenses as general dealers."[20]

In Johannesburg, too, African Methodism attracted what one might label an African petty bourgeoisie, albeit a singularly precarious one. Luke Nyokana, for example, grew up at the American Board station at Groutville, the son of a prominent member of the Natal *amakolwa*. Like many members of his class, the elder Nyokana pursued a two-pronged strategy, conveying land and cattle to his elder son and an education to Luke. In the 1890s, however, oppor-tunities for educated Africans were dwindling. After completing Standard V, Luke moved to Johannesburg, where he found a low-paying teaching job. He soon fell in with the Ethiopians, eventually returning to Natal as an ordained AME minister. (Nyokana eventually fell out with the church, but his encoun-ter with black America was inscribed in the name of his son: Booker T. Washington Nyokana.) Marshall Maxeke, a future founder of the South Afri-can Native National Congress, had a broadly similar pedigree. After passing the industrial course at Lovedale, he settled in Johannesburg, working as an apprentice harnessmaker alongside James Yapi Tantsi, son of Ethiopian Church founder J. Z. Tantsi. With no prospects for increasing his education or advancing beyond the status of apprentice, Maxeke seemed a lad of few pros-pects. A year later, he and young Tantsi were en route to Wilberforce Univer-sity in the United States, whence they returned to distinguished political careers.[21]

What all this suggests is a link between African Methodism and an older mission community struggling to reproduce its class position in an urban setting. At the same time, however, one ought not impute too narrowly elite a character to the church. Most surviving data about church membership pertains to the exceptional, to future ministers and teachers, whose backgrounds may not have been typical of African Methodist rank-and-file. There is also countervailing evidence, admittedly fragmentary, that suggests that the AME Church reached quite deeply into urban communities, especially in the years after the Anglo-Boer War. In 1901, for example, an AME local preacher named Hosea Siyinas opened a church and school among railway workers at Pretoria station and was reported preaching on trains up and down the line. At about the same time, "Ethiopians" in several communities on the Rand were accused of preaching "social equality" to domestic servants. Perhaps the best evidence of all is the host of AME night schools planted in Pretoria and Johannesburg in the wake of the South African War—schools that taught, among other things, English, the language of the Transvaal's new rulers. Such schools were of little value to mission school products such as Nyokana and Maxeke, but to new arrivals, entering the city without education or skills, they were a vital resource.[22]

In sum, the urban consituency of the AME Church cannot be captured in ready-made categories like "petty bourgeoisie" or "proletariat." Probably a more helpful distinction is between permanent city dwellers and migrants, between those who had more or less severed their rural ties and those who remained economically and psychologically rooted in the countryside. Aside from a handful of Shangaan mineworkers, the church failed to make much impression on the latter group. In part, this failure reflected the difficulty church leaders had gaining access to mine compounds, but it also probably bespoke the lower priority that migrant workers placed on education and urban church affiliation. Among those who had cast their lot permanently in the city, however, the AME Church represented a precious resource. In vice-ridden slums, where dissolution stalked the unwary, African Methodism offered direction and discipline, much as it had in antebellum American cities like Philadelphia and Baltimore. To people who spent their weeks isolated behind shop counters or in white kitchens, the church provided a sense of belonging, a point of structure and community around which one could begin to construct an urban identity. The church also offered education in English, which in a city like Johannesburg was often the only thing separating a respectable clerk or "messenger boy" from a descent into criminality or, worse, the mines.[23]

Prior to the South African War, the AME Church appears to have played little overt political role in the Transvaal. Obviously, seceding from white missions and allying with a black American church represented political acts, but within the circumscribed world of the Z.A.R. there was little scope for projecting that impulse onto a broader political canvas. In this as in so many other ways, the war had a transforming effect. British rule touched off extraordinary political ferment in the Transvaal, beginning in Johannesburg, where jubilant Africans welcomed the first imperial troops by burning their passes. Innumerable congresses, committees, and "vigilance associations" sprouted to take advantage of the new channels for organized political activity that British rule afforded. The AME Church shaped and was shaped by this new political reality. As in the United States a century earlier, the church provided black people with a foundation for political action, as well as an arsenal of ideas and images with which to confront a revolutionary transformation.

In the immediate aftermath of the war, African Methodists were prominent in the chorus hailing the British as liberators. Despite their own experiences in missions, most AME leaders and adherents retained considerable faith in British liberalism and anticipated a new liberal order that would, at a minimum, extend the protections and privileges enjoyed by Africans in the Cape. British wartime propaganda fueled such expectations, highlighting the suffering of blacks under Boer rule. Needless to say, the promised liberal order never materialized. The central objective of imperial reconstruction, as Shula Marks, Stanley Trapido, and others have shown, was to establish the gold industry on a firm and profitable footing. This was no easy task. The deposits that underlay the Witwatersrand, while unusually dependable, were generally low grade and extremely deep and required immense infusions of capital to recover. Between this exacting cost structure and gold's internationally fixed price, South African mineowners could prosper in only one way: by relentlessly squeezing down the cost of labor. Imperial officials bent themselves to the task, most dramatically by underwriting the temporary importation of sixty-thousand Chinese laborers in 1903. At the same time, Lord Milner's administration laid the foundations of a strong central state, capable of producing a sufficient supply of cheap labor closer to home. Between 1901 and the retrocession of "responsible self-government" to the Boers in 1907, imperial officials unleashed the power of a modern bureaucratic state, bringing white authority into even the most intimate domains of African life. To be sure, the administration never openly renounced its liberal professions; it continued to entertain African petitions and delegations, and elite Africans continued to appeal to British justice and "fair play." The preeminent themes of the postwar period, however, were hypocrisy and disillusionment.[24]

The victims of imperial reconstruction were legion, from distillers and dynamite manufacturers, who lost profitable concessions they had enjoyed under the Z.A.R. government, to skilled British miners, who faced deskilling and eventual replacement by cheaper black and Afrikaner labor. Imperial betrayal, however, bore most cruelly on Africans. The same people who welcomed the British Army by burning their passes found themselves subject to onerous new taxes and master-servant laws, new restrictions on land tenure, and an intensified pass law system, all designed to compel blacks into the labor market. Exemptions were offered for the educated, but criteria were so stringent that only a few dozen Africans in the entire colony—mostly ministers in white mission churches—qualified. The crowning betrayal came in the Act of Union, which failed to extend even the limited Cape franchise to the former Boer republics.[25]

One of the first targets of imperial authorities was the AME Church. Under the Z.A.R. government, the church had been left more or less to its own devices. In a few instances, AME ministers encountered opposition or harassment, but in the main republican officials were content to follow the dictum of President Paul Kruger, who, when told of the new church, allegedly said, "Let the kaffirs preach to the kaffirs." Kruger, in fact, seems to have entertained a hope that the church would become a counterweight to British missions, to which end he cordially received Bishop Turner during his 1898 visit to Pretoria. With the accession of the British, this relative tolerance evaporated. Given their social engineering proclivities, imperial authorities naturally looked askance at an institution like the AME Church, which by its very nature challenged the necessity of European control. While reluctant to legislate against the church directly, they sought to impede it in indirect ways. Pass exemptions available to African ministers in mission churches were withheld from African Methodists, on the grounds that no European missionaries had signed their applications. Similar pretenses were found to deny grants to AME schools, to nullify African Methodist marriages, even to bar AME ministers from purchasing wine to celebrate communion. Most important, officials conspired with their colleagues in Natal and the Orange River Colony to exclude church leaders from the interior, relying first on martial law and later on a "permit" system deliberately designed to discriminate against African Americans. While African Methodists in the Transvaal continued to draw energy from their association with black America, they spent the decade after 1898 without direct American supervision.[26]

Far from stifling the AME Church, the state campaign served only to invest the church with greater political energy. "Before the war our Church enjoyed all such privileges as were accorded to all Churches in the Transvaal at that time," an uncharacteristically sardonic Mangena Mokone wrote in 1904. "Since the war and under the present Glorious British Government our Church is differentiated against and we are visited with nothing but disabilities." Mokone focused on discrimination against the church, but such grievances had a way of broadening into more fundamental issues. It was difficult to plead for a school grant, for example, without reflecting on the character of an administration that collected half a million pounds per year in direct taxes from Africans while investing less than five thousand pounds in black education. At the same time, the state offensive against the AME Church made it a powerful symbol of the dashing of postwar expectations, and thus a rallying point for all Africans of whatever religious persuasion. A host of groups, from the Germiston Native Vigilance Association to the infant Transvaal Native Congress, seized on the church's predicament to highlight the hypocrisy of a regime that professed to value Christianity and "civilisation" while suppressing churches and schools.[27]

The most obvious index of African Methodism's political significance lay in the prominent role church leaders played in the various "proto-national" movements that so vexed imperial administrators in the years after the war. Mangena Mokone canvassed for the African Political Union and served on no end of deputations to state officials. H. R. Ngcayiya served as an officer of the Transvaal Native Congress. The Transvaal Native Vigilance Association was virtually an AME front, at least at the leadership level. Over time, church leaders seem to have played less and less of a direct political role, for reasons we shall explore, but as late as 1912 they were still well represented in the national movement. Marshall Maxeke and James Tantsi, back from Wilberforce University in the United States, were both prominent at the inaugural meeting of the South African Native National Congress; Tantsi helped preside at the first session. At least a dozen other Congress founders had been touched by the church, directly or indirectly. Ngcayiya, who by that time had left the AME Church, was the Congress's first chaplain. Edward Tsewu, one of the nominees for president, had likewise spent several years in the AME ministry before breaking away to found his own independent church. Senior Treasurer Alfred Mangena studied at an AME school in Cape Town before pursuing his legal studies in Britain. Pixley Seme, founder of the Congress newspaper, *Abantu Batho,* and later A.N.C. president, took advantage of the channel opened by the AME Church to go to college in the United States. Seme spoke for all the assembled when he looked out on the delegates at the inaugural meeting and announced that Ethiopia was at last stretching forth its hands to God.[28]

All this suggests that "Ethiopianism" did indeed play a prominent role in the birth of African nationalism, confirming an hypothesis advanced by George Shepperson and at least a dozen historians since. Yet to stop there, as scholars have been wont to do, is to miss most of what was distinctive about African Methodism's political thrust. In the first place, the AME Church was not a congress or a vigilance society but a Christian church. Obviously this fact did not preclude political activity, but it shaped church leaders' forays into the political arena in distinctive ways. Early nationalist leaders, steeped in the conventions of Cape liberalism, typically appealed to British justice and spoke of what the black man might become; AME Church leaders were more apt to speak of God's justice and of what Africans already were: creatures fully equal to whites in the eyes of their creator. Secure in their own worth, many AME leaders explored a kind of racial populism quite foreign to the Congress tradition. Edward Tsewu, for example, pointedly ignored established channels for communicating with the Pretoria administration on the grounds that one did not need "to go through the Pope to get to God." He once left a Native

Commissioner sputtering by walking into his office and addressing him directly, in English, rather than through his interpreter. Simon Sinamela, choir leader of the original Marabastad Ethiopian Church and later an AME presiding elder, likewise flouted the elaborate protocol that was so much a part of early African nationalists' political repertoire. According to one anxious official, Sinamela encouraged his congregants to address Europeans by their names, rather than as "Baas." He was also alleged to have sent a tax collector packing in 1904, informing him that he had one God already and did not need another "in the shape of a European." This was hardly the stuff of early African nationalism, and a number of early national leaders, including John Tengo Jabavu and Solomon Plaatje, were quick to condemn the "Ethiopians" as intemperate.[29]

This populist posture was reinforced by the AME Church's structural position within urban communities. Ultimately, the various congresses and committees of the pre-Union period engaged only a narrow stratum of elite Africans, but the AME Church reached to the roots, drawing thousands of congregants from across the urban spectrum. Put differently, AME ministers were accountable to a much broader constituency than their nationalist counterparts—to a constituency, moreover, whose Sunday contributions constituted their subsistence. This fact conditioned church leaders' political sensibilities, simultaneously broadening and narrowing their political range: broadening in the sense that it forced them to address the needs of urban Africans of all classes; narrowing in that ministers tended to invest their political energies on immediate, local issues that impinged directly on the lives of their congregants. The question of preferred railroad facilities for "the better class of natives," which exercised elite political organizations in the early years of the century, seems to have engaged AME leaders little if at all. But on issues such as state aid to schools, pass exemptions for scholars, or the right of urban Africans to be secure in their homes, African Methodists stood in the van.[30]

In the Transvaal as elsewhere in South Africa, African Methodists became involved in a host of local campaigns and struggles, involving everything from liquor raids to laundress licenses. Broadly speaking, however, the church's political energies were focused on two issues: education and land. Of the two, education was probably more fundamental to the church's appeal, yet it was the land issue that seized Africans' imaginations. Insofar as Ethiopianism embodied a rejection of European control, it inevitably raised the question of control of the land, which stood as the ultimate emblem of European domination. At least some AME ministers encouraged such speculations. Simon Sinamela allegedly told the members of his eastern Transvaal congregation "that some day with the help of their Ethiopian brothers in America they will become the possessors of South Africa." His colleague Abel Gabashane traveled through the western Transvaal and northern Cape, heralding the coming of a black king, descended of Solomon and Sheba, who would arrive at the head of a great army and restore the land to its rightful owners. While the urban Transvaal produced nothing so spectacular, the land issue remained volatile. Historically, Africans in places like Marabastad and Johannesburg held no property rights, living as squatters or renters in private or municipally owned locations. Indeed, under the Z.A.R., Africans were legally debarred from holding property in their own names, a policy that left them dependent on the good offices of white intermediaries, most often missionaries. Even before the South African War, this arrangement rankled Africans, who on more than a few occasions found themselves expelled from land purchased by their subscriptions.[31]

With the coming of the new regime, blacks expected a new dispensation; as in American Reconstruction, rumors of confiscation and redistribution abounded. Once again, however, African aspirations were dashed. Imperial officials, eager to placate the Boers on one hand and to expand the supply of mine labor on the other, had no interest in expanding African landownership, especially on the Rand where the question of land title was tied up with the subsurface rights of mining companies. In the end, they opted more or less to continue the policy of the Z.A.R., establishing a special government trustee to hold title to African lands. Floating a line that would be used to justify the South African Natives Land Act a decade later, officials described trusteeship as necessary to protect naive Africans from unscrupulous whites. Not surprisingly, the betrayal provoked a torrent of protest.[32]

African Methodists played a prominent role in the agitation. In the immediate aftermath of the war, AME congregations all along the Rand held teas and bazaars, raising money in anticipation of the day when they could own their own churches. Such campaigns were encouraged by American church leaders in the Cape, who portrayed property ownership as the key to black Americans' vaunted prosperity. J. Z. Tantsi, pastor of a large congregation in downtown Johannesburg, badgered the Pretoria administration on the issue, demanding not only freehold rights but the right of Africans to be compensated fairly for property lost in evictions and removals. When their efforts proved unavailing, church leaders resorted to the courts. In 1905 Edward Tsewu, seconded by four current or future AME ministers—Marshall Maxeke, D. H. Hlati, John Mtshula, and J. Z. Tantsi's son James—formally challenged the refusal of the Registrar of Deeds to register land in Africans' names. The case of *ex parte Tsewu* represented perhaps the greatest African political victory in the entire reconstruction period. In a delightfully ironic twist, the Supreme Court determined that a 1901 ordinance repealing Z.A.R. restrictions on British owners had also vacated the prohibition against black landownership. Africans were thus entitled to buy property anywhere in the Transvaal Colony and to hold it in their own names.[33]

Ex parte Tsewu sparked jubilation among Africans and panic among colonial officials. Fearing both an African land rush and a Boer backlash, colonial

officials quickly gazetted a new ordinance, explicitly sanctioning the practice
of holding African land "in trust." At the same time, the Department of
Native Affairs launched a campaign against Tsewu, charging him with involvement in the illegal liquor trade and threatening to deport him. Tsewu,
they assured themselves, was the leader of a small band of "impertinent" and
"lightly educated natives" who were "spreading discontent" among urban
Africans, the mass of whom continued to "appreciate the assistance of the
Department and the protection which trusteeship affords." Once again, however, the state had mismeasured its opposition. Hlati and Tantsi immediately
began raising funds for a lawyer to defend Tsewu; colonial officials, staring at
another embarrassing defeat, abandoned the prosecution. The new ordinance
lasted scarcely longer. While Mtshula led "secret prayer meetings" against the
ordinance, a group of his colleagues, including Hlati, Mangena Mokone,
Marcus Gabashane, Simon Sinamela, and two ministers from the Orange River
Colony, joined Tsewu at a mass meeting in Johannesburg, where they drafted a
formal protest to the imperial authorities in London. Downing Street, uncomfortable with the plainly discriminatory intention of the law and alarmed by
the depth of opposition it had provoked, disallowed the ordinance, providing
the second African victory in six months. Admittedly, victory proved fleeting:
a 1908 ordinance reimposed restrictions on African land purchases in urban
areas, while the 1913 Land Act put paid to the whole question. In the short
run, however, the victory secured access to land for dozens of African individuals and syndicates, most notably Pixley Seme's African Farmers' Association.
It also doubtless enhanced the AME Church's visibility and prestige on the
Rand and across South Africa.[34]

As important as the land issue was, the church's chief focus in the urban
Transvaal and, indeed, throughout southern Africa, remained education. It is
hard today to appreciate the value of education to Africans settling permanently in the city, or how difficult it was for them to obtain. As late as 1905
there were barely two hundred African students enrolled at government-aided
mission schools in Johannesburg, and still fewer in Pretoria. Total state grants
for African education in the colony hovered at about five thousand pounds per
annum. Once again the AME Church stepped into the breach. By 1904 the
church was operating thirty-eight schools in the Transvaal, including at least
half a dozen on the Rand. Inevitably, these schools became points of controversy. Missionaries and government officials fretted that the schools, which
were unaided and thus not subject to state inspection, served as clearinghouses
for Ethiopian propaganda. Africans, in turn, grew bitter at the state's thinly
veiled efforts to force the schools closed. The effect of the collision was once
again to propel the AME Church into the political arena.[35]

Conflict initially focused on an AME school at the new location of
Klipspruit, the first piece in the vast urban jigsaw that would become Soweto.
Klipspruit's origins dated to 1903, when authorities began to demolish the

slumyards around Johannesburg and to remove their African inhabitants to a farm ten miles southwest of the city. As in Cape Town and Port Elizabeth, removal was preceded by a plague scare and enacted in the name of "sanitation," though it is difficult to see how the interests of sanitation were served at Klipspruit, which had previously served as a municipal sewerage farm. For the AME Church, however, the site offered fertile ground. For the first two or three years, neither the government nor established missions made any provision for opening churches in the location, conferring on the more decentralized and responsive AME Church the advantage of a temporary monopoly. More broadly, removal, which entailed a loss of economic opportunities, higher rents, and vastly increased transportation costs, left many Africans profoundly alienated from white authority. Particularly after 1906, as the local economy buckled beneath a sharp, gold-induced depression, the residents of Klipspruit were almost uniquely attuned to the racial populism of the AME Church.[36]

By early 1904 an AME chapel had risen above the tin and mud shacks of the new location. A school was opened in the church under the direction of J. Z. Tantsi's daughter Adelaide, another in the line of young Africans returning from Wilberforce University in the United States. Within weeks, the school was oversubscribed, not only by African Methodists, but by the children of mission adherents and non-Christians, all of whom were welcome. The only problem was finding money to keep the school open. Tuition fees produced almost no income; even a shilling or two a month was beyond the reach of many Klipspruit residents. Government aid was not forthcoming, given the school's affiliation with an "unrecognised" denomination. In mid-1905, J. Z. Tantsi led a delegation to the Department of Native Affairs to discuss the situation. Having vainly sought official recognition for the AME Church, the delegates tried a different tack, arguing that the state itself had an obligation to provide free education to urban Africans. The appeal was based primarily on the gulf between the state's vast intake from African taxes and its paltry outlay on African education. The delegates also capitalized on the precedent the administration had set in providing free schools to whites and, more recently, to Coloureds, neither of whom faced the tax liabilities of Africans. In the following months, identical demands came from AME schools in Marabastad and Boksburg.[37]

Tantsi's proposal received an unexpectedly sympathetic hearing from Godfrey Lagden, Chief Native Commissioner of the Transvaal and chairman of the South African Native Affairs Commission. A career native administrator, Lagden was certainly no friend of Ethiopianism; nor was he prepared to jettison existing state policy, in which native education was funded indirectly through grants-in-aid to European mission societies. Nonetheless, he concluded that an exception could plausibly be made in places such as Boksburg and Klipspruit, where the demand for education far outstripped the resources of white missions. Underlying this conclusion was profound uneasiness with the world

Lagden saw emerging along the Reef, a world where Africans from a "confused mass of nationalities" mingled together without churches, schools, or even the most rudimentary "tribal restraints." In such a setting, any school, even an Ethiopian one, promised to provide a much needed point of structure and stability. In the Klipspruit case, a well-appointed school would also lubricate the process of removal and "encourage the creation and contentment of a labouring class of natives." Finally, such a policy would ensure government oversight of the school, which was otherwise not subject to inspection. "The best way to counteract mischievous tendencies," Lagden concluded, "is to bring the school underfoot. . . ."[38]

Lagden's logic provoked a visceral response from European missionaries, who were fixated on "Ethiopianism" and blind to the broader problems of urban administration. "In centres like Marabastad and Klipspruit Ethiopianism flourishes," one missionary declared, as if that alone proved the folly of Lagden's plan. Undergirding missionaries' opposition was fear that state education, especially if offered without charge, would end their own educational monopoly and undermine their control over converts. "All of us who are engaged in Native work do not consider the time ripe for free native education," one missionary intoned. Many, in fact, argued that school fees should be raised, on the grounds that Africans were too unsophisticated to appreciate something unless they paid dearly for it.[39]

For the next three years, the Klipspruit school was caught in a crossfire between the Native Affairs Department, missionaries, and the missionary-dominated Native Education branch of the Transvaal Education Department. After nearly two years of infighting, Lagden negotiated a compromise, which provided for a free public school in Klipspruit under the supervision of a board of European missionaries. The agreement was scuttled, however, by the return of "responsible self-government" to the Transvaal in 1907. Skeptical of both Ethiopianism and potentially expensive precedents, the new colonial secretary, J. C. Smuts, decided that fees at the Klipspruit school should be set at more or less normal mission school levels. In the meantime, European missionaries, appalled to learn that the new school was to be held in an "Ethiopian" building, resigned en masse from the Klipspruit board.[40]

As the saga unfolded, the Klipspruit school became the vehicle for a remarkable community-wide mobilization. In September 1906 Klipspruit residents convened the first in a series of mass meetings, to discuss not only the status of their application for government aid but the broader problem of urban education. Early in 1907, as the economy plummeted deeper into recession, residents launched the Klipspruit Native Location Free School Committee. The committee, under the chairmanship of J. Z. Tantsi, organized deputations and mass meetings, increasingly placing the education issue within the broader context of urban Africans' economic plight. A 1907 petition, for example, included a detailed breakdown of the cost of living in Klipspruit, to show that residents simply could not afford to pay school fees. (According to the group's figures, necessities alone—lodging, food, taxes, and commuting costs—consumed about six pounds per family per month, easily twice the average family income in the location.) The petition apparently had some effect—a few months later, the state cut poll taxes on urban Africans from two pounds to one pound—but opposition to free government education persisted. So did the Klipspruit school, though it was ultimately moved to a building owned by the Free Church of Scotland. For the next half century, Klipspruit boasted the only state-run African school in the Transvaal.[41]

In Marabastad, too, the AME Church's fight for a school grant precipitated a broad-based community movement. From Lagden's perspective, the demands for free education here were more easily dismissed. The location was an established one, with a handful of mission schools already in operation. Among Marabastad Africans, however, the education issue proved to have extraordinary staying power, at least in part because of the proximity of one of the state's free Coloured schools. Midway through 1907, residents of Marabastad and nearby Schoolplaats convened a series of mass meetings, chaired by Mangena Mokone and probably held in the AME Church. The meetings produced the most far-reaching statement of urban African grievances of the entire period. The central demand remained free education, a demand that was at last being picked up by "proto-national" organizations such as the Transvaal Native Congress and the African National Political Union. Marabastad residents, however, went much further, demanding a moratorium on evictions, provision of relief for the unemployed, and a reining in of police, who routinely broke into homes without the formality of warrants or even knocking. ("Surely this is not the much-praised English liberty?" the residents asked with ill-concealed sarcasm.) Many of the participants in the meeting were women, who also demanded an end to laundry licenses and surcharges for use of the municipal washhouse, both of which made it difficult for them to compete with "coolies"—presumably a reference to Indian washermen in Pretoria's Asian Bazaar.[42]

It is hard to look at such protests without being struck by their intense localism, their rootedness in the experiences and grievances of particular communities at specific historical moments. This does not mean, however, that African Methodism's association with black America was immaterial or irrelevant. On the contrary, the sense of membership in a broader black community was central to the AME Church's appeal and to the character of popular politics in the urban Transvaal. African protesters frequently invoked African American experience, measuring their own predicament against the experience of another group of black people who had overcome oppression and disunity to achieve power and prosperity. In other cases, the transatlantic bond was expressed metaphorically, in references to the Israelites or to a biblical Ethiopia of which black South Africans were a part. In either case, the sense of connection energized African politics, endowing even the most parochial disputes with broad, surpassing significance.

Take the case of Boksburg, a squalid mining town on the far East Rand. The AME Church's presence in the city dated to at least 1905 or early 1906, when Marshall and Charlotte Maxeke, two of the Wilberforce University contingent, opened a small school. Like their colleagues in Klipspruit, they petitioned for state support and, in the absence of any European mission schools, received a favorable hearing from Godfrey Lagden. Once again, however, the promised subsidy never arrived, due to a zealous local pass officer who refused to hand over the money after hearing that Marshall Maxeke was involved in buying and selling unwrought gold. (The rumor, typical of the kind of allegations that attached to independent Africans, proved unfounded.) When an official arrived for a scheduled inspection, he found the school deserted and promptly canceled the grant.[43]

The Maxekes moved on after the episode, but the school was revived by another Wilberforce graduate, Charles Msikinya. Articulate and persuasive, Msikinya quickly established himself as a leader in the community. In addition to pressing the education issue, he marshaled opposition to the municipality's plans to remove Africans to a location several miles outside town. When that campaign failed, he led the fight to ensure that Boksburg Africans were fairly compensated for lost property. Msikinya's influence, and the influence of the broader transatlantic connection he embodied, was clearly registered in a 1908 petition from the newly formed Boksburg Native Vigilance Association. Having been rebuffed by European authorities, the signers of the petition resolved to pursue "the only course still open . . . to petition God." To that end, they declared the upcoming Empire Day a day of national humiliation and prayer.

> We feel that our sympathies should be broad enough to include the whole of the African race when we approach our Maker. For instance, the atrocities which our brethren are suffering under the administrators of the Congo Free State should appeal to us with a loud voice for our sympathy and prayers. Undoubtedly the time has come for the sons of Africa to stretch forth their hands unto God unitedly, as was prophesied of us in Psalms 68 verse 31.

If prayers were offered "in the right attitude and spirit," the declaration concluded, "He will bless us and send us a wave of his Spirit, which will pass through the whole of Africa from the Cape to Egypt, the effects of which will be felt even by our brethren in America, who come from the same original stock as ourselves. God grant this to His people."[44]

In the short term at least, prayer proved as unavailing as protest. Indeed, insofar as AME-sponsored initiatives aimed at forcing the Transvaal adminstration to assume some responsibility for the welfare of urban Africans, they were almost wholly unsuccessful. Yet here was one of those cases where the medium was the message, where the very act of struggle was itself a kind of victory. In a sense, Godfrey Lagden, who preferred even "Ethiopian" schools to the chaos of ill-administered, ethnically diverse urban locations, missed the point. The deputations he entertained, the endless petitions and mass meetings, were themselves proof that urban communities, even those caught in processes of removal, were capable of acting with extraordinary unity and cohesion. There is a lesson here for South African historians, who have been so preoccupied with portraying the dissolution of communities through the experience of removal and relocation that they have neglected the institutions and networks that enabled communities to recohere and survive. In places such as Klipspruit and Boksburg, the AME Church was one such institution.

The episodes here also raise questions about the character of African politics in the reconstruction Transvaal. At least on issues of education and land, arguably the two most crucial issues of the period, the notion of "nationalist" politicians mobilizing the masses is singularly misleading. On the contrary, the impetus for action bubbled up from communities themselves, often leaving elite leaders scrambling to catch up. Leaders of the Transvaal Native Congress, for example, were distinctly uneasy with the tone adopted at the mass meeting convened by Edward Tsewu and his lieutenants to protest the 1906 land ordinance and withdrew their endorsement from its resolutions. They were also slow to respond to the free education issue, asserting themselves only in late 1907, more than two years after the campaign had been launched by African Methodists in Klipspruit.[45]

Finally, the episodes here help qualify some of the standard assumptions about the social and political character of African Methodism. Clearly, the AME Church attracted many members of the educated, urban elite, yet it also embraced individuals and interests across a much wider urban spectrum. Similarly, African Methodism contributed to the rise of nationalism, at the level of both personnel and ideology, yet at the same time it became entwined with other political impulses that had little to do with what historians usually think of as African nationalism. At risk of stretching a point, one can discern in the early AME Church the first stirrings of urban mass politics, a politics that would reappear in the dramatic upheavals of 1919–1921. Yet we have only begun to sample the church's social and political range.

The AME Church in the Orange Free State

Even before its affiliation with the AME Church, Ethiopianism had begun to spread. Mokone's 1895 recruiting trip gave the movement a foothold in the eastern Cape, a position consolidated with the entrance of James Dwane. Dwane's efforts were seconded by J. Z. Tantsi, who spent the years before the South African War in Queenstown district, and by the young H. R. Ngcayiya, a future founder of the South African Native National Congress, who sowed

African Methodist congregations all through the eastern Cape and Transkei. A. A. Morrison, a West Indian ordained by Bishop Turner in 1898, organized a Coloured congregation in Cape Town before venturing north to the diamond fields. Morrison's itineracy eventually carried him to the Bafokeng people in the northwestern Transvaal, a passage memorialized in Naboth Mokgatle's classic *Autobiography of an Unknown South African.* At the same time, Ethiopianism emanated South and West from its base in Pretoria and Johannesburg. By the end of 1897 Marcus Gabashane and his son Abel had established a chain of AME churches all along the northern bank of the Vaal River, from Potchefstroom through Klerksdorp and Bloemhof to Christiana in the far southwestern Transvaal. Abel continued west to Vryburg, while his father embarked on a thousand-mile trek up the entire length of the Bechuanaland Protectorate. Meanwhile, Jacobus Xaba, the youngest of the original Ethiopians, organized the first AME congregations in the Orange Free State. It was here, in the sleepy towns and dusty farmlands of the southern highveld, that African Methodism would have its most enduring success.[46]

If the urban Transvaal was South Africa's crucible, the expansive, level plains of the southern highveld were its crossroads. Raiders and refugees traversed the region during the *mfecane;* in their wake came Griqua pastoralists, Dutch-speaking trekboers, and a motley collection of European, mostly British, missionaries. With the onset of the Great Trek in the middle 1830s, upwards of ten thousand Boers entered Transorangia, accompanied by thousands of slaves and dependents. Decades of upheaval ensued, punctuated by an international wool boom, an abortive British annexation, and an endless series of raids and skirmishes, culminating in the Basotho-Boer Wars of the 1860s, which established the borders of the modern Orange Free State. The discovery of diamonds at Kimberley and the subsequent opening of the Witwatersrand goldfields wrought perhaps the greatest transformation of all, transforming a colonial economy still largely organized around the provision of wool and skins into the granary of an industrializing nation.[47]

This history of upheaval bequeathed to the Orange Free State a singularly polyglot black population. By far the largest contingent was Sotho, a category that included not only people from Basutoland but groups like the Tlokoa, who settled in the region before the *mfecane,* and later arriving refugees like the Bakwena and Bangwato. The Barolong, the second largest African group in the Free State, were likewise refugees and lived with their chief Moroka in an enclave around Thaba 'Nchu. A substantial Zulu population lived in the republic, especially in the districts bordering Natal, while smaller Mfengu and Xhosa contingents were dispersed across the farms in the south. Sprinkled among these groups were Dutch-speaking *oorlams* and *inboekselings,* as well as more recently captured slaves and "apprentices" from north of the Vaal. Of all South Africa's diverse populations, these people were perhaps the most thoroughly deracinated and dispossessed. By the mid-1880s, all independent chiefdoms in the Free State, and virtually all indigenous claims to land, had been extinguished.[48]

By the time the AME Church arrived a decade later, somewhere between 80 and 90 percent of Free State blacks lived on white-owned farms, often in extended kin groups, working under various tenancy arrangements. Probably the most common arrangement was sharecropping, a system whose dynamics have been admirably explored by Tim Keegan, Charles van Onselen, and others. As in the United States, the system represented a kind of compromise between white and black patriarchs: the former controlled land but lacked the means to exploit it profitably; the latter commanded skills, implements, draught power, and large amounts of labor, but lacked independent access to land. Terms of tenure were generally negotiated verbally and varied widely, depending on the productive resources of the contracters. Typically, sharecroppers handed over half of what they harvested; they might also pay additional rent, usually in the form of family members' labor, for the privilege of grazing their stock. In contrast to the United States, where sharecropping spiraled into a system of virtual peonage, many Free State sharecroppers did very well indeed, accumulating large flocks of sheep and cattle and reaping hundreds of bags of grain per year. Most privileged of all were those who cropped for absentee landlords, usually urban speculators or land companies that had bought up farms for the potential mineral rights. The most famous example was Vereeniging Estates, a collection of twenty-two farms in the southern Transvaal and northern Free State, owned by mining magnate Sammy Marks. In their heyday, the Estates housed 250 sharecropping families, most of whom went their daily rounds without so much as a by-your-leave to white authority.[49]

Several aspects of this world are worth noting. As a group, sharecroppers were remarkable for their openness to "progressive" ideas and values. The experience of migration and ethnic mixing, along with decades of involvement in the colonial economy, had eroded traditional identities. Few sharecroppers retained meaningful loyalty to chiefly authority; many, most notably Bakwena and Bangwato families re-entering the republic from Basutoland, settled on white farms precisely to escape chiefly exactions. While highveld sharecroppers continued to exchange bridewealth, a crucial underpinning of patriarchal power, customs such as initiation, more directly related to chiefly authority, waned. The vast majority of men took only one wife. This alienation from traditional society was both reflected in and reinforced by the spread of mission Christianity, which enjoyed a bountiful harvest on the southern highveld. At a time when perhaps 10 percent of black South Africans might be classified as Christian, close to half of blacks in the Free State were regular churchgoers. The Wesleyans enjoyed particular success, attracting almost fifty thousand members by the 1890s. In many cases, conversion was accompanied by a rudimentary education, often in small farm schools erected by tenants themselves.[50]

Part of the secret to sharecroppers' success lay in their capacity to generate nonfarm income, a necessity that grew as the century progressed. Standard scholarly dichotomies such as urban and rural, "townsman" and "tribesman," cannot comprehend the world of highveld sharecroppers, most of whom had considerable exposure to town life, and to working for wages. Probably the most common pattern was for one or two members of a sharecropping family— usually young men, sometimes young women—to migrate to town during periods of crisis or in the lulls between planting and reaping to earn money to pay taxes, buy stock, and meet other cash needs. Sharecroppers rode transport and worked on railroads and diamond diggings; they came to town to sell wood and skins and to ply trades they had mastered on the farms, from smithing to carpentry to cobbling. By the end of the century, some individuals and families had begun settling permanently in town, but even they tended to keep a foot on the land, maintaining a few cattle and sheep on the farms of kinfolk and contributing labor during sowing and harvest. This interpenetration of rural and urban worlds shaped Free State politics in manifold ways. Municipal policies toward African tradesmen, for example, had a direct effect on white farmers' capacity to recruit and control black labor, a fact lost on none of the actors involved. African popular movements, in turn, had to come to terms with these same linkages. The movements that would enjoy success on the southern highveld—the AME Church and later the Industrial and Commercial Workers' Union—were those that spanned town and countryside, that recognized and spoke to the varied experience and eclectic consciousness of Free State Africans.[51]

Finally, this was a world where the "political economy of white supremacy" was peculiarly fragile, as Tim Keegan's work powerfully demonstrates. Even though blacks had been almost completely dispossessed, white farmers remained dependent on their skills, energy, and productive resources, a circumstance that no amount of racist bluster could obscure. Worse still, many sharecroppers appeared to be growing increasingly prosperous and independent, expanding herds and acreage even as more and more whites slipped into poverty and landlessness. When natural and economic disasters struck the highveld, as they so frequently did in the late nineteenth century, it was usually debt-strapped whites who buckled first, while Africans, embedded in networks of reciprocity and able to call upon the labor of extended kin groups, endured and recovered. The result, in terms of race relations, was a structure both precarious and paradoxical, ever poised between mutual dependence and competition, paternalism and violence, intimacy and loathing. In moments of great stress, that balance could topple, triggering "moral panics," great populist spasms targeting all the farmers' perceived enemies: foreign capitalists, Jewish speculators, and, above all, independent Africans. At such moments, any sign of black prosperity or self-reliance became a provocation. Special ordinances gave whites authority to arrest and detain Africans. Schools were closed, and black churchgoers were harassed and assaulted.[52]

Significantly, African Methodism's appearance coincided with just such a period. Even by the unforgiving standards of the highveld, the 1890s were hard times. Between 1891 and 1893, the Free State experienced a devastating sequence of drought and locusts, accompanied by an outbreak of foot-and-mouth disease. The next few years were bountiful, producing a dramatic improvement in sharecropper fortunes, but drought returned in 1896–1898. The rinderpest epizootic arrived hard on its heels, destroying entire herds of cattle and propelling thousands of Boer families off the land and into the swelling white proletariat of Johannesburg and Bloemfontein. The spectacle of white debt and dispossession, projected against Africans' apparent prosperity and "idleness," enflamed racial sensibilities and ushered in yet another populist assault. As one Volksraad member put it, "the poor whites are being wholly oppressed by the accumulation of too many loose Kaffirs." The centerpiece of the assault was Ordinance 4 of 1895, which reimposed restrictions on the number of black "squatters" on white farms in order to secure a more equal distribution of black labor. Insofar as the Ordinance purported to assist struggling white farmers, it failed almost totally: the limit of five black families per farm remained ill enforced, and absentee landlordism persisted; poor whites were extruded from the land in ever greater numbers. The importance of the law, however, was not lost on Africans, particularly on sharecroppers, who faced new exactions from landlords, as well as a wave of racist harassment.[53]

It is not difficult to imagine the appeal of African Methodism in such a context. In a period of escalating racial tension, the AME Church offered a haven, embodying aspirations for independence and respectability that were under assault in the broader society. This appeal was doubtless enhanced by the church's association with black American, which existed for most Africans as an almost mythical land of progress and prosperity. (Such beliefs were seemingly confirmed by Bishop Turner's celebrated 1898 visit to Bloemfontein.) The church also had the benefit of an extraordinary collection of African leaders, many of whom were peculiarly well attuned to the values and aspirations of highveld sharecroppers. Jacobus Xaba, who established the first AME congregations in the northern Free State in 1896–1897, was a product of the prosperous peasant community at Edendale, as was Benjamin Kumalo, who became leader of the church in the Free State after Xaba's premature death. Marcus Gabashane, Xaba's counterpart north of the Vaal, was himself a former Free State sharecropper, from Thaba 'Nchu district. These ministers' efforts were seconded by an army of unordained lay preachers, recruited from the ranks of local leaders and sensitive to popular concerns. It was through the agency of these local preachers, Xaba reported in 1898, "that the machinery of our church is moving on."[54]

As in other areas, the church's initial catch came primarily at the expense of the Wesleyans. Posted to Vereeniging by Mokone, Xaba trolled the mid-Vaal region, netting hundreds of his erstwhile coreligionists, including the Wesleyan congregation he had pastored at Heilbron. By early 1898 the AME Church boasted circuits—collections of rural outstations organized around central towns—all across the region: not only in Vereeniging and Heilbron but in Parys, Kroonstad, Viljoensdrift, and Vredefort, precisely the areas with the highest rates of absentee landownership and the most prosperous sharecropping population. In at least some of these places, the church opened schools. Exactly how many people joined the movement is impossible to establish, but the numbers were clearly substantial. A British administrator arriving in 1901 at Viljoensdrift, in the heart of the old Vereeniging Estates, estimated, doubtless with some exaggeration, that half the Africans in the district had defected to the new church.[55]

African Methodism's increase, however, was confined neither to the northern districts nor exclusively to the farms. The economic disasters of the mid-1890s stimulated a distinct townward drift all across the Free State, as African tenants and sharecroppers began the laborious task of restocking. While this townward trickle never rivaled the cataract of African urbanization on the Rand, it nonetheless badly overstressed existing facilities. In most municipal locations, housing was inadequate, and churches and schools, if they existed at all, were swamped by new arrivals. As in the Transvaal, European mission societies were slow to react to this new demand, leaving the more decentralized AME Church to fill the breach. By the beginning of the South African War in October 1899, AME churches had been established in towns and cities all across the republic. In Bloemfontein, the capital and a burgeoning rail center, the church attracted several hundred adherents, including an entire congregation of former Anglicans. In Kroonstad, further up the line of rail, African Methodism seems virtually to have swept the location. By mid-1899, the Kroonstad AME Church boasted a substantial brick building, day and night schools, regular weekly classes, and an active women's prayer union, all under the leadership of the ubiquitous Simon Sinamela. (Not surprisingly in light of Sinamela's background, the Kroonstad church was especially noted for its choir.) In tiny Smithfield, in the heart of the so-called Conquered Territory excised from Basutoland, Jacobus Xaba accepted more than 170 new members in a single day. The people, he informed church leaders in America, "flocked into our church like a swarm of locusts entering contumacious Pharaoh's palace."[56]

The AME Church was thus firmly planted in the Orange Free State by the beginning of the South African War, a conflict that was to have a dramatic impact on the church's scope and character. Of all the upheavals that remade the southern highveld in the nineteenth century, the war proved the most disastrous. While relatively unscathed by the opening campaigns of 1899–1900, the Free State—rechristened the Orange River Colony by its imperial conquerors—bore the brunt of the two years of guerrilla fighting that followed. By the coming of peace in mid-1902, vast swaths of the countryside had been depopulated and laid waste. Productive assets of every kind—farm buildings, herds, ploughs, implements, wells—had been smashed in the British army's relentless scorched-earth campaign. A dozen towns and untold hundreds of farms lay in ashes.[57]

In contrast to the trauma of the Boers, long a staple of South African history texts, the wartime experience of Africans has only recently begun to engage historians. Peter Warwick, Bill Nasson, and Jeremy Krikler have all shown how the war presented Africans with new possibilities and new perils. In the Transvaal, many chiefs used the conflict to reclaim land, accumulate arms, and commandeer stock, often with the connivance of the British. Reasserting state control over such chiefdoms, in fact, became one of the central tasks of imperial administrators during reconstruction. Free State Africans, in contrast, rarely profited from the crisis. In a few isolated pockets—in the mountainous regions of Bethlehem district and in a protected enclave around Thaba 'Nchu—Africans continued to sow and reap "as regularly as if no war existed." Other sharecroppers were fortunate enough to find refuge in Basutoland, husbanding herds and resources for a later return. The bulk of the black population, however, was whipsawed between the Boers and the British, and lost everything. Boer commandos raided African settlements, stealing stock and grain and impressing men and boys into service as grooms, scouts, and servants. British troops did much the same thing, though usually with promises of compensation—promises that, in the case of stock compensation at least, were honored more in the breach than the observance. By mid-1901, tens of thousands of Free State peasants had given up the struggle and fled to town, where the presence of British garrisons at least ensured the availability of wage work. Most of the rest—close to sixty thousand men, women, and children—were rounded up, with their stock and whatever possessions they could carry, and herded into two dozen "refugee camps" strung along the lines of rail. These camps, largely neglected by historians, were to become crucial staging areas in the dissemination of African Methodism.[58]

It takes nothing from the suffering of the Afrikaner women and children who died in the notorious British concentration camps to say that conditions in the African refugee camps were generally worse. While the object of the Boer camps was relatively straightforward, the African camps served a variety of purposes: they were strategic hamlets, labor depots, victualing stations for the British army, and in one British administrator's memorable words, schools "to inculcate the principle of self-help, and to teach the Kaffir the dignity of labour." In actual practice, they were fetid rural slums, where thousands struggled to scratch out a life without adequate food, water, shelter, or sanitation. In contrast to Boer internees, African refugees were required to provide their own shelter, which in many cases consisted of little more than mealie bags stitched together. Africans were also expected to feed themselves, either by cultivating grain or by purchasing it at government stores, which enjoyed monopolies in each camp. Men were encouraged to accept work with the British army: those who did were paid one shilling per day, or about one pound four shillings per month, one pound of which was deducted as rent for dependents left in the camps. Between inadequate rainfall, Boer raids, and the voracious appetite of the British army, starvation stalked several of the camps. In Boschhoek, a camp near Harrismith, residents were reduced to eating rinderpest carcasses. Medical facilities were virtually nonexistent, and various pestilences—measles, smallpox, leprosy, typhus, pneumonia—ran rampant. Total mortality never equaled that in the white concentration camps, where nearly thirty thousand people—a tenth of the Boer population—lost their lives. Mortality rates, however, were generally higher in the African camps. In the worst month, December 1901, the annual mortality rate among black refugees in the Free State was 436 per thousand.[59]

Beyond the brute facts of death and deprivation, surviving evidence records little about the consciousness or experience of those who passed through the camps. Obviously this first encounter with British authority did little to instill confidence in the region's new rulers. The experience also probably increased Africans' alienation from white mission churches, which prior to 1902 made virtually no effort to minister to their converts in the camps. AME ministers, in contrast, managed to reach most if not all of the camps, braving impressment and even execution by Boer commandos to do so. Samuel Mabote, one of Bishop Turner's ordinees, secured a permit to hold services in three of the largest camps, Honing Spruit, Geneva, and Boschrand, which together housed more than seven thousand Africans. Nicholas Makone, an AME minister twice ejected from Lindley location before the war, spent the duration at Heilbron camp, holding services, delivering sacraments, and burying the dead. John Kubedi, one of the church's more outspoken leaders, was sufficiently conspicuous at the Virginia and Holtfontein camps to be judged a nuisance by British authorities. John Phakane, ordained a deacon a few months before the outbreak of the war, preached at three camps—Kopjes, Vredefort Road, and Roodevaal Spruit. AME ministers were also reported at Rhenoster and Taaibosch, the enormous camp on Vereeniging Estates. It is impossible to know how many new adherents the AME Church gained in the camps, but thousands of people were exposed to the church, and that at a moment of profound duress and disillusionment. As the refugees dispersed after the war, many carried African Methodism with them.[60]

The refugee camps represented one staging area for African Methodism; towns and cities were another. During the guerrilla phase of the war, urban locations, already swollen from the upheavals of the 1890s, experienced explosive growth—growth that showed little sign of abating at war's end. Bloemfontein's black population swelled from about three thousand in the mid-1890s to fifteen thousand during the war to more than twenty thousand in 1904–1905. Dozens of other Free State towns experienced similar influxes, albeit on a smaller scale. By 1904 British officials, eager to revive agricultural production, were complaining of desperate shortages of rural labor. "The two great needs in [the rural] part of this district are stock and labour," the resident magistrate at Bloemfontein reported. "Kaffir labour is in many cases absolutely unobtainable." "It is worth seeing Bethany," added a colleague, "for here one sees the natural native population of a whole district congregated together while the surrounding district is destitute of labour." In Edenburg, home to a large British garrison, the resident magistrate was startled to find entire farms with "not even one Native." Farmers were so strapped for workers that they found themselves paying the fines of Africans convicted of pass law violations or other crimes, a predicament that accounted, at least in part, for demands for a return to the republican practice of flogging.[61]

Not all Africans, of course, left the land. On many farms, sharecropping relationships were quickly reconstituted. Families that had passed the war in Basutoland or otherwise managed to husband their resources through the crisis often extracted advantageous terms from white landlords. On the whole, however, agricultural recovery lagged as thousands of former refugees headed for already overcrowded municipal locations. For desperate white farmers, this exodus was just more proof of Africans' penchant for idleness. Imperial officials, with even less insight into this class of rural accumulators, attributed blacks' refusal to return to the land to inflated wartime expectations: as one administrator put it, the "native mind" had been "a good deal unhinged by the war." In fact, African sharecroppers' move to town was characteristic and calculated. Postwar cities and towns offered abundant opportunities to work, often at unprecedentedly high wages. Africans found work in construction or cartage, servicing garrisons, or working on the railways, which became a source of protected employment for blacks who had served the British army and who faced reprisals if they returned to their farms. The enlarged African population itself opened a market for black shopkeepers and contractors, as well as an outlet for the kind of artisanal skills that many rural Africans possessed.[62]

The countryside, in contrast, offered little but more suffering. Without seed, draught, or assets of any kind, most Africans had little hope of getting a crop into the ground or surviving long enough to harvest it. Money was scarce, and few white farmers were in a position to pay wages. With the Witwatersrand mired in recession, demand for foodstuffs slumped; at the very same moment, cheap American wheat began to flow into the interior along reconstructed railroads. Nature, characteristically, added its mite to the misery. Drought returned in 1903–1904, and what rains did fall brought forth swarms of locusts. In such circumstances, Africans had little incentive to return to the land, whether to returning Boer landlords or to the new British settlers sprinkled through the countryside by the reconstruction administration. Imperial officials could perhaps have encouraged a return by dispensing resettlement funds to African producers or by at least offering blacks a share of the food relief set aside for indigent whites. For the most part, however, they declined to do so, lest they antagonize white landlords and encourage Africans' alleged taste for idleness. Of the £14.5 million spent by Britain on reconstructing the South African countryside, scarcely 1 percent found its way into African hands. In the Orange River Colony, just twenty-seven thousand pounds was spent repatriating black refugees.[63]

As urban centers grew, African Methodism flourished. By 1904, the first year for which statistical evidence is available, the AME Church possessed substantial congregations in virtually every city and town in the colony, from Boshof in the west to Bethlehem in the east. In most of these communities, the church opened schools, a vital resource not only to those who hoped to remain in town permanently but to sharecropping families increasingly dependent on nonfarm earnings. At a time when only four or five thousand Africans attended school in the entire Orange River Colony, the AME Church maintained two dozen schools, catering to close to twelve hundred students. Even where other churches and schools existed, African Methodists carved out a niche for themselves. In Bloemfontein, for example, home to eight European denominations and more than a dozen mission schools, the AME Church sustained four congregations and four thriving schools. Membership in the colony as a whole is impossible to establish with any precision, but it was substantial and growing. The generally unreliable Orange River Colony census of 1904 ranked the church as the fourth largest denomination in the colony, with about thirty-seven hundred full adult members. Typically, "members" accounted for between a third and a half of AME adherents, suggesting a following in the colony of about ten thousand people. Even that figure, however, seems conservative. Probably closer was the calculation of an AME presiding elder, who reported a membership of seventy-three hundred in 1906, serviced by two dozen ministers and more than two hundred lay preachers.[64]

Establishing who precisely these people were is difficult, but again some inferences are possible. The vast majority of African Methodists were already Christian converts when they entered the church. By far the largest contingent came from the Wesleyan Church, though every white church experienced defections, including the Dutch Reformed Church, which had previously enjoyed a religious monopoly in many small towns. In gender terms, the church seems to have been fairly evenly divided between women and men, a pattern consistent with Free State mission churches, though somewhat at odds with the pattern in reserves, where women often predominated. Ethnically, AME adherents appear to have represented a fair cross-section of Free State

Africans. The majority of those who can be identified were of Sotho origin, but the church also boasted a large Setswana-speaking contingent, as well as individuals of Zulu, Xhosa, and Mfengu descent. The occasional surfacing in church records of names such as Johannes, Paulus, and Botha also suggests that some members possessed *oorlams* origins. People of different ethnic backgrounds mixed freely within congregations, and there is little evidence of friction. In 1905 or 1906 a group of Setswana speakers in Bloemfontein cleaved off and organized a Bechuanaland Methodist Church, but the proximate cause of the schism was less ethnicity than a dispute over the authority of a newly arrived African American bishop.[65]

Given the diversity of congregations and the church's policy of assigning ministers without regard to ethnic background, language differences occasionally posed a problem. As in the Transvaal, the church seems to have encouraged the use of English, which in the wake of British victory represented a valuable skill for Africans. English, however, remained very much a minority language in the Free State, especially on the farms, where most people spoke an amalgam of Sesotho, Setswana, and Afrikaans. Given the remarkable linguistic facility of so many black South Africans—visiting African Americans were constantly stunned by their charges' ability to speak several languages—it was usually possible for a preacher and his congregation to find some common medium. In cases where it was not, the church developed a remarkable system of simultaneous translation, in which one or two congregants stood beside the preacher, translating his remarks as he went along, reproducing not only words but inflections and gestures. Musical selections were offered in any number of different languages, and members either learned them or simply pitched in in their own tongues, producing a cacophony that white observers and visiting African Americans alike found oddly compelling.[66]

Characterizing the church's constituency in class terms is even more problematic. In a society like South Africa's, where all blacks remained members of a subordinate caste, the membrane between classes was indistinct and often porous. This was doubly the case in the cities and towns of the postwar highveld, where people of disparate backgrounds and experiences had been tossed together and faced in common a range of oppressive barriers and regulations. One did not need to be a member of a particular class to resent municipal pass laws that compelled children to work and rendered women vulnerable to arbitrary searches, though obviously the terms in which such grievances were expressed could differ. In such a context, one would expect an institution like the AME Church to have attracted blacks across a wide economic spectrum, and it appears to have done so. In Bloemfontein, for example, the city with the largest African population and the most well-developed class structure, the church attracted close to eight hundred adherents, from boardinghouse owners to "railway boys." In short, African Methodism cannot be reduced to a simple class label in the Free State any more than in the Transvaal.[67]

To say that the church attracted a diverse class constituency, however, is not to say that it appealed equally to all classes or that it was class-neutral in its politics. In the Free State even more than on the Witwatersrand, the church made its deepest impression on, and was in turn most shaped by, what might loosely be termed an aspirant petty bourgeoisie—a broad stratum of teachers, clerks, tradesmen, artisans, and those who, in the words of one AME sponsored petition, hoped "to do a little business." In Smithfield, for example, the church's most zealous adherent was Petrus Mothibi, a bricklayer and contractor who built the large AME Church in the location. A. A. and Theophilus Mareka, two young brothers who joined the AME Church in Ladybrand in the late 1890s, possessed broadly similar pedigrees. Born on a Free State mission station, they had trained as tradesmen at Bensonvale, a Wesleyan school in the Cape, before joining the church. By 1899 A. A. Mareka was an ordained AME minister; Theophilus continued to labor for several years as a carpenter before tightening municipal restrictions on African tradesmen drove him into the ministry as well. In other towns, too, African Methodism seems to have become the province of a relatively skilled and educated stratum of Africans, including many former sharecroppers who had first encountered the church on farms before the war.[68]

This was not some tiny elite; on the contrary, the cities and towns of the postwar Free State were literally bursting with such people. Some, like Mothibi, had carved out permanent niches for themselves in the city; others saw working in town as the shortest route back to the land. Whatever their trajectory, however, such people shared a congeries of qualities: they were enterprising, resourceful, "improving." Most possessed a smattering of education and invested in the education of their children. While adept in the ways of the white world, they continued to cherish their independence from it—a value that the AME Church embodied. Certainly this was how white observers saw matters. "Their followers here are all well known to me, and they consist of the worst class of natives, generally found in a location," the vice chairman of the Bethulie town council informed the colonial secretary; "they are idle and most of them unemployed—their ideas being above that of the ordinary wage earning native—and they certainly have as a class given a great deal of trouble to the authorities." The chairman of the council concurred, adding that Africans' desire for autonomy had been exacerbated by imported "American ideas and notions"—notions that had no place in a "country swarming with an easily excitable native population," and still less in municipal locations, which had been designed as labor reservoirs for local whites rather than as "full native towns."[69]

To an extraordinary extent, politics in the Orange River Colony came to center precisely here, on the question of what municipal locations would and would not be. While the immediate issues at stake were often local and mundane, the struggle had vast ramifications, embracing the whole question of agrarian reconstruction and the terms under which Africans would return to the land. Inevitably, the AME Church became implicated in the struggle. As the sole independent black institution in most towns, the church became a nodal point, an institutional precipitant around which popular grievances and demands could coalesce. For whites, on the other hand, African Methodism symbolized a world gone awry. Having been allowed into town to service the needs of white residents, blacks were making municipal locations their own, establishing schools, businesses, and their own churches, "squatting in idleness" while farmers in the surrounding countryside were starved of labor.

Contours of this confrontation could already be discerned in the year or so preceding the outbreak of the war, especially after Bishop Turner's 1898 tour. African Methodism's rapid spread placed republican officials in a quandary. While scarcely sympathetic to black aspirations for autonomy, most Boer officials recognized the difficulties of suppressing the movement, especially given their limited administrative and police resources. Determined to make the best of a bad situation, the state secretary sought guarantees of the church's good behavior from Turner, offering in exchange official "recognition," a nebulous term whose precise meaning would be debated for the better part of a decade. A year later, however, the republican government passed a law regulating African marriages, a device that may have been intended, and was certainly later used, to discriminate against African Methodists. Municipal officials, with a more immediate perspective on the problem, tended to be more direct. Several towns ejected AME ministers and teachers on the grounds that municipal locations were reserved for those earning an "honest livelihood"—that is, working for whites. ("They asked me who was my Baas," an indignant minister complained after being expelled from Heilbron.) Other municipalities refused to grant the church stands in their locations, unwittingly conferring greater visibility on African Methodists by forcing them to meet outdoors. One or two towns barred AME services entirely. For all of that, however, official opposition to the church remained unfocused and uneven. African Methodists worked without obstacle in several locations, often erecting prominent churches. In one or two instances, AME ministers overcame local prohibitions by appealing directly to republican authorities.[70]

With the accession of the British, even this small measure of flexibility disappeared. Determined to cut the movement off from the baneful "Negro" influences that allegedly sustained it, Orange River Colony officials, working with their colleagues in Pretoria, enacted a series of travel restrictions designed to keep African American church leaders out of the conquered colonies. With the exception of a brief meeting in Bloemfontein in 1907, no AME bishop entered the Free State between Turner's visit and the establishment of Union twelve years later. O.R.C. officials also discriminated against African churchmen, often in the guise of maintaining fidelity with preexisting law. Thus, a number of ministers were prosecuted under the 1899 marriage law, despite evidence that African Methodists had not been uniformly barred from conducting marriages by the act. In other cases, republican precedent counted nothing. AME ministers and teachers applying for exemption from the 1903 pass law, for example, were routinely denied on the grounds that their church had never been "recognised" by the republican government, a position flatly contradicted by documents in officials' possession. The new administration also declined to review local restrictions on the church on the grounds that control of urban locations was solely a municipal prerogative.[71]

The message was not lost on municipalities, which proceeded to launch a virtual assault on the AME Church. Their common weapon was the municipal pass system, established by the Volksraad and refined by O.R.C. ordinance but administered and policed at the local level. The system empowered each municipality to restrict entry into its location to those with employment, a requirement that most towns interpreted to mean employment by "white masters." In the first decade of the century, at least a dozen municipalities, several of which had previously acceded to the presence of the AME Church, denied permits to the church's ministers and teachers. In Wepener, where the AME Church had been established in 1899, the town council determined in 1903 that the minister was "without means or subsistence other than such as could be begged from the inhabitants" and summarily ejected him. Other towns refused to grant stands to the church or denied permission to occupy lots already granted. Municipalities whose by-laws prevented them from ejecting the church invented other devices. The Springfontein council declared the AME Church's large, unburnt brick building in violation of municipal building codes and ordered it torn down. The Thaba 'Nchu council contented itself with fining the local minister's "idle" wife. In Rouxville, police broke up an AME service, citing an 1893 law that empowered municipalities to regulate location "meetings."[72]

This assault was aimed not solely at the AME Church but at the broader principle of African autonomy and self-possession that it embodied. Using a tangle of republican laws, imperial ordinances, and local by-laws, municipalities endeavored to restore black dependency and exorcise the specter of racial competition that they saw emerging in the postwar era. Self-employment taxes, prohibitions against trading within locations, and special restrictions on black artisans all attacked African independence at the source. "The primary object of the Locations is to provide homes for natives who are employed amongst the Citizens in the Town," a Bloemfontein official wrote in 1904, outlining new residence and registration requirements. They "are not meant as convenient places for natives to come from all over the Colony to carry on trades and speculate, and generally come into competition with white inhabitants." Such policies, while rarely 100 percent effective, could reverse an individual's fortunes with brutal swiftness. Contractor Petrus Mothibi, for example, prospered in the first months after the war, having just built Smithfield's new AME Church, as well as the home of the new resident magistrate. When imperial officials promulgated the new pass law in the middle of 1903, he readily invested two pounds for the "tradesman's license" that served as his exemption. A few days later, however, Mothibi learned of a new municipal tax of five shillings per month on blacks not employed by Europeans. The tax, ten times the corresponding levy on Africans with white employers, amounted to a surcharge of three pounds per year, not only on Mothibi himself, but on every person in his employ. The bill included his daughter, a teacher at the local AME school, and two AME ministers, all of whom had been registered as his employees in order to circumvent local residence restrictions. Mothibi protested to the colonial secretary, who regretted his inability to interfere in municipal affairs.[73]

Much of the postwar assault focused on schools, which white officials recognized as wellsprings of African accumulation and community life, as well as a central source of the AME Church's appeal. African Methodist teachers were harassed and ejected from locations; various pretenses were sought to close church schools, even in towns where no alternatives existed. The question of offering government grants to AME schools, which acquired such salience in Transvaal Colony politics, never arose. The debate, rather, was over whether the state should make any provision for African education at all. The conclusion of municipal and imperial officials alike was a nearly unanimous no. (The only prominent dissenter, South African Native Affairs Commission member J. Q. Dickson, had little interest in black education per se but saw a system of state subsidies as a way to undercut the AME Church's appeal.) Through the entire reconstruction period, state grants for African education in the Orange River Colony never exceeded two thousand pounds per annum, far and away the lowest figure in South Africa and scarcely a twentieth of what the Cape provided in annual grants-in-aid to mission schools. Most galling of all, O.R.C. and municipal officials conspired to uphold the old republican policy of issuing labor passes to all Africans when they reached their sixteenth (in some municipalities, their fourteenth) birthdays, ensuring that education, even for those lucky enough to acquire it, could never proceed beyond the elementary level.[74]

If such policies were intended to dampen enthusiasm for African Methodism or to restore municipal locations to some kind of pristine status quo ante, they missed their mark. As in the Transvaal, the campaign against the AME Church, and against the broader interests and aspirations which it represented, served only to propel the church into the political arena. African Methodists stood in the forefront of a dozen different local campaigns, targeting the residential permit system, restrictions on trading, and the hated pass laws, particularly those affecting women and students. When petitions failed, AME leaders had recourse to the courts, winning at least two important judgments.

In 1904 John Phoukoutsi, an AME minister, won a case establishing that the term *employment* in the O.R.C.'s new municipal enabling legislation did not necessarily mean employment by a European. At about the same time, A. A. Mareka successfully appealed his conviction for living in Smithfield location without a permit. The High Court of the Orange River Colony, having determined that Mareka was a bona fide minister, ruled that the municipality had no cause to deny him a residential permit and thus no cause to arrest him. While of less moment than the *ex parte Tsewu* decision in the Transvaal, these cases represented the most significant legal victories won by Free State Africans in the entire reconstruction period.[75]

The AME Church gained a particularly high political profile in Bloemfontein, where ministers Benjamin Kumalo and Edward Mpela launched the Orange River Native Vigilance Association, the forerunner of the Orange River Native Congress. Kumalo in particular became an administration nemesis, the archetypal Ethiopian agitator. While his endless petitions and protests frequently betrayed his mission elite origins—he professed his faith in the "glorious" British Empire and his desire to go down to the "hovels of ignorance" to spread the light of Christianity—they also represented the interests of a broad stratum of town dwellers, a thousand of whom subscribed to one of his petitions. Like his counterparts in Johannesburg, Kumalo insisted on blacks' right to own property and to attend churches of their own choice. He also seized on more local grievances: prohibitions on trading in locations; failure to pay adequate compensation to homeowners uprooted by the opening of a new municipal quarry; burdensome municipal pass laws, especially those aimed at women. Kumalo was especially trenchant on the subject of education. "We are accused of having a little education, which is spoiling us," he complained to the South African Native Affairs Commission. Yet the very people making the accusation did everything in their power to ensure that an African could never "reach that point in education which will not spoil him." Kumalo added a special plea for "industrial education"—not the aimless hammering that prevailed in mission schools but genuine artisanal training, which would help Africans "improve" and compete economically.[76]

Weighed in the great scales of history, these municipal struggles were fleeting and largely ineffectual. Imperial officials had no intention of fostering racial competition, and the Boer government which came to power in 1907–1908 was even more grudging of black rights. Measured in the lives of those who waged them, however, the campaigns of African town dwellers were momentous and profoundly liberating. Consider the case of Bethulie, a small settlement in the south, near the confluence of the Caledon and the Orange rivers. Despite the town's proximity to water, the district as a whole was dry and unpromising, and labor was perennially scarce. Not coincidentally, the local council was as restrictive as any in the Free State. Even before the arrival of the AME Church, Bethulie moved to tighten the controversial pass law on teenagers. The same ordinance required individuals to obtain explicit, written permission from at least three municipal council members, including the chairman, before convening any public meeting, dance, or party, under penalty of a twenty-shilling fine or two weeks' hard labor.[77]

Not surprisingly, Bethulie authorities took a dim view of the AME Church. When a minister arrived from nearby Smithfield in 1899, they refused even to entertain his applications for a residence permit and church site, forcing him to take refuge in the hills outside town, whence he returned at night to preach. Several other ministers apparently visited the village during the war years, vainly petitioning for permission to settle and to open a church. Matters came to a head in 1902. Like other Free State towns, Bethulie experienced a postwar infusion of "refugees" and "idle natives," whom the municipal council determined "to get rid of . . . as soon as possible." Late in the year a new AME minister, Joseph Chou, arrived to take over the Bethulie circuit. Chou approached the clerk of the municipality for a residential pass and was refused; he applied again a few days later and was refused again. Later that same day he returned to the office with several other AME ministers, including A. A. Mareka of Smithfield and Edward Mpela of Bloemfontein. The group handed the clerk a terse note: "We let you know we are going to preach tonight at the Location. We have been advised to acquaint you." The stunned clerk replied with a note of his own, pledging to take "the necessary steps" to stop them.[78]

Both parties kept their words. That evening a group of about twenty people convened a prayer meeting in a private hut in Bethulie location. White constables twice entered the house and "told those there if they did not stop the meeting at once they would be arrested." The group continued to pray and sing. The constables, nonplussed by this act of nonviolent defiance, retired outside and waited for the group to emerge before arresting the lot. After an urgent meeting of the municipal council, the town decided to prosecute four AME ministers for instigating an unauthorized meeting. The local magistrate hearing the case accused the four of "practically hurling a challenge at the head of the Municipality" and imposed the maximum fine of twenty shillings on each, adding an additional twenty-shilling fine for contempt of court. On appeal, the High Court remitted the fines for contempt but let the convictions stand. Ultimately, however, what mattered to the people of Bethulie was less the legal outcome, which most understood to be a foregone conclusion, than the fact that white authority had been directly confronted and, in an elusive but unmistakable way, faced down. What the magistrate correctly read as contempt might equally have been read as assurance, almost serenity. "We held a prayer meeting," Edward Mpela testified. "Trooper Mallet warned us during the prayer meeting we must stop. We continued the meeting and we shall continue." Joseph Chou was blunter still: "I came to live in Bethulie; I have got my appointment and I must stay here. That is all I have to say." In the harsh and enclosed racial world of the southern highveld, this kind of assurance was something new under the sun.[79]

Even as such struggles continued, the constellation of factors that made them possible had begun to shift. From about 1905 onward, district officials across the colony reported an accelerating movement of Africans back to the countryside. The phenomenon, as always, was most pronounced in Bloemfontein, whose black population fell by more than half, from a postwar high of more than twenty-five thousand in 1906 to about twelve thousand five years later. No single cause animated the movement. Municipal harassment doubtless helped pry some Africans out of town. More important was the gradual recovery of the countryside, a product of adequate rainfall, the repatriation of Boer prisoners of war, and massive infusions of state assistance. Whatever their motivations, thousands of blacks returned to the farms, helping to trigger a remarkable economic revival. Holdings in livestock and implements soared, as did acreage under cultivation. Maize production alone increased more than threefold between the censuses of 1904 and 1911, until nearly half a million morgen were under the plough.[80]

Beneath these benign statistics, however, lay a more sinister reality. With agricultural recovery came the first significant stirrings of rural capitalization, a process marked by the increasing prevalence of wage labor relations, especially in the more prosperous eastern districts. Large, highly skilled sharecropping families, long the backbone of agricultural production in the Free State, found old landlords unwilling to take them on and were increasingly pushed to the drier, less capitalized districts in the north and west. Many were told to cull their herds or trek. Labor exactions intensified, and landlords increasingly demanded service from wives and children—demands that exacerbated tensions within families, precipitating flight and further eroding the position of household heads. The campaign against independent Africans reached a crescendo following the reaccession of the Boers in 1907–1908. Act 42 of 1908, for example, disingenuously dubbed the "Rights of Coloured Persons in Respect of Fixed Property Act," took direct aim at African "squatters." The act required that tenants sign contracts, bringing them within the ambit of the law, and that they register wives and children as servants, ostensibly to secure their rights on the land. The act also outlawed the common practice by which "indigent" whites fronted for black sharecroppers in land purchases. In a letter to the secretary of state in London, the colonial secretary conceded that the act would have a "demoralising" impact on some Africans, particularly those who possessed large herds and disdained working for whites. "This class is, however, a small one, considerably advanced in years," he consoled.[81]

Rural Africans protested, drawing on political skills and experiences acquired in the postwar municipal campaigns. A number of districts saw mass meetings and petition drives protesting against landlords who assaulted tenants and "enslaved" their children. Among surviving petitions, the most remarkable came from the Eastern Branch Native Vigilance Association in Bethlehem, a district with a substantial AME presence. At a mass meeting in late 1908, the association submitted a list of grievances to the Free State government, capturing accumulating Africans in suspension between urban and rural worlds. While most of the articles reiterated the familiar demands of better-off town dwellers—relief from pass laws, a voice in the making of municipal by-laws, removal of restrictions on the AME Church—others spoke directly to the concerns of African sharecroppers. The association demanded, among other things, protection from violence, laws to ensure that children were paid for their labor, and an end to mid-season evictions, by which tenants were deprived of their just share of a crop. As a final index of their desperation, the subscribers advocated the establishment of a special "reservoir" where Africans could administer their own affairs under the rule of state-appointed headmen.[82]

The new administration, however, had little intention of taking counsel from Africans, especially from what it took to be "an entirely artificial movement engineered . . . from outside the borders of this Colony." Determined to speak "plainly to these native claims" and "so called grievances," Prime Minister Abram Fischer penned a blistering response to the Bethlehemites. Municipal passes, he wrote, were necessary "to counteract the natural tendency of natives generally to lead lives of idleness resulting in evils amongst which it would seem that latterly would have to be included the one of harbouring and raising a class of native agitators." Pass exemptions for scholars were uncalled for: Africans should not be idle once they "arrived at an age to do honest labour." As for the plight of rural Africans, Fischer regarded the association's allegations as "impudent" and unworthy of comment. Under his regime, the campaign against independent Africans accelerated, compressing sharecroppers into labor tenancy and labor tenants into the ranks of the proletariat. The culmination, of course, came in the South African Natives Land Act of 1913, a bill whose antisquatting provisions were rigorously enforced only in the Orange Free State.[83]

Thus began the "great dispersal" of the Free State tenantry. The story has been eloquently told by Solomon Plaatje, but it is worth examing again, for it provides several final clues to the social composition and political nature of African Methodism on the southern highveld. Many sharecropping families were ejected from farms or remained in declining circumstances, which doubtless increased their alienation from white authority, and perhaps enhanced the appeal of a separatist church. Among his informants, Tim Keegan found several who joined the AME Church after 1913, as their fortunes fell and they lost that "social optimism" and "faith in self-improvement" that had once defined sharecroppers as a class. Others elected to leave the land, using the resources they still retained to carve out respectable positions for themselves and their children in town. Many found a lifeline in Evaton, a small community north of Vereeniging and one of a handful of places in the Transvaal where Africans were still permitted to own freehold property. Residents of the community, which remained practically self-governing through the 1940s, paid twenty pounds for one-acre lots, which entitled them to grazing rights on the commonage. Evaton's appeal, however, lay not only in the autonomy it offered but in the availability of education: the town boasted Wilberforce Institute, an AME-sponsored industrial and teacher-training school founded and staffed by South African graduates of Wilberforce University in the United States.[84]

Obviously, the "great dispersal" represented a rupture in the history of the highveld, yet tracing patterns of movement among particular families reveals significant continuities, in both economic and political terms. Take the case of Jacob Nhlapo. The son of a substantial sharecropper, Nhlapo spent his childhood on a farm outside Reitz. While most in the family had some exposure to location life, they looked down on those who had settled permanently in town. "I well remember how my father and other farm dwellers would ridicule the location dwellers as 'Bushmen' who possessed no cattle and had to depend on their rural cousins and on buying everything for their living," Jacob later recalled. By 1912, however, the pressures on the family had grown so great that his parents saw no alternative but to sell their assets and move to Reitz location, where the children would at least have the benefit of regular schooling. From Reitz Jacob proceeded on to Bensonvale and Lovedale, where he qualified as a teacher. Eventually, he received a Ph.D. in education, earned by correspondence through a black American university. In the 1920s he and his brother became prominent organizers of the Industrial and Commercial Workers' Union in the Free State. Two decades after that, he settled in Evaton as principal of Wilberforce Institute. "I feel we are closer to America here at Evaton than anywhere else in South Africa," he once remarked.[85]

Some families refused to relinquish the land, moving into poorer districts north and west, searching for eddies in the currents of capitalization where sharecroppers could still survive. Within the Free State, the most frequent destination was Hoopstad, a zandveld district in the northwestern corner of the province. Given its marginal rainfall (the district perched on the twenty-inch isohyet), its distance from railways, and the virtual absence of improved roads, this "sandy waste" had long been the least settled and developed district on the southern highveld. That very fact, however, represented an opportunity to black sharecroppers, some of whom managed to negotiate agreements, technically illegal, with struggling white landlords. By the 1920s Hoopstad had become one of the major maize-producing districts in the entire province. If African Methodism was indeed the church of this class of rural accumulators, one would anticipate an increase in church membership in the district, and that is precisely what one observes. Indeed, by 1920 tiny Hoopstad boasted one of the largest AME circuits in the entire Free State.[86]

An even more common destination for those with the personal and material resources to keep sharecropping was the southwestern Transvaal, especially the so-called "Maize Triangle" defined by Bloemhof, Wolmaransstad, and Schweizer-Reneke. In this flat, dry, undercapitalized triangle of farms, just across the Vaal River from Hoopstad, African sharecroppers continued to plough—and, in some cases, to prosper—right up until 1948. Here again, the link between independent Africans and African Methodism is unmistakable. The church, first introduced in the late 1890s by Marcus Gabashane, blossomed in the 1910s and '20s into one of the most important institutions in the region. Christiana, Bloemhof, Schweizer-Reneke, even tiny Makwassie, all anchored AME circuits, catering to close to five hundred people. (Wolmaransstad also boasted a congregation but had no church building, due to the persistent opposition of the local council.) Over the ensuing decades, this seemingly remote and insignificant corner of the world offered a breeding ground for some of black South Africa's most militant political movements, including the Industrial and Commercial Workers' Union, the Communist Party of South Africa, and the Pan-African Congress. The AME Church remains a substantial presence in the region to this day.[87]

6

African Methodism
as a Social Movement, II

The AME Church in the Reserves

In August 1903 a short letter appeared in *Koranta ea Beacona,* the English-Setswana newspaper edited by future South African Native National Congress founder Solomon Plaatje. The letter came from Segale Pilane, a Bakhatla chief and one of Britain's most important allies in the just completed South African War. Like other Africans, Segale and his people had expected British victory to usher in a new liberal order for Africans in the Transvaal. They had also hoped for a restoration of Bakhatla lands in the western Transvaal that had been stolen by the Boers in the 1880s. Needless to say, both expectations proved unavailing, leaving Segale bitter and resentful. While in this attitude, he somehow came across a copy of *The Voice of the People,* an African American emigrationist newspaper published by AME Bishop Henry Turner. The paper, essentially a catalog of racial oppression around the globe, struck an immediate chord with the chief, prompting him to write. Segale was particularly enraged by a story of an African minister in the Orange Free State who had been defrocked by white missionaries "only because he is black." "I say: Pray, Natives, do hear the cry of your own 'People'," he wrote. "They even despise our own creation and say that they cannot allow the Book in black hands. I say, let us leave them alone." As a parting shot, he added that, in any future war, Africans should aid the Boers.[1]

Segale's outburst touched off a flurry of meetings and memos in imperial circles. While officials somehow overlooked the AME connection, they well appreciated the danger of such sentiments, especially coming from an erstwhile ally. The local magistrate immediately confronted editor Plaatje, who explained that he had been out of town when the issue in question went to press and promised that future letters would be more carefully screened. The episode was eventually forgotten.[2]

Several historical themes run through this little exchange. Segale Pilane's career highlights Africans' participation in the South African War, as well as their immense sense of betrayal in the war's aftermath. Imperial administrators' fevered response to a seemingly insignificant letter betrays their own uneasiness as they watched the spreading ripples of African disenchantment. Solomon Plaatje's meek response provides yet another illustration of the "ambiguities of dependence" in early African nationalist politics. For historians of African Methodism, however, the episode raises unexpected questions. How had a Georgia newspaper found its way into the hands of a chief in a reserve on the Bechuanaland border? What possible interest could a hereditary African leader have in a Christian, pan-ethnic movement such as the AME Church? How are we to understand Segale's call to "leave them alone" when at the very same moment African Methodists in Pretoria and Johannesburg were leading movements to win Africans inclusion and equality within colonial society?[3]

Nor was Segale an isolated case. On the contrary, dozens of African traditional leaders became involved with Ethiopianism in the late nineteenth and early twentieth centuries. The subscription list from the dedicatory service of the first Ethiopian chapel in Marabastad included the names of two Transvaal chiefs, Mosebi and Kekana. When Mangena Mokone went to Johannesburg a year later to dedicate the first Ethiopian church on the Rand, he was accompanied by chief Hans Makapan, a descendant of the Ndebele chief killed in the Boers' murderous siege at Makapansgat forty years before. Pedi paramount chief Sekukuni also had close links with the early independent church movement, having spent the years of his exile in Marabastad living as the ward of African Church founder Joseph Kanyane Napo. The fact that he was not a Christian himself did not prevent Sekukuni from encouraging the spread of African Methodism in his realm following his restoration by the British.[4]

Traffic between chiefs and "Ethiopians" increased further following the entrance of the AME Church. During the inaugural meeting of the Transvaal Annual Conference in Pretoria in 1898, Bishop Turner was joined on the platform by "two kings and a chief": apparently Sekukuni; Ramoghopa, a minor northern Sotho chief who later sponsored an AME school; and Samuel Moroka, the exiled claimant to the Seleka Barolong chieftainship at Thaba 'Nchu. At least a dozen traditional leaders, including virtually all of the major paramount chiefs in southern Africa, attended a reception in Cape Town in 1901 to welcome the newly arrived AME resident bishop, Levi Coppin. While not all of these chiefs identified themselves with the church, many did, apparently seeing no contradiction between involvement in a pan-ethnic Christian church and their own position as traditional leaders.[5]

The presence of African chiefs in the front ranks of the independent church movement poses paradoxes within paradoxes. As we have already seen, Ethiopianism both reflected and hastened the erosion of ethnic identities and loyalties, especially after the movement's association with black America. At the very same time, in reserves from Pondoland to Barotseland, the AME Church was becoming implicated in local neotraditional movements aimed at reviving indigenous authority. Stranger still, these movements often brought together chiefs, the bulk of whom were not Christian, and Christian converts, many of whom had initially gravitated to Christianity precisely to escape chiefly exactions. Befitting this odd social base, these rural movements wove together seemingly incompatible intellectual strands: Christian universalism and racial nationalism; demands for incorporation and calls for separation; paeans to progress and valorizations of "tradition." Clearly, we still have some way to go before we fully comprehend African Methodism's social and political range.[6]

To unravel the problem, it is necessary to return to nineteenth-century missions, specifically to the changing place of mission Christianity within chiefly society. It is by now a truism that many chiefs initially welcomed the arrival of missionaries. Missionaries offered access to valuable skills and technology, notably medicine and education, and their facility with the ways of the colonizers made them useful intermediaries. Chiefs were generally less receptive to the specifically religious component of missionary teachings, a fact constantly lamented in mission sources, but most missionaries were prepared to accept their contingent status within chiefdoms in order to gain access to the people there. Chiefs, in turn, extended the missionaries protection, in the belief that their presence on the whole enhanced traditional authority.[7]

Missionaries and chiefs sustained this relationship of convenience with varying degrees of success. Ultimately, however, conflict was inevitable. In the first place, African societies and European missions embodied two distinct systems of hierarchy, each in its own way all-encompassing. By preaching a doctrine of spiritual equality and offering preferment without regard to birth or ascriptive status, missionaries could undermine existing relations of patronage and dependence within host societies. Indeed, the bulk of early converts appear to have been dependents or refugees who settled on mission stations to escape obligations to chiefs or patrons or traditional restrictions on accumulation. Many were women fleeing unwanted marriages or the operation of the levirate system, which consigned a widow to the control of her husband's brother. More broadly, missionaries promoted new conceptions of community, individuality, and obligation that could be profoundly subversive of chiefly authority. A chief in Kuruman district, for example, restocking in the wake of the rinderpest, was convicted of cattle raiding in the late 1890s on the testimony of one of his subjects, a London Missionary Society convert. The political and cultural dimensions of the case escaped the local missionary, who saw only a convert's laudable commitment to truth and private property. The chief suffered no such myopia: he expelled the L.M.S. and burned its church to the ground.[8]

Missionaries and "traditionalists" collided most frequently on issues of ritual and custom. By mission standards, practices such as circumcision, rainmaking, polygamy, and "beer-drinks" were "vestiges of heathenism" to be eradicated. To chiefs, on the other hand, they represented critical mechanisms for expressing ritual authority, asserting control over labor, conducting diplomacy, and lubricating relationships of patronage and clientage. Conflict most often came to a point on the question of *lobola,* the payment of brideprice. Where Africans recognized a fundamental prop of generational and chiefly authority, missionaries saw a barbarous system of female slavery, the material base of African indolence and sexual wantonness. While different mission societies adopted slightly different policies on the custom, all worked to suppress it, kindling conflicts all across the subcontinent. Among the Bapedi, for example, the arrival of the Berlin Mission Society at the capital immediately ignited protests from elders, who complained that Christianity undermined their control over women. And it was the Society's success among royal wives, crucial markers in the extension of the paramountcy, that precipitated the Berliners' expulsion by the elder Sekukuni in 1865.[9]

The removal of the B.M.S. from Sekukuniland, however, was as much a conscious decision by missionaries to draw more closely into the orbit of the Z.A.R. government as it was an expulsion. In making that decision, the Society charted a course that missionaries all over southern Africa would follow in the last third of the nineteenth century. The missionary's transformation from "native advocate" to "colonial agent" is familiar enough and needs little recitation here. Suffice to say that as the process of colonial conquest advanced, the balance of power between missionaries and chiefs shifted. Many missionaries found that they no longer needed chiefly sponsorship but could fare as well or better under the auspices of a vigorous colonial state. What is significant for our purposes is the degree to which European missionaries became implicated in colonial campaigns to undermine traditional authorities. In both Thembuland and Pondoland, Wesleyan missionaries played vital roles in defusing chiefly resistance in the run-up to annexation. L.M.S. officials supported the British war against Lobengula and extended hospitality to the troops dispatched to put down the subsequent rebellion. Missionaries everywhere helped to enforce the mounting exactions of the colonial state—hut taxes, labor levies, and the like—often at the expense of traditional obligations. In Qumbu, the Presbyterian mission station housed the new district jail, a "comfortable and commodious" facility, confining Africans who violated any of the new colonial ordinances.[10]

Chiefs were generally astute enough to appreciate what was happening; like the founders of the Ethiopian Church, they routinely distinguished between sympathetic "old" missionaries and their mettlesome successors. The most obvious recourse was simply to expel mission societies, as old Sekukuni had done, but this option became less viable as the century progressed. If anything, the encroachment of settler society made mission resources such as literacy and education all the more valuable. Moreover, the close relationship between missionaries and colonial authorities made direct confrontation risky. When Thembu paramount chief Dalindyebo lent his support to an independent church in the 1880s, for example, Wesleyan missionaries protested to the Cape Native Affairs Department, which immediately called the young chief onto the carpet. The changed balance of power was matter-of-factly acknowledged in a turn-of-the-century exchange of letters between a Bechuanaland official and the superintendent of the London Missionary Society, discussing what action to take in a local chieftainship dispute. When the superintendent observed that the L.M.S. operated in the area on the reigning chief's sufferance, the official pointedly replied: "That is true in theory, but again I say that the day is gone by when a native Chief may dictate to the Government on that or any other point."[11]

Obviously, these processes unfolded across the subcontinent at different times and in different ways. In the Transvaal, the real subsumption of traditional authority came not with the end of formal conquest in 1879 but during imperial reconstruction, by which time missionaries had become much more marginal politically. In the Cape and the Transkei, the process of incorporation took place earlier and over a longer period of time, with missionaries playing a vital part. The situation was further complicated by the introduction of a stratum of state-appointed location headmen, as well as by the Cape administration's penchant for replacing troublesome leaders with "loyal," often Christian, chiefs. Yet even granting this variety, the general pattern remains clear: in the late nineteenth and early twentieth centuries, traditional leaders across southern Africa found their authority increasingly circumscribed by colonial authority, operating in league with white missionaries and, more often than not, African mission converts.

Chiefs responded to the erosion of their authority in different ways. Some collaborated with their conquerors, enforcing colonial taxes and ordinances in exchange for healthy stipends and the security of state recognition. A few rebelled. Most steered courses between these extremes, eschewing outright resistance while struggling to retain some room for maneuver within the tightening colonial noose. It takes little imagination to see the appeal of African Methodism in such a context. Here was a church whose leaders were Africans, who challenged colonial authority and spoke of black people's right to control their own destinies. The "Ethiopian" vision of a great black civilization existing prior to the coming of whites was easily appropriated to a defense of precolonial authority, while the idea of captives returning from exile to reclaim their birthright provided a potent idiom for asserting traditional claims to the land. Above all, African Methodism promised access to the ostensibly vast economic and educational resources of black America, offering all that white missions offered and more, with none of the apparent costs.

One question remains. Granting that many chiefs were open to African Methodism, why was it open to them? How did the AME Church avoid the conflicts that marred European missionaries' relationship with chiefs? To missionaries, the answer was patent and could be stated in one word: indiscipline. The presence of "barbarous" chiefs in the front ranks of Ethiopianism was only further proof that the movement lacked "standards," that African Christians, freed from strict European governance, were "reverting to heathenism." Missionaries spun no end of variations on the theme, which served to vindicate their own stringency, as well as their increasingly pessimistic assessment of African potential. "The gospel of Ethiopianism," ran one of the more colorful variations,

> presents an emasculated Christ in the centre of a very abbreviated Decalogue. It countenances polygamy and certain other highly undesirable native customs, including the disgusting beer-fests, and, while requiring acquiescence in the narrowest literal interpretation of the first six commandments, regards the remainder as suggestions admirable indeed, but impracticable.

Ethiopians, in other words, might honor the sabbath and eschew graven images, but when it come to conduct—to lying, stealing, murder, and adultery—it was back to the law of the jungle. [12]

By now it should be clear that the appeal of Ethiopianism and, later, of African Methodism flowed from something deeper than lax standards. We should not dismiss the question too quickly, however. While the evidence is inevitably anecdotal, there is ample reason to believe that the AME Church did in fact adopt a more flexible position on matters of ritual and custom than white mission churches, especially where traditional authorities were concerned. African Methodists first gained a foothold in Port St. Johns, for example, when they agreed to baptize the infant child of a local headman; the Wesleyans had refused on the grounds that the child was the issue of a polygamous union. Chief Robert Moepi of the Bakhatla ba Mocha was an ardent African Methodist and a graduate of an AME school in Cape Town, none of which deterred him from staging great hunts to bring the rain or from perpetuating the custom of circumcision among his people. We can probably dismiss as hyperbole missionary reports of an AME local preacher in Bizana with ten wives, but the general point—that the church was more tolerant of traditional practices than its predecessors and thus better able to accommodate traditional leadership—is sound. [13]

To some extent at least, this relative flexibility was a function of race, though not in the way in which the church's critics imagined. Reading mission sources today, it is impossible not to be struck by the burden of whiteness that nineteenth-century European missionaries bore. Almost from the moment they disembarked in Africa, missionaries were beset by fears of degeneration, fears that the process of "conversion" was superficial, even that it might somehow be reversed and that they themselves would revert to savagery. While the last fear seems to have ebbed over the course of the nineteenth century, doubts about Africans' "convertibility" continued to rise as new, ever more pessimistic racial ideologies percolated into the mission world. By the end of the century, many missionaries had become so preoccupied with the "savage" lurking beneath the convert's "veneer" of "civilisation" that they all but renounced the evangelical enterprise. Many made a fetish of "standards," finding little comfort even in instances of great piety and devotion. Thus the strange lament of an L.M.S. superintendent in the northern Cape: "Christianity has undoubtedly a strong hold upon a large number of Bechuanas, and is exerting a certain influence upon their lives."

> But I fear that it is principally as a religion that Christianity has been embraced. Probably it would be difficult to find anywhere a people more entirely devoted to the Christian religion as a creed and a charm. . . . It must, however, be admitted that the Christianity of Christ and the New Testament—that is to say a Christianity which enters into all the ramifications of domestic and social relationships, is a thing which is rather conspicuous by its absence. Self-denial in any shape or form is a very rare quality among the Bechuanas. The gratification of the appetites and passions of their animal nature is, alas, all too prominent. . . .

This particular missionary was more optimistic than most. The work would yet bear fruit, he predicted, but only "when the power of these worthless chieftains is at an end, the tribes as such are broken up and scattered, and each individual is compelled to look to the sweat of his own brow for a livelihood." In the meantime, all a missionary could do was keep a weather eye to protect the church from the "unworthy."[14]

African Methodism could scarcely have been more different. Fired by prophecy, AME ministers traversed the countryside, determined to bring all Africans under their banner. Would-be converts were rarely if ever subjected to formal examinations; accessions from other denominations were accepted without benefit of "removal certificates," devices used by missionaries to prevent individuals under discipline in one church from moving to another. A host of colonial proprieties went by the board. European missionaries, for example, regarded the move from round huts to square homes, with properly demarcated and private rooms, as an essential step on the road to "civilisation." Most were loath to enter congregants' huts, and they certainly never held services in them. AME ministers, on the other hand, routinely lived and preached in private huts; indeed, given their difficulties in obtaining residence permits and church sites, they often had no alternative. Church leaders took a similarly pragmatic approach on questions of chiefly authority. If accommodating a chief or headman was the price of admission into a particular location, most AME ministers were quite prepared to pay it—so prepared, in fact, that the first resident bishop sent out from America was forced to issue a special directive against accepting polygamous chiefs into membership.[15]

In sum, African Methodists were open to chiefs' participation in ways that white missionaries typically were not. In cultural or psychological terms, AME ministers were less threatened by the rituals and customs through which chiefly power flowed. In structural terms, they were of necessity more sensitive to the practices and loyalties of local congregations, which paid their salaries. Simply in practical terms, African Methodists' inability to call on the protection of the colonial state prevented them from setting themselves up in opposition to chiefly authority, even had they wished to. On the contrary, the AME Church offered embattled chiefs a potential weapon in their struggles against internal rivals and an intrusive colonial state.

How and whether particular chiefs availed themselves of this new weapon depended on a host of variables, from patterns of preexisting factional division within chiefdoms to idiosyncracies of individual temperament. The range of possibilities can be graphically illustrated by taking a journey with Ethiopian Church founder Marcus Gabashane, the minister who planted the first AME churches in the towns and farmlands of the western Transvaal. Late in 1898 Gabashane and his son, Martin Luther, embarked on an eight-week, thousand-mile circuit, from their home outside Klerksdorp, through the western Transvaal and British Bechuanaland, and up the length of the Bechuanaland Protectorate. The pair stopped at every major Tswana settlement along the way to preach and herald the coming of the AME Church. In the different responses of chiefs we can discern many of the factors conditioning African Methodism's spread.[16]

The occasion of the Gabashanes' journey was the trek of the "Samuelites," the followers of exiled Seleka Barolong chief Samuel Moroka, who were traveling to a new location they had been promised in northern Bechuanaland. Exiled from his home at Thaba 'Nchu in the wake of a violent succession dispute, Samuel was one of African Methodism's first chiefly patrons and one of the three traditional leaders who shared the rostrum with Bishop Turner at the church's inaugural conference in Pretoria. Samuel's interest in African Methodism is easy enough to fathom, for few chiefs had suffered quite so directly from the intersection of white missions and colonial authority. As the sole surviving son of the first house of Moroka, the chief who had led the Seleka to Thaba 'Nchu during the *mfecane,* Samuel considered himself the legitimate heir to the chieftainship, but he was outmaneuvered by Tshipinare, a brother from a junior house whose mother was not even Seleka but Tshidi. Tshipinare, no doubt aware of the shakiness of his traditional claim, cultivated a close relationship with Wesleyan missionaries and Free State officials, who supported his elevation to the chieftainship following old Moroka's death in 1880.[17]

Samuel, characterized by a contemporary as "irascible, implacable and obdurate in temperament," was endlessly enterprising in his efforts to secure his birthright. He concluded alliances with neighboring chiefs and established himself as a patron of Thaba 'Nchu's Sotho minority, many of whom had never forgiven the Barolong for their role in the Basotho-Boer wars. (The Gabashanes were prominent members of this community.) Samuel even made an early foray into religious separatism, sponsoring an Anglican mission in direct opposition to the Wesleyans. When all these measures failed to secure his accession, Samuel and his followers resorted to arms, launching an attack in 1884 that left Tshipinare and several of his followers dead. The rebellion was quickly put down by an armed force from the Free State, which proceeded formally to annex Thaba 'Nchu. Samuel was forced into exile. Given this bitter personal history, the chief was immediately receptive to African Methodism. With its rejection of meddling missionaries, its assertion of Africans' right to the land, and its unique capacity to wed a defense of tradition with a vision of black education and progress, African Methodism virtually mirrored Samuel's own aspirations. The fact that the church counted one of his followers among its leaders doubtless enhanced its appeal. [18]

Samuel spent the years before his northward trek at Khunwana, a dusty location perched on the border of the Transvaal and British Bechuanaland, and this was the Gabashanes' first stop. Khunwana was home to the Ratlou Rolong, who lived under their aging chief, Moshette. Moshette's alliance with Samuel was probably enough to dispose him favorably toward the AME Church, but it is clear that he also entertained a serious grievance against the London Missionary Society, which boasted the location's only church. The Khunwana mission had been opened amid much fanfare in the mid-1880s, but in the years that followed the village was shamefully neglected. L.M.S. missionaries visited only once or twice a year; in about 1896 they stopped coming altogether, apparently due to the shortage of draught following the rinderpest. A black local preacher with almost twenty years experience was stationed in the village, but he was not empowered to dispense the sacraments; according to local tradition, the L.M.S. refused to ordain him because he spoke no Latin. Residents seeking a Christian marriage or the baptism of a new child were forced to travel over a hundred miles of sandy, rutted roads to the L.M.S. station at Kanye. ("It is said that one span of oxen just collapsed under the yoke while taking people to Kanye," an old informant recalled.) Moshette urged L.M.S. officials to station a minister in the village, but they refused. [19]

The chief was thus receptive when Abel Gabashane first visited Khunwana in mid-1898 and positively enthusiastic when Abel's father and brother arrived a month or two later. While no record of these first encounters survives, we can draw some firm inferences about what was said. Moshette obviously described the plight of the L.M.S. local preacher. "Still a probationer!" Gabashane raged in his report to the *Voice of Missions*. "Nineteen years a Probationer! Probation for life!! That is how we native ministers are treated in Africa!!!" Gabashane, in turn, doubtless referred to Bishop Turner's just completed visit and to the college that Turner had pledged to build. He also presumably mentioned his young son, Henry, who was even then en route to America for training as a medical doctor. The L.M.S. was routed. By the end of 1898 the new AME church in Khunwana counted more than two hundred members, including the erstwhile L.M.S. probationer, soon to be an ordained minister. The church's most noted convert was Moshette himself: Marcus Gabashane baptized the blind and halt chief shortly before his death, apparently untroubled by his continuing attachment to "vestiges of heathenism." "On the outside he is not a Christian," Gabashane conceded in a letter to the *Voice of Missions,* "but internally he is a great Christian."[20]

During old Moshette's decline, the duties of the chieftainship increasingly devolved upon his son, Aaron, under whose sponsorship the AME Church became a political force in the region. It was Aaron's lot to rule at Khunwana during the period of postwar reconstruction. Like chiefs throughout the Transvaal Colony, he found himself facing a concerted assault on what he took to be his traditional prerogatives. In 1902 the acting chief, by all accounts a formidable drinker, ran afoul of the new Transvaal liquor laws, which, in deference to the interests of mineowners, made it an offense for Africans to possess spirits. A year later the Transvaal Native Affairs Department prevented the chief from disposing of a portion of his location on the grounds that no title for the land had been registered in Z.A.R. archives. In 1904 a native constable stationed by the government in Khunwana reported that Aaron was selling wood from the location; the state, looking to the possibility of mining in the location and anxious to preserve local timber, ordered him to desist. Increasingly, the chief's bitterness focused on the government constables. He complained that they were "outsiders" (one was Ndebele, another Zulu); that they ignored his labor exactions; that they enforced the new pass regulations with such vigor that residents of the part of Khunwana location that fell in British Bechuanaland were arrested for crossing into the Transvaal. He ordered one of the constables flogged, a decision that did not endear him to the Native Affairs Department, which responded by holding in abeyance his application for a rifle. In 1908 the Department declared that Khunwana location would henceforth be held in trust for the tribe by the Commissioner for Native Affairs, a device that firmly established state control over the disposal of land and timber. As a final indignity, the government refused to register the title until Moshette and his people had paid a substantial transfer duty.[21]

In these roiled circumstances, African Methodism flourished. In 1902 J. S. Moffat, scion of L.M.S. pioneer John Moffat and a Bechuanaland administrator, reported that Marcus Gabashane was back at Khunwana, illegally solemnizing marriages and preaching against the whites. In the same letter Moffat complained of chiefs who persecuted mission loyalists. A few years later a missionary of the Church of England protested that Aaron Moshette refused to allow him to open a church or school in the location. Long after the end of imperial reconstruction, officials continued to fret about the AME Church's monopoly in "this lonely part of the Colony" and about their apparent inability to break it. As late as 1910 a native commissioner at Lichtenburg warned his superiors of the continuing spread of "Ethiopianism" in the area, estimating that 50 percent of Africans in his district had already joined. The "root of this evil," he added, "is Kunana Location, where this doctrine reigns supreme."[22]

After leaving Khunwana, the Gabashanes trekked to Mafeking in British Bechuanaland, where they were hosted by Tshidi Rolong chief Montsioa. From there, they proceeded up the Protectorate, traveling by wagon and by rail, stopping off at Kanye, capital of the Ngwaketse, and Phalapye, capital of chief Khama's Ngwato. Everywhere, they were well received by chiefs, many of whom had spent the last several years pressing the L.M.S. to build them a college. Bathoen, paramount chief of the Ngwaketse, entertained the travelers for a week, offering his son for training in the United States, as well as a parcel of land for construction of the promised AME college. The Gabashanes do not appear to have met Khama, but they did meet one of his brothers, who volunteered two of his sons for American education. Khama himself later evinced considerable interest in African Methodism. In mid-1902, shortly after relocating his capital from Phalapye to Serowe, he contacted leaders of the AME Church and offered them the abandoned L.M.S. mission at his old capital for the planned college. "All these Kings have one voice!" Marcus Gabashane wrote in his initial report to the *Voice of Missions*. "One cry: Education! Education!" They wanted "trades of any kind," "business," and "the way of making money," and they wanted to learn these things from "no other people but Africans." "Show that you were made stronger and healthier than the opposite race," he challenged African Americans. "Sun cannot scorch you any blacker than you are."[23]

Yet even as African Methodism flourished in Khunwana, it had begun to wither in Bechuanaland. Khama, perhaps the most politically astute chief of his generation, enjoyed relatively good relations with the Bechuanaland administration, which had sustained him through a series of bruising factional disputes in the 1880s and '90s. He was also well aware of the advantages of imperial protection, which shielded him and his people from the exactions and indignities endured by their counterparts in South Africa. Finally, Khama, for all his frustration with the limitations of L.M.S. education, appreciated the Society's metropolitan links. Just a few years before, in fact, L.M.S. superintendent W. C. Willoughby had escorted him and two other Tswana chiefs to London in a successful effort to stave off the annexation of Bechuanaland by Cecil Rhodes's British South Africa Company. After weighing all this in the balance, the chief chose the politic course. When Willoughby approached him with reports about the AME college, the chief denied having made any offer.

When questioned about "Ethiopianism" by the South African Native Affairs Commission, he blandly lied. He had "heard the name," he conceded, "but so far there are no Ethiopians in my country."[24]

Bathoen attempted a similar reversal, but with less success. As with Khama, Bathoen's ardor for African Methodism cooled once he perceived its political costs. The AME Church made no effort to take up his offer of a college site, and the chief made no effort to revive the idea. That might have been the end of it but for the presence of Tsime, Bathoen's brother-in-law and a singularly ambitious rival. Tsime seems initially to have positioned himself as a traditionalist, condemning the spread of the white man's religion and, by implication, the chief's cozy relationship with the L.M.S. No sooner had Bathoen doffed the mantle of Ethiopianism than Tsime donned it. The chief was in a quandary. Clearly, the presence of the church inflated his rival's standing; on the other hand, any attempt to suppress it would only confirm allegations that he himself was a white tool. "It is ostensibly a Church row, and Bathoen tries (somewhat unsuccessfully) to persuade himself that it is merely that," Willoughby reported. "It is much more. It is an attempt on the part of Tsime to secure the chieftainship for his son." Tsime even endeavored to have one of his followers ordained, an idea that Willoughby found singularly repugnant. "Bathoen tries to sit on the fence," he concluded, "but that is an accomplishment that few men can successfully acquire."[25]

Ultimately, nothing came of Tsime's ambition; Bathoen continued to be dogged by Ethiopian dissidents, but his grip on the chieftainship remained secure. Yet even as events in Bechuanaland wound down to their anticlimactic end, an even more spectacular "Ethiopian Episode" was erupting in Barotseland, across the Zambesi. As African Methodism spread north, word somehow reached Lozi paramount chief Lewanika, who promptly issued a call to the church. The schism became particularly notorious in mission circles, for it came at the expense of the Paris Evangelical Mission and its revered head, François Coillard. Established after almost twenty years of struggle, the Barotseland mission was hailed across Africa as the acme of missionary "enterprise and courage," as well as the crowning achievement of Coillard's long career. The territory itself bulked large in imperialist dreams, as both an entrepot for migrants headed south to the mines and a staging post in the planned Cape-to-Cairo railroad. Lewanika himself was widely regarded as the epitome of the "friendly" chief. While inhibited from converting by more conservative subchiefs, he regularly attended P.E.M. services and exhibited a "considerable ability to absorb the better influences of civilisation." He even visited London for Edward's coronation, apparently cutting quite a figure in a white frock coat given him by the new king. The intrusion of the AME Church into this seemingly idyllic world dealt a devastating blow to missionary aspirations and left Coillard a broken man. His death a short time later provided European missionaries with their first martyr to Ethiopianism.[26]

Colonial responses to the schism revealed all the predictable blindspots.
R. T. Coryndon, the administrator for the British South Africa Company,
resorted to the language of indiscipline, warning Lewanika that the Ethiopians
taught "wrong things." "The 'Ethiopian' is not a good church," he wrote.
"You like them because the missionaries are black people and because they talk
nicely to you and do not tell you when you do wrong as Mr. Coillard did."
Missionaries took a similar line, suggesting that the impressionable chief had
been duped by clever Ethiopians. In fact, Lewanika's dissatisfaction with the
P.E.M. was long-standing. Conflict centered initially on the issue of education. While the paramount and the Lozi elite both welcomed mission schools,
they resented Coillard's insistence that only the children of converts could
attend, and they objected strenuously to the P.E.M. curriculum, which emphasized singing and Bible reading rather than the technical and industrial
skills needed by people facing an advancing colonial world. They also opposed
the P.E.M. policy of teaching in vernacular languages rather than English,
which, paradoxically, represented a vital resource in the Lozi struggle for
independence. The importance of these issues was driven home in the wake of
the 1890 Coryndon Concession, which consigned Barotseland to the dubious
protection of the British South Africa Company. Significantly, Coillard played
a leading role in persuading Lewanika to sign the concession.[27]

Even before the appearance of the AME Church, Lewanika had issued a call
for "new missionaries" to replace the P.E.M. He also sponsored a short lived
English-medium school, under the direction of Willie Mokalapa, a Sotho
evangelist who had been dismissed from the P.E.M. for opposing the Coryndon Concession. When word of African Methodism reached Barotseland, it
must have seemed like a dream come true. The chief immediately dispatched
Mokalapa to Cape Town with an invitation to begin work in his territory.
AME leaders, not surprisingly, were receptive to the paramount's offer, especially when they learned of his interest in "industrial" education. They were
equally taken with Mokalapa, who possessed all the earmarks of a first-rate
missionary. An experienced and ardent evangelist, he was multilingual, accustomed to privation, and possessed by the dream of African redemption. His
close relationship with a "heathen" chief in the African interior—proof in itself
of his unfitness in the eyes of his European supervisors—was by African Methodist standards a superb credential. In early 1903, Mokalapa returned to
Barotseland as an ordained AME minister, bearing vague promises to build an
industrial college. Thus was the AME Church's "Zambesi Mission" born.[28]

When Coillard got wind of the planned AME school, he confronted
Lewanika. The paramount sent a stinging reply:

> What do we want with all that rubbish heap of fables that you call the Bi-
> ble? . . . What does your school do for us? . . . it is a purposeless and un-
> profitable folly. What I want is missionaries . . . who build big workshops and

teach us all the trades of the white man. . . . What I want is carpenters, blacksmiths, armourers, masons. . . . That's what I want, industrial missionaries; that is what all the chiefs want. We laugh at all the rest.

No single statement better reveals the contextual nature of ideas or Africans' and African Americans' remarkable facility for simultaneously talking to and past each other. Born of accommodation to southern segregation, industrial education remained a controversial doctrine among African Americans, especially among African Methodists, who had pioneered black university education. Many AME leaders, however, embraced industrial education in the mission field as appropriate to Africans' needs and current stage of development. For Lewanika, industrial education represented something else altogether—an opportunity to break the white monopoly on skills and technological resources and restore traditional control over the economic development of his realm. In Barotseland, industrial education represented a formula not of accommodation but of liberation, a way to restore the old while seizing the new.[29]

It is in this context that the chief's eventual falling out with the AME Church must be placed. Lewanika had long dreamed of developing commerce and communications along the Zambesi and had extracted several promises in this regard from the B.S.A. Company. When these promises went unheeded, he turned to the AME Church. In 1905 he dispatched Mokalapa and a Lozi royal back to Cape Town with seven hundred pounds raised from a tribal levy, with instructions to use the church's connections to purchase wagons and boats. Mokalapa's contact in Cape Town was A. Henry Attaway, a black American and AME General Superintendent, second-in-command to the resident bishop. We shall have occasion in a later chapter to assay Attaway's South African career: suffice to say that he was something of an entrepreneur, whose ventures occasionally verged on sharp practice. Attaway accepted the money and dispatched Mokalapa back to Barotseland with some clothes, a box of books, and a new church bell. The boats and wagons, supposedly to follow, never arrived. As for the seven hundred pounds, Attaway allegedly entrusted it to a business partner, who promptly declared bankruptcy. An enraged Lewanika ordered Mokalapa to "clear out of his country," and the curtain fell on the AME Church's Zambesi Mission.[30]

Tracing each of these episodes helps illuminate the variables that shaped chiefly responses to the AME Church. Ultimately, however, the church's "northern frontier" remained something of a sideshow. While African Methodism's passage through the region awakened considerable alarm among colonial observers, its influence, outside the Khunwana case, was fleeting and scarcely felt beyond the rarefied world of chiefly politics. To weigh the church as a social movement it is necessary to focus within South Africa itself, on areas that had been more thoroughly Christianized and that had borne the full brunt of settler colonialism. And there is no better place to begin than the densely settled reserves of the eastern Cape and Transkei, the heartland of nineteenth-century mission Christianity.[31]

Reconstructing African Methodism's exact range in the region is difficult, due both to the fragmentary nature of the evidence and to the multiplicity of separatist sects in the region. In most of the places we have discussed, the AME Church enjoyed a monopoly on independent Christianity, at least initially. In the eastern Cape and Transkei, on the other hand, it overlapped with three other independent churches, all typically rendered "Ethiopian" in the sources. Among the Mfengu, the largest church was the African Presbyterian Church, founded in 1899 by P. J. Mzimba after a bitter dispute with Free Church of Scotland officials at Lovedale. By the early twentieth century, Mzimba's church claimed more than ten thousand adherents in Victoria East alone; it also surfaced in Transkeian locations with substantial Mfengu populations. Jonas Goduka's African Native Church, a lineal descendent of the original Tile Thembu Church, was also active in the region, particularly in Herschel district. Goduka met Ethiopian Church founder Mangena Mokone during his visit to the eastern Cape in 1894–1895, and the two leaders pulled in harness for a time, but on the ground the two movements remained distinct. The picture was further muddled by the presence of the Order of Ethiopia, established by James Dwane after his secession from the AME Church in 1899, an episode we shall examine in Chapter 7. The Order was largely confined to the Ciskei, where most of Dwane's original followers were based, but it also took over AME congregations in the districts of Willowvale and Xalanga.[32]

Last but not least was the AME Church itself, the most geographically extensive and ethnically diverse of the independent churches in the region. Ethiopianism's initial base of operations was in Middledrift, outside Kingwilliamstown, home of James Dwane and his chiefly patron, Kama. By 1896 it had spread into Queenstown district, an old stronghold of the Wesleyan Methodist Missionary Society. A revival begun in Queenstown in 1897, after the amalgamation with the AME Church, carried the church all across the eastern Cape and Transkei. By the beginning of the twentieth century AME ministers were active in a dozen different districts: in Herschel, Peddie, and Indwe in the Cape; in Xalanga and Cofimvaba in Emigrant Thembuland and Engcobo in Thembuland proper; in Qumbu and Matatiele in East Griqualand; and in all four districts of Eastern Pondoland. At least one Ethiopian preacher of the "American Methodist variety" was reported operating across the Transkeian border in southern Natal.[33]

As in the Transvaal and the Orange Free State, the AME Church entered the region in a period of social and political upheaval—upheaval that, in retrospect, seems almost calculated to propagate Ethiopianism. Mokone's 1894 visit coincided with both the annexation of Pondoland and the passage of Cecil Rhodes's Glen Grey Act. In symbolic terms, the annexation of the last nominally independent chiefdom in South Africa was of greatest moment, but it was Glen Grey that galvanized Africans across the region. The explicit purpose of the act was to hasten the process of proletarianization in the Transkei through the imposition of new taxes and a novel system of primogeniture. (If plots were entailed to eldest sons, Rhodes reasoned, other Africans would have no alternative but to enter the colonial labor market.) At the same time, the Glen Grey Act froze Transkeians out of the broader colonial polity, continuing an alarming trend begun with the franchise restrictions of 1887 and 1892. In a harbinger of the Nationalists' "bantustan" policy, the Act channeled African political participation into local "self-government," embodied in district councils and a Transkeian *Bunga,* both of which were crafted to ensure the dominance of state-appointed headmen. While extended piecemeal and never fully implemented, the Glen Grey Act provided the clearest possible signal that Africans—even Christian, "civilised" Africans—would be barred from full economic and political participation in colonial society.[34]

At the best of times, such initiatives would have sparked resistance, but the 1890s were far from the best of times. All across the region, colonial officials reported severe overcrowding and commented on once-prosperous peasants' inability to find land on which to settle their sons. Often the hardest hit were Christians, who had committed themselves most fully to the market economy and who bore the additional expense of a "progressive" lifestyle. Magistrates reported a burgeoning population of "idle school natives," of "half-educated" young Africans pestering them for jobs as constables—a position that "formerly none but the uneducated native sought." Nature added its characteristic contribution, bringing searing drought, locusts, and, in 1896–1897, rinderpest. Almost as an afterthought, the region was scoured by human diseases, carried back by labor migrants who left the district in ever increasing numbers. Smallpox, influenza, whooping cough, and a virulent strain of measles erupted in dozens of locations, seemingly capriciously, producing "unprecedented heavy mortality," especially among children.[35]

As disaster piled upon disaster, colonial officials reported a profusion of "superstitions" and "imaginary grievances." One ubiquitous rumor held that European traders were selling "poisoned goods" with the aim of exterminating Africans and stealing their land. Another held that rinderpest had been deliberately introduced by whites "with the object of impoverishing the natives to such a degree as would compel them to go to work." (In this instance at least, popular epidemiology had considerable basis in fact: the vaccine used to inoculate cattle was often as deadly as the disease itself.) Such effusions emerged even in districts such as Tsomo and Qumbu, home to the "loyal" Mfengu. One Tsomo magistrate heard district residents denouncing the Glen Grey Act as a plot to steal the land of "their fathers." "The question as to how and from whom they obtained the land they now call that of 'their fathers' does not seem to occur to them," he added, without conscious irony.[36]

What the magistrate might have remarked, but did not, was the way such beliefs crossed the normal social boundaries of nineteenth-century society. Africans of different ethnic groups, chiefs and commoners, Christians and traditionalists, were brought together by desperation and a shared suspicion of all things white. This pervasive disillusionment did not portend an imminent "native uprising," as several magistrates fretted. Nor did it mean that African Christians were renouncing their faiths or, in missionary parlance, "reverting to tribalism." What it did betoken was a broad and quite understandable sense that the reign of missionaries and magistrates had failed to deliver on its promise. Across the social spectrum, Africans yearned, if not for the past, then at least for a different future, where blacks could again exercise a degree of control over their own lives. It is difficult to conceive a more fertile field for African Methodism.

Determining who precisely joined the church is, as always, difficult. As elsewhere, the composition and character of African Methodism varied from district to district, even from location to location. In many districts, the movement enjoyed chiefly patronage, but in others it was arrayed against chiefs, especially those regarded as too subservient to colonial authority. Probably the surest thing one can say is that most who joined the church were Christian already. African Methodism did win some "converts"—one eastern Cape minister counted 114 former "red heathens," including five "witchdoctors," in his district—but in general traditionalists were far outnumbered by defectors from the missions. (In one location in Kingwilliamstown, traditionalists spearheaded opposition to the AME Church, less on principle than out of concern that another building would consume already scarce commonage needed for grazing.) African Methodism appears to have made even less headway among the mission elite—that narrow stratum of teachers, ministers, interpreters, and petty civil servants who managed, through collaboration with whites, to escape the fate befalling their countrymen. A few disgruntled government headmen joined the movement, and the prospect of an American education was enough to entice a few mission workers; ultimately, however, most members of the incorporated elite were too dependent on white patronage to risk affiliation with a separatist church, especially one reputed to be seditious. The conclusion one reaches, almost by elimination, is that African Methodism attracted the mission rank-and-file, the forgotten thousands who had embraced the missionaries' vision of progress and mobility only to see it go aglimmering.[37]

As in the Transvaal and Free State, the AME Church became entangled in a host of local campaigns and struggles. Inevitably, however, the church was drawn toward the land question. No other issue encompassed so many frustrations or lent itself so naturally to treatment in an "Ethiopian" idiom. All across the region, AME ministers declaimed on the subject, portraying Africa as the "divine Portion" of the black man and demanding its return to its "rightful Owners." A minister in the eastern Cape besought God to "deter white people from finding the glistening Gold and silver of the children of Ham." Others were heard to pray, "Grant that our land be not the inheritance of other nations; that it be the inheritance of our children." Several officials detected rumors of invading black armies coming to restore the land to its ancestral owners, rumors eerily reminiscent of the millenarian prophecy that triggered the 1856 Xhosa cattle killing.[38]

The Reverend Elijah Makiwane, a Free Church loyalist and an unusually astute observer of independent churches, underscored these themes in a 1901 report on Ethiopianism, written at the behest of the Cape administration. "It is a fact that those who have urged me to join the movement have based their argument mainly on the consideration that Africa was intended for the Africans and that it is now in the hands of the white men," he wrote. Makiwane noted several biblical texts that Ethiopians adduced to bolster their argument. One of the most common was the tale of Esau and Jacob, in which Esau, "the elder and stronger, the one to whom the first place belonged by birth," was deprived of his inheritance by his more cunning sibling. Another text, which resonated more directly with the experience of a pastoral people, was the tale of the ram and the goat from the book of Daniel. "The ram with two horns is said to represent the Africans who in former days pushed Northward and Southward and became a great people," Makiwane explained. "The he-goat is the European who with his one horn (i.e. union) has been able to destroy or rather cast down the ram and trample upon him." Ethiopianism promised to rectify this injustice by stimulating African unity and self-assertion.[39]

Such arguments were particularly appealing in Eastern Pondoland. On the surface, Pondoland was not the most likely setting for African Methodism. The last annexed of the so-called Transkeian Territories, it was also the most socially intact: the Mpondo were never conquered, while the presence of powerful chiefs had slowed the growth of an accumulating peasantry. Labor migrancy, destined to transform Pondoland in the twentieth century, remained relatively limited. Yet here too the extension of colonial jurisdiction and the incorporation of the region into the wider economy had chipped away at the traditional order. Mpondo chiefs were unusually enterprising in their efforts to defend their position, none more than Mhlangaso, the paramount chief in the 1880s. On the diplomatic front, Mhlangaso attempted to circumvent colonial authority by communicating directly with the imperial government and, in one instance, with Bismarck's Germany. On the economic front, he imposed levies on trade to and from the Cape, while working to promote autonomous economic development within his realm. He attempted to open an industrial school and encouraged a range of local enterprises, including a gunpowder industry. The chief even made a brief foray into independent religion, sponsoring a short-lived Pondoland Methodist Church in the early 1880s, with himself as the head.[40]

Sigcau, who emerged as paramount in the late 1880s, was initially more inclined to cooperate with the colonial authorities, largely because of his rivalry with Mhlangaso. Yet he too struggled to retain some room for maneuver. He remained committed to developing local industries, and granted a series of mining concessions to a British company alleged to have political influence with the imperial government. Such initiatives, however, could not stave off annexation in 1894, a year etched in local memories as marking the end of independence. In the years that followed, Sigcau remained, in the polite lexicon of officialdom, "disaffected." He objected when his mining concessions were abrogated and his power to collect duties on trade nullified. He protested bitterly when the area traditionally administered from the Great Place was balkanized and divided among government-appointed headmen. In 1896 he was implicated in resistance to the new hut tax, leading to his arrest and to a costly legal battle. As a local magistrate put it, Sigcau did not understand that "the Government is now the Paramount Chief."[41]

All these injuries coalesced in Sigcau's mind into one burning grievance. An AME missionary who passed through Pondoland around the turn of the century later recalled an evening spent listening to the embittered chief recount "the true story of how the Pondos lost their freedom." Sigcau's tale began in the early 1890s with the arrival of half a dozen wagons from the Cape, carrying thirty "Europeans garbed as missionaries." Beneath the benign disguise, the men were agents of Cecil Rhodes, sent to provoke a crisis and provide a pretense for annexation. The tale ended with Sigcau emerging from jail, bereft of ninety thousand of his one hundred thousand cattle. As "history," the account had several flaws: the time scale was enormously compressed; the disguised agents, for better or worse, were real missionaries; the cattle loss figure collapsed Sigcau's fines and the ravages of rinderpest. As an account of lived experience, however, the tale was concise and compelling. The chief's embrace of the AME Church must be seen as part of his continuing search for some alternative locus of power outside this colonial prison, outside the world of Rhodes and the missionaries. Like so many of his contemporaries, Sigcau believed that black Americans possessed great wealth and education and all the technological mastery of Europeans. The AME Church thus offered a model of black progress and development outside the colonial context, as well as a new conduit to skills and resources previously monopolized by missions.[42]

The first AME representative to arrive in Pondoland was Samson Mtintso, one of the sixty men ordained by Bishop Turner during his 1898 tour. Judging from surviving correspondence, Mtintso was well educated, probably at Shawbury, a Wesleyan school in Qumbu district. Mpondo himself, he settled at Qaukeni, Sigcau's Great Place, in late 1898, pointedly neglecting to report to the resident magistrate at Lusikisiki. He remained there for the next twenty years, serving as teacher, chaplain, and royal counselor. By all accounts, he was untroubled by Sigcau's continuing attachment to "heathenism," participating in great hunts and beer-drinks and laboring unceasingly to promote the paramountcy. According to the local magistrate, Mtintso also preached self-government and the virtues of making arms from minerals—presumably a reference to the gunpowder industry.[43]

Early in 1900 Mtintso was joined at Qaukeni by Conrad Rideout, an African American attorney and the first in a series of volunteers coming out to work in the AME Church's newest mission field. Like his mentor, Henry Turner, Rideout had held political office during Reconstruction, serving as a justice of the peace and briefly as a member of the Arkansas legislature. He was converted to emigrationism in the wake of southern "Redemption." When Turner put out a call in the *Voice of Missions* for skilled hands for the South African work, the "Judge" and his family hastened to answer. Rideout's first letters home, mailed from Cape Town, were positively rapturous; here at last was a land with "no scullianism." Africans, he reported, were engaged in "all departments of business—thousands of them, comfortably situated, healthy, happy, and contented." All they lacked was a bit of education, which the AME Church was well placed to provide.[44]

Rideout was soon disabused of such ideas and returned to the United States. In his time, however, he cut quite a swath through South Africa, what with his "high silk hat," his Prince Albert coat, and his reliance on elaborate "legal phraseology" to convey even the most pedestrian observations. "He is the first man of this kind in these parts of South Africa," an awed Mangena Mokone reported.

> We never saw a black Judge in our lives, only Judge Rideout. . . . We never saw a black member of Parliament, only Hon. Rideout, who is Hon. C. A. A. Rideout, M.P. Well, well, Heavens above. We are now waiting for M.D., M.A., B.A., L.L.B., B.S.C., V.S. We want a man who will be useful to us here in Africa. . . . one who will fight for the equal rights for the race on the face of the globe. . . .

Rideout was quick to divine Africans' desire for educational facilities, especially of a technical or "industrial" kind. "[T]he different paramount chiefs of large African tribes are begging for our church to come to their different territories and establish schools," he reported to the *Voice of Missions*. One such chief was Sigcau, and Rideout was soon ensconced at Qaukeni. In a series of urgent letters home, he reported that Sigcau had donated a large tract of land for an AME industrial school and urged church leaders to arrange with Booker T. Washington for the immediate posting of a doctor, carpenter, blacksmith, and practical agriculturalist to Pondoland.[45]

Within months, the assistant Chief Magistrate of the Transkei was reporting renewed "signs of restlessness" at Qaukeni. Typically, he reached for the agitator theory, oblivious to what his own narrative implied about the direction of Sigcau's and Rideout's exchange.

> On inquiry, I found that [Sigcau] is under the influence of an Ethiopian Missionary—an American Negro . . . who has succeeded in persuading the Chief, that he does not receive the treatment from Government, which such a very important person as the head of the Pondo nation has a right to expect. That the subsidy he receives, is absurdly small, and should be increased to at least four thousand [pounds] a year, and that much more power should be allowed him, with regard to ruling the Pondos, &c. &c.; and he was led to believe that if he would visit England, the Queen would speedily right matters for him.

Sigcau, the local magistrate added, had already initiated a tribal levy to pay for his trip to Britain. More menacing still, he announced his intention to send his heir, Marelane, to an AME college in the United States for education, a suggestion that produced virtual distemper among colonial officials, who saw "Negro" education as a breeding ground for agitators.[46]

Before any of this could come to pass, Rideout left Pondoland for Basutoland, in response to an invitation from Basotho paramount chief Lerotholi. Like Sigcau, Lerotholi pined for greater control over the political and economic development of his realm, an aspiration reflected on one hand in his quest for a Basotho National Council and on the other by his fascination with "industrial education." Both campaigns were supported by African Methodists, who were active throughout his realm. By the beginning of the twentieth century, the AME Church had more than thirty local preachers active in Basutoland, at least one of whom was a relative of the paramount. Lerotholi welcomed Rideout to Mafeteng and later extended a warm reception to AME Bishop Levi Coppin, who addressed a throng of almost two thousand people at the capital. According to Rideout's letters, the chief pledged a staggering four thousand pounds for construction of an industrial college, to be staffed by African Americans. Like his counterparts in Bechuanaland, however, Lerotholi soon had occasion to reconsider his offer. For all his frustration with the inefficacy of mission education, he enjoyed unusually equable relations with local missionaries, who, as Frenchmen, were less entangled with state authority than Sigcau's Wesleyans. He also was reluctant to do anything to jeopardize the special dispensation his territory enjoyed, especially at a time when many voices were clamoring for the inclusion of the imperial protectorates in the emerging Union of South Africa. Like Ngwato chief Khama before him, he ended up choosing the politic course. When confronted by authorities, he denied any knowledge of the AME Church.[47]

Back in Pondoland, Sigcau waited anxiously for Rideout, who had left without beginning work on the promised school. The judge seems never to have returned; at last report, he was en route to visit chief Khama in Bechuanaland. His seat was soon occupied, however, by another African American, the colorful Harry Dean. A ship's captain by trade, Dean was a black Trader Horn, an adventurer and raconteur who sailed the seven seas on a self-proclaimed quest to found an "Ethiopian Empire." He came by his calling honestly: he was the great-grandson of Paul Cuffe, the pioneer emigrationist who had transported the first group of African American émigrés to Sierra Leone almost a century before. The 1890s found Dean in South Africa, ferrying Mpondo migrants between Port St. Johns, Port Elizabeth, and Cape Town. In Cape Town, he fell in with a group of well-to-do Coloured citizens who were prominent in the local AME Church. He met Bishop Coppin—the two had apparently been acquainted in Philadelphia—and came away from the encounter with an appointment as missionary to Sigcau. Between their mutual interest in promoting black economic self-reliance and their intense hatred of colonialism, Sigcau and Dean became fast friends. During his brief stay, Dean fanned the chief's interest in industrial education, while dabbling in various commercial schemes, including woodcutting (significant at a time when the chief and colonial authorities struggled over control of forests) and gun-running. Dean's most grandiose scheme envisioned the construction of a wagon road to transport produce from Basutoland, Rideout's current base, to Port St. Johns, where it would be loaded onto his ship, enabling blacks to reach colonial markets without recourse to white merchants and middlemen.[48]

Ultimately, the passages of Rideout and Dean through Pondoland produced more spectacle than substance. The industrial college they promoted was chimerical, as was the broader idea that the AME Church would liberate the Mpondo from colonial dependence. The road from Basutoland was never built. Dean drifted back to the Cape and eventually to Kimberley, whence he was deported on what he claimed were trumped-up charges of illicit diamond buying. There was, however, an additional, internal dimension to Sigcau's predicament, and here African Methodism proved somewhat more efficacious. As elsewhere in Africa, colonial authority in the Cape and Transkei hinged on a system of indirect rule in which local magistrates worked closely with "loyal" chiefs and state-appointed location headmen. Often recruited from the missions and subsidized by the state, these individuals were responsible for enforcing hut taxes, labor levies for road building, scab and dipping ordinances, and all the mounting exactions of the colonial state. Inevitably, such offices became points of political contention, and charges of collaboration flew, especially in cases where the state nominee had no prior claim on popular loyalties. It was not uncommon for such conflicts to persist for generations, opening cleavages between rival families and different chiefly factions. African Methodism added an explosive new element to these ongoing struggles.[49]

Sigcau was characteristically quick to appreciate the possibilities. As we have already seen, he bitterly resented the introduction of state headmen into his realm. Headmen exercised powers that he considered chiefly, including the

power to distribute land. They collaborated with missionaries, and undermined his position as the sole intermediary between the people and the administration, historically an important prop to the power of the paramountcy.
Much of postannexation politics in Pondoland centered on Sigcau's campaign
against the headmen. He vainly asserted his right to nominate candidates and
angrily declined the large "location" reserved for him. In one disputed location
in Flagstaff district, he resorted to witchcraft accusations to try to unseat the
state appointee.[50]

African Methodism provided yet another way to hammer the usurpers.
Employing a variant of the paramountcy's timeworn tactic of "placing out"
sons and supporters, Sigcau encouraged the spread of the AME Church into
contested locations, often by dispatching Samson Mtintso. One such place
was Gqubeni, a location in Lusikisiki, traditionally administered by the paramount but placed by the government under a headman named Nzozo. Within
weeks an AME church had risen on the commonage in defiance of both the
headman and the local magistrate. Nzozo faced Hobson's choice. If he acceded
to the church, he risked alienating white patrons, while giving his rival a
platform in the location. To resist, on the other hand, required that he pub-
lically align himself with white authority against the paramount. After considerable hesitation, he elected to resist, charging AME supporters in the magistrate's court with building an unauthorized church. The act loosened his
already tenuous grip on popular loyalties, as Sigcau had doubtless calculated.
To make matters worse, the case was dismissed on a technicality—the magistrate, as presiding judge, was unable to testify that he had not in fact autho-
rized construction of the church—leaving African Methodists free to operate in
the location.[51]

Events in Pondoland illustrate the relationship between the AME Church
and traditional authorities in an unusually graphic way, given both Sigcau's
prominence and his singularly instrumental attitude toward the church. Yet
the processes evident in Pondoland unfolded in less dramatic ways all across the
region. Colonial sources are rife with reports of "Ethiopians" conspiring with
disaffected chiefs, flouting government headmen, driving their cattle through
the crops of mission loyalists, and generally "working against the school
natives." Everywhere, incorporated Africans were derided as *mlungu*—white
men. For state appointees, even for hereditary chiefs who identified too closely
with the state, the situation was fraught with peril. To permit the church to
operate was to underwrite a doctrine that, in its rejection of colonial authority,
implicitly challenged their right to rule. Refusal, on the other hand, exposed
the real sources of the headman's authority and rent the mantle of "traditional'
legitimacy which even government appointees needed to maintain order in
their locations. A magistrate in Butterworth, having followed the spread of
African Methodism in his own district, explained the dilemma succinctly.
"Ethiopians," he wrote, first

go to the Headman and ask his permission [to open a church]; . . . Should the headman refuse his consent or cooperation, as generally happens, the reply is "Ah, you are on the side of the white man, my work lies with my fellow Africans. I will go direct to them without consulting you," and in approaching his fellow Africans the same string is harped upon.

The result in such locations was usually a kind of religious guerrilla warfare, with constant sniping over schools, grazing, water, wood—all the nodes of a headman's authority.[52]

A few individuals managed, through a combination of prevarication and personal adroitness, to mediate the dilemma. Probably the most spectacular example was Enoch Mamba, the Idutywa headman whose career has been traced by Colin Bundy. During one remarkable period early in the century, Mamba managed simultaneously to serve as a government headman, to sponsor an AME school, and to run a profitable business as a labor recruiter, all without a shred of traditional legitimacy. In 1904 Mamba stunned the members of the South African Native Affairs Commission by expressing his support for African Methodism: he had not joined the church, he explained, but he intended to send his children to an AME college in the United States, where they would develop the "republican spirit." A short time later, he sponsored an AME school in his location, staffed by two of the returning graduates from Wilberforce University, in direct competition with the Wesleyan school which he himself had opened a decade before. All the while, Mamba managed to make himself sufficiently indispensable to the local magistrate and to accumulate a substantial enough popular following that the administration could not risk replacing him.[53]

Others were less supple. Bokleni, the paramount chief of Western Pondoland, had impeccable traditional credentials but was too closely associated with colonial authority to risk affiliation with the AME Church. Historically, Mpondomise chiefs had been much more cooperative in their dealings with colonial authority than their Mpondo counterparts, none more than Bokleni. He zealously enforced colonial taxes and dipping ordinances and entrusted the raising of his son and heir to a Wesleyan missionary, an act that naturally endeared him to colonial officials. He thus wanted no part of the AME Church, recognizing that its volatile mix of racial chauvinism and neotraditionalism could all too easily be turned back against him. When an AME congregation surfaced in Libode district, he quietly asked the Cape administration to remove it.[54]

The administration received an identical request from a self-described group of "Chiefs, Headmen and leading men" in Willowvale, in Gcalekaland. Ethiopianism's entry point in the district was Bangcolo location, home of Pearse Magaba, one of the most outspoken of the early AME ministers and later a leader of James Dwane's Order of Ethiopia. Magaba's charisma and his large local following placed him several steps above the location headman, a state appointee who doubled as a Wesleyan local preacher and a detective for the resident magistrate. By the beginning of the century, AME and Order of Ethiopia congregations had sprouted all across Willowvale, eliciting a desperate petition from the district's "leading men." The petitioners begged the administration to "take steps" against "Ethiopianism," in accordance with the "universal wishes of our Ministers, Headmen and people." Obviously, the very existence of the petition belied the final claim, as did the authors' decision to send it anonymously.[55]

Cape officials were sympathetic to such appeals; unfortunately, there was little they could legally do. While the administration could and usually did deny AME applications for church sites, there were no laws to prevent individuals from entering a district or from opening churches in private homes. The administration acquired somewhat greater leverage after 1914, but even then it eschewed the kind of blatantly discriminatory legislation needed to exclude Ethiopians. It is worth noting in passing how important this lack of effective "influx control" was in producing the extraordinarily rich and eclectic political culture of the eastern Cape and Transkeian reserves. Between the limitations of state authority and the sheer scale of migrancy, these ostensibly "remote" and "isolated" reserves were permeated by a dizzying array of political ideas and movements in the first half of the twentieth century. The point, for present purposes, is that state and local officials lacked any means to stem the spread of independent Christianity. In effect, all that Ethiopians needed to enter an area was a sponsor, even in the face of objections from chiefs, headmen, magistrates, and missionaries. Surely the most ironic illustration of the principle came from Kingwilliamstown district, where African Methodists had the temerity to open a church on a Wesleyan mission station. The Wesleyans, it seems, had deeded the land to individuals a generation before, an initiative intended to instill ideas of acquisitiveness and private property. They were thus without any legal recourse when one of the landowners conveyed his plot to the AME Church. African editor and political leader J. T. Jabavu led a group of local Wesleyans in protesting to the administration, but officials were stymied.[56]

Probably the most common pattern was for the AME Church to seep into locations along existing factional lines. In Kamastone location in Queenstown, the church became entangled in a feud between two branches of the Sishuba family, each of which claimed to be the senior line and hence entitled to the headmanship. The claimants favored by the government naturally remained loyal Wesleyans, while their rivals gravitated to African Methodism, supplying the church with two of its most distinguished early ministers. In Lower Izeleni, near Kingwilliamstown, the church's entrance also coincided with a headmanship dispute. Followers of a deceased headman, Pahlana, were enraged when the administration elevated not Pahlana's son but Tonyella, a leader of the incorporated community in the district and, in the local magistrate's words, "an ardent Wesleyan." Sixty families, led by the younger Pahlana, promptly moved into the AME Church, triggering a long-running conflict in the location. The fact that it was a state appointment at stake did not prevent the AME faction from framing its claims in the language of heredity and tradition.[57]

Ultimately, the AME Church seems to have had its most enduring impact in Herschel, a high-lying district wedged into the vertex of the Free State and Basutoland. Herschel had initially been demarcated as the Wittebergen Native Reserve, and its population at the turn of the century was still more than 99 percent black, making it more like a piece of the Transkei than the Cape proper. With an ethnically diverse population, several well-established mission stations, and a dearth of powerful chiefs, Herschel offered fertile ground for the emergence of an accumulating Christian peasantry in the mid-nineteenth century; in the ensuing decades, it provided the most spectacular example of that peasantry's decline. By the end of the century, it was a blighted place—overcrowded, overgrazed, scarred by erosion, extruding an endless stream of migrant workers. This barren economic surface, however, concealed remarkable political vitality. Between its central location and the steady flow of migrants in and out, Herschel played host to a range of political influences, including independent Christianity. By 1905 the AME Church boasted at least a half dozen congregations in the district.[58]

The "headquarters of Ethiopianism" in Herschel, according to a local missionary, was Ndofela, in the northern corner of the district, where the AME Church established a congregation in 1898. The first minister to arrive seems to have been H. R. Ngcayiya. Ngcayiya gathered a large congregation on what had been a Wesleyan outstation and applied to the Cape administration for a church site. He claimed, probably with some exaggeration, that 250 people in the location had joined the AME Church, leaving just three Wesleyan loyalists. The application was endorsed by the local headman and, through an apparent oversight, approved by the Superintendent of Locations. AME adherents proceeded to erect a church on the commonage, on a site designated by the headman, just a few feet from the old Wesleyan chapel. It took six months for Wesleyan missionaries to discover what had happened—proof in itself of how badly the community had been neglected—but when they did they immediately protested to the resident magistrate, who confronted the headman. The headman, choosing the better side of valor, claimed to know nothing about the church, and the magistrate ordered the building torn down. He also allegedly promised to do everything in his power to prevent African Methodists "from putting foot in this District." If this was indeed the magistrate's intention, he failed miserably. In fact, government suppression turned the church into a rallying point for aggrieved Africans. Ngcayiya mustered a protest delegation and submitted a petition condemning the magistrate's action as a violation of Africans' rights as taxpayers. By 1900 attendance at the church had doubled.[59]

African Methodism had an even stormier career in Tugela location, the main Hlubi settlement in Herschel and another Wesleyan stronghold. Even before the arrival of the AME Church, the location was rife with conflict, centered around two lines of the Mehlomakulu family, both descended from the chief who had led the AmaHlubi into the district during the *mfecane*. The colonial administration awarded the headmanship to Joel Mehlomakulu, head of what was allegedly the junior line; the AME Church, predictably, coalesced around the other line, led by Joel's brother, Ngesman, and an ambitious nephew named Makobeni. The immediate point of contention, according to a local missionary, was an AME school that Makobeni had opened in direct competition with the Wesleyan school patronized by Joel. By portraying the Wesleyan school as a white man's school, Makobeni hoped to siphon off enough students to deprive it of its government grant, which depended on maintaining a certain minimum enrollment. Those in the location who wished to educate their children would thus have no alternative but to acknowledge Makobeni's line. How realistic the scenario was is unclear, but Joel was sufficiently unnerved to send a string of letters to the Cape administration, accusing the "Ethiopians" of "stirring up family strife" and "working against me."[60]

By 1910 the AME congregation at Tugela had swelled to more than two hundred, and the headmanship dispute showed no signs of abating. Joel Mehlomakulu continued to rail against outsiders and "new Comers" and denied a newly arrived AME minister a plot in the location; his brother responded by taking the minister into his own home. As we shall see in a later chapter, the dispute was passed intact to the next generation, acquiring new political dimensions along the way. By the mid-1920s, African Methodists in Herschel stood at the center of a broad popular movement opposing land registration and demanding Makobeni Mehlomakulu's recognition as a full Hlubi chief. The seemingly endless conflicts evoked a nostalgic reverie from the local Wesleyan superintendent. "Until the Ethiopian movement started at Ndofela years ago, there was peace and contentment amongst the people," he recalled. "Since then there has been strife and confusion, division and quarreling, which continue until today."[61]

As in most flights of nostalgia, the sentiment was both appealing and somewhat at odds with the facts. Obviously, the coming of the AME Church intensified "conflict" in many places, a few of which may indeed have been harmonious prior to its arrival. In most cases, however, Ethiopianism was as much the consequence of "division and quarrelling" as its cause. Chiefs like Sigcau and Makobeni Mehlomakulu did not fall "under the influence" of Ethiopianism; they sought the movement out, shaping it to their own concerns and needs. Everywhere, the AME Church spread along existing lines of cleavage, especially cleavages opened by the process of colonial incorporation. In this respect, the church's explosive growth in reserves across southern Africa offers the most compelling index imaginable of African distress.

This is not to suggest that the AME Church was politically insignificant, some kind of institutional cipher overlaying preexisting grievances. In providing a vehicle for African discontent, the church also transformed it, focusing and channeling disparate beliefs and aspirations, investing local struggles with new layers of ideological and political significance. At the institutional level, the church served as a network, connecting local communities to one another and to the broader struggles of black people across the world. At the imaginative or symbolic level, it contributed a range of new concepts and contexts, enabling generations of black South Africans to comprehend and act upon their world in new ways. The fact that the church so rarely equaled the immediate expectations it unleashed in no way obviates the significance of that contribution.

Conclusion

There is an old folktale in which a group of blind men are positioned around an elephant and asked to determine what it is. Not surprisingly, they report very different conclusions. The South African AME Church presents a similar problem: a single institution, whose specific shape and texture depend very much on where one is standing. Forged in the crucible of South Africa's industrial revolution, African Methodism found a home on highveld farms, in fetid wartime refugee camps, and in reserves across the breadth of the subcontinent. In one context, it appeared as a movement of urban dwellers, struggling to carve out a permanent niche for themselves in the city; in another, as a church of sharecroppers, doggedly clinging to the land; in still others, as a movement of disaffected chiefs, defending their authority against an encroaching colonial state. Examining additional contexts would doubtless reveal still more variety. To grasp this fact is, to paraphrase a standard AME catechism, to grasp the "genius" of African Methodism. Erected on strong intellectual and institutional foundations, the AME Church was nonetheless sufficiently decentralized and flexible to adapt to diverse local circumstances and to accommodate a range of different meanings and interpretations.

In exploring this diversity, however, several generalizations emerge—generalizations that take us back to the questions with which this elephantine discussion began, two chapters ago. For all its neotraditional overtones, African Methodism was primarily a movement of Christians. While precise statistics are unavailable, it seems likely that 80 or 90 percent of the church's early adherents entered not as "converts from heathenism" but as accessions from other denominations. Adherents tended to come en masse—like "locusts," in Jacobus Xaba's memorable Old Testament image. Entire communities followed the lead of African ministers and local preachers, a pattern that attests yet again to the centrality of black mission workers in the dissemination of Christianity in Africa. While the Wesleyans were hardest hit by Ethiopianism, all the major European societies—the Anglicans, the London Missionary Society, the Free Church of Scotland, the Paris Evangelical Mission, the Berlin Mission Society, the American Board, and the Dutch Reformed Church—experienced defections.

While there was no specific "recipe" for Ethiopianism, secessions tended to coincide with periods of social and economic crisis. Everywhere, African Methodism's coming was heralded by drought, depression, and disease, as well as by an intensifying political assault on Africans' autonomy and small measure of prosperity. The church's spread was further facilitated by the upheaval of the South African War and by the uncertainties of postwar reconstruction, with its legacy of inflated hopes and crushed aspirations. In a world of turmoil and disillusionment, African Methodism, and the broader black American connection it embodied, offered aggrieved Africans hope, dignity, and a renewed sense of possibility.

That African disillusionment broke first over the heads of missionaries was perhaps unfair but it is not, in retrospect, surprising. Missionaries, after all, were the avatars of the colonial order. It was they who had instilled the expectations of "progress" and individual mobility that were so cruelly dashed in the decades after the mineral discoveries. Missionaries also engaged in practices that struck their more literal-minded converts as distinctly un-Christian. Probably the most frequent charge was neglect. Between their aversion to cities, their unwillingness to travel, and their growing reluctance to invest religious authority in Africans, European mission societies effectively abandoned tens of thousands of their adherents in the late nineteenth century. Itinerating African Methodists were constantly shocked to find Christian communities that had gone years without pastoral visits or benefit of the sacraments. People thus treated needed little prodding to join the AME connection. At the other end of the spectrum were Africans who saw all too much of missionaries and felt the sting of racial disdain. Sources from the period are full of tales of missionary arbitrariness—of white superintendents zealously enforcing "discipline," declining to baptize candidates brought forward by African mission workers, and otherwise acting in ways that called into question their evangelical commitment.

Inevitably, missionaries justified such restrictiveness in terms of "standards," but the very frequency with which they invoked the term suggests that something more was at work. As new, more pessimistic racial ideologies seeped into the mission world, many missionaries came to doubt whether Africans could ever truly be "converted." Africans, they complained, lacked the "initiative" to see through "the reconstruction of their social and tribal habits"; while "inclined to delight in the consolations of the Christian faith," they had yet to appreciate the "tremendous importance of its moral demands." Many missionaries became so concerned with defending standards that they seem almost to have taken pride in their dearth of converts.[62]

One does not need to resuscitate the old saw about "natives" and "standards" to acknowledge that the AME Church was a very different kind of institution. Religious independence unleashed extraordinary evangelical energy, all the more potent for having been so long bottled up within white missions. Convinced that their church was the instrument of Africa's long-prophesied redemption, AME leaders set out to collect all Africans under the church's banner. While European missionaries confined their energies to established fields, men such as Jacobus Xaba, Henry Ngcayiya, and Marcus Gabashane itinerated with gusto, heralding the coming of African Methodism at every village and farm. At a time when white societies were reluctant to allow Africans to operate without European supervision, the AME Church invested authority in scores of black ministers and an army of unordained local preachers—more than two hundred in the Orange Free State alone. While missionaries routinely subjected would-be converts to searching examinations, African Methodists generally accepted members on a profession of faith, trusting the seed of the Word to do the rest. In short, Africans across a broad social spectrum found in the AME Church an acceptance and an inclusivity they no longer found in white missions, if indeed they ever had. Ironically, it was one of the church's most implacable foes, Lovedale principal James Stewart, who put the point best. Ethiopianism's errors were all the more "regrettable," he observed in 1902,

> since there can be no question as to the high missionary qualities of the men connected with this Society. Their genuine religious warmth, their directness of effort, their gentleness and patience with their converts and adherents, are known to all who have come into contact with them.

Such a concession, coming from one of African Methodism's chief critics, provides a compelling testament to the church's character and appeal.[63]

All this helps explain the AME Church's great initial success in South Africa, as well as its breathtaking social diversity. Ultimately, however, such explanations take us only so far. While they help explain why the church became an outlet for antimission sentiment, they cannot explain the enthusiasm it unleashed, the extraordinary avidity with which Africans across southern Africa rallied to its banner. Clearly, there was something more, something intrinsic to African Methodism's message, that struck a chord with Africans. What was it?

The question admits no single answer, because African Methodism conveyed no single message. At the most basic level, the church embodied the idea of independence, or "freedom"—the vision, in the words of one AME leader, of "black men controlling their own affairs independently of white tutelage." The immediate points of contention were usually churches and schools, the terrain occupied by European missions. Freedom and independence, however, are promiscuous ideas, particularly in a place like turn-of-the-century South

Africa, where blacks found themselves ever more circumscribed by white authority. In such a context, "Ethiopianism" became an idiom for articulating a range of different aspirations and grievances. Not surprisingly, some adherents pushed the logic of the movement in the direction of inclusion, arguing that Africans, as coequal children of God, were entitled not only to run their own churches but to move without pass restrictions, to hold title to land in their own persons, to enjoy all the rights and immunities of citizens. Others pushed in precisely the opposite direction, hailing independent churches as the first step toward racial separation, even a restoration of the precolonial order. Many African Methodists pushed in both directions simultaneously, arguing at once for autonomy and for blacks' right to share in South Africa's bounty.[64]

The movement's association with black America, far from promoting unity of interpretation, exploded the imaginative possibilities. Just as Africa functioned as a kind of metaphor in African American life, conjuring up a range of ideas and images, so did black America evoke different meanings among Africans—meanings that were often unfettered by any actual contact with African American realities. America was the place where blacks had attained their "freedom," a place where black people became judges, bishops, doctors, and "members of Parliament." How all this had come to pass, and precisely what lessons Africans might draw from it, would remain subjects of considerable debate. African American progress was variously ascribed to unity, education, defiance, cooperation, political assertion, and political submission. What united all the different interpretations was their positive tone. The less pleasant aspects of African American experience—Jim Crow, disfranchisement, the horror of lynch law, all peaking at precisely the moment the AME Church entered South Africa—rarely entered African accounts. America remained an enchanted place, the stuff that dreams were made of.

Amid all the competing images and interpretations, two themes surface again and again. The first is education. Even as they rejected mission governance, African Christians retained many missionary assumptions, especially about the relationship between education and racial progress. Indeed, much of the popular resentment against European missions stemmed from the perceived inefficacy of their schools. Missionaries were accused of artificially limiting African educational preferment, of relying too heavily on vernacular languages, of dispensing pablum rather than the knowledge and skills that blacks needed to survive in the emerging colonial order. Black Americans, renowned in South Africa for their educational attainments, offered an alternative source of this vital resource. Precisely what education Africans hoped to acquire, as always, varied. While some envisaged universities where their children could train as doctors and lawyers, others coveted "Negro"-style industrial schools to help Africans reassert control over their own economic lives. Yet whatever the different visions, the equation of African Methodism and education was well-nigh universal.

As fundamental as education was to the church's appeal, it was the land question that gave African Methodism its sharp political edge. In a country like South Africa, with its long history of migrations, wars of conquest, dispossession, and forced relocation, there is a sense in which all politics reduces to competing claims to the land. Certainly this was the case in the late nineteenth century, a period that saw not only the completion of colonial conquest but the opening of the diamond and goldfields, the imposition of the Glen Grey Act in the Transkei, and a steady ratcheting up of taxes and antisquatting legislation, with the explicit goal of loosing Africans from the land. The century ended in the last great imperial war, a war that spawned rumors of confiscation and redistribution, just as the American Civil War had done four decades before. The whole period was alive with agitation over land.[65]

African Methodism played an important part in the popular ferment. Insofar as the church embodied a rejection of European control, it inevitably highlighted control of the land, which stood as both emblem and substance of white domination. The land question also easily lent itself to treatment in a religious idiom: the Old Testament, after all, is a story of a people dispossessed, struggling to regain their birthright. With the arrival of African Americans on the scene, the whole issue acquired an immediacy and concreteness it had never before possessed. Here were modern-day Israelites, returned from captivity, coming to reclaim the land of their ancestors. Anxious colonial officials across the breadth of the subcontinent detected millenarian rumors, often explicitly linking independent Christianity with a restoration of the land. Significantly, even these rumors were locally specific, betraying again that conceptual elasticity that was Ethiopianism's hallmark. Thus, in Oudtshoorn, a Cape district with a predominantly Coloured population, the heralded black king was transmogrified from a descendent of Solomon and Sheba into Hendrik Witbooi, the Nama guerrilla leader battling the Germans in Southwest Africa. According to one version of the story, Witbooi would sweep into South Africa at the head of a great army, accompanied by "three black Bishops."[66]

Finally, and perhaps most important, African Methodism was distinguished by a certain tone, a militant, distinctly racial temper that characterized the church in all its different incarnations. The word that recurs in each of the cases examined here is *populist*. Everywhere the AME Church went, it engendered a strong conception of shared oppression, a belief that blacks constituted a people whose rights and interests were being traduced by a powerful white world. This populist vision could, of course, be taken in different directions, but it was always present: in Sigcau's dreams of autonomous economic development; in Edward Tsewu's insistence on addressing white officials directly, by their names, rather than through the medium of interpreters; in that extraordinary act of passive resistance mounted by African Methodists in tiny Bethulie, in the Free State. Everywhere, Africans who declined to join the movement were derided as traitors, quislings, and "white men."

While nationalist in the most literal sense of the term, this potent racial populism was a far cry from what historians conventionally think of as "African nationalism," that patient, self-consciously respectable protest tradition embodied by the South African Native National Congress. If one is looking to trace descendance, a more promising place to begin is with the militant Industrial and Commercial Workers' Union, which swept across South Africa in the decade after World War I. As in the AME Church, the combination of inadequate resources and state harassment produced within the I.C.U. a proliferation of highly localized branches with only tenuous links to national headquarters. This practical decentralization, in turn, enabled the Union, like African Methodism before it, to span town and countryside, to speak simultaneously to urban workers, embattled sharecroppers, and Africans in the reserves. Finally, the I.C.U., like the AME Church before it, broadcast an extraordinarily eclectic message, blending racial chauvinism and assertions of Christian brotherhood, calls for separation and demands for equal rights, paeans to "progress" and appeals to the ancestral land, all frequently underscored with the authority of African American experience.[67]

Yet therein lay a difference. While I.C.U. leaders had the luxury of invoking black America as a kind of free-floating signifier, African Methodists had also to contend with African Americans of the flesh-and-blood variety. In 1901 the AME Church in the United States dispatched an African American, Levi J. Coppin, to serve as resident bishop of South Africa. Coppin's efforts were seconded by a small handful of African American missionaries and, later, by a stratum of Africans returning from AME colleges in the United States. These people came to South Africa—or, in the case of the students, returned to it—with their own vision of African Methodism and their own ideas about the relationship of African to African American experience. The resulting collisions would fundamentally transform the character of the South African AME Church.

BOOK THREE

By the rivers of Babylon, there we sat down, yea, we wept, when we remembered Zion.

We hanged our harps upon the willows in the midst thereof.

For there they that carried us away captive required of us a song; and they that wasted us required of us mirth, saying, Sing us one of the songs of Zion.

How shall we sing the LORD's song in a strange land?

If I forget thee, O Jerusalem, let my right hand forget her cunning.

If I do not remember thee, let my tongue cleave to the roof of my mouth; if I prefer not Jerusalem above my chief joy.

Remember, O LORD, the children of Edom in the day of Jerusalem; who said, Rase it, rase it, even to the foundation thereof.

O daughter of Babylon, who art to be destroyed; happy shall he be, that rewardeth thee as thou hast served us.

Happy shall he be, that taketh and dasheth thy little ones against the stones.

PSALM 137

7

The Making of a Religious Institution

Reading contemporary colonial descriptions of African Methodism, one imagines swarms of "Negro" agitators—"alien demagogues of colour"—"stumping the country," spreading their "hatred of the white man" throughout the furthest reaches of the subcontinent, poisoning "the good relations which have hitherto existed between Europeans and Natives." In fact, African Americans were few and far between in the South African AME Church. Aside from Bishop Turner's six-week visit in 1898, the church spent its formative years with no direct supervision from the United States. While the church drew much of its energy and meaning from its association with black America, it remained a distinctly "Ethiopian" movement.[1]

That situation began to change in the early years of the twentieth century. In 1901 an African American Bishop, Levi J. Coppin, arrived in Cape Town to assume control of the newly designated Fourteenth Episcopal District of the AME Church. He was followed by a handful of African American ministers and teachers, as well as by the first returning South African graduates of Wilberforce University. Initially, the influence of this "American Colony"—the characterization was Coppin's—was more or less confined to the Cape, thanks to the war in the interior and to postwar restrictions on travel. Gradually, however, American church leaders asserted their authority, gathering the burgeoning Ethiopian movement into the institutional confines of African Methodism. In so doing, they touched off a series of bitter disputes and schisms that ultimately carried thousands of disillusioned Africans out of the AME Church.

The chapter that follows examines these processes through a close study of the careers of the first African American missionaries in South Africa. Chronologically, the chapter covers much the same period as the previous two chapters, and it is in some ways intended as a counterpoint to them. In simplest terms, it seeks to show how the diverse and dynamic popular movement we

have been discussing evolved into an established institution, an institution
that, by the early 1920s, was widely hailed as the most "stable" and "respectable" of South Africa's independent churches.

From the outset, the South African AME Church rested on a series of unresolved questions. African American church leaders, for example, took it for
granted that they had been called to "redeem" Africa, but what precisely did
that mean? What was the nature of their kinship with Africans? How would
authority be parsed in the new church? Would the Ethiopians continue to
oversee their own affairs, or would they now be subject to American governance? Such questions brooked no easy answers. For all their talk of racial
affinity and providential reunion, most African Americans continued to think
of Africans as "benighted" and "backward"; given the information about
Africa they had at their disposal, it would be astonishing had they not. The
very concept of mission work presumed the need for external stimulus, for
some outside agency to "emancipate" Africans from the "bondage" of "heathenism." American church leaders sympathized with the Ethiopians' rejection
of European missionary tutelage, and they were impressed with James Dwane
when he visited the United States in 1896. At the same time, however, they
were acutely aware that leaders like Dwane were only a few decades removed
from heathenism themselves. Indeed, this was part of Dwane's cachet: as the
Voice of Missions put it, he had "never lost touch with kaffir sympathies." Such
men would require a thorough apprenticeship before being entrusted with full
ecclesiastical authority.[2]
South Africans were equally ambivalent about their relationship to black
America. Most accepted the stereotype of the wealthy, cultured black American and keenly felt their own relative backwardness. "Behold the truth was
never told," Jacobus Xaba wrote in an early letter to the *Voice of Missions*. "We
never dreamed that [African Americans] recognized us as their fellow country
people originally, they having succumbed in the privileges of education,
Christianity and civilisation, and we, still under the kingdom of ignorance
and heathenism." Others conveyed the perceived gulf in generational terms:
J. Z. Tantsi, fast approaching fifty, addressed Bishop Turner in his letters as
"Venerable Father" and signed himself "Your dutiful son." Other correspondents characterized themselves as "children," a "set of little boys" at the
bishop's feet. Mangena Mokone invoked a similar image in a letter sketching
African Methodism's boundless prospects: "[T]he AME Church will be the
father and mother of the whole of Africa." Beneath such self-deprecating
imagery, however, was an iron belief in African capacity, which had been
forged and tested in the long battle with European missionaries. "I am sure we
are not inferior to anyone—only ignorant," Mokone observed in the same
letter. The early Ethiopians knew what it was to be patronized, and they were
unlikely long to abide it.[3]

Similar uncertainties surrounded the question of church finance. Given their ideas about African American wealth and progress, Africans expected affiliation with the AME Church to unleash a rain of resources—money for churches and schools and trained teachers and artisans to staff the promised South African college. Most African American church leaders, on the other hand, recognized their limited resources and remained wary of exhausting them in Africa. The problem manifested itself as early as 1898, in the wake of Bishop Turner's visit. Aware of his colleagues' skepticism, Turner portrayed the South Africans as mature, virtually self-sufficient churchmen who asked only for some temporary help on the educational front. "Not one man asked for a penny," he declared in his report. He even went so far as to suggest that Africans would one day support the AME Church in America, a claim he bolstered with descriptions of South Africa's vast mineral wealth and Africans' distinctly promising phrenology. At the very same time, however, Turner fueled African expectations with several ill-considered financial pledges. He promised Mangena Mokone one thousand dollars to erect a new church in Cape Town. He also assured James Dwane that the ten thousand dollars appropriated for the South African college would be forthcoming as soon as returns from the annual Easter Day mission collection had been counted. Africans naturally took such promises at face value, laying the seeds of future disillusionment. (They might have been alerted to the real state of affairs when Turner was forced to borrow money to pay train fare.)[4]

Disillusionment was not long in appearing. The 1898 Easter Day collection, conducted while Turner was away, netted scarcely ten thousand dollars total, a third of which was reserved by law for home missions. Several ministers, uncomfortable with developments in the African field, contributed no money at all. Given other pressing commitments, Secretary of Missions H. B. Parks had no choice but to defer any investment in South Africa. In the wake of Park's announcement, a clearly anxious J. Z. Tantsi wrote a long letter to AME Bishop Abraham Grant, ostensibly a friend of the South African mission, stressing the importance of the college. "Except the African Methodist Episcopal Church take the whole matter of education on herself our work will not be successful," he wrote. In reply, he received a pledge of five pounds and a homily on self-help. Remember, Grant wrote, "no race or people can become great who do not depend on their own resources."[5]

Hard on the heels of that letter came another, this one from Bishop Wesley Gaines, an ardent booster of the New South and a long-time Turner nemesis. Gaines naturally took a dim view of the African interest, which he believed diverted blacks from the expanding opportunities awaiting them at home. Turner's irregular promotion of James Dwane to the office of "vicar bishop" gave Gaines just the weapon he needed. In a letter to the *Christian Recorder,* published in December, 1898, he denounced Dwane's appointment as *ultra vires* and ill-conceived and demanded a full debate at the 1900 General Conference. To make matters worse, the letter somehow came to the attention of Cape officials, who were already casting about for ways to rein in the independent church movement. In early 1899 the Cape administration announced that it would neither entertain AME applications for church and school sites on Crown land, nor recognize marriages conducted by AME ministers, pending clarification of the church's status. In a society where marriage by Christian rites represented a central marker of legal and social identity, this last prohibition dealt an especially severe blow to the church's legitimacy.[6]

In a desperate attempt to regain the mission's momentum, Bishop Turner invited Dwane back to the United States. The visit, timed to coincide with the round of AME annual conferences, would provide a practical apprenticeship in episcopal administration, answering at least one of Gaines's objections. At the same time, the tour offered Dwane and Turner an opportunity to stump for the South African college prior to the 1899 Easter Day collection. As in 1896, Dwane spent several months in the United States, visiting conferences and addressing audiences across the South. In a meeting with the assembled House of Bishops, he sketched an ambitious plan to build a chain of missions along the proposed Cape-to-Cairo railroad, to be staffed by graduates of the AME college. He also mentioned plans to send missionaries to Abyssinia, the historical cradle of Ethiopianism. By all accounts the bishops were impressed with the presentation, but in the end they deferred any decision on Dwane's status until the upcoming General Conference. On top of it all, the 1899 Easter Day collection proved disastrous. Despite energetic promotion by the *Voice of Missions,* which portrayed the South African college as all that stood between Africans and a spiral of "drink and death," the collection netted just a third of its projected thirty thousand dollars. Once again, the college was put on hold.[7]

A bitter Dwane returned to South Africa in mid-1899. A few months later he and three dozen ministers of the Cape Annual Conference convened at Queenstown and voted to sever their ties with the AME Church. About half the seceders were deacons, ordained by Dwane in his capacity as vicar bishop, but several, including Ethiopian Church founder Mangena Mokone, were established church leaders. To the consternation of church leaders in America, only four ministers at the meeting voted to remain African Methodists. More bewildering still, the seceders voted to affiliate themselves with the Anglican Church of the Province of South Africa, where they were to be gathered into a self-governing "Order of Ethiopia," with Dwane as their bishop. The only cheering news was the confinement of the rebellion to the Cape, due to the nearly simultaneous outbreak of the South African War. Nonetheless, the incident represented a devastating setback. Overnight, the AME Church lost a quarter of its South African ministry and several thousand of its adherents.[8]

European observers responded to the Ethiopians' return to the mission fold with predictable derision. "No one who has watched the erratic development of the Ethiopian Church movement could take these people seriously," opined Dudley Kidd, South Africa's leading expert on "native" psychology. "A ship will run into any port in a storm, and it is probably a good thing that these unstable people are now under the strong control of rigid ecclesiastical authorities." Missionaries fastened, inevitably, on the issue of ambition, portraying Dwane as "restless" and prepared to do anything to ensure his elevation to the episcopacy. Stung by such allegations, Dwane did his best to portray the schism in doctrinal terms. He described himself as much vexed to discover, while perusing an AME catechism during his second visit to America, that the church rejected the doctrine of apostolic succession. After further research, he concluded that the "catholic" church alone possessed valid orders and immediately began negotiating with the Anglicans. Alas, this explanation is no more plausible than the one it was intended to rebut. The AME Church made no secret of its position on apostolic succession. The circumstances of Bishop Allen's original investiture were discussed in the "historical introduction to the AME *Discipline,* which Dwane had presumably read; the question was also frequently debated in church periodicals. Had he been so concerned with the issue, he would never have joined the AME Church.[9]

Ultimately, the secession of 1899 had less to do with apostolic succession or personal ambition than with Africans' growing disenchantment with the AME Church. From the first exchange of letters in 1895, South Africans had received an endless chain of promises from America, few of which had been honored. At the same time, affiliation with a black American church, far from conferring legitimacy on the movement, had fueled white suspicions, leading to the current ban in the Cape. In such circumstances, African church leaders had little incentive to retain their American affiliation and considerable reason to jettison it, especially if they hoped to participate in imperialism's march into the interior. In Dwane's own case, disillusionment went still deeper. During his second U.S. visit, he began to detect troubling undercurrents beneath the smooth surface of African American unity and progress. "I found amongst the coloured themselves that the darker ones were looked down upon by the lighter-coloured ones," he testified to the South African Native Affairs Commission; "this was carried to such an extent, that in appointing a minister, it became a very difficult matter. The lighter ones would not have a very dark man. . . ." He began to doubt the wisdom of introducing African American missionaries and teachers into South Africa, lest they infect Africans with this disdain for blackness. In America, he concluded, "they are doing all they can to get white."[10]

While less explicit on the issue, Dwane also feared that exposure to black America would estrange Africans from their culture. He questioned, for example, the church's policy of sending young Africans to U.S. colleges for missionary training. When students "come back here after having been to America they feel at a loss," he explained. "They won't care for their home. They will be

above their people. I do not believe in taking a young man away from his
country, and teaching him different ways and customs." In part, this position
reflected the residual respect that Dwane, the son of a tribal counselor, maintained for African tradition. More important, however, it reflected his growing
conviction that Africans "filled with Western ideals and aspirations" were
useless in his grand plan for redeeming the continent. "The people to whom
[our missionaries] are to be sent are heathens," he explained in a 1901 letter to
an Anglican bishop. "[U]nless they can feel that their teachers are bone of their
bones & flesh of their flesh who are in thoroughly sympathy [*sic*] with them &
eat the food they eat & are satisfied with accommodation given them our
Mission as an Ethiopian Society will not accomplish much. We do not want to
Europeanize our men. . . ." In a later letter, Dwane wrote poignantly of his
own education, which had alienated him from the people he wanted so desperately to save. African Americans, by extension, were even more ill suited for
mission work. In effect, Dwane inverted the whole ideology of African American missions: far from a providential preparation, the culture and "civilization"
that black Americans had acquired in the "hard school" of slavery disqualified
them for the task of African redemption.[11]

The irony, of course, is that Dwane's fear of "Europeanizing" Africans did
not prevent him from leading his followers into a European church. If the
object was to forge a united African church, why truck with Anglicanism? The
best one can say is that Dwane saw the Church of the Province as a flag of
convenience. Affiliation would remove the onus of government suspicion in
South Africa and in the other colonial territories the Ethiopians hoped to enter.
The C.P.S.A. was also far wealthier than the AME Church, and its leaders
were quick to promise money for an African "theological college," the linchpin
of Dwane's evangelical vision. In return, the Anglicans appeared to ask little.
They assured the Ethiopians that they could maintain their "corporate character" and exercise virtual autonomy in church matters. Members of the Order
would be subject not to parish priests but to their own leaders, including
Bishop Dwane. In short, the Order of Ethiopia, while linked with Anglicanism at the episcopacy, promised to be a genuinely African church in a way
that the AME Church was not.[12]

The travails of the Order would make a chapter in themselves. While
initially solicitous, Anglican authorities had no intention of granting Dwane
and his followers autonomy. The constitution of the Order of Ethiopia, published by the C.P.S.A. Council of Bishops after nearly a year's delay, was a
model of missionary restrictiveness. Europeans assumed title to all Ethiopian
properties and controlled all decisions on membership and discipline. Adherents of the Order were to be subjected to intense individual examinations by
white priests before being accepted for confirmation. (Of the first seven hundred candidates offered by Dwane, just fifty-three were confirmed.) All AME
ordinations were voided. After four months of intensive theological training,

Dwane, the erstwhile bishop, was made a deacon. A few of his colleagues were installed as provisional catechists, an office with no sacerdotal responsibilities. The rest were stripped of all office. The "theological college" that the Anglicans opened was little more than a charade. On the rare occasions it was open, ministerial candidates spent more time toiling in fields and brickyards than studying theology. After a decade, the Order still possessed no priest of its own, forcing adherents to eschew the sacraments or to accept them from white hands. Needless to say, Dwane was not elevated to the bishopric, nor was any other African for the next sixty years. [13]

In the wake of Dwane's secession, chaos reigned in the South African AME Church. The fact that the church survived at all was a testament to the energy of a small group of loyalists in the Cape who labored tirelessly to check the spread of the rebellion. Led by J. Z. Tantsi and Francis Gow, a Coloured lay preacher from Cape Town, the loyalists instituted legal proceedings to regain properties claimed by the seceders and began the task of rebuilding shattered circuits. They also rallied their ministerial colleagues in the interior, a task made more difficult by the problems of wartime communication but eased by the resentment that many of the original Ethiopians had always entertained toward Dwane. Between loyalist lobbying and Anglican authoritarianism, seceders began to drift back to the AME Church. Dwane himself chafed against his European supervisors and was for a time suspended, but ultimately he remained within the Anglican fold. Not so Mangena Mokone, who wrote a contrite letter to Bishop Turner asking him "to forgive and forget and treat me as before." "I feel very small about these things," he confessed in a later letter. "I don't feel so brave as before." [14]

AME loyalists sent a flurry of cables to Turner in the months after the secession, begging him to return to South Africa to help bolster the church's flagging credibility. With the General Conference imminent, Turner declined, sending in his stead I. N. Fitzpatrick, an AME pastor from Arkansas and one of the candidates he was touting in the upcoming episcopal elections. Fitzpatrick arrived in Cape Town in early 1900 and immediately wired the *Voice of Missions:* "Money in urgent demand; people rejoicing. They thank God I came." For the next two months, he traveled the Cape, denouncing the "arch-fiend" Dwane, reassuring Africans of African American support, and negotiating with colonial officials for removal of the embarrassing marriage ban. Turner gave his movements full play in the *Voice of Missions.* [15]

Shortly before returning to the United States, Fitzpatrick convened the reconstituted South African Annual Conference and delivered an "eloquent and timely address," the text of which was reprinted in the *Voice of Missions.* No other speech or sermon so admirably captured nineteenth-century African American mission ideology or better exposed the layers of misapprehension and self-reference that underlay the AME Church's outreach to Africa. Like so many of his intellectual mentors, Fitzpatrick began by rehearsing the continent's glorious—and incipiently Christian—history. It was Africans, he declared, "who taught proud Rome her alphabet," who "gave to the world art, science, literature and mechanism," who "sheltered the infant babe of Bethlehem" and "furnished the world with the first Christian Queen," Candace of Ethiopia. In his next breath, however, he offered up a prayer for the benighted continent's "complete emancipation from error and sin." More jarring still, Fitzpatrick continued to spin tales of African American wealth and power, apparently unaware that it was precisely these exaggerated notions that had precipitated Dwane's revolt. Tracing the providential plan that had carried black Americans into and out of slavery, he announced:

> God sends us back to you, not in chains of iron and steel but chains of gold, bracelets set with pearls and diamonds; not nude but clothed in cashmeres, broadcloth, linens of India and France, with Bibles and banking houses, colleges and seminaries, publishing houses, doctors and lawyers, judges, statesmen and soldiers, preachers and teachers, with property approximating half a billion dollars, besides school and church properties with a large banking account.

"Are you glad to see us, my brethren?" he concluded. [16]

Thus the South African AME Church weathered its first crisis. By the end of 1900 the church had recovered the bulk of its membership and property and at least some of its equilibrium. Most of its fundamental problems, however, remained unresolved. Fitzpatrick's memorable address did little to clarify the issue of ecclesiastical governance, now posed more sharply by Dwane's departure. His description of colleges and cashmere obviously did nothing to reduce Africans' inflated ideas about black American prosperity. The South African college remained a bone of contention. All these issues would resurface in the years to come.

In retrospect, the real significance of Fitzpatrick's visit lay somewhere else entirely. The fifteen months between Bishop Gaines's letter and Fitzpatrick's arrival witnessed a subtle but decisive shift in state policy toward the AME Church and the transatlantic connection it embodied. First in the Cape and then in other colonial capitals, white officials began to entertain the notion that African Methodism, properly conceived and administered, might be no menace but rather a useful channel for containing African aspirations. To appreciate this transformation, it is necessary to focus directly on an issue that has already surfaced several times in our narrative: the making of colonial policy toward African independent churches.

We have already had occasion to observe colonial officials' attitudes toward African Methodism. In the Transvaal and the Orange Free State, for example, we saw the Boer governments' generally laissez-faire approach—"Let the kaffirs preach to the kaffirs," in President Paul Kruger's pungent phrase—give way to the bureaucratic obstructionism of the reconstruction administration. While reluctant to legislate directly against African Methodism, imperial officials invented no end of devices to impede its progress. AME ministers were denied the pass exemptions available to African ministers in mission churches, allegedly because of their lower educational qualifications. Similar pretenses were found to withhold school grants, rights of marriage, access to church sites, even the right to purchase sacramental wine. When these devices failed, administrators condoned all manner of local discriminatory ordinances, ostensibly in deference to "municipal prerogatives." Perhaps most important, Transvaal and Orange River Colony officials conspired to enforce the travel restrictions that kept African American church leaders from entering the former republics. [17]

Natal officials were more forthright in their hostility. The colony with proportionally the smallest white population, as well as the most recent memories of colonial conquest, Natal had no intention of accommodating independent black churches of whatever stripe. From 1900 on, AME ministers were deported from the colony or turned away at the border. Those ministers who did manage to organize congregations in the colony, thanks to a legal loophole for Natal-born Africans, were stymied by a law requiring direct European supervision at all mission stations. (Ironically, the white mission societies that championed the law were sometimes its victims; Wesleyans in particular often relied on African ministers and local preachers to oversee rural outstations.) Natal officials even mooted a proposal to prohibit all religious assemblies of Africans, retreating only after objections from colleagues in other colonies. [18]

Taken on their own terms, the policies pursued in Natal and the conquered republics were failures. Imperial officials, in eschewing direct legislation, hoped to have the best of both worlds: to check the spread of African Methodism without compromising their own liberal credentials. Manifestly this did not happen. On the contrary, Africans rallied to the church, seizing on each petty obstruction as proof of British hypocrisy and betrayal. By 1903 or '04, imperial officials were confronting precisely what they had hoped to avoid: a spreading popular movement, infused with the "energy of martyrdom." Natal's policy was superficially more successful. While a few AME congregations emerged in the colony, particularly among the small African landholding communities along the Transvaal border, the church never really gained a foothold in Natal. In the long run, however, the policy of repression did not so much stem independent church activity as drive it underground. By the 1920s officials found themselves confronting a raft of sects and movements, many with no discernible hierarchy or structure.

The most far-sighted policy—and the one that provided the blueprint for state policy in the emerging Union of South Africa—emanated from the Cape Colony. Perhaps because of their longer experience with organized African political activity, Cape officials were largely immune to the rumor-mongering and racist doomsaying that consumed their counterparts in other colonies.

Secretary of Native Affairs Walter Stanford, for example, had been a magistrate in Thembuland during the rise of the Tile Thembu Church, more than a decade before the AME Church's entrance on the scene. Renowned for his "safety valve" approach to native administration, Stanford immediately rejected the idea of repression, which promised only to enhance African Methodism's appeal or to so fragment the movement as to render it impossible to control. Stanford's cautious approach found a ready constituency among his colleagues in the Cape administration, most of whom regarded white missionaries' clamoring for repression as impolitic and more than a little unseemly. "The intolerant articles in the Christian Express must be to the natives a revelation," Prime Minister W. P. Schreiner commented in the margin of a memo in late 1898; "the sneers at the lack of education of one of these native ministers contained in the articles are a humourous commentary on the sincerity of those who profess to preach the doctrines [and] revere the lives of the fishermen of Galilee." He concluded with an admonition from Gibbon: "[T]o the magistrate, all religions are equally useful."[19]

Cape policy, already emerging in the late nineteenth century, was set out most systematically in a 1901 memo by Walter Stanford. In contrast to colleagues in other colonies, who routinely attributed the independent church movement to baneful "Negro" influences, Stanford portrayed it as an inevitable product of Africans' racial evolution. The danger, he continued, lay not in the movement itself but in its lack of institutional cohesion, which had thus far prevented colonial officials from gaining any effective purchase on it. Once the movement had been contained within regular institutional channels, Stanford was confident that he and his colleagues could control it, through the judicious dispensing of school grants, church sites, marriage rights, and other privileges essential to the institution's survival. Implicit in this argument was a new perspective on the transatlantic connection, a suggestion that African American leadership, far from being a menace, might provide a salutary source of structure and cohesion. "I see no reason to doubt," he concluded presciently, "but that this Church will quietly find its own place in the Christian system."[20]

When Cape officials spoke of channeling the church along "harmless" lines, they had quite specific ideas in mind. Churches were structured, stable affairs, overseen by men of education and character. They had clear lines of leadership and established procedures for disciplining the wayward. They did not traffic with disaffected chiefs or open churches on the doorsteps of existing missions. In a word, they confined themselves to "religion," which emerged in administrative discourse as the antithesis of the netherworld of "politics." What Cape administrators did not yet know was how neatly these conceptions dovetailed with the assumptions and priorities of African American church leaders. Under the leadership of men such as Daniel Payne, the AME Church had been defined by its preoccupation with structure and order, by its commitment to an educated ministry, and by its suspicion of ministers who dabbled in politics. The whole church had been conceived as an exemplary institution for demonstrating blacks' maturity and capacity for self-government to skeptical whites. Thus, a politics born of opposition to American slavery became, a century later and half a world away, the basis for an unexpected accommodation.[21]

Bishop Gaines's letter provided Cape officials with their first opening. Citing the uncertainty of Dwane's position, they suspended all the AME Church's privileges, essentially gathering in the chips they hoped later to dispense. When Fitzpatrick arrived some months later, he was cordially received by Prime Minister Schreiner. At a time when officials in other colonies were hailing the end of African American influence in the region, Schreiner pursued precisely the opposite tack, offering the AME Church full "recognition," on two conditions: first, that the church be "domiciled" in the Colony; second, that it have "on the spot some fully competent authority"—that is, an African American bishop. All communications between the church and administration would travel through the bishop, and applications for church sites, school grants, and the right to perform marriages would be entertained only if they bore his endorsement. In turn, the bishop would be held responsible for the actions of his African subordinates. In essence, the Cape administration put the onus for controlling the church squarely on the shoulders of its African American leaders.[22]

Over the next several years, Cape officials elaborated the policy, working to cultivate the loyalty of African Methodist church leaders while restraining the more reactionary instincts of their counterparts in other colonies. In endless memos and discussions, they noted the inevitability, even the desirability, of some organized African political activity, as well as the absurdity of holding African American church leaders responsible for activities in colonies from which they were barred. The gradual triumph of the Cape perspective was registered in the work of the 1903–1905 South African Native Affairs Commission, an assembly of "native experts" deputed to draw up a blueprint for African administration in the emerging Union of South Africa. While witnesses and commissioners traded in Ethiopian rumors, Walter Stanford, one of the two Cape representatives, worked patiently to separate fact from fantasy. While others dreamed of a future South Africa where an endless and undifferentiated supply of docile African workers would cater to white needs, Stanford stressed the importance of leaving outlets for "more advanced Natives." The Commission's conclusions on the subject of the "Church Separatist Movement" ratified Cape policy. After discussing the sources of the movement and the potential dangers of entrusting authority to immature or ambitious men, the Report concluded:

> [T]he course which commends itself to the Commission is to accord recognition to such Native Churches as are possessed of sufficiently stable organisation to

control their pastors and enforce discipline where necessary and to ensure the appointment to the ministry of reliable and worthy men only.

With proper cultivation, the commissioners predicted, the Ethiopian Movement "will grow in the fulness of time to be a power for good."[23]

To be sure, implementation of this recommendation was neither smooth nor even. Conciliatory gestures toward the AME Church by officials in Cape Town or Pretoria were often scuttled by local magistrates and pass officers, who either had not heard of the new Ethiopian policy or disapproved of it. We saw in Chapter 5, for example, how the missionary-dominated Transvaal Education Department obstructed Chief Native Commissioner Godfrey Lagden's efforts to grant an educational subsidy to an AME-sponsored school. Shifts in the locus of political authority further complicated matters, requiring almost constant renegotiation of agreements. Thus, church leaders found themselves briefly back at square one following the retrocession of authority to the Boers in the Transvaal and the Orange Free State and again as the four colonies negotiated the creation of a Union Native Affairs Department. The Natal administration, for its part, remained committed to repression, especially after the 1906 Bambatha rebellion, which spawned a new wave of anti-Ethiopian hysteria. The AME Church fully emerged from the bureaucratic briar patch only in the years after Union. Nonetheless, there is no mistaking the drift of state policy. By the end of imperial reconstruction, many colonial officials had concluded that this venerable African American church represented "no menace to temporal authority" but a valuable potential ally.[24]

Initially at least, African church leaders agreed on the necessity of an American bishop. The Dwane debacle demonstrated the danger of entrusting ecclesiastical authority to "halfly-educated men," an uncharacteristically self-deprecating H. R. Ngcayiya declared in a letter to the *Voice of Missions* early in 1900. Samuel Brander and Simon Sinamela, two Ethiopian stalwarts in the Transvaal, agreed that "an African Bishop for the present is a failure" and urged church leaders to appoint a bishop from America. In part, these men saw an American appointment as a way to patch over the ethnic and regional jealousies aroused by Dwane's rapid promotion and subsequent rebellion. Another letter—unsigned, but probably written by Sinamela—warned of ethnic tensions within the church, while simultaneously partaking of that consciousness. "We are no longer prepared to have supervisors of the Kaffir [Xhosa] tribe," the author declared. "Send out, in the name of God in Heaven, ministers straight from America to have the full control of the church, but no other amongst us."[25]

AME leaders in the United States concurred. Dwane's secession had brought to the surface all the lingering doubts about African capacity. Critics of the mission seized on the schism as proof of Bishop Turner's folly in annointing an

African bishop and insisted that the church either withdraw from the South African field or take steps to bring it under proper governance. Even mission supporters conceded that they might have acted hastily in entrusting authority to untested African leaders. A sober editorial in the AME *Church Review,* while counseling against overreaction, questioned Africans' ability to grasp the genius of African Methodism without some apprenticeship in denominational usages. Virtually all agreed, at a minimum, on the necessity of appointing an American bishop to superintend the South African church. [26]

Consensus thus reigned on the importance of assigning American bishops to mission fields. The Committee on Bishops at the 1900 General Conference recommended the election of five bishops, two to fill vacancies in the United States and one each for South Africa, West Africa, and the West Indies. The only contention concerned the bishops' terms of assignment. A faction led by Henry Turner advocated separate elections for "missionary" bishops to prevent the election of men not committed to the work. Turner also urged the conference to suspend the usual policy of quadrennial rotation, on the grounds that mission bishops needed more than four years to fathom Africa's distinctive conditions and needs. Events would reveal the wisdom of this counsel, but church leaders at the time refused to tamper with existing procedure. In the end, candidates were all elected from one pool, and all were, in Turner's derisive words, "stereotyped candidates." (I. N. Fitzpatrick, the leader of Turner's slate of candidates, fell short of election and never returned to Africa.) For South Africa, now designated the Fourteenth Episcopal District, the General Conference tapped Levi J. Coppin of Philadelphia. [27]

Insofar as Levi Coppin was a stereotypical AME leader, he reminds us just how remarkable most church leaders were. Born in 1848, he began his church career as an adolescent choirmaster in a tiny congregation in Cecilton, Maryland, during Reconstruction. Over the ensuing decades, he rose to become one of the church's most respected divines—composer of several standard hymns, editor of the AME *Church Review,* and author of a popular guide to scriptural interpretation. At the time of his election, he was pastor of Philadelphia's Mother Bethel Church, occupying the pulpit once held by Richard Allen. Coppin's wife, the former Fanny Jackson, was even more remarkable. Born a slave and freed through the industry of a devoted aunt, she received her first education working as a domestic servant in a white home. She proceeded to Oberlin, where she overcame both racial and sexual prejudice to graduate at the top of her class. From 1868 to 1902 she served as principal of the Institute for Colored Youth, training ground of Philadelphia's black elite. She was also a founder of the National Association of Colored Women. In short, the Coppins occupied the very pinnacle of nineteenth-century African American society. [28]

What distinguished the Coppins from many members of their class was their fascination with Africa. Possessed of an acute sense of history, Levi Coppin embraced Africa as his generation's field for heroism. He promoted mission work in the *Church Review,* and his Philadelphia congregation was unmatched in annual Easter Day giving. If his personal library is anything to judge by, he read voraciously on the subject, everything from the missionary memoirs of Livingstone and Moffat to the travel accounts of H. M. Stanley to the complete works of Martin Delany and Alexander Crummell. (Among Coppin's papers is a Crummell autograph.) While many of his successors viewed the South African assignment as four years in the wilderness, Coppin actively pursued the post. Fanny Jackson Coppin fully shared this commitment. A past president of the Woman's Mite Missionary Society, she joined her husband in South Africa in late 1902 after her retirement from the Institute for Colored Youth. Despite failing health, she remained in the country for a year, traveling as far as Bulawayo to organize chapters of the W.M.M.S.[29]

Aside from a few comments in her memoirs and a single surviving speech, little evidence remains of Fanny Jackson Coppin's passage through South Africa. (The speech, delivered to the 1903 South African Annual Conference, focused on home training, the virtues of domestic service, and the plight of young women in cities, all concerns central to her work in the United States.) Levi Coppin, on the other hand, wrote constantly. He sent dozens of long letters from the field, which were later collected and published, together with a book of South African "Observations." On the surface, there was little to distinguish the bishop's writing from any of a hundred other late-nineteenth-century "Dark Continent" travel accounts. He exploited all the usual conventions of African reportage—descriptions of the long sea voyage and of strenuous overland journeys, accounts of the different physical "types" of African—and indulged all the standard missionary oppositions—light and darkness, civilization and heathenism, and so forth. While not oblivious to the evils of colonialism, Coppin tended to see Africans' predicament in evolutionary rather than political terms, as a function of backwardness rather than oppression. He frequently invoked black American experience, suggesting that Africans too could lift themselves through patience, industry, and education.[30]

In other respects, however, Coppin did not fit the stereotype of the black Victorian. Blunt and occasionally acerbic, he refused to play the apologist for white racism. While most AME clerics referred to Africa as a "Fatherland," he pointedly called it his "Motherland," a not too subtle reminder of centuries of involuntary miscegenation. He noted the depredations of Africa's "boasted civilized Governments" and observed the dissolution and anomie that often greeted Africans who had imbibed the "so-called advantages" of western civilization. Coppin also proved an unusually sensitive observer of African culture. Unlike European missionaries, who typically described chieftaincy as despotic and cruel, he quickly perceived the consensual dimensions of chiefly rule, characterizing it as a kind of "Constitutional Monarchy." He also rejected missionaries' instinctive equation of polygamy and sexual wantonness. "It is altogether a mistake to regard the custom of plural marriage among the heathen people as evidence of a want of moral restraint, or, a sign of a low standard of morals," he wrote. On the contrary, he suggested that Americans, white and black, had a great deal to learn from African chastity and marital fidelity. In such passages, Coppin came as close as anyone in his generation to a genuine cultural relativism.[31]

Ultimately, however, Coppin could take such speculations only so far. He was, after all, a Christian missionary, for whom the universal validity of "Christian civilization" was an article of faith. "That civilization betters the condition of a people is not an open question," he declared in a chapter titled "Christianity vs. Heathenism." Spreading its blessings was "the indispensable duty of the Christian Church." As convinced as he was of the integrity of African culture, he could find no warrant for polygamy, even in contexts where a slight compromise might yield a harvest of souls. (In at least one case, the church lost access to an entire community because of Coppin's refusal to sanction the baptism of a polygamous chief.) In the end, the best the bishop could do was hope that the transition to civilization could be accomplished without undue violence to African life, that somehow the "inclination to multiply their wives" would wither as Africans moved into the light of Christianity. At his most optimistic, he portrayed the transformation almost organically, as a process of racial evolution.[32]

Coppin needed all the optimism he could muster as he confronted the South African church's manifold problems. The outbreak of the South African War had severed communication between the Cape and the interior, cutting him off from the lion's share of AME adherents. In the Cape itself, the church still reeled from Dwane's secession. Many congregations had been lost to the seceders, and others were torn between seceders and loyalists. Everywhere morale was at a nadir. Even those who had remained faithful to African Methodism agreed that the church had failed to honor its financial commitments, and they waited to see what the new bishop would bring. Unfortunately, Coppin had little to show when he arrived; if anything, the Dwane episode had made African American church leaders even more skeptical about committing resources to South Africa. Amid the enthusiasm of the General Conference, church leaders reiterated their commitment to build the South African college "as soon as possible," but they appropriated no money. Coppin was forced to embark on a personal fund-raising tour, to save himself the embarrassment of arriving in South Africa "with empty hands." Atop it all, the church confronted the skepticism of colonial officialdom and the outright hostility of European missionaries.[33]

Coppin thus possessed at least three different briefs as he disembarked in Cape Town. He needed somehow to persuade his colleagues in the United States that the South African church was viable and worthy of financial support. At the same time, he needed to shore up skeptical Africans' faith in the transatlantic connection. Finally, he needed to remove the various legal obstacles to the church's operation. It is a measure of Coppin's temperament that he saw no conflict among these different tasks. To his mind, the problem was simply one of institution building. Once the South African church had been properly organized, Africans would recognize the transparent genius of African Methodism and become devoted adherents. Church leaders in America, assured of Africans' loyalty, would open their hearts and wallets. Colonial officials would appreciate the AME Church for what it was—not some sinister cabal but just another Christian church, ready to take its "place among other agencies for the redemption of the world."[34]

This institutionalizing impulse defined virtually everything Coppin did from his arrival in South Africa early in 1901 to his final departure late in 1903. One of his first acts as resident bishop was to commission a history of the South African church, from its formation in Marabastad in 1892 to his own arrival. Like the historical introduction to the AME *Discipline,* the history would provide a charter linking future generations to those who had come before. Coppin also commanded congregations to buy property and erect permanent churches. Meeting outdoors or in private homes promoted instability, he warned; with proper churches, on the other hand, "the people will become settled down, and the growth will be permanent." Most important, Coppin took steps to stabilize the church's ministry. There had been too much "rapid itineracy," he argued, too heavy a reliance placed on uneducated men who went about "preaching to the people and turning them loose." The time had come to build up a proper ministry, composed of educated men with at least some grounding in AME doctrine and usages. In contrast to Bishop Turner, who ordained sixty Africans in six weeks, Coppin exercised considerable caution, ordaining only thirty during his entire tenure. The price of his approach, he conceded, was reduced growth, but he was more than willing to pay it. "This is the planting and ploughing season, and we must be content to wait for the harvest," he declared, employing a familiar missionary metaphor.[35]

Gathering the harvest, however, required at least the tacit support of South African authorities. "The first and most important thing to do," Coppin wrote, "is to win the confidence of the Government, and thereby overcome the unnecessary opposition by the missionaries of the other churches." On arrival, he presented himself to Cape officials, submitting a host of testimonials and letters of introduction, including one from the U.S. State Department. The Cape administration, in keeping with the letter if not the spirit of its agreement with Fitzpatrick, allowed the bishop to nominate a dozen marriage officers but adopted a wait-and-see attitude on further recognition. For his part, Coppin took every opportunity to impress the government with the soundness and moderation of his views. In several well-publicized sermons and speeches, he enjoined his listeners to cultivate a spirit of submission to authority, invariably underscoring his argument with the authority of African American experience. In a lecture titled "From Bondage to Freedom," delivered in

Cape Town's Metropolitan Hall and later circulated through the Cape in pamphlet form, Coppin used the "Negro" to illustrate the duties of subject to ruler. In a sermon at the Kimberley Opera House, he preached from Romans 13, the Pauline text on authority once cherished by American slaveholders. Again, he underscored the lesson with U.S. experience, arguing that "not a single instance could be pointed out where the American black man was a rebel." The implication, of course, was that Africans, by cultivating a spirit of patience and forebearance, could scale the social and economic heights allegedly attained by African Americans. The secondary message, for any whites who happened to be listening, was that the AME Church represented no threat to authority and social order.[36]

For the next quarter century and beyond, AME Church leaders in South Africa continued to sound this moderate, apolitical refrain. One could scarcely count the missives sent to colonial officials by Bishop Coppin and his successors, all scrupulously disavowing political intent. To some extent, this was a pose, forced on African Methodists by the exigencies of working in a colonial setting. Clearly, however, most church leaders accepted the merits of the approach, which reflected not only their estimation of Africans' capacities and needs but their understanding of their own history. In essence, African Americans saw the bulk of Africans as they imagined their own foreparents three centuries before, at the commencement of the long journey from slavery to freedom. Such assumptions led African American churchmen to define their priorities in more or less conventional missionary terms. Africans needed churches to eradicate "heathenism," schools to dispel "ignorance." While not oblivious to the political implications of a black-run church in South Africa, most AME leaders were distinctly uneasy with the political proclivities of their African charges, which tarnished the church's reputation while diverting Africans from the true path of racial evolution.

Even at the time, there were individuals who warned against this accommodationist turn, who begged AME Church leaders not to allow political caution or their doubts about African capacity to overshadow the goal of full racial equality. Probably the most explicit statement came in an open letter to Bishop Coppin by a correspondent from Cape Town, published in the South African *Spectator,* the city's chief clearinghouse for information about black America. (The editor of the *Spectator,* Gold Coast–born F. Z. S. Peregrino, was himself a product of the transatlantic connection, having edited a paper in New York before settling in South Africa.) Uplifting "benighted" races was all well and good, the author began, but the real challenge of the age was to break down racial barriers. The "only way to do this," the author charged, "is for the men of culture and intellect who are to be found in your ranks to take a progressive step, and claim as a God-given right the educational, social, religious and political equality that must be conceded if men are to do their duty as God has directed and to fulfill their calling in life." It was compelling advice, which unwittingly called African Methodists back to their own roots, to founders such as Richard Allen and Daniel Coker, who had fused revolutionary liberalism and Christian universalism into a radical equalitarian creed. It was advice that Allen's successors, a century later, could neither recognize nor heed.[37]

A more immediate problem loomed. While Coppin's conciliatory refrain was doubtless music to the ears of colonial officials, it rang discordantly to many in his church. Coming from a society where the structures of white control were so interwoven, Africans found it nearly impossible to draw any neat conceptual line between religion and politics. Whatever the conscious intentions of the original Ethiopians, their rejection of missionary tutelage was a profoundly political act, which inevitably spilled into other spheres. Everywhere the new church went, it ignited expectations of a day when Africans would control their own lives, enjoy the full benefits of citizenship, even reclaim the land itself. Affiliation with black America, far from dampening such beliefs, only infused the movement with greater expectancy and militance; America, after all, was the place where blacks were free. Precisely what Africans expected African Methodism to accomplish varied from place to place, as we discussed in the preceding chapters, but all agreed that a pivotal moment in the history of the race was at hand. In short, Africans had their own ideas about the meaning of religious independence, which had very little to do with Coppin's bromides about submission and authority.

Tensions between Coppin and his flock surfaced most clearly on the issue of proselytizing, or "sheep stealing." Of all the charges that attached to the church, the most common was that it gathered its adherents from other churches rather than from "heathendom." Broadly speaking, the charge was true. While African Methodists often responded to "calls" from local congregations, they were not above entering areas uninvited, sometimes opening churches and schools within feet of existing European missions. Nor were AME adherents above pressuring mission loyalists, taunting those who refused to join them as "slaves" and *mlungu*. Such conduct was not always endorsed by African church leaders, but it was certainly consistent with their sense of urgency and righteousness. "Ethiopianism" to these people was not simply a question of denominational preference; it was a crusade to reassert Africans' control over their own social and religious lives.

Coppin anguished over the proselytism issue. On one hand, he appreciated the grievances that had prompted many mission converts to turn to the AME Church. These were not "ambitious and ungrateful people," he argued, in an oblique rebuttal of missionary allegations; rather, "they were people who had been literally driven away from the church either by unchristian discrimination, or by being severely let alone." Everywhere he traveled, he found unmarried couples and unbaptized children, a testament to European missionaries' "utter neglect" of their nominal converts. In such circumstances, Coppin believed that the church had an obligation to respond, the demands of missionary comity notwithstanding. He was also clearly moved by the spirit of the church's would-be adherents, by their sense of "coming to their own." "It mattered not how vehemently we refused to receive them," he later recalled. "One old lady at one of the places where we were being importuned to organize, said: 'you may bring your Church here, or not, but I will never step my foot inside of another white man's church so long as I live.'" How could he turn such people away? On the other hand, Coppin recognized the dangers of proselytizing. He remained wary of the church overextending itself and feared a loss of institutional integrity through the constant infusion of new members from different denominational traditions. He also understood that the AME Church would never win the confidence of European missionaries or colonial officials so long as it was seen to fish in mission waters. In the end, he saw no alternative but to adopt a strong public posture against proselytizing.[38]

That posture brought him into conflict with some of his own ministers, most notably Henry Reid Ngcayiya, an original Ethiopian and, as it happens, one of the men who had pressed for the appointment of an American bishop in 1900. Since casting his lot with Ethiopianism in 1895, Ngcayiya had remained a thorn in the side of European missionaries. Posted to the eastern Cape, he immediately began organizing congregations in Oxkraal and Tsitsikama, two of the most densely populated locations in Queenstown district and both long-time Wesleyan strongholds. By 1898 he had moved into Herschel district, where he again worked at the Wesleyans' expense. A year later he surfaced at Cisira, near Peddie. In each instance, missionaries protested to Cape officials, who ordered Ngcayiya to desist. All they received in reply was a series of protests and petitions defending religious freedom and accusing the administration of traducing the rights of African taxpayers. The arrival of another Ngcayiya-inspired petition in 1902 provided Cape officials with an opportunity to put Coppin's moderate professions to the test.[39]

The bishop passed with flying colors. On hearing that one of his ministers was involved in "Ethiopian" activities, Coppin promised an immediate investigation, adding a personal pledge to defrock the culprit. "No act of insubordination to the Government by any of our missionaries will go unpunished [in] the A.M.E. Church," he proclaimed. While he ultimately failed to defrock Ngcayiya, he ordered him to sever all ties with the dissident congregation in Peddie (which he dismissed as a vestige of "Ethiopianism") and to refrain from communicating with the Cape administration except through his office. With Coppin's support, officials ordered the African Methodist chapel in Peddie torn down.[40]

Significantly, the intervention seems to have made more of an impression on Cape authorities than on the people in Peddie. As the first resident bishop of a still ill-organized church, Coppin commanded little practical authority. His power was further circumscribed, ironically, by the very *Discipline* he sought to implement, which imposed precise limits on episcopal authority. (The power to defrock a minister, for example, was vested in the annual conference.) For his part, Ngcayiya ignored the bishop's order: he moved the Peddie congregation into a private hut, beyond the statutory reach of the Cape administration, and fired off yet another petition. Even so, the spectacle of an African American bishop and the Cape Native Affairs Department working in tandem to tear down a church building spoke volumes about the changing institutional face of African Methodism.[41]

Coppin's troubles with the indigenous ministry were exacerbated by continuing controversy over the proposed South African college. Despite the renewed pledge from the General Conference, money for the school never materialized, leaving Coppin to secure a site with a few thousand dollars he had raised before coming. He located a suitable building in the heart of Cape Town's District Six, but between an unfavorable exchange rate and dramatic wartime inflation he needed all the money he had simply to place a down payment. Bethel Institute, more a high school than a college, opened on the site in late 1901, but the school soon tottered on the edge of bankruptcy. Coppin managed to stave off foreclosure in 1902 by embarking on another fund-raising tour during a U.S. furlough, but the future remained cloudy. Worse still, Coppin's decision to locate the school in Cape Town, where he could supervise it personally, infuriated African ministers in the interior, who were still smarting from Dwane's rapid promotion and who regarded this as one more case of American favoritism toward the Cape. A "heated discussion" on the issue erupted at the South African Annual Conference in December 1901, pitting the bishop against ministers who had traveled down to the Cape from the Free State and the Transvaal.[42]

What made the lack of support from America especially galling to Africans was Coppin's simultaneous insistence that they meet all their obligations to the central church. In addition to annual collections on behalf of various church departments—the Easter Day collection for the Missionary Department, Endowment Day for the Board of Church Extension, and so forth—all South African congregations were expected to raise the equivalent of one dollar per person for the church's General Fund. By General Conference decree, a third of this "Dollar Money" could be dispensed locally, but the balance was to be sent to America to maintain superannuated bishops, connectional schools, church newspapers, and various other agencies that South Africans had never seen. Enforcing these obligations, from Coppin's perspective, was part and parcel of the process of establishing "church fealty," but to South Africans it seemed a rank injustice. Why should they pay into the coffers of a wealthy black American church when it neglected its obligations to them? Many South African congregations simply ignored the required subscriptions, introducing more tension into the transatlantic relationship.[43]

As Coppin's troubles mounted, he came increasingly to doubt the capabilities of African ministers. Native churchmen possessed great initial enthusiasm, he explained in letters home, but they lacked the maturity and experience to sustain the church beyond its "formative period." As a group, they were still too inclined to "polemical indiscretions" and to flouting denominational policies and procedures. Such problems, Coppin conceded, were not unique to South Africa: in the American South, too, the AME Church had initially been forced to rely on the leaders it found in the field, with much the same results. The South African situation, however, was too precarious for half-trained men. The church urgently required "wise and competent" leaders, leaders "who know the discipline, doctrine and polity of the Church and have experience in governing"—leaders, in plain language, from the United States.[44]

Coppin put out the first call for volunteers in mid-1901. By the time he left South Africa two and a half years later, half a dozen African American men and women had answered the summons, creating what the bishop whimsically called his "American Colony." The colony's leader was A. Henry Attaway, a thirty-one-year-old minister from Kansas who arrived in Cape Town at the end of 1901, accompanied by Charlotte Manye and Henry Msikinya, the first South African graduates of Wilberforce University. A delighted Coppin immediately appointed Attaway principal of Bethel Institute and South African General Superintendent, an office just below bishop.[45]

Far from settling the South African situation, however, Attaway's appearance generated almost instant controversy. A rigid Social Darwinist, he calculated that Africans were at least sixteen hundred years behind Europeans in the race of "civilization," an assessment that placed him far closer to colonial officialdom than to his African flock. "The native has natural aspirations, but he does not know in many cases really what he requires," he explained to the South African Native Affairs Commission. "He sees the effect of civilisation upon others, and he is very anxious, as far as possible, to keep pace with those things. But, as I see it, his salvation lies in his availability as a labouring asset." Lest such statements be dismissed as mere fodder for a white audience, Attaway said precisely the same thing to Africans, ending one well-publicized lecture with the admonition "Learn to labor and to wait." The curriculum that he installed at Bethel Institute reflected the prescription, overlaying the standard Cape Colony mission syllabus with a veneer of Tuskegee-style "practical" work. The combination naturally recommended itself to Cape officials, but it did not satisfy the church's African adherents, who continued to yearn for the promised college.[46]

Attaway showed scarcely greater sensitivity to African political aspirations. Because he conceived Africans' handicaps in evolutionary rather than political terms, he tended to dismiss political action as irrelevant or even counterproductive. The AME Church's only object, he declared in a letter to Lord Milner, was to "heartily cooperate with His Majesty's Government (wherever requested) in bringing the benign benefits of the world's greatest civilization to an hitherto unfortunate people." To African ministers, Attaway was considerably blunter, threatening to expel anyone who dabbled in "Etheopian [sic] Propaganda" or otherwise transgressed the line between religion and politics. In one circular, written after Coppin's departure in December 1903, Attaway ordered African ministers entering new areas to report to local magistrates and to render "all possible help in the administration of law, and the maintenance of order." Given the practical limitations of his authority, such commands were mostly hot air. Nonetheless, they further alienated African ministers from African American authority.[47]

African disenchantment was hastened by the transparent opportunism of several of the central church's representatives. Like most black Americans, missionaries who ventured to Africa had been taught to see the continent in a kind of parallax, as a field of service and of opportunity. Emigrationists and mission advocates alike argued that African Americans, in uplifting their benighted brethren, would raise their own social and economic standing. Inevitably, some took this harmony of aims as an entrepreneurial license. Thus, the early African Methodist missionaries in Liberia devoted much of their time and energy to coffee plantations and steamboat concessions. AME emissary Harry Dean engaged in various commercial ventures during his years in South Africa, while I. N. Fitzpatrick returned from his short visit promoting "The Wonder of the Age: African Limbless Cotton." It was Attaway, however, who most fully explored Africa's commercial possibilities, launching a dozen different schemes, invariably to the detriment of his church. The AME Church's Barotseland mission, for example, collapsed when a Cape Town agency business with which he was associated went bankrupt, taking with it seven hundred pounds that Lozi paramount chief Lewanika had raised to buy boats and wagons. So suspicious was Attaway's role in the affair—he accepted the money only days before the company declared bankruptcy—that the Cape administration considered prosecuting him for fraud, eventually retreating for want of any proof of intent.[48]

African Methodism's reputation was further tarnished by Attaway's involvement in the ill-fated Chatsworth Normal, Mechanical and Industrial Institute. The scheme originated in 1904, when Attaway acquired an option on a ten thousand-acre parcel of land forty miles north of Cape Town. Using the promise of an African American–staffed industrial institute as a lure, he proposed to offer small plots to land-hungry African and Coloured families on an installment basis. In his promotional campaign, he portrayed Chatsworth as the foundation of an independent black community, with its own schools, farms, and factories. In the context of the time, this was heady stuff, and AME congregations all across South Africa held bazaars, tea meetings, and concerts to raise funds, sending the proceeds directly to Attaway. In late 1904, more than five hundred people made the journey from Cape Town to watch the general superintendent, in full Masonic regalia, lay the cornerstone of the school. More than one hundred plots were knocked down on the spot. Unfortunately, the scheme came with more than its share of fine print. In contrast to most mortgage arrangements, the deal gave purchasers no title until all installments had been paid; missing a single monthly payment meant forfeiture of one's entire investment. In the absence of title, even those who kept up payments had no legal standing, leaving them without recourse when the scheme went belly up in early 1905.[49]

Bankruptcy, however, did not end Attaway's association with the project. Chatsworth's new owners, a group of white Cape Town businessmen, had seen the commercial appeal of the black American connection and asked him to stay on as a front man. For the next two years, Attaway promoted the school across the eastern Cape, exhibiting a salesman's sense of customers' frustrations and desires. Peasants in impoverished Herschel district, for example, could scarcely help but respond to charges that white traders were "doing" them, buying wool for sixpence a pound and selling it back as blankets at six times the price. At Chatsworth, Attaway averred, skilled teachers from America would show Africans "how to convert wool into clothes and hides into shoes." While assuring colonial officials that Chatsworth was "in no sense connected" with Ethiopianism or any other "Denominational Religion," he moved along AME networks, and most Africans naturally assumed the school was still associated with the church, rather than an enterprise of white businessmen. Few understood the implications of the installment plan. If the testimony of disgruntled investors is to be admitted, Attaway also failed to provide receipts for the numerous "deposits" he collected, in both cash and kind. When Chatsworth returned to bankruptcy court in 1908, it left a trail of aggrieved Africans, including at least one prominent chief. Attaway, still unbowed, resurfaced in Basutoland, touting another fanciful scheme to build a literary, mechanical, and industrial academy "not unlike Tuskegee Institute of which Dr. Booker T. Washington is Principal." He finally returned to the United States in about 1910, leaving more than a dozen unsettled claims behind.[50]

Not all members of the American contingent behaved so appallingly. John Albert Gregg, the twenty-seven-year-old minister whom Attaway recruited to oversee the school at Chatsworth, acquitted himself honorably and earned Africans' esteem and affection. Gregg, who later returned to South Africa as a resident bishop, arrived in 1904, accompanied by his new wife, Celia, a classmate from the University of Kansas. Together, the Greggs opened a two-room school, which, if it failed to match advance billing, at least became a going concern. Unlike Attaway, Gregg showed considerable sensitivity to Africans' plight. In a brief, recently discovered memoir, written a few years after his return to the United States, he portrayed South Africa in unstinting terms, describing a world where Africans were dispossessed and brutalized and accused of sedition the moment they sought to assert themselves. Whites' preoccupation with African Methodism, Gregg noted perceptively, was just further evidence of their "willful blindness" to "the real cause of Native unrest."[51]

Yet for all his manifest sympathy for Africans, the young minister shared his mentors' limited conception of the AME Church's role, as well as their skepticism about Africans' capacity for self-government. "We may have been a little too prodigal in giving our commissions to preachers over our work out there in the beginning," he suggested, adding that "Dwane's advancement in the church was a little too much for him and completely turned his head." (Dwane, of course, had left the AME Church long before Gregg arrived.) Other African ministers had become "over zealous" and "too visionary as regards the object of the A.M.E. Church," interpreting its message of liberation in "temporal" rather than "spiritual" terms. The church, Gregg insisted, had no interest in "the political side of the matter whatever" and represented "a most loyal ally to the government." He would continue to propound that analysis during his tenure as South African resident bishop two decades later, at a time when African ministers and church members were again becoming immersed in politics.[52]

Carleton M. Tanner, the twenty-seven-year-old son of AME Bishop Benjamin Tanner, advanced much the same analysis, but without Gregg's sensitivity. A former student of Fanny Jackson Coppin's at the Institute for Colored Youth, Tanner accompanied the Coppins back to South Africa in December 1902. While his very presence in Africa distinguished him from his virulently antiemigrationist father, young Tanner clearly shared the old man's haughty manner. He was also a stickler for AME procedures, having just published a manual for church probationers. Within a month of his arrival, he had been appointed a member of the executive board of Bethel Institute and presiding elder of one of the church's most populous districts. Tanner also served as editor of the church's first periodical, the South African *Christian Recorder,* modeled on the Philadelphia paper once edited by his father. From his editorial desk, he discoursed freely on the prospects and problems of the South African AME Church, particularly on the limitations of the indigenous ministry.[53]

Tensions between U.S. church leaders and African ministers built all through 1903, finally coming to a head in December at a joint session of the Transvaal and Cape Annual Conferences. The conference convened at Aliwal North—African American churchmen were still not permitted across the Orange River—and marked the end of Coppin's stay in South Africa. It also represented the first time that most of the church's leaders in the interior had met their African American supervisors. Events got off to a dismal start. On the very day the conference convened, Carleton Tanner published an article advocating tighter American control over the church. African ministers, he alleged, were ill educated and often illiterate; they lacked financial sense; they possessed no understanding "of the laws and genius of the church" or of the need for circumspection when dealing with white authorities. Too often, he wrote, "we hear of things being done (not maliciously, but ignorantly) in the name of our church that cause us apprehension and trouble." Tanner proposed introducing a layer of African American general superintendents between the resident bishop and African ministers to ensure that episcopal edicts were enforced on the ground. "These superintendents must travel at large throughout the country wherever we have work," he wrote. "They must represent our church to the government officials; they must see to the transfer of all properties, call together and instruct the men who are out on the field at work, and in general have complete control of the district to which they are assigned."[54]

Tanner's article set the tone for the entire conference. On the very first day, Coppin antagonized Africans by proposing that they elect only two representatives to the upcoming General Conference in America instead of the eight to which they were entitled. The balance of the South African seats, he assured delegates, would be assumed by responsible ministers from the United States, at a considerable savings to the church. The issue that tore the conference apart, however, was the Tanner proposal and Coppin's suggestion that Tanner himself be appointed as the first of these new intermediate superintendents. Furious African ministers responded that they would abide no system of governance not consistent with AME discipline and that under no circumstances would they accept Tanner. The conference ended in disarray, with many African ministers openly questioning their American supervisors. Free State minister Benjamin Kumalo spoke for many of his colleagues when he suggested that "Bishop Coppin's head" was "not so good as some of ours."[55]

In the wake of the conference, a group of African ministers, including Kumalo, Henry Ngcayiya, J. Z. Tantsi, and Samuel Brander, drafted a letter of protest to the AME General Conference. "Much has been said of Africa by strangers," they began, in a not too subtle swipe at African American church leaders; the time had now come for Africans to speak for themselves. Most of the letter focused on Tanner, a "new man in Africa," who presumed to speak as an expert on South Africa despite never having left the Cape. The authors rebutted Tanner's characterization of the African ministry, reminding him that his own district had been organized and sustained "by one he despises as illiterate and incompetent to manage the affairs of the church." The proposal to introduce African American supervisors, they noted perceptively,

> places us under the same condition which forced us to leave the white churches, to be placed under the superintendency of men who are ignorant of the people, their customs, traditions, and life in general; these men will have to require interpreters wherever they go, and they do not always seem to have sympathy with the people, having been disappointed with the state in which they found them.

"[W]e are not prepared to take a secondary place, nor do we care to be the instruments of promoting ambitious adventurers," the authors concluded.[56]

Even before the missive reached America, the church was wracked by another schism. In early 1904 Samuel Brander, a pioneer Ethiopian and one of the authors of the protest letter, resigned from the AME Church and with a handful of followers established the Ethiopian Catholic Church in Zion. As the name suggests, the new church adopted catholic usages, in deference to Brander's early training in the Church of England. Brander himself assumed the office of archbishop. The roots of the secession, however, lay in neither doctrine nor desire for office but in a profound sense of betrayal. "We were united to the Americans because we thought they would help us," Brander explained to the South African Native Affairs Commission a few months later. "They told us, 'Look here; we will show you and teach you and bring you equal in education with the whites, so they will recognize you'. . . ." All they had provided, however, was a cohort of "men from America," and a chain of broken promises.

> They promised that they would give us a school from America at their own expense, with teachers and all, and this they did not do. . . . We had to support schools and everything here ourselves, and at the same time collect our yearly income, and also take collections for Easter Day, contingent moneys, and all that money had to be forwarded to America. When we asked for help when we were in debt, or anything, they refused to help us. . . . [T]hree times I sent an application to America for them to help us, and they said they could not. . . .

"[W]e thought as they were our own colour, they would help us up," he concluded, "but we found they helped us down. . . ."[57]

By the time the AME General Conference assembled in Chicago in 1904, most American church leaders had grasped Africans' desire for greater autonomy. Carleton Tanner's reorganization plan was shelved, and Tanner either chose or was asked not to return to South Africa. With the exception of Attaway, who remained in the field as a quasi-independent entrepreneur, all the original members of Bishop Coppin's American Colony were back in the United States by the end of 1906. For the next thirty years, all major church offices, save the office of bishop itself, were entrusted to Africans, though often to Africans educated in America.[58]

Some lessons, however, had yet to be absorbed. While conceding greater scope for African self-government, U.S. church leaders still endorsed the thrust of Coppin's administration, with its emphasis on institutionalization and political conciliation. A "Bishops' Declaration" drafted during the General Conference pledged "fraternity and co-operation" with European missions, as well as "loyalty and obedience to lawfully constituted authority." "It is no part of our business to concern ourselves with politics," the bishops wrote. "We shall strictly confine our endeavors to civilization, education and christianiza-tion." In return, all the church asked was an opportunity to "help bring the heathen to a knowledge of the true God." Unbeknownst to the bishops, it was precisely this crabbed conception of the church's mission that had precipitated much of the turmoil of the previous quadrennium.[59]

As in 1900, controversy swirled over the terms of assignment for missionary bishops, with Bishop Turner's faction again arguing for separate elections and extended appointments. Missions would never prosper, the *Voice of the People* warned, so long as the church posted bishops who knew no more of Africa than of "Neptune." Once again, however, a majority of delegates refused to tamper with established procedures. Bishop Coppin was reassigned to the Seventh Episcopal District in South Carolina. South Africa, still widely regarded as a hardship post, was entrusted to one of the junior bishops, Charles Spencer Smith.[60]

By any light, it was a bizarre appointment. Autocratic and uncompromising, the Canadian-born Smith viewed African mission work with something between skepticism and outright hostility. This was the same man who had sailed to West Africa in 1894 to locate a homeland for returning African Americans, only to experience a kind of colonialist epiphany along the way. Smith's account of the voyage, *Glimpses of Africa,* published at the very moment the Ethiopians were voting to amalgamate with the AME Church, read like a colonial primer: Africans were childlike and indolent; imperialism was a boon, awakening a torpid people to the blessings of sustained industry; "civilization" was "a plant of slow growth" that, in the first few generations, was more likely to turn Africans into rogues than into responsible adults. Given such presumptions, Smith naturally took a dim view of Ethiopianism. To him, the rebellion against European missionary authority exemplified African immaturity and ingratitude, while American church leaders' intrusion in the affair betrayed lamentable ignorance. At a time when African ministers pressed for greater autonomy, Smith was frankly skeptical of their capacity. As he put it in a later book, "It is impossible for any people only one generation removed from barbarism to comprehend and successfully grapple with the genius and multifarious ramifications of an ecclesiastical organism." Had the General Conference acted intentionally, it is hard to imagine it finding a man more ill suited for the South African field. To make matters worse, a layer of personal animosity was added when the South African delegation became implicated in the Turner faction's vicious campaign to discredit Smith and block his appointment.[61]

Smith served as resident bishop of South Africa for eighteen tumultuous months. During that time, a government informant noted approvingly, he was not "a whit behind any white missionary in impressing upon the people the fact that they are as yet unprepared for self-government." Within days of his arrival in October 1904, he assembled the church's presiding elders and read them the riot act. African ministers were to desist from all provocative action, including "proselytizing and meddling with politics and sometimes taking the side of the Chiefs who had been deposed by the Government." To publicize the new regime, Smith requested an audience with the South African Native Affairs Commission, which had just finished taking testimony. He submitted the Bishops' Declaration and added a personal promise to expel any minister "who used the pulpit for political purposes." When queried about the activities of AME ministers in the interior, Smith took refuge behind the government travel ban, which prevented him from "exercising ecclesiastical supervision." Pressed further, he disavowed the whole movement. "I do not intend to hold any official relation or correspondence with the men in Rhodesia, Transvaal, Orange River Colony, Natal, Basutoland, and Bechuanaland," he announced, lest it "be construed as being done in contempt of the governing authorities of those Colonies." Beyond the borders of the Cape, "I regard it that our Church has ceased to exist."[62]

Smith's impromptu disavowal did not deter him from trying to bring African church leaders in the interior to heel. One of his first targets was Benjamin Kumalo, the Bloemfontein-based presiding elder and one of the authors of the 1904 protest petition. By Smith's lights, the outspoken Kumalo embodied the evil of Ethiopianism: he chaired the Orange River Native Vigilance Society, an organization that mobilized Free State town dwellers in the years after the South African War; he was also a regular guest of the Basotho paramount chief Lerotholi. Smith began by reassigning the Basutoland work from the Orangia to the Cape District, taking the country out of Kumalo's circuit. Later, he supported an attempt by a group of disaffected Sotho local preachers to bring charges against Kumalo. Eventually he resorted to ridicule, accusing Kumalo of conflating Zulu "Fetishism" and Christianity. "I once heard him praise the ancient civilisation of his people over that of the British," Smith scoffed in a published pamphlet.

> I pointed out to him that before the advent of the European in South Africa there was no written language; no books or newspapers; no organized commerce, banks or clearinghouses; no churches or schools; no shipping industry; no railroads, postal, telegraph or telephone facilities; no codified laws or constitutional protection for life and liberty; nothing but wild barbarism accentuated by the fierce growl of untamed beasts.

"The A.M.E. Church stoutly repudiates all such wild vagaries," Smith concluded, "and has no place in its ministry for such 'Ephraims' as Kumalo."[63]

Conflict within the church was compounded by continuing controversy over money matters. Smith's term coincided with another of South Africa's periodic recessions and a severe financial crisis in the local church. In following Bishop Coppin's injunction to build permanent houses of worship, many congregations had fallen deeply into debt. Coppin himself, for all his emphasis on prudence, had undertaken substantial obligations in the church's name, in anticipation of support from America. In the western Cape alone, the church faced encumbrances on at least ten properties, including Bethel Institute and a large house that Coppin had purchased as an episcopal residence. As in 1900, Africans anxiously awaited the new bishop and the will-o'-the-wisp of American dollars.[64]

While the dearth of church records makes a definitive accounting impossible, enough fragments survive to piece together Bishop Smith's financial administration. He appears to have arrived with at least two thousand dollars in hand, earmarked by the General Conference for the episcopal residence. To Africans' astonishment, however, he refused to hand over the money. Nor did he raise a finger as a succession of church properties fell under the hammer, including the AME chapel in Pretoria, the birthplace of Ethiopianism. In retrospect, Smith seems almost to have welcomed the church's humiliation, which provided further proof of the folly of the whole enterprise. In January 1905, after just three months in the country, he sailed back to the United States. His object, according to a white missionary in whom he confided, was to persuade his colleagues in the AME House of Bishops to withdraw from South Africa entirely.[65]

Smith had still not returned in March, when the 1905 South African Annual Conference assembled in Kimberley. In the bishop's absence, confusion presided. Some delegates labored under the belief that Smith had gone on a fundraising tour and would return with money to redeem Bethel Institute; others doubted that he would return at all. Both camps were partially correct. A "humiliated" Smith arrived back in Cape Town in April, having been ordered back to his post by his fellow bishops. He did not, however, bring any money, or if he did he refused to part with it. Instead, he gathered the leaders of the AME Church in Cape Town and delivered yet another homily on self-help. African Americans could provide Africans with "advice, encouragement, and moral support," he stated, but ultimately "the colored people of America cannot fight your battles." Africans should rather look to the British, under whose benign trusteeship colored peoples the world over were making the difficult transition from barbarism to civilization. Ironically, Smith concluded his sermon with an account of the strides black Americans had made under the self-help regime, thus conserving stereotypes about African American progress and prosperity even as he sought to disabuse Africans of any hope of support from that quarter.[66]

Resentment soon swelled into rebellion. A few weeks after the Cape Town fiasco, a tribunal of leading African ministers convened and formally suspended Smith from office. While suspension of a sitting bishop was unprecedented in the church's history, the rebels followed procedures specified in the AME *Discipline.* They began by charging Smith with maladministration, presenting him with a list of specific offenses. (The central allegation was that Smith had refused "to interest himself with the debts and liabilities of the A.M.E. Church with intent to ruin the Church in South Africa.") The committee allowed the bishop time to answer the charges and suspended him only after the prescribed period had passed. At the conclusion of the proceedings, they mailed the records of the case to the House of Bishops in the United States for final adjudication. After nearly a decade of broken promises, African churchmen still retained a residuum of faith in the AME Church and in the connection with a broader black world that it embodied.[67]

Smith, however, proved a formidable adversary. A graduate of the hard school of AME Church politics, he had little difficulty finding irregularities in the rebels' action, the most serious of which was their failure to submit the issue to an annual conference. Dismissing his suspension as invalid, he convened a committee of his own and suspended his accusers; he later rammed a resolution through what remained of the South African Conference expelling them formally. The bishop also availed himself of the power of the pen, issuing a stream of pamphlets and letters, the bulk of them directed at whites, whom he saw as natural allies in his fight. In a circular letter to native affairs officials in all four South African colonies, Smith portrayed the rebels as a threat to "the sanctity of the Christian ministry and moral discipline." In an additional letter to imperial officials in the Transvaal and the Orange River colonies, he cast himself as a bulwark against "Ethiopianism" and stressed "how necessary it is that I should have the cooperation of the Governments of the various colonies so as to enable me to get rid of the 'Undesirables.'"[68]

South African officials, while careful to maintain a facade of impartiality, stood by the bishop. In the Transvaal, S. J. Mabote, a member of the tribunal that had suspended Smith, was denied relief from the pass laws on the grounds that he was no longer a minister. In the Cape, four of Smith's accusers were struck from the roll of marriage officers. Government permission to erect a church in Peddie district, H. R. Ngcayiya's old stomping ground, was rescinded after Smith withdrew his endorsement. In Pondoland, where the AME Church had long trafficked with paramount chief Sigcau, authorities rejected a series of AME applications, again at the bishop's behest. Matters had come full circle: where once Cape officials looked to black Americans to help them domesticate the independent church movement, an African American bishop now turned to the state to shore up his nonexistent authority.[69]

The ensuing months brought unremitting upheaval. Everywhere, the AME Church, hailed so recently as a focus of African unity, was riven by "rebel" and "loyal" factions. In Thaba 'Nchu, African Methodists remained divided for the next twenty years, in congregations known locally as AME and AME Smith. In Bloemfontein, a running conflict between Solomon Molotsi, a Barolong minister loyal to Smith, and opposition leaders Kumalo and Ngcayiya tore the church along ethnic lines. Molotsi and several hundred Setswana-speaking congregants eventually seceded from the AME Church to form the Bechuanaland Methodist Church. Violence erupted in a congregation in nearby Ladybrand, propelling more people into the Bechuanaland church. In Cape Town,

Smith himself was nearly assaulted when he attempted to replace Francis M. Gow, the popular pastor of Bethel Church, with J. J. Pearce, a newly arrived African American.[70]

Smith returned to the United States in late 1906, convinced that "nothing more could be done." The House of Bishops convened to discuss the matter a few months later. The bishops had little difficulty concluding that Smith's suspension was invalid, but they also recognized the folly of returning him to the field. In the end, they settled on a switch, posting Smith to West Africa and West Africa's William Derrick to Cape Town. The expedient solved little. Smith was no better disposed to West Africans than to South Africans, and he quickly became embroiled in new conflicts. Bishop Derrick, on leave in the United States at the time of his reassignment, was allegedly too ill to take up his new post. He reached South Africa only late in 1907 and remained just a few weeks.[71]

During the interregnum, the South African AME Church continued to hemorrhage. Without clear direction, stable leadership, or financial resources—without institutional resources of any kind—there was nothing to hold the church together, nothing to prevent differences of opinion from escalating into schism. A number of AME adherents were snapped up by the Apostolic Faith Mission, an American pentecostal church that entered the southern African field in 1906 and immediately began trolling the roiled waters of "Ethiopianism." With its emphasis on healing, possession, and baptism by immersion, the A.F.M. enjoyed a bountiful catch, especially among those seeking a more distinctively African Christianity than that offered in the AME Church. In 1909 the leader of the Apostolic Mission claimed, doubtless with some exaggeration, to have netted sixty "Ethiopian" congregations in the Transvaal alone. Many of these congregations soon spun out of the Apostolic Faith Mission and coalesced into new sects, completing the first round in the extraordinarily fissiparous history of South African independent Christianity. The Zion Apostolic Church, the Native Baptist Church, the Brethren Mission Church of South Africa, and a dozen other churches and sects were founded by leaders who had passed through the AME Church.[72]

Bishop Derrick's belated arrival did little to staunch the bleeding. While more committed to mission work than Smith, he shared most of his predecessor's assumptions about Africans and the need for careful supervision. Raised under the Union Jack—he was born in Antigua and first came to the United States as a sailor—Derrick exuded an unshakeable faith in Britain's essential beneficence, especially toward the world's "darker peoples." He also accepted the by now universal conviction that success in South Africa required placating white authorities. British High Commissioner Selborne, who permitted Derrick to come to Bloemfontein for an interview, came away from their meeting positively rapturous. "He is white, not black, to look at," Selborne wrote the Governor of Natal:

If I had met him anywhere, I should have taken him for a Spaniard or a Portuguese. He is enthusiastically British and strikes me all around very favourably
as a really good sensible man. He deplores the vagaries of certain members of his
Church in South Africa, and assured me that his only object in seeking leave of
the South African Governments to look after his congregations in the various
Colonies, was to wheel them into line, to make them good Christians and
thoroughly loyal to the Government.

Selbourne happily gave Derrick permission to remain in Bloemfontein to hold
a "Reconciliation Conference" of the entire South African AME Church.[73]

Africans, however, proved difficult to reconcile. Ministers who had remained loyal to Bishop Smith resented the restoration of rebel leaders, while
several of the rebels were unhappy with their new appointments, accusing
Derrick of punishing them with "dry circuits." The pressure continued to
build even as Derrick returned to the United States, where he triumphantly
announced that the crisis in South Africa was over. As the 1908 General
Conference assembled, the South African AME Church was wracked by one
more schism. H. R. Ngcayiya, Isaiah Sishuba, and Benjamin Kumalo—all
ministers in the original Ethiopian Church and members of the tribunal that
had suspended Bishop Smith—resigned from the AME Church and rees-
tablished the Ethiopian Church of South Africa. About a dozen ministers and
several thousand adherents joined them. The essence of the new church was
embedded in its name. In proclaiming themselves Ethiopians, the seceders
sought to reappropriate the mantle of Mangena Mokone's original Ethiopian
Church and, by extension, to lay claim to the independent Christian lineage
that Mokone had found in a biblical Ethiopia. The irony, of course, was that
their assertion of independence was directed not against European missionaries
but against a black American church.[74]

The Ethiopian secession of 1908, coming a dozen years after the founding of
the South African AME Church, provided the final concussion in African
Methodism's explosive early history. In the months and years that followed,
the church finally reached a kind of equilibrium, reflected in both a stabilizing
of membership and a cessation of conflict between African and African American church leaders. At least part of the credit for this new equilibrium belonged to American church leaders, who took several long overdue steps.
Belatedly heeding Bishop Turner's advice, the 1908 General Conference chose
missionary bishops from a distinct pool of candidates, each of whom committed to three four-year terms in the field. In the event, the bishop assigned to
South Africa, Canadian-born John Albert Johnson, served only two terms.
Even so, Johnson's tenure lent the South African church some desperately
needed continuity, while his quiet patience helped restore African faith in
African American leadership.[75]

American church leaders also finally opened their wallets. During Johnson's first term, the AME Church committed more than six thousand dollars to the field, including two thousand dollars to remove the "annoying and embarrassing" debt on Bethel Institute. Money continued to trickle in during the following quadrennium, including a five-thousand-dollar grant for Wilberforce Institute, a new teacher training center in the Transvaal. To be sure, investment never matched the inflated expectations of the early Ethiopians; pledges continued to outstrip remittances, and Bethel and Wilberforce occasionally struggled. Nonetheless, South Africans at last had something tangible to show for their affiliation with black America. Equally important, the AME House of Bishops exempted the Africans from financial obligations to the central church, removing a long-standing grievance. From 1914 on, proceeds from Easter, Endowment Day, and other regular church collections could be kept and dispensed locally.[76]

South African officials contributed to the equilibrium. In 1909, the governments of the Transvaal and the Orange Free State finally lifted the ban on interior travel, giving African American church leaders leave to travel more or less freely through the country. With the establishment of the Union Native Affairs Department in 1911, even Natal opened its doors to the AME Church, though by the time it did so the social space the church would likely have found had been occupied by a multitude of other churches and sects. In 1913 a special interprovincial Select Committee formally certified the AME Church as one of three independent churches of "sufficient magnitude and stability" to warrant official "recognition." From that moment on, African Methodists enjoyed virtually all the privileges of their counterparts in white mission churches—relief from pass laws, discounted railroad fares, the right to purchase sacramental wine, and access to school grants and church sites. (To prevent proselytizing, the Union government imposed a three mile radius rule on all new church site applications.) Unlike European missionaries, AME ministers were required to apply individually for recognition as marriage officers, but most had no difficulty meeting the educational requirement or obtaining the necessary endorsements from local officials. By the early 1920s the AME Church, once vilified as seditious and "intensely anti-European," was hailed as far and away "the most respectable of the purely Native Churches in South Africa." Several colonial officials and white missionaries wondered aloud whether there might be some way to steer South Africa's proliferating independent sects into the safe harbor of African Methodism.[77]

Few appreciated the layers of irony in that suggestion. Had missionaries and officials had their way at the turn of the century, the South African AME Church would not have existed in the 1920s. That it did was a testament not only to the determination and loyalty of African churchpeople but to the perspicacity of policymakers such as the Cape's Walter Stanford, who saw beyond the cries for repression to the long-term possibilities of a black American church in South Africa. Policymakers' very success, however, produced a curious defeat. As African Methodism evolved from movement to institution, it shed many of its adherents and hence lost much of its value as an agency of social control. By the 1920s white officials confronted precisely the situation Stanford had most feared: a profusion of independent sects without apparent structure or "responsible" leadership. The dangers of such a situation were demonstrated vividly on the fields of Bulhoek in early 1921, when eight hundred followers of Enoch Mgijima, a charismatic prophet indirectly descended from the AME Church, defied a government order to disperse. When the standoff finally ended, nearly two hundred Africans lay dead, and the South African government faced its first—not its last—international scandal.[78]

Thus, the years produced dramatic changes in the institutional face of African Methodism, transforming a diverse, dynamic popular movement into a more or less conventional mission church. Having traced that transformation, however, it is important to note that the South African AME Church never completely lost its vitality or its political edge. Even as African American church leaders won plaudits for their "balance" and "moderation," the concept of black America retained its imaginative potency among black South Africans. Moreover, the AME Church remained enmeshed in a system of racial domination in which the very existence of an independent black church could, in certain circumstances, assume profound political significance. We shall return to these themes in the final chapter. Before doing so, however, it is worth examining a group of people who experienced the ambiguities and paradoxes of the transatlantic connection even more acutely than African American church leaders.

8

"The Seed You Sow in Africa"

During the height of the Ethiopian panic in the early twentieth century, white South Africans leveled every variety of charge against the AME Church. The church was blamed for the Bambatha rebellion in Natal, for impertinent farm laborers in the Free State, and for restive domestic servants on the Rand. Nothing so exercised white observers, however, as the spectacle of guileless young Africans being dispatched to the United States for education. A European missionary, writing in 1904, admirably summarized the case, packing a universe of racist assumptions into two short paragraphs:

> Each year an increasing number of young men and women are sent from Africa, at the expense of the American Methodist Episcopal body, to study in the Negro universities of the United States. There they obtain a superficial veneer of knowledge, while breathing the atmosphere of race hatred which pervades these so-called seats of learning.
>
> After the attainment of a more or less worthless degree, these students return to their own country to preach, with all the enthusiasm of youth and the obstinate conviction of the half-taught mind, a gospel usually far more political than religious.[1]

So pervasive were such beliefs that the 1903–1905 South African Native Affairs Commission adopted "Ethiopianism" and the specific problem of AME-sponsored education as explicit objects of inquiry. After hearing grim prophecies of half-taught agitators loose among their uneducated, "impressionable" countrymen, the Commission recommended the creation of a local college for Africans—a recommendation that issued, twelve years and several commissions later, in the Inter-State Native College at Fort Hare. Fort Hare, as a Scottish missionary later conceded, was conceived as a matter of "self-defence": unless the state provided higher education at home, Africans would continue "going to America in search of it," returning "with notions which were not suited for South Africa."[2]

Who were the students who traveled to America? What "notions" did they absorb there, and how were these suited or unsuited for colonial Africa? While little work has been done specifically on South Africans, the transatlantic educational traffic has occasioned a substantial literature. Broadly speaking, scholars have advanced two contradictory hypotheses. Several historians have portrayed exposure to America as a radicalizing experience, citing the experience of American-educated African Nationalist leaders such as Nnamdi Azikiwe of Nigeria, Kwame Nkrumah of Ghana, and Nyasaland rebel John Chilembwe. Others have emphasized the depoliticizing, even reactionary, effects of American education; the stock figure for this interpretation is Gold Coast–born James Aggrey, who returned to Africa in the 1920s as an apostle of "sound," "adapted" education, along the lines of Booker T. Washington's Tuskegee Institute. A few individuals have served historical double duty. Thus, President-for-Life Hastings Kamuza Banda of Malawi, celebrated in the nationalist historiography of the 1960s for his role in the coming of independence, is portrayed today as the epitome of a stilted, authoritarian conservatism.[3]

Such studies share certain flaws, notwithstanding their different emphases. With few exceptions, scholars have focused on the careers of returned students, taking their backgrounds and experiences in America more or less as read. We thus have no way of explaining why American education produced the effects it did, even if we could agree what those effects were. Equally important, most studies of émigré students remain embedded in the "nationalist" historiographical tradition and share its characteristic deficiencies: the impulse to generalize on a continental scale; the reliance on paradigmatic figures and overly stark dichotomies; the elevation of politics over other kinds of action and consciousness and of nationalism over other kinds of politics. The limitations of such an approach are obvious as soon as one descends from the world of neat labels to the complexities of ideas in action. Kwame Nkrumah, for example, quintessential African nationalist, counted conservative James Aggrey as a formative influence. To take an example closer to home, Natalian John Dube, first president of the South African Native National Congress, was a leading advocate of Tuskegee-style industrial education, and later a proponent of a conservative, deeply patriarchal Zulu nationalism.[4]

This chapter attempts to address some of these paradoxes by examing the social origins, American experiences, and subsequent careers of about three dozen black South Africans who studied in the United States under the auspices of the AME Church between 1894 and 1914. While small in number, these students had a profound impact on their home country. Virtually an entire generation of AME leadership, including the church's first African-born bishop, were drawn from their ranks. Several also capitalized on the prestige conferred by their American diplomas to become leaders in secular politics. All the tensions and ambiguities that defined the South African AME Church, and the broader transatlantic traffic it facilitated, were expressed in the lives of these few dozen men and women.

It is a little-known fact that the first black students to matriculate at an American college were Africans. Bristol Yamma and John Quamine, two Gold Coast sailors, entered the College of New Jersey (Princeton) in 1774. Their enrollment was the brainchild of a pair of New England divines, Samuel Hopkins and Ezra Stiles, who envisioned them returning home as educated Christian missionaries. Revolution interrupted the experiment, but the idea endured, most dramatically at Ashmun Institute, later Lincoln University. Founded by a group of Princeton graduates in 1854, the Institute was designed to train black students, African and African American, for missionary service in the "Dark Continent." Many black Americans were alienated by the school's linkages with the American Colonization Society, but Lincoln did attract several dozen African students, mostly Americo-Liberians, in the decades after the Civil War.[5]

The flow of African students to the United States swelled with the growth of the African American mission movement. By the 1880s black American missionaries, working under the auspices of both black and white denominations, had established themselves all along the west coast of Africa and in the Congo. Like their European counterparts, these missionaries occasionally brought promising young converts home with them to be trained as ministers and teachers. Given the difficulty of recruiting missionaries for the African field, the policy was an expedient one, but it was also consistent with the ideology of African American evangelism, particularly with the notion that blacks themselves had been tapped for the task of redeeming Africa. For black Americans convinced by arguments about "providential destiny" but reluctant to venture to Africa themselves, American-trained Africans offered ideal substitutes. Indeed, African students who came to the United States were often portrayed as recapitulating African American experience, complete with the literal and metaphorical middle passage between savagery and civilization.[6]

By the end of the century, most white denominations had retreated from the idea of training African mission workers in the United States. By that time, however, African students were scattered through U.S. colleges. Orishatukeh Faduma, destined to become a leading intellectual of the embryonic pan-African movement, enrolled at Yale in 1891. In Nashville, Fisk University and Central Tennessee College both trained about half a dozen Liberian and Sierra Leonean students during the last quarter of the nineteenth century. The AME Church, after educating a group of Haitian "missionary students" in the 1870s, sponsored a handful of Americo-Liberian students in the 1880s and '90s, at both Wilberforce University and Huntsville (Alabama) A&M. The

AME Zion Church followed suit. James Aggrey, the most celebrated product of the educational trade, was one of four Fanti students brought to the United States in 1898 by an AME Zion missionary working in the Gold Coast.[7]

Because early Afro-American mission activity was concentrated in West Africa, South African students entered the educational pipeline relatively late. With the exception of John Dube, who came to the United States in 1887 under the auspices of the American Board of Missions, it is impossible to identify any black South African students in American colleges prior to 1894, the year the members of the African Jubilee Choir commenced their North American tour. A previous chapter has discussed the origins of the ill-fated choir, and traced the chain of events that brought the stranded singers into the arms of the AME Church. The upshot of the encounter was the enrollment of half a dozen South Africans at Wilberforce University as church-sponsored "missionary students."[8]

Charlotte Manye, whose letters home precipitated the union of the Ethiopian and AME churches, epitomized the early émigré students. Her father, remembered in the sources only by his European name of Jan, hailed from the eastern Transvaal, from the same part of Sekukuniland as Mangena Mokone. Sometime in the 1860s Jan Manye migrated to the eastern Cape, intending to work long enough to purchase a gun. Like so many migrants, he was converted to Christianity along the way, probably at a Free Church mission station. He married another convert, an educated Presbyterian woman of Mfengu stock whose name does not surface in the documentary record. The couple settled near Uitenhage, outside Port Elizabeth, a center of the Cape Christian elite. Charlotte, their first child, was born in the early 1870s; her sister, Kate, followed a few years later. In the 1880s the Manyes joined the trek of elite Africans from the eastern Cape to the Kimberley diamond fields, where the two sisters became stalwarts of the Free Church choir, which performed under the baton of future Ethiopian leader Simon Sinamela. Blessed with a rich contralto voice, Charlotte became the star attraction of the choirs which toured Britain and America in the early 1890s. She enrolled at Wilberforce in the winter of 1894–1895 and earned a B.Sc. in 1901, a distinction that qualified her as black South Africa's first female college graduate.[9]

Four or five other choir members joined Manye at Wilberforce: Magazo Fanele Sakie, James Nxanixani Kolombe, John Boyana Radasi, Edward Magaya, and perhaps Thomas Katiya. While less is known of them, their pedigrees were apparently similar to Manye's. All hailed from well-worn eastern Cape mission fields. Sakie and Kolombe, of Xhosa descent, came from Ngqika, near Queenstown, long a stronghold of the Wesleyan Methodist Missionary Society. Radasi, the oldest of the singers at twenty-eight, and Magaya, the youngest at twenty-one, came from Seymour and Cradock, respectively. Both were Mfengu and probably adherents of the Free Church of Scotland. Katiya's origins remain obscure. None of these students appears to have earned a Wilberforce degree. Kolombe was apparently driven back to South Africa by ill health. Magaya and Katiya transferred to Lincoln University, drawn perhaps by its Presbyterian affiliation, and graduated in 1903. Sakie's and Radasi's fates are unclear. [10]

Contrary to the assumptions of contemporaries (and some later historians), these first students were not blank slates upon which African American aspirations and sensibilities could be inscribed. On the contrary, they were products of a specific class at a particular historical moment. In mission parlance, they were "school people," members of a narrow, highly conscious Christian elite that first took root in the eastern Cape and later blossomed on the diamond fields. What evidence we have suggests that they shared the characteristic attitudes of their class—the devotion to education, the preoccupation with respectability, the ambivalent feelings of duty and disdain toward their "uncivilised" cousins. In the students' own terms, they were "progressive" Africans, a word that conveyed not only their commitment to Western-style progress but their sense of themselves as a racial vanguard. Indeed, choir members nightly reenacted the passage from "barbarism" to "civilisation," performing the first half of their program in traditional dress and vernacular languages and the second half in English and Victorian costume. All these attributes made the students uncannily receptive to African American mission ideology, especially to the idea that blacks themselves would carry the light of Christian civilization into Africa. Within a month of their arrival, one of the students, probably Magazo Sakie, wrote a letter to the *Voice of Missions,* pledging to use his education to help uplift his people. "To think of their condition almost breaks my heart," he confessed. The same missionary sensibility was evident in Charlotte Manye's first college essay: "I wish there were more of our people here to enjoy the privileges of Wilberforce and then go back and teach our people so that our home may lose that awful name, 'the Dark Continent,' and be properly called the continent of light." [11]

Just as she played a key role in introducing African Methodism to South Africa, so did Charlotte Manye help extend the "privileges of Wilberforce" to other members of her class. Spurred by her letters home, two of her Kimberley contemporaries, Chalmers Moss and Henry Msikinya, embarked for Wilberforce, arriving in 1896. The pair represented two of the most distinguished African families on the diamond fields. Chalmers Moss was the son of Joseph Singapy Moss, interpreter to the High Court of Griqualand West and one of the wealthiest Africans in Kimberley. A Lovedale graduate and devout Presbyterian—Chalmers was named for a pioneering Scottish missionary—"Mr. Interpreter Moss" exemplified the unflagging faith in education that was the signature of the nineteenth-century African elite. In Kimberley he was renowned for his defense of classical education, and he no doubt leapt at the opportunity to obtain a university training for his son. Henry Msikinya came from an equally illustrious family. His brother Jonas was court interpreter at

Beaconsfield; his brother John was an ordained minister in the Primitive Methodist Church; yet another brother, David, was a minister in the Wesleyan (and later the AME) Church. While the elder Msikinyas schooled at Lovedale, Henry followed David to Healdtown, the premier Methodist training institute in South Africa. At the time of his departure for America, he was a twenty-six-year-old schoolteacher, respected in the community for his work directing the Wesleyan Church choir and for his formidable skills as a debater. Tragically, Chalmers Moss died after a year in the United States, but Msikinya completed his degree and returned to South Africa in 1901.[12]

Two other students, Charles Dube and Theodore Kakaza, arrived at Wilberforce at about the same time as Msikinya and Moss. Both only eighteen years old, the two were younger than their compatriots, but their backgrounds were much the same. Dube was the son of an ordained American Board minister and the younger brother of John Dube, who had already begun to carve out a name for himself among Natal's *amakolwa* community. Like his more famous brother, Charles had studied at the Congregational mission at Amanzimtoti before coming to America. Kakaza was also the son of an ordained minister, Gana Kakaza, who headed a Wesleyan congregation in Port Elizabeth. Like Msikinya, he was a graduate of Healdtown. How the two young men came to be at Wilberforce is not clear. Dube was apparently dropped off at the school by his brother, who traveled to the United States in 1896 to raise money for what eventually became Ohlange Institute. Kakaza probably enrolled at the school through the intercession of his father, who, despite his Wesleyan affiliation, was an outspoken AME sympathizer.[13]

James Tantsi and Marshall Maxeke, who arrived at the end of 1896, were the first students to come to Wilberforce with the explicit intention of training as AME missionaries—they were, in fact, the two aspiring teachers referred to in Mangena Mokone's initial letter to Bishop Turner. In class terms, they were indistinguishable from their predecessors. Tantsi, eldest son of Ethiopian Church founder J. Z. Tantsi, had studied at Cape Town's Zonnebloem College; Maxeke had trained at Lovedale, apparently in the industrial department. The two were working together in Johannesburg as apprentice harnessmakers and AME evangelists when the opportunity to travel to America presented itself. With their arrival, the total number of South Africans enrolled at Wilberforce had grown to nearly a dozen.[14]

As word of Wilberforce filtered back across the Atlantic, African Christians from Cape Town to Bechuanaland determined to send their children. The enthusiasm was encouraged by itinerant AME ministers, at least some of whom lubricated their entry into old mission communities by promising free American education to the children of local notables. By the time of the 1900 AME General Conference, the traffic had grown so large that church leaders moved to restrict it, resolving to support only five students per year, and only those who had been African Methodists for at least one year before arriving.

The Conference further required that students sign pledges committing themselves to return home as AME missionaries after graduation. Even with these restrictions, however, the flow of students continued to increase. By 1904 the church was sponsoring about thirty South African students, two-thirds of them at Wilberforce, at an annual cost of about thirty-five hundred dollars. Virtually all of those who can be identified emerged from the same elite stratum that had produced the first students. John Manye was evidently a relative of Charlotte's. Mbulaleni Kuzwayo, Albert and David Sondezi, and Stephen Gumede all represented prominent Natal *amakolwa* families. Sebopioa Molema, a graduate of Lovedale, was one of the Mafeking Molemas; his uncle and sponsor, Silas, was South Africa's first black attorney. Judging from a few surviving letters, Sebopioa—in America, he used the Christian name Stephen—took great pride in his family's role as "instigator of civilisation" in South Africa. Here again was that missionary consciousness that would grow so luxuriantly in the soil of Wilberforce.[15]

A number of AME ministers took advantage of their positions in the church to arrange scholarships for their children. J. Z. Tantsi sent three children to Wilberforce: Harsant arrived in early 1898, two years behind James; later that same year Tantsi prevailed upon the visiting Henry Turner to take his daughter Adelaide back to America, scraping together one hundred pounds to cover her expenses. West Indian photographer and AME presiding elder Francis Macdonald Gow, a leader of Cape Town's emerging Coloured community, likewise sent three children to America: Hannah, who enrolled at Wilberforce around the turn of the century; Francis Herman, who followed a decade later; and Levi Coppin, who traveled to America in the wake of World War I. (Levi Coppin Gow was obviously the namesake of the first AME resident bishop, while his brother, Francis Herman, was destined to become the church's first African-born bishop.) Marcus Gabashane's son, Henry Barton, was only seventeen in 1898, when he arrived at Bishop Turner's Atlanta home with a dream of becoming a medical missionary. Younger still was Patrick Ngcayiya, who was scarcely thirteen when he accompanied his father to the 1904 General Conference in America. The lad remained behind at Wilberforce and eventually earned a bachelor's degree, long after his father had left the AME Church to reestablish the Ethiopian Church of South Africa. Last but not least was Jonathan Mokone, son of the AME Church's South African founder. Mokone enrolled at Wilberforce in about 1911, having graduated with the inaugural class at Wilberforce Institute, the school established outside Johannesburg by the first returning students.[16]

Enthusiasm for African American education exposes again the basic paradox that underlay the South African AME Church's rise. On one hand, the rush of students to U.S. colleges bespoke enormous frustration with European mission education, which had produced scarcely a dozen black matriculants in the previous fifty years. At the same time, however, elite Africans continued to subscribe to many missionary prescriptions, especially the idea that education was the key to individual and racial progress. Reinforcing that conviction were the exaggerated notions of Afro-American wealth and attainment that distinguished black South African perceptions of the United States in the nineteenth century. In this context, "Negro" education emerged as a kind of panacea, which would wrench open all the doors that mission education had promised, but failed, to open. Everywhere, the departure of students for America was portrayed in providential terms, as the germinal event in the birth of a new African civilization. Ethiopian Church founder Marcus Gabashane captured African expectations in a letter to Bishop Turner that accompanied his son Henry to America: "My Lord, remember again that this young man is the very seed you are going to sow in Africa."[17]

Enthusiasm for American education soon spilled beyond the banks of the AME Church. In 1901 P. J. Mzimba, founder of the African Presbyterian Church, arrived in America with eight young men whom he enrolled at Lincoln University. By 1903 close to two dozen of Mzimba's followers were studying in the United States, not only at Lincoln but at Tuskegee, where their presence stunned the visiting James Stewart, Mzimba's former superintendent. Dozens of other young Africans embarked for America as individuals, seeking professional training not available in South Africa: the most conspicuous examples were Pixley Seme and A. B. Xuma, both future presidents of the African National Congress. In contrast to their AME-sponsored counterparts, these students were generally responsible for their own passages and tuition, which ensured that they too were drawn from elite ranks. Gordon Dana, for example, one of the young men sent to America by Mzimba's church, was the son of a prosperous Mfengu farmer in Qumbu district. Melrose Sishuba and John Sonjica, who sailed to America in 1910, were the scions of two of the most successful "progressive" farming families in the eastern Cape; both men's fathers were former AME ministers. What evidence there is suggests that these students shared the sense of personal exceptionalism and racial obligation so characteristic of their class. As Sonjica and Sishuba explained in a letter to Booker T. Washington, "What we desire is to obtain education and go back to Africa and be a light to our people."[18]

Life could be quite precarious for those who arrived in America without institutional affiliation or sponsorship. Gordon Dana, for example, was unable to raise tuition after his father's death and returned to South Africa without the law degree he coveted. A. B. Xuma eventually completed his medical degree, but only by interspersing his studies with long stretches working in stables, coalyards, and boiler rooms. Sishuba and Sonjica had trouble even finding a school that would accept them. They vainly canvassed for scholarships at black American colleges before enrolling briefly at a Canadian business college. Sonjica's fate is uncertain, but Sishuba, his savings exhausted, ended up working as a railroad porter in Washington, D.C. He eventually hooked up with a Baptist association, which sponsored his training at a small school in Tennessee. He returned to South Africa after World War I.[19]

The year 1914 marked a watershed in the educational traffic. With the outbreak of war, most Africans had no way of reaching the United States, while those already there were stranded for the duration. After the armistice, government officials made a concerted effort to stem the traffic. From 1920 on, would-be emigrants to America were required to submit lengthy passport applications, including European character references and a fifty-pound (later one-hundred-pound) bond against the costs of possible repatriation. The new policy was prompted primarily by the specter of Garveyism, which rekindled fears of "Negro agitators" and provoked a brief ban on black American travelers. At the same time, the availability of "higher education" locally, at the new Inter-State Native College at Fort Hare, gave state officials a rationale for acting against the transatlantic traffic, a not insubstantial consideration for an administration concerned with projecting an appearance of even-handed justice and "fair play."[20]

The effect of the new policy was to slice the number of students traveling to America, while ensuring that those who did make the journey came from only the most respectable sectors of black society. Several students were actually sponsored by the South African government, acting through the medium of American philanthropic agencies like the Phelps-Stokes Fund. Sibusisiwe "Violet" Makhanya won the attention of Native Affairs Commissioner C. T. Loram for her work as a teacher and founder of the Bantu Purity League, an organization designed to lift the "moral standards" of African womanhood. In 1927 she and a colleague, Amelia Njongwana, received scholarships to study at Tuskegee and the South Carolina Penn School, headquarters of the "Jeanes teaching" system of vocational training. Reuben Caluza, destined to become one of black South Africa's most celebrated composers, and his fellow Natalian Q. M. Cele likewise found comparatively safe harbor at Hampton Institute. The AME Church, having recovered its hard-earned reputation for moderation and balance, continued to sponsor a handful of students at Wilberforce, all drawn from relatively middle-class backgrounds. Eli Nyombolo was the son of AME minister Chalmers Nyombolo, one of the founders of the Congress movement in the eastern Cape; Eva Mahuma was a schoolteacher; Pearl Ntsiko was apparently the daughter of one of Mangena Mokone's original Marabastad parishioners. The most famous Wilberforce product, Hastings K. Banda, future president of Malawi, worked as a clerk at a Witwatersrand goldmine before coming to America. Capitalizing on his uncle's status as an AME minister, he succeeded in persuading the local AME bishop to sponsor him to Wilberforce in 1924.[21]

Given the spottiness of the documentary record, it is impossible to establish the size of the transatlantic traffic with any precision, but clearly it was considerable. In early 1904 F. Z. S. Peregrino, a Cape Town newspaper editor and sometime government informant, reported that eighteen students had passed through the city en route to America in the previous month alone. Seven years later a Cape education official estimated that one hundred Africans from Cape Colony alone were in or had recently returned from the United States. A more conservative estimate would place the total number of South African students passing through the United States between 1894 and 1914 somewhere between 100 and 150, perhaps 50 of whom traveled under the auspices of the AME Church. Probably another two or three dozen made the passage in the 1920s. With the onset of the depression, even that small trickle more or less evaporated. By that time, however, dozens of black South Africans had made the pilgrimage to America. What had they found?[22]

One generalizes about African students' experiences in America at one's peril. South Africans enrolled in at least twenty colleges and institutes between 1894 and 1914. A few of the host schools—places like Oberlin and Columbia—were "white" institutions, with few African American students, let alone Africans. Some, like Lincoln and Howard, had black students bodies but largely white faculties and administrations. A few had black student bodies and were black-run. In terms of curriculum, institutions ran the gamut from Howard, which maintained a full slate of university liberal arts courses, to Hampton, the wellspring of industrial education, then emerging as America's racial panacea. The most popular destination, however, was Wilberforce University, an AME Church-sponsored institution just outside Xenia, Ohio. Black America's oldest college, Wilberforce hosted at least three dozen South African students before World War I.

Geographically and historically, Wilberforce and the surrounding countryside stood at the crossroads of North and South. While a part of the Old Northwest, the tranquil rivers and gently rolling hills of southwestern Ohio possessed a distinctly southern flavor. The region's first white settlers were Virginians, who were deeded farms in sixteen counties of southern Ohio for service in the revolutionary army. Xenia, one of a number of small commercial and manufacturing centers in the region, was founded in 1803 and settled primarily by migrants from Kentucky. Many farmers in the area planted tobacco, which was tended and harvested by gangs of slaves brought from across the Ohio River. The southern ambiance was sustained by the occasional columned portico and by the annual passage of southern planters, who arrived each summer to take the waters at several resorts in the area. One of the most popular, Tawawa Springs, stood on the future site of Wilberforce University.[23]

Racial practice in Ohio was shaped by the state's position at the crossroads of North and South. The state constitution, enacted in 1802, denied blacks the franchise, though mulattoes (those of at least 50 percent white parentage) were classed as white and entitled to vote. In the years that followed, the Ohio legislature passed the young nation's most notorious "Black Codes," essentially classifying all African Americans as aliens and denying them the normal protections of citizenship. (The codes required, for example, that African Americans carry proof of freedom and post bonds of up to five hundred dollars as guarantees of good conduct.) Though irregularly enforced, the codes left free people of color vulnerable to harassment and periodic outbreaks of racial violence, most dramatically in the Cincinnati riots of 1829. At the same time, however, Ohio was home to a more liberal racial tradition. The populous counties of the Western Reserve boasted a long antislavery heritage and provided fertile soil for the Liberty, Free Soil, and Republican parties. (In 1849 abolitionists in the Free Soil Party managed to secure the repeal of most of the state's Black Codes.) Ohio's facilities for black higher education were unique in America. Oberlin College was founded in 1833 and began to accept students "without regard to color" two years later. Wilberforce University was founded in 1856. That same year in nearby Yellow Springs, blacks were admitted to Antioch College at the instigation of the school's young president, educational reformer Horace Mann. During Reconstruction, Ohio was one of the first states to install a nonracial franchise.[24]

Black settlement in southwestern Ohio was pulsed by changes in the slave South. The majority of antebellum black settlers came from the upper South, especially Virginia, Kentucky, and North Carolina. A few were fugitives, but the vast majority were free people of color, borne northward by a rising tide of racist harassment. Many had acquired facilities for self-purchase in the afterglow of the American Revolution, and entered Ohio as individuals or in small family groups. Others came as entire communities. The Long community, the history of which was first documented by W. E. B. Du Bois, was composed of blacks, Indians, and a few Germans who were hounded out of Virginia and settled in Darke County, just north of Cincinnati. In a few cases, entire plantations of slaves were resettled in Ohio. Virginian John Randolph, for example, provided land in Mercer County for more than five hundred of his former slaves in the 1840s; another southern planter settled more than nine hundred former slaves on two sites in Brown County. The majority of black settlers seem to have established themselves as farmers, but some drifted to towns, where they worked as casual laborers or plied trades learned under slavery. In Xenia, about 17 percent of the town's pre–Civil War population— about eight hundred people in a populace of just over four thousand—were black. In proportional terms, Xenia possessed the largest African American population in Ohio; in absolute terms, its black population ranked behind only nearby Cincinnati's.[25]

Sprinkled within this growing black population was a substantial percentage of mulattoes, the product of unions between southern planters and black slaves. In several cases, planters who vacationed at Tawawa Springs settled their slave mistresses and offspring on farms in the area, several of which later became waystations on the underground railroad. (The concentration of "the dusky shades of society" around the Springs drew a scathing comment from the Cincinnati *Gazette* in 1854: "[T]he colored elite are in excellent health, though complexions aren't specially improved.") It is yet another index of the peculiarity of the "Peculiar Institution" that Wilberforce University, America's first black college, was largely built from the subscriptions of southern planters, who saw an opportunity to secure the education that their "dusky" sons and daughters were denied in their native South. Indeed, the school's first crisis came in 1861, when the Civil War drove its "chief patrons into the rebel army."[26]

The flow of blacks into southwestern Ohio swelled with emancipation. Freedmen and women from across the upper South flooded across the Ohio to pursue education, to locate lost relatives, or simply to shake the dust of bondage from their feet. By 1870 Xenia's black population had more than doubled. African Americans were drawn to Xenia and to neighboring towns like Chillicothe, Springfield, and Yellow Springs by a unique combination of educational and economic opportunities. In contrast to the cities and towns of the state's Western Reserve, southwestern Ohio attracted relatively little European immigration, leaving blacks to fill occupational niches occupied elsewhere by immigrants. In Springfield, for example, blacks worked in the iron foundries that opened in the 1880s. Xenia's small Irish population, descended of the navvies who brought the railroad in the 1840s, dominated the local shoe factory, but blacks composed the bulk of workers in the town's distillery, cordage factories, and tobacco-sorting plant. In the absence of white competition, a few blacks flourished as artisans; others took advantage of the substantial black market to open restaurants, barbershops, and a range of small businesses. Those with the wherewithal to buy a horse or wagon worked as hackers and draymen. To southern blacks caught in the punishing cycle of tenancy and debt peonage, the reports that filtered back from southwestern Ohio must have strained belief. As a pioneer sociologist studying the region in 1904 put it, "[A]ll negroes in Virginia, the Carolinas, and Kentucky know of Xenia and Springfield. . . . They regard these places as mecca."[27]

By the mid-1890s, when the train bearing the first of the South African students lurched into Xenia station, the town represented a curious amalgam of racial patterns and practices. At a time of accelerating urbanization, when most of rural and small-town Ohio was being drained of black settlement, the proportion of African Americans in the city continued to grow. While places like Cleveland and Cincinnati possessed only embryonic ghettos, Xenia showed a well-established pattern of racial segregation, with 90 percent of blacks crammed into a twenty-block-square area known to locals as the East End. The community possessed a tiny "old elite," made up of a few professionals who lived on the border of the East End and worshipped in white churches, as well as a more substantial postsegregation elite, rooted in black businesses and institutions. In addition to a massive AME Church, black Xenia boasted two Baptist congregations and at least a dozen lodges and fraternal orders. In contrast to the pattern in the South, however, the development of the internal resources of the black community in Xenia implied no political retreat. On the contrary, the concentration of people in a single city ward, together with the persistence of a vital Republican Party, enabled blacks to exercise substantial political power. Xenia blacks maintained a member on the city council and a representative on the local board of education; on one occasion, Greene County sent a black man, AME Bishop Benjamin Arnett, to the Ohio legislature. It was Arnett who introduced the 1887 bill rescinding the last remnants of the notorious Black Codes, a bill that marked the high-water mark in the postbellum struggle for racial justice in the state. Ironically, the major provision of the Arnett bill—integrating public schools—proved ineffectual in Xenia, where the concentration of blacks in the East End enabled local politicians to gerrymander segregated school districts. In tacit compensation, however, the town funded black education relatively generously.[28]

Exposure to Xenia probably did little or nothing to unsettle the inflated ideas about black American "progress" that the arriving students carried with them from South Africa. The town may not have been Mecca, but compared to the conditions they had seen in South Africa—compared, for that matter, to the condition of blacks in the rest of the United States—it presented a picture of remarkable prosperity. Houses in the East End were tidy, if sometimes overcrowded, and streets were alive with flowers. Most families owned their own homes. The people, on the whole, seemed sober and industrious; a few boasted professional degrees and substantial fortunes. Education was clearly a precious value to Xenia blacks, and virtually all residents, aside from the newest southern migrants, possessed some schooling. (The literacy rate in the East End was only marginally below the national average for all races and a full third higher than the Afro-American average.) Adults could improve themselves by attending classes and lectures offered in the evening by teachers from nearby Wilberforce, while a local compulsory schooling ordinance ensured the nearly universal education of the young. At a time when most towns in Ohio offered only rudimentary elementary education for African Americans, Xenia boasted a well-equipped black high school, which annually graduated about a dozen students, better than a quarter of the total number of black matriculants in the entire state of Ohio. Taken as a whole, there was little in the town's aspect to indicate that African Americans were but three decades removed from slavery.[29]

Socially, politically, and intellectually, black Xenia was oriented toward Wilberforce University, and twice a year, on Founders' Day and on Commencement Day, the entire community set out on the two-mile journey to the campus. By the 1890s a remarkable elite community had coalesced around the university, representing some of black America's most distinguished families.

The family of Thomas and Francis Brown was representative. In the 1840s the Browns left their Pittsburgh home and joined the black expatriate community in Canada. They returned after the Civil War and settled at Wilberforce, drawn by the prospect of obtaining education for their children. The oldest child, Jere, moved to Cleveland, where he distinguished himself as a lawyer and state legislator; the youngest, Hallie Quinn, traveled widely but eventually resettled at Wilberforce, where she lectured in elocution and organized a chapter of the elite National Association of Colored Women. At least two other founders of the N.A.C.W., Anna Julia Cooper and Mary Church Terrell, also taught at Wilberforce in the last decades of the century. (Cooper's classic *A Voice from the South* was published in Xenia and dedicated to AME Bishop Benjamin Arnett.) Martin Delany, the pioneer pan-Africanist, spent his retirement at Wilberforce; his wife and children still lived in the community when the first South Africans arrived. Campbell Maxwell, a Xenia attorney and a former U.S. ambassador to Santo Domingo, was a fixture at the school, as was poet Paul Laurence Dunbar, who traveled from nearby Dayton to give readings. At a time when most African Americans were stalked by poverty and debt, the average family at Wilberforce held about twenty-five hundred dollars in personal property. The air of affluence and respectability was further enhanced by the annual passage of the cream of black Ohio society, which came to Wilberforce each summer to share in the cultural life of the community and to take the waters once enjoyed by southern planters. Without question, this was the most educated and affluent black community in America, and the South African students were quickly gathered into its folds.[30]

The faculty to which the arriving students were exposed included some of America's foremost black intellectuals. W. E. B. Du Bois, recently returned from Germany and still affecting the gloves and cane of the continental intellectual, lectured the first students in English, German, and Classics. William S. Scarborough, who taught classical languages in the newly opened Payne Theological Seminary, had risen from slavery to become one of America's premier philologists. Edward Clarke (later the namesake of Marshall and Charlotte Manye Maxeke's first child) lectured in Latin, while the venerable John G. Mitchell, one of the school's pioneers, remained as dean of the seminary. The school's military science department, established in 1894 with a special federal grant, was headed by Lieutenant Charles Young, a graduate of West Point and at the time the only black commissioned officer in the U.S. Army. In the early years of the century, the faculty was supplemented by Theophilus Gould Steward, the politician, theologian, and pioneering Reconstruction missionary, and by sociologist and future Bishop R. R. Wright, Jr. All these men were prominent members of the American Negro Academy.[31]

The president of the university was Samuel T. Mitchell, but affairs at the school were overseen by the resident bishop, Benjamin Arnett. Largely forgotten today, Arnett in his time may have been the most influential black man in

America. Born free in Kentucky and trained first as a schoolteacher, he had by the 1890s accumulated a resumé that virtually defined the ambit of the post-bellum northern black elite: bishop and financial secretary of the AME Church; secretary to the National Convention of Colored Men; national vice president of the Anti-Saloon League; grand director of the Grand Order of Odd Fellows. A canny and ambitious man, Arnett was unswerving in his loyalty to the Republican Party, denouncing the Liberal schismatics in 1872 and expediently endorsing the party's retreat from Reconstruction four years later. His fealty eventually won the attention of Marc Hanna, chief Republican fixer in Ohio and the power behind Governor William McKinley. Hanna valued voters of any color, and he saw in the ambitious bishop of America's largest and most affluent black church a bridge to African American voters, North and South. He cultivated Arnett throughout McKinley's march to the White House; it was Arnett who delivered the invocation and benediction at the 1896 National Republican Convention and who supplied the Bible on which McKinley swore the presidential oath of office. In the five years before McKinley's assassination, federal patronage to blacks was funneled through the bishop's Wilberforce home, in much the same way that McKinley's successor, Theodore Roosevelt, channeled patronage through Tuskegee. Arnett, then in his glory, took a special interest in the newly arrived South African students, especially Charlotte Manye, whom he and his wife treated almost as a daughter. The South Africans were always welcome at his home, where they could chat with his guests, including Hanna, or avail themselves of his substantial personal library.[32]

The individual who wielded the greatest influence over the young Africans, however, was a man that none of them ever met. Daniel Payne, the senior AME bishop and a fixture at Wilberforce since its founding, died a year before the arrival of the first South Africans. It was Payne who helped launch the college in 1856 as a joint venture between the AME Church and the Cincinnati Conference of the white Methodist Episcopal Church. When the school languished six years later, it was he who redeemed it, buying the whole facility in the name of the AME Church for the cost of its debt. When a bitter southern sympathizer burned the school to the ground in 1865, Payne patiently rebuilt it. Even after resigning the presidency of the university in 1877, Payne maintained his episcopal see at Wilberforce, running the school, and for a time the entire AME Church, as a virtual fiefdom. One of his last acts at the school was to join Frederick Douglass and Governor McKinley in inaugurating Payne Theological Seminary, the culmination of his lifelong quest for an educated black ministry. One of the explicit objects of the new seminary, according to its first catalog, was to prepare "missionaries for the redemption of Africa and other foreign lands."[33]

All of Payne's attributes—his piety, his obsession with self-improvement, his unswerving belief in the transforming power of education—were infused into the very structure of the school he built. In the true spirit of liberal education, the Wilberforce experience aimed to develop all an individual's faculties, moral, physical, and intellectual. Student life was governed by a rigid code of conduct, beginning with mandatory attendance at morning chapel. Students provided whatever labor was necessary to maintain buildings and grounds. Physical culture was a required course for men and women alike. Long before the rise of Booker T. Washington, Payne stressed the virtues of manual labor, the obligation to racial service, and the need for a balanced education that trained head, hands, and heart in concert.[34]

What distinguished Wilberforce from Hampton or Tuskegee was its underlying faith in African Americans' intellectual potential. Students in both preparatory and collegiate divisions confronted a full classical curriculum, featuring ancient and modern languages, mathematics, and science, which Payne understood as a kind of natural theology. Rhetoric and composition bulked large in the curriculum, and frequent recitations encouraged proper elocution—a skill that Payne saw as necessary to blacks' eventual assimilation into the mainstream of American society. Candidates for the ministry received training in everything from systematic theology to Hebrew, and the school even boasted a small law department. Four degrees were awarded: a bachelor of arts degree for those who completed the classical curriculum; a bachelor of divinity degree for graduates of Payne Seminary; and bachelors' degrees in science and in law.[35]

It is tempting to portray the Wilberforce of the 1890s as the last bastion of black higher education in the dawning age of Booker T. Washington, but the truth is more complex. Despite the presence of a seminary and a few law courses, Wilberforce's claim to university status was always something of a pretension, as Payne (and, later, Du Bois) freely admitted. Throughout the nineteenth century, the bulk of students at the school were enrolled in the preparatory, or secondary, division; in all, the school awarded no more than fifty bachelors' degrees in its first half century. Even those who completed the collegiate course rarely found their way into the professions but instead gravitated toward teaching, just like their counterparts at "industrial" schools like Hampton and Tuskegee. What prevented Wilberforce from reaching the academic heights envisioned by Payne and later attained by Howard University was simply lack of money. While Howard received upwards of half a million dollars a year from its white governors, Wilberforce depended almost solely on the mites of AME Church members. In a good year, the AME Education Department might raise twenty thousand dollars for higher education, and even that had to be divided among a dozen church-sponsored colleges, each of which jealously guarded its apportionment. At the same time, Wilberforce's continuing commitment to higher education was enough to alienate the philanthropic capital that transformed humble Tuskegee into such a showplace.

Aside from a small Carnegie library, built in 1904, the Wilberforce campus boasted no monuments to white philanthropy.[36]

AME Church leaders found a partial solution to the problem in 1888, when Ohio's Republican-controlled legislature, in a blatant act of political patronage, established a commercial, normal, and industrial department on the Wilberforce campus. Under the terms of the department's charter, each state legislator awarded one scholarship to Wilberforce per year, enabling hundreds of young African Americans to qualify as teachers or to obtain certificates in subjects such as carpentry, bookkeeping, and domestic science. In the long term, the presence of a state-supported training institute on the campus of a church-run university generated profound questions about the school's mission, as well as nearly insuperable problems of academic governance. In the more immediate term, however, the C.N.I. Department brought tens of thousands of dollars in state aid to Wilberforce, enabling the school to maintain a full slate of university courses at a time when most black schools were being pushed toward more "practical" curricula. During the era of the South African students, the relationship between Wilberforce and the C.N.I. Department apparently ran smoothly. State-funded normal students completed all their liberal arts prerequisites within the university, while university students were able to avail themselves of industrial courses.[37]

The records of Wilberforce University have endured more than their share of fires and tempests, making it almost impossible to reconstruct the reception or day-to-day experiences of the South African students. On a campus of about four hundred students, they were undoubtedly conspicuous, doubly so since Africa was already the subject on every tongue. (The very month the first Africans arrived, Wilberforce was visited by a self-styled "African Explorer," who showed astonished students the scars that established her as a "blood brother" of a particular "tribe.") Sermons, essay contests, and monthly missionary meetings all dwelt on Africa. While few at the school endorsed Bishop Turner's emigrationist schemes, most seem to have accepted that black Americans possessed a distinct, providential obligation toward the continent, which was alternately portrayed as a garden uncorrupted by man and a jungle befogged by ignorance and vice. The reception of the first students reflected such preconceptions. Theodore Kakaza later indignantly recalled that a few of his fellow students "had the nerve to examine our anatomy, to see if they could observe the remnants of our forest ancestors." More subtle but no less revealing, groups of church women "adopted" a number of the Africans, despite the fact that most were well into their twenties. The women of the North Ohio Conference of the Woman's Mite Missionary Society, for example, adopted "that Rare Jewel," Charlotte Manye, and, later, Adelaide Tantsi, "our dear sweet African daughter." Magazo Sakie was likewise adopted by local churchwomen, who, in the best missionary tradition, renamed him Daniel Payne, in honor of their late bishop.[38]

Such attitudes seem to have persisted even after the South African students were ensconced at the school, despite the obvious fact that they were neither children nor savages. The winner of the 1899 Eliza Turner prize, awarded each year for the best student essay on Africa, characterized the continent as "an uncouth, rugged child," peopled by a "slumbering" race. At monthly mission meetings, students prayed for the future of "civilization" in Africa and read of the heroic labors of Livingstone, Moffat, and the other missionary pioneers who had first carried light into Africa's pagan gloom. In part, such attitudes could persist because the South African students did little to challenge them. On the contrary, the image of a slumbering continent, just stirring to life, accorded quite well with their own preconceptions, with the proviso, of course, that they counted themselves among the awakened. The several surviving speeches and essays of Charlotte Manye, for example, all remain well within the "Dark Continent" tradition of African reportage, a reflection no doubt of her deference to audience expectations but also of her own distance from African customary life. In later life, Charlotte would evince considerable respect for the African past—like many black elite spokespeople in South Africa in the 1920s and '30s, she came to portray the precolonial past as a lost idyll of order, harmony, and generational control—but her 1890s accounts resounded with lurid tales of ritual killings, live burials, and snake-bedecked "witchdoctors." Hearing such accounts, listening to the South African students' renditions of fearful native "war songs," students at Wilberforce doubtless came away even more persuaded of the urgency of African "redemption."[39]

AME leaders were quick to appreciate the South African students' value in promoting the cause of foreign missions. The African Choir was reconstituted on campus and carted to no end of conventions and conferences. South African singers performed at Commencement and Founders' Day celebrations and at the 1898 convention of the predominantly white Student Volunteer Movement. (Henry Msikinya addressed the Volunteers on "The Condition of My People.") The students also performed at the 1900 AME General Conference, following a vernacular selection with the African Methodist missionary standard "Breathe a Prayer for Africa." Black Americans, many of whom had never laid eyes on a native-born African, clamored to see and hear and touch them. Church periodicals printed rapturous descriptions of their humility, piety, and intelligence. In the students, such articles implied, African Americans could glimpse Africa's future, as well as something of their own past. For a group of young people fresh from Africa, this was bracing stuff, which no doubt did much to intensify the convictions of duty and destiny that they had brought with them to America.[40]

The daily round that the South African students experienced still followed Bishop Payne's spartan regime, with its emphasis on self-control, punctuality, and hygiene. Payne was a notoriously early riser, and students at his school were up by 5:30 each morning, tidying their rooms and fetching coal and water for the day. Morning chapel commenced at 8:00. Classes followed, interrupted only by lunch and physical culture, which in the case of men consisted of marching about the parade ground under the watchful eye of Lieutenant Young. Students enjoyed an hour of free time after dinner before being dispatched to their rooms for a mandatory study period. Lights out—lanterns out, actually, since the school was without electricity—came at 9:00 P.M. Weekends offered little respite from the routine, aside from a Saturday night bath and a second chapel service on Sundays. Missionary meetings, a monthly temperance lecture, and regular elocution contests completed the circuit of the days. The iron routine was broken only by "mixers," closely chaperoned affairs that consisted of students marching up and down hallways to the strains of martial music, and by the annual revival, when, in best Methodist fashion, labor was suspended and the spirit given reign.[41]

A battery of rules helped create an atmosphere of rigid propriety. Use of alcohol or tobacco, gambling, profanity, insubordination, even leaving the school grounds without permission were all offenses warranting expulsion. "Associating" between the sexes was likewise a dismissable offense, a testament to Payne's preoccupation with eradicating any vestigial promiscuity left from slave days. Male and female students walked to recitation halls through different hallways, and when their paths did cross they were obliged to pass without speaking. (It is a testament to the human spirit that romance blossomed even in this sere environment: Marshall Maxeke and Charlotte Manye were betrothed while at Wilberforce, as were Adelaide Tantsi and Charles Dube.) Not all students adapted well to the Wilberforce regimen. In the most notorious case, a female student expelled in the 1880s retaliated by setting fire to the school's main block, destroying tens of thousands of dollars worth of property. For their part, the South African students seem to have adjusted well, thanks perhaps to their previous experience in European mission schools. Surviving records of the school's Disciplinary Board reveal no cases involving Africans.[42]

It is difficult to establish what courses of study individual students pursued, due both to the loss of records and to the curricular overlap between the preparatory, collegiate, and C.N.I. departments. All of the arriving students, save Henry Msikinya, were placed initially in preparatory classes, apparently to improve their English. Msikinya, a graduate of the premier Wesleyan mission school in South Africa, enrolled directly in Payne Theological seminary, graduating with a B.D. in 1901. Charlotte Manye, after a year of remedial English, pursued the "scientific" curriculum and earned a B.Sc., also in 1901. Both returned to South Africa a short time later, he as an ordained minister and she as a teacher. Their peers took somewhat longer to complete their studies. Theodore Kakaza graduated with a B.Sc. in 1902 and proceeded to Toronto to study medicine. Marshall Maxeke earned a bachelor of arts degree in 1903, the same year that Edward Magaya and Thomas Katiya, who had transferred from

Wilberforce to Lincoln, obtained their arts degrees. Charles Dube and Adelaide Tantsi completed B.Sc. degrees in 1904 and 1905, and Sebopioa Molema took a law degree in 1906. James and Harsant Tantsi both studied divinity, graduating in 1905 and 1907, respectively. Probably a dozen other South Africans earned Wilberforce degrees prior to or during World War I, but it is difficult to specify when or in what fields.[43]

The evidence permits a few generalizations. It appears that about half of the students who came to Wilberforce completed bachelors' degrees, though they frequently took seven or eight years to do so. Obviously students who came at a younger age or with less preparation spent a longer time in the preparatory division and thus took longer to earn diplomas. Patrick Ngcayiya, just thirteen when he arrived in 1904, took five years to qualify for the collegiate course and another five to finish his degree. Michael Seganoe spent twelve years at Wilberforce before failing eyesight drove him home without a degree. Equally striking is the concentration of South African students in teaching and ministerial tracks. Only two of the early students, Sebopioa Molema and Stephen Gumede, pursued law degrees, and only one, Theodore Kakaza, proceeded to medical school. Finally, all of the students had some exposure to "industrial education" and were doubtless familiar with the arguments advanced on its behalf. (Looking to the students' future as missionaries, the 1900 AME General Conference resolved that all African students should receive training in at least two branches of industry.) Charlotte Manye and Adelaide Tantsi took courses in domestic science, while Charles Dube completed a course in carpentry, which undoubtedly helped prepare him for his future work at Ohlange Institute. Thomas Kalane, who enrolled at Wilberforce in 1906, earned a printing diploma. Nonetheless, the Wilberforce students were clearly not devotees of "practical" education. They saw industrial training not as the essence of their educations but as an adjunct to it, to help prepare them for the responsibilities they would shortly assume back in South Africa.[44]

How did they define those responsibilities? How did Wilberforce shape their sense of themselves and of their future role in South Africa? Again, it is difficult to say, because the South African students were exposed to a range of political opinion. They apparently never met Frederick Douglass, a frequent visitor at the school prior to his death in February 1895, but they did hear the eulogy to Douglass that W. E. B. Du Bois delivered in the Wilberforce chapel a few weeks later. Benjamin Arnett bestrode the campus, a walking advertisement for political pragmatism. The students met the venerable Alexander Crummell at the 1896 commencement, and Booker T. Washington two years later. Bishop Turner, still breathing the fire of African emigration, was a regular visitor to the campus and never failed to stop and visit the South Africans, especially after his 1898 tour of their homeland. The entire AME House of Bishops, including Benjamin Tanner, Turner's great adversary, descended on the school at least once a year.[45]

All the arguments and questions that defined African American politics at the end of the nineteenth century were embodied in this roster. Should blacks capitalize on their votes and on existing antidiscrimination laws to push for full equality, or should they eschew politics in favor of economic development? What was the role of the black intellectual? Did the future of the race lay in America at all? The South African students no doubt confronted all these questions at Wilberforce. Withal, the dominant influence on their outlook remained what one might call the "moral assimilationism" of Daniel Payne. While Payne never renounced equality or full political participation for blacks, he remained convinced that they would come only when African Americans themselves had demonstrated the intelligence, character, and moral fiber essential to responsible citizenship. The whole culture of Wilberforce—the structured regimen, the elocution contests, even the concern with hygiene—reflected that conviction.

Probably the most important purveyor of Payne's analysis, at Wilberforce if not in the United States as a whole, was the young W. E. B. Du Bois. Du Bois's 1895 eulogy for Douglass and his classic "Conservation of Races," published by the American Negro Academy two years later, clearly bore the stamp of both Payne and Alexander Crummell, whom he ranked as nineteenth-century black America's two greatest leaders. (In his *Autobiography*, published almost seventy years later, Du Bois still remembered the reverence he felt when he met the aged Crummell at the 1896 Wilberforce Commencement.) The paradox in Du Bois's thought, of course, was that his vision of "civilization," and his commitment to black assimilation in America, coexisted with a kind of mystical racialism—a belief in the genius and distinct destiny of the black race that owed more than a little to his youthful encounter with German philosophy. Eventually, these convictions would lead Du Bois back to Africa, where he lent his name to Kwame Nkrumah's experiment in "African Socialism." In the 1890s, however, Du Bois still spoke the Wilberforce language of racial uplift, with its distinctly bourgeois cadences. In "The Conservation of Races," for example, he wrote, "We believe that the first and greatest step toward the settlement of the present friction between the races . . . lies in the correction of the immorality, crime and laziness among the Negroes themselves, which still remains as a heritage of slavery."[46]

Three other aspects of the political culture of Wilberforce warrant special remark. First and most obvious, the assimilationist project was to be pursued within separatist institutions. As much as Payne and his successors valued their contacts with whites, virtually all of the institutions that flourished within the Wilberforce community—the Masons and Odd Fellows, the National Association of Colored Women, the American Negro Academy—were segregated or forthrightly racial. Obviously, the university was a racial institution, as was the AME Church itself. The solution to this apparent paradox lay in seeing separate institutions as church leaders since Richard Allen had seen them: as means rather than ends in themselves. For most of the nineteenth century, separatist institutions were judged to offer blacks the best opportunity to hone their leadership and organizational skills, and to exhibit those qualities of civility upon which their assumption into the dominant society was presumed to depend. Benjamin Arnett, who subscribed to dozens of elite racial organizations, put the matter succinctly when he described the black Order of Odd Fellows as a "moral normal school" for the race. He might have added, but did not, that such institutions freed blacks from the affronts and indignities they were forced to endure in interracial organizations.[47]

Second, the vision articulated by Payne, Crummell, and the young Du Bois was unapologetically elitist, with the educated elite—what Du Bois in 1897 called "the better classes"—cast as both vehicle and vanguard of racial progress. Prominent individuals, through the conspicuousness of their attainments, would show skeptical whites (as well as the downtrodden of their own race) what blacks could achieve when given the opportunity. At times, this analysis conduced to an almost biographical conception of racial progress, as evidenced by such books as Kletzing's and Crogman's *Progress of a Race* and W. J. Simmons's massive *Men of Mark: Eminent, Progressive and Rising.* This elite self-conception was reinforced at Wilberforce in endless sermons and lectures, which stressed students' exceptionalism and exhorted them to take up their burden of "racial service." Implicit in all this was a distinct ambivalence toward the black masses. Acculturated leaders constantly fretted that their efforts would be subverted by the lower classes, whose poverty, vice, and penchant for enthusiasm reinforced the very prejudices that the elite was struggling to break down. Few suggested that the masses might be capable of "uplifting" themselves, still less that they might possess attributes meriting respect and preservation.[48]

Finally, the political culture of Wilberforce was almost staggeringly optimistic. Ultimately, the whole formula rested on the by now familiar assumption that prejudice was susceptible to reason, that at a certain point the dominant society would recognize its folly and throw open its doors, at least to the more meritorious members of the race. Bishop Arnett expressed that conviction in a metaphor characteristic of the age: "If a man is worth a dollar, he will be treated as a dollar." Obviously, such optimism could only be sustained outside the southern states. Indeed, it was increasingly difficult to sustain even in the privileged world of Wilberforce. The 1890s witnessed half a dozen lynchings in southern Ohio, at least one of which occurred after the South African students had arrived at Wilberforce. The passage of a tough state antilynching bill in 1898 helped restore black Ohioans' confidence, but it was shaken again by outbreaks of mob violence against blacks in Akron in 1900 and in nearby Springfield four years later. Even Jim Crow seemed to be crossing the Ohio. Delegates to the 1900 AME General Conference in Columbus, where the African Choir performed, were chagrined to find themselves

refused accommodation in the city's best hotels. In the long run, such developments would divest Du Bois and leaders like him of many of their liberal
assimilationist assumptions. In the short term, however, the gathering clouds
of racist reaction made the task of racial uplift seem all the more urgent.[49]

What is significant for our purposes is how neatly the notions of respectability and racial uplift that characterized Wilberforce dovetailed with the
assumptions the first South Africans had brought with them to America.
Indeed, it is difficult to conceive a more congenial intellectual climate for the
students. Terminology differed: where progressive South Africans spoke of
the "civilised" and the "barbarous," progressive African Americans contrasted
the "enlightened" and the "ignorant." One group lamented the vestiges of
heathenism, the other the vestiges of slavery. Nonetheless, the essential idea,
of an acculturated elite lighting the path to racial progress, was identical. Long
before they reached Wilberforce, educated Africans such as Henry Msikinya,
Charles Dube, and Theodore Kakaza had imbibed a sense of their own exceptionalism and had learned to equate their own advancement with the progress
of the race.

Seen from this vantage, the remarkable fact about the Wilberforce experience is not the way in which it transformed African students' consciousness but
the way in which it honed an already developed self-conception. This is not to
say that the effect of the visit was minimal or unimportant; human beings
generally are more forcibly impressed by phenomena which appear to confirm
existing convictions than by those which challenge them. For these students,
passing through Wilberforce at this particular moment, exposure to black
America offered priceless vindication, a confirmation of the future that had
been charted for them and their race. Shielded as they were from the more
intractable realities of Afro-American life, they left the school with all the
articles of their nineteenth-century creed—their devotion to "civilisation,"
their beliefs in education and progress, their faith in the essential reasonableness of the colonial order—intact. For them, as for many of their mentors at
Wilberforce, the long journey of disillusionment was just beginning.

The first two Wilberforce graduates, Charlotte Manye and Henry Msikinya,
returned to South Africa in September 1901, to a rapturous welcome in Cape
Town's Metropolitan Hall. Over the next quarter century, they were joined by
scores of other American-educated black South Africans. By the mid-1920s,
South Africa boasted a whole stratum of American graduates, embedded not
only in the AME Church but in the broader world of African education and
politics. What roles did these returning students play? What was the nature of
their kinship with black America, and with the world they had left behind?
How did they respond when Africa's golden future, the providential awakening of which they were to be the instrument, failed to materialize?[50]

As always, there are no single answers to these questions; the paths the students followed after leaving America were at least as various as those that led them there initially. Nonetheless, certain generalizations suggest themselves. Clearly, American education did not have the transformative effect that its early proponents had envisioned. While there was never any real consensus as to what African American education could or would do, most of its advocates assumed that it would enhance African mobility, enabling blacks to aspire to something beyond the ministerial and teaching careers that remained the ceiling for most mission school graduates. "We have been sending our children to these schools where they have been trained to be Evangelists and school teachers," Transkeian headman Enoch Mamba complained to the South African Native Affairs Commission in 1904. "There are too many of the school teachers and they cannot get work, they are not trained for anything else, whereas in America they will get into a place where they will get cheap education, and wider education than they get in these Mission schools." In short, an American diploma would throw open the professional doors that mission education had promised, but failed, to open.[51]

Ironically, however, it was precisely to the ministry and teaching that the vast majority of the returning students gravitated. Among the Wilberforce contingent alone, the roster of future clerics included Henry Msikinya, Marshall Maxeke, James and Harsant Tantsi, Edward Magaya, Jonathan Mokone, and Abraham Lawrence. Virtually all the students devoted considerable chunks of their lives to African education. Msikinya taught at AME schools in the western Cape and Transvaal before his premature death in 1912. Marshall Maxeke and his wife, Charlotte Manye Maxeke, opened a succession of schools in the northern Transvaal, on the East Rand, and in the Transkei. Adelaide Tantsi taught at the controversial "Ethiopian" school at Klipspruit before moving to Natal to join her betrothed, Charles Dube, who served until his death as headmaster of his brother John's Ohlange Institute. Msikinya, the Tantsi brothers, Maxeke, Magaya, and future AME bishop Francis Gow all occupied the principalship of Wilberforce Institute, the teacher-training school south of Johannesburg that became the focus of AME educational efforts in the subcontinent. For the next half century, the upper echelons of AME leadership in South Africa were recruited almost exclusively from the ranks of the American-educated.[52]

To some extent, the students' gravitation toward teaching and the ministry was dictated by their African American mentors. From the outset, AME Church leaders in the United States conceived the South Africans as "missionary students," and they directed their educations accordingly. Equally important, however, was the subtle and not-so-subtle channeling students experienced after returning to South Africa. The experience of Sebopioa Molema was fairly typical. The product of one of black South Africa's most distinguished families, Molema earned a bachelor's degree in law at Wilberforce and went on to qualify as an attorney. He returned to South Africa to open a practice, but his career was stymied when the Cape administration declined to recognize his U.S. credential. While Cape officials were prepared to accept the validity of British degrees—they tended, after all, to be graduates of British universities themselves—they viewed American diplomas in general, and African American diplomas in particular, as worth little more than the paper on which they were printed. They also viewed the recipients of such degrees as politically "unsound," which helps explain their refusal to help Molema locate a London law firm where he could complete the articles necessary for certification. Molema ultimately ended up working as a magistrate's interpreter and later as a clerk in a small business, precisely the niches he would likely have found had he never gone to America.[53]

Aspiring doctors were likewise required to possess British certificates, a policy with far less intrinsic logic than the policy for lawyers. Black physicians also faced a battery of legal and customary prohibitions on everything from treating white patients to employing white nurses. The only American-educated student to run this professional gauntlet successfully was A. B. Xuma, who supplemented his American training—he studied at Tuskegee and Minnesota before earning a Northwestern University medical degree—with residencies in Edinburgh and Hungary. Wilberforce graduate Hastings Banda also completed the necessary British credential and was poised in the late 1930s to come to South Africa to oversee an AME health clinic, but World War II intervened, stranding him in Britain. For better or worse, he returned after the war not to South Africa but to his native Nyasaland, where he led the fight for Malawian independence and subsequently installed himself as president-for-life. None of the other U.S.-educated medical doctors appears ever to have practiced in South Africa.[54]

For all of that, it would be singularly misleading to imply that all the returning students entered the ministry and teaching out of expediency or because more attractive professional outlets were blocked. Among the Wilberforce contingent at least, what is striking is not how many students were frustrated in their ambitions to become doctors and lawyers but rather how few evinced those ambitions. In all, only two of the AME-sponsored students, Molema and Stephen Gumede, majored in law, while only Theodore Kakaza, Henry Gabashane, and, later, Hastings Banda studied medicine. Virtually all the rest entered Payne Theological Seminary or pursued liberal arts programs, with an eye to teaching. For them, as for generations of educated Africans before them, such familiar occupations represented callings commensurate with their sense of themselves, with the feelings of personal exceptionalism and racial duty that the years in America had done so much to sharpen.

All this leads to another problem. In bringing Africans to the United States to be trained as missionaries, AME Church leaders risked effacing precisely those qualities that had first recommended the students for the task. In a word, there was a danger that African students would become deracinated, so imbued with the values and attitudes of their African American mentors that they would "lose touch" with African life. Virtually every major evangelical church had experienced instances where African students brought to the metropole for missionary training had refused to return home after completing their studies. Wilberforce itself had experienced a similar case in the 1870s involving four Haitian "missionary students." Given their class background and their obvious affinity for African American life, the South African students might conceivably do the same. Such concerns lay behind the 1900 General Conference resolution requiring pledges from all African students supported by church funds affirming their commitment to return home.[55]

Despite such assurances, many émigré students found pretenses to tarry in the United States. Francis Gow stayed in America to teach at Tuskegee's Phelps Hall Bible Training School, returning home only in the early 1920s. Hannah, his sister, married an African American and settled permanently in the United States. John Manye did the same. Theodore Kakaza proceeded from Wilberforce to medical school in Toronto before opening a practice in Indianapolis; Stephen Gumede last surfaces in the record as an apprentice attorney in Ann Arbor, Michigan. Patrick Ngcayiya, son of A.N.C. founder Henry Reid Ngcayiya, remained in the United States as a schoolteacher, a decision that devastated his father. At one point in the 1920s, the elder Ngcayiya resorted to writing to Marcus Garvey, asking him to remind African students of their responsibilities to the countries they had left behind.[56]

More tragic still were those students who returned home but found themselves unable to readjust to South African life. Harsant Tantsi returned to South Africa in about 1908 and taught for a year or two at Wilberforce Institute before sailing back to the United States. He settled in the Midwest, pastoring several AME congregations while holding office in the African Student Union, a Tuskegee-based network of émigré students. Melrose Sishuba, who spent nearly a dozen years in the United States pursuing his education, returned to South Africa in the mid-1920s; within months he began vainly applying for a passport to return to America. Most heartwrenching of all was the case of Jonathan Mokone, son of the South African church's founder and himself an ordained AME minister. Mokone married a black American woman and postponed returning home for the better part of twenty years. In deference to his dying father, he returned to South Africa in 1930, pastoring a series of congregations in South Africa and Rhodesia, but his experience was an unhappy one. In 1943 he attached a plaintive note to a passport application, in which he professed a lack of affinity with African people and complete ignorance of African languages. By way of explanation, he noted that he was "a descendant of slaves," presumably a reference to his father's *inboekseling* past but one that suggests just how thoroughly he had internalized African American history and culture. "All my friends, school-mates and acquaintances are in America," Mokone concluded. "I have lost every contact with my people here (the natives) who regard me as a foreigner"—a term, he added, which "would cover volumes."[57]

Even those who successfully negotiated their return to South Africa—and the vast majority of U.S.-educated students did—continued to cherish their association with black America. They cultivated American correspondents, flocked to welcome visiting African Americans, and responded with alacrity when opportunities for return visits arose. No one illustrates the paradoxes of this situation better than A. B. Xuma, the physician and political leader destined to become the most famous product of the educational traffic between South Africa and the United States. Xuma today is rightfully remembered as the man who sustained the African National Congress through some of its darkest days. Acceding to the presidency of a destitute and faction-ridden Congress in 1940, he patiently rebuilt the organization, bequeathing— reluctantly—a rejuvinated institution to the "Young Turks" of the A.N.C. Youth League nine years later. What historians have sometimes forgotten is how thoroughly African-Americanized this leading African nationalist had become. In his institutional affiliations, his speech and demeanor, even his musical and sartorial tastes, Xuma was as much African American as African.[58]

Xuma never formally joined the AME Church, preferring the greater status that came with being one of the only black officers in the white Methodist Church. Nonetheless, he had close ties to African Methodism. His first wife, Americo-Liberian Amanda Mason, was a graduate of Wilberforce University, who spent the years before her marriage working as an AME missionary in Liberia and Sierra Leone. (The two apparently met through the African Student Union, of which Mason was the Wilberforce representative.) Almost from the moment of their arrival in South Africa in 1927, the Xumas labored for the AME Church. While Amanda became a leader in the local Women's Missionary Society, A. B. served on the board of Wilberforce Institute, the Evaton-based school founded by his American-educated predecessors. He also offered his professional services at Crogman Clinic, the community health center attached to the school. Indeed, through much of the 1930s Xuma almost singlehandedly kept both institute and clinic afloat, paying teachers and creditors out of his own pocket to spare the church embarrassment. "I am deeply concerned over the work of the AME Church, because it is an institution that is run by non-whites," he declared, in a passage worthy of Richard Allen or Daniel Payne. "I would like to see every department of it run according to recognised standards." The fact that the church was associated with the United States made its success doubly important to him. "I feel very keenly any criticism levelled at people from American Institutions," he confessed in another letter. Having been "moulded into manhood" by such institutions, he was anxious to see their "high standards" preserved.[59]

It was in the context of personal tragedy that the depth of Xuma's affinity with black America was most dramatically illustrated. Amanda Mason Xuma died during childbirth a few years after traveling to South Africa with her husband. With small children to care for, Xuma was determined to remarry, yet he showed little interest in marrying an African. Instead, he determined to win an African American bride, to the extent of asking a female friend traveling to Wilberforce in the United States to apprise him of suitable candidates. The friend dutifully complied, sending letters describing the various women she met, detailing both professional distinctions and personal appearances. Astonishingly, the gambit succeeded: the correspondent referred Xuma to Madie Hall, the daughter of a leading black family in North Carolina and an officer in the black Y.W.C.A. Xuma launched a determined courtship, initially through the mails and later during an extended visit to the United States, ostensibly undertaken to study public health policy. By 1940 Ms. Hall had become the second Mrs. Xuma. The moral of the story, of course, rests in Xuma's conviction that only in America could he find a wife who shared his perspective and experience, not to mention his social status. More broadly, the episode illustrates the extraordinary self-consciousness of the returning students, their unflagging sense of personal exceptionalism. The result, in Xuma's case, was profoundly paradoxical. Here was a man so conscious of his position as a "leader of the race," so preoccupied with vindicating African potential in his own life, that he could no longer conceive marrying an African. [60]

Given their feelings of personal exceptionalism, as well as the enormous prestige that their American degrees conferred, it was probably inevitable that the returning students would play prominent political roles. This phenomenon, in South Africa and in Africa generally, has led a number of historians to posit a kind of causal link between American education and African nationalism. Exposure to the United States, the argument goes, provided African students with a broader perspective on problems of race and colonialism, enabling some at least to question the legitimacy of white rule. Equally important, America presented Africans with the spectacle of a black population undivided by language or ethnicity, a crucial model for aspiring nationalists. The case is typically forwarded by the multiplication of examples, including luminaries such as Nkrumah, Azikiwe, Xuma, and Dube. [61]

In broad terms, the equation of American education and nationalist consciousness is appropriate. Exposure to America does seem to have reinforced students' tendency to think in pan-ethnic terms. Many returning students became involved with the Congress movement—three of the A.N.C.'s first six presidents were American-educated—and virtually all invoked black America as a model of unity to be emulated. While many expressed respect for Africa's "traditional" past, none, save John Dube, regarded ethnic affiliation as a legitimate basis for political organization. "Extinguish that spirit of *tribal-*

ism," Charlotte Manye Maxeke commanded in her last public address; it is an "animal that will tear us to pieces."[62]

As so often, however, the nationalist label conceals as much as it reveals. In the end, what distinguished the American contingent was less their opposition to "tribalism," a common enough sentiment among educated Africans, than their commitment to what one might call "representative" politics—a politics of elite representation and mediation nurtured in the nineteenth-century missions and sustained by exposure to "the best" of black America. Again, A. B. Xuma provides the exemplary figure. Writing in a black Johannesburg newspaper shortly after his return from America, the young doctor went so far as to portray overseas education as a prerequisite for progressive political leadership. After detailing the achievements of the Maxekes, John Dube, and Cambridge-educated D. D. T. Jabavu, Xuma concluded:

> These people are well educated, civilised, and, above all, cultured. They more fully appreciate the people's aspirations as well as their limitations because they themselves have a broader outlook and wider experience. . . . They plead the cause of the Bantu with dignity and consideration. They have a sincere and heartfelt sympathy for their backward brother and would like to see him rise up to their own level, at least, in outlook. They voice his legitimate claims and interpret his wishes to the white man intelligently and rationally.

Given all this, the overseas contingent represented "the safest bridge for race contact in the present state of race relations in South Africa."[63]

Xuma developed the argument further in a short biographical sketch of Charlotte Maxeke, written at about the same time and titled "What an Educated African Girl Can Do." In the pamphlet, he measured Mrs. Maxeke's contribution along three dimensions: in the spur her example provided to fellow Africans; in her tireless efforts to serve and uplift the lowly of her race; and in the model of respectability and achievement that she presented to white South Africans, a contribution confirmed by a string of testimonials from Europeans hailing her grace, character, and "well-balanced mind." For a foreward, Xuma turned to W. E. B. Du Bois, who had taught the young Charlotte Manye at Wilberforce and followed her subsequent career with interest. After praising Maxeke's achievements in the face of both racial and sex prejudice, Du Bois wrote: "I think that what Mrs. Maxeke has accomplished should encourage all men, and especially those of African descent. And in addition to that, it should inspire the white residents of South Africa and of America to revise their hastily-made judgments concerning the possibilities of the Negro race." Here again was that extraordinary convergence of elite African and African American political thought. In South Africa as in the United States, educated black people bore the burden of racial vindication, and shared the awful "second sight" that came with it.[64]

Most of the American graduates' defining political attributes flowed from their conception of themselves as "representatives" of the race. All placed enormous faith in education and saw political leadership as the province of the educated. Insofar as they conceived progress as a process of racial "upliftment," they tended to be gradualists. Quasi-millenarian movements such as Garvey- ism and the Industrial and Commercial Workers' Union, which swept through southern Africa in the 1920s, held little appeal for Xuma and his ilk. Perhaps most important, the American students, especially those from Wilberforce, were marked by a certain political style. No matter how keenly felt the griev- ance, they insisted on presenting it with moderation and decorum, the better to demonstrate their own maturity and balance, and, by extension, the innate capacity of Africans as a whole. In this respect, they stood much closer to the founders of the AME Church in America than to the founders of the South African Ethiopian Church.

Given their sense of themselves as "bridges" between the races, the erstwhile students were naturally well represented in the various interracial initiatives thrown up by South African liberalism in the decades between the wars. American graduates were prominently represented, for example, in the Joint Council movement, a movement modeled on the Inter-Racial Committees of the American South and designed to bring together enlightened Europeans and Africans to discuss South Africa's racial problems in a congenial and construc- tive atmosphere. During one period in the 1920s, the Johannesburg Joint Council boasted three Wilberforce graduates—James Tantsi and Charlotte and Marshall Maxeke. Mrs. Maxeke also became a stalwart in the Joint Conferences of Europeans and Bantu, which convened annually during the 1930s. For his part, Marshall Maxeke served as editor of *Umteteli wa Bantu,* the black news- paper launched by the Chamber of Mines in 1920 to cultivate "responsible" African opinion.[65]

No one better epitomized this style of politics than future AME bishop Francis Gow, who returned to South Africa in the early 1920s to assume the principalship of Wilberforce Institute. Under Gow's leadership, Wilberforce became the very model of "sound," "adapted" education, along the lines of Tuskegee, where he had spent the better part of a decade. By the mid-1920s, the Institute boasted an industrial education curriculum, a substantial state subsidy, and a bevy of white liberal patrons, including American Board mis- sionaries Ray Phillips and J. Dexter Taylor, Joint Council chairman Howard Pim, and South African Institute of Race Relations founder J. D. Rheinhallt Jones. The entire group descended on the Institute on Sunday evenings for vesper services, to hear the Wilberforce Singers, under Gow's baton, perform superb renditions of Afro-American sorrow songs. Returning to his native Cape Town in the 1930s, Gow continued to plough the same furrow, meeting regularly with white leaders while assembling community meetings to discuss problems such as liquor and juvenile delinquency, or "skollyism." Later, he served as chairman of the "Coloured Advisory Committee," a controversial

wartime agency denounced by many black Capetonians as an attempt to cana-
lize black grievances.[66]

Trafficking with white liberals provided a measure of legitimation, confirming students in what they took to be their historical role as "bridges" between
the races. Ultimately, however, such activities could not protect them from
the deeper contradictions of their position. In effect, the students were seeking
to bridge two receding shores. White South Africans, for their part, evinced
little interest in would-be black mediators. Amid the upheavals of 1919–
1921, there was considerable talk of cultivating the "better class of natives,"
but little of it ever found its way onto the statute books. On the contrary, the
thrust of postwar native administration, as Adam Ashforth and Saul Dubow
have both shown, was to silence black voices, to establish the "native problem"
as the province of "neutral" (white) experts, rather than of educated Africans,
who, depending on one's predilections, were either too close to or too remote
from the problems of the African masses to contribute meaningfully. The
progress of this campaign can be measured in any number of ways: in the
indifference to elite African concerns in 1920s urban areas legislation; in
the scientific, scrupulously apolitical language of the 1932 Report of the Native Economic Commission; in the decade-long battle over the Hertzog Bills,
which culminated in 1936 with the excision of the last vestiges of the Cape
African franchise. Liberal initiatives such as the joint councils and the location
advisory boards continued to exist and to attract their quota of "representative"
race leaders, but they were increasingly driven to the political margin, especially after the "Black Peril" election of 1929.[67]

In economic terms, too, the former students endured all the mounting
agonies of their class—the restrictions on property ownership, the rising "colour bar," the desperate financial insecurity. Indeed, a considerable portion of
their political energies was consumed trying to shore up their own economic
position against state initiatives deliberately designed to foreclose avenues of
independent African accumulation. John Dube and Pixley Seme both played
pivotal roles in resistance to the 1913 Natives Land Act: Dube in his capacity
as the first president of the South African Native National Congress and leader
of the Congress delegation to Britain; Seme as the editor of the Congress's
newspaper, *Abantu Batho,* and founder of the African Farmers' Association.
Charles Dube testified to the 1916 Beaumont Commission on behalf of native
landowners. In the 1920s James Tantsi led a deputation protesting government plans to repeal the tax relief traditionally enjoyed by "exempted" natives.
Later, he helped author the Johannesburg Joint Council pamphlet attacking
the Hertzog Bills, especially the provisions strengthening tribal tenure and
barring cooperative land purchases by westernized Africans. Such provisions,
the pamphlet argued, "do not take into account the progressive Native (a large
and increasing class) who had become detribalised and for whom tribal conditions are a mark of barbarism from which he has emerged." From the perspec-

tive of a man like Tantsi, the attack on "progressive" Africans menaced the very foundation of racial progress. At a more immediate level, it made it increasingly difficult for him and for people like him to provide for their families. By the 1930s several of the American graduates were living in dire poverty.[68]

Even as state legislation bore down on them from above, the emergence of new, more militant political organizations menaced the erstwhile students from below. Given their commitment to interracial cooperation and the importance they attached to respectability and protocol, American-educated leaders tended to view an organization like the Industrial and Commercial Workers' Union with distinct uneasiness. The ubiquitous Charlotte Maxeke surfaced at the first national conference of the Union in 1920, but beyond that it is impossible to identify any Wilberforce graduate in the ranks of the I.C.U. On the contrary, several former students were prominent in the opposition. In Natal, Charles Dube earned the gratitude of white officials—and, if papers in his estate are to be believed, title to a small sugar farm—for his work rallying African opposition to the Union. In Johannesburg, Marshall Maxeke directed a steady stream of fire from his editorial desk at *Umteteli wa Bantu,* accusing the I.C.U. and kindred organizations of destroying "that better understanding between white and black which is vital to our progress." One exasperated I.C.U. sympathizer was finally moved to ask, "Who is the editor? Is it Mr. Maxeke" or his white patrons?[69]

The predicament of a host of American-trained leaders, and indeed of a whole political tradition, was distilled in that one question. Like generations of elite black leaders in both the United States and South Africa, the returning students had positioned themselves between two quite incompatible masters: Europeans, whom they sought to influence, and Africans, whom they presumed to lead. Lacking even that leverage that an attenuated franchise conferred on African Americans, they were forced to subsist on a diet of white concessions, concessions that could be extracted only through the most craven demonstrations of "balance" and "maturity." This posture, together with its manifest lack of results, left them vulnerable to the rise of new, more populist leaders, who derided their methods and impugned their motives. From their own perspective, they were victims of the race's inability to discern its true leaders; A. B. Xuma developed that lament into a virtual soliloquy. From the historian's perspective, they were the first victims of the remorseless dialectic of twentieth-century South African black politics. They would not be the last.

Through it all, the students continued to steer to the course they had charted at Wilberforce. To do otherwise required acknowledging that their entire lives had been organized around a fiction, and that is something few of us are prepared to do. Most busied themselves with church work, with participation in various deputations and interracial conferences, and with occasional visits to the United States, where they could again bask in effusions of attention and praise. Despite American education's failure to fulfill its promise in their own lives, most continued to place great stock in it, even to the extent of sending their own children to the United States. At least two of the South Africans at U.S. colleges in the 1920s were second-generation students. Frederick Dube, the son of Charles and Adelaide Tantsi Dube and Uncle John's heir apparent at Ohlange Institute, ventured to America in 1926, studying at Morehead State and briefly at Columbia Teachers College. His life recapitulated the frustrations of his elders. His marriage fractured when his African American wife proved unable to adjust to life in South Africa. His professional aspirations were derailed when a group of Ohlange's erstwhile white patrons took over the school and appointed a European principal and headmaster. Fate was scarcely kinder to Edward Clarke Maxeke, the only child of Marshall and Charlotte Manye Maxeke. Maxeke enrolled at the AME Church's Morris Brown College in 1923 and remained in the United States through 1938. He returned briefly to South Africa to accept a post at Wilberforce Institute, but he was soon disillusioned and returned to America. He died in the early 1940s, a few years after his mother.[70]

Thus rendered, the careers of the returned students seem studies in futility. South Africa in 1962, the year of A. B. Xuma's death, was no further down the road toward justice and inclusion than it had been in 1912, the year of Henry Msikinya's premature death, despite a half century of effort by would-be black "bridges" and brokers. In fairness to the students, the fault lay less in them than in the South African state, which proved time and again to be nothing if not impervious to reason. Yet somehow the sense of personal failure lingers, perhaps because of the enormous expectations that accompanied the first students to America.

Ultimately, however, such a conclusion does justice neither to the students' character nor to their achievements. History is long, and individuals' contributions are often not to be measured in their own lifetimes. In Xuma's case, for example, we can focus so much on the struggles that led to his deposal as A.N.C. president in 1949 that we forget that it was largely due to his energy and resourcefulness that the Congress survived at all. Similarly, one can become so preoccupied with the political gulf between him and his Youth League successors—on issues such as mass action, civil disobedience, and, ultimately, armed struggle—that one forgets just how much of his imprint remains on the A.N.C. today. At a more human level, there is a danger, in our concern with results, of reducing the returned students to caricatures. It becomes all too easy to paint them as "naive," to dismiss their enduring convictions about respectability and reasonableness as quaint and more than a little self-serving. But what of their other qualities—their courage and compassion, their commitment to service, their abiding dignity in the face of endless provocation and disappointment? Surely these too belong in the balance.

Perhaps the best way to recover these qualities is with a brief reprise of the life of Charlotte Manye Maxeke, the first of the students to arrive at Wilberforce University and the one whose early correspondence precipitated the formation of the South African AME Church. No one better embodied the character and values of Wilberforce than Maxeke; no one better exemplified its contradictions and essential tragedy. If any individual provides an opportunity for a balanced assessment of the transatlantic traffic, it is she.

The details of Maxeke's early life have already emerged. Almost from the moment of her birth, she was a "representative" figure. The child of devoted Christian converts, she received the best early education the missions could afford. (According to T. D. Mweli Skota's 1932 *African Yearly Register,* which Maxeke helped to compile, her teachers in Uitenhage and Port Elizabeth were Paul Xiniwe and Isaac Wauchope, two of the leaders of the eastern Cape "school" community.) She proceeded to Kimberley, the cradle of South Africa's black middle class, where she completed her education and began working as a schoolteacher. It was there that she heard Orpheus McAdoo's touring Jubilee Singers, which launched her on a course to the United States, from which she returned as South Africa's first black female college graduate.[71]

By every account, Maxeke—"Mother Maxeke," as she became known to generations of black South Africans—was a person of extraordinary warmth and generosity. Yet there were steelier qualities as well, qualities less well registered in popular memory: immense personal ambition, courage, and an uncanny ability to gauge the expectations and sensibilities of her audience, whether a convention of African American churchwomen or a conference of South African white liberals. There was nothing naive or feckless about Charlotte Maxeke: she knew what she wanted and was adept at obtaining it. It is clear, for example, that she was a favorite of the African Choir's white promoters; indeed, much of the turmoil that engulfed the choir during its first British tour seems to have stemmed from her peers' resentment of her privileged status. Much the same thing happened at Wilberforce. Among all the South African students, it was Charlotte whom African American women rushed to adopt and whose memory they most cherished. She was their "Rare Jewel," their "African girl of beloved memory."[72]

Maxeke spent the first decade and a half after her return from America working as a teacher in AME schools. With Henry Msikinya, she served on the faculty of Bethel Institute, the Cape Town school opened by Bishop Coppin. With the end of martial law in the interior, she traveled to the northern Transvaal, to the village of Dwaar's River, near her father's boyhood home. She was soon joined by her fiance, Marshall, a newly ordained AME minister. Together, they launched the first Wilberforce Institute, on land donated to the church by Ramoghopa, one of the chiefs encountered by Bishop Turner during his whirlwind 1898 tour. If the actions of other chiefs trafficking with African Methodism at the time offer any guide, Ramoghopa saw the school as an instrument to reassert traditional control over his society's political and economic development. He thus probably envisioned a curriculum emphasizing industrial and clerical skills. The Maxekes, on the other hand, deliberately set out to pattern the school after its American namesake, offering education for head, hands, and heart. While advertisements for the institute noted that "teachers take special care to teach manual work," the couple also offered a full complement of liberal arts courses. On the school's letterhead, they represented themselves as "Rev. Marshall Maxeke, B.A. Principal & Professor of Mathematics, Greek and Latin; Mrs. Charlotte Maxeke, B.Sc. Lady Principal and Instructor in Science, English and Sewing."[73]

During their time in Dwaar's River, the Maxekes probably won more converts to Christianity than at any other period in their lives. Their educational work, however, fell far below expectations. Given the previous government's suspicion of *uitlander* missionaries, few in the village had attended school, certainly not English-medium schools. Of the handful of mission schools in the postwar Transvaal, none taught beyond Standard III save Kilnerton Institute, which offered a four-week teacher training course each summer. There was little constituency here for a university curriculum. There was also little money. Few families in the area could afford to pay school fees, and government support was not forthcoming, particularly at a time when the entire region was convulsed by an "Ethiopian" panic. The Transvaal administration provided a glimmer of hope in 1905, when it provisionally recognized Wilberforce, but the promised grant was withdrawn after officials learned that the Maxekes proposed to teach beyond Standard III. The couple solicited contributions from America, describing their work in this "dark" corner of the Transvaal in terms calculated to appeal to African American subscribers. (The editor of the *Voice of Missions,* with a poor sense of geography but not without a certain poetic aptness, headlined one of their letters "An Appeal from the Jungle.") Some money did trickle in, mostly from churchwomen's groups, but not enough to sustain the school.[74]

By 1906 the Maxekes had left Dwaar's River and settled on the Witwatersrand. They may have played some role in the launching of a second Wilberforce Institute in Evaton, on a plot of land purchased by Transvaal church leaders in 1905. There is also some evidence of a school in Klerksdorp, a mining town on the West Rand. They surface for certain only in 1906–1907, when they applied for government support of a school they had opened in Boksburg, on the eastern edge of the goldfields. As we saw in Chapter 5, their application gained a sympathetic hearing from Transvaal Chief Native Commissioner Godfrey Lagden, who saw the squalid, ill-administered slums sprouting along the Reef as breeding grounds of social unrest. Given the virtual absence of white mission activity on the East Rand, Lagden negotiated a regular mission subsidy for the Maxekes' school, but he imposed stringent conditions: the school must accept white superintendence, limit instruction to Standard

III, and follow the Department of Education's prescribed syllabus for African education, which emphasized sewing, singing, and "native" crafts. Even then, the grant was withheld by a local pass officer, and the school languished.[75]

In the wake of the Boksburg fiasco, the Maxekes left the Witwatersrand and traveled to the Transkei. They opened a school in Idutywa under the patronage of controversial headman Enoch Mamba, then engaged in one of his periodic battles with Wesleyan missionaries. So successful was their work in Idutywa that they received an invitation from Dalindyebo, paramount chief of the Thembu, to open a school under his patronage. The couple agreed, and spent the next several years in Thembuland. According to A. B. Xuma, whose father knew the Maxekes during this period, Charlotte quickly "endeared and ingratiated" herself "to the whole tribe of the Tembus." She regularly attended the chief's court, traditionally a province of male elders, winning a reputation for "courage and eloquence." As in so many of the places she lived, her memory endured in Thembuland long after she had gone.[76]

The Maxekes returned to the Witwatersrand in the last years of World War I, apparently because of Marshall's ill health. (For the last decade of his life Marshall was debilitated by heart disease.) They settled in Nancefield, in Soweto, where they would remain for the rest of their lives. Closing fast on her fiftieth birthday, Charlotte was a far different person from the "missionary girl" who had sailed back to Cape Town in 1901. A decade and a half of labor had exposed her to aspects of African life from which her education had sheltered her, enlarging her natural empathy, while sanding down that edge of condescension so many students carried back from America. Working in the mushrooming slums of the Witwatersrand had given her a first hand view of the wages of South Africa's industrial revolution, as well as a new appreciation of the complexity of the "civilising" project. At the same time, her experiences in the northern Transvaal and Thembuland had endowed her with new respect for African traditional life, not in evidence at Wilberforce, where she entertained African Americans with tales of snakes and witchdoctors. While she remained a committed Christian evangelist, she denied that Africans had been pagans before the coming of the missionaries; Africans had worshipped God "in our own way," she insisted. She defended customary marriage in similar terms, wondering aloud whether it or its western counterpart better ensured female chastity, parental authority, and the sanctity of the marriage relation.[77]

One ought not exaggerate Maxeke's transformation. Her developing cultural relativism remained bounded not only by her Christianity but by her abiding faith in the ideals, if not the practice, of "British civilisation." Her belief in her own exceptionalism, and in the obligations and duties it entailed, remained unshaken. What the years had given her was more elusive— generosity of spirit, humility, a common touch. "She took it as a matter of course," an acquaintance recalled, "that no African could live within the law . . . in the conditions created in South Africa" and was hence inclined to

reserve judgment. While many of her class fretted about the absence of preferred railroad facilities for the "better class of natives," she simply boarded the
third-class coach. (Maxeke once stunned her Women's Missionary Society
colleagues by arriving for a convention after an overnight ride in an open
railroad car with a group of migrant workers.) Of all the American-educated
students, she was the most approachable, the least given to airs.[78]

The Maxekes returned to the Rand during a period of intense political
ferment. The betrayal of black rights in the 1910 treaty of Union and the
subsequent promulgation of the Natives' Land Act galvanized black political
leadership. Responding to a call from American-educated Pixley Seme, African
leaders from across the subcontinent assembled in Bloemfontein in early 1912
to launch the South African Native National Congress, later the African National Congress. Given the prominence they enjoyed as college graduates and
as leaders of the AME Church, the Maxekes naturally attended the inaugural
meeting, remaining active Congress supporters through the war and the upheavals of the postwar period. Like most Congressmen, Marshall Maxeke seems
to have focused on the Land Act, which menaced elite Africans' economic
position even as it mocked their dreams of common citizenship. (As a leader of
the Transvaal Native Congress branch, Marshall was elected in 1918 to the
second Congress delegation sent to Britain to protest the act, but poverty and
poor health prevented him from making the journey.) Charlotte devoted herself to gender issues, specifically to fighting the state's recently announced
plans to bring women under the rubric of the pass laws. All the convictions and
contradictions that defined Charlotte Maxeke as a person and a politician
intersected in this decades-long struggle.[79]

The impetus for women's passes emerged from an ongoing debate over the
place of African "houseboys" in white homes. It is a singular fact of South
Africa's industrial development that domestic labor in the urban Transvaal
initially became the province of men. At the most basic level, the predominance of male domestics was a function of their greater supply, which in turn
reflected the prevailing division of labor within African households and the
way in which those households responded to the pressures of proletarianization. At the same time, whites' preference for male domestics reflected enduring stereotypes about African women, who were widely stigmatized as unreliable, slovenly, and disease-ridden. As with so many racial stereotypes, the
portrayal of black women as vectors of social disorder had a wonderfully self-
fulfilling logic. As more and more African women came to town in the early
twentieth century—to search for husbands who had absconded, to avoid unwanted marriages, or simply to escape the pressures of rural poverty—they
found themselves shut out of the labor market. Many were forced to resort to
prostitution, beer brewing, and other illicit activities to support themselves,
all of which confirmed the original stereotype, justifying their continued
exclusion.[80]

"Houseboys," however, brought problems of their own, which first came into focus during the years of imperial reconstruction. At the most obvious level, the spectacle of men cooking, cleaning, and minding children violated gender assumptions that Lord Milner and his minions had brought with them from Britain, assumptions that informed the whole "Anglicization" project. Equally important, domestic service bottled up workers, a cardinal offense at a time when mining capital cast desperately about for supplies of cheap, exploitable labor. Perhaps most important of all, the presence of mature black men moving in the most intimate corners of white life menaced the imperialists' vision of racial order, raising the awful specter of miscegenation—a specter engraved in the ubiquitous image of a hulking African man carrying morning tea into the boudoir of a scantily clad white mistress. All these streams converged during the economic upheavals of 1906–1912 as a series of alleged assaults on white women on the Witwatersrand ignited a full-blown moral panic.[81]

The most obvious product of the "Black Peril" agitation and the subsequent *Report of the Commission appointed to Enquire into Assaults on Women* was a concerted campaign to "replace the houseboy." Such a campaign could not begin, however, until the state had done something to rein in urban black women, who, in the absence of an influx of British women, represented the only viable alternative source of domestic labor. Various proposals were put forth. While mission groups spoke of erecting hostels and "industrial schools," where single women would be under proper supervision and control, editors and politicians demanded that all black women entering the city be subjected to "medical inspections"—pelvic examinations—to ensure that they were "disease-free." Virtually all whites agreed on the need for enabling legislation to allow municipalities to bring black women within the net of the pass laws. Pass laws promised to bring order and accountability to a dangerous, floating population, driving disreputable women out of the city while channeling their respectable counterparts into the labor market.[82]

The Union government's announcement of its intention to extend the pass laws ignited a firestorm, especially among elite African women, who suddenly confronted a choice between working in white kitchens or being expelled from urban areas. Charlotte Maxeke quickly moved to the van of the resistance. While there is no direct evidence, she was almost certainly one of the women who tabled an antipass petition at the inaugural meeting of the S.A.N.N.C., a petition that ultimately garnered more than five thousand signatures. She also played a minor role in the protests of 1912–1913, when thousands of women in the southern Transvaal and Orange Free State took to the streets in a successful effort to forestall pass legislation. Institutionally, the chief product of the campaign was the Bantu Women's League, which Maxeke established as the female affiliate of the National Congress. In her capacity as president of the League, she traversed the country, speaking at countless meetings and leading deputations to government officials, including at least two to Prime Minister Louis Botha. (Anxious to preserve African support for the war effort, Botha assured her late in 1917 that the government "had not the remotest idea of introducing a compulsory Pass Law for women.") Over the next decade, she continued to marshal resistance to women's passes and to the even more obnoxious idea of medical inspections.[83]

Locating the "real" Charlotte Maxeke in this period is a difficult task. The explosion of black militancy on the Witwatersrand at the end of World War I—the transport and sanitation workers' strikes, the abortive antipass campaign, and the 1920 mineworkers' strike—placed enormous pressure on black petty bourgeois leadership, producing all kinds of contorted political postures. Maxeke was no exception. Even by the standards of her class, her range of institutional affiliations was dizzying. She attended the inaugural national meeting of the Industrial and Commercial Workers' Union in 1920, yet months later she and her husband joined the Johannesburg Joint Council, established by white liberals precisely to wean African leaders away from "irresponsible" organizations like the I.C.U. While rooted in the AME Church, she enjoyed a close relationship with white missionaries, especially with American Board missionaries such as Ray Phillips, J. Dexter Taylor, and Francis Bridgman, with whom she shared not only an American connection but a distinct sociological analysis, linking urban vice to the erosion of parental and generational authority in the countryside. Aside from the AME Church, Maxeke's deepest allegiance was doubtless to the Congress movement, but she could be sharply critical of Congress leadership. Women would not be in their predicament, she declared, but for the cowardice of male leaders, who had "submitted tamely" to the initial imposition of passes and later acceded to the 1919 "compromise" on registration that streamlined the system.[84]

The difficulty is further compounded by Maxeke's remarkable capacity to speak different political languages, a facility which became one of the defining features of her leadership. When the occasion demanded, she could wax defiant. African women "would all go to prison" before submitting to pass laws, she told a meeting in Bethlehem in 1918. She was even more outspoken a year later, during the wave of mass meetings convened by the Congress to protest the harsh sentences meted out to Johannesburg's striking sanitation workers. "What sort of sentence is this?" she roared to a thousand-strong crowd in Ebenezer Hall. "A native is handcuffed for asking for bread." In her interactions with whites, however, Maxeke was ever at pains to present herself as "sound," "moderate," "balanced"—"in no sense an agitator," as an approving white journalist put it. She never failed to assert her loyalty to the Crown, trading on her connection with Queen Victoria, for whom she had performed a quarter century before. (When the Prince of Wales toured South Africa in 1925, Maxeke presented him with a kaross.) "The natives are my people," she told an interviewer from the Johannesburg *Star*, "and if I attempt to explain the case, and plead in their favour, you are not to interpret my remarks as savouring of an anti-white policy. I am a British subject, and I am very proud to owe allegiance to the flag, so I trust no one will misconstrue my motive."[85]

All these tensions and ambiguities were reflected in Maxeke's approach to gender issues. She firmly believed in women's equality, in their right to education and to full political participation. She bitterly resented the 1919 constitution of the S.A.N.N.C., which excluded women from full membership, and was distinctly unmollified by the acceptance of the Bantu Women's League as an affiliated organization. ("They needed us to help by making the tea," she told a friend.) At the same time, however, Maxeke subscribed to many of the assumptions that underlay women's marginalization. Her attacks on women's passes, for example, remained safely within the confines of domestic ideology, with its interlocking ideas about women's distinctive nature and role. Pass laws, she argued, stripped women of "the respect to which they are entitled," leaving them vulnerable to personal searches and sexual molestation by lower-class policemen. They undermined parental control, driving mothers out of the home and away from their children. Even women returning from evening church services were not safe from harassment. How, she asked rhetorically, could "one of the most civilised Christian nations in the world . . . so take advantage of the weaker sex as to forget all that was meant by the words, mother, wife and sister?" Obviously such rhetoric was tailored to her audience, but it was also heartfelt, and consistent with the ideas about women's purity and "natural sphere" that she had imbibed at Wilberforce.[86]

If there was a common thread running through these conflicting priorities and principals, it lay in Maxeke's unshaken conviction about her own role as a "representative" leader of the race, a "bridge" between white and black worlds. The erosion of racial comity she witnessed in the aftermath of World War I clearly alarmed her. "If there is a White League," she warned, referring to a vigilante organization established to protect white women, "there will be a Black League," until the entire country was polarized between white "lynchers" and black "conspirators." To forestall such an outcome, she offered herself as a broker, granting interviews, meeting with "influential" whites, and appearing before countless government commissions, all to help whites better understand "the viewpoint of the native." In her testimony to the 1918 Moffat Commission, called to investigate the causes of the first strike wave on the Rand, she delineated the predicament of urban women, proffering figures on wartime inflation, wage cuts, and escalating transport costs. She was the first African to appear before the Native Pass Laws Commission. When the Local Government Commission of 1919–1921 neglected to call her, she requested permission to give evidence. "I think I understand the exact condition and needs of my people," she wrote, "especially in regard to medical inspection of women and girls."[87]

In all her testimony, Maxeke strove to be polite and reasonable, but she was also fearless and ever prepared to speak truth to power. When a member of the Moffat Commission floated the old colonial canard about education producing rogues, she replied, "Yes, you will find that in London where there are the largest schools in the world." ("Do not give London a bad name," the enraged commissioner sputtered.) Another commissioner who tried to bully her into conceding that African women were excluded from the domestic labor market because they were lazy and unreliable also discovered her mettle. The real problem, Maxeke explained, her words dripping with innuendo, was that "the boys are generally great favourites with the mistresses, far more so than the girls. I cannot explain why it is so but it is so." Maxeke was even less delicate when a member of the Pass Laws Commission suggested that passes were necessary to "protect" black women. If this were true, she noted, then perhaps they were also needed to "protect the European women and girls who went about at all hours of the night in doubtful places, so much so that many of them were arrested and fined £10." Whites eager to save Africans from urban vice, she suggested, should remember the old adage "Charity begins at home."[88]

Ultimately, however, mediating between European and African worlds represented only one aspect of Maxeke's leadership. The role of "representative" race leader also entailed "racial service," an obligation to help lift the ignorant and lowly into the light of "Christian civilisation." Again, Maxeke was true to her calling. On returning to the Rand, she secured permission to hold religious services in Johannesburg Jail. Her personal warmth and freedom from sanctimony quickly won her the trust of women prisoners, for whom she became an adviser and confidante. Even by the standards of South Africa, the treatment of African women awaiting trial was appalling. They were allowed no visits, parcels, or even messages; they had no means to contact families, procure legal advice, or make provision for their children. Treatment of juveniles was still worse: given the "uneconomical" nature of reformatories, young African offenders were routinely sentenced to corporal punishment. Maxeke stepped into the breach. She began to follow cases through the courts, contacting detainees' friends and employers, organizing legal help, and rendering whatever other assistance she could. She made provision for the children of female prisoners, usually by taking them into her own home. Eventually, magistrates began calling her in to counsel women and children, often releasing first-time offenders to her care.[89]

Maxeke labored as "native probation officer" from 1919 to 1922. On weekends she continued to hold religious services, extending her mission to include jails in Krugersdorp, Boksburg, and Germiston. She received no remuneration for her work, save the gratitude of women and children and a small allowance to cover travel costs. Late in 1922 the Native Affairs Department arranged a small "sub rosa" payment of five pounds per month, channeled through Johannesburg's "Helping Hand Club." At the end of 1923 she was formally ap-

pointed "native welfare officer," a newly created post that came with an office
in an unwhitewashed shed outside the Magistrate's courts and a monthly salary
of about twelve pounds per month. The raise was doubtless welcome, given the
Maxekes' burgeoning household and Marshall's persistent ill health. For its
part, the South African government parlayed its paltry investment into a
public relations triumph, citing the existence of posts such as native welfare
officer and native probation officer as proof of the adequacy of African legal
facilities. The dilemma of generations of black reformist leadership was distilled in that self-serving claim.[90]

To her credit, Maxeke realized that prison work addressed the symptoms
rather than the root cause of urban African women's plight, which remained
women's exclusion from the labor market. Any mother in the world would
turn to vice, she argued, in a characteristically maternalist turn of phrase, if
offered no other means to provide for her children. Her solution to the problem, launched in 1923, was a domestic registration agency—in effect a labor
bureau for female domestic workers. For a small fee, African women could
register with Maxeke, who would check their bona fides and then use her
contacts with white South Africans to find them suitable employment. To
Maxeke, the benefits of the system were obvious. Whites reluctant to employ
black women would have the comfort of knowing that their domestic worker
had been vetted "as to her character, health, and general fitness." This assurance would help break down resistance to employing African women and
eliminate the need for pass legislation. In turn, African women, many fresh
from the countryside, would have a network in the city to place them in
positions where they would be assured of regular wages and proper accommodation. Like her Mite Missionary mentor Fanny Jackson Coppin, who rose
from domestic service to become one of black America's most prominent
educators, Maxeke argued that the very experience of working in respectable
white homes would redound to black women's advantage, exposing them to
the manners and mores of "civilised" society. ("From the better class of European woman the native girls would learn how to conduct themselves with
propriety," she explained to a white journalist. They would "receive instruction in domestic science and housecraft generally, and thereby become useful members of society.") Needless to say, the scheme won the "patronage
of influential Europeans," who wished to see some control exerted over the
movements of African women but recoiled from passes and medical inspections.[91]

All the ambiguities of Maxeke's position, already visible in her service as
native welfare officer, exploded into prominence. While posed as an alternative
to passes and medical inspections, the registry system exploited prevailing
stereotypes about African urban women, implying that no respectable white
family would take a black woman into its home unless she had been thoroughly
vetted. "Although we have no condition as to medical inspection," Maxeke

explained to a white interviewer, "I myself had training as a nurse in connection with missionary work in America and elsewhere, and, as a result, I can always tell whether the women are free from blemish or otherwise. You can take it from me that before I recommend any girl I shall satisfy myself that she is beyond reproach in every respect." Worse still, the scheme forced Maxeke to partake of the agitation against "houseboys," who remained the chief obstacle to female domestics. "Nature itself ordains that the European woman's handmaid should be one of her own sex, and not a member of the opposite sex," she argued. "It is ridiculous to think of a big, able-bodied man moving about a house and ousting a woman from her natural duties." On a few occasions, she went even further, indulging in the worst kind of Black Peril imagery. Imagine "what state of mind is induced in those raw, uneducated boys," she asked one interviewer, when "they are permitted, as is very frequently the case, to enter with morning tea or coffee the bedrooms of their European mistresses, who may be in bed, or perhaps, *en deshabille.*" All human action is morally ambiguous, but rarely are the tradeoffs so agonizingly apparent. In her campaign "to beat down the unjust prejudice" against African women, Maxeke was forced to indulge the most vicious racial stereotypes about African men. And, insofar as she succeeded in opening the labor market to black women, she helped propel black men into the maw of the mines.[92]

For better or worse, little came of Maxeke's scheme. While the agency idea enjoyed a brief vogue among liberals in the mid-1920s, those looking to secure "control over the movements of Native women" ultimately found their solution not in domestic registration but in a system of de facto rural registration. Amendments to the Urban Areas Act in 1930 empowered municipalities to require women entering urban areas to present certificates from magistrates in their home districts, certificates that were to be issued only with the consent of husbands, fathers, or guardians. Thus were African patriarchs and white liberal reformers reconciled to the previously unpalatable idea of women's passes. How Maxeke felt about this "compromise" is not entirely clear. In most respects, she probably welcomed it. The certificate system was less than a pass law, while the parental consent clause was consistent with long-held beliefs about authority and appropriate generational control. (A 1925 proposal from the Johannesburg Joint Council, adopted during her tenure on the council and endorsed by the Bantu Women's League, included virtually all the provisions contained in the 1930 legislation.) On the other hand, Maxeke knew all too well where such a system could lead. Subjected to the rule of frequently ill-educated parents and guardians, herded into unwanted marriages, young women would continue to flee to the city, where they would now be doubly vulnerable. The cycle of vice and harassment would continue, eventually issuing in what she had always opposed: women's passes.[93]

By the mid-1920s, Charlotte Maxeke had established herself as one of the half dozen most respected and influential black leaders in South Africa. Prestige alone, however, could not save her from the vortex of poverty and degradation that claimed so many members of her class. Marshall's health continued to deteriorate. Aside from his brief stint as editor of *Umteteli wa Bantu,* he spent the last decade of his life confined to his home. While he remained an ordained AME minister, he did no pastoral work and received no pension from the church. He died in 1928 at the age of fifty-four. During most of the years on the Rand, the family depended on the salary that Charlotte brought home for her work as native welfare officer. It was never enough, particularly in a household that included not only the Maxekes' own son, Clarke, but Marshall's mother, an elderly aunt, and half a dozen "waifs and strays." Maxeke's own health, which she had always neglected, was also failing. Her stout frame had become fat, and she moved with difficulty and much labored breathing. She had lost several teeth.[94]

At about the time of her husband's death, Maxeke received an invitation to return to the United States under the auspices of the Women's Home and Foreign Missionary Society. She leapt at the offer, which enabled her to renew old acquaintances and to visit Clarke, who was just finishing his studies. Characteristically, she saw the trip as an opportunity to research developments in American prisons, hostels, and reformatories, and on that basis she applied for and received a six-month leave of absence from her job at the courts. While few details of the visit remain, Maxeke clearly relished her time in America. African American churchwomen, on the other hand, were appalled by the state in which they found her. At her hosts' insistence, she extended her visit an extra month in order to regain her strength and undergo extensive dental work, paid for by the Mite Missionary Society.[95]

Once back in South Africa, Maxeke's fortunes resumed their downward spiral. In 1930 the state eliminated the native welfare position. According to the Public Service Commission that ordered the closure, the post was no longer economical, given the opening of a separate juvenile court in Auckland Park and the dispersal of other native cases to suburban courts. Worse, Maxeke learned that in extending her stay in America beyond the agreed period she had technically broken her service and was thus not eligible for a state pension. Eventually, her white liberal friends succeeded in steering a special condonation bill through Parliament, which entitled her to thirty-seven pounds in benefits, paid in one lump sum. (To claim the award, Maxeke was required to submit a petition explaining that she had no income and seven dependents, including four orphans, aged six to eight, whom she had adopted.) Beyond that single payment, she weathered the worst years of the Depression with no regular income. Howard Pim, a friend from the Joint Council days, helped her with thirty shillings per month through about 1935, when she accepted an offer to serve as matron of the girls' hostel at Wilberforce Institute in Evaton. Unfortunately, the Institute was itself caught in the throes of the Depression, and her salary was ever in arrears. Rarely did she receive more than five or ten pounds per year, usually out of the pocket of her American-educated comrade, A. B. Xuma, Wilberforce's de facto treasurer.[96]

Still, her reputation endured. In 1937 Maxeke was elected president of the newly created National Council of African Women. Spawned by the All-Africa Convention, the Council was intended as a successor to the moribund Bantu Women's League. In her presidential address, one of her last public addresses, Maxeke enjoined delegates to take up the burden of racial service that she had borne so well. "The work is not for yourselves," she declared. "Kill that spirit of 'self' and do not live above your people, but live with them. If you can rise, bring someone with you." Above all, she concluded, "love one another as brothers and sisters."[97]

For young women in the audience, including several who would later distinguish themselves in the grueling battle against apartheid, it was a rare opportunity to see and hear and touch a living legend. For those who had known Maxeke before, however, the spectacle was limned with sadness. "I was shocked by her appearance," South African Institute of Race Relations founder J. D. Rheinallt Jones wrote in a letter to the chief native commissioner of Johannesburg. "She is evidently suffering great privation, but still tries to do her best to help her people." Surely, he added, some small grant could be arranged "to keep her in food and decency." Dorothy Maud, a Sophiatown social worker, agreed. "She is very poor, and I was shocked to see her appearance, and to know that she had been through real privation, real poverty." At that moment, she added, Charlotte was keeping five children in her home, paying for their food and school fees.[98]

Two years later she was dead. Her body was buried in Evaton, at Wilberforce Institute. The last reference to Charlotte Maxeke in the South African government archives is a 1941 solicitation from the Women's Missionary Society, aimed at raising money to purchase a headstone for her grave. This campaign, at least, succeeded. A few months later, her friends gathered at the graveside to raise the stone and recommit her to Africa.[99]

Like all the Wilberforce students, Charlotte Manye Maxeke was a creature of the gloaming. In her consciousness and character, she represented the finest flower of South Africa's nineteenth-century mission culture. She could scarcely have been better suited for the world of Wilberforce, which was, in its own way, in twilight. By the time she and the first group of students returned home, Crummell had joined Payne in death, while Du Bois, disillusioned, had begun an intellectual trek that would eventually carry him back to Africa. South Africa, in the students' absence, had been transformed utterly, by war and an imperial reconstruction that mocked their dreams of a social order based on character rather than race. As the decades passed, Maxeke and her peers were marginalized politically and ground down economically. It was a singularly cruel fate for people who had once dared imagine themselves the instruments of Providence.

Yet taken on its own terms, the life of Charlotte Maxeke was not spent in vain. Faithful to her calling, she lifted hundreds of people, mostly women and children, from the wretchedness to which a casually brutal society had otherwise consigned them. Her determined efforts to bridge black and white worlds, however flawed and seemingly ineffectual, helped sustain a fragile tradition of nonracialism in South Africa, a tradition that, against all odds, survives today. Perhaps most important, Maxeke's example of dignity, service, and simple humanity remains to inspire another generation of South Africans, who struggle in their own way to redeem their nation from the darkness of its history. At such a moment, it is well to heed the lesson of her friend and teacher W. E. B. Du Bois, and strive to see in the shadows which engulfed her life not the coming night, but the Dusk of Dawn. [100]

9

Middle Passages

By the beginning of World War I, African Methodism's unique moment in the intertwined history of the United States and South Africa had more or less passed. Henry Turner, the driving force behind the AME Church's African outreach, went to his rest in 1915, the same year as Benjamin Tanner, his great antagonist. Questions about Africa and its relationship to African American life, which had consumed AME councils for the better part of a century, were crowded aside by a host of concerns closer to home—by war, by renewed spasms of racial violence, and by a massive northward migration that depopulated whole swaths of the church's southern heartland. While AME leaders continued to endorse African missions and occasionally to support them financially, Africa was clearly becoming a sideshow within the church. In the face of the East St. Louis race riot of 1917 and the explosion in Chicago two years later, it was hard to see Africa as the primary challenge for black Christianity, the field on which the future of the race would be determined.

In South Africa, the AME Church had finally reached a kind of equilibrium, after years of tumult. The patient stewardship of John Albert Johnson, resident bishop from 1908–1916, soothed tensions between the church's African and African American branches and helped stem the seemingly endless schisms and secessions that had plagued the movement since its early days. Politically, the church had lost much of its vitality and moment, a process reflected in and reinforced by the emergence of new, more secular political movements such as the South African Native National Congress. By the time of Johnson's departure, little remained of that extraordinary expectancy that had greeted the AME Church when it first entered South Africa. African adherents continued to value their affiliation with black America, but few were naive enough to expect liberation from that quarter.

This transformation was observed and appreciated by South African officials, who after all had played a pivotal role in steering the church away from politics to the safe harbor of religion. A survey of magistrates and white missionaries in the early 1920s brought ringing endorsements of the church's work. African Methodists were described as "well behaved," "quiet," and "civil in all respects." "Leaders American Negroes," a Cape Town magistrate reported. "Highly intelligent and exceptionally loyal. Doctrine excellent." The resident magistrate at Ficksburg in the Free State, a town that had tried to expel the church in the early twentieth century, agreed: the local minister "is of good character, and preaches the Gospel only, without introducing political or other inflammatory matter."[1]

It all makes for a tidy ending. Once again, the "sect" had become a "church"; African Methodism, vilified at the turn of the century as seditious and antiwhite, had become "far and away the most respectable of the purely Native churches in this country." Ultimately, however, such a conclusion does justice neither to the church nor to the complexity of subsequent events. At the very moment that AME leaders in the United States were turning away from Africa, the revival of the Pan-African movement and the simultaneous eruption of Marcus Garvey's Universal Negro Improvement Association catapulted the continent back into the center of African American intellectual and political life. In South Africa, too, black America remained a ubiquitous imaginative presence. The political eclipse of African Methodism did not so much end popular interest in "the Negro" as fragment it, enabling new actors and movements to contest for the mantle of African American authority. Given the nature of their institution and their history, African Methodists were inevitably drawn into these renewed debates, in unexpected, sometimes contradictory ways. Thus, as the curtain fell on one historical episode, a new, more diffuse drama commenced.[2]

Just as emancipation, the epochal event of nineteenth century African American history, helped establish the AME Church as the center of an emerging national African American community, so the Great Migration, the epochal event of the twentieth century, inaugurated the church's slow disestablishment. Between 1915 and 1920, half a million blacks abandoned the South for northern cities, the first wave in a demographic shift that would fundamentally transform the economic and political landscape of the United States. Migration wrought profound changes in African American Christianity in general, and in African Methodism in particular. In states such as Georgia and South Carolina, home to the bulk of the church's adherents since Reconstruction, entire congregations evaporated in the space of months. In the north, the influx of thousands of new migrants, some with no previous exposure to urban life, strained church resources, while opening new gulfs of class, education, and experience within congregations. More broadly, migration coincided with and contributed to an ongoing process of secularization, which challenged the church's primacy in black life. New forms of association and recreation, from political machines to music halls, competed with the church for African Americans' patronage and scarce resources.[3]

AME Church leaders were slow to respond to these new circumstances. Even as southern ministers reported declines in church membership of up to 80 percent, Senior Bishop Benjamin Lee continued to urge migrants to remain in the South, recycling arguments about rolling stones and cast-down buckets that his predecessors had directed against African emigration. "We beg to advise you who are still in the South to remain on the farms, and buy small or large tracts of land while you can, and practice honesty, industry and frugality," Lee urged Alabamans in 1916. "Practice the habit of saving . . . [and] cultivate a friendly relationship with all races." By the end of 1917, however, most church leaders realized that the exodus would continue, with or without them, and that the church must adapt or perish. Migration presented "obligations and opportunities which can neither be avoided or ignored," AME *Church Review* editor Reverdy Ransom declared. "The church must create new forms of service and new lines of activity to meet the instant demands of a new situation." At the most mundane level, the sudden shift of population required the reallocation of personnel and resources, as well as reapportionment of the General Conference. At the same time, the church needed to respond to new secular and religious rivals, as well as to the surging tide of racial animosity. Above all, the church had somehow to assimilate tens of thousands of northern migrants—not simply to meet their religious needs but to facilitate their adaptation to urban, industrial society.[4]

While such priorities did not necessarily conflict with African missions, they consumed energy and attention that might otherwise have been devoted to mission activity. The 1916–1920 quadrennium produced a raft of new institutions within the church, including a Labor Commission, a Committee on Negro Migration, a Social Services Commission, a Committee on Negro Troops, and a Committee on After-War Problems. Church leaders' decision to convene the 1920 General Conference in St. Louis, across the river from the scene of one of the era's bloodiest race riots, itself bespoke their growing preoccupation with the problems of urban life. The Board of Church Extension, long a poor relation of the AME Missionary Department, experienced a new lease on life, consolidating southern congregations and overseeing the expansion of overburdened northern facilities. In the early 1920s the Board raised twenty-five thousand dollars to help construct homes for new migrants, money that, in a previous decade, might well have been earmarked for Africa. Such efforts were mirrored at the congregational level in employment and housing bureaus, libraries, athletic clubs, and relief campaigns. Philadelphia alone supported half a dozen initiatives, from an interdenominational ministers' committee to defend black civil rights to the Richard Allen Home, founded in 1923, as a halfway house for new migrants.[5]

The shift in institutional priorities was reflected in the character of church leadership. For the better part of two generations, Africa represented one of the surest avenues of advancement in the highly competitive world of AME politics. Henry Turner, Richard Cain, William Heard, Levi Coppin, H. B. Parks, even that arch-antiemigrationist Charles Smith—all rode their experience in or expertise on Africa to the episcopacy. Dozens of other church leaders capitalized on the issue to promote themselves to national office. By the early 1920s, however, the pathway to office increasingly ran not through Africa but through urban America. No one better illustrates the shift than Bishop Reverdy Ransom, a man best remembered today as the great orator of the Niagara Movement. Like many churchmen born too late to participate in the epochal events of emancipation and Reconstruction, Ransom first sought distinction in the cause of African missions. In 1893 he hosted the first national convention of the Woman's and Parents' Mite Missionary Society at his Cleveland church, working closely with his wife, Emma, editor of the Society's short-lived journal *Women's Light and Love for Heathen Africa.* A year later, he sponsored the enrollment of the first South African students at Wilberforce, his alma mater, thereby contributing to the formation of the South African AME Church. With his transfer to Chicago a few years later, however, Ransom began to shift direction. Influenced by the social gospel currents sweeping through American Protestantism, he founded the Institutional Church and Settlement House, the AME Church's first concerted response to the problem of black urbanization. Located along the rail line that carried southern migrants into Chicago, the Institutional Church embraced a two-thousand-seat tabernacle, an employment bureau, a day care center, regular public forums and classes, and the first African American rescue home, modeled on Jane Addams's nearby Hull House. At the same time, Ransom carried the church into urban politics with his attacks on vice and his attempts to mediate the 1904 stockyard strike. His coreligionists were somewhat slow to appreciate his contributions, but in 1912 they elected him editor of the AME *Church Review,* providing him a national forum. In 1924 he was elected to the bishopric.[6]

R. R. Wright, Jr., perhaps the most distinguished of the AME Church's twentieth-century bishops, traced a similar path. Born in 1878, Wright was the son of the famous "black boy of Atlanta," the young freedman whose words to Freedmen's Bureau head O. O. Howard—"Tell them we are rising"—were immortalized in verse by James Greenleaf Whittier. By the time Richard, Jr., was coming of age, his father had risen from slavery to become president of Georgia State Industrial College and a prominent Republican Party spokesman. Wright took his first degree at Georgia State but thereafter left the South. He eventually landed at the University of Chicago, where he took a master's degree in sociology while working as an assistant at Ransom's Institutional Church. He assisted W. E. B. Du Bois in the Atlanta University series on the Negro and, after a sojourn in Germany to take additional courses in sociology, completed a Ph.D. at the University of Pennsylvania. (His disserta-tion, "The Negro in Pennsylvania," was intended as a sequel to Du Bois's classic work on black Philadelphia.) All the while, Wright retained his interest in urban issues, penning a series of pathbreaking essays on black migration in the *Southern Workman*. Like Ransom, Wright defended migrants' right to come north and advocated a dramatic "institutional reordering of priorities" within African Methodism to cope with the new situation. Appointed editor of the *Christian Recorder,* he urged his coreligionists to "throw open the arms of welcome to every Negro who desires to come," portraying the exodus not as a problem but as an unparalleled opportunity to transform black people's place in American society. He himself helped launch the Citizen and Southern Bank of Philadelphia, an institution catering to southern migrants that quickly grew into the largest black-owned bank in America. He was finally elected to the bishopric in 1936.[7]

Leaders such as Ransom and Wright were certainly not averse to African mission work. Having sponsored the first Wilberforce students, Ransom fol-lowed the development of the South African AME Church with lively interest. Wright published a study guide for prospective missionaries and actually spent his first episcopal tour as resident bishop of South Africa, where he established himself as a popular and effective leader. Neither man, however, saw African missions as the church's most pressing priority or regarded his own destiny as inextricably linked with the continent. Wright, who clearly enjoyed his years in South Africa, was forthright on the matter. "I am an American," he declared in the opening pages of his autobiography. "I love Africa . . . yet I am not African in education, religion, language, social concepts, nor in general out-look." For Wright and Ransom, as for a whole rising generation of AME leadership, blacks' "promised land" lay not in Africa but in full civic participa-tion in northern cities like Chicago and Philadelphia.[8]

The irony, of course, is that African Methodism's retreat from Africa coin-cided with a dramatic resurgence of African interest in broader African Ameri-can society. The 1919 Pan-African Congress, convened in Paris to coincide with the Versailles Peace Conference, revived transatlantic linkages, while reestablishing Africa as one of the fields on which the future of the world would be determined. At the same time, Marcus Garvey's Universal Negro Improve-ment Association and African Communities League began its meteoric rise. Born of the same demographic shifts that were remaking African Methodism, Garveyism drew hundreds of thousands of black men and women to the banner of African redemption. By the early 1920s interest in Africa had spilled into every corner of African American intellectual life, most notably in the so-called "New Negro" movement. The poetry of Langston Hughes and Countee Cul-len, the criticism of Alain Locke, and the graphic art of Aaron Douglas all addressed Africa's legacy in America, posing the question of African Ameri-cans' relationship to their ancestral continent.[9]

For the most part, the AME Church stood outside the Africanist revival. African Methodists were conspicuous by their absence at the 1919 Pan-African Congress, especially given the predominance of churchmen in the founding of the movement in 1899–1900. While the old rhetoric of regeneration occasionally resurfaced at the 1919 Congress, postwar Pan-Africanism was a distinctly secular affair, which conceived Africa's plight in terms of colonialism rather than "civilization." As for the U.N.I.A., most church leaders were actively hostile, discerning in Garvey's militant appeals a threat not only to racial comity but to their own status and authority. The whole Garvey movement, as E. Franklin Frazier observed in 1926, revolved around a "half-acknowledged antagonism toward Negro preachers, and the sleepy religion they served to the masses with dreams of a land to come." AME leaders more than reciprocated the antagonism, denouncing Garvey as a demagogue, capitalizing on roiled postwar conditions for his own ends. Leading the charge was Bishop Charles Spencer Smith, who remained one of African Methodism's resident sages on Africa, despite his own disastrous tour of duty there. "I can furnish a list of more than a dozen reliable, intelligent colored Americans, now at home, who have studied Africa in Africa," Smith declared, modestly including himself. Any one of them, he argued, knew more about Africans' real interests and needs than Garvey or fellow "delusionists and dreamers" like W. E. B. Du Bois.[10]

Beneath this surface antagonism, however, Garveyism and African Methodism had a great deal in common, which may paradoxically account for the stridency of church leaders' attacks. Both movements competed for African Americans' loyalty and resources, while striving, in different ways, to establish themselves as the primary bridge between black America and Africa. There were also significant continuities in terms of images and ideas, as Randall Burkett has persuasively argued. Echoes of the nineteenth-century African evangelical movement pervaded Garvey's rhetoric—in the constant invocations of Ethiopia; the assertions of racial "manhood"; the image of a providential hand leading African Americans into and through the furnace of slavery, steeling them for the task of African redemption. Even the Black Star Line had ample precedents in African Methodist history, from the *Azor* debacle of 1877 to the various steamship schemes of Henry Turner. Certainly this was how many churchpeople saw matters. Despite the admonitions of bishops and presiding elders, several AME ministers and an untold number of laypeople rallied to the U.N.I.A., accepting its emphasis on African redemption as perfectly in keeping with their own denominational traditions. Like the return of the repressed, Africa reemerged in African Methodism, even as church leaders turned away.[11]

The situation on the other side of the Atlantic was even more complex and seemingly contradictory. As students of South African history well know,

World War I ushered in a decade and a half of political turbulence. In addition to the dislocations occasioned by the war itself, the period witnessed two armed rebellions by poor whites and an unprecedented wave of African militance, expressed in the upheavals on the Witwatersrand and in the electric spread of the Industrial and Commercial Workers' Union through the South African countryside. One unexpected consequence of all this turmoil was a renewal of popular interest in black America. African politicians across the political spectrum compared their own predicament to that of their brethren in America, adducing African American experience in support of a dizzying range of political prescriptions. White missionaries and officials also partook of the interest, harnessing the "Negro" to proposals of their own. For a time it was virtually impossible to open a South African newspaper, African or European, without coming across some reference to the United States, usually accompanied by implicit or explicit "lessons" for South Africa. In an elusive but important sense, the meaning of American, and specifically African American, experience became one of the central issues in South African postwar politics.[12]

The most obvious manifestation of African interest in black America was Garveyism, which continued to reverberate through South Africa long after it had begun to wane in the United States. South African officials first detected the U.N.I.A.'s "seditious and unwholesome teachings" in mid-1920, in the wake of the First International Conference of Negro Peoples of the World in New York. Not surprisingly, the movement first took root in ports, especially in Cape Town, home to several hundred West Indians as well as a substantial floating population of black seamen. By the end of the year, the city boasted its own Garveyite newspaper, *The Black Man,* edited by a mercurial Transkeian named S. M. Bennett Ncwana. At about the same time, copies of Garvey's *Negro World* were discovered on the Witwatersrand, allegedly circulated through a network of African American sailors and cooperative African warehousemen. Word of mouth did the rest, carrying reports of black fleets and armies to the far corners of the subcontinent. "[E]ven from the backwood hamlets rings the magic cry *'Ama Melika ayeza'*—the Americans are coming"—a worried D. D. T. Jabavu reported in early 1922.[13]

Like all manifestations of black America in Africa, Garveyism was as much a metaphor as a movement, an imaginative vehicle for a diverse range of African grievances and aspirations. At the broadest level, it expressed a vision of liberation, most vividly in the idea of a returning black army, coming to restore the land to its rightful owners. Garveyism also provided an outlet for Africans' pervasive disenchantment with existing authorities—not only colonial officials and European missionaries but collaborating chiefs, "rubber stamp" editors, and all the "backboneless, spineless African leaders" who placed their sinecures above the interests of their supposed constituents. Such ideas clearly overlapped with and drew strength from earlier "Ethiopian" traditions; as in the United States, one could argue that Garveyism flowed through channels first carved by independent Christianity. A South African correspondent to *The Negro World,* for example, described Garvey as a "true Moses" coming "to emancipate the children of Ethiopia from the fetters of bondage," language that uncannily echoed Africans' initial response to the AME Church. [14]

What ultimately distinguished Garveyism from African Methodism was its amorphousness. For all its decentralization, the South African AME Church remained recognizably a single institution, bound by structures, procedures, and hierarchies, all of which became stronger over time. Not so the U.N.I.A., which remained more a specter than a functioning institution. At best, it represented a loose aggregation of local movements, organized around particular leaders, peddling their own distinctive versions of Garveyite doctrine. In the long run, this lack of structure and cohesion ensured the U.N.I.A.'s fragility and eventual dissolution. In the short run, however, it facilitated the movement's expansion, enabling it to find a niche in diverse settings. The African American presence was less obvious but ultimately no less important in the Industrial and Commercial Workers' Union. Like the U.N.I.A., the I.C.U. first emerged in Cape Town, during the dockworkers' strike of 1919. African workers, caught between spiraling inflation and shrinking real wages, responded enthusiastically to the organization's distinctive brand of racially charged unionism, and branches opened in Johannesburg and Bloemfontein and across the eastern Cape. The Union appeared to be in decline by 1922 or 1923, but the launching of a rural organizing drive in 1925 lent it a new lease on life. While the struggle for higher wages remained central to the I.C.U. appeal, organizers in the countryside explored a more broad-based racial populism attacking everything from pass and dipping laws to local ordinances that prohibited Africans from walking on sidewalks. Everywhere they sounded the clarion call of land, insisting on black people's right to live and work on the land of their ancestors. By the end of 1927 the Union boasted more than one hundred branches and a membership exceeding one hundred thousand. [15]

While the I.C.U. had no direct links with black America, the figure of the "Negro" surfaced again and again in Union rhetoric and ideology. Union speakers addressed their audiences as "Fellow slaves," often explicitly contrasting their plight with that of their "cousins" in the United States, who had fought for and won their "freedom." So frequent were such invocations, Natal activist Gilbert Coka recalled, that many "country people" assumed "that the I.C.U. leaders were American Negroes who had come to deliver them from slavery." Clements Kadalie, the Nyasaland clerk who founded the Union and served as its general secretary, seems actively to have fostered that perception, to the point of affecting an American accent. Kadalie, who ascribed his commitment to "public life" to a youthful encounter with Booker T. Washington's *Up From Slavery,* cultivated links with black America throughout his life. In Cape Town, he identified openly with Garveyism, speaking at U.N.I.A.

meetings and rallies and also serving briefly as managing editor of *The Black Man*. "My essential object is to be the great African Marcus Garvey," he confided to his co-editor, Bennett Ncwana, in a letter requesting a copy of the U.N.I.A. constitution. Although he later distanced himself from Garvey, Kadalie retained his American interest, hobnobbing with African Methodist leaders—his son Alexander became an AME minister—and with Africans returning from U.S. schools. He also somehow made contact with A. Philip Randolph, the head of the Brotherhood of Sleeping Car Porters, black America's most powerful union. From 1923 to 1927, he served as South African correspondent for *The Messenger*, the Brotherhood's monthly journal. [16]

Kadalie was not the only African leader of the period to find a political cachet in black America. His partner, Bennett Ncwana, invented an African American alter ego, W. O. Jackson, under which name he proselytized for the U.N.I.A. and launched a series of dubious business ventures. James Thaele, Ncwana's partner in several enterprises, was cut from much the same cloth. Born in Basutoland, Thaele was one of the last southern African students to make the passage to the United States before the outbreak of World War I, enrolling at Lincoln University and later at the University of Pennsylvania. Returning to South Africa as a self-styled "professor," he used his alleged connections with Garvey and other "prominent Negro persons and Associations" to secure election as president of the Western Cape branch of the African National Congress. Thaele's flamboyance and his penchant for inflammatory statements quickly scandalized more moderate Congressmen. D. D. T. Jabavu, for example, angrily disavowed Thaele's suggestion that Africans remove pictures of Queen Victoria from their homes, a disavowal that the "professor" dismissed as typical of his "me-too-boss attitude." "Mr. Jabavu has (unfortunately) received his education in England, not in America," he explained. "English education is too circumscribed and tends to specialization; American, encyclopaedic and perspective [*sic*]." [17]

Certainly the most accomplished of these "mimetic American Negroes" was Wellington Buthelezi, alias Dr. Wellington. Born on a Natal mission station in the 1890s and educated briefly at Lovedale, Buthelezi spent the early 1920s in the Transkeian Territories, peddling patent remedies and occasionally passing himself off as a medical doctor. By 1925 he had fashioned an entirely new identity: he was now the Chicago-born Dr. Butler Hansford Wellington, Oxford-trained physician and emissary of Marcus Garvey's U.N.I.A. From that time until his mysterious disappearance in 1937, "Dr. Wellington" won thousands of adherents in the Transkei, preaching a distinctive blend of Garveyism, independent Christianity, and New Testament millenialism. Probably his most significant initiative was the so-called "American School movement." As in earlier African Methodist ventures, adherents were urged to move their children from European missions to independent schools, where they would allegedly acquire all the knowledge and technological mastery of African Americans. While little ultimately came of such proposals and prophecies, colonial officials regarded them as sufficiently serious that they attempted to deport Buthelezi—to the United States! The attempt failed when he produced witnesses attesting to his birth in Natal.[18]

Given their overlap in ideas and their shared preoccupation with the United States, the political movements of the 1920s inevitably became comingled on the ground. Probably the most spectacular example came in Pondoland, where the ideas of Garveyites and Wellingtonites combined with indigenous prophetic traditions and the enthusiasm unleashed by a massive I.C.U. organizing campaign to ignite a sweeping millenarian movement. While specific beliefs varied across time and place, the movement revolved around the core idea of African Americans arriving in airplanes and raining fire from the sky. Depending on the particular variation, the only people destined to survive were those who rid themselves of European commodities, killed their pigs, or held up their red I.C.U. membership cards at the moment the holocaust began. Beneath the manifest influence of Garveyism lay entire universes of knowledge and history. The idea of fire falling from the sky had a long history in local eschatology, as did the notion of ancestors returning to reclaim the land. Pig killings, a traditional mechanism for eliminating pollution, had broken out sporadically in the region for decades; in several instances in the late nineteenth and early twentieth centuries, they unfolded alongside boycotts of European goods. The idea of passover bespoke the influence of the Old Testament, while the belief in African Americans' technological prowess, vividly expressed in the image of airplanes, hearkened back at least to the turn of the century, to Pondo paramount chief Sigcau's abortive sponsorship of an African Methodist industrial school. The entire history of colonialism was distilled in the millenialists' cry *"Mayibuye iAfrika"* [Let Africa return].[19]

It is easy, in retrospect, to dismiss men like Bennett Ncwana, Professor Thaele, and Dr. Wellington as freaks and charlatans, capitalizing on African desperation to advance their own ends. Such a perspective, however, begs the question of their success. Just as Ethiopianism spoke to the hopes and frustrations of Africans at the opening of the century, so impulses such as Garveyism, the I.C.U., and the American School movement touched a taproot of popular militancy in the 1920s. Whatever their individual motives, these latter-day prophets spoke to Africans' grievances: their resentment of meddlesome missionaries and colonial officials; their disillusionment with established African leadership; their yearning for an Africa before the coming of passes, poll taxes, and white landlords. They also understood the extraordinary imaginative power that black America still commanded among black South Africans. In an atmosphere of upheaval and despair, African Americans continued to provide a model, a vision of progress, dignity, and power outside the colonial relationship. America remained the place where blacks were free.

Among white South Africans, postwar upheaval and the revival of transatlantic linkages combined to produce a recrudescence of fears of "Negro agitators" and "unnatural" political combinations. Colonial officials could scarcely miss the Pan-African Congress, convening as it did alongside the Versailles Conference, or overlook its potential significance, particularly given their interest in the new African mandates. Garveyism, while somewhat slower to engage official attention, appeared even more sinister. In the wake of the International Conference of Negro Peoples of the World in the summer of 1920, colonial administrations all across Africa were bombarded with rumors of the imminent arrival of African American colonists, even of Garvey himself. At about the same time, South African officials awoke to the widespread circulation of both *The Negro World* and its local offspring, *The Black Man.* Characteristically reaching for the agitator thesis, they responded by trying to throw an intellectual quarantine around the entire country. Citing a clause in a 1913 immigration law regulating the entry of persons "unsuited to the requirements of the Union," the state prohibited the entry of "coloured persons of whatever nationality who are not domiciled in the Union of South Africa." (One particularly obtuse official enquired whether the ban was meant to apply to African mineworkers, the majority of whom still migrated from beyond the Union's borders.) Officials even mooted a plan to confine visiting black sailors to their ships, an idea without warrant in either national or international law.[20]

Yet even as such fears reached a crescendo, a remarkable reassessment of the possibilities of the "transatlantic connection" had begun to unfold. Spurred by a small knot of American-trained missionaries and educators, South African officials began seriously to entertain the notion that African American experience—properly understood and packaged—might offer solutions to their own country's worsening "race problem." Not surprisingly, they evinced special interest in the work of the late Booker T. Washington, who appeared to have perfected an approach that harmonized the demands of capitalist development, political stability, and white supremacy. In effect, white South Africans sought to wrest the figure of the "Negro" from its African purveyors, transforming a symbol of resistance and liberation into a model of racial cooperation and "good sense."

At the core of white interest in black America lay the idea of "industrial education," a term with a long and problematic history in both the British Empire and the United States. The origins of the concept, in both incarnations, lay in the transition from slavery to free labor, and in the perceived need for some form of labor discipline to replace the compulsion of slavery. R. Hunt Davis dates the idea to an 1847 report of the Committee of the Privy Council on Education, addressing the problem of creating a viable free labor system in the West Indies. Drawing on earlier debates about appropriate schooling for the English working class, the committee stressed the importance of inculcating "habits of self-control and moral discipline" in an indigenous population presumed to be inherently indolent. The idea was refined by Sir George Grey, whose efforts to introduce industrial schools among the Maori of New Zealand provided a model for "native education" within the empire. It was Grey, appointed colonial governor of Cape Colony in 1855, who brought industrial education to South Africa. Grey's ideas found a ready constituency among European missionaries, who at the time still envisioned their converts developing into an independent Christian yeomanry. By the late 1850s, when American industrial education pioneer Samuel Chapman Armstrong's father was refining his ideas on a Hawaiian mission station, most South African mission schools included some manual and agricultural training in their curricula. When the younger Armstrong arrived at Hampton Institute a decade later, Lovedale already boasted a full industrial curriculum, featuring masonry, carpentry, wagon making, and printing.[21]

Yet even as industrial education emerged as a racial panacea in the United States, it was fast falling from favor in South Africa. As we have already seen, the mineral revolution in the late nineteenth century provoked a fundamental reassessment of Africans' place in South African society. Mineowners and capitalizing farmers, grappling alike with crippling shortages of cheap labor, had little interest in native education, particularly education designed to enhance African autonomy. White artisans and tradesmen, themselves caught in the swelling currents of proletarianization, had even less interest in schemes that promised to promote racial competition and undercut white wages. The growing association of the idea with black America only further inflamed white opposition, especially during the Ethiopian panic that followed the South African War.[22]

Ironically, the aspect of industrial education that whites in South Africa found most objectionable was precisely that which their counterparts in the United States most welcomed: the idea of black "self-help." Booker T. Washington's insistence that African Americans see to their own development was music to the ears of white Americans—to white southerners who resented paying taxes to support black education and to northerners seeking some reasonably dignified way to jettison their historical commitment to the freedmen. In South Africa, on the other hand, the upheaval of war and the exigencies of reconstruction generated an obsession with European control of all things African. In that context, even long-time proponents of industrial training exhibited new caution. Free Church missionary James Stewart, for example, presided over an enormous expansion of Lovedale's industrial departments in the 1870s and '80s, effectively dismantling all facilities for higher education. He visited Tuskegee in the 1890s and came away singing Washington's praises. A 1903 visit, however, left him considerably more circumspect, no doubt in part because of an unexpected encounter with several of his former students, deposited there by African Presbyterian Church founder P. J. Mzimba. In his testimony before the South African Native Affairs Commission later that year, Stewart continued to defend industrial education against charges that it promoted racial competition, but warned of the dangers of African autonomy and insisted that even industrial schools needed white supervision to succeed. When one of the commissioners offered Tuskegee as a counterexample, Stewart reminded him that "Booker Washington's father is believed to have been a white man."[23]

To be sure, industrial education never fell entirely from favor. At the very time Stewart was discoursing on Washington's parentage, the British South Africa Company was inviting the Tuskegeean to Rhodesia to help devise a system to "raise, educate, and civilise the black man," an invitation that Washington apparently considered seriously. E. B. Sargent, supervisor of native education in the Transvaal during reconstruction, corresponded briefly with Washington, as did planners of the Inter-State Native College at Fort Hare, a singularly ironic turn given the original conception of the school as an antidote to American education. Needless to say, such correspondents were less interested in the core idea of "self-help" than in secondary attributes such as docility and industriousness, which an industrial curriculum allegedly promoted. Even then, nothing came of the exchanges. In the uncertain circumstances of pre-Union South Africa, the issues raised by industrial education were simply too explosive for any such program to be seriously entertained.[24]

Official interest in black America, and Tuskegee in particular, revived in the decade and a half after Union, a period that witnessed the emergence of segregation as both ideology and policy. Given the thrust of recent exercises in comparative history, it is worth emphasizing at the outset that "segregation" implied fundamentally different things in the United States and in South Africa. In the United States, segregation permitted, indeed, encouraged, the emergence of a middle class within the racial caste; in South Africa, on the other hand, the major pieces of segregationist legislation were crafted to curtail elite accumulation and hasten the process of proletarianization. More basic still, segregation in South Africa underpinned a system of migrant labor, a function that distinguished it utterly from its American counterpart. Cape Town and Johannesburg did produce their share of Jim Crow trams, but ultimately South African segregation was primarily a mechanism for ensuring the reproduction of cheap labor power.[25]

Historians are correct, however, to note the overlap in segregationist ideology between America and South Africa and to emphasize the way in which the United States served as an explicit model for South African segregationists. Like their counterparts in the United States, South African proponents cast their program in essentially liberal terms. Segregation facilitated "cooperation," they argued, by eliminating unhealthy economic and political competition between the races. It respected the "genius" of different peoples. It allowed blacks to develop at their own evolutionary pace, without fear of being swamped by the more advanced white race. Such arguments, of course, dovetailed neatly with the canons of industrial education: the idea that blacks were by nature a rural people and should remain so; the faith in "evolution" and the corresponding distrust of politics; the belief that education should be sensitive to the needs and distinctive genius of "backward races," as defined, of course, by whites.[26]

The first individual to draw all these threads together was Maurice Evans, a transplanted Englishman and member of the Natal Native Affairs Commission. In two pioneering works of comparative sociology, *Black and White in South East Africa: A Study in Sociology,* published in 1911, and *Black and White in the Southern States: A Study of the Race Problem in the United States from a South African Point of View,* published four years later, Evans systematically mined American experience for solutions to South Africa's racial predicament. In each book, premise and conclusion were one and the same: segregation was the only way to avert racial conflict and save blacks from falling forever into a sink of despair and vice. Evans's travels in America led, inevitably, to Hampton and Tuskegee, where he participated in the 1912 International Conference on the Negro. To Evans, Washington's program conjured up a cornucopia of possibilities. It promised, simultaneously, to steer Africans back to the countryside and away from the corrosive city; to encourage native progress without provoking racial competition; to remove racial issues from the political arena; and (by way of insurance) to reinforce ethnic divisions between Africans, all while satisfying the country's need for black labor. For a white liberal, this was very heaven.[27]

Evans's ideas had their greatest impact in the decade between 1914 and 1924, as the governments of Louis Botha and Jan Smuts laid the foundations of the segregationist edifice. Among Evans's readers was Colonel F. W. Stallard, author of the 1923 Urban Areas Act, the cornerstone of urban segregation in twentieth-century South Africa. Africans, in the terms of the act, were essentially rural creatures, who entered the city as temporary sojourners and remained only insofar as they "ministered to the white man's needs." Evans's work had an even more profound impact on C. T. Loram, at the time an inspector of schools in Natal. In 1914 Loram took leave from his post and, on Evans's advice, accepted a scholarship from the Union Government for graduate study in the United States. While completing a doctorate in education at Columbia Teachers College, Loram conducted extensive research on Afro-American education, traveling to Hampton, Tuskegee, and other historically black colleges. In 1917 he published *The Education of the South African Native,* one of the most influential books on African education ever written. Part history, part segregationist tract, the book was above all an elaboration of the potential value of American educational models in Africa. Loram proceeded from two premises: first, that segregation allowed blacks to develop at their own pace and thus offered a prudent middle path between the twin follies of repression and racial equality; second, that education should be adapted to the circumstances and needs of the host society, including, in the case of South Africa, the need for black labor. Loram's recommendations flowed from these premises: curricula should be weighted toward industrial and practical arts, with a carefully chosen diet of higher education offered to future African leaders; use of vernacular languages in instruction should be increased, though the "ultimate supremacy of the European language" should be preserved; education should recognize Africans' rural proclivities and "induce the educated Natives to return to the land."[28]

Returning to South Africa, Loram assumed the newly created post of chief inspector of native education in Natal. With its substantial American missionary presence, Natal offered a congenial climate for Loram's ideas, and he quickly brought native education into line with his blueprint. His ideas had an equally dramatic impact on education policy in the Cape, where a 1919 provincial commission endorsed virtually all the conclusions of *The Education of the South African Native.* "The overstress on scholasticism in the curriculum," the commissioners intoned, in a passage worthy of Booker T. Washington, "has had lamentable effects on the attitude of Natives towards education and subsequent vocation, and it should be impressed upon all that the earning of an honest livelihood in any capacity is not beneath the dignity of an educated person." The report advocated the appointment of a chief inspector of native education in the Cape to oversee the introduction of a new curriculum for government-aided mission schools, featuring compulsory courses in religious and moral instruction, hygiene, and civics, as well as agricultural, domestic, and industrial training. By 1923 the recommended changes were largely in place. In the interim, Loram accepted an appointment as one of the three members of a new, permanent Native Affairs Commission, an office that gave him a national constituency for the first time. Throughout the period, he maintained close links with the United States, serving as chief South African contact for U.S. philanthropic agencies such as the Phelps-Stokes Fund and the Carnegie Foundation.[29]

In the Transvaal, Loram's efforts were seconded by a coterie of white liberals, including several American Congregational missionaries. F. B. Bridgman, head of the American Board on the Witwatersrand, Clara Bridgman, Ray Phillips, and James Dexter Taylor, Americans all, pioneered social settlement work in the cauldron of the postwar Witwatersrand. Like Loram, they believed that U.S. experience, properly understood, offered valuable lessons for containing racial conflict in South Africa—lessons whose importance was driven home in the aftermath of World War I by a massive black miners' strike and the palpable disaffection of the Rand's Western-educated African elite. Capitalizing on their linkages with American philanthropic capital and on the access they enjoyed, through Loram, to the Smuts government, the "American lobby" came to exercise considerable influence in the early 1920s, launching a host of initiatives aimed at bringing together "responsible" white and black leaders on issues of mutual concern. Seen in the broad sweep of South African history, the liberals' reign proved fleeting: the election of the Nationalist-Labour Pact in 1924 weakened their position, while the Nationalists' outright triumph in the 1929 "Black Peril" election more or less put paid to the whole movement. (C. T. Loram, deposed from his post on the Native Affairs Commission, spent the last years of his life in America, at Yale University's new Institute of Human Relations.) In its time, however, this small liberal caucus played a leading role in debates on African education and administration and in the ongoing reassessment of black American history and experience.[30]

The most energetic member of the American lobby was missionary and social worker Ray Phillips. Like so many white liberals of his day, Phillips was overwhelmed by what he took to be the "demoralization" of blacks when they came into contact with urban life. He developed the theme in two books, *The Bantu Are Coming* and *The Bantu in the City,* both of which stressed the need for new agencies of social control to replace the "tribal restraints" that Africans had left behind in the reserves. Phillips's solution, as Tim Couzens has noted, was to sponsor a series of initiatives aimed at "moralizing leisure time" for urban Africans, many of which drew on American models. It was Phillips who arranged for the introduction of American-made films into Rand mining compounds, a move that he credited with keeping black miners quiescent during the 1922 white miners' strike. To create a forum for "responsible" African opinion, Phillips organized the Gamma Sigma Club, a debating society modeled on a similar institution in the United States. The club eventually blossomed into the Bantu Men's Social Centre, in whose library many of black South Africa's most prominent political and literary figures first encountered the musical and literary world of black America. At the same time, Phillips contributed a weekly "Social Service" column to *Umteteli wa Bantu,* the newspaper founded in 1920 by the Chamber of Mines to cultivate elite African opinion. In his column, Phillips provided profiles of famous African Americans—Benjamin Banneker, George Washington Carver, and, of course, Booker T. Washington—as proof of what blacks could achieve if they devoted themselves to education and eschewed politics.[31]

The apogee of American interest occurred with the celebrated tours of the Phelps-Stokes Commissions on African Education in 1921 and 1924. Founded in 1911 but with roots going back to the New York Colonization Society, the Phelps-Stokes Fund became one of the dominant influences in spreading the gospel of industrial education in both the United States and Africa. The Fund's two-volume survey, *Negro Education: A Study of the Private and Higher Schools for Colored People in the United States,* remained a standard reference on Afro-American education from its publication in 1917 until at least World War II. A commendation in the survey, or in one of the periodic updates published by the Fund, ensured a struggling southern school access to the coffers of a bevy of northern foundations; a lukewarm review—an implication that instruction was "bookish" or that agriculture was neglected—spelled doom. The director of the Fund, and the chief author of the American survey, was Thomas Jesse Jones, a transplanted Welshman and head of the Research Department at Hampton Institute. An energetic and singularly uncompromising man, Jones labored throughout his life to exorcise any lingering conviction that blacks should be accorded the same education as whites. Proper education, he insisted, was "adapted" to the needs of particular peoples and societies—needs that were naturally best understood by people like himself, with expertise in emerging social sciences such as psychology and anthropology. In the case of African Americans, Jones argued, what was needed was an educational system that instilled a taste for rural life, political quiescence, and a mind to work.[32]

Such ideas had already begun to filter into South Africa, thanks largely to Loram. It was only in 1920, however, that American philanthropic capital addressed itself explicitly to the problem of African education, when the trustees of the Phelps-Stokes Fund voted to undertake an African sequel to *Negro Education*. The decision was partly dictated by the terms of the Fund's original bequest, which specified, in good colonizationist fashion, that money be devoted to "the education of Negroes both in Africa and the United States." At the same time, the end of World War I and the creation of African mandates at Versailles had raised a host of questions about the future of Africa, of which education was one of the most pressing. To oversee the new project, the trustees naturally turned to Jones, recently returned from France, where he had implemented a program of industrial training for blacks in the U.S. Army. Jones was joined on the commission by five others who shared his perspective on African education. Mr. and Mrs. Arthur Wilkie headed the Free Church of Scotland mission in the Gold Coast. Dr. Henry Hollenbeck had served for a dozen years as an American Board medical missionary in Angola, where, in the words of Anson Phelps Stokes, he "rendered peculiarly valuable service, not only in health and hygiene, but in promoting practical education, especially in agriculture and animal husbandry." Leo Roy, the secretary of the commission, had a long association with the Phelps-Stokes Fund, and had most recently supervised a government program for training black soldiers. The final and most conspicuous member of the commission was James E. Kwegyir Aggrey, an African educated in black American schools. Born among the Fanti of the Gold Coast, Aggrey had been brought to America in 1900 by a missionary of the AME Zion Church. He spent most of the next two decades as a student and teacher at the church's Livingstone College, earning a reputation as a "balanced" and "sensible" educational spokesman, of a distinctly Washingtonian stripe.[33]

Aggrey's inclusion lent the Phelps-Stokes Commission a certain legitimacy, but the overall composition demonstrates that the group was intended not to produce a new educational formula but to proselytize for an existing one. Revealingly, the commissioners' first destination was not Africa but Europe, where they discussed their terms of reference with colonial officials, missionaries, and assorted experts on native education. Late in August 1920 the commission began a five-month journey down the west coast of Africa, highlighted by stops in Sierra Leone and Liberia, a trip into the Nigerian interior, and an emotional visit to Aggrey's natal village. In February 1921 the first two commissioners, Jones and Roy, arrived in Cape Town. Aggrey remained temporarily behind in Angola with Hollenbeck, apparently out of concern that his appearance might unsettle Africans or provoke a white backlash.[34]

Jones saw South Africa as an ideal field for his vision. With its tremendous natural endowments and relatively sparse population, the country had an urgent need for the efficient, disciplined labor force that industrial training promised to provide. The political turmoil that had engulfed the country since the end of the war also suggested the need for some readjustment of African expectations and aspirations, which was what "adapted" education was all about. Jones's convictions were bolstered by Loram, who served as the commissioners' guide during their stay. Predictably, the two men saw eye-to-eye on most issues, and Jones quoted extensively from Loram's book in preparing his eventual report, published in 1922 as *Education in Africa*. (When a second Phelps-Stokes Commission was appointed in 1924 to visit areas the first tour had missed, Loram served as its secretary.) In the space of seven weeks, Loram and Jones traveled more than seven thousand miles, evaluating dozens of schools in the Union, the Protectorates, and Rhodesia. Each school was evaluated using essentially the same criteria employed in the Phelps-Stokes survey of Afro-American education. Was instruction "related to the hygenic, economic, and character needs of a people emerging from a primitive state"? Were South African educators sensitive to their role in developing reliable native leaders, and to the importance of nurturing in them a commitment to serving their own communities? Was agriculture sufficiently emphasized? While troubled by the lack of investment in native education in the interior, and by a general lack of attention to gardening, Jones emerged sanguine about South Africa's educational future. His report endorsed virtually all the recommendations of the 1919 Cape Education Commission and lavished special praise on the social welfare work of the American Board missionaries in Johannesburg.[35]

The commissioner who excited the most comment, however, was Aggrey, who arrived in South Africa a month behind Jones and Roy. Entering South Africa in a period of economic depression and profound social stress, Aggrey embarked on a speaking tour of the Union, lecturing Europeans and Africans alike on the virtues of "toleration and cooperation." Everywhere he employed his famous piano metaphor, arguing that harmony could be produced only by playing white and black keys together. Taking the metaphor on its own terms, the harmony that Aggrey extolled was in a strictly C-major mode, with white keys carrying the tune. Not surprisingly, it was music to the ears of white liberals, at whose behest Aggrey remained in South Africa an extra three months. To liberals like C. T. Loram and Ray Phillips, struggling to build up a "moderate" middle ground in a polarized racial environment, Aggrey was a gift from the gods. Well-spoken and urbane, he could be held up to impatient Africans as proof that education and political moderation would eventually yield results. At the same time, he provided a flesh-and-blood rebuttal to white mossbacks, who saw all African education as unnecessary and dangerous. Loram was positively effusive about the man. "Aggrey is all that you described him, and more," he wrote to Jones. "I looked closely at his shoulders to see if wings were growing. . . . Now I see why the meek shall inherit the earth."[36]

Fears that Aggrey would provoke a European backlash proved unfounded. In fact, the only unpleasantness Aggrey encountered during his travels through southern Africa came from occasional African hecklers, who derided him as a European lackey. Probably the most ironic episode took place during a 1924 visit to Livingstonia, the main Free Church of Scotland mission in Nyasaland and the site, a decade before, of the Chilembwe rising, a brief but bloody rebellion led by an American-educated African. On learning that a "Negro" was coming to speak—Aggrey was constantly mistaken for an African American during his tour—an enthusiastic crowd of Africans turned out. Most apparently assumed that Aggrey was an emissary from Marcus Garvey, and they responded with bewilderment when he launched instead into a speech on racial harmony. According to Loram, who witnessed the episode, the people "were sorely disappointed when, instead of telling them to fight the White, Dr. Aggrey reminded them that in order to obtain harmony it was necessary to play both the black and white bars of a piano."[37]

Loram enjoyed recounting the episode later in life, presenting it as evidence of both Aggrey's poise and Africans' impressionability. But there was a deeper meaning to the event. Even as liberals sought to portray the "Negro" as a model of "good nature and cooperativeness," the concept of black America continued to convey a range of different messages and meanings to Africans. The venerable AME Church, still the most substantial African American presence in South Africa, inevitably became one of the arenas within which this contest over meaning was waged.[38]

Church leaders at the 1920 AME General Conference were eager to restore links with their coreligionists in South Africa, who, because of the war, had gone the previous quadrennium with virtually no supervision from the United States. After a typically fierce episcopal election, the General Conference appointed William Tecumseh Vernon to the post of resident bishop of South Africa. Superficially, Vernon represented something of a departure for the church. Three of the first four AME resident bishops had grown up under the Union Jack—Charles Smith and J. A. Johnson in Canada, William Derrick in the West Indies—a qualification that allegedly equipped them to negotiate constructively with South Africa's British rulers. Vernon was born in Missouri, a child of former slaves. He was also of decidedly unmixed black parentage, which, in a South African context, sharply distinguished him from his light-skinned predecessors. "The bishop is a man of enormous bulk, with one of the blackest skins I have ever seen," a South African official reported. According to another African American missionary, even Africans were startled by Vernon's complexion.[39]

In other respects, however, the new bishop came from the same mold as his predecessors. Vernon attended Wilberforce University in the early 1890s—he was acquainted with several South African students—and qualified as a minister and teacher. He first won political prominence at the turn of the century, when, as president of Western University, a small black college in Quindaro, Kansas, he helped marshal black opposition to the Populist insurgency. In the years that followed, Vernon solidified his reputation as a moderate, stressing the virtues of "frugality," "industry," and "money getting," while warning of the "virus" of socialism and of "the wily demagogue," who played upon the "incapacity of the Negro to know his needs." "I say, agitations of civil rights bills are folly," he declared in one speech. "Such schools as Tuskegee and Hampton will do more to solve this great problem than resolutions, agitations and soldiery." A speech delivered at the Kansas statehouse somehow came to the attention of President Theodore Roosevelt, who appointed Vernon registrar of the Treasury, traditionally the highest black patronage post in the federal government. Vernon remained in the office under Roosevelt's successor, William Howard Taft, returning to church work following the Democratic victory in 1912.[40]

Given his conspicuous political moderation, Vernon represented a valuable potential ally to the Union government and to all those promoting the "responsible" version of African American history. Ironically, however, the government nearly denied itself his services. According to the new immigration policy, promulgated to check the spread of Garveyism, the bishop was a prohibited immigrant. He was accordingly denied permission to land when he arrived in Cape Town with his wife and child in January, 1921. Vernon's insistence that he had nothing to do with Garvey left port authorities unmoved, as did the passel of white testimonials he presented. (Former President Taft, never one given to rhetorical excess, stated that Vernon had served "most acceptably" at the Treasury.) After long negotiations and interventions by C. T. Loram and the American consul in Cape Town, the Vernons were permitted to disembark, only hours before their ship was due to sail. Even then, immigration officials determined to keep a "watch" on the bishop, "with a view to determining the real object of his work."[41]

Not surprisingly, they liked what they saw. In speeches, sermons, and newspaper interviews, Vernon dismissed political agitation as "inexpedient," offering instead the values of "law and order," "sanity and moderation." An inspector of native education in the Cape heard him deliver a two-hour speech titled "The History of the World," during the whole of which "the Bishop did not touch on the colour question." Another official, who heard him address the 1921 AME Annual Conference, was even more effusive. Vernon, he reported, is "a man of high education and polished manners," who

> seems to hold the view that the natives of this country have been wrongly led away by prejudiced ideas and notions and inclined rather to be more of a political combination than that of a Christian people. He stated that the natives must at all times loyally obey the laws of the Government and laid great emphasis on this remark.

Vernon's presence, he concluded, "will do much good in sobering down the minds of those whose idea is Black versus White in this country."[42]

Occasional echoes of Henry Turner and an older African evangelical tradition surfaced in Vernon's speeches, but with a distinctly conservative twist. Like all of his predecessors, the bishop held out black America as a model of unity and progress for Africans to emulate, yet he was quick to disavow any idea of "trying to institute remedies on parallel lines." "He recognizes that he is working with raw material here, while in America the Negro is the product of hundreds of years of civilizing influence and environment," an interviewer from the Johannesburg *Star* reported approvingly. "[T]o use the bishop's own expression, the native must measure up to the American standard before he can expect to obtain the privileges he desires." Vernon likewise invoked the "providential" theory of African American slavery, but he rejected what had long been its corollary: the belief that black Americans had a special role to play in the unfolding destiny of Africa. While not mentioning Garvey by name, he worked to disabuse Africans of any expectation of liberation from America. "The agitation now in America among some, if well meaning, certainly mistaken elements who are now preaching the doctrine of Africa for the Africans is making for a false and misleading hope among the credulous, suffering Natives, rendering less easy the task of those from abroad who seek to elevate the Natives," he complained in an early letter home.[43]

Many African ministers, particularly those in the upper echelons of church leadership, endorsed Vernon's approach, contrasting their own "responsible" race leadership with that provided by organizations like the I.C.U. and U.N.I.A. By a singular coincidence, South African delegates returning from the 1920 AME General Conference were passing through New York at the very moment that Garveyites were preparing the first International Conference of Negro Peoples. The entire delegation, led by long-time Cape presiding elder Francis M. Gow, made a special visit to the British consul-general in the city to assure him of their loyalty as "British subjects" and to disclaim "all connection" with the upcoming conference. One of the delegates, Wilberforce graduate James Tantsi, made a further point of reporting to the Bloemfontein

superintendent of locations on returning home. Tantsi, whom the superintendent described as "a very well affected Native Wesleyan parson and teacher,"
emphasized that he had taken no interest in the Garvey agitation, which the
"better class Negro is keeping away from." Garvey, he added, in a comment
profoundly revealing of his own political assumptions, "is simply working on
the Negroes' passions and anti-white feelings."[44]

The South African government naturally appreciated such sentiments and
strove to enhance the AME Church's influence. Even during the postwar surge
of anti-American sentiment, the church continued to enjoy all the privileges of
religious "recognition"—access to church sites, school grants, and the like—
and church leaders' signatures sufficed on documents such as visa applications
and repatriation bonds, which technically required European endorsement.
Bishop Vernon was granted an audience with Prime Minister Smuts, who
endorsed the church's work and apologized for the misunderstanding that had
soured the bishop's arrival in the country. On the few occasions that AME
leaders encountered local opposition, Union officials were quick to intervene
on their behalf, quite a change from the early years of the century, when
imperial administrators professed their helplessness in the face of "municipal
prerogatives." Probably the clearest indication of African Methodism's privileged status among independent churches came in the wake of the 1921
Bulhoek massacre, an event that briefly rekindled fears of independent
churches. Both the permanent Native Affairs Commission, which tried unsuccessfully to mediate the standoff at Bulhoek, and the Native Churches Commission, appointed in the wake of the massacre, went out of their way to praise
the AME Church. Several commissioners went so far as to suggest that "the
virile African Methodist Episcopal Church" might become the center of a unity
movement among African independent churches. Placing South Africa's proliferating sects and churches under such a "strong, properly articulated organization," the Native Churches Commission argued, would ensure "better internal discipline and more cordial relations with the Government. . . ."[45]

Once again, however, matters were more complex than they seemed. If one
point should by now be clear, it is that AME leaders, however carefully they
chose what they said, could not control what their listeners heard. Particularly
on a subject as laden with popular hopes and expectations as black America,
Africans had a way of filtering out unwanted aspects of the message, with
sometimes bizarre results. I.C.U. founders Clements Kadalie and George
Champion, for example, were two of the decade's most "notorious native
agitators," yet both were professed admirers of Bishop Vernon. Champion,
interviewed in his dotage by a South African historian, went so far as to place
Vernon alongside Garvey among his formative influences.

> I read a lot about the newspaper of Marcus Garvey. It inspired me a great
> deal. . . . I have [also] met some Bishops of the AME Church, in the early days

I met Bishop Vernon when the African Congress was at its height. One of the things that impressed me, he said in carrying out work black men are like three monkeys when they want to get oranges and have no ladder one must climb on the shoulders of another and the other on the shoulders of another who reaches the oranges. In saying so he meant to say when we want to go to heaven we must combine God the Father, Jesus the son and [the] Holy Spirit; also when we want to liberate the nation we must cling to one another like monkeys. . . .

Lest one dismiss the recollection as the ramblings of a no longer lucid mind, Champion proceeded to contrast both Garvey and Vernon with Dr. Aggrey, whom he had also met. How, he asked pointedly, could Africans and Europeans be expected to "work together as notes of [a] piano" in a society cleaved by a "colour bar"?[46]

George Champion was obviously unusual; even by the generous standards of interwar African nationalism, he was erratic, veering wildly between seemingly contradictory political principles. Presumably most of Vernon's African flock understood quite well what he was driving at. Even then, however, there was little assurance that they would obey. As always in the AME Church, there was no neat or easy alignment between the official church policy promulgated by bishops and presiding elders and the beliefs and activities of people on the ground. African Methodism remained a site of struggle, as leaders and laypeople, men and women, African Americans and Africans pursued their competing visions. Compared to other black churches in the United States and South Africa, AME leaders had substantial institutional resources at their disposal and enjoyed considerable success in imposing their vision, yet their victory was never, and could never be, entirely complete. So it was in the 1920s. Braving the sanction of their superiors, a handful of AME ministers and an untold number of their congregants cast their lot with the I.C.U. and the U.N.I.A.

Inevitably, such participation is difficult to measure or document. In contrast to church leaders' pronouncements, the arguments of the often illiterate men and women who rallied to postwar popular movements rarely found their way into the documentary record. Initially, then, the case must be built from inference—from similarities in the regional and class bases of movements, from continuities in ideology and language, from passing observations in magistrates' reports or in the recollections of oral informants. It is clear, for example, that the I.C.U. enjoyed some of its most enduring success in areas that had previously been "burned over" by African Methodism: in Free State towns such as Kroonstad, Heilbron, and Parys, AME strongholds since the late 1890s; in the reserves of Eastern Pondoland, scene of a celebrated turn-of-the-century "Ethiopian episode"; in the "maize triangle" of the southwestern Transvaal, where the last vestiges of an independent African sharecropping class clung doggedly to the land. One elderly informant in the last area went so far as to portray the I.C.U. and African Methodism as two sides of the same coin, recalling occasions when entire congregations filed from church directly into Union meetings. "They talked about freedom," she declared, when asked of African Methodist sermons from the period. "During A.M.E. [services] we sang *'Nkosi Sikelela.'* That is why I am saying that those priests were working together with the I.C.U." For what it is worth, contemporary white farmers shared her interpretation. After years of relative harmony, African Methodist itinerants in 1926–1927 found themselves barred from farms all over the highveld, amid an escalating white counteroffensive against the Union. Several old sharecroppers recalled new pressure from employers to leave the *"kaffir kerk"* and return to the Dutch Reformed fold.[47]

African Methodism's linkages with the U.N.I.A. were generally more tenuous, yet some ministers and members did hearken to Garvey, expressing anger and puzzlement at their leaders' attacks on a movement that seemed so akin to their own. A letter in the Cape *Argus,* apparently from a teacher at an AME school, denounced "our leaders" who, in disavowing Garvey, had "blotted" the name of African Methodism. "[W]e pray day and night that the Africans in America may come," the author declared. Such sentiments were fanned by *The Black Man,* whose editors were incensed by the visit that F. M. Gow and the other South African General Conference delegates had paid to the British consul-general in New York, details of which Gow reported to Cape Town's leading white newspaper. "No sane leader of any nation will ever allow himself to be the instrument of the enemies of his race, like Rev. Gow and Co.," the paper declared.

> We would like to know how many of the members of this denomination are in favour of Africa, our only hope, being made a White man's country. If not, then why allow these divine gentlemen, who purport to represent you and who, thirty-five years ago, championed the cause of severing relations with the White man's Church, to publish in the White man's papers such low and disgraceful statements to the detriment of the general welfare of our race here and abroad?

On at least one occasion, the dispute within the South African church found its way into the columns of Garvey's *Negro World.* In 1927 a South African correspondent reported the formation of a local U.N.I.A. chapter in Evaton, the home of Wilberforce Institute and a community in which the AME Church enjoyed a virtual monopoly. "The native ministers are against us," he explained. "They don't allow us to hold any meetings in churches or schools because they have this spirit of a white man, keep nigger down." The AME minister in Evaton at the time was Gow's son, Francis Herman, a future AME bishop, back in South Africa after a stint at Tuskegee.[48]

Evidence of overlap between African Methodism and the more overtly political movements of the postwar period is also to be found in the papers of the Union Criminal Investigation Department. With its network of African informants, the C.I.D. accumulated reports, sometimes verbatim transcripts, of thousands of political assemblies in the 1920s, producing a massive (and still largely unexploited) encyclopedia of African politics. These records attest to African Methodism's continuing political vitality, even after more than two decades of conservative African American stewardship. At the most obvious level, AME churches frequently served as venues for meetings, evidence of at least tacit support from ministers and congregations. Some ministers went further, sharing podiums with Garveyites, I.C.U. organizers, Native Congressmen, even the eccentric Wellington Buthelezi, delivering invocations that fused postwar concerns with older independent church traditions. One AME minister opened a mass meeting in Johannesburg, convened to protest the arrest of striking black sanitation workers, with a classically "Ethiopian" appeal to the land. "During his prayer he cried for assistance," a police constable reported, "and said the land had been taken from the black man by the white man. He asked Almighty God to be kind enough to give the land back. . . ." In a world of neat ideological and political boundaries, such an appeal might seem a non sequitur, coming as it did in a meeting about sanitation workers; in the world of black South African politics, it struck a deep, resonant chord.[49]

A few AME ministers became sufficiently immersed in the political movements of the day to win inclusion on the C.I.D.'s numerical list of "native agitators," a kind of reverse honor roll that eventually included more than a hundred names. Agitator No. 39, for example, was Nimrod Tantsi, youngest of Ethiopian Church founder J. Z. Tantsi's ministerial sons and, perhaps significantly, the only one who did not travel to America for his education. Born in Johannesburg in 1895, Nimrod Tantsi completed his education in Thembuland, at the Idutywa school founded by Charlotte and Marshall Maxeke. He worked for a time as an insurance agent in the eastern Cape before returning to Johannesburg, where he met Clements Kadalie. Through the mid-1920s, he worked as an organizer for both the I.C.U. and the A.N.C., all while studying for the AME ministry. As if that combination were not taxing enough, Tantsi began attending the new Communist Party training school in Ferreirastown, established in 1925 as part of the Party's campaign to develop indigenous leadership. (Among Tantsi's classmates was future S.A.C.P. general secretary Moses Kotane.) He remained an active Party member through the Native Republic campaign and was elected vice chairman of the League of African Rights in 1929. While his brother James distinguished himself on Johannesburg's ultra-respectable Joint Council of Europeans and Natives, Nimrod helped orchestrate the abortive 1930 general strike. He is also remembered as co-author of *"Mayibuye iAfrika,"* an anthem, sung to the tune of "Clementine," which became one of the short-lived League's signatures. Tantsi studied for the ministry throughout the period and was ordained an AME elder in 1930.[50]

Edward Khaile, Agitator No. 30, blazed an equally remarkable political trail through the 1920s, holding office in the I.C.U., the A.N.C., and the

Communist Party, all while serving as an AME ministerial probationer. Like Tantsi, Khaile was a second-generation minister; his father, Joseph, was ordained into the AME ministry in 1905, two years after Edward's birth, and went on to hold a series of important pulpits in the Cape, Free State, and western Transvaal. Edward attended Wilberforce Institute in Evaton and earned his junior certificate, with concentrations in commerce and theology. He spent the early 1920s in Port Elizabeth, working as a bookkeeper while pursuing studies in commercial law through a London correspondence college. He dreamed of attending Wilberforce University in the United States and even applied for a passport, but his growing political involvement prevented him from making the trip.[51]

Khaile was first drawn into organized politics during his years in the eastern Cape. In 1925, having just passed his twenty-second birthday, he was appointed secretary of the Port Elizabeth branch of the I.C.U. Later that same year he was elected national financial secretary, a promotion that entailed a move back to the Transvaal. Khaile's introduction to Marxism is more obscure, but by the time of his election he was an avowed communist, constituting with James LaGuma, John Gomas, and Thomas Mbeki a core of Party members on the I.C.U. national executive. Within a year, however, Khaile and his comrades were locked into a vicious factional struggle with Clements Kadalie, which, depending on one's point of view, stemmed from the general secretary's determination to keep the Union free of domination from Moscow or from their determination to prevent a corrupt and incompetent leader from "[selling] out the Union to the bourgeoisie." Late in 1926 Kadalie succeeded in ramming a resolution through a national committee meeting that prohibited communists from holding office in the I.C.U.; when Khaile, LaGuma, and Gomas refused to resign from the Party, they were expelled. Undaunted, Khaile immediately moved on to the national executive of the South African Communist Party. He was also a member of the communist slate that won control of the African National Congress a few months later, assuming the office of general secretary. (Just twenty-five years old at the time, Khaile remains the youngest general secretary in the history of the A.N.C.) All the while, he studied for the AME ministry, consistently topping his class in year-end examinations. He was ordained in 1930, the same year as Nimrod Tantsi.[52]

Through one of those bits of serendipity upon which historical research so often turns, an enterprising C.I.D. detective, deputed to watch Khaile in 1926, "secretly snatched his letter and correspondence bag" and recorded its contents. He hoped to find "communistic matter," but what he discovered was rather more interesting. Some of Khaile's reading material was indeed communistic—a pamphlet on Party doctrine, another on organizing women, a third on "building *Uncele,*" or communist cells. Also in the case, however, were various minutes of AME conferences; a collection of essays on the native separatist church movement, edited by a white missionary; and a copy of the AME Church *Discipline,* including Richard Allen's "Historical Preface," with all its bourgeois verities. Two self-improvement books, *The Art of Lecturing* and *Personality as a Business Asset,* and a compendium of socialist songs rounded out the collection. The case stands as a monument not only to one man's intellectual eclecticism but to the general porousness of political and ideological boundaries in 1920s South Africa.[53]

Khaile's few surviving speeches exhibit the same eclecticism. A fiery orator, he attacked the "bosses"—the Chamber of Mines and politicians such as Smuts and Hertzog—and insisted that their power could be broken only by organizing workers across the color line. At the same time, he trafficked in a kind of prophetic racial nationalism, which bore the unmistakeable imprint of Ethiopianism. "Most of Khaile's address was out of the Bible," reported a detective who heard him speak in the eastern Transvaal town of Middelburg, a center of African Methodism in the early years of the century and an I.C.U. stronghold twenty-five years later. He "told the meeting that Africans should today bind themselves together to become one people," sketching a vision of a future day of "freedom" when blacks would control their own country and "cease carrying passes." Like his Ethiopian forebears, Khaile reserved his worst venom for African mission loyalists. "The ministers and teachers are working for the white people, and do not care what happens to the black people so long as they get their money," he declared. A "policeman or a detective is better than they are . . . they are like snakes in the grass."[54]

As remarkable as Khaile was, it was another minister, Timothy Hlaba Mngqibisa, who most fully explored the diverse political potentialities that continued to exist within African Methodism. Like Khaile and Tantsi, Mngqibisa grew up in the bosom of the independent church movement. His father, Abraham, was one of the founders of the original Ethiopian Church in 1893–1894; his brother-in-law, Enoch Sontaga, was a founding member of P. J. Mzimba's African Presbyterian Church and the composer of *"Nkosi Sikelel' iAfrika,"* the hymn that became the anthem of African nationalism in the subcontinent. More than any other individual, Mngqibisa carried the legacy of that first generation into the battles of the postwar period. Driven by a prophet's righteous anger, he poured himself into dozens of local struggles, earning a well-deserved reputation as one of South Africa's most implacable "native agitators."[55]

Few details remain of Mngqibisa's early life. Born sometime in the 1880s and modestly educated, he began working as an AME evangelist in the eastern Cape shortly after the South African War. He was apparently expelled from a location near Grahamstown in 1906, for reasons that remain obscure. A colonial official, writing a few years later, alleged that he had put a woman "in family way," but such charges, like charges of liquor selling and illicit diamond buying, frequently attached themselves to independent Africans and must be taken with a grain of salt. In 1909 he and his father were reportedly in Natal, preaching and illegally solemnizing marriages around Dundee and Newcastle, the center of the colony's small African landholding elite. Natal officials revoked Timothy's inward pass—Abraham had apparently not bothered to obtain one—and circulated descriptions of both men. Of Timothy they wrote: "Tall, light complexion, heavy build, large features, weak chin, age about 35."[56]

Mngqibisa returned to the Rand shortly before the beginning of World War I, settling in Benoni, where he remained for the better part of a decade. According to Benoni's location superintendent, he was "constantly in trouble," neglecting his religious duties while indulging in politics, litigation, and—inevitably—liquor selling and gold buying. In 1919 Mngqibisa emerged as a leader in the Transvaal Native Congress's antipass campaign, organizing several deputations to local officials. A year later he joined the I.C.U. Compared to other petty bourgeois leaders on the Rand, Mngqibisa was scarcely in need of "radicalisation," yet the upheavals of the postwar period left a profound mark. He saw African protesters shot in the streets of Benoni location. He also professed to have been present "spiritually" at the massacre of twenty-three I.C.U. marchers in Port Elizabeth in October 1920. By his own account, the sermon he delivered on that occasion so frightened his superiors in the AME Church that he was denied a ministerial assignment at the next annual conference. Significantly, his suspension seems to have coincided with Bishop William Vernon's arrival in South Africa.[57]

Mngqibisa apparently spent the next several years in Benoni, though he also surfaced at least once in Bloemfontein, where he delivered an inflammatory speech that once again brought him into conflict with white officials and leaders of his own church. In 1924 or 1925, Bishop Vernon or his successor, Bishop J. A. Gregg, transferred him to Herschel, a mountainous district wedged between the Cape, Free State, and Basutoland. Once a center of a thriving Christian peasantry, Herschel had become so impoverished by the 1920s that historian William Macmillan chose it as a case study for his classic *Complex South Africa.* Land was scarce and overgrazing rampant; most homesteads survived on the small remittances of migrant workers. Because of its peculiar history as a "native reserve," Herschel boasted no cities, and the white population remained infinitesimal. The district was also something of an administrative backwater, which meant there were few officials around to antagonize. To AME Church leaders, weary of Mngqibisa's defiance, the opening of a pastorate in this quiet, rural district must have seemed a heaven-sent solution to a vexing problem.[58]

They could not have been more wrong. Precisely because of the peculiarities of its situation and history, Herschel remained one of the most politically dynamic districts in all South Africa. At the end of the nineteenth century, the region was scoured by independent churches, including both the AME Church and Jonas Goduka's African Native Church. In the AME case in particular, independency became coupled with chiefly politics, spawning that distinctive neotraditionalist racial populism that was the hallmark of Ethiopianism. In contrast to other districts, the sectarian strife in Herschel did not run its course but continued to rumble through World War I. The main antagonists remained the two rival branches of the Mehlomakulu family, descendants of the chief who led the AmaHlubi into the district during the *mfecane*. As in the early years of the century, state officials and mission loyalists allied themselves with Joel Mehlomakulu, who held the headmanship despite his dubious traditional claim, while African Methodists, traditionalists, and a diverse collection of disaffected location dwellers rallied around his rival, Makobeni Mehlomakulu.[59]

The dispute, which festered through the 1910s, acquired new sharpness in the early 1920s. On Joel Mehlomakulu's death, the local magistrate appointed his son, Read, to the headmanship, once again bypassing Makobeni. (Lest there be any doubt about Joel's loyalties, Read was the namesake of a European missionary.) As if this were not provocation enough, the state also announced plans to begin registering land in the district, a first step on the road from communal to private tenure, as well as plans to install a new Glen Grey-style district council, to be supported by new taxes. Herschel exploded. Boycotts of white schools and trading stores engulfed the district, spearheaded by the *amafelandawonye*—the diehards—a group of Makobeni's female followers, most of them African Methodists. In 1923 the local magistrate, hoping to co-opt opposition, permitted the people of Tugela location to elect their own headman, ensuring Makobeni's elevation. Makobeni, however, remained obstreperous, forcing the magistrate to depose him, a move that elicited a new wave of protest, demanding not only his reinstatement as headman but his recognition as a proper Hlubi chief. This was the world into which unwitting AME leaders had deposited Timothy Mngqibisa.[60]

Mngqibisa's predecessor in Herschel, William Mtimka, had apparently tried to maintain some distance between himself and the diehards. He made his home some distance from Tugela and refused to join the local vigilance society, a decision that so enraged his *amafela* congregants that they attempted to starve him out. Mngqibisa suffered no such qualms. He settled in Tugela location and commenced holding services in Makobeni's kraal. He also became "very active" in the vigilance society, enraging the local magistrate with his opposition to land registration, the planned district council, and everything else "proposed by the Government for the uplift and progress of the natives." He spearheaded the continuing boycott of mission churches and schools, deriding loyalists as traitors and blaming them for the proposed new taxes. Mngqibisa was also reported "stumping the District with Makobeni Mehlomakulu," pressing the case for chiefly recognition. Echoes of turn-of-the-century Ethiopianism reverberated through his speeches. "The Herschel

Reserve is a native country," he allegedly told one audience. "What are the white men doing here? They have been here long enough."[61]

Colonial officials fully reciprocated Mngqibisa's disdain. As in the early part of the century, however, they lacked any statutory basis for proceeding against him. As a duly appointed minister of a recognized church, Mngqibisa had a right to reside in the district. Expelling him without warrant only invited an embarrassing lawsuit. Taking a page from their predecessors' book, state officials turned to the local AME bishop. In November 1925 the secretary of native affairs in Pretoria penned a letter to Bishop John Albert Gregg, recounting Mngqibisa's activities in Herschel, as well as his earlier career in Benoni, and requesting the bishop's "sympathetic consideration." Mngqibisa, he explained, "is not confining his activities to church work but is exerting an undesirable influence upon the Natives by political agitation."[62]

Bishop Gregg was a more complex character than most of his predecessors. He had spent several years in South Africa at the beginning of the century, an experience that gave him some perspective on the "agitator" question, on the way in which whites blamed outsiders as a way to avoid confronting the "real cause of Native unrest." At the same time, however, Gregg accepted the now time-honored distinction between "religion" and "politics" and the importance of cultivating good relations with colonial authority. (His first act on arriving in South Africa was to send a missive to the Union government, pledging to maintain Bishop Vernon's policy of "loyalty" to constituted authority.) In the end, Gregg acceded to the secretary's request. "According to my promise, I brought Mngqibisa before the bar of the Annual Conference," he wrote in early 1926. "I gave him a public reprimand . . . [and] threatened to call in his appointment if he continued." In the meantime, Mngqibisa was posted out of Herschel to Port Elizabeth, where the local presiding elder had agreed to take him in. State officials, who had hoped to see him unfrocked, were somewhat disappointed with Gregg—"the Bishop is too weak to assert himself," one complained—but at least now they had the rationale they needed to move against Mngqibisa. After a standoff of several months, Mngqibisa finally left Herschel in late 1926. Significantly, he left the bulk of his congregation not to his AME successor but to his nephew, Joubert, who had just arrived in the district as a minister of the reconstituted Ethiopian Church of South Africa.[63]

If Bishop Gregg expected Mngqibisa simply to fade from view, he was sadly mistaken. Port Elizabeth, his new pastorate, was home to one of the oldest I.C.U. chapters in South Africa, the chapter that had produced the twenty-three protesters whose deaths had so affected Mngqibisa in 1920. In the years since, the chapter had suffered all the slings and arrows endured by other I.C.U. branches—intense factionalism, financial mismanagement, and subversion by state informants and spies. Nonetheless, it survived, and Mngqibisa soon made its acquaintance. He attended his first meeting in May 1927, offering his newly completed church building free of charge for meetings. Over the next two years he spoke at dozens of Union functions: at concerts and receptions; at mass meetings on the windswept *kopje* outside Korsten, where the local branch had been born; at a moving memorial ceremony for the twenty-three martyrs. Fortunately or unfortunately, the chief interpreter at most of these gatherings, A. A. Toba, happened also to be a singularly efficient police spy. After each meeting, Toba filed a lengthy report, providing synopses of each speaker's remarks. In the process, he produced not only the finest extant record of a single I.C.U. branch but the testament of one of African Methodism's most singular ministers.[64]

From the moment Mngqibisa began his first speech, his auditors realized that he was no ordinary parson. Disdaining English, he addressed the crowd in his native IsiXhosa, recounting his long allegiance to the I.C.U. as well as his more recent ejection from Herschel. "The powers-that-be expelled me from Herschel because I was accused of having caused a strike in the churches and schools," he explained. "I admit . . . I was responsible for the strike there, and, I maintain, I was right and perfectly justified having done so." He lambasted African mission loyalists, repeating his charge that they were responsible for the poll tax, and stressed that I.C.U. members were the only "truly religious" people. He then launched into a defense of plural marriage, based on the Biblical injunction to be fruitful and multiply. "I encourage polygamy," he explained, "because you must beget many women and men and soldiers for our people. . . . When you have begat many soldiers, we [will] gradually squeeze the Europeans out of Africa." The effect was electric. The branch secretary, a Coloured man, urged all in attendance to leave white churches, with their "white Gods," and join Mngqibisa's church. "We must have our own ministers and churches, and go back to the customs of our forefathers, and leave the customs of the foreigners," he declared. The meeting closed with the singing of *"Nkosi Sikelel' iAfrika."*[65]

In the months that followed, Mngqibisa continued to amaze crowds, mixing South African and biblical history, traditional lore, and homespun parables into a potent political brew. On one occasion, he offered a revisionist account of the Reverend James Ayliff, explaining how the missionary pioneer had used lies and deceit to divide the Mfengu and the Xhosa and facilitate Africans' reduction to vassalage. On another, he offered a novel reading of the Lord's Prayer, citing the phrase "Give us this day our daily bread and forgive us our sins" as proof of the priority of industrial over religious organization. (A Christian's first obligation, he explained, was to acquire his daily bread, which, in the circumstances of South Africa, meant supporting the I.C.U. Then one could worry about praying for forgiveness.) Most of his biblical references, however, came from the Old Testament. A four-hundred-strong crowd heard of prophets like Nehemiah, "a slave in a foreign land" who required "a Pass from the king to proceed to his Native country," and Ezekiel,

who transformed dry bones into a "united and very strong race." In one
sermon, Mngqibisa recounted how Jacob, "the greatest thief ever born," stole
the birthright of his elder brother, Esau, a favorite text of turn-of-the-century
Ethiopians. "There was no peace between the posterity of Esau and Jacob
until . . . the former had revenged themselves," he declared. He himself
was "daily devising ways and means to steal from the white man what he had
stolen from our fore-fathers."[66]

On a few occasions, Mngqibisa advocated "retaliation," but generally he
stressed political unity as the path to salvation. "You must break your kerrie
and throw your revolvers away," he declared in one sermon, "and fight the
white man, who is a very clever man, with 'Unification'." "Unite yourselves
very solidly, and squeeze the white man gradually until he reaches the sea." He
underscored the lesson in a variety of ways—invoking the unity of the Trinity,
the history of the Israelites, even physically drawing out members of the crowd
and pressing them together. Like generations of African Methodists, however,
he found the highest expression of unity in the figure of the African American.
"The American Negroes were forcibly taken away from this country, shipped
to Europe and sold there as slaves," he explained, slightly bending the facts to
suit his purpose. "They obtained their emancipation not by force of arms, but
by Unification. Today, they are a terror to the white man; and the white man
does not want them to return to their fatherland Africa, because if they do,
they would with our assistance forcibly drive the Europeans out of Africa."[67]

The irony, of course, was that African American church leaders had assisted
colonial officials in driving Mngqibisa out of Benoni and Herschel. On a few
occasions, he acknowledged his differences with AME leaders. The "Ethiopian
Church of America" had erred in attempting "to organize our people reli-
giously instead of industrially," he once noted. In another instance, he brought
several fellow ministers to an I.C.U. meeting but warned the crowd in advance
of their temperateness. "You must also bear in mind, that the ministers are
under a certain contract, and cannot exceed certain limits in their speeches," he
explained, neglecting to say why such "limits" did not apply to him as well. In
perhaps his boldest move, he organized an I.C.U. reception for Bishop Gregg,
who was in the eastern Cape to dedicate a church building. Gregg arrived at
the meeting, accompanied by the local presiding elder, to hosannahs from the
crowd. Mngqibisa, in the chair, led a hymn and delivered an invocation, but
just as he launched into his sermon, recounting black Americans' journey from
slavery to freedom, the bishop rose and fled the room. Word soon arrived that
Gregg had taken ill and would not return, and the meeting proceeded without
him.[68]

We will probably never know whether Gregg's hasty withdrawal was occasioned by "gastric distress," as his spokesman professed, or by distress at what
he was about to hear. More is the pity. As the bishop walked up the aisle of
Mngqibisa's church, surrounded by cheering Africans, amid banners bearing

legends such as *"Nkosi Sikelela iAfrika"* (God Bless Africa), *"Mayibuye iAfrika Madoda"* (Let Africa Come Back, Men) and *"Umfela Ndawonye"* (To Die Together), the scene was set for a final confrontation over the meaning of African Methodism, a confrontation between the two divergent impulses whose struggle has been traced throughout this book. In another sense, however, the irresolution is apposite. Ultimately, African Methodism embodied both tendencies—rebellion and respectability, freedom and authority, "liberty" and "order." These twined impulses emerged from the same realities; both represented responses to the same cruel dilemmas. Clearly by the late 1920s a man like J. A. Gregg was a more "representative" African Methodist than Timothy Mngqibisa, who even among African churchmen was something of an anachronism. The fact that only a handful of AME ministers made it onto the Criminal Investigation Department's "Native Agitator" list in the 1920s was itself proof of how respectable the South African AME Church had become since its founding three decades before. And yet the African Methodism of Vernon and Gregg could never fully extinguish the African Methodism of Mngqibisa and Khaile, any more than the African Methodism of Daniel Payne could completely eclipse the African Methodism of Henry Turner. So long as black Americans and black South Africans remained strangers in the lands of their births, so long would the AME Church and the broader transatlantic connection that it embodied inspire dreams of freedom.[69]

Epilogue

The revival of the Port Elizabeth branch of the I.C.U. represented one of the last rumbles in an earthshaking decade. With the enactment of draconian restrictions on political activity in the amended Native Administration Act in 1929 and the simultaneous onset of economic depression, African politics entered a period of relative quiescence, from which it fully emerged only after World War II. Yet even in this period of transition, the transatlantic conversation continued. The AME Church in the United States dispatched bishops to South Africa, who continued to sound a conservative, apolitical refrain. G. B. Young, D. H. Sims, and R. R. Wright, Jr., resident bishops between 1928 and 1940, addressed Rotary Clubs and missionary conferences, holding up the AME Church as a model of "the very best of the American Negro." Their efforts were seconded by Johannesburg's embattled white liberal community and by American philanthropic organizations such as the Carnegie and Phelps-Stokes foundations, which continued to sponsor educational exchanges and other "constructive" responses to the problem of race relations in the United States and Africa.[1]

Among Africans, black America remained a ubiquitous imaginative presence, still capable of awakening the old dreams of freedom and achievement. Scattered U.N.I.A. branches persisted through the 1930s, while assorted "native agitators" stumped the country, enjoining their "fellow slaves" to follow the example of their "emancipated" brethren in the United States. At the level of popular culture, black America remained the touchstone of sophistication in everything from music to dress to hair culture. Black South Africa, in the words of a contemporary handbill, was "bubbling in a cloud of Harlem rhythm." So pervasive was African admiration for African Americans that Fannie Glass, a Communist Party organizer and No. 15 on the Criminal Investigation Department's list of "agitators," finally lost patience. "Some people from America tell you that the Negroes are free, that they have the highest education," she roared to a group of Johannesburg workers in 1930, "but they do not tell you that they are the most exploited people. They keep on telling you there is no colour bar in America, [but] in America the laws are much more harsh than in South Africa. Russia [is] the place where a worker [is] welcome, white or black."[2]

No one better appreciated the ironies of the situation than Ralph Bunche, a professor of political science at Howard University and, for a time at least, one of black America's leading radical voices. Bunche visited South Africa in 1937 as part of a two-year world research tour sponsored by the Social Science Research Council. Ostensibly studying anthropological field methods, he devoted most of his energy to a planned book on indigenous people's responses to colonialism, a project that emerged, in direct and indirect ways, from his experiences as a black scholar and activist in the United States. The book never materialized. With the outbreak of World War II, Bunche went into government service and from there to the United Nations, where his efforts to mediate the Arab-Israeli conflict garnered him the 1950 Nobel Peace Prize. All that remained of the visit to South Africa was a collection of detailed daily note cards recording observations and conversations with a diverse collection of interlocuters. Recently published, Bunche's travel notes throw a spotlight on one of the twentieth century's most elusive political figures, while illuminating the continuing human and imaginative traffic between black America and black South Africa.[3]

From the moment of his arrival, Bunche was amazed by black America's salience in South African life. Walking along Cape Town Parade the day after disembarking, he heard two different soapbox speakers discoursing on the virtues of American Negroes, who "have brains and wealth and don't stand for foolishness." Political leaders of every stripe sought him out, seeking the moral authority that he, as an African American, conferred. White liberals such as Ray Phillips and J. D. Rheinallt Jones, head of the South African Institute of Race Relations, a liberal clearinghouse established with a grant from the Carnegie Foundation, endeavored to take Bunche under their wings, to ensure that he—and, presumably, his philanthropic sponsors—received a "balanced" picture of South African society. Author and educator D. D. T. Jabavu, son of John Tengo Jabavu, one of the early AME Church's most outspoken African opponents, escorted him to a chapter meeting of the Cape African Teachers Association. Jabavu often traded on a youthful tour of the United States, and he used Bunche's appearance to extol black Americans, in terms that Bunche himself found more than a little bizarre. "Jabavu again took occasion to disparage, for my benefit, the policy of the African holding on to his old culture," he recorded in his notes. "He said it would be better for the African to be, like the American Negro, with no cultural roots, and therefore willing and eager to clutch at every new idea, leader or movement. He praised the gullibility of the American Negro and his eager attendance at meetings, etc. He also laid emphasis on the tremendous amount of organizations among the American Negroes, which he regards with envy."[4]

AME Church leaders fared little better in Bunche's unstinting assessment. He spent several days with Francis Herman Gow, the Tuskegee-trained minister and future bishop who had, by the late 1930s, acceded to his father's position as leader of Cape Town's Coloured elite. Bunche attended a community meeting that Gow had organized on juvenile delinquency, a shared obsession of black and white liberals in the interwar years. He listened with astonishment to a Gow-directed quartet singing old plantation songs about "coons" and "pickanninies." He saw Gow cruelly snubbed by the white moderator at a Dutch Reformed Mission Church synod. In his notes, Bunche reflected on Gow's "not too subtle kow-towing," his flight from politics, his preoccupation with winning the respect of an imaginary white audience. "He asked me if I 'had yet met any of Cape Town's more solid and substantial citizens,'" Bunche noted in one entry. "Typical of Negro intellectuals everywhere—tho these here have difficulty enumerating their 'solid and substantial citizens,' since they lack businessmen, professional men, public office-holders, etc."[5]

Everywhere, Bunche was enthusiastically received by black South Africans. Africans prevailed upon him to speak and solicited his opinion on issues of the day, as though he somehow held the key to South Africa's predicament. Much to his own bemusement, Bunche was drawn into the transatlantic dialogue, delivering impromptu lectures on African American experience to instruct and inspire Africans. On several occasions he found himself preaching the virtues of "group chauvinism," a prescription far different from the one that he and other radical intellectuals dispensed in the United States. After one particularly taxing day in the eastern Cape, Bunche noted the irony of his position. "I insisted to Scallon at South Africa House in London, that I am not a missionary," he wrote, referring to a South African consular official who had tried to dissuade him from visiting the Union. "But any American Negro visiting South Africa *is* a missionary whether or not he wills it."[6]

And so it goes, unto our own time: reflections and refractions, Africans and African Americans fashioning each other as they refashion themselves. With the emergence of global media, images move instantaneously, yet they remain limned with irony and paradox. Consider the case of Nelson Mandela, who, for millions of Americans, embodies black South Africans' long struggle for justice. In June 1990, a few months after emerging from a twenty-seven-year stay in prison, Mandela toured the United States. In the course of eleven hectic days, he visited eight different cities, receiving rapturous welcomes in each. In Washington, D.C., he lunched at the White House with President George Bush and addressed a joint session of the United States Congress. In New York he addressed the General Assembly of the United Nations and enjoyed a massive ticker tape parade down Fifth Avenue. Americans marveled at his self-possession, his freedom from rancor, his unshaken sense of purpose. Mandela, a jaded New Yorker told a reporter, was "among the two or three undisappointing figures in the world."[7]

African American leaders, many of whom had long pressed for Mandela's release from prison, embraced him as one of their own. New York City Mayor David Dinkins called him a "modern-day Moses," employing the very image that black South Africans had used to describe Henry Turner and the first visiting African American churchmen ninety-odd years before. Other speakers compared Mandela to Martin Luther King—King, who was campaigning in Montgomery in 1961, when the leadership of the African National Congress made the decision to resort to armed struggle, and in Birmingham two and a half years later, when Mandela went on trial for his life. Still others draped him in the mantle of the martyred Malcolm X, whose memory was even then undergoing an extraordinary historical revival. Indeed, Mandela's visit seems to have contributed to a kind of posthumous reconciliation between the two slain leaders. In several cities, Mandela was greeted by young African Americans wearing tee shirts emblazoned: "Martin, Malcolm, Mandela and Me."[8]

Mandela himself actively encouraged the process of identification. In an interview with *Ebony* magazine, published a month before his visit, he stressed the links between South Africa's liberation struggle and blacks' ongoing quest for justice and equality in America. "Yes, you are correct, there are many similarities between us," he explained. "We have learned a great deal from each other. It is important, especially now, that these bonds remain strong and committed." One of the most moving stops on his tour was Atlanta, where he laid a wreath on King's grave and paid homage to the leaders of America's Civil Rights Movement. In all his speeches and interviews, he invoked famous African Americans, from Booker T. Washington and George Washington Carver to W. E. B. Du Bois and Joe Louis, often tailoring his references for particular audiences. In his speech to the U.S. Congress, for example, Mandela spoke of American "freedom fighters" such as King, Sojourner Truth and Frederick Douglass. Addressing a one hundred thousand-strong crowd in the streets of Harlem, he invoked the names of Marcus Garvey, Adam Clayton Powell, Jr., and Malcolm X. "I am here to claim you because . . . you have claimed our struggle," he declared. "Harlem signifies the glory of resistance." In Detroit he confessed a love for the music of Motown, which he said had sustained him through his long incarceration. He even quoted the words of "What's Goin' On," a Motown classic by the late Marvin Gaye: "Mother, mother, mother, there's far too many of you crying. Brother, brother, brother, there's far too many of you dying."[9]

As so often in the history of the transatlantic connection, the visit became entangled with preexisting disputes and conflicts, producing moments of high drama and low comedy. Officials in the Bush White House were reportedly "apoplectic" when congressional Democrats tried to schedule a vote on the

1990 Civil Rights Bill, which the President had pledged to veto, to coincide with Mandela's arrival. Mayor Richard Daley of Chicago, son and political heir of the man who had hounded Martin Luther King out of his city in 1966, sent a letter to the A.N.C. protesting Chicago's exclusion from Mandela's itinerary. Tour organizers in New York were so irritated by Jesse Jackson's attempts to share Mandela's spotlight that they ostentatiously excluded him from the list of speakers for the Harlem rally. [10]

With the appearance on the scene of film director Spike Lee, events veered still further toward the postmodern. Lee joined actors Eddie Murphy and Robert DeNiro in hosting a five thousand dollar-a-plate dinner in New York to benefit the A.N.C. The relationship between the African elder statesman and the young African American filmmaker culminated two years later in Lee's film biography of Malcolm X, in which Mandela made a cameo appearance. Mandela may or may not have heard of the controversies that swirled around the making of the film: of Lee's struggle with Norman Jewison, a white director, over the rights to Malcolm's story, and of subsequent attacks by black nationalist Imamu Amiri Baraka, who accused Lee of sanitizing Malcolm's life for the benefit of whites and a nonrevolutionary brown bourgeoisie. He almost certainly heard of Lee's confrontation with white studio heads over funding and artistic control of the film. In any case, he lent his considerable prestige to the project. *Malcolm X* ends not with the assassination in the Audubon Ballroom but with Nelson Mandela—the real Nelson Mandela—tutoring Soweto schoolchildren on Malcolm's importance to them.

To the surprise of many, Lee's film successfully navigated South Africa's censorship board and went into wide release in the country. While only a modest box office success, the movie contributed to a popular rediscovery of Malcolm's life and legacy by South Africans, white and black. After nearly a quarter century on the banned book list, Alex Haley's *The Autobiography of Malcolm X* appeared in libraries and bookstores. Betty Shabazz, Malcolm's widow, made a much-publicized tour of South Africa, speaking at meetings and appearing on talk shows. (In one last, horrifying irony, Shabazz's visit was sponsored by Soft Sheen, South Africa's largest distributor of hair-straightening products.) Probably the most obvious sign of popular interest in Malcolm's life was the ubiquitous "X" logo, which blossomed on shirts and caps in townships across South Africa.

It is worth reflecting upon that logo. X: the quintessential variable, a symbol, like Africa itself, capable of conveying different meanings and values at different times. In the case of adherents of the Nation of Islam, who adopted it as a surname, X symbolized enslavement, the historical rupture that prevented African Americans from ever knowing their true names. Strictly speaking, the symbol is not apt for South Africa. Despite all the decades of brutality, all the mind-numbing attempts to classify and categorize, black

South Africans today know who they are and where they come from. In a more than metaphorical sense, it is this knowledge that has enabled them to survive. Yet who can question that X speaks to their experience? Who can deny their claim to it?

Echoes of African Methodism are still occasionally audible in the transatlantic conversation. In late 1991 a group of thirty-three African American "celebrities and leaders" embarked on a three-day visit to Johannesburg, dubbed the "Democracy Now Tour." Lindiwe Mabuze, the A.N.C.'s chief representative in the United States and one of the organizers, described the tour's significance in terms uncannily reminiscent of late-nineteenth-century evangelical ideology. "Here are sons and daughters of Africa whose ancestors left the continent as slaves coming back to say to their brothers and sisters in South Africa who are undergoing another form of slavery, 'We are coming back not shackled, not weak, but strong because we have learned over the centuries that in order to make it we must stand together.'" ("God sends us back to you, not in chains of iron and steel but chains of gold," I. N. Fitzpatrick declared in 1900. "Are you glad to see us, my brethren?") AME Bishop John Hurst Adams, one of the delegates, described the visit with an image straight from "Stretch Forth Thy Hands," the missionary hymn penned by his predecessor Levi Coppin a century before. "This trip has [sealed] the relationship between Black Americans and Black South Africans," Adams told a reporter. "Our hands stretched south and the hands of South Africa reached north and somewhere over the ocean they clasped. Never again will we be separated by the distance, for we are forever connected by the struggle."[11]

As always, however, connection meant different things to different people. In early 1993, a century after the founding of the Ethiopian Church and two centuries after Richard Allen's celebrated exit from St. George's Methodist Church, Harry Schwarz, South Africa's ambassador to the United States, accepted an invitation to speak at the First African Methodist Episcopal Church of Los Angeles. Long a bastion of the black community in south central Los Angeles, First AME had received international exposure a year before, when several television networks used it as a forward area in their coverage of the Los Angeles riots. (Media currents momentarily reversed, images of brutal white policemen and unquenchable black rage beamed from America into the living rooms of South Africa.) Schwarz began with a meditation on connectedness, on the ties that bound the members of First AME to his own country's history. Alas, he took as his example Cecil Rhodes, whose bequest in establishing the Rhodes scholarships had enabled one of the congregation's pastors to study at Oxford. That Schwarz chose the nineteenth century's most notorious mining magnate to illustrate the historical relationship between black America and black South Africa is indicative of many things, not least the distance that

South Africa has still to travel before arriving at anything like a just appreciation of its past. That he did so while standing in a tabernacle of the AME
Church only pours salt into the historical wound. [12]

Not all historical memories are so foreshortened. In late 1993 I returned from
South Africa to my home in Chicago. I carried a more or less finished manu-
script, having two days before completed the sketch of Charlotte Maxeke that
concludes Chapter 8. Strolling through the concourse at Johannesburg's Jan
Smuts Airport, killing time before my flight, I encountered a group of elderly
African women, dressed in vibrant colors, singing. The placards and banners
they bore identified them as members of the National Council of African
Women, an organization that Maxeke helped found a year before her death.
("The work is not for yourself," she reminded delegates in her presidential
address. "Do not live about your people, but live with them. If you can rise,
bring someone with you.") The women were at the airport to welcome members of a sister organization of African American women from, of all places,
Chicago.
    I inhabit a world that speaks of coincidence rather than Providence, but this
was too providential a coincidence to ignore. I introduced myself to several of
the women, and—how often this happened, amid all apartheid's madness—
they gathered me into their celebration. We spoke of their organization, which
is headquartered in an AME church in downtown Johannesburg, a church that
somehow slipped through the cracks of the Group Areas Act. We spoke of
ministers we knew in common. Mostly we spoke of Charlotte Maxeke. None of
them had known her—she has been dead for more than half a century now—
but they all knew of her and had stories to share. I asked where her body was
buried. Several people had told me she lay in Nancefield cemetery, near her
Soweto home, but I had never been able to find the spot. No, the women told
me, Maxeke was buried in Evaton, at Wilberforce Institute. They still tend her
grave.

Abbreviations Used in the Notes

C.A.D.	Cape Archives Depot, Cape Town
N.A.D.	Natal Archives Depot, Pietermaritzburg
O.A.D.	Orange Free State Archives Depot, Bloemfontein
T.A.D.	Transvaal Archives Depot, Pretoria
ABX	A.B. Xuma Papers, University of the Witwatersrand
AG	Papers of the Cape Attorney General, C.A.D.
BNS	Papers of the Bureau of Immigration, T.A.D.
CMT	Papers of the Chief Magistrate of the Transkei, C.A.D.
CO	Papers of the Colonial Secretary, Orange River Colony, O.A.D.
CS	Papers of the Colonial Secretary, T.A.D.
G	Papers of the Governor of the Orange River Colony, O.A.D.
GG	Papers of the Governor-General, T.A.D.
GH	Government House Papers, C.A.D.
GNLB	Papers of the Director of Native Labour, T.A.D.
GOV	Papers of the Governor of the Transvaal, T.A.D.
GRD	Papers of the Director of Government Relief, Orange River Colony, O.A.D.
GS	Papers of the Goewermentsekretaris, Orange Free State Republic, O.A.D.
HG	Papers of the Recorder of the High Court of South Africa, Orange Free State, O.A.D.
JUS	Papers of the Minister of Justice, T.A.D.
K	Government Commissions, T.A.D.
LC	Papers of the Legislative Council, T.A.D.
LD	Papers of the Law Department, T.A.D.
LHT	Papers of the Resident Magistrate, Harrismith, O.A.D.
LND	Papers of the Lands Department, C.A.D.
LTG	Papers of the Lieutenant Governor, T.A.D.

MBL	Papers of the Municipality of Bloemfontein, O.A.D.
MHG	African Estates, Transvaal, T.A.D.
MOH	Papers of the Medical Officer of Health, C.A.D.
MSCE	African Estates, Natal, N.A.D.
NA	Papers of the Cape Native Affairs Department, C.A.D.
NAB	Papers of the Adviser to the Native Affairs Branch, Orange River Colony, O.A.D.
NSNA	Papers of the Natal Native Affairs Department, N.A.D.
NTS	Papers of the Union Department of Native Affairs, T.A.D.
PAE	Papers of the Cape Education Department, C.A.D.
PAS	Papers of the Provincial Administrator, C.A.D.
S	Papers of the Resident Commissioner of Basutoland, National Archives of Lesotho
SNA	Papers of the Secretary of Native Affairs, Transvaal Colony, T.A.D.
SS	Papers of the Staatssekretaris, South African Republic, T.A.D.
SSA	Papers of the Staatssekretaris afdeling Buitelandse Sake, South African Republic, T.A.D.
TAD	Papers of the Transvaal Education Department, T.A.D.
TOD	Papers of the Union Department of Education, T.A.D.
TPB	Papers of the Administrator of the Transvaal, T.A.D.
1/BIZ	Papers of the Resident Magistrate, Bizana, C.A.D.
2/SPT	Papers of the Bantu Affairs Commissioner, Herschel, C.A.D.

Notes

Preface

1. W. E. B. Du Bois, *The Souls of Black Folk* (1903, reprint ed., New York, 1969), p. 217.

2. The "names controversy" is discussed in detail in Chapter 3. On Daniel Payne and debates over appropriate worship, see Chapter 2.

3. Olaudah Equiano, *The Interesting Narrative of the Life of Olaudah Equiano or Gustavus Vassa, the African, Written by Himself* (1789, reprint ed., Leeds, 1814) in Henry L. Gates, ed., *Classic Slave Narratives* (New York, 1987), p. 60.

4. Book-length studies include J. Mutero Chirenje, *Ethiopianism and Afro-Americans in Southern Africa, 1883–1916* (Baton Rouge, La., 1987); Carol Page, "Black America in White South Africa: Church and State Reaction to the AME Church in Cape Colony and Transvaal" (Ph.D. diss., University of Edinburgh, 1978); and Josephus R. Coan, "The Expansion of Missions of the African Methodist Episcopal Church in South Africa, 1896–1908" (Ph.D. diss., Hartford Theological Seminary, 1961). My debts to and disagreements with these and other works are reflected in the footnotes that follow.

5. Ralph Ellison, *Shadow and Act* (New York, 1953), p. 253; C. Eric Lincoln and Lawrence H. Mamiya, *The Black Church in the African American Experience* (Durham, N.C., 1990), p. 8; Gary B. Nash, *Forging Freedom: The Formation of Philadelphia's Black Community, 1720–1840* (Cambridge, Mass., 1988), p. 100; Gayraud Wilmore, *Black Religion and Black Radicalism* (New York, 1972), p. 137.

6. See, for example, H. R. Ngcayiya, "Opportunities for the Negro in South Africa and America Compared," *AME Church Review* 21, 2 (1904), pp. 141–145. For recent scholarly comparisons, see George Fredrickson, *White Supremacy: A Comparative Study in American and South African History* (New York, 1981); John Cell, *The Highest Stage of White Supremacy: The Origins of Segregation in South Africa and the American South* (New York, 1982); Howard Lamar and Leonard Thompson, eds., *The Frontier in History: North America and South Africa Compared* (New Haven, Conn., 1982).

7. All these cases are discussed below.

Chapter 1. Vindicating the Race

1. African American Christianity has spawned a rich literature, much of it preoccupied with determining its degree of "Africanness." To W. E. B. Du Bois, who pioneered the field, the black church was "the most characteristic expression of African character" in the United States, a "remnant of the African forest." See *The Souls of Black Folk* (Atlanta, 1903); *The Philadelphia Negro: A Social Study* (Philadelphia, 1899); and *The Negro Church: Report of a Social Study made under the direction of Atlanta University* (Atlanta, 1903). Du Bois's claim received support in the work of anthropologist Melville Herskovits, especially in his classic *The Myth of the Negro Past* (New York, 1941). The case for cultural discontinuity is associated with E. Franklin Frazier, who characterized the middle passage as "The Death of the Gods." See Frazier, *The Negro Family in the United States* (Chicago, 1939); and *The Negro Church in America* (Liverpool, 1964). Recent contributions to the debate include Eugene Genovese, *Roll, Jordan, Roll: The World the Slaves Made* (New York, 1976); Lawrence Levine, *Black Culture and Black Consciousness* (New York, 1977); Albert J. Raboteau, *Slave Religion: The "Invisible Institution" in the Antebellum South* (New York, 1978); Mechal Sobel, *Trabelin' On: The Slave Journey to an Afro-Baptist Faith* (Westport, Conn., 1979); Sterling Stuckey, *Slave Culture: Nationalist Theory and the Foundations of Black America* (New York, 1987); and Margaret Creel, *"A Peculiar People": Slave Religion and Community-Culture Among the Gullahs* (New York, 1988).

For the institutional history of black Christianity, the best place to begin is still Carter G. Woodson, *The History of the Negro Church*, 2nd ed. (New York, 1945). Woodson's contribution, and the state of the field as a whole, is assayed in Albert J. Raboteau and David W. Wills, with Randall K. Burkett, Will B. Gravely, and James Melvin Washington, "Retelling Carter Woodson's Story: Archival Sources for Afro-American Church History," *Journal of American History* 77, no. 1 (1990), pp. 183–99.

2. Winthrop Jordan, *White Over Black: American Attitudes Toward the Negro, 1550–1812* (Chapel Hill, N.C., 1968), pp. 93, 180–83; George Fredrickson, *White Supremacy: A Comparative Study in American and South African History* (New York, 1981), p. 82; Jon Butler, *Awash in a Sea of Faith: Christianizing the American People* (Cambridge, Mass., 1990), pp. 132–41; Joseph Miller, *Way of Death: Merchant Capitalism and the Angolan Slave Trade, 1730–1830* (Madison, Wis., 1988), pp. 402–04. For comparisons of the church's role in Latin America and in North America, see Frank Tannenbaum, *Slave and Citizen: The Negro in the Americas* (New York, 1946); Stanley M. Elkins, *Slavery: A Problem in American Institutional and Intellectual Life*, 3rd ed. (Chicago, 1976); and Herbert S. Klein, *Slavery in the Americas: A Comparative Study of Cuba and Virginia* (Chicago, 1967).

3. Raboteau, *Slave Religion*, pp. 94–150; Peter Wood, *Black Majority: Negroes in Colonial South Carolina from 1670 through the Stono Rebellion* (New York, 1974), p. 189; Gayraud Wilmore, *Black Religion and Black Radicalism* (New York, 1972), p. 35; Butler, *Awash in a Sea of Faith*, pp. 149–50.

4. Quoted in Jordan, *White Over Black*, p. 212; "The Carolina Chronicles of Dr. Francis Le Jau, 1706–1717," in Milton C. Sernett, ed., *Afro-American Religion: A Documentary Witness* (Durham, N.C., 1985), pp. 24–32; Sobel, *Trabelin' On*, pp. 99–108. On the awakeners and slavery, see Stephen J. Stein, "George Whitefield on Slavery: Some New Evidence," *Church History* 42, no. 2 (1973), pp. 243–56; and James D. Essig, *The Bonds of Wickedness: American Evangelicals Against Slavery* (Philadelphia, 1982). The precise proportion of slaves who converted to Christianity remains imponderable. William Freehling estimated that only one in twenty black slaves in the 1830s was formally a communicant; such a statistic, however, says little about the absolute number of black Christians. Albert Raboteau, following Du Bois, puts

the number of slave Christians in 1859 at nearly half a million. The debate is summarized in Stuckey, *Slave Culture*, pp. 37–38, 367 fn. 89.

5. Milton C. Sernett, *Black Religion and American Evangelicalism: White Protestants, Plantation Missions, and the Flowering of Negro Christianity, 1787–1865* (Metuchen, N.J., 1975); Albert J. Raboteau, "The Slave Church in the Era of the American Revolution," in Ira Berlin and Ronald Hoffman, eds., *Slavery and Freedom in the Age of the American Revolution* (Urbana, Ill., 1986). On the rise of evangelicalism in Virginia, see Rhys Isaacs, *The Transformation of Virginia, 1740–1790* (Chapel Hill, N.C., 1982).

6. *The Life Experiences and Gospel Labors of the Right Reverend Richard Allen* (1833; reprint ed., Philadelphia, 1887). Biographies include Charles H. Wesley, *Richard Allen: Apostle of Freedom* (Washington, D.C., 1935); Carol V. R. George, *Segregated Sabbaths: Richard Allen and the Emergence of Independent Black Churches, 1760–1840* (New York, 1973); and Albert J. Raboteau, "Richard Allen and the African Church Movement," in Leon Litwack and August Meier, eds., *Black Leaders of the Nineteenth Century* (Urbana, Ill., 1988). On the politics of black autobiography, see William L. Andrews, *To Tell a Free Story: The First Century of Afro-American Autobiography, 1760–1865* (Urbana, Ill., 1986).

7. Gary B. Nash, "New Light on Richard Allen: The Early Years of Freedom," *William and Mary Quarterly* 46, no. 2 (1989), pp. 332–40; Allen, *Gospel Labors*, p. 6.

8. Allen, *Gospel Labors*, p. 5.

9. Allen, *Gospel Labors*, pp. 6–8; Nash, "New Light on Richard Allen," pp. 336–38; Sidney Kaplan and Emma Nogrady Kaplan, *The Black Presence in the Era of the American Revolution*, 2nd ed. (Amherst, Mass., 1989), p. 97.

10. While adoption of a surname was standard practice among manumitted slaves, the source of "Allen" remains unclear. Nash traces it to William Allen, Chief Justice of the Pennsylvania Supreme Court and an associate of Richard's original master. See "New Light on Richard Allen," p. 335.

11. The quotations are from "To the People of Color" and "An Address to those who keep Slaves, and approve the Practice," annexures to A. J. [Absalom Jones] and R. A. [Richard Allen], "A Narrative of the Proceedings of the Black People During the Late Awful Calamity in Philadelphia, in the Year, 1793: And a Refutation of Some Censures, Thrown Upon Them in Some Late Publications," in Dorothy Porter, ed., *Negro Protest Pamphlets* (New York, 1969).

12. Allen, *Gospel Labors*, p. 6 ff.

13. Allen, *Gospel Labors*, pp. 8–13. The testimonial is reproduced in Nash, "New Light on Richard Allen," p. 339.

14. Allen, *Gospel Labors*, pp. 13–14. On Philadelphia, see Gary B. Nash, *Forging Freedom: The Formation of Philadelphia's Black Community, 1720–1840* (Cambridge, Mass., 1988). AME historian Benjamin Tanner argued that Allen was posted to Philadelphia by Francis Asbury, who was jealous of his evangelical prowess and wished to confine him to one place; see Tanner, *An Outline of Our History and Government for African Methodist Churchmen, Ministerial and Lay* (n.p., 1884), p. 150. This tradition appears to have originated with Lorenzo Dow, a contemporary white evangelist, and probably says less about Allen's experience than about Dow's struggles with Methodist authorities.

15. Nash, *Forging Freedom*, pp. 17, 23–24, 29–31, 72–74, 135–43 ff. On Quakers and slavery, see David Brion Davis, *The Problem of Slavery in the Age of Revolution, 1770–1823* (Ithaca, N.Y., 1975). Jordan's suggestion that Allen himself attended Benezet's school appears to be unfounded; see *White Over Black*, p. 422.

16. Allen, *Gospel Labors*, pp. 13–14; Raboteau, "Richard Allen and the African Church Movement," pp. 2–3; Nash, *Forging Freedom*, pp. 95–96.

17. "A Pioneer Negro Society, 1787," in Herbert Aptheker, ed., *A Documentary History of the Negro People in the United States* (1951; reprint ed., New York, 1990), pp. 17–19; William Douglass, *Annals of the First African Church in the United States of America, Now Styled the African Episcopal Church of St. Thomas, Philadelphia* (Philadelphia, 1862), p. 19; Wilmore, *Black Religion and Black Radicalism*, p. 114.

18. Douglass, *Annals of the First African Church*, pp. 22–24.

19. Allen, *Gospel Labors*, pp. 14–18; Nash, *Forging Freedom*, pp. 109–19. The precise sequence of events has occasioned considerable confusion among historians. An introductory note to the original 1817 AME *Discipline*, authored by Allen, Coker, and James Champion, dated the episode in St. George's to 1787, helping to foster the idea that black independent churches began as a reaction to segregation. Milton C. Sernett, however, has shown that the episode could not have occurred prior to 1792—that is, after the launching of the African Church initiative. See C. M. Tanner, ed., *Reprint of the First Edition of the Discipline of the African Methodist Episcopal Church* (Atlanta, 1917), p. 11; and Sernett, *Black Religion and American Evangelicalism*, pp. 117–18, 219–20. On the question of origins, see Will B. Gravely, "The Rise of African Churches in America (1786–1822): Re-examining the Contexts," in Gayraud S. Wilmore, ed., *African American Religious History: An Interdisciplinary Anthology* (Durham, N.C., 1989).

20. Allen, *Gospel Labors*, pp. 18–21; Tanner, *Outline of Our History and Government*, pp. 145–149; *Articles of Association of the African Methodist Episcopal Church of the City of Philadelphia . . .* (1799; reprint ed., Philadelphia, 1969); Wesley, *Richard Allen*, pp. 81–90. "Bethel" is the place where God addressed Jacob in Genesis 28. By significant coincidence, a white minister chose the same text to dedicate South Africa's first "Ethiopian" church a century later; see chapter 4, below.

21. Allen, *Gospel Labors*, pp. 18–19; Raboteau, "Richard Allen and the African Church Movement," p. 8 ff.

22. *Articles of Association of the AME Church;* Allen, *Gospel Labors*, pp. 20–21. A copy of the "African Supplement" is appended to the 1887 edition of Allen's *Gospel Labors*, pp. 25–28.

23. Allen, *Gospel Labors*, pp. 21–23; Daniel A. Payne, *History of the African Methodist Episcopal Church* (1891; reprint ed., New York, 1968), p. 318; Nash, *Forging Freedom*, pp. 192–99, 228–29. Some of these episodes are recounted in a February 1816 letter from Allen to Daniel Coker, reprinted in Tanner, *Outline of Our History and Government*, pp. 152–55.

24. Tanner, *Outline of Our History and Government*, pp. 152–55; Daniel Coker, "Sermon Delivered Extempore in the African Bethel Church in the City of Baltimore . . . to which is annexed a list of the African Preachers in Philadelphia, Baltimore, &c. who have withdrawn under the charge of the Methodist Bishops and Conference (But Are Still Methodists)," in Aptheker, *Documentary History of the Negro People*, pp. 67–69; George, *Segregated Sabbaths*, pp. 83–86 ff.

25. Because of the circumstances of his birth, much of Coker's early life remains elusive. This account is based primarily on Payne, *History of the AME Church*, pp. 3, 88–91; and David Smith, *Biography of Rev. David Smith of the A.M.E. Church* (Xenia, Ohio, 1881), pp. 25–28, 34–36.

26. Daniel Coker, "A Dialogue Between a Virginian and an African Minister, Written by the Rev. Daniel Coker, A descendant of Africa . . . 1810," in Porter, *Negro Protest Pamphlets;* Coker, "Sermon Delivered Extempore in the African Bethel Church," pp. 67–69. On Coker's career in Africa, see Chapter 3, below.

27. Allen, *Gospel Labors*, pp. 19, 24; Smith, *Biography of Rev. David Smith*, pp. 31–33; Payne, *History of the AME Church*, pp. 3–10 ff; Wesley, *Richard Allen*, pp. 161–77. On the AME Zion Church, see Christopher Rush, "Rise of the African Methodist Episcopal Zion Church," in Sernett, *Afro-American Religion: A Documentary Witness.* By the early nineteenth

century, white Methodists had moved decisively away from abolition toward the idea of amelioration. Twice, in 1800 and 1808, the MEC General Conference was challenged to enforce the ban against slaveholders and refused. Later, the church circulated an expurgated copy of its *Discipline* in the South, without any antislavery references. See Gravely, "The Rise of African Churches in America," pp. 311.

28. Smith, *Biography of Rev. David Smith*, pp. 31–34; Daniel Payne, *Recollections of Seventy Years* (1888; reprint ed., New York, 1968), pp. 100–01; Payne, *History of the AME Church*, pp. 15, 28–29; Coker, "Dialogue Between a Virginian and an African Minister," p. 39. The exact chronology of events remains unclear. Allen's autobiography refers only to the first gathering in 1816, and most commentators have dated his election to this meeting. David Smith, a participant in the events but one whose account is often unreliable, recalled three meetings: an initial gathering at Bethel Church, an annual conference in Philadelphia in 1817, and a second session in Baltimore the following spring, at which Allen was elected.

29. See, for example, Gordon Wood, *The Radicalism of the American Revolution* (New York, 1992); and Joyce Appleby, *Capitalism and a New Social Order: The Republican Vision of the 1790s* (New York, 1984). Robert H. Wiebe, *The Opening of American Society: From the Adoption of the Constitution to the Eve of Disunion* (New York, 1984), charts many of the same developments, while suggesting a different periodization. The ramifications of America's revolutionary transformation in the realm of religion are explored in Nathan O. Hatch, *The Democratization of American Christianity* (New Haven, Conn., 1989).

30. The most conspicuous exception is Wilson J. Moses. See *The Golden Age of Black Nationalism, 1850–1925* (Hamden, Conn., 1978); *Alexander Crummell: A Study of Civilization and Discontent* (New York, 1989); and *The Wings of Ethiopia: Studies in African-American Life and Letters* (Ames, Iowa, 1990).

31. On slavery and the "contagion of liberty," see Bernard Bailyn, *The Ideological Origins of the American Revolution* (Cambridge, Mass., 1967), pp. 232–46. On the intersection of slavery, race, and revolution see Jordan, *White Over Black;* Davis, *The Problem of Slavery in the Age of Revolution;* and Duncan J. MacLeod, *Slavery, Race and the American Revolution* (New York, 1974).

32. Jordan, *White Over Black*, pp. 294–304, 406–07. On the meaning of emancipation, see Gary B. Nash and Jean Soderlund, *Freedom by Degrees: Emancipation in Pennsylvania and its Aftermath* (New York, 1991); and Shane White, *Somewhat More Independent: The End of Slavery in New York City, 1770–1810* (Athens, Ga., 1991).

33. Jordan, *White Over Black*, pp. 26, 97, 269–311 ff.; James Campbell and James Oakes, "The Invention of Race: Rereading *White Over Black*," *Reviews in American History* 21, no. 1 (1993), pp. 172–83. It is worth noting in this context that women, the other major group explicitly excluded from the revolutionary compact, were also the objects of intense scientific scrutiny in this period—scrutiny that likewise served to "fix" their nature and rationalize a distinct social role; see Thomas Laqueur, *Making Sex: Body and Gender from the Greeks to Freud* (Cambridge, Mass., 1990).

34. Davis, *The Problem of Slavery in the Age of Revolution*, pp. 306–42; Jordan, *White Over Black*, pp. 328, 375–402.

35. Jay Fliegelman, *Prodigals and Pilgrims: The American Revolt Against Patriarchal Authority, 1750–1800* (New York, 1982); Jordan, *White Over Black*, pp. 281–94 ff. These influences were limpidly displayed in Jefferson's *Notes on the State of Virginia*, which, paradoxically, also marked a watershed in the developing science of race; see below.

36. See, for example, Anthony Benezet, *Some Historical Account of Guinea, Its Situation, Produce and the General Disposition of Its Inhabitants. With an Inquiry into the Rise and Progress of the Slave-Trade, Its Nature and Lamentable Effects* (Philadelphia, 1771); Benjamin Rush, *An*

Address to the Inhabitants of the British Settlements in America, upon Slave-Keeping (Philadelphia, 1773); Samuel Stanhope Smith, *An Essay on the Causes of the Variety of Complexion and Figure in the Human Species. To Which Are Added, Animadversions on Certain Remarks Made on the First Edition of this Essay*, 2nd ed. (1810; reprint ed., Cambridge, Mass., 1965). See also Davis, *The Problem of Slavery in the Age of Revolution*, pp. 328–29; and Jordan, *White Over Black*, pp. 508–18, 533–38.

37. Thomas Jefferson, *Notes on the State of Virginia* (1785; reprint ed., New York, 1982), pp. 138–42.

38. Jefferson, *Notes on the State of Virginia*, p. 143.

39. James Oakes, *Slavery and Freedom: An Interpretation of the Old South* (New York, 1990), pp. 62–64 ff; Jordan, *White Over Black*, pp. 295–96, 375–402; Davis, *The Problem of Slavery in the Age of Revolution*, p. 276. The comment by Thomas Rodney is from James A. Monroe, *Federalist Delaware*, quoted in Susan Hawes, "Caesar Rodney: A Biography" (B.A. (Hons.) thesis, Northwestern University, 1991).

40. Jordan, *White Over Black*, pp. 403–26, 577–78; Gary Nash, *Forging Freedom*, pp. 272–79 ff; Leon Litwack, *North of Slavery: The Negro in the Free States, 1790–1860* (Chicago, 1961). On free blacks and colonizationism, see Philip J. Staudenraus, *The African Colonization Movement, 1816–1865* (New York, 1961); and Chapter 3, below. On race and proslavery ideology, see George M. Fredrickson, *The Black Image in the White Mind: The Debate on Afro-American Character and Destiny, 1817–1914* (New York, 1971), pp. 71–96.

41. Tanner, *Outline of Our History and Government*, pp. 145–49; Douglass, *Annals of the First African Church in the United States*, p. 94; Coker, "Sermon Delivered Extempore in the African Bethel Church," p. 68; Wesley, *Richard Allen*, pp. 79–80. The broadside for the African Church is quoted in Nash, *Forging Freedom*, pp. 113–14.

42. Benedict Anderson, *Imagined Communities: Reflections on the Origins and Spread of Nationalism*, 2nd ed. (New York, 1991).

43. Allen and Jones, "To the People of Color," pp. 21–23; Wesley, *Richard Allen*, pp. 108–09; Nash, *Forging Freedom*, pp. 186–89.

44. Nash, *Forging Freedom*, pp. 153–54, 318 fn. 35. On the perils of debt and the importance of keeping clear title to church properties, see Payne, *History of the AME Church*, p. 60. AME congregations often celebrated triumph over debt with "Jubilee" ceremonies, highlighted by the burning of mortgage papers. On church leaders' attitude toward white patrons, see Allen and Jones, "A Short Address to the Friends of Him who hath no Helper," annexed to "A Narrative of the Proceedings of the Black People During the Late Awful Calamity in Philadelphia," p. 23.

45. Tanner, *Outline of Our History and Government*, pp. 145–49; Wesley, *Richard Allen*, 79–80; Payne, *History of the AME Church*, pp. 9–10.

46. Charles Wiltse, ed., *David Walker's Appeal, in Four Articles; Together with a Preamble, to the Coloured Citizens of the World, But in Particular, and Very Expressly, to Those of the United States of America* (1829; reprint ed., New York, 1991), pp. 14–15. The idea that slaves were creatures "devoid of Logos" stretched back to the ancient world; see David Brion Davis, *The Problem of Slavery in Western Culture* (Ithaca, N.Y., 1966), pp. 62–90. Predictably, this idea acquired a racial gloss in the United States; thus the ubiquitous epigram on slave narratives: "Written by Him/Herself." See Houston A. Baker, Jr., "Autobiographical Acts and the Voice of the Southern Slave," in Charles T. Davis and Henry Louis Gates, Jr., eds., *The Slave's Narrative* (New York, 1985).

47. Allen and Jones, "An Address to those who keep Slaves," pp. 19–21. Benjamin Banneker employed similar logic in his famous 1791 letter to Thomas Jefferson; see Kaplan and Kaplan, *The Black Presence in the Era of the American Revolution*, pp. 139–44.

48. Quoted in Kaplan and Kaplan, *The Black Presence in the Era of the American Revolution*, pp. 115–16. See also John Marrant, "A Narrative of the Lord's Wonderful Dealings with John Marrant, A Black, (Now Gone to Preach the Gospel in Nova Scotia) . . . 1802," in Dorothy Porter, ed., *Early Negro Writing, 1760–1837* (Boston, 1971).

49. Daniel Coker, "A Dialogue Between a Virginian and An African Minister," pp. 14–21.

50. Allen and Jones, "An Address to those who keep Slaves," p. 23.

51. Richard Bland, quoted in Bailyn, *Ideological Origins of the American Revolution*, p. 307. On the intersection of slavery and liberalism, see Oakes, *Slavery and Freedom*, pp. 40–79.

52. "Petition of Absalom Jones and Twenty-Three Others," in Porter, *Early Negro Writing;* Kaplan and Kaplan, *The Black Presence in the Era of the American Revolution*, pp. 267–71.

53. Kaplan and Kaplan, *The Black Presence in the Era of the American Revolution*, pp. 273–76. For congressional responses to the petition, see Jordan, *White Over Black*, pp. 328–29.

54. Allen and Jones, "To the People of Color," pp. 22–23.

55. Prince Saunders, "An Address, Delivered at Bethel Church, Philadelphia; on the 30th of September, 1818. Before the Pennsylvania Augustine Society . . . To Which is Annexed the Constitution of the Society," in Porter, *Early Negro Writing;* Tanner, *Outline of Our History and Government*, pp. 143–44; Wesley, *Richard Allen*, pp. 91–92, 117–18 ff; George, *Segregated Sabbaths*, pp. 76, 126; Raboteau, "Richard Allen and the African Church Movement," pp. 13–14; Raboteau, "The Black Experience in American Evangelicalism: The Meaning of Slavery," in Leonard I. Sweet, ed., *The Evangelical Tradition in America* (Macon, Ga., 1984), p. 191.

56. W. E. B. Du Bois, *The Souls of Black Folk* (1903; reprint ed., New York, 1969), p. 45.

57. See Allen and Jones, "A Narrative of the Proceedings of the Black People During the Late Awful Calamity in Philadelphia." On Rush, a leading environmentalist and a man preoccupied with improving the manners and morals of lower-class Philadelphians, see Eric Foner, *Tom Paine and Revolutionary America* (New York, 1976), pp. 137–38; Nash, *Forging Freedom*, pp. 111–20; and Allen and Jones, "A Short Address to the Friends of Him who hath no Helper."

58. Allen and Jones, "An Address to those who keep Slaves," p. 21; "A Narrative of the Proceedings of the Black People During the Late Awful Calamity in Philadelphia," pp. 5–9 ff. Carey's attack is recounted by Nash, who attributes it to the competition and antipathy between blacks and the city's growing Irish working class; see *Forging Freedom*, pp. 121–25, 129.

59. Richard Allen, "Confession of John Joyce, alias Davis, who was Executed on Monday, the 14th of March, 1808. For the Murder of Mrs. Sarah Cross; With an Address to the Public, and People of Colour," in Porter, *Early Negro Writing;* Allen and Jones, "A Narrative of the Proceedings of the Black People During the Late Awful Calamity in Philadelphia," p. 11. On the persistence of African dancing in northern cities, including Philadelphia, see Foner, *Tom Paine and Revolutionary America*, pp. 93–94; and Stuckey, *Slave Culture*, pp. 22–24. Ira Berlin argues that certain African practices actually survived better in the urban North than in the slave South, where there was more overt repression; see Berlin, "Time, Space, and the Evolution of Afro-American Society on British Mainland North America," *American Historical Review* 85, no. 1 (1980), pp. 44–78. Shane White notes the centrality of dancing in black recreation in New York City but portrays it as a syncretic cultural product rather than an African one; see White, *Somewhat More Independent*, pp. 95–101.

60. Jordan, *White Over Black*, pp. 328–29.

61. Jordan, *White Over Black*, pp. 452–54 ff. For the exchange between Banneker and Jefferson, see Kaplan and Kaplan, *The Black Presence in the Era of the American Revolution*, pp. 139–47.

62. Quoted in Emma Jones Lapansky, "'Since They Got Those Separate Churches': Afro-Americans and Racism in Jacksonian Philadelphia," *American Quarterly* 32, no. 1 (1980),

pp. 54–78. On racist caricaturing of elite blacks, see Nash, *Forging Freedom*, pp. 254–59, 275.

63. John Runcie, "'Hunting the Nigs' in Philadelphia: The Race Riot of August, 1834," *Pennsylvania History* 29, no. 2 (1972), pp. 187–218; Nash, *Forging Freedom*, pp. 213, 227, 273–79; Lapansky, "Since They Got Those Separate Churches," pp. 75–78. Litwack, *North of Slavery* describes similar patterns all through the antebellum North.

64. James Forten, "A Philadelphia Negro Condemns Discriminatory Proposals, 1813," in Aptheker, *Documentary History of the Negro People*, pp. 59–66; Nash, *Forging Freedom*, pp. 180–82; John Bracey, August Meier, and Elliot Rudwick, eds., *Blacks in the Abolition Movement* (Belmont, Calif., 1971). On colonization, see Chapter 3, below.

65. See Eric Foner, *Nothing But Freedom: Emancipation and its Legacy* (Baton Rouge, 1983), p. 40 ff. Foner pursues this insight in *Reconstruction: America's Unfinished Revolution, 1863–1877* (New York, 1988).

Chapter 2. Harnessing the Spirit

1. W. E. B. Du Bois, *The Souls of Black Folk* (1903; reprint ed., New York, 1969), p. 217. On antebellum church membership, see Daniel A. Payne, *History of the African Methodist Episcopal Church* (1891; reprint ed., New York, 1968), pp. 26–27, 33, 125. A few sources put membership at half a million in the 1870s, but conference statistics, which counted only full, adult members, suggest that AME rolls reached that level only in the 1890s, by which time the church was one of the ten largest denominations in America. See *AME Church Review* 24, no. 4 (1908), p. 411. According to the Bureau of the Census, the AME Church counted 497,777 members in 1906.

2. David Smith, *Biography of the Rev. David Smith of the A.M.E. Church* (Xenia, Ohio, 1881), p. 60; Daniel A. Payne, *The Semi-Centenary and Retrospection of the African Methodist Episcopal Church in the United States of America* (1866; reprint ed., New York, 1972), p. 24; Payne, *History*, pp. 97, 109–32.

3. L. L. Berry, *A Century of Missions of the African Methodist Episcopal Church 1840–1940* (New York, 1942), pp. 49–55; R. R. Wright, Jr., *Bishops of the A.M.E. Church* (Nashville, 1962), pp. 283–86; Wright, *The Encyclopedia of the African Methodist Episcopal Church*, 2nd ed. (Philadelphia, 1947), p. 596. Cf. Daniel A. Payne, *Recollections of Seventy Years* (1888; reprint ed., New York, 1968), p. 102, which characterizes Quinn as West Indian.

4. Payne, *History*, pp. 170–71 ff; Sarah J. W. Early, *Life and Labors of Rev. Jordan W. Early* (Nashville, 1894), pp. 23–26; Berry, *Century of Missions*, pp. 49–55; Wright, *Bishops of the AME Church*, pp. 283–86; Payne, *Recollections*, p. 102. On Quinn's antislavery work, see W. Paul Quinn, "The Origins, Horrors, and Results of Slavery, Faithfully and Minutely Described, in a Series of Facts, and its Advocates Pathetically Addressed . . . 1834," in Dorothy Porter, ed., *Early Negro Writing, 1760–1837* (Boston, 1971).

5. Smith, *Biography of Rev. David Smith*, pp. 41–42, 69–72 ff. See also Payne, *Recollections*, pp. 106, 111–12, 123; and Payne, *History*, p. 97. On African Methodism's subsequent career in Ohio, see Chapter 8, below.

6. Early, *Life and Labors of Jordan Early*, pp. 50–52; Smith, *Biography of Rev. David Smith*, pp. 57–60, 69–77, 86. (The comment on lower-class whites is on p. 74.)

7. Smith, *Biography of Rev. David Smith*, pp. 23–24, 52–53; Early, *Life and Labors of Jordan Early*, pp. 20–33; Payne, *History*, pp. 53–54, 110, 171, 222, 344, 408; Payne, *Recollections*, pp. 122–28; W. H. Mixon, *History of the African Methodist Episcopal Church in Alabama, with Biographical Sketches* (Nashville, 1902), p. 29.

8. Payne, *Semi-Centenary and Retrospection*, pp. 23–24; Ulrich B. Phillips, *American Negro*

Slavery (New York, 1918), pp. 419–21; Charles H. Wesley, *Richard Allen: Apostle of Freedom* (Washington, 1935), pp. 185–88; Milton C. Sernett, *Black Religion and American Evangelicalism: White Protestants, Plantation Missions, and the Flowering of Negro Christianity, 1787–1865* (Metuchen, N. J., 1975), pp. 128–40; Gayraud Wilmore, *Black Religion and Black Radicalism* (New York, 1972), pp. 83–85.

9. See John Oliver Killens, ed., *The Trial Record of Denmark Vesey* (1822; reprint ed., Boston, 1978). For interpretations of the conspiracy, see Richard Wade, "The Vesey Plot: A Reconsideration," *Journal of Southern History* 30, no. 2 (1964), pp. 143–61; Robert S. Starobin, *Denmark Vesey: The Slave Conspiracy of 1822* (Englewood Cliffs, N.J., 1970); Sterling Stuckey, *Slave Culture: Nationalist Theory and the Foundations of Black America* (New York, 1987), pp. 43–53.

10. Payne, *History*, pp. 101–02, 140, 184, 211, 247, ff; Payne, *Recollections*, p. 136.

11. Richard Niebuhr, *The Social Sources of Denominationalism* (New York, 1929).

12. On transformations in British Methodism, see David Hempton, *Methodism and Politics in British Society, 1750–1850* (Stanford, 1984); W. R. Ward, *Religion and Society in England* (New York, 1973); and E. P. Thompson, *The Making of the English Working Class* (New York, 1963), pp. 350–400. For the American case, see Nathan O. Hatch, *The Democratization of American Christianity* (New Haven, Conn., 1989), pp. 8, 81–93; and Niebuhr, *Social Sources of Denominationalism*, pp. 165–76. On revivalism and American character, see Perry Miller, *The Life of the Mind in America: From the Revolution to the Civil War* (New York, 1965), pp. 3–35.

13. This paragraph, and the several that follow, draw heavily on David W. Wills, "Womanhood and Domesticity in the A.M.E. Tradition: The Influence of Daniel Alexander Payne," in Wills and Richard Newman, eds., *Black Apostles at Home and Abroad: Afro-Americans and the Christian Mission from the Revolution to Reconstruction* (Boston, 1982). See also Payne, *Recollections*, pp. 12–17, 34–38, 59–64, 74–81; and Payne, *History*, pp. 200, 221, 276–78.

14. Payne, *History*, pp. 9–10; Payne, *Recollections*, pp. 253–57 ff; Wills, "Womanhood and Domesticity," pp. 135–36.

15. Payne, *History*, pp. vii, 16–17, 97–100, 115–19, 127, 393; Payne, *Recollections*, pp. 64, 220–21; Smith, *Biography of Rev. David Smith*, pp. 42–43. For early educational initiatives, see Benjamin T. Tanner, *An Outline of Our History and Government for African Methodist Churchmen, Ministerial and Lay* (n.p., 1884), pp. 143–44. For representative resolutions on education, see "Minutes of the Four Last Annual Conferences of the African Methodist Episcopal Church . . . 1834," in Porter, *Early Negro Writing.*

16. The quotations are drawn from Payne's account in *Recollections*, pp. 75–76, 137, 220–23; and *History*, pp. 141–44, 154–56, 329. Payne's 1842 resolution is quoted in Wills, "Womanhood and Domesticity," pp. 136.

17. Payne, *History*, pp. 101–07, 121–25, 132, 138, 154–68, 262, 284, 396–402; Payne, *Recollections*, pp. 104, 225, 239.

18. Payne, *History*, pp. 176–79, 269–73; Payne, *Recollections*, pp. 81, 92–93, 253–57. On praying bands, see below.

19. Quoted in Gary B. Nash, *Forging Freedom: The Formation of Philadelphia's Black Community, 1720–1840* (Cambridge, Mass., 1988), pp. 194–95.

20. Richard Allen, "Spiritual Song," in Porter, *Early Negro Writing.* For Allen and the F.A.S., see Chapter 1, above.

21. Payne, *Recollections*, pp. 68–69.

22. Payne, *History*, pp. 194, 457; Payne, *Recollections*, pp. 233–37.

23. Richard Allen, *A Collection of Hymns and Spiritual Songs from Various Authors* (1801; reprint ed., Nashville, 1987); Eileen Southern, *The Music of Black America: A History*, 2nd ed. (New York, 1983), pp. 30–31, 75–88; Southern, "Musical Practices in Black Churches of New

York and Philadelphia, ca. 1800–1844," *Afro-Americans in New York Life and History* 4, no. 1 (1980), pp. 61–77.

24. Quoted in Southern, *Music of Black America*, p. 79. Lawrence Levine, in an astute discussion of the problem of African "survivals," notes the affinity between African call and response patterns and the practice of lining out hymns; see *Black Culture and Black Consciousness* (New York, 1977), p. 33. On the context and performance of spiritual songs, see the introduction to the 1987 edition of Allen's *Hymns and Spiritual Songs*.

25. Southern, *Music of Black American*, pp. 79–82; Southern, "Musical Practices in Black Churches," pp. 69–71; Payne, *Recollections*, pp. 233–37; Allen, *Hymns and Spiritual Songs*, p. xxxiv.

26. Payne, *Recollections*, pp. 233–37; Payne, *History*, p. 452. The debate over instrumental music had a long history in American Protestantism. Puritans, for example, accepted vocal music as a natural phenomenon but regarded "singing with Instruments" as "ceremoniall worship" and forbade it. See Charles E. Hambrick-Stowe, *The Practice of Piety: Puritan Devotional Disciplines in Seventeenth-Century New England* (Chapel Hill, N.C., 1982), p. 113.

27. Payne, *Recollections*, pp. 92–94, 233–37; Payne, *History*, pp. iii–iv, 452–57; Southern, "Musical Practices in Black Churches," pp. 67–68.

28. Daniel A. Payne, *A Treatise on Domestic Education* (Cincinnati, 1889), p. 71. Though published at the end of his life, the treatise represented a compilation of observations and notes Payne had accumulated over the course of his long career. See also Wills, "Womanhood and Domesticity," pp. 137–42; Payne, *Recollections*, pp. 137–38; Payne, *History*, pp. 56, 87, 160 ff; Berry, *Century of Missions*, pp. 36–39; Anna Julia Cooper, *A Voice from the South* (1892; reprint ed., New York, 1988); and Fanny J. Coppin, *Reminiscences of School Life and Hints on Teaching* (Philadelphia, 1913). For an introduction to domesticity and its paradoxes, see Barbara Welter, "The Cult of True Womanhood, 1820–1860," *American Quarterly* 18, n. 2 (1966), pp. 151–74; Nancy F. Cott, *The Bonds of Womanhood: Woman's Sphere in New England, 1780–1835* (New Haven, Conn., 1977); and Carroll Smith-Rosenberg, "The Female World of Love and Ritual: Relations Between Women in Nineteenth-Century America," *Signs* 1, no. 1 (1975), pp. 1–29.

29. This paragraph, and much of what follows, draws on the introduction and collected spiritual narratives in William L. Andrews, ed., *Sisters of the Spirit: Three Black Women's Autobiographies of the Nineteenth Century* (Bloomington, Ind., 1986). See also Payne, *History*, pp. 40–41, 179; and Payne, *Recollections*, p. 81 ff.

30. For examples, see Andrews, *Sisters of the Spirit*, pp. 16–17, 33, 163, 192, 208, 229.

31. See Harold Lindstrom, *Wesley and Sanctification* (London, 1950). For examples of the debate in AME circles, see *Repository of Religion and Literature* 3, no. 2 (1861), pp. 55–58. (Scattered copies of the *Repository* can be found in the Daniel Payne Papers, Wilberforce University.) Zilpha Elaw refers to her "ethereal attendant" in Andrews, *Sisters of the Spirit*, p. 75.

32. Jarena Lee, *The Life and Religious Experience of Jarena Lee* (Philadelphia, 1836), in Andrews, *Sisters of the Spirit*. See also Lee, *Religious Experience and Journal of Mrs. Jarena Lee, Giving an Account of Her Call to Preach the Gospel* (Philadelphia, 1849). On the British case, see Deborah M. Valenze, *Prophetic Sons and Daughters: Female Preaching and Popular Religion in Industrial England* (Princeton, N.J., 1985).

33. Jean M. Humez, "Visionary Experience and Power: The Career of Rebecca Cox Jackson," in Wills and Newman, *Black Apostles at Home and Abroad*. See also Humez, ed., *Gifts of Power: The Writings of Rebecca Jackson, Black Visionary and Shaker Eldress* (Amherst, Mass., 1981). For Joseph Cox's role in the founding of Bethel Church, see Payne, *History*, pp. 177–78.

34. Julia Foote, *A Brand Plucked from the Fire: An Autobiographical Sketch by Mrs. Julia A.*

J. Foote (Cleveland, 1879); and Zilpha Elaw, *Memoirs of the Life, Religious Experience, Ministerial Travels and Labors of Mrs. Zilpha Elaw* (London, 1846), both in Andrews, *Sisters of the Spirit*. See also Amanda Smith, *An Autobiography: The Story of the Lord's Dealings with Mrs. Amanda Smith, the Colored Evangelist* (1893; reprint ed., New York, 1988).

35. Elaw, *Ministerial Travels and Labors*, pp. 61–62, 75, 79, 84; Foote, *A Brand Plucked from the Fire*, pp. 197, 201, 217; Smith, *Autobiography*, pp. 42–43, 58–72; Humez, "Career of Rebecca Cox Jackson," pp. 110–12. These women, it should be noted, never completely freed themselves from prevailing assumptions about gender, producing some extraordinary tensions in their work. Thus, Elaw followed the passage quoted here with an endorsement of patriarchy: "That woman is dependent on and subject to man, is the dictate of nature. . . ." It is also worth noting how these women's insistence on their submission to a will greater than their own subverted the conventions of the other African American autobiographical genre of the era, the slave narrative. The whole object of the slave's narrative was to chart the author's movement from subjection to self-ownership, from object of another to bourgeois subject.

36. Lee, *Life and Religious Experience*, p. 45; Smith, *Autobiography*, pp. 97–109 ff; Elaw, *Ministerial Travels and Labors*, p. 76.

37. Lee, *Life and Religious Experience*, p. 36; Elaw, *Ministerial Travels and Labors*, pp. 75, 92, 124; Foote, *A Brand Plucked from the Fire*, pp. 164, 208.

38. Lee, *Life and Religious Experience*, pp. 36–37, 48; Elaw, *Ministerial Travels and Labors*, pp. 111, 144; Foote, *A Brand Plucked from the Fire*, pp. 205–09, 227. See also Smith, *Autobiography*, pp. 29–30, 70.

39. Elaw, *Ministerial Travels and Labors*, p. 107; Smith, *Autobiography*, pp. 58–62, 76–80, 94, 107–12, 117, 132.

40. Elaw, *Ministerial Travels and Labors*, pp. 52, 74, 118.

41. "Some letters of Richard Allen and Absalom Jones to Dorothy Ripley," *Journal of Negro History* 1, no. 4 (1916), pp. 436–43; Payne, *Recollections*, p. 102.

42. Lee, *Life and Religious Experience*, pp. 35–36, 42–45.

43. Humez, "Career of Rebecca Cox Jackson," pp. 113–15; Payne, *History*, pp. 256, 273; Smith, *Autobiography*, pp. 80–86, 109–12, 132, 146; Andrews, *Sisters of the Spirit*, p. 6; Foote, *A Brand Plucked from the Fire*, pp. 185–87, 212–13. Lee's complaint is quoted in Wills, "Womanhood and Domesticity," p. 138. "There surely can be little doubt," Wills comments, "that the segment of the city's A.M.E. community that wished to push Jarena Lee out significantly overlapped with the segment that would shortly draw Daniel Alexander Payne in."

44. Payne, *History*, pp. 237, 273; Jualynne E. Dodson, "Women's Collective Power in the A.M.E. Church" (Ph.D. diss., University of California, Berkeley, 1984) pp. 145–49. The 1848 petition is reproduced in Tanner, *Outline of Our History and Government*, pp. 185–87.

45. *Christian Recorder*, quoted in Payne, *History*, p. 298; Tanner, *Outline of Our History and Government*, p. 186; E. Weaver, "Woman—Her True Sphere," *Repository of Religion and Literature* 1, no. 2 (1858), pp. 57–61.

46. See David Leverenz, *Manhood and the American Renaissance* (Ithaca, N.Y., 1989).

47. Payne, *History*, p. 12; W. J. Gaines, *The Negro and the White Man* (1897; reprint ed., New York, 1969), pp. 26–28; Benjamin T. Tanner, *An Apology for African Methodism* (Baltimore, 1867), p. 16. For similar invocations of manhood in postbellum churchmen's writings, see Wesley J. Gaines, *African Methodism in the South, or Twenty-Five Years of Freedom* (1890; reprint ed., Chicago, 1969), pp. 206, 231; Levi J. Coppin, *Unwritten History* (New York, 1919), pp. 74–75, 227; Smith, *Biography of Rev. David Smith*, p. 135; W. H. Mixon, *A Methodist Luminary* (Selma, Ala., 1871), pp. 8–9; Reverdy Ransom, *The Mission of the Religious Press* (New York, 1912), p. 7; and Payne's editorial in the inaugural edition of the *AME Church Review* 1, no. 1 (1884), pp. 1–3.

48. Cf. Dodson, "Women's Collective Power," pp. 106, 122–23, 148–54.

49. Abraham Grant, *Deaconess Manual of the African Methodist Episcopal Church* (n.p., 1902), pp. 7, 12, 26–31.

50. Berry, *Century of Missions,* p. 36. On women's missionary work, see Chapter 3, below.

51. Daniel Payne, "Welcome to the Ransomed," in Milton C. Sernett, ed., *Afro-American Religious History: A Documentary Witness* (Durham, N.C., 1985), pp. 217–26.

52. E. Franklin Frazier, *The Negro Church in America* (New York, 1964), pp. 16, 20.

53. Clarence Walker, *A Rock in a Weary Land: The African Methodist Episcopal Church During the Civil War and Reconstruction* (Baton Rouge, 1982), pp. 49–50, 64–65; Payne, *History,* pp. 467–69; William Seraile, *Voice of Dissent: Theophilus Gould Steward (1843–1924) and Black America* (New York, 1991), pp. 9–14. On Port Royal, see Willie Lee Rose, *Rehearsal for Reconstruction: The Port Royal Experiment* (New York, 1964); on Lynch, see William B. Gravely, "James Lynch and the Black Christian Mission During Reconstruction," in Wills and Newman, *Black Apostles at Home and Abroad.* At the time, Payne was an officer of the American Missionary Association, which pledged to pay Lynch's and Hall's salaries. The Association apparently failed to honor the pledge, the first of many misunderstandings between the A.M.A. and the AME Church. See Joe M. Richardson, *Christian Reconstruction: The American Missionary Association and Southern Blacks, 1861–1890* (Athens, Ga., 1986), pp. 141–60.

54. Eric Foner, *Reconstruction: America's Unfinished Revolution* (New York, 1988), pp. 88–102; Walker, *Rock in a Weary Land,* p. 85 ff; Joel Williamson, *After Slavery* (Chapel Hill, N.C., 1965), pp. 180–208; Coppin, *Unwritten History,* pp. 122–24; T. G. Steward, *Fifty Years in the Gospel Ministry* (Philadelphia, 1915), p. 33. See also William G. Montgomery, *Under Their Own Vine and Fig Tree: The African-American Church in the South, 1865–1900* (Baton Rouge, 1993), which unfortunately appeared after these pages were written.

55. A. W. Wayman, *My Recollections of African Methodist Episcopal Ministers, or Forty Years' Experience in the African Methodist Episcopal Church* (Philadelphia, 1881), pp. 90–91; R. H. Cain, quoted in Walker, *Rock in a Weary Land,* p. 51; Coppin, *Unwritten History,* p. 120. The one notable exception was pioneer missionary James Lynch, who regarded a separate black church as a temporary expedient necessitated by slavery. Lynch resigned from the AME Church after emancipation. See Gravely, "James Lynch and the Black Christian Mission During Reconstruction."

56. Gaines, *Negro and the White Man,* pp. 26–31; Seraile, *Voice of Dissent,* p. 19. For similar attitudes among white missionaries, see Robertson, *Christian Reconstruction;* and Jacqueline Jones, *Soldiers of Light and Love: Northern Teachers and Georgia Blacks, 1865–1873* (Chapel Hill, N.C., 1980).

57. Payne, *History,* pp. 465–70; Payne, *Recollections,* pp. 161–63; T. G. Steward, *My First Four Years in the Itineracy of the African Methodist Episcopal Church* (Brooklyn, N.Y., 1876), pp. 9–18; Seraile, *Voice of Dissent,* p. 11.

58. Wesley J. Gaines, *African Methodism in the South,* pp. 8–17, 19 ff. Gaines's book is supplemented by several state studies, which provide valuable information on the church's southern spread. See Israel L. Butt, *History of African Methodism in Virginia, or Four Decades in the Old Dominion* (Hampton, Va., 1908); Revel A. Adams, *Cyclopedia of African Methodism in Mississippi* (n.p., 1902); and Mixon, *History of the African Methodist Episcopal Church in Alabama.*

59. Gaines, *African Methodism in the South,* pp. 23–24, 74, 151, 266–67; Steward, *My First Four Years,* pp. 34–46; Walker, *Rock in a Weary Land,* pp. 71–74. On postwar urbanization, see Foner, *Reconstruction,* pp. 81–82; on Turner's subsequent career, see Chapter 3, below.

60. Coppin, *Unwritten History,* pp. 117–23, 158.

61. Coppin, *Unwritten History,* pp. 119–20, 123, 141, 149, 158, 163.

62. Coppin, *Unwritten History*, 117, 144–47; Seraile, *Voice of Dissent*, pp. 12–14, 35–37. Bishop Wayman frequently preached in MEC, South churches in the late 1860s, apparently in the belief that African Methodists would soon take control of them. On such occasions, local AME members were invited to attend the sermons—in the gallery. At least one AME minister, future bishop William B. Derrick, refused to allow his congregation to so demean themselves. See Wayman, *Recollections of African Methodist Episcopal Ministers*, pp. 98, 171.

63. Walker, *Rock in a Weary Land*, pp. 76–77; Steward, *Fifty Years in the Gospel Ministry*, p. 33. For insight into the social origins of southern ministers, see the biographical sketches in Butt, *History of African Methodism in Virginia*, pp. 63–74, 110–14, 159–67.

64. Payne, *Recollections*, pp. 262, 285, 294; Payne, *History*, pp. 420–21; Wayman, *Recollections of African Methodist Episcopal Ministers*, pp. 248–49; Seraile, *Voice of Dissent*, pp. 22, 34–35. David Wills dates Payne's declining influence to his failure to prevent the election of Turner and Cain in 1880; see Wills, "Womanhood and Domesticity," p. 137.

65. Foner, *Reconstruction*, pp. 93–94; Walker, *Rock in a Weary Land*, pp. 116–22; Payne, *History of the AME Church*, pp. 469–70; John Hope Franklin and Alfred A. Moss, Jr., *From Slavery to Freedom: A History of Negro Americans*, 6th ed. (New York, 1988), p. 211. On the social origins of African American political leadership in South Carolina, see Thomas Holt, *Black Over White: Negro Political Leadership in South Carolina During Reconstruction* (Urbana, Ill., 1977), p. 88.

66. Russell Duncan, *Freedom's Shore: Tunis Campbell and the Georgia Freedmen* (Athens, Ga., 1986); Gaines, *African Methodism in the South*, p. 25; Vernon Lane Wharton, *The Negro in Mississippi* (Chapel Hill, N.C., 1947), pp. 149–51. Eric Foner advances the argument about localism in *Nothing But Freedom: Emancipation and its Legacy* (Baton Rouge, 1983).

67. Payne, *History*, pp. 470–71, 476; Payne, *Recollections*, pp. 67–68, 262, 329–30; Butt, *History of African Methodism in Virginia*, p. 95.

68. Payne, "Welcome to the Ransomed," p. 218. For a classic example of this ambivalence, see *Christian Recorder*, May 30, 1863.

69. See Gaines, *African Methodism in the South*, p. 258; Gaines, *Negro and the White Man*, pp. 135–36; Walker, *Rock in a Weary Land*, p. 54; and Payne, "Welcome to the Ransomed." The belief that the poor will not labor without compulsion, an idea as old as capitalism itself, acquired a distinctly racial form during Reconstruction; see Foner, *Reconstruction*, pp. 133, 146 ff. For comparative perspectives, see Foner, *Nothing But Freedom*, pp. 15–16, 29–30; and Thomas C. Holt, *The Problem of Freedom: Race, Labor, and Politics in Jamaica and Britain, 1832–1938* (Baltimore, 1992), pp. 55–79.

70. Gaines, *Negro and the White Man*, pp. 78–79, 178–83; Gaines, *African Methodism in the South*, pp. 31, 54, 176; Payne, *Semi-Centenary and Retrospection*, p. 36; Glenn Sisk, "The Negro Colleges in Atlanta," *Journal of Negro Education* 33, no. 4 (1964), pp. 404–08.

71. Coppin, *Unwritten History*, pp. 39, 54, 125–28; Gaines, *Negro and the White Man*, pp. 30, 80, 143–47; Seraile, *Voice of Dissent*, p. 19; Frazier, *Negro Church in America*, pp. 37–40. Cf. Herbert Gutman, *The Black Family in Slavery and Freedom, 1750–1925* (New York, 1976). The comment of the *Christian Recorder* is quoted in Walker, *Rock in a Weary Land*, p. 38.

72. Gaines, *Negro and White Man*, pp. 187–89; Coppin, *Unwritten History*, pp. 163–65 ff; Frazier, *Negro Church in America*, pp. 35–37; Seraile, *Voice of Dissent*, pp. 55, 101. On ring shouts, see Stuckey, *Slave Culture*, pp. 24–57 ff.

73. Payne, *Recollections*, pp. 93–94, 253–57. The episode has been recounted, to quite different ends, by a dozen different historians. See, for example, Stuckey, *Slave Culture*, pp. 92–95; and Wilson J. Moses, *The Wings of Ethiopia: Studies in African-American Life and Letters* (Ames, Iowa, 1990), pp. 163–64.

74. Payne, *Recollections*, pp. 255–56; Coppin, *Unwritten History*, pp. 165, 197–98; Foner, *Reconstruction*, p. 92.

75. Walker, *Rock in a Weary Land*, pp. 50, 71–75, 90; Gaines, *African Methodism in the South*, pp. 21–22. On Baptists and "Africanisms," see Melville Herskovits, *The Myth of the Negro Past* (1941; reprint ed., Boston, 1958), pp. 207–60; and Mechal Sobel, *Trabelin' On: The Slave Journey to an Afro-Baptist Faith* (Westport, Conn., 1979).

Chapter 3. Through the Looking Glass

1. The best one volume treatment of the A.C.S. remains Philip J. Staudenraus, *The African Colonization Movement, 1816–1865* (New York, 1961).

2. Thomas Jefferson, *Notes on the State of Virginia* (1785; reprint ed., New York, 1982), pp. 162–63. On Hopkins's scheme, see Lorenzo J. Greene, *The Negro in Colonial New England* (New York, 1942), pp. 277–79; Staudenraus, *African Colonization*, pp. vii–viii, 1–5; Imanuel Geiss, *The Pan-African Movement: A History of Pan-Africanism in America, Europe and Africa* (New York, 1974), p. 131; and Bernard Bailyn, *The Ideological Origins of the American Revolution* (Cambridge, Mass., 1967), pp. 234–44. Hopkins did succeed in enrolling Yamma at Princeton, but the scheme was interrupted by the Revolution; see Chapter 8, below.

3. Absalom Jones, "A Thanksgiving Sermon, Preached January 1, 1808, In St. Thomas's, or the African Episcopal Church, Philadelphia: On Account of the Abolition of the African Slave Trade," in Dorothy Porter, ed., *Early Negro Writing, 1760–1837* (Boston, 1971), pp. 335–42. On the Massachusetts petition, see Herbert Aptheker, ed., *A Documentary History of the Negro People in the United States* (1951; reprint ed., New York, 1979), pp. 7–8; on Wheatley, see John C. Shields, ed., *The Collected Works of Phillis Wheatley* (New York, 1988), pp. 18, 43–50, 175–84. See also Wilson J. Moses, "African Redemption and the Decline of the Fortunate Fall Doctrine," in *The Wings of Ethiopia: Studies in African-American Life and Letters* (Ames, Iowa, 1990).

4. Olaudah Equiano, *The Interesting Narrative of the Life of Olaudah Equiano or Gustavus Vassa, the African, Written by Himself* (1789; reprint ed., Leeds, 1814), in Henry L. Gates ed., *Classic Slave Narratives* (New York, 1987), pp. 3, 22–24, 167–69.

5. Charles H. Wesley, *Richard Allen: Apostle of Freedom* (Washington, D.C., 1935), p. 67; Lamont D. Thomas, *Rise to Be a People: A Biography of Paul Cuffe* (Urbana, Ill., 1986), pp. 19–21. Prince Hall's petition is reproduced in Sidney Kaplan and Emma Nogrady Kaplan, *The Black Presence in the Era of the American Revolution* (Amherst, Mass., 1989), pp. 207–09. On the origins of the Sierra Leone colony, see Christopher Fyfe, *A History of Sierra Leone* (London, 1962).

6. Paul Cuffe, *Memoir of Captain Paul Cuffe, A Man of Colour: To Which is Subjoined The Epistle of the Society of Sierra Leone, in Africa, &c.* (London, 1811); Cuffe, *A Brief Account of the Settlement and Present Situation of the Colony of Sierra Leone in Africa* (1812; reprint ed., New York, 1970); Hollis R. Lynch, "Pan-Negro Nationalism in the New World, Before 1862," in August Meier and Elliot Rudwick, eds., *The Making of Black America* (New York, 1969), pp. 46–47; Fyfe, *History of Sierra Leone*, pp. 112–13; Thomas, *Rise to Be a People*, pp. 24–26.

7. Thomas, *Rise to Be a People*, pp. 35, 83–119; Staudenraus, *African Colonization*, pp. 9–11.

8. Quoted in Staudenraus, *African Colonization*, p. 28; Carol V. R. George, *Segregated Sabbaths: Richard Allen and the Rise of Independent Black Churches, 1760–1840* (New York, 1973), pp. 137–38.

9. "Resolutions of a meeting at Bethel Church," in Aptheker, *Documentary History of the Negro People*, pp. 17–19; Gary B. Nash, *Forging Freedom: The Formation of Philadelphia's Black*

Community, 1720–1840 (Cambridge, Mass. 1988), pp. 236–42. Allen pursued the theme of reversion in a classic 1827 letter against colonization, published in *Freedom's Journal* and quoted in Wesley, *Richard Allen*, pp. 277–78. Forten's letter is quoted in Kaplan and Kaplan, *Black Presence in the Era of the American Revolution*, p. 162. See also Ray Billington, "James Forten: Forgotten Abolitionist," in John Bracey, August Meier, and Elliot Rudwick, eds., *Blacks in the Abolitionist Movement* (Belmont, Calif. 1971). Cf. Nash, *Forging Freedom*, p. 240, which argues, largely on the basis of Forten's letter, that black elites were duped by the A. C. S. but were saved by "the intuitive understanding of the unlettered black masses."

10. George, *Segregated Sabbaths*, pp. 149–53; Staudenraus, *African Colonization*, pp. 193–206. See also William Lloyd Garrison, *Thoughts on African Colonization* (1832; reprint ed., New York, 1968); and Garrison, *An Address Delivered Before the Free People of Color in Philadelphia and New York, and other Cities, during the Month of June, 1831*, 2nd ed. (Boston, 1831).

11. Daniel Coker, *Journal of Daniel Coker, A Descendent of Africa . . . on a Voyage to Sherbro, in Africa* (1820; reprint ed., New York, 1970). Recall that Coker's relationship with other AME leaders was already strained, apparently because of the disputed episcopal election in 1816–1817. He was even briefly suspended from the church, though he had been reinstated prior to his departure. See Daniel Payne, *History of the African Methodist Episcopal Church* (1891; reprint ed., New York, 1968), pp. 15, 29; and Chapter 1, above.

12. Coker, *Journal*, pp. 37–39, 44; Matei Markwei, "The Rev. Daniel Coker of Sierra Leone," *Sierra Leone Bulletin of Religion* 7, no. 2 (1965), pp. 41–48; Payne, *History*, pp. 88–93; Christopher Fyfe, "The West African Methodists in the Nineteenth Century," *Sierra Leone Bulletin of Religion* 3, no. 1 (1961), pp. 22–28, and Fyfe, *History of Sierra Leone*, pp. 132–33.

13. Payne, *History*, pp. 90–91; George, *Segregated Sabbaths*, pp. 119–20. Lott Carey, a Baptist minister and the man after whom the largest black Baptist missionary connection is named, sailed to West Africa a year behind Coker. He was killed in an explosion during preparations for an attack on a nearby African village. For his life, see Leroy Fitts, *Lott Carey: First Black Missionary in Africa* (Valley Forge, Pa., 1978).

14. See Leon Litwack, *North of Slavery: The Negro in the Free States, 1790–1860* (Chicago, 1961), esp. pp. 64–112.

15. Staudenraus, *African Colonization*, pp. 81–84. On the dissemination of news about events in Haiti, see Julius S. Scott, "The Common Wind: Currents of Afro-American Communication in the Era of the Haitian Revolution" (Ph.D. diss., Duke University, 1986).

16. Payne, *History*, pp. 55, 65–67, 85, 132, 140–41, 476–77; Lewellyn L. Berry, *A Century of Missions of the African Methodist Episcopal Church, 1840-1940* (New York, 1942), pp. 43–46.

17. Berry, *Century of Missions*, pp. 43–46; Payne, *History of the AME Church*, pp. 104–06, 475–83; Staudenraus, *African Colonization*, pp. 84–85.

18. Litwack, *North of Slavery*, pp. 72–74. The standard work on the Canadian settlements is Robin W. Winks, *The Blacks in Canada: A History* (New Haven, Conn., 1971); see pp. 355–60 for the AME Church. In 1840 the Canadian AME congregations were organized into a separate conference; later they severed their links with the AME Church entirely. See Payne, *History of the AME Church*, pp. 128–32.

19. George, *Segregated Sabbaths*, p. 148; Wesley, *Richard Allen*, pp. 277–78; Geiss, *The Pan-African Movement*, p. 136.

20. "The Pioneer National Negro Convention," in Aptheker, *Documentary History of the Negro People*, pp. 98–107. The dream of an exodus to the countryside persisted within the AME Church, and within the broader political culture. By the end of the nineteenth century, it was taken as a truism that blacks were rural creatures whose manners and morals were corroded by urban life. This idea was to have a profound effect on segregationist ideology in both the United States and South Africa; see Chapter 9, below.

21. The minutes of the third and fifth conventions are excerpted in Aptheker, *Documentary History of the Negro People*, pp. 145–59. On the "names controversy," see Sterling Stuckey, *Slave Culture: Nationalist Theory and the Foundations of Black America* (New York, 1987), pp. 193–244.

22. Payne, *History*, pp. 138, 148–51, 236; "Prospectus of the African Methodist Episcopal Church Magazine, September, 1841," in Aptheker, *Documentary History of the Negro People*, pp. 209–11. Church leaders' attitudes toward African missions are discussed in detail below.

23. Staudenraus, *African Colonization*, pp. 240–42; Geiss, *The Pan-African Movement*, pp. 88–92; Litwack, *North of Slavery*, pp. 257–62. On the deteriorating legal position of free people of color in the period, see Don E. Fehrenbacher, *The Dred Scott Case: Its Significance in American Law and Politics* (New York, 1978).

24. This paragraph, and the several which follow, rely heavily on Wilson J. Moses, *Alexander Crummell: A Study of Civilization and Discontent* (New York, 1989). See also Alfred Moss, "Alexander Crummell: Black Nationalist and Apostle of Western Civilization," in Leon Litwack and August Meier, eds., *Black Leaders of the Nineteenth Century* (Urbana, Ill., 1988), pp. 236–51; and George U. Rigby, *Alexander Crummell: Pioneer in Nineteenth-Century Pan-African Thought* (Westport, Conn., 1987).

25. See Alexander Crummell, *The Future of Africa* (New York, 1862); and Crummell, *Africa and America* (New York, 1891). The concept of civilizationism is developed in Moses, *The Golden Age of Black Nationalism, 1850–1925* (Hamden, Conn., 1978).

26. Edward Blyden, *Liberia's Offering: The Call of Providence to the Descendents of Africa in America* (New York, 1862). For a fine account, see Hollis R. Lynch, *Edward Wilmot Blyden: Pan-Negro Patriot, 1832–1912* (New York, 1970).

27. For Blyden's development, see Lynch, *Edward Wilmot Blyden*. Some of the changes in his thinking were already registered in *Christianity, Islam and the Negro Race* (London, 1887), published twenty-five years after *Liberia's Offering*.

28. Martin R. Delany, *The Condition, Elevation, Emigration and Destiny of the Colored People of the United States. Politically Considered* (Philadelphia, 1852); Lynch, "Pan-Negro Nationalism in the New World," pp. 54–56. See also Nell Ivrin Painter, "Martin R. Delany: Elitism and Black Nationalism," in Litwack and Meier, *Black Leaders of the Nineteenth Century*, pp. 148–71.

29. "Proceedings of the National Emigration Convention of Colored People . . . August, 1854," in Aptheker, *Documentary History of the Negro People*, pp. 363–66; Geiss, *The Pan-African Movement*, pp. 86–90. See also Lynch, "Pan-Negro Nationalism in the New World," pp. 57–59, which discusses the impact of Bowen's and Livingstone's books. Delany's disdain for Liberia was one of the factors distinguishing him from Henry Highland Garnet, another convert to African emigration in the 1850s. See Sterling Stuckey, "A Last Stern Struggle: Henry Highland Garnet and Liberation Theory," in Litwack and Meier, *Black Leaders of the Nineteenth Century*, pp. 128–47, and Stuckey, *Slave Culture*, pp. 138–92.

30. M. R. Delany, *Official Report of the Niger Valley Exploring Party*, and Robert Campbell, *A Pilgrimage to My Motherland: An Account of a Journey Among the Egbas and Yorubas of Central Africa, in 1859–60*, in Howard H. Bell, ed., *Search for a Place: Black Separatism and Africa, 1860* (Ann Arbor, Mich., 1969). (The quotations are taken from pp. 105–06, 110, emphasis in original). See also Lynch, "Pan-Negro Nationalism in the New World," pp. 59–60 ff.

31. See Don E. Fehrenbacher, *Abraham Lincoln: Speeches and Writings, 1859–1865* (New York, 1989), pp. 357–58.

32. Moses, *Alexander Crummell*, pp. 134–45; Daniel Payne, *The Semi-Centenary and Retrospection of the African Methodist Episcopal Church in the United States of America* (1866; reprint ed., New York, 1972), pp. 129–31; Payne, *Recollections of Seventy Years* (1888; reprint ed.,

New York, 1968), pp. 144–46; "The Negro on Lincoln's Colonization Plan, 1862," in Aptheker, *Documentary History of the Negro People,* pp. 471–75; James M. McPherson, "Abolitionist and Negro Opposition to Colonization During the Civil War," *Phylon* 26, no. 4 (1965), pp. 391–97; Staudenraus, *African Colonization,* p. 246. On the Freedmen's Bureau, see William McFeely, *Yankee Stepfather: O.O. Howard and the Freedmen* (New Haven, Conn., 1968). The nature and duration of Lincoln's interest in colonization has occasioned considerable confusion, largely due to spurious testimony by contemporaries. Claims that Lincoln remained committed to removing blacks at the time of his death appear unfounded. For the debate, see George M. Fredrickson, "A Man But Not a Brother: Abraham Lincoln and Racial Equality," in *The Arrogance of Race: Historical Perspectives on Slavery, Racism, and Social Inequality* (Middletown, Conn., 1988); Don E. Fehrenbacher, "Only His Stepchildren," in *Lincoln in Text and Context* (Stanford, 1987); and Mark E. Neely, "Abraham Lincoln and Black Colonization: Benjamin Butler's Spurious Testimony," *Civil War History* 25, no. 1 (1979), pp. 77–83.

33. Quoted in Clarence A. Bacote, "'Negro Proscriptions,' Protests and Proposed Solutions in Georgia, 1880–1908," in Charles E. Wynes, ed., *The Negro in the South Since 1865: Selected Essays in American Negro History* (New York, 1968). The standard work on emigrationism is Edwin S. Redkey, *Black Exodus: Black Nationalist and Back-to-Africa Movements, 1890–1910* (New Haven, Conn., 1969). While the book remains essential, it probably exaggerates the degree to which "back-to-Africa" was a "mudsill" movement. Atlanta's Bethel Church, for example, was one of the most prosperous AME congregations in the South.

34. All of these themes are explored below.

35. George Brown Tindall, *South Carolina Negroes, 1877–1900* (Columbia, S.C., 1952), pp. 153–68; Redkey, *Black Exodus,* p. 22.

36. Tindall, *South Carolina Negroes,* pp. 153–68. On Cain, see R. R. Wright, *The Bishops of the AME Church* (Nashville, 1963), pp. 119–22; Thomas Holt, *Black Over White: Negro Political Leadership in South Carolina During Reconstruction* (Urbana, Ill., 1977), pp. 126–32. For Cain's career, see the eulogies in *AME Church Review* 3, no. 4 (1887), pp. 337–45.

37. Walter L. Williams, *Black Americans and the Evangelization of Africa, 1877–1900* (Madison, Wis., 1982), p. 40; Wright, *Bishops of the AME Church,* p. 112; Donald Franklin Roth, "Grace Not Race: Southern Negro Church Leaders, Black Identity, and Missions to West Africa, 1865-1919" (Ph.D. diss., University of Texas, 1975), pp. 74–76.

38. Tindall, *South Carolina Negroes,* pp. 161–68.

39. Henry Turner, "Letter to the American Colonization Society, July 18, 1866," and "Speech on the Eligibility of Colored Members to Seats in the Georgia Legislature, September 3, 1868," in Edwin S. Redkey, ed., *Respect Black: The Writings and Speeches of Henry McNeal Turner* (New York, 1971), pp. 13–28. See also John Dittmer, "The Education of Henry McNeal Turner," in Litwack and Meier, *Black Leaders of the Nineteenth Century;* Wright, *Bishops of the AME Church,* pp. 329–41; Redkey, *Black Exodus,* pp. 24–29; and Moses, *Alexander Crummell,* pp. 142–43.

40. Theophilus G. Steward, *The End of the World; or, Clearing the Way for the Fullness of Gentiles* (New York, 1888); James Theodore Holly, "The Divine Plan of Human Redemption, in its Ethnological Development," *AME Church Review* 1, no. 2 (1884). On Swedenborg's influence among African Americans, see Albert Raboteau, "The Black Experience in American Evangelicalism: The Meaning of Slavery," in Leonard I. Sweet, ed., *The Evangelical Tradition in America* (Macon, Ga., 1984), pp. 195–97; and William Seraile, *Voice of Dissent: Theophilus Gould Steward (1843–1924) and Black America* (New York, 1991), pp. 90–91. (Special thanks to George Fredrickson for alerting me to this theme.) Daniel Payne, it should be noted, went out of his way to distance himself and the church from Steward's theology; see Payne, *Recollections,* p. 239.

41. See speeches and writings in Redkey, *Respect Black*. "The Barbarous Decision" was reprinted in the *Christian Recorder*, December 13, 1883.

42. *Voice of the People* began publication in February 1901, following Turner's transfer from the Fourth to the Sixth Episcopal District. *Voice of Missions* continued publication under a different regime.

43. Quoted in Gayraud Wilmore, *Black Religion and Black Radicalism* (New York, 1972), p. 187.

44. See Turner, *Emigration of the Colored People of the United States. Is it Expedient? If so where to?* (Philadelphia, 1879). (Copy in the Benjamin Arnett Papers, Wilberforce University, v. 76.) Turner attributed his free status at birth to an obscure British law against the keeping of royal-blooded slaves in South Carolina. In fact, he probably owed his free birth—and his very fair complexion—to a white maternal grandmother; see Redkey, *Black Exodus*, p. 45.

45. For Turner's letters home from Africa, see *AME Church Review* 8, no. 4 (1892), pp. 446–98. The letters are reproduced in Redkey, *Respect Black*, pp. 85–134.

46. Turner, "Letters," *AME Church Review* 8, no. 4 (1892), pp. 453, 462–63, 476, 488.

47. Turner, "Letters," pp. 467, 478, 482–84. Black church leaders' attitudes toward European imperialism are examined in detail in Williams, *Black Americans and the Evangelization of Africa*, pp. 133–40.

48. Alfred Lee Ridgel, *Africa and African Methodism* (Atlanta, 1896), pp. 39, 45 ff; Indianapolis *Freeman*, August 5, 1893, quoted in Williams, *Black Americans and the Evangelization of Africa*, p. 111.

49. Charles Spencer Smith, *Glimpses of Africa: West and South-West Coast (Containing the Author's Impressions and Observations during a Voyage of Six Thousand Miles from Sierra Leone to St. Paul de Loanda, and Return)* (Nashville, 1895); Wright, *Bishops of the AME Church*, pp. 317–22. On Smith's career in South Africa, see Chapter 7, below.

50. Smith, *Glimpses of Africa*, pp. 5–13, 54, 70–81 ff; Redkey, *Black Exodus*, pp. 206–21.

51. W. J. Gaines, *African Methodism in the South; or, Twenty-Five Years of Freedom* (Atlanta, 1890), pp. 27–28, 258–65; Gaines, *The Negro and the White Man* (1897; reprint ed., New York, 1969), pp. 135–36, 203–13.

52. Classic examples of this "progressive" school of postbellum black history are William J. Simmons, *Men of Mark: Eminent, Progressive and Rising* (1887; reprint ed., New York, 1968), and H. F. Kletzing and W. H. Crogman, *Progress of a Race . . . or . . . the Remarkable Advancement of the Afro-American* (1897; reprint ed., New York, 1969). Needless to say, both books prominently featured the achievements of AME Church leaders.

53. The antiemigrationist position was already in place by the late 1870s; see William H. Yeocum, *Lecture #2: The Exodus Movement: Reasons Why We Should Not Emigrate to Africa* (Providence, 1879). (Copy in Benjamin Arnett Papers, Wilberforce University, v. 76.) The debate reached a peak in the *Christian Recorder* in January and February 1883; the comments cited above appeared in the Jan. 4 and Jan. 18 editions. See also R. R. Downs, "Causes and Effects of the African Agitation," *AME Church Review* 12, no. 4 (1896); Redkey, *Black Exodus*, pp. 30–40, 102–07, 121–26; and the passionate denunciation of emigration in the 1895 AME Episcopal Address, signed by no fewer than seven bishops, in *Voice of Missions*, August, 1895. On Tanner, see Wright, *Bishops of the AME Church*, pp. 323–26.

54. *AME Church Review* 2, no. 1 (1885), p. 72; *AME Church Review* 4, no. 3 (1888), p. 317. Frederick Douglass made an identical argument in a rejoinder to Turner, published in the *Christian Recorder*, February 1, 1883.

55. Several African Methodists left accounts of the Liberian work. See William Henry Heard, *The Bright Side of African Life* (Philadelphia, 1898); Heard, *From Slavery to the Bishopric of the AME Church: An Autobiography* (Philadelphia, 1924); T. McCants Stewart, *Liberia: The*

Americo-African Republic (New York, 1886); and Ridgel, *Africa and African Methodism*. See also Turner, "Letters," pp. 446–98. The existence of slavery is acknowledged in Heard, *Bright Side of African Life*, p. 96. For the debate on the issue within the AME Church, see Williams, *Black Americans and the Evangelization of Africa*, pp. 100–01.

56. J. Dunmore Clark, "An Eye Opener, Based Upon Twelve Years' Experiences on the West Coast of Africa and Seven Years as a Missionary in the A.M.E. Church," *AME Church Review* 33, no. 2 (1916), pp. 63–68; Heard, *Bright Side of African Life*, pp. 100–79 ff.

57. Turner, "Letters," pp. 484–87. See also T. McCants Stewart, "Conditions in Liberia," *AME Church Review* 32, no. 1 (1915), pp. 1–14.

58. Christopher Fyfe, "The Countess of Huntingdon Connexion in Nineteenth-Century Sierra Leone," *Sierra Leone Bulletin of Religion* 4, no. 2 (1962), pp. 53–61; Fyfe, *History of Sierra Leone*, pp. 31–38.

59. Payne, *History*, pp. 486–90; Turner, "Letters," pp. 453, 468–75; Fyfe, *History of Sierra Leone*, pp. 468, 532; Williams, *Black Americans And the Evangelization of Africa*, pp. 46–47, 51; Lynch, *Edward Wilmot Blyden*, pp. 218–19, 245–46. Cf. Alfred Ridgel's interpretation of Islam in his letter to *Voice of Missions*, January 1894.

60. "Interview with Rev. C. Max Manning," *AME Church Review* 14, no. 3 (1898), pp. 374–78. See also "Liberia Mission Lagging," *AME Church Review* 22, no. 1 (1905), pp. 89–90; Redkey, *Black Exodus*, p. 92; Ridgel, *Africa and African Methodism*, p. 21; and Roth, "Grace Not Race," pp. 93–94.

61. *Voice of Missions*, January 1894; Ridgel, *Africa and African Methodism*, pp. 9, 60, 90; J. M. Townsend, *Quadrennial Report of the Missionary Board of the African M. E. Church, 1884–1888* (New York, 1888); Turner, "Letters," p. 471; Henry Turner, *An Appeal for Africa, From the African Methodist Episcopal Church* (Atlanta, 1883). (Copy in Benjamin Arnett Papers, Wilberforce University, v. 76). See also Roth, "Grace Not Race," pp. 78–85.

62. Daniel Payne, "The Past, Present and Future of the A.M.E. Church," *AME Church Review* 1, no. 4 (1885), pp. 317–19; Payne, *Recollections*, pp. 229–32, 299, 306, 312; *History*, pp. 33, 54, 91, 138, 150–51, 210, 236, 293, 318–19, 332, 483–92; Williams, *Black America and the Evangelization of Africa*, pp. 38–39.

63. This argument follows Williams, *Black Americans and the Evangelization of Africa*. On the Congress on Africa, see Frederic Perry Noble, *The Redemption of Africa: A Story of Civilization*, 2 vols. (Chicago, 1893).

64. Williams, *Black Americans and the Evangelization of Africa*, pp. 1–29. For parallel developments within British Protestantism, See Douglas M. Thornton, *Africa Waiting, or the Problem of Africa's Evangelisation* (London, 1898).

65. Williams, *Black Americans and the Evangelization of Africa*, pp. 6–8, 19–29 ff; Roth, "Grace Not Race," pp. 131–63; J. W. E. Bowen, ed., *Africa and the American Negro: Addresses and Proceedings of the Congress on Africa Held Under the Auspices of the Stewart Missionary Foundation for Africa of Gammon Theological Seminary in Connection with the Cotton States and International Exposition* (Atlanta, 1896). White propaganda also had a profound impact on black Baptists, who launched two major missionary societies in the 1890s; see Lewis G. Jordan, *Up the Ladder in Foreign Missions* (Nashville, 1901).

66. On colonial responses to black missionaries, see Lillie M. Johnson, "Missionary-Government Relations: Black Americans in British and Portuguese Colonies," in Sylvia Jacobs, ed., *Black Americans and the Missionary Movement in Africa* (Westport, Conn., 1982); and Chapter 7, below.

67. L. L. Berry, *A Century of Missions of the African Methodist Episcopal Church, 1840–1940* (New York, 1942), pp. 101–14 ff; *Journal of the Twentieth Session of the General Conference of the African Methodist Episcopal Church, Wilmington, North Carolina, May 4–22, 1896* (Phila-

delphia, 1896), pp. 31–32; *Minutes, Reports and Addresses of the First Woman's Day and Special Conference of the Woman's Missionary Society of the African Methodist Episcopal Church. Held in Columbus, Ohio, May 18–19, 1900* (n.p., 1900); Jualynne E. Dodson, "Women's Collective Power in the A.M.E. Church" (Ph.D. diss., University of California, Berkeley, 1984), pp. 130–33, 156–64. On the W.H.F.M.S., see Sara J. Duncan, *Progressive Missions in the South and Addresses* (Atlanta, 1906). For the Baptist case, see Evelyn Brooks Higginbotham, *Righteous Discontent: The Women's Movement in the Black Baptist Church, 1880–1920* (Cambridge, Mass., 1993), which unfortunately appeared after these pages were written.

68. "Early Minutes of the Third District W.M.M. Convention," in Berry, *Century of Missions*, pp. 101–14, 312–23; *Minutes of the Fifth Annual Convention of the Ohio Conference Branch Woman's Mite Missionary Society of the African Methodist Episcopal Church* (Xenia, Ohio, 1900); Duncan, *Progressive Missions in the South*, ff. Copies of the *Missionary Searchlight* and *Women's Light and Love* appear to be virtually nonexistent. Fortunately something of their character and tone can be gleaned from articles reprinted in other periodicals, including *Voice of Missions*, the *Christian Recorder*, and *The Women's Era*.

69. Berry, *Century of Missions*, pp. 103–04, 317; Duncan, *Progressive Missions in the South;* Hallie Quinn Brown, *Homespun Heroines and Other Women of Distinction* (Xenia, Ohio, 1926). On Coppin, who served briefly in South Africa, see Fanny Jackson Coppin, *Reminiscences of School Life, and Hints on Teaching* (Philadelphia, 1913); Linda M. Perkins, *Fanny Jackson Coppin and the Institute for Colored Youth, 1865–1902* (New York, 1987); and Chapter 7, below. Other denominations offered more space for female missionaries; see Sylvia Jacobs, " 'Say Africa When You Pray': The Activities of Early Black Baptist Women Missionaries Among Liberian Women and Children," in Darlene Clark Hine, ed., *Black Women in American History: The Twentieth Century*, vol. 3 (Brooklyn, N.Y., 1990).

70. Anna Julia Cooper, *A Voice from the South* (Xenia, Ohio, 1892), p. 28; Berry, *Century of Missions*, p. 105. On the ambiguities of domestic ideology among African American women, see Paula Giddings, *When and Where I Enter: The Impact of Black Women on Race and Sex in America* (New York, 1984). The chapter in Corinthians states: *Though I speak with the tongues of men and of angels, and have not charity . . . it profiteth me nothing. Charity suffereth long, and is kind; charity envieth not, is not puffed up, Doth not behave itself unseemly, seeketh not her own. . . .* In short, charity, like virtue, was a woman.

71. Berry, *Century of Missions*, pp. 70–71, 110 ff; Amanda Smith, *An Autobiography: The Story of the Lord's Dealings with Mrs. Amanda Smith, the Colored Lady Evangelist* (Chicago, 1893); Dodson, "Women's Collective Power," p. 160. Women enjoyed somewhat greater opportunity to pursue missionary vocations in the National Baptist Convention; see Higginbotham, *Righteous Discontent*.

72. See for example R. H. Cain's comments in the *Christian Recorder*, July 12, 1883. Vital statistics of AME bishops are collected in an appendix to Wright, *Bishops of the AME Church*, p. 383. Benjamin Tanner, elected to the bishopric in 1888, clearly represents an exception.

73. Wright, *Bishops of the AME Church*, pp. 146–50, 264–65. The idea that African missions offered an opportunity to reenact the heroism of an earlier generation is suggested in Roth, "Grace Not Race," pp. 95–96; and Williams, *Black Americans and the Evangelization of Africa*, pp. 107–08. For a contemporary statement, see C. S. Smith's letter in the Nashville *Evening Standard*, January 25, 1890. Smith, who later recanted the sentiment, included the letter in the introduction of his 1895 *Glimpses of Africa*, as evidence of his own initial naiveté about Africa. For Coppin's later career in South Africa, see Chapter 7, below.

74. Parks, "The Redemption of Africa the American Negroes' Burden," in *Voice of Missions*, March 1899. For Mason's comment, see Bowen, *Africa and the American Negro*, p. 146.

75. *Voice of Missions*, March 1899; Levi Coppin, "The Negro's Part in the Redemption of

Africa," *AME Church Review* 19, no. 2 (1902), pp. 506–11. Edwin Redkey, "The Meaning of Africa to Afro-Americans, 1890–1914," *Black Academy Review* 1, no. 1 (1972), p. 14 ff; Redkey, *Black Exodus,* pp. 270–76.

76. Walter Thompson, "The Missionary Work of the A.M.E. Church, as it Relates to Africa," *AME Church Review* 20, no. 1 (1903), pp. 58–59.

77. *Voice of Missions,* March 1899; *The African Methodist Episcopal Hymn and Tune Book* (Philadelphia, 1898), pp. 203–15; Williams, *Black Americans and the Evangelization of Africa,* pp. 42, 104–21, 161–75; Coppin, "The Negro's Part in the Redemption of Africa," p. 511. Camphor's hymn is reproduced in Bowen, *Africa and the American Negro,* p. 236.

78. See Benjamin Arnett, "Africa and the Descendants of Africa," *AME Church Review* 10, no. 2, pp. 231–38. The other quotations are culled from *Voice of Missions,* March 1899; *Voice of the People,* March 1901, May 1902; *AME Church Review* 18, no. 2 (1901), pp. 156–57; and Williams, *Black Americans and the Evangelization of Africa,* p. 107.

Chapter 4. Stretch Forth Thy Hands

1. Some terminological housekeeping: probably no word in African history, save perhaps "nationalism," has been used so frequently and with so little precision as "Ethiopianism." While the use of the term apparently originated with Mokone's movement, anxious colonial officials quickly transformed it into a generic label for anything smacking of black independence and self-determination, and it was in this context that the term spread through the British Empire. Not surprisingly, colonial attempts to demonize the term only enhanced its power among Africans, who invoked Ethiopia in the names of hundreds of different churches. For examples of this usage, to quite different ends, see Daniel Thwaite, *The Seething African Pot: A Study of Black Nationalism, 1882–1935* (London, 1936), and Jomo Kenyatta, *Facing Mt. Kenya* (1938; reprint ed., New York, 1965), both of which stress the role of Ethiopian churches in the rise of African nationalism. Among scholars of African religion, the term has somewhat greater specificity, thanks to Bengt Sundkler's *Bantu Prophets in South Africa,* 2nd ed. (London, 1961), which distinguished between "Ethiopian" and "Zionist" independent churches. Sundkler's typology, however, has problems of its own, not least the tendency to lump movements that need to be examined individually and historically. This chapter addresses some of these concerns by closely examining the origins of the eponymous Ethiopian Church.

2. J. Du Plessis, *A History of Christian Missions in South Africa* (London, 1911), pp. 29–35, 50–60, 91–119. For a broader context, see Andrew Porter, "Religion and Empire: British Expansion in the Long 19th Century, 1780–1914," Inaugural Lecture, University of London, 1991. Missionary memoirs are legion. Among the more interesting to South Africanists are Robert Moffat, *Missionary Life and Labours in Southern Africa* (London, 1834); John Edwards, *Reminiscences of the Early Life and Missionary Labours of the Rev. John Edwards, Fifty Years a Wesleyan Missionary in South Africa* (1886; reprint ed., Graaff-Reinet, 1988); and R. L. Cope, ed., *The Journals of Rev. T. L. Hodgson: Missionary to the Seleka-Rolong and the Griquas, 1821–1831* (Johannesburg, 1977).

3. See Jean Comaroff and John Comaroff, *Of Revelation and Revolution: Christianity, Colonialism, and Consciousness in South Africa* (Chicago, 1991), esp. pp. 1–48.

4. On paternalism and missionary authoritarianism, see Peter Delius, *The Land Belongs to Us: The Pedi Polity, The Boers and the British in the Nineteenth-Century Transvaal* (Johannesburg, 1983), pp. 108–25; H. A. C. Cairns, *Prelude to Imperialism: British Reactions to Central African Society, 1840–1890* (London, 1965), pp. 43–45, 84; and Landeg White, *Magomero: Portrait of an African Village* (New York, 1990), pp. 23, 37, 76. White cites one case in Nyasaland where a missionary flogged an African to death.

5. *Africa's Golden Harvests: The Organ of the South African Compounds and Interior Mission* 18, no. 12 (1923), p. 84. On horticultural metaphors, see Comaroff and Comaroff, *Of Revelation and Revolution*, pp. 80, 170–75, 206–07 ff.

6. For various aspects of mission life, see Norman Etherington, *Preachers, Peasants and Politics in Southeast Africa, 1835–1880: African Christian Communities in Natal, Pondoland and Zululand* (London, 1978); Jeff Guy, *The Heretic: A Study of the Life of John William Colenso, 1814–1883* (Johannesburg, 1983); and Thomas Beidelman, *Colonial Evangelism: A Socio-Historical Study of an East African Mission at the Grassroots* (Bloomington, Ind., 1982).

7. Quoted in Cairns, *Prelude to Imperialism,* p. 241; Etherington, *Preachers, Peasants and Politics,* pp. 68–70, 91, 98 ff; Delius, *The Land Belongs to Us,* pp. 112–20. On the problem of conversion, see Robin Horton, "African Conversion," *Africa* 41, no. 2 (1971), pp. 85–108; Horton, "On the Rationality of Conversion," *Africa* 45, nos. 3–4 (1975), pp. 219–35, 372–99; and John Peel, "Conversion and Tradition in Two African Societies—Ijebu and Buganda," *Past and Present* 76, no. 1 (1977), pp. 108–41. On the cattle killing and its aftermath, see J. B. Peires, *The Dead Will Arise: Nongqawuse and the Great Xhosa Cattle-Killing Movement of 1856–7* (Johannesburg, 1989). The relationship of missionaries to colonial conquest is considered further in Chapter 6, below.

8. On missions and the emergence of an accumulating peasantry, see Colin Bundy, *The Rise and Fall of the South African Peasantry* (London, 1979), pp. xi, 32–44 ff. On the world of the mission elite, see Brian Willan, *Sol Plaatje: A Biography* (Johannesburg, 1984). The bourgeois assumptions of British missionaries are explored in Comaroff and Comaroff, *Of Revelation and Revolution*, pp. 49–85.

9. Richard Gray, "Problems of Historical Perspective: The Planting of Christianity in Africa in the Nineteenth and Twentieth Century," in C. G. Baeta, ed., *Christianity in Tropical Africa* (London, 1968).

10. Joan Anne Millard, "The Role of the Methodist Local Preachers and Other Laity in Potchefstroom, Pretoria and Johannesburg Before 1900" (M.A. thesis, University of South Africa, 1986), pp. 25, 58, 45–48, 86–87. From 1882 on, Methodists in the Cape, Natal, and the Orange Free State operated under the rubric of the Wesleyan Methodist Church of South Africa, while the Transvaal and Swaziland work remained under the Wesleyan Methodist Missionary Society in Britain. In day-to-day practice, the organizations were of a piece and are so treated here.

11. Norman Etherington, "An American Errand into the South African Wilderness," *Church History* 39, no. 1 (1970), pp. 62–71.

12. See the statements of Edward Jacottet in *Report of the Proceedings of the Second General Missionary Conference for South Africa, July 5–11, 1906* (Morija, 1906), pp. 48–49, for a representative statement of missionary ambivalence about surrendering ecclesiastical control to Africans. The best work on the nineteenth-century African ministry is W. G. Mills, "The Role of African Clergy in the Reorientation of Xhosa Society to the Plural Society in the Cape Colony, 1850–1915" (Ph.D. diss., University of California, Los Angeles, 1976).

13. T. D. Mweli Skota, *The African Yearly Register: Being an Illustrated National Biographical Dictionary (Who's Who) of Black Folks in Africa* (Johannesburg, 1932), pp. 34–35, 74–75, 90–94, 250–51; R. Hunt Davis, "School vs. Blanket and Settler: Elijah Makiwane and the Leadership of the Cape School Community," *African Affairs* 78, no. 1 (1979), pp. 12–31; Mills, "The Role of African Clergy," pp. 9, 35–40; Chris Saunders, "The New African Elite in the Eastern Cape and Some Late Nineteenth Century Origins of African Nationalism," in *Collected Seminar Papers of the Societies of Southern Africa in the Nineteenth and Twentieth Centuries,* vol. 1 (London, 1971).

14. Mills, "The Role of African Clergy," pp. 31–33, 41.

15. Mills, "The Role of African Clergy," pp. 25–30; Skota, *African Yearly Register*, pp. 83, 208–11; Millard, "The Role of Methodist Local Preachers," pp. 3, 25.

16. J. M. Mokone, *The Life of Our Founder* (Johannesburg, 1935), p. 10; Mills, "The Role of African Clergy," pp. 19–20; testimony of J. Scott to *South African Native Affairs Commission, 1903–5*, 5 vols. (Cape Town, 1904–5) [hereafter *SANAC*], vol. 4, p. 332.

17. *Africa's Golden Harvests* contains innumerable admonitions against spoiling African mission workers, especially in the years after the South African War, as the society endured a series of "Ethiopian" secessions.

18. *Chronicle of the London Missionary Society*, June 1897; Mills, "The Role of African Clergy," pp. 30, 33; Mokone, *Life of Our Founder*, pp. 10–11.

19. Dozens of such statements can be found in GNLB 205 1697/14/110, which contains the results of questionnaires circulated by the Native Churches Commission. In their report, the Commissioners noted the "numerous complaints from natives regarding the attitude of the present day European missionary toward them, with touching references enhanced no doubt by the passage of time, to the patience, energy, brotherliness and absence of colour feeling of the old time European missionary." *Report of the Native Churches Commission* (Cape Town, 1925), p. 21.

20. GNLB 205 1697/14/110; Cairns, *Prelude to Imperialism*, pp. 34, 51–70; Mills, "The Role of African Clergy," p. 20. On the refusal of missionaries to embrace children at baptism, see interview with Selloane Legobathe by M. T. Nkadimeng, March 1986 (University of the Witwatersrand, African Studies Institute, Oral History Project, ref. 543/544); and interview with Ruth Machwisa by J. Campbell and M. Ntoane, March 2, 1986 (transcript in author's possession).

21. Comaroff and Comaroff, *Of Revelation and Revolution*, pp. 118–25; Cairns, *Prelude to Imperialism*, p. 8 ff.

22. See Thomas C. Holt, *The Problem of Freedom: Race, Labor and Politics in Jamaica and Britain, 1832–1938* (Baltimore, 1992); George M. Fredrickson, *The Black Image in the White Mind: The Debate on Afro-American Character and Destiny, 1817–1914* (New York, 1971); Richard Cope, "Civilisation and Proletarianisation: The 'New Native Policy' of the 1870s," paper delivered to the History Workshop, University of the Witwatersrand, February 1987. South African perspectives on U.S. race relations are explored in John Cell, *The Highest Stage of White Supremacy: The Origins of Segregation in South Africa and the American South* (New York, 1982), pp. 21–33; and in Chapter 9, below.

23. Quoted in Moitsadi Thoane Moeti, "Ethiopianism: Separatist Roots of African National-ism in South Africa" (Ph.D. diss., Syracuse University, 1981), p. 155. See also Stewart's comments on "race development" in *SANAC*, vol. 4, p. 899. Cf. Cairnes, *Prelude to Imperial-ism*, pp. 89–93, 237, which stresses Central African missionaries' relative indifference to racial theories. On the Free Church and the remedial power of education, see George Shepperson, "External Factors in the Development of African Nationalism, with Particular Reference to British Central Africa," *Phylon* 22, no. 3 (1961), pp. 207–25.

24. Stanley Trapido, "'The Friends of the Natives': Merchants, Peasants and the Political and Ideological Structure of Liberalism in the Cape, 1854–1910," in Shula Marks and Anthony Atmore, eds., *Economy and Society in Pre-Industrial Africa* (London, 1980). On the social and political ramifications of the mineral revolution, see Charles van Onselen, "The World the Mineowners Made," in *Studies in the Social and Economic History of the Witwatersrand, 1886–1914*, vol. 1, *New Babylon* (London, 1982).

25. Testimony of E. Farmer to *SANAC*, vol. 4, pp. 652–67. For similar statements by missionaries, see *SANAC*, vol. 4, pp. 404–07, 604, 900. See also R. Hunt Davis, "Nineteenth-Century African Education in the Cape Colony: A Historical Analysis" (Ph.D. diss., University of Wisconsin, 1969).

26. *Report of the Proceedings of the First General Missionary Conference. Held at Johannesburg, July 13–20, 1904* (Johannesburg, 1905), p. 111.

27. Edward Jacottet, *The Native Churches and their Organisation* (Morija, 1905), pp. 10–11 (emphasis in original).

28. Quoted in Davis, "School vs. Blanket," p. 25; testimony of J. Stewart to *SANAC,* vol. 4, p. 906.

29. The standard work on independent churches in South Africa remains Sundkler's *Bantu Prophets.* On Tile, see C. C. Saunders, "Tile and the Thembu Church: Politics and Independency on the Cape Eastern Frontier in the Late Nineteenth Century," *Journal of African History* 11, no. 4 (1970); on the Taung secession, see Q. N. Parsons, "Independency and Ethiopianism in the late 19th and early 20th Centuries," in *Collected Seminar Papers of the Societies of Southern Africa,* vol. 1 (London, 1970); on the Mpondo church, see Mills, "Role of African Clergy," pp. 221–27. The Lutheran Bapedi Church, African Church, and African Native Church await investigation. Information on these and other independent churches can be found in GNLB 205 1697/14/110.

30. *Voices of Missions,* April 1896.

31. Mokone, *Life of Our Founder.* For the context of Mokone's youth, see Peter Delius, "Migrant Labour and the Pedi, 1840–80," in Marks and Atmore, *Economy and Society;* Delius and Stanley Trapido, *"Inboekselings* and *Oorlams:* The Creation and Transformation of a Servile Class," in Belinda Bozzoli, ed., *Town and Countryside in the Transvaal* (Johannesburg, 1983); and Delius, *The Land Belongs to Us.* Mokone's son later characterized himself as a "descendent of slaves" who grew up speaking Dutch, lending credence to the *inboekseling* theory; see NTS 2719 394/301; and Chapter 8, below.

Here and elsewhere, I use the term *mfecane* in a more or less orthodox way. Cf. Julian Cobbing, "The Case Against the Mfecane," paper presented to the African Studies Institute, University of the Witwatersrand, March 5, 1984; and Cobbing, "The Mfecane as Alibi: Some Thoughts on Dithakong and Mbolompo," *Journal of African History* 29, no. 2 (1988), pp. 487–519. For recent interventions in the debate, see J. D. Omer-Cooper, "Has the Mfecane a Future? A Response to the Cobbing Critique"; and J. B. Peires, "Paradigm Deleted: the Materialist Interpretation of the Mfecane," both in *Journal of Southern African Studies* 19, no. 2 (1993), pp. 273–313. A collection of essays on the subject, edited by Carolyn Hamilton, is forthcoming.

32. MHG 77776; Mokone, *Life of Our Founder,* p. 7; Skota, *African Yearly Register,* pp. 209–210.

33. Mokone's early career is rehearsed in several secondary sources, including J. R. Coan, "The Expansion of Missions of the African Methodist Episcopal Church in South Africa, 1896–1908" (Ph.D. diss., Hartford Theological Seminary, 1961); Edward Roux, *Time Longer than Rope: A History of the Black Man's Struggle for Freedom in South Africa,* 2nd ed. (Madison, Wis., 1964); and Carol Page, "Black America in White South Africa: Church and State Reaction to the AME Church in Cape Colony and Transvaal, 1896–1910" (Ph.D. diss., University of Edinburgh, 1978).

34. Mokone, *Life of Our Founder,* pp. 8–9; NSNA 1/1/440 2647/09; Millard, "Role of Methodist Local Preachers," pp. 119, 134. The Wesleyan presence in the Transvaal actually reached back to the 1820s, when Samuel Broadbent began work among the Seleka Rolong at Makwassie. During the *mfecane,* the Seleka Rolong migrated to Thaba 'Nchu, which became Methodism's headquarters in the interior; see below.

35. Mokone, *Life of Our Founder,* pp. 9–10; Millard, "Role of Methodist Local Preachers," pp. 135–36. See also "Synopsis of the Early History of the AME Church in South Africa," in *Journal of Proceedings of the Sixth Session of the South African Annual Conference of the AME*

Church, January 21–27, 1903 (Cape Town, 1903). The social composition of the Marabastad church is examined in Chapter 5, below.

36. Mokone, *Life of Our Founder*, pp. 10–12. Unfortunately, the original document does not survive.

37. Mokone, *Life of Our Founder*, pp. 10–12; Coan, "Expansion of Missions," pp. 88–93.

38. Ethiopia's imaginative power increased still further after the Abyssinians' victory over the Italians at Adwa in 1896; indeed, many colonial officials, unaware of the origins of Mokone's movement, assumed that this was the root of the church's name. See Sundkler, *Bantu Prophets*, pp. 56–57.

39. "Historical Preface" to the *Constitution and Canons of the Ethiopian Catholic Church in Zion* (Bloemfontein, 1919). (A copy of this pamphlet is in NTS 1420 5/214.) See also testimony of S. Brander to *SANAC*, vol. 4, pp. 519–24.

40. The E.C.C. in Zion's "Historical Preface" recounts the falling out with the Anglicans. On his later break with the AME Church, see Chapter 7, below.

41. Sundkler, *Bantu Prophets*, p. 39. The composition of the Johannesburg church is discussed in Chapter 5, below.

42. Mokone, *Early Life of Our Founder*, p. 17. On Tantsi, see Skota, *African Yearly Register*, pp. 105–06. On Mngqibisa, see NSNA 1/1/428 1909/1068, NSNA 1/1/388 3801/07; and MHG 25720; on Timothy Mngqibisa, Abraham's son, see Chapter 9, below. My thanks to William Beinart for information about the conversion of the original Mngqibisa in the 1830s.

43. CO 225 1195/03; MSCE 28 134/1904; *Voice of Missions*, December 1899. On the Edendale community, see Sheila Meintjies, "Family and Gender in the Christian Community at Edendale, Natal, in Colonial Times," in Cherryl Walker, *Women and Gender in Southern Africa to 1945* (Cape Town, 1990).

44. CO 78 4499/01, CO 311 5477/03; Mokone, *Early Life of Our Founder*, pp. 16–17; *Voice of Missions*, November 1898; MSCE 28 134/1904. See also Chapter 5, below. Xaba died, apparently of diabetes, while in the United States for the 1904 AME Church General Conference. His final days are described in Sara J. Duncan, *Progressive Missions in the South and Addresses* (Atlanta, 1906).

45. Skota, *African Yearly Register*, pp. 21, 60–65; MHG 13066. The history of Thaba 'Nchu is meticulously reconstructed in Colin Murray, *Black Mountain: Land, Class and Power in the Eastern Orange Free State 1880s–1980s* (Johannesburg, 1992).

46. S. M. Molema, *Methodism Marches into the Midlands* (Mafeking, 1956), p. 6; testimony of J. Scott to *SANAC*, vol. 4, p. 329; James Stewart, *Lovedale: Past and Present. A Register of Two Thousand Names* (Lovedale, 1887), p. 181; MHG 13066; Murray, *Black Mountain*, pp. 33–40, 165 ff. For an example of Gabashane's attitude toward missionaries, see *Voice of Missions*, February 1899.

47. G. Z. Lethoba, "The African Methodist Episcopal Church in South Africa," unpublished manuscript, 1967, pp. 19–20; *Christian Express*, August 1898. See also "Synopsis of Early History," in *Journal of Proceedings . . . 1903*.

48. NSNA 125 1890/593, NSNA 1/1/323 1967/05; Stewart, *Lovedale: Past and Present*, p. 512; MSCE 27948/1915; testimony of E. Mpela, B. Kumalo, and others to *SANAC*, vol. 4, pp. 368–79.

49. *Voice of Missions*, December 1897, December 1898; Coan, "Expansion of Missions," pp. 115–24; testimony of J. Dwane to *SANAC*, vol. 2, pp. 708–22. On the Amagqunukhwebe, see J. B. Peires, *The House of Phalo: A History of the Xhosa People in the Days of their Independence* (Johannesburg, 1981).

50. *Voice of Missions*, December 1989. On Dwane's subsequent secession from the AME Church, see Chapter 7, below.

51. Missionary interpretations of Ethiopianism and the persistence of those interpretations in the historical literature are examined in Chapter 5, below.

52. Alan Gregor Cobley, "The Caribbean in Africa—A Case Study: Black Political Consciousness and the Afro-Caribbean Community in South Africa," paper delivered to the African Studies Association meeting, St. Louis, November 1991. See also M. Cohn and M. K. H. Platzer, *Black Men of the Sea* (New York, 1978); and Fiona Spiers, "Black Americans in Britain and the Struggle for Black Freedom in the United States," in Jagdish Gundara and Ian Duffield, eds., *Essays on the History of Blacks in Britain* (Aldershot, 1992). For examples, see Harry Dean, *The Pedro Gorino: The Adventures of a Negro Sea-Captain in Africa and on the Seven Seas in his Attempts to Found an Ethiopian Empire* (Boston, 1929); and Owen Mathurin, *Henry Sylvester Williams and the Origins of the Pan African Movement, 1869–1911* (Westport, Conn., 1976). The idea of an African American slave fleeing to sea—in this case on a slave ship—is the starting point of Charles Johnson's remarkable novel *Middle Passage* (New York, 1991).

53. Special thanks to Dr. Atkins, whose research promises to render much of this discussion obsolete. These examples are drawn from Atkins, "Questionable Haven: African American Emigrants in South Africa," paper delivered to the African Studies Association Meeting, St. Louis, November 1991.

54. Clement Keto, "Black Americans and South Africa, 1890–1910," *Current Bibliography on African Affairs* 5, no. 2 (1972), pp. 383–406; E. de Waal, "American Black Residents and Visitors in the S.A.R. Before 1899," *South African Historical Journal* 6, no. 1 (1974), pp. 52–55; Harry Dean, *The Pedro Gorino;* Report of the *SANAC,* vol. 1, pp. 12, 65; Charles van Onselen, *Chibaro: African Mine Labour in Southern Rhodesia, 1900–1933* (London, 1976), pp. 24, 137; *Voice of Missions,* October 1898; R. R. Wright, Jr., *The Encyclopedia of the African Methodist Church* (Philadelphia, 1947), p. 319. For cases revolving around African Americans' uncertain legal status, see SNA 310 627/06, SNA 370 2012/07, SNA 464 1450/10, SNA 471 2256/10; and NTS 1423 12/214.

55. Saunders, "The New African Elite in the Eastern Cape," p. 46; R. Hunt Davis, "School vs. Blanket," p. 23.

56. David Coplan, *In Township Tonight: South Africa's Black City Music and Theatre* (Johannesburg, 1985), p. 38; Veit Erlmann, " 'A Feeling of Prejudice': Orpheus M. McAdoo and the Virginia Jubilee Singers in South Africa 1890–1898," *Journal of Southern African Studies* 14, no. 3 (1988), pp. 331–40. See also Erlmann, *African Stars: Studies in Black South African Performance* (Chicago, 1991). On the Christy Minstrels and local imitators, see Cape *Argus,* August 21, 1863, August 26, 1863, and November 2, 1873. (Thanks to Dr. Erlmann for these and other references.) On minstrelsy, see Robert C. Toll, *Blacking Up: The Minstrel Show in Nineteenth-Century America* (New York, 1974).

57. Erlmann, "A Feeling of Prejudice," pp. 332–38 ff; Cape *Times,* July 5, 1897. On the birth of the Jubilee style, see J. B. T. Marsh, *The Story of the Jubilee Singers with Their Songs* (Boston, 1880).

58. Erlmann, "A Feeling of Prejudice," p. 341; Kimberley *Daily Independent,* August 4, 1890, August 15, 1890, November 11, 1890; Cape *Argus,* July 1, 1890, October 8, 1896; Transvaal *Advertiser,* February 2, 1891, February 9, 1891.

59. Erlmann, "A Feeling of Prejudice," p. 346; Burghersdorp *Gazette,* November 6, 1890; *Imvo Zabantsundu,* December 11, 1890; *Voice of Missions,* June, 1896; MHG 77776.

60. Levi J. Coppin, *Observations of Persons and Things in South Africa, 1900–1904,* 2 vols. (Philadelphia, 1905), vol. 1, p. 140; Sara Duncan, *Progressive Missions in the South,* pp. 94–100; N. B. Tantsi, *Historical Sketch of the AME Church in Southern Africa* (n.p., n.d.). For the text of "Kgoshi Sekukuni," see Mokone, *Early Life of Our Founder,* p. 3.

61. Coplan, *In Township Tonight,* pp. 27–37.

62. Coplan, *In Township Tonight*, pp. 32–36, 44–46; John Knox Bokwe, *Ntsikana: The Story of an African Convert* (Lovedale, 1914); T. D. M. Skota, *The African Who's Who* (Johannesburg, 1966), p. 78.

63. See Richard Alan Waterman, "African Influence on the Music of the Americas," in Sol Tax, ed., *Acculturation in the Americas* (New York, 1952). Waterman's seminal article helps explain Africans' ready appropriation, or reappropriation, of Afro-American music.

64. Erlmann, "A Feeling of Prejudice," pp. 333, 338–43 ff.

65. Coplan, *In Township Tonight*, pp. 135–39 ff; Tim Couzens, "'Moralizing Leisure Time': The Transatlantic Connection and Black Johannesburg," in Shula Marks and Richard Rathbone, eds., *Industrialisation and Social Change in South Africa: African Class Formation, Culture and Consciousness, 1870–1930* (London, 1982). For contention over the black American "model," see Chapter 9, below.

66. Quoted in Erlmann, "A Feeling of Prejudice," p. 344.

67. Clifford Geertz, "Religion as a Cultural System," in *The Interpretation of Cultures* (London, 1975), p. 105. On I.C.U. rhetoric, see Chapter 9, below.

68. Brian Willan, *Sol Plaatje*, pp. 28–57; Willan, "Sol Plaatje, DeBeers and an Old Tram Shed: Class Relations and Social Control in a South African Town," *Journal of Southern African Studies* 4, no. 2 (1978); Erlmann, "A Feeling of Prejudice," p. 346. The evening's program is reproduced in Coplan, *In Township Tonight*, p. 41.

69. *Christian Express*, February 2, 1891, May 1, 1891, November 2, 1891, August 1, 1892; *Imvo Zabantsundu*, December 11, 1890, March 17, 1892.

70. Interview with Kate Manye Makanya by Margaret Nixon, ca. 1962; thanks to Veit Erlmann for sharing a typescript of this interview. On Ransom, see David Wills, "Reverdy C. Ransom: The Making of an A.M.E. Bishop," in Randall K. Burkett and Richard Newman, eds., *Black Apostles: Afro-American Clergy Confront the Twentieth Century* (Boston, 1978); and Chapter 9, below. The Wilberforce students are examined in Chapter 8, below.

71. *Voice of Missions*, September, 1895; "Synopsis of Early History," in *Journal of Proceedings . . . 1903*.

72. Ironically, the misleading chronology of events in the historical introduction of the AME *Discipline* probably contributed to the sense of recognition. By dating the episode in St. George's Church to 1787, Allen and his co-authors gave the impression that the AME Church began as a response to segregation. African churchmen, confronting new forms of segregation in European missions, could scarcely but respond.

73. *Voice of Missions*, December 1895, March 1896, July 1897.

74. *Voice of Missions*, June 1896, July 1896, August 1896; "Synopsis of Early History," in *Journal of Proceedings . . . 1903*. A photograph of the amalgamation ceremony was printed on the frontispiece of the *AME Church Review* 13 no. 3 (1897).

75. *Voice of Missions*, August 1896, September 1896, December 1897, January 1899, February 1899, March 1899.

76. *Voice of Missions*, March 1897, May 1897, July 1897, September 1897, November 1897; Tantsi, *Historical Sketch of the AME Church*, p. 6.

77. Henry Turner, "My Trip to South Africa," *AME Church Review* 15, no. 4 (1899), pp. 809–13; *Voice of Missions*, March 1897, June 1898. Turner's visit was reported, with predictable derision, in Lovedale's *Christian Express*, August 1, 1898.

78. Turner, "My Trip to South Africa," pp. 811–13; Cape *Argus*, April 23, 1898; *Voice of Missions*, June 1898, July 1898, October 1898; Wright, *Encyclopedia*, p. 319.

79. *Voice of Missions*, June 1898. A copy of the ordination list was reprinted in the *Christian Express*, August 1, 1898. In fairness to Turner, many of those he ordained were experienced evangelists who had been denied ordination in missions on racial grounds. On Edward Tsewu

and his falling out with the Free Church of Scotland, see *Defence of the Rev. Tsewu of Johannesburg on Dispute in Church Matters* (Johannesburg, 1897). (Copy in SNA 48 1680/1902.)

Chapter 5. African Methodism as a Social Movement, I

1. *Voice of Missions*, December 1895.

2. Unfortunately, there are no records to provide an accurate count of AME membership in South Africa. The first Union census in 1911 counted more than sixty thousand AME members, but that number appears to include adherents of all independent churches. Allen Lea's *The Native Separatist Church Movement in South Africa* (Cape Town, 1926) estimated AME membership at just over twenty thousand, a figure which seems unduly conservative.

3. SNA 207 533/04; SNA 221 1258/04; SNA 222 1258/04; testimony of E. H. Hogge to *SANAC*, vol. 4, pp. 462–463; testimony of A. Wilson to *SANAC*, pp. 310–14. For a recent interpretation of the eastern Transvaal episode, see Jeremy Krikler, "Social Neurosis and Hysterical Pre-Cognition in South Africa: A Case Study and Reflections," *South African Historical Journal* 28, no. 1 (1993), pp. 65–97.

4. Examples of this logic are too numerous to mention. The quotations above are culled from *Report of the Proceedings of the First General Missionary Conference. Held at Johannesburg, July 13–20, 1904* (Johannesburg, 1905), pp. 26, 130, 177; testimony of J. Stewart to *SANAC*, vol. 4, pp. 680–85; SNA 39 1300/02; SNA 125 970/03; SNA 207 533/04; *Natal Mercury*, August 23, 1902; AG 1387 1259; NA 497 a96; NA 498 a96; *Christian Express*, December, 1901.

5. Leonard Thompson and Monica Wilson, eds., *The Oxford History of South Africa* (Oxford, 1971), pp. 432–36. The chief purveyor of this interpretation, though in a much more nuanced way, has been George Shepperson; see his "Ethiopianism and African Nationalism," *Phylon* 14, no. 1 (1953), pp. 9–18; and "Notes on Negro American Influences on the Emergence of African Nationalism," *Journal of African History* 1, no. 2 (1960), pp. 299–312. For earlier versions of this interpretation, see Daniel Thwaite, *The Seething African Pot: A Study of Black Nationalism, 1882–1935* (London, 1936); and Edward Roux, "The Ethiopian Movement," *Trek* 10, no. 2 (1945), pp. 9–13. More recent examples include Andre Odendaal, *Vukani Bantu! The Beginnings of Black Protest Politics in South Africa to 1912* (Cape Town, 1984); Badra Lahouel, "Ethiopianism and African Nationalism in South Africa before 1937," *Cahiers d' Etudes africaines* 26, no. 4 (1984), pp. 681–88; and J. Mutero Chirenje, *Ethiopianism and Afro-Americans in Southern Africa, 1883–1916* (Baton Rouge, 1987). The tendency "to place all twentieth-century religious movements into a proto-nationalist/nationalist sequence" has been astutely criticized by T. O. Ranger, one of the founders of the nationalist historiography; see Ranger, "Religious Movements and Politics in Sub-Saharan Africa," *African Studies Review* 29, no. 2 (1986), pp. 1–67.

6. The three ministers/officers were H. R. Ngcayiya in the Transvaal, Benjamin Kumalo in the Orange River Colony, and Chalmers Nyombolo in the Cape. See SNA 242 2701/04; SNA 481 3170/10; GH 35/81 31; and CO 666 2899/06. On African Methodists and the S.A.N.N.C., see below.

7. With the exception of the Cape Town example, all these cases are discussed below. For Cape Town, see the columns of the *South African Spectator*, which regularly reported on the progress of the AME Church. On the emergence of a self-conscious "Coloured" community, see Ian Goldin, "Coloured Identity and Coloured Politics in the Western Cape Region of South Africa," in Leroy Vail, ed., *The Creation of Tribalism in South Africa* (London, 1989); and Gavin Lewis, *Between the Wire and the Wall: A History of South African 'Coloured' Politics* (Cape Town, 1987).

8. J. Du Plessis, *A History of Christian Missions in South Africa* (London, 1911), p. 457; James Stewart, *Dawn in the Dark Continent, or Africa and its Missions* (London, 1903), p. 131.

9. See Charles van Onselen, "The World the Mineowners Made: Social Themes in the Economic Transformation of the Witwatersrand, 1866–1914," in *Studies in the Social and Economic History of the Witwatersrand, 1886–1914,* vol. 1, *New Babylon* (Johannesburg, 1982).

10. Special thanks to Michelle Friedman, whose ongoing study of Marabastad promises to fill a major lacuna in South African history. Scattered materials on the community can be found in the papers of the Z.A.R. Staatssekretaris and the Transvaal Colony's Secretary of Native Affairs; see, for example, SNA 131 1184/03. For a linguistic survey, see G. K. Shuring, "Die Omgangs-Sotho van die Swart Woongebiede van Pretoria" (Ph.D. diss., Rand Afrikaans University, 1984).

11. Michelle Friedman, "African Urbanisation in Pretoria, 1902–1924," paper delivered to the Postgraduate Seminar, University of the Witwatersrand, July 28, 1993; and Friedman, "African Urbanisation in Pretoria Prior to 1902," unpublished paper.

12. Friedman, "African Urbanisation in Pretoria Prior to 1902," pp. 14–23; Peter Delius, *The Land Belongs to Us: The Pedi Polity, the Boers and the British in the Nineteenth-Century Transvaal* (Johannesburg, 1983), pp. 108–125. On the rural proclivities of missionaries, see Chapter 4, above.

13. The history of the African Church remains obscure. It appears to have been absorbed into the AME Church along with the Ethiopian Church; Kanyane Napo hosted Bishop Turner during his 1898 visit and was appointed an AME presiding elder. By 1902 or so, the church had regained its corporate character, though it seems to have worked amicably with local African Methodists. By the 1920s the African Church had split into several fragments. See SS 2433 9617/90; SNA 79 2698/02; SNA 243 2822/04; LTG 144 120/03; GNLB 205 1697/14/110, files 1, 17.

14. Johannesburg Gezondheids Comite, *Census* (Johannesburg, 1896), pp. 13–15. It was another fifty years before black Johannesburg again boasted such a high proportion of Christians.

15. SNA 243 2889/04; T. D. M. Skota, *The African Yearly Register: Being an Illustrated National Biographical Dictionary (Who's Who) of Black Folks in Africa* (Johannesburg, 1932), pp. 105–106; *Voice of Missions,* June 1898, July 1898. The problems of evangelization were reduced in Kimberley, a missionary at the 1904 General Missionary Conference opined, because natives were kept "under proper control." See *Proceedings of the First General Missionary Conference . . . 1904,* pp. 32–34. For a similar perspective on the problem of urban missions, see testimony of E. C. Farmer to *SANAC,* vol. 4, pp. 652–667.

16. David Coplan, *In Township Tonight: South Africa's Black City Music and Theatre* (Johannesburg, 1985), pp. 56–89 ff. For a stunning evocation of Marabastad life in the 1920s, see Ezekiel Mphahlele's *Down Second Avenue* (Johannesburg, 1963).

17. Kimberley drew almost as diverse a population in the 1870s and '80s but contributed less to the emergence of these new forms of identity. The explanation, at least in part, lay in urban geography: in Kimberley, Africans were segregated along class lines, with workers, who often migrated to the diamond fields in ethnic cohorts, housed in closed compounds, away from the small "detribalised" elite. The gulf was reinforced by Cape law, which sharply differentiated the "civilised" from the "uncivilised." In short, Kimberley could be comprehended in the categories of nineteenth-century missions in ways that the urban Transvaal could not. The net effect was to make Kimberley less conducive to Ethiopianism.

18. Unidentified clipping, ca. 1904, in SNA 207 533/04; SNA 75 2569/02; NA 497 a96; James Stewart, *Dawn in the Dark Continent,* p. 131.

19. The subscription list is reproduced in Mokone, *The Life of Our Founder,* pp. 14–16. See also Friedman, "African Urbanisation in Pretoria Prior to 1902," pp. 6–8. The point about

youth ought not be pushed too far. At the leadership level, at least, much of the Ethiopians'
support came from older mission workers who had been passed by for promotion; see chapter 4,
above.

20. SS 5403 r5661/96. On *oorlams*, see Peter Delius and Stanley Trapido, "*Inboekselings* and
Oorlams: The Creation and Transformation of a Servile Class," in Belinda Bozzoli, ed., *Town and
Countryside in the Transvaal* (Johannesburg, 1983).

21. Skota, *African Yearly Register*, pp. 70, 105–106, 267; NSNA 1/1/340 1375/1906; SNA
28 930/02; NTS 2726 501/301.

22. SNA 39 1300/02; SNA 128 1114/03; testimony of M. Mokone, J. Z. Tantsi and S. J.
Mabote to *SANAC*, vol. 4, pp. 473–76; *South African Spectator*, April 26, 1902; Charles van
Onselen, "The Witches of Suburbia: Domestic Service on the Witwatersrand, 1890–1914," in
Studies in the Social and Economic History of the Witwatersrand, 1886–1914, vol. 2, *New Nineveh*
(Johannesburg, 1982), p. 43.

23. A number of independent churches sprouted on the mines in the first decade of the
twentieth century, especially among Mozambican migrants, but they seem essentially to have
been burial societies, organized to repatriate the bodies of men killed on the job. In a few cases, the
founders of these churches passed through the AME Church. See the various "Gaza" churches in
GNLB 205 1697/14/110, especially file 9; and *Africa's Golden Harvests: The Organ of the South
African Compound and Interior Mission*, April 1907, October 1907. By the 1910s, the AME
Church was active on a few mines, but for the most part mineowners managed to keep "Ethio-
pian" churches out of the compounds. See GNLB 216 150/15/317; and the testimony of Andrew
Reid Ngcayiya to the 1913 Native Grievances Commission, Transvaal Archives Depot, K358.

24. Shula Marks and Stanley Trapido, "Lord Milner and the South African State," in
P. Bonner, ed., *Working Papers in Southern African Studies* (Johannesburg, 1981). Cf. Donald
Denoon, *A Grand Illusion* (London, 1973). On the exigencies of gold production, see Frederick
Johnstone, *Class, Race and Gold: A Study of Class Relations and Racial Discrimination in South
Africa* (London, 1976); Peter Richardson and Jean Jacques Van-Helten, "Labour in the South
African Gold Mining Industry, 1886–1914," in Shula Marks and Richard Rathbone, eds.,
*Industrialisation and Social Change in South Africa: African Class Formation, Culture and Con-
sciousness, 1870–1930* (London, 1982); and van Onselen, "The World the Mineowners Made."

25. Information on new legislation, and on African responses to it, can be found in the Papers
of the Transvaal Secretary of Native Affairs, Transvaal Archives Depot. See, for example SNA 48
1619/01 (Transvaal Native Vigilance Association), SNA 286 2640/05 (Transvaal Basuto Committee), SNA 337 2868/06 (African National Political Union), and SNA 452 4121/09 (Transvaal Native Congress).

26. On Z.A.R. policy toward the AME Church, see SSA 840 ra3515/99; SS 7747 r3566/99;
LD 141 ag4544/02; Henry Turner, "My Trip to South Africa," *AME Church Review* 15, no. 4
(1899), pp. 809–13. On postwar policy, see, *inter alia*, LTG 144 120/07; SNA 10 393/01;
SNA 143 1475/05; SNA 187 3088/04; SNA 207 533/04; and SNA 247 3105/04. The evolution of state policy toward the AME Church is examined in greater detail in Chapter 7, below.

27. SNA 93 191/03; SNA 207 533/04; SNA 243 2889/04; SNA 411 2392/08.

28. SNA 242 2701/04; SNA 481 3170/10; Odendaal, *Vukani Bantu*, pp. 84–85, 141–42,
272–73 ff; Peter Walshe, *The Rise of African Nationalism in South Africa* (London, 1970),
pp. 44–48. On the political careers of U.S.-educated students, see Chapter 8, below.

29. SNA 287 2893/05; SNA 334 2565/06; testimony of E. H. Hogge to *SANAC*, vol. 4,
p. 463; Brian Willan, *Sol Plaatje: A Biography*, (Johannesburg, 1984), p. 122. On the nationalist interpretation, see footnote 5, above.

30. These issues are elaborated below. On railroad facilities, see R. Ellsworth, "'The
Simplicity of the Native Mind': Black Passengers on the South African Railways in the Early

Twentieth Century," paper delivered to the African Studies Institute Seminar, University of the Witwatersrand, March 14, 1983. AME leaders did pester railway officials, but their concern was not with preferred facilities for elite Africans but with obtaining the concessionary fares available to ministers of other denominations; see SNA 331 2445/06; SNA 341 3294/06.

31. For Sinamela's alleged comment, see Robert A. Hill and Gregory A. Pirio, "Africa for the Africans: The Garvey Movement in South Africa, 1920–1940," in Marks and Rathbone, *Industrialisation and Social Change,* p. 210; for Gabashane's, see SNA 334 2565/06. The village of Schilpadfontein, north of Pretoria, provides a classic case of an African community finding its way into the AME Church amidst a dispute over land title with white missionaries; see J. Campbell, "Chiefly Authority and the AME Church," in *Collected Seminar Papers of the Societies of Southern Africa in the Nineteenth and Twentieth Centuries,* vol. 15 (London, 1990), p. 41. The land issue is discussed further in Chapter 6, below.

32. SNA 287 2893/05.

33. SNA 181 2764/03; SNA 192 63/04; SNA 263 842/05; SNA 287 2893/05; LD 656 ag 1407/04; LD 1038 1295/05; Johannesburg *Star,* April 5, 1905.

34. SNA 287 2893/05; SNA 294 3249/05.

35. SNA 176 2413/03; SNA 242 2889/04; SNA 399 579/08. The statistics on enrollment and funding are culled from *Epitome of the Principal Statistical Figures of the Colony (Transvaal) for the Years 1902–1906* (Pretoria, 1907).

36. Klipspruit's history remains to be written. A few references can be found in van Onselen, "The Witches of Suburbia"; and Coplan, *In Township Tonight.* On the origins of segregation in Cape Town and Port Elizabeth, see Maynard Swanson, "The Sanitation Syndrome: Bubonic Plague and Urban Native Policy in the Cape Colony, 1900–1909," *Journal of African History* 18, no. 3 (1977), pp. 387–410.

37. TPB 690 talg 1856; SNA 276 1591/05; SNA 313 732/06, vol. 1; SNA 325 1722/06.

38. TPB 690 talg 1856; SNA 313 732/06, vol. 1; SNA 407 1754/08. Lagden's position was consistent with the recommendations of the South African Native Affairs Commission, which concluded that independent churches should gradually be brought under administrative control rather than repressed; see Chapter 7, below.

39. Testimony of S. Weigall to *SANAC,* vol. 4, p. 412; SNA 313 732/06, vol. 1–2; TPB 690 talg 1856.

40. TPB 690 talg 1856; SNA 407 1754/08; Transvaal Native Affairs Department, *Annual Report for the Year Ended 30th June, 1908* (Pretoria, 1909), p. 9. The Transvaal Superintendent of Native Education during most of the conflict was a Wesleyan missionary; see testimony of W. E. C. Clarke to *SANAC,* vol. 4, pp. 601–608.

41. SNA 313 732/06 vol. 1–2; SNA 357 957/07; SNA 407 1754/08; GNLB 310 125/19/48. The existence of the Klipspruit school was noted by Ralph Bunche in 1938; see Robert Edgar, ed., *An African American in South Africa: The Travel Notes of Ralph J. Bunche, 28 September 1937–1 January 1938* (Johannesburg, 1992), p. 201.

42. TPB 690 talg 1856; SNA 404 1134/08; SNA 434 2050/09; SNA 470 2129/10; LD 1588 ag 1059/08. On competition over control of the laundry industry in the urban Transvaal, see Charles van Onselen, "*Amawasha*: The Zulu Washermen's Guild of the Witwatersrand, 1890–1914," in *New Nineveh.*

43. TOD 122 E2041. On the Maxekes, see Chapter 8, below.

44. Quoted in Odendaal, *Vukani Bantu,* pp. 110–11; SNA 459 579/10. On Msikinya, see Chapter 8, below.

45. SNA 287 2893/05; SNA 434 2050/09.

46. *Voice of Missions,* October 1895, August 1896, March 1897, July 1897, August 1898; SNA 331 2445/06; SNA 334 2565/06; *South African Spectator,* February 23, 1901, June 15,

1901. On Morrison, see Naboth Mokgatle, *The Autobiography of an Unknown South African* (London, 1971), pp. 66–69; and Belinda Bozzoli, *Women of Phokeng: Consciousness, Life Strategy, and Migrancy in South Africa, 1900–1983* (London, 1991), pp. 66–67. On Marcus Gabashane's trek, see Chapter 6, below.

47. See Timothy J. Keegan, *Rural Transformations in Industrializing South Africa: The Southern Highveld to 1914* (Johannesburg, 1986). Special thanks to Dr. Keegan for sharing his insights into African Methodism in the Free State, as well as a thick stack of references.

48. Tim Keegan, "White Settlement and Black Subjugation on the South African Highveld: The Tlokoa Heartland in the North Eastern Orange Free State, ca. 1850–1914," in William Beinart, Peter Delius and Stanley Trapido, eds., *Putting a Plough to the Ground: Accumulation and Dispossession in Rural South Africa, 1850–1930* (Johannesburg, 1986); Colin Murray, *Black Mountain: Land, Class and Power in the Eastern Orange Free State, 1880s–1980s* (Johannesburg, 1992); William Lye and Colin Murray, *Transformations on the Highveld: The Tswana and Southern Sotho* (Cape Town, 1980).

49. On sharecropping, see Charles van Onselen, *Chameleon Among the Boers: the Life Story of Kas Maine* (New York, 1995); Keegan, *Rural Transformations*, esp. Chapter 3; Stanley Trapido, "Putting a Plough to the Ground: A History of Tenant Production on Vereeniging Estates, 1896–1910," in Beinart, Delius, and Trapido, *Putting a Plough to the Ground*; and Helen Bradford, *A Taste of Freedom: The ICU in Rural South Africa, 1924–1930* (Johannesburg, 1987), esp. Chapter 1. On the emergence and transformation of sharecropping in the American South, see Roger Ransom and Richard Sutch, *One Kind of Freedom: The Economic Consequences of Emancipation* (New York, 1977). For comparative perspectives, see A. F. Robertson, *The Dynamics of Productive Relationships: African Share Contracts in Comparative Perspective* (New York, 1987).

50. Timothy Keegan, *Facing the Storm: Portraits of Black Lives in Rural South Africa* (Cape Town, 1988); Keegan, *Rural Transformations*, pp. 53–54, 74–84, 238fn.7; Ted Matsitela, "The Life Story of Nkgoma Mma-Pooe," in Marks and Rathbone, *Industrialisation and Social Change*; Colin Bundy, *The Rise and Fall of the South African Peasantry* (London, 1979), pp. 212–37.

51. The epitome of this species of rural entrepreneur is Kas Maine, the subject of van Onselen's *Chameleon Among the Boers*. For an exploration of the gender and generational tensions inherent in this movement between town and country, see van Onselen, "The Social and Economic Underpinnings of Paternalism and Violence on the Maize Farms of the South-Western Transvaal, 1900–1950," *Journal of Historical Sociology* 5, no. 2 (1992), pp. 127–160.

52. Keegan, *Rural Transformations*, pp. 18–24, 57–60, 243fn. 97. See also Charles van Onselen, "Race and Class in the South African Countryside: Cultural Osmosis and Social Relations in the Sharecropping Economy of the South-Western Transvaal, 1900–1950," *American Historical Review* 95, no. 1 (1990), 99–123; and van Onselen, "Underpinnings of Paternalism and Violence." The concept of 'moral panic' comes from G. A. Cohen, *Folk Devils and Moral Panics* (New York, 1972).

53. Keegan, *Rural Transformations*, pp. 56–61, 70–73 ff. (The quotation is on p. 58.)

54. NAB 3 238/06; NAB 4 288/06; *Voice of Missions*, November 1898. Xaba's final comment was clearly intended to echo "The Church is Moving On," a popular AME hymn.

55. CO 78 4499/01; CO 110 1562/02. The church at Viljoensdrift was finally removed, along with the remnants of the community it served, in the early 1980s. See Keegan, *Facing the Storm*, pp. 3–4.

56. *Voice of Missions*, August 1898, October 1898, September 1899; NA 497 a96; GS 1797 r1796/98.

57. The best one-volume treatment of the South Africa War is Thomas Pakenham, *The Boer War* (London, 1979).

58. CO 75 4353/01; CO 81 15/02; G. B. Beak, *Aftermath of War: An Account of the Repatriation of Boers and Natives in the Orange River Colony* (London, 1906), pp. 76, 159 ff; S. B. Spies, *Methods of Barbarism? Roberts and Kitchener and Civilians in the Boer Republics, January, 1900–May, 1902* (Cape Town, 1977). For the wartime experience of Africans, see Peter Warwick, *Black People and the South African War, 1899–1902* (Johannesburg, 1983); Bill Nasson, *Abraham Esau's War: A Black South African War in the Cape, 1899–1902* (New York, 1991); and Jeremy Krikler, *Revolution from Above; Rebellion from Below: The Agrarian Transvaal at the Turn of the Century* (Oxford, 1993).

59. Quoted in Beak, *Aftermath of War,* pp. 25–26. Aside from chapters by Warwick and Spies and a few references in Matsitela's "Life Story of Nkgoma Mma-Pooe," the history of the refugee camps remains virtually unwritten. Material on the camps is scattered through the papers of the O.R.C. Colonial Secretary; see, for example, CO 47 2611/01; CO 58 3377/01; CO 81 29/02; and CO 90 586/02. See also LHT 2/2/1/25.

60. LHT 2/2/1/25; CO 73 4262/01; CO 79 4553/01; CO 81 15/02; CO 97 935/02; CO 98 104/02; CO 104 1251/02; CO 236 1727/03; CO 316 5478/03.

61. *Corporation of Bloemfontein Year Book* (Bloemfontein, 1905) [hereafter *CBYB*], p. 40; CO 311 5447/03; CO 379 8851/03; CO 416 1783/04; CO 454 3652/04; CO 471 4521/04.

62. Quoted in Beak, *Aftermath of War,* pp. 158–59; GRD 23 705/02; CS 1019/01; CO 165 4316/02; CO 466 4252/04; Keegan; *Rural Transformations,* pp. 61–64.

63. Warwick, *Black People and the South African War,* p. 161; Matsitela, "Life Story of Nkgoma Mma-Pooe," pp. 220–22; GRD 13 318/02; GRD 23 705/02; CO 437 2813/04; *CBYB,* 1905, p. 40.

64. *Census of the Orange River Colony* (Bloemfontein, 1904), pp. 120, 136–37; NAB 3 238/06. For the church's postwar expansion, see NAB 4 288/06; G 71 196/1; CO 73 4262/01; CO 255 2655/03; CO 292 4544/03; CO 311 5447/03; CO 316 5448/04; CO 484 5199/04; *CBYB,* 1906, p. 70.

65. NAB 1 26/a/05; CO 311 5447/03; CO 679 3257/06; SNA 412 2441/08. On the origins of the Bechuanaland church, see Chapter 7, below.

66. This portrayal is derived from the recollections of oral informants, contemporary observations, and scattered bits of documentary evidence. See, for example, NTS 1423 12/214; L. J. Coppin, *Observations of Persons and Things in South Africa, 1900–1904,* 2 vols. (Philadelphia, 1905), vol. 2, pp. 2, 40, 78–79 ff; and Coppin, *Unwritten History* (New York, 1919), p. 318.

67. MBL 4/1/1/1 176/07; CO 165 4316/02. Details about Bloemfontein's African population are scattered through the Corporation of Bloemfontein's Annual Year Books, 1904–1908.

68. CO 321 5973/03; NTS 1423 12/214; T. D. M. Skota, *African Yearly Register,* p. 50.

69. CO 311 5447/03; CO 316 5748/03.

70. GS 1797 r1976/98; GS 2067 r4278/99; CO 79 4553/01; CO 260 2917/03; CO 316 5478/03; CO 484 5199/ 04; CO 525 7238/04; NA 497 a96.

71. NAB 4 288/06; PAS A29 58/3; PAS A29 64/1; CO 128 2477/02; CO 292 4544/03; CO 316 5748/03; CO 349 7385/03; CO 425 2221/03.

72. PAS 607 1486; NAB 3 238/06; CO 292 4544/03; CO 311 5447/03; CO 316 5748/03; CO 344 7130/03; CO 349 7385/03; CO 484 5199/04.

73. MBL 4/1/1/16 183/7; CO 321 5973/03; *CBYB,* 1904, p. 31.

74. NAB 4 288/06; CO 128 2477/02; CO 292 4544/03; CO 311 5447/03; CO 344 7130/03; CO 523 7127/04; CO 695 3654/06; PAS A30 64/2.

75. HG 4/1/3/1/1 Appeal 11/1904; NAB 4 397/06; NAB 5 666/06; CO 562 9092/4; CO 679 3257/10/06; CO 843 113/7; CO 844 113/4.

76. Testimony of E. T. Mpela, B. Kumalo, and others to *SANAC,* vol. 4, pp. 368–79; CO 666 2899/06; NAB 1 79/a/05; NAB 3 180/6; NAB 4 288/06; MBL 4/1/1/16 178/1908; G 67 103/1. The conflict over women's passes proved particularly enduring, as the work of Julia Wells shows. The state's attempt in 1913 to bring women formally within the rubric of the pass laws produced explosive protests in both Bloemfontein and Potchefstroom—protests led by women, including several prominent African Methodists. See Wells, "A History of Black Women's Struggle Against the Pass Laws in South Africa, 1900–1960" (Ph.D. diss., Columbia University, 1982); and Chapter 8, below.

77. HG 4/1/3/1/1 no. 144–147; CO 316 5748/03.

78. HG 4/1/3/1/1/ no. 144–147; G. Z. Lethoba, "The African Methodist Episcopal Church in South Africa," p. 19. My thanks to the Rev. Lethoba for sharing this unpublished manuscript.

79. HG 4/1/3/1/1 no. 144–147. Significantly, when the AME Church's first resident bishop appeared before the South African Native Affairs Commission in 1903, he was pointedly questioned about the "Bethulie incident"; see testimony of L. J. Coppin to *SANAC,* vol. 2, p. 223. The AME Church survived in Bethulie, though municipal officials conceded the church a site in the location only in 1935; see PAS 329 570/55.

80. *CBYB,* 1907, p. 80; CO 311 5447/03; Keegan, *Rural Transformations,* pp. 210–11.

81. G 110 444/1; Keegan, *Rural Transformations,* esp. Chapter 5; Matsitela, "Life Story of Nkgoma Mma-Pooe," pp. 223–25, 231–32.

82. Keegan, *Rural Transformations,* pp. 137–39; G 71 1968/1; G 110 444/1; G 110 444/5; NAB 1 26/1/05.

83. G 110 444/5; CO 917 933/3.

84. Sol T. Plaatje, *Native Life in South Africa* (1916; reprint ed., Johannesburg, 1982), pp. 78–90; Keegan, *Rural Transformations,* pp. 137–39, 166-95; Keegan, "Crisis and Catharsis in the Development of Capitalism in South African Agriculture," *African Affairs* 84, no. 4 (1985), pp. 371–98; Keegan, *Facing the Storm,* pp. 135–36. On Wilberforce Institute, see Chapter 8, below.

85. The papers of Jacob Nhlapo are deposited at the University of the Witwatersrand Archives. The quotations are from a handwritten biographical fragment in file C8. Barney Ngakane, one of the subjects in Keegan's collection of life histories, followed a broadly similar path; see *Facing the Storm,* pp. 83, 93.

86. CO 403 1123/04; NTS 1434 28/214 vol. 1; Keegan, *Rural Transformations,* pp. 99–100, 103.

87. SNA 229 1869/04; TPB 1004 ta4/7420; NTS 1434 28/214 vol. 1. On political continuities in the region, see van Onselen, *Chameleon Among the Boers;* and Chapter 9, below.

Chapter 6. African Methodism as a Social Movement, II

1. *Koranta ea Beacona,* August 8, 1903, copy in SNA 186 3034/03. On Segale's contributions to the British war effort, and his subsequent disillusionment, see Peter Warwick, *Black People and the South African War, 1899–1902* (Johannesburg, 1983), pp. 40, 46, 176–77.

2. SNA 186 3034/03. In fairness to Plaatje, *Koranta* was consistently critical of imperial policy in the former Boer republics; see Brian Willan, *Sol Plaatje: A Biography* (Johannesburg, 1984), pp. 98–140.

3. See Shula Marks, *The Ambiguities of Dependence in South Africa: Class, Nationalism and the State in Twentieth-Century Natal* (Johannesburg, 1986). On the ambiguities of Plaatje's career, see Brian Willan, "Sol Plaatje, DeBeers and an old Tram Shed: Class Relations and Social Control in a South African Town, 1918–1919," *Journal of Southern African Studies* 4, no. 2 (1978), pp. 195–215; and Willan, *Sol Plaatje.*

4. J. M. Mokone, *The Early Life of Our Founder* (Johannesburg, 1935), pp. 15, 17. On Sekukuni's involvement, see SS 3904 9606/93; SS 5846 r14967/96; SNA 140 1406/03; SNA 189 3216/03; SNA 254 457/06; SNA 341 3257/06; *Annual Report by the Commissioner for Native Affairs for the Year Ended 30 June, 1903* (Pretoria, 1903), p. B38.

5. H. M. Turner, "My Trip to South Africa," *AME Church Review* 15, no. 4 (1899), pp. 809–13; *Voice of Missions*, June 1898, July 1898, January 1899, February 1899, July 1899; *South African Spectator*, September 7, 1901. On Samuel Moroka, see below; on Ramoghopa, see Chapter 8, below.

6. Beinart and Bundy, speaking of the 1920s, dub this eclectic ideology "rural Africanism" and identify it with "Ethiopian" churches. See William Beinart and Colin Bundy, *Hidden Struggles in Rural South Africa: Politics and Popular Movements in the Transkei and Eastern Cape, 1890–1930* (Johannesburg, 1987), pp. 22–23, 34.

7. The literature on relations between chiefs and missionaries is vast. See, for example, Leonard Thompson, *Survival in Two Worlds: Moshoeshoe of Lesotho, 1786–1870* (Oxford, 1975).

8. *Chronicle of the London Missionary Society*, April 1894. On the epistemological gulf between missionaries and chiefs, see Jean Comaroff and John Comaroff, *Of Revelation and Revolution: Christianity, Colonialism and Consciousness in South Africa* (Chicago, 1991).

9. Peter Delius, *The Land Belongs to Us: The Pedi Polity, the Boers and the British in the Nineteenth-Century Transvaal* (Johannesburg, 1983), pp. 113–21. On the importance of such control, see Claude Meillassoux, "From Reproduction to Production: A Marxist Approach to Economic Anthropology," *Economy and Society* 1, no. 1 (1972), pp. 93–105.

10. Delius, *The Land Belongs to Us*, pp. 193–96; Cape of Good Hope, *Blue Book on Native Affairs* (Cape Town, 1893), p. 86; A. J. Dachs, "Missionary Imperialism—The Case of Bechuanaland," *Journal of African History* 13, no. 4 (1972), pp. 647–58. The classic statement of the thesis is N. Majeke, *The Role of Missionaries in Conquest* (1952, reprint ed., Cumberwood, 1986).

11. NA 497 a96. On Dalindyebo, see C. C. Saunders, "Tile and the Thembu Church: Politics and Independency on the Cape Eastern Frontier in the Late Nineteenth Century," *Journal of African History* 11, no. 4 (1970), pp. 553–70.

12. Clipping from *Chambers Journal*, ca. 1904, copy in Grant scrapbook, Papers of the Archbishop of Cape Town, Archive of the Church of the Province of South Africa, University of the Witwatersrand. For a similar assessment, see F. Suter, "The Ethiopian Movement," in *Report of the Proceedings of the Second General Missionary Conference for South Africa. Held at Johannesburg July 5–11, 1906* (Morija, 1907).

13. NTS 533 3/78; NTS 483 6/64; 1/BIZ 6/74 N2/3/3/22. For the case of Moepi, see J. Campbell, "Chiefly Authority and the AME Church, 1896–1910," in *The Societies of Southern Africa in the Nineteenth and Twentieth Centuries*, vol. 15 (London, 1990), p. 41.

14. *Chronicle of the London Missionary Society*, June 1897.

15. These observations are based on a wealth of documentary and oral evidence; see, for example, *Voice of Missions*, November 1898, February 1899. The intervention of the resident bishop, Levi Coppin, is examined in detail in Chapter 7, below. On architecture and the organization of space within European missions, see Brigid Lambourne, "Methods of Mission: The Ordering of Space and Time, Land and Labour on Methodist Mission Stations in Caffraria, 1823–1835," paper presented to the African Studies Institute Seminar, University of the Witwatersrand, August 24, 1992; and Comaroff and Comaroff, *From Revelation to Revolution*, pp. 33, 200–06 ff.

16. Marcus Gabashane reported his trip in *Voice of Missions*, November 1898, February 1899.

17. On the trials of Samuel Moroka, see Colin Murray, *Black Mountain: Land, Class and Power in the Eastern Orange Free State, 1880s to 1980s* (Johannesburg, 1992), pp. 19–32.

18. Murray, *Black Mountain,* pp. 20–22, 30–32, 91–95. Whether or not a church was ever opened is not clear. Gabashane clearly stayed in contact with Samuel and led a campaign to permit him to return to South Africa following the collapse of the Bechuanaland settlement; see SNA 192 45/04.

19. Interview with Shadrach Leshomo by J. Campbell and M. Ntoane, January 10, 1986; interview with Ruth Machwisa by J. Campbell and M. Ntoane, March 2, 1986 (transcripts in author's possession); *Voice of Missions,* November 1898, February 1899; Murray, *Black Mountain,* pp. 21, 91.

20. *Voice of Missions,* November 1898, February 1899; Transvaal Native Affairs Department, *Annual Reports for the Year Ended 30th June, 1905* (Pretoria, 1906), p. B35.

21. SNA89 100/03; SNA 230 2030/19; SNA 263 873/05; SNA 299 3537/05; SNA 448 3687/09; LD 1652 2607/08; NA 498 a96. On liquor legislation, see Charles van Onselen, "Randlords and Rotgut, 1896–1903," in *Studies in the Social and Economic History of the Witwatersrand, 1886–1914,* vol. 1, *New Babylon* (London, 1982).

22. CS 185 15733/02; SNA 328 2059/06; SNA 334 2565/06; Transvaal Native Affairs Department, *Annual Report for the Period 1st July, 1909 to 31st May, 1910* (Pretoria, 1911), p. 11. As late as 1924 a local magistrate estimated that the AME Church counted three thousand adherents in the district that embraced Khunwana; see NTS 1434 28/214 vol. 1; and NTS 1423 12/214.

23. *Voice of Missions,* February 1899; *Chronicle of the London Missionary Society,* January 1896; NA 497 a96.

24. NA 497 a96; Warwick, *Black People and the South African War,* pp. 42–43; *Chronicle of the London Missionary Society,* November 1895, December 1895, January 1896; testimony of Khama to *SANAC,* vol. 4, p. 252. The church had a similarly abortive career in Mafeking. After initially welcoming the church, chief Montsioa disavowed it, lest he jeopardize his close relationship with the Wesleyan mission, which served as a kind of established church among the Tshidi elite. An AME Church did survive in Mafikeng stadt, but it remained largely the province of Mfengu emigrants and other "outsiders." See testimony of Badrile Montsioa to *SANAC,* vol. 4, p. 259.

25. NA 497 a96; *Chronicle of the London Missionary Society,* December 1898.

26. The significance of the episode was first noted in a seminal article by T. O. Ranger, "The 'Ethiopian Episode' in Barotseland, 1900–1905," *Rhodes-Livingstone Journal,* 37, no. 1 (1965), pp. 26–41. See also J. Mutero Chirenje, *Ethiopianism and Afro-Americans in Southern Africa, 1883–1916* (Baton Rouge, 1987), pp. 146–49; and Carol Page, "The Sigcau/Lerothodi/ Lewanika Response to the A.M.E. Church," unpublished paper. For the importance of the Barotseland mission in church circles, see James Stewart, *Dawn in the Dark Continent, or Africa and its Missions* (Edinburgh, 1903), pp. 255–59. For missionary responses to the schism, see *Christian Express,* April 1904, June 1904, July 1904; and *Report of the Proceedings of the First General Missionary Conference. Held at Johannesburg July 13–20, 1904* (Johannesburg, 1905), p. 14 ff.

27. Quoted in Robert Rotberg, *The Rise of Nationalism in Central Africa: The Making of Malawi and Zambia, 1873–1964* (Cambridge, Mass., 1965), pp. 59–60. See also *Christian Express,* April 1904; SNA 207 533/04; and Ranger, "Ethiopian Episode," pp. 27–31. Coryndon's private correspondence, it is worth noting, emphasized not indiscipline but African Methodism's "pernicious" doctrines, not least "the practical equality of white and black races." See Gervais Clay, *Your Friend, Lewanika: The Life and Times of Lubosi Lewanika, Litunga of Barotseland, 1842–1916* (London, 1968), pp. 119–120.

28. SNA 207 533/04; Ranger, "Ethiopian Episode," pp. 31–33. According to a derisive Coillard, Mokalapa's full title on his return was "Arch-Elder, Director of Training Institution,

Presiding Elder, British Barotseland Upper Zambezi and Central Africa"; see *Christian Express,* April 1904.

29. Quoted in Clay, *Your Friend, Lewanika,* p. 94.

30. SNA 207 533/04; NA 497 a96; LTG 144 120/07; Chirenje, *Ethiopianism and Afro-Americans,* p. 149. The Cape administration investigated a charge of fraud against Attaway but determined that there were no grounds to prosecute, since he had apparently placed an order for the materials. See AG 1572 1557/05; and Chapter 7, below.

31. Such a focus also enables us to mine the extraordinarily rich historiographical vein opened up by William Beinart and Colin Bundy. See Bundy, *The Rise and Fall of the South African Peasantry* (London, 1979); Beinart, *The Political Economy of Pondoland* (New York, 1982); and Beinart and Bundy, *Hidden Struggles in Rural South Africa.* While these works rarely discuss the AME Church, they provide a vital context for understanding the church's appeal.

32. All three of these movements await systematic treatment. For information, see NA 497 a96; NA 498 a96; JUS 64 20470/09; GNLB 205 1697/14/110 f12–15, 53; and various documents in the Papers of the Chief Magistrate of the Transkei, Cape Archives Depot. On Dwane's secession from the AME Church, see Chapter 7, below.

33. *Voice of Missions,* March 1897, November 1897; NA 497 a96; NA 498 a96; CMT 3/636; NSNA 297 2677/1902.

34. See Bundy, "Mr. Rhodes and the Poisoned Goods: Popular Opposition to the Glen Grey Council System, 1894–1906," in *Hidden Struggles.*

35. The best sources on the crisis in the region are annual reports by local magistrates, collected in Cape of Good Hope, *Blue Book on Native Affairs* (Cape Town, published annually). See for example *Blue Book* (1893), pp. 55, 64–65; *Blue Book* (1895), pp. 41–42, 57–60, 79–83; *Blue Book* (1897), pp. 30–83. With starvation stalking several districts, officials in Cape Town vacillated on the question of food relief, reluctant to do anything that might encourage the natives' alleged penchant for idleness or otherwise reduce the flow of labor out of the region. The link between locusts and proletarianization is made explicitly by the Chief Magistrate of the Transkei in *Blue Book* (1896), p. 85. For the broad context on the Christian peasantry's decline, see Bundy, *Rise and Fall of the South African Peasantry.*

36. *Blue Book,* pp. 63–64; Bundy, "Mr. Rhodes and the Poisoned Goods," pp. 143–45, 152–55 ff; Charles van Onselen, "Reactions to Rinderpest in Southern Africa, 1896–97," *Journal of African History* 13, no. 3 (1972), pp. 473–88. The tradition that whites introduced rinderpest to force blacks to work survives today, even among educated Africans; see interview with the Rev. D. Segwai, by J. Campbell, December 3, 1985 (transcript in author's possession).

37. NTS 578 6/94 (I); *Voice of Missions,* March 1897, May 1897. On the problem of rural differentiation, see Beinart, *Political Economy of Pondoland,* pp. 131–51; and Beinart and Bundy, *Hidden Struggles,* pp. 10–12.

38. GH 35/84 31; AG 1387 1259; SNA 221 1258/04; *South African Spectator,* August 10, 1901. On the prophecies of Nongqawuse, see J. B. Peires, *The Dead Will Arise: Nongqawuse and the Great Xhosa Cattle-Killing Movement of 1856–7* (Johannesburg, 1989). See also Chapter 9, below.

39. Makiwane, "Notes on the Ethiopian Movement," in GH 35/84 31.

40. Beinart, *Political Economy of Pondoland,* pp. 9–41, 138, 153. On the Mpondo church, see W. G. Mills, "The Role of African Clergy in the Reorientation of Xhosa Society to the Plural Society in the Cape Colony, 1850–1915" (Ph.D. diss., University of California, Los Angeles, 1975), pp. 221–27.

41. *Blue Book* (1896), p. 153; *Blue Book* (1897), pp. 114–19; Beinart, *Political Economy of Pondoland,* pp. 34–39.

42. Harry Dean, *The Pedro Gorino: The Adventures of a Negro Sea Captain in Africa and on the*

Seven Seas in his Attempts to Found an Ethiopian Empire (Boston, 1929), pp. 174–76. On Dean's passage through Pondoland, see below.

43. NTS 132 f243; NA 497 a96; Dean, *The Pedro Gorino*, p. 186; Beinart, *Political Economy of Pondoland*, pp. 153–54.

44. *Voice of Missions*, August 1899, February 1900. See also Page, "The Sigcau/Lerothodi/ Lewanika Response to the AME Church."

45. *Voice of Missions*, February 1900, April 1900; Dean, *The Pedro Gorino*, p. 205; NA 497 a96; GH 35/85 31; LTG 144 120/07.

46. NA 686 2610; Beinart, *Political Economy of Pondoland*, pp. 104–105. Much to officials' relief, Sigcau died before dispatching Marelane to America. The administration, acting with the support of the regent, Mhlanga, bundled him off to the more temperate climate of Lovedale. On U.S. education, see Chapter 8, below.

47. S 3/9/2/5; S 3/16/4/7; SNA 75 2569/02; NA 497 a96; NAB 4 288/06; testimony of Lerothodi, Molapo, Theka, Maama, and other chiefs and counsellors to *SANAC*, vol. 4, pp. 382–98; Coppin, *Observations of Persons and Things in South Africa, 1900–1904*, 2 vols. (Philadelphia, 1905), vol. 1, pp. 150–80; Page, "The Sigcau/Lerothodi/Lewanika Response to the AME Church."

48. Dean, *The Pedro Gorino*, pp. 139–45, 174–252 ff; NA 497 a96. Rideout seems never to have reached Bechuanaland.

49. On headmen, see W. D Hammond-Tooke, *Command or Consensus: The Development of Transkeian Local Government* (Cape Town, 1977); Max Gluckman, *Order and Rebellion in Tribal Africa* (London, 1963); and Colin Bundy, "A Voice in the Big House: The Career of Headman Enoch Mamba," in *Hidden Struggles*.

50. Beinart, *Political Economy of Pondoland*, pp. 17, 36–39 ff. Among the Mpondo, witchcraft accusations often provided a mechanism for restricting accumulation of wealth and power by individuals, especially individuals of common birth.

51. NTS 132 f243. Marelane, Sigcau's heir, later employed an identical tactic in a disputed location in Tabankulu district; see CMT 3/938 784; and Beinart, *Political Economy of Pondoland*, p. 116.

52. NA 497 a96; NA 498 a96; GH 35/85 31; NTS 132 f243; NTS 239 f570.

53. Testimony of Enoch Mamba to *SANAC*, vol. 4, pp. 1032–49. (The comment about American education is on p. 1043.) While noting Mamba's testimony, Bundy overlooks his involvement with the AME Church; see "Voice in the Big House," in *Hidden Struggles*. On the AME school, see Chapter 8, below.

54. NA 497 a96; Beinart, *Political Economy of Pondoland*, p. 112.

55. NA 498 a96. On Magaba, see Papers of the Archbishop of Cape Town, Church of the Province of South Africa Archives, University of the Witwatersrand, Aa1.1.

56. NTS 578 6/94; NTS 483 6/64; NA 497 a96; NA 498 a96. The Cape administration would soon find support from an unexpected quarter: African American church leaders. See Chapter 7, below.

57. NTS 576 B1290; NTS 578 6/94 (I); GH 35/85 31; NA 497 a96; *Voice of Missions*, June 1900. For a similar case in Peddie district, which persisted into the 1930s, see NA 498 a96; and NTS 598 8/101–10/101.

58. Herschel illustrates the process of rural impoverishment so well that historians have made a cottage industry out of writing about it. William Macmillan's *Complex South Africa* (London, 1930) includes a close study of the district, as does Bundy's *Rise and Fall of the South African Peasantry*.

59. NA 497 a96; NA 498 a96.

60. LND 1/840 L15043; NA 497 a96; NA 498 a96.

61. NTS 299 1351/1912/f799; NTS 483 6/64; NA 497–498 a96; 2/SPT 16 N1/9/2 (Mng-qibisa). While Beinart acknowledges the presence of the AME Church in Herschel, he overlooks the church's central role in the upheavals of the 1920s, as well as in the twenty years of conflict that preceded them. His contention that African Methodism "had not attracted many followers in Herschel" prior to the 1920s is not accurate. See William Beinart, "Women in Rural Politics: Herschel District in the 1920s and 1930s," in Belinda Bozzoli, ed., *Class, Community and Conflict: South African Perspectives* (Johannesburg, 1987); and Beinart, "*Amafelandawonye* (the Diehards): Popular Protest and Women's Movements in Herschel District in the 1920s," in *Hidden Struggles.* We will return to Herschel in Chapter 9, below.

62. *Chronicle of the London Missionary Society,* December 1893, December 1895.

63. Stewart, *Dawn in the Dark Continent,* p. 132.

64. NTS 574 7/92; excerpt from a speech by C. S. Smith, *AME Church Review* 23, 2 (1906), pp. 186–87.

65. On the political salience of land in South Africa—"the fastest short-cut through South African history imaginable"—see Helen Bradford, *A Taste of Freedom: The ICU in Rural South Africa, 1924–1930* (Johannesburg, 1987), pp. 34–35, 113 ff; and Chapter 9, below.

66. GH 35/84 31; AG 1601 4282; SNA 221 1258/04. See also Chapter 9, below.

67. Links between the I.C.U. and the AME Church are examined in detail in Chapter 9, below.

Chapter 7. The Making of a Religious Institution

1. See SNA 125 970/03; SNA 207 533/04; NA 498 a96; AG 1387 1259; NGH 1547. Colonial responses to the AME Church are discussed in more detail in Chapter 5, above.

2. *Voice of Missions,* March 1899. See also Chapters 3 and 4, above.

3. *Voice of Missions,* December 1895, April 1896, July 1897, October 1898, November 1898.

4. *Voice of Missions,* July 1896, June 1898, July 1898, November 1898; H. M. Turner, "My Trip to South Africa," *AME Church Review* 15, no. 4 (1899), pp. 809–10. On Turner's visit, see Chapter 4, above.

5. *Voice of Missions,* March 1898, June 1898, November 1898; *Journal of the Twenty-First Quadrennial Session of the General Conference of the African M.E. Church. Columbus, Ohio, May 7–25, 1900* (Philadelphia, 1900), p. 450.

6. *Christian Recorder,* December 1, 1898, December 15, 1898, December 29, 1898; GH 35/84 (31); NA 497 a96. The controversy is discussed in detail in J. R. Coan, "The Expansion of Missions of the African Methodist Episcopal Church in South Africa, 1896–1908" (Ph.D. diss., Hartford Theological Seminary, 1961), pp. 177–92.

7. *Voice of Missions,* January 1899, February 1899, March 1899; GH 35/84 (31); Coan, "Expansion of Missions," pp. 192–208; Paul O. Hentsch, "The Separate Churches Among the Coloured People of South Africa," *AME Church Review* 33, no. 2 (1916), p. 136; Bengt Sundkler, *Bantu Prophets in South Africa,* 2nd ed. (Oxford, 1961), pp. 40–41.

8. *Voice of Missions,* December 1899; January 1900, February 1900; NA 497 a96. The minutes of the secessionary conference are included in "Resolutions of the Synod of the Bishops of the Province of South Africa, August 22, 1900," in Papers of the Archbishop of Cape Town, Church of the Province of South Africa Archives, University of the Witwatersrand, Aa1.1.

9. Dudley Kidd, *The Essential Kaffir* (London, 1904), p. 407; testimony of J. Dwane to *SANAC,* vol. 2, pp. 709. The catechism in question, Henry Turner's *The Genius and Theory of Methodist Polity, or the Machinery of Methodism* (Philadelphia, 1885) actually fudged the issue, disavowing the principle of apostolic succession while simultaneously maintaining that the

church possessed valid orders, through Absalom Jones, an ordained Anglican minister and one of the men who laid hands on Allen. For contemporary debates on the issue, see Daniel Payne, *History of the African Methodist Episcopal Church* (1891; reprint ed., New York, 1968) pp. 244–45; Payne, *Recollections of Seventy Years* (1888; reprint ed., New York, 1968), p. 299.

10. Testimony of J. Dwane to *SANAC,* vol. 2, pp. 709–10.

11. Testimony of J. Dwane to *SANAC,* vol. 2, p. 716; Papers of the Archbishop of Cape Town, Aa1.1, Aa1.5.

12. African expectations are discussed further in T. D. Verryn, *A History of the Order of Ethiopia* (Cleveland, Transvaal, 1972); and Elizabeth Tuckey, "The Order of Ethiopia: A Study of African Church Independency, 1900–1916" (B. A. (Hons.) thesis, University of the Witwatersrand, 1977).

13. See correspondence and documents in the Papers of the Archbishop of Cape Town, especially *The Order of Ethiopia: The Compact of 1900, Constitution and Form of Admission* (Queenstown, 1900); and *Pastoral Letter Issued by the Archbishop and Bishops, August, 1900* (Cape Town, 1900). On the Order's subsequent history, see Verryn, *A History of the Order of Ethiopia.*

14. *Voice of Missions,* December 1899, January 1900, February 1900, April 1900; C. Nontshinga-Citashe, *Brief Outline of the History of the Ethiopian Church of South Africa* (Morija, 1957), pp. 22–24.

15. *Voice of Missions,* December 1899, March 1900, April 1900, May 1900.

16. *Voice of Missions,* May 1900.

17. See Chapter 5, above.

18. NSNA 1/1/320 1905/1159; NSNA 1/1/323 1905/1767; NSNA 1/1/329 1905/2948; NSNA 1/1/340 1906/1375; NSNA 1/1/373 1907/2066; NSNA 1/1/427 1909/937; NSNA 1/1/428 1909/1068; NSNA 1/1/439 1909/2491; NTS 132 f243; GOV 1160 ps56/1/08.

19. GOV 1160 ps56/1/08; NA 497 a96; NA 498 a96; GH 35/85 (31). On the Thembuland Church, see C. C. Saunders, "Tile and the Thembu Church: Politics and Independency on the Cape Eastern Frontier in the Late Nineteenth Century," *Journal of African History* 11, no. 4 (1970), pp. 553–70.

20. GH 35/85 (31).

21. GOV 1160 ps56/1/08.

22. GH 35/85 (31); NA 497 a96. The agreement was summarized in a memorandum from the Cape Colonial Secretary, reprinted in *Voice of Missions,* May 1900.

23. Report of the SANAC, vol. 1, pp. 63–65. For examples of Stanford's role on the Commission, see his cross examination of witnesses in vol. 4, pp. 313, 463; and his dissent from the conclusions on African landownership, vol. 1, p. 36. On the Commission, see Adam Ashforth, *The Politics of Official Discourse in Twentieth-Century South Africa* (Oxford, 1990), pp. 22–68; on the spread of Cape policy, see SNA 75 2569/02; SNA 75 2557/02; SNA 207 533/04; CS 45 6077/01; GOV 1160 ps56/1/08.

24. SNA 241 2649/04; SNA 313 732/06; SNA 397 523/08; SNA 407 1754/08; TPB 690 talg1854; CO 417 1825; CMT 3/637 65/3; NTS 132 f243; NTS 133 4035/f243; NTS 242 2981/12/f572; NTS 1423 12/214. On Lagden and the "Ethiopian" school at Klipspruit, see Chapter 5, above. On the role of "Ethiopianism" in the Bambatha rebellion, see Shula Marks, *Reluctant Rebellion: The 1906–08 Disturbances in Natal* (Oxford, 1970).

25. *Voice of Missions,* April 1900, May 1900, June 1900.

26. *AME Church Review* 16, no. 3 (1900), pp. 382–83.

27. *Journal* of the 1900 General Conference, pp. 122, 142–43, 174–78, 403; *Voice of Missions,* June 1900, September 1900.

28. On the bishop, see Levi J. Coppin, *Unwritten History* (Philadelphia, 1919); Coppin, *The*

Key to Scriptural Interpretation (Philadelphia, 1895); R. R. Wright, Jr., *The Bishops of the A.M.E. Church* (Nashville, 1963), pp. 146–50; and Chapter 2, above. On Mrs. Coppin, see Fanny Jackson Coppin, *Reminiscences of School Life, and Hints on Teaching* (Philadelphia, 1913); and Linda M. Perkins, *Fanny Jackson Coppin and the Institute for Colored Youth* (New York, 1987).

29. The bishop's library and a few surviving papers are housed at the Wilberforce University Archives. For his role in Easter Day collections, see *Voice of Missions*, June 1898. For F. J. Coppin's travels, see Coppin, *Unwritten History*, pp. 297, 359–63.

30. Levi Coppin, *Observations of Persons and Things in South Africa, 1900–1904*, 2 vols. (Philadelphia, 1905), vol. 1, pp. 21, 59–64, 73 ff. One of the most embarrassing moments of Coppin's tenure came during his initial voyage, as he was discoursing on the church's work among the "Kaffirs." A white Methodist missionary pointedly informed him that no such group existed, that *kaffir* was a term of derogation. Coppin never used it again; see *Unwritten History*, pp. 313–14. For Fanny Jackson Coppin's speech, see "Minutes of the Sixth Session of the South African Annual Conference of the African Methodist Episcopal Church, held at Port Elizabeth, January 21–27, 1903." (The handwritten [and unpaginated] minutes of this and other early AME conferences can be found in the D. P. and E. M. Gordon Papers, University of the Western Cape Archives. Thanks to J. Joubert for granting me access to this uncatalogued collection.)

31. Levi Coppin, "The Negroes' Part in the Redemption of Africa," *AME Church Review* 19, no. 2 (1902), pp. 506–12; and *Observations*, vol. 1, pp. 67–78, 113–14, ff. In his autobiography, Coppin perceptively noted that missionaries perpetuated images of "poor benighted Africa" to capitalize on "the credulity of those from whom they hope to receive larger donations." See *Unwritten History*, p. 320.

32. Levi Coppin, "The Outlook in the Fourteenth District," *AME Church Review* 20, no. 3 (1904), pp. 237–42; and *Observations*, vol. 1, pp. 111–13, 118–30. How strictly the prohibition against polygamy was enforced remains, of course, problematic; see Chapter 6, above. The problem of episcopal authority is discussed in more detail below.

33. *Journal* of the 1900 General Conference, pp. 192–94; *Voice of Missions*, August 1900.

34. Coppin, "The Negroes' Part in the Redemption of Africa," p. 510.

35. Coppin, *Observations*, vol. 1. pp. 7–15, 27; Coppin "The Outlook in the Fourteenth District," pp. 237–42. See also Coppin's letter to the *South African Spectator*, May 31, 1902; his opening address in "Minutes" of the 1903 South African Annual Conference; and the editorial in the *AME Church Review* 18, no. 3 (1902), pp. 263–64.

36. Coppin, *Observations*, vol. 1. pp. 16–18, 100, 202–03; SNA 207 533/04; *South African Spectator*, May 4, 1901, June 1, 1901, August 24, 1901, September 21, 1901. (For the text of Coppin's lecture, "From Bondage to Freedom," see the June 1 edition of the *Spectator*.)

37. *South African Spectator*, February 8, 1902. On Peregrino, who often doubled as a government informer, see C. C. Saunders, "F.Z.S. Peregrino and the South African Spectator," *South African Library Quarterly Bulletin* 32, no. 1 (1977–78), pp. 81–91; and SNA 405 1304/08.

38. See Coppin, *Observations*, vol. 1. pp. 109–12, 123; vol. 2, p. 27; Coppin, *Unwritten History*, pp. 314–15. See also the bishop's injunctions against proselytizing in "Minutes" of the 1903 South African Conference.

39. NA 497 a96; NA 498 a96; NTS 299 1351/1912/f799; NTS 483 6/64; NTS 598 8/101. On Ngcayiya, see T. D. M. Skota, *An African Yearly Register: Being an Illustrated National Biographical Dictionary (Who's Who) of Black Folks in Africa* (Johannesburg, 1932), p. 78; and Chapter 4, above.

40. NA 497 a96.

41. NA 497 a96.

42. *South African Spectator,* July 27, 1901, December 7, 1901; May 31, 1902; *Voice of Missions,* June, 1900; Coppin, *Observations,* vol. 2, pp. 127, 193–202. The handwritten "Minutes of the Fourth Session of the South African Annual Conference, Held at Cape Town, December 18–20, 1901" can be found in the Gordon Papers.

43. See Coppin's address in "Minutes" of the 1903 South African Conference.

44. Coppin, *Observations,* vol. 2, pp. 130–34, 148, 178–80.

45. Coppin, *Observations,* vol. 2, pp. 178–85; *South African Spectator,* September 7, 1901, September 21, 1901, October 5, 1901, December 7, 1901, February 22, 1902; *Voice of the People,* June 1903. For a biographical sketch, see R. R. Wright, Jr., *Who's Who in the General Conference, 1912* (Philadelphia, 1912), p. 136.

46. Testimony of A. H. Attaway to *SANAC,* vol. 2, pp. 252–61; *South African Spectator,* November 9, 1901, November 23, 1901, April 26, 1902, May 31, 1902. (The Nov. 23 issue of the *Spectator* includes the text of Attaway's lecture.) On Bethel's curriculum, see testimony of L. J. Coppin to *SANAC,* vol. 2, pp. 215–16.

47. *South African Spectator,* November 23, 1901; LC 145 302/299/04; SNA 40 1312/02.

48. On the Liberian mission, see Chapter 3, above; on Dean and the Lewanika fiasco, see Chapter 6. Fitzpatrick advertised his wonder in the columns of *Voice of Missions* and *Voice of the People.*

49. NTS 2963 136/305; NA 497 a96; NSNA 1/1/311 891/04; LC 145 302/04/279; R. R. Wright, Jr., *The Encyclopedia of African Methodist Church* (Philadelphia, 1947), p. 322.

50. LC 260 712; NA 497 a96; MOH 390 L56h; SNA 390 4024/07; S3/9/2/5. For more on Attaway's peculations see Andrew Paterson "Contest and Co-optation: The Struggle for Schooling in the African Independent Churches of the Cape Colony, c. 1895–1920 (Ph.D. diss., University of Cape Town, 1992). Attaway continued his entrepreneurial career after returning to the United States. See A. H. Attaway, *The Race Question: Another Angle. A Tract of the Negro Co-operative Health and Education Congress* (Jackson, 1918).

51. Dennis C. Dickerson, ed., *The Land of the Southern Cross: John A. Gregg and South Africa* (North Adams, Mass., 1990), pp. 18–22, 27, 34 ff. Special thanks to Dr. Dickerson for a copy of this valuable pamphlet. See also Wright, *Encyclopedia of the African Methodist Church,* pp. 122, 320.

52. Dickerson, *Land of the Southern Cross,* pp. 27, 31–33. On Chatsworth school, which survived through the 1930s, see PAE 45 cms96/10. On Gregg's episcopal career, see Chapter 9, below.

53. C. M. Tanner, *A Manual of the African Methodist Episcopal Church: Being a Course of Twelve Lectures for Probationers and Members* (Philadelphia, 1900); *South African Spectator,* March 1903, October 1903, February 1904; Coppin, *Reminiscences of School Life,* pp. 165–66. See also "Minutes of the 1903 South African Conference"; and "Minutes of the Convention of the Cape District Held in Bethel Church, February 24, 1904," with Tanner presiding, in the Gordon Papers. Unfortunately, I have been unable to locate any copies of the S.A. *Christian Recorder* from this period.

54. Tanner's article was reprinted in *Voice of the People,* February 1904. See also Coppin, *Observations,* vol. 1, pp. 53, 199; and "Minutes of the Combined South African and Transvaal Conference, Held at Aliwal North, December 2–6, 1903," in the Gordon Papers.

55. "Minutes" of the 1903 Combined South African and Transvaal Conference; testimony of M. Makgatho to *SANAC,* vol. 4, pp. 199–205; testimony of M. M. Mokone, J. Z. Tantsi, and S. J. Mabote to *SANAC,* vol. 4, pp. 473–76.

56. "A protest against a dangerous, misleading information [*sic*] and erroneous spirit by Revd. C. M. Tanner . . . ," and accompanying petition, in CO 460 3970/04.

57. Testimony of S. J. Brander, J. M. Mphela and S. Nguato to *SANAC,* vol. 4,

pp. 519–24. See also "Historical Preface" to *The Constitution and Canons of the Ethiopian Catholic Church in Zion* (Bloemfontein, 1919), copy in NTS 1420 5/214.

58. See Chapter 8, below.

59. "Declaration of the Bishops of the African Methodist Episcopal Church, 1904," copy in SNA 241 2649/04. See also the editorial in the *AME Church Review* 20, no. 3 (1904), pp. 298–99.

60. *Voice of the People*, February 1903, August 1903.

61. Charles Spencer Smith, *A History of the African Methodist Episcopal Church* (Philadelphia, 1922), p. 224; LTG 144 120/07; NA 497 a96; Wright, *Bishops of the A.M.E. Church*, pp. 317–22. On the 1894 voyage, see Smith, *Glimpses of Africa: West and Southwest Coast (Containing the Author's Impressions and Observations during a Voyage of Three Thousand Miles from Sierra Leone to St. Paul de Loando, and Return).* (Nashville, 1895); and Chapter 3, above.

62. Testimony of C. S. Smith to *SANAC*, vol. 4, pp. 957–66; LTG 144 120/07.

63. SNA 48 1680/02; SNA 75 2569/03; testimony of E. T. Mpela, B. Kumalo, and others to *SANAC*, vol. 4, pp. 368–79; C. S. Smith, *Blue Book of the AME Church in South Africa*, copy in S3/9/2/5. On Kumalo, see Chapters 4 and 5, above; on Lerotholi, see Chapter 6.

64. Coppin, *Observations*, vol. 1, pp. 24–25; SNA 207 533/04; Wright, *Encyclopedia of the African Methodist Church*, pp. 321–22.

65. LTG 144 120/07; SNA 207 533/04; GH 35/85 (31). See also "Memorandum" by H. A. Fortuin in the Gordon Papers.

66. "Minutes of the Eighth Annual Conference of the Cape Colony held at Kimberley, March 15–20, 1905," in the Gordon Papers; SNA 207 533/04; C. S. Smith, *Excerpts from a Sermon by Bishop C. S. Smith, May 21, 1905*, copy in NAB 1 26/1/05.

67. SNA 207 533/04; SNA 241 2649/04; SNA 279 1997/07; LTG 144 120/07. The tribunal apparently consisted of Benjamin Kumalo, H. R. Ngcayiya, Abel Gabashane, Henry Msikinya, J. Z. Tantsi, Isaiah Sishuba, and Samuel Mabote.

68. See C. S. Smith, *The Government of Cape Colony, South Africa, Sustains Bishop C. S. Smith;* Smith, *Extracts from a Sermon;* and Smith, *Blue Book of the AME Church*, copies in LTG 144 120/07. See also SNA 207 533/04; and NAB 1 26/1/05.

69. LTG 144 120/07; NTS 598 8/101; NA 497 a96; GH 35/84 (31).

70. SNA 412 2441/08; NTS 1434 28/214 v.1; CO 679 3257/06; CO 988/08; NAB 1 26/a/04; NAB 4 397/06; NA 497 a96. Cf. B. A. Pauw, *Religion in a Tswana Chiefdom* (London, 1960), which portrays the Bechuanaland Church schism as a "language dispute."

71. SNA 353 358/07; NAB 4 288/06; CO 679 3257/06; Wright, *Bishops of the AME Church*, pp. 155–57, 317–22.

72. GNLB 205 1697/14/110 f9; SNA 322 1475/06; NAB 4 288/06. The standard work on Apostolic or "Zionist" churches is Bengt Sundkler's *Zulu Zion, and Some Swazi Zionists* (London, 1976).

73. NSNA 1/1/388 3801/07; SNA 441 1177/08; GOV 1096 ps56/5/07.

74. SNA 279 1997/05; SNA 399 585/08; S3/9/2/5; Nontshinga-Citashe, *Brief Outline of the History of the Ethiopian Church*, pp. 28–29 ff; Bloemfontein *Friend*, April 3, 1907.

75. *Journal of the Twenty-Third Quadrennial Conference of the African Methodist Episcopal Church, Norfolk, Virginia, May 4–21, 1908* (Nashville, 1908), pp. 168–69; Smith, *History of the AME Church*, p. 270; Wright, *Bishops of the AME Church*, pp. 234–35. See also Solomon Plaatje's obituary of Johnson in *Umteteli wa Bantu*, January 12, 1929.

76. *Twenty-Fifth Quadrennial Report of the Parent Home and Foreign Missionary Department of the African Methodist Episcopal Church, 1912–1916* (n.p., n.d.), p. 21; *Annual Report of the Home and Foreign Missionary Department . . . for the Year Ending March 31, 1914* (n.p., n.d.), p. 11;

Journal of the Twenty-Fifth Quadrennial Session (Being the Centenary Session) of the General Conference of the African Methodist Episcopal Church, Philadelphia, May 3–23, 1916 (Nashville, 1916), pp. 382–84; *Journal* of the 1908 General Conference, p. 307; *Quadrennial Report of the Financial Board to the Twenty-Fourth Session of the General Conference . . .* (Nashville, 1912), p. 14; *Journal of Proceedings of the Fifteenth Session of the Transvaal and Natal Annual Conferences of the African Methodist Episcopal Church, October 14, 1913* (Cape Town, n.d.), pp. 11, 21–27.

77. NTS 1420 3/214; NTS 1423 12/214; NTS 1424 12/214 vol. 3; NTS 1425 12/215 vol. 4; NTS 1434 28/214 vol. 1; GNLB 205 1697/14/37; GNLB 208 1777/14/198; GNLB 216 150/15/317; J. Dexter Taylor, ed., *Christianity and the Natives of South Africa: A Year-Book of South African Missions* (Lovedale, 1927), pp. 301–02. On the radius rule, see Department of Native Affairs, *Occupation of Church, School and Mission Sites in Native Areas* (Pretoria, 1918), copy in GNLB 216 150/15/317.

78. On Bulhoek, where police opened fire on unarmed Africans, see Robert Edgar, *Because They Chose the Plan of God: The Story of the Bulhoek Massacre* (Johannesburg, 1988). It is worth noting that the *Christian Express* endorsed the shooting. No "responsible person," the paper argued, could deny that "the Government had behaved with great patience and finally with necessary firmness." *Christian Express*, July 1, 1921.

Chapter 8. "The Seed You Sow in Africa"

1. "The Menace of Ethiopianism," undated clipping from *Chambers' Journal*, ca. 1904, in Papers of the Archbishop of Cape Town, Church of the Province of South Africa Archives, University of the Witwatersrand.

2. Dr. Robert Laws, quoted in George Shepperson and Thomas Price, *Independent African: John Chilembwe and the Nyasaland Rising of 1915* (Edinburgh, 1958), p. 366; *SANAC*, vol. 1, pp. 73–74. See also *Report of the Select Committee on Native Education* (Cape Town, 1908); and K. A. Hobart Houghton, *Native Higher Education* (Lovedale, n.d.). On Fort Hare's continuing linkages with black America, see Z. K. Matthews, *Freedom for My People. The Autobiography of Z. K. Matthews: Southern Africa 1901 to 1968* (Cape Town, 1981); and Cynthia Kros, "'Deep Rumblings': Z. K. Matthews, Witness to the Eiselen Commission of Enquiry into Native Education, 1934–1949," paper delivered to the History Workshop, University of the Witwatersrand, February, 1990.

3. See Kenneth J. King, *Pan-Africanism and Education: A Study of Race Philanthropy and Education in the Southern States of America and East Africa* (Oxford, 1971); Richard Ralston, "A Second Middle Passage: African Student Sojourns in the United States During the Colonial Period and their Influence Upon the Character of African Leadership" (Ph.D. diss., University of California, Los Angeles, 1972); R. Hunt Davis, "The Black American Education Component in African Responses to Colonialism in South Africa, ca. 1890–1914," *Journal of Southern African Affairs* 3, no. 1 (1978), pp. 65–83; Walter L. Williams, *Black Americans and the Evangelization of Africa, 1877–1900* (Madison, 1982); Edwin W. Smith, *Aggrey of Africa: A Study in Black and White* (New York, 1929); Robert Rotberg, *The Rise of Nationalism in Central Africa: The Making of Malawi and Zambia, 1873–1964* (Cambridge, Mass., 1965); Thomas C. Howard, "Black American Missionary Influence on the Origins of University Education in West Africa," in Sylvia Jacobs, ed., *Black Americans and the Missionary Movement in Africa* (Westport, Conn., 1982); and Shepperson and Price, *Independent African*.

4. "It was through [Aggrey] that my nationalism was first aroused." Nkrumah recalled. See *The Autobiography of Kwame Nkrumah* (London, 1957). On Dube, see William Manning Marable, "African Nationalist: The Life of John Langalibalele Dube" (Ph.D. diss., University of Maryland, 1976); R. Hunt Davis, "John L. Dube: A South African Exponent of Booker T.

Washington," *Journal of African Studies* 2, no. 4 (1976); Shula Marks, "John Dube and the Ambiguities of Nationalism," in *The Ambiguities of Dependence in South Africa: Class, Nationalism, and the State in Twentieth Century Natal* (Johannesburg, 1986); and Marks, "Patriotism, Patriarchy and Purity: Natal and the Politics of Zulu Ethnic Consciousness," in Leroy Vail, ed., *The Creation of Tribalism in Southern Africa* (Berkeley, 1989).

5. Horace Mann Bond, "The Origin and Development of the Negro Church-Related College," *Journal of Negro Education* 29, no. 3 (1960), pp. 217–26; Ralston, "A Second Middle Passage," pp. 3–4. On the context of Hopkins's and Stiles's experiment, see Chapter 3, above.

6. See Williams, *Black Americans and the Evangelization of Africa*, pp. 141–60, 191–93; and Chapter 3, above.

7. Reverdy C. Ransom, *Preface to History of A.M.E. Church* (Nashville, 1950), pp. 184–85; *Voice of Missions*, June 1897; Smith, *Aggrey of Africa*, pp. 56–66; Walter L. Yates, "The History of the African Methodist Episcopal Zion Church in West Africa, Liberia and Gold Coast, 1880–1900" (Ph.D. diss., Hartford Theological Seminary, 1963). For representative articles by Faduma, see *AME Church Review* 9, no. 1 (1892), and 12, no. 1 (1895).

8. See Chapter 4, above. Dube, the son of an ordained African minister, persuaded a missionary of the American Board to bring him to the United States for education in 1887. He studied for about two years in Oberlin's preparatory school and later traveled the Great Lakes region on the chatauqua circuit before returning to South Africa in 1892.

9. Details of Manye's early life can be gleaned from an interview with her sister, Kate, conducted ca. 1963 by Mrs. Margaret Nixon; I am grateful to Veit Erlmann for sharing this typescript with me. See also Erlmann "'A Feeling of Prejudice': Orpheus M. McAdoo and the Virginia Jubilee Singers in South Africa 1890–1898," *Journal of Southern African Studies* 14, no. 3 (1988), pp. 331–50; T. D. Mweli Skota, *The African Yearly Register: Being an Illustrated National Biographical Dictionary (Who's Who) of Black Folks in Africa* (Johannesburg, 1932), pp. 194–95; and Chapter 4, above.

10. Xenia *Daily Gazette*, December 6, 1894; *Voice of Missions*, February 1895, March 1895; Davis, "Black American Education Component," p. 73; Williams, *Black Americans and the Evangelization of Africa*, p. 191. While Manye later recalled being joined by four of her comrades, a contemporary photo shows six African students, including Katiya; see W. H. Mixon, *History of the African Methodist Episcopal Church in Alabama, with Biographical Sketches* (Nashville, 1902), p. 50.

11. *Voice of Missions*, February 1895, November 1898.

12. Brian Willan, *Sol Plaatje: A Biography* (Johannesburg, 1985), pp. 33–41; James Stewart, *Lovedale: Past and Present. A Register of Two Thousand Names* (Lovedale, 1887), pp. 230–39; J. R. Coan, "The Expansion of Missions of the A.M.E.Church in South Africa, 1896–1906" (Ph.D. diss., Hartford Theological Seminary, 1963), pp. 455–57.

13. *Voice of Missions*, December 1898, January 1900; Coan, "Expansion of Missions of the A.M.E. Church," p. 455; Marable, "African Nationalist: The Life of John Langalibalele Dube," pp. 85, 106–07. Gana Kakaza earned considerable notoriety in mission circles in the 1880s for his defense of certain African customs; see Wallace George Mills, "The Role of African Clergy in the Reorientation of Xhosa Society to the Plural Society in the Cape Colony, 1850–1915" (Ph.D. diss., University of California, Los Angeles, 1975), pp. 56, 314.

14. *Voice of Missions*, September 1895, August 1897, September 1897; Skota, *The African Yearly Register*, pp. 70, 105–106, 267; Marshall Maxeke, "South African Graduates," *Christian Recorder*, July 14, 1927.

15. *Journal of the Twenty-First Quadrennial Session of the General Conference of the African M.E. Church, Columbus, Ohio, May 7–25, 1900* (Philadelphia, 1900), pp. 192–94, 342; *Voice of Missions*, March 1899, April 1900, July 1901; testimony of L. J. Coppin to *SANAC*, vol. 2,

p. 221; Coan, "Expansion of Missions," pp. 455–57; SNA 241 2694/04. On Molema, see the Plaatje-Molema Papers, University of the Witwatersrand Archives, Aa1, Aa2.22, Ac. Kuzwayo was probably the son of Mbiya Kuzwayo, a graduate of Lovedale; see Stewart, *Lovedale: Past and Present*, p. 132. The Sondezi brothers were apparently the sons of Joseph Sondezi, a leader of the Driefontein land-buying syndicate; see NSNA 219 555/1896.

16. *Voice of Missions*, July 1898, October 1898, November 1898, October 1899, March 1900; Sara J. Duncan, *Progressive Missions in the South and Addresses* (Atlanta, 1906), p. 206; *Fifth Quadrennial Report of Payne Theological Seminary, Wilberforce, Ohio* (n.p., 1912), copy in Benjamin Arnett Papers, Wilberforce University Archives, ARC 287.8 G327. See also J. M. Mokone, *The Life of Our Founder* (Johannesburg, 1935).

17. *Voice of Missions*, November 1898; *Report of the Proceedings of the Second General Missionary Conference for South Africa, Held at Johannesburg, July 5–11, 1906* (Morija, 1907), p. 84.

18. Quoted in Davis, "Black American Education Component," p. 81 fn 51; SNA 15 272/02; GH 35/84 31; Stewart, *Lovedale: Past and Present*, pp. 37, 338, 524; testimony of J. Stewart to *SANAC*, vol. 4, pp. 898–913.

19. C. Nontshinga-Citashe, *Brief Outline of the History of the Ethiopian Church of South Africa* (Morija, 1957), pp. 92–94. The material on Dana is drawn from a 1976 interview; my thanks to William Beinart for sharing the transcript. On Xuma, see Skota, *African Yearly Register*, pp. 282–83. See also Davis, "Black American Education Component," pp. 72–73.

20. GNLB 305 19/19/72; NTS 2692 4/301/1, vol. 1. Given the absence of a college curriculum at Fort Hare, the official rationale rang somewhat hollow. On the revival of "Negro" fears after World War I, see Chapter 9, below.

21. NTS 2692 4/301/1 vol. 1; GNLB 305 19/19/72; NTS 2709 79/301; King, *Pan-Africanism and Education*, pp. 226–28; AME *Church Review* 46, no. 1 (1929), pp. 33–37. Makhanya is one of the principals in Shula Marks's haunting *Not Either an Experimental Doll: The Separate Worlds of Three South African Women* (Bloomington, Ind., 1987). On the Jeanes experiment, see R. Hunt Davis, "Producing the 'Good African': South Carolina's Penn School as a Guide for African Education in South Africa," in A. T. Mogomba and N. Nyaggah, *Independence without Freedom: The Political Economy of Colonial Education in Southern Africa* (Santa Barbara, Calif., 1980).

22. SNA 217 995/04; NTS 132 f243; GH 35/84 31; Davis, "Black American Education Component," p. 70.

23. R. R. Wright, Jr., "The Negroes of Xenia, Ohio: A Social Study," *Bulletin of the Bureau of Labor*, no. 48 (September 1903), pp. 1006–44.

24. This paragraph and much of what follows is culled from David Gerber's excellent *Black Ohio and the Color Line* (Urbana, Ill., 1976).

25. W. E. B. Du Bois, "Long in Darke," *Independent* 67 (October, 1909), pp. 917–18; Wright, "The Negroes of Xenia," pp. 1014–16; Gerber, *Black Ohio*, pp. 15–19. See also Jennie Braddock, "The Colored People and Greene County, Ohio," unpublished manuscript in the Greene County Public Library, Xenia, Ohio.

26. Daniel Alexander Payne, *Annual and Retrospect of the First Decade of Wilberforce University* (Cincinnati, 1873), p. 4; Payne, *Recollections of Seventy Years* (1888, reprint ed., New York, 1968), pp. 149–57; Frederick McGinnis, *A History and Interpretation of Wilberforce University* (Wilberforce, 1941); Cincinnati *Gazette*, quoted in Braddock, "Colored People and Greene Country," p. 79. The original 1856 subscription book for the "Ohio African University" is deposited at the Greene County Public Library.

27. Wright, "The Negroes of Xenia," pp. 1009–11, 1023–30 ff; Gerber, *Black Ohio*, pp. 62–69, 278.

28. Helen Hoover Santmyer, *Ohio Town* (Columbus, 1962), pp. 81–109; Wright, "The Negroes of Xenia," pp. 1012, 1040–43; Gerber, *Black Ohio,* pp. 98–99, 158–61, 240–43.

29. Wright, "The Negroes of Xenia," pp. 1020–23, 1031–40; Gerber, *Black Ohio,* p. 396.

30. Hallie Q. Brown, *Homespun Heroines and Other Women of Distinction* (Xenia, Ohio, 1926), pp. 71–80, 90–91; William J. Simmons, *Men of Mark: Eminent, Progressive and Rising* (1887, reprint ed., New York, 1968) pp. 113–17; Nell Irvin Painter, "Martin R. Delany: Elitism and Black Nationalism," in Leon Litwack and August Meier, eds., *Black Leaders of the Nineteenth Century* (Urbana, Ill., 1988); Anna Julia Cooper, *A Voice from the South* (Xenia, Ohio, 1892).

31. *Ninth Quadrennial Report of Wilberforce University* (Wilberforce, 1900), copy in Benjamin Arnett Papers, Wilberforce University Archives, vol. 83; *The Wilberforce Calendar* (Wilberforce, 1895), copy in Greene County Public Library; W. E. B. Du Bois, *The Autobiography of W. E. B. Du Bois: A Soliloquy on Viewing My Life from the Last Decade of its First Century* (New York, 1968), pp. 183–93; Du Bois, "The Future of Wilberforce University," *Journal of Negro Education* 9, no. 4 (1941), pp. 553–70; Francis P. Weisenburger, "William Sanders Scarborough: Early Years and Life at Wilberforce," *Ohio History* 71, no. 3 (1962), pp. 203–26, and 72, no. 1 (1963), pp. 25–50. On the A.N.A., see Alfred A. Moss, *The American Negro Academy: Voice of the Talented Tenth* (Baton Rouge, 1981). On the creation of the Military Science Department, see Xenia *Daily Gazette,* December 6, 1894; and Wilson Jeremiah Moses, *The Golden Age of Black Nationalism 1850–1925* (Hamden, Conn., 1978), p. 75. Moses attributes the "militarization" of black higher education, evident at Tuskegee and Hampton as well as at Wilberforce, to a contemporary stereotype of blacks as an "effeminate" and "dreamy" race that needed discipline to survive in the modern world. That perception also provided one of the rationales for industrial education.

32. Simmons, *Men of Mark,* pp. 883–91; Gerber, *Black Ohio,* pp. 214–20, 350–55; R. R. Wright, Jr., *The Bishops of the A.M.E. Church* (Nashville, 1963), pp. 78–82. For the broader context of Arnett's life, see August Meier, *Negro Thought in America, 1890–1915: Racial Ideologies in the Age of Booker T. Washington* (Ann Arbor, Mich., 1963).

33. See *Catalogue of the Directors, Officers and Students of Payne Theological Seminary, Wilberforce Ohio, 1893–94* (n.p., n.d.), pp. 6, 14; Payne, *Annual and Retrospect of the First Decade of Wilberforce University;* and Payne, *Recollections of Seventy Years.* See also Simmons, *Men of Mark,* pp. 1078–85; Wright, *Bishops of the A.M.E. Church,* pp. 266–79; J. R. Coan, *Daniel Alexander Payne: Christian Educator* (Philadelphia, 1935); and Chapter 2, above.

34. Unlike most white universities, Wilberforce was coeducational from the outset. Far from precluding women's education, Payne's commitment to the idea of "separate spheres" made it seem all the more important: it was women, after all, who would nurture the future leaders of the race. See Payne, *Treatise on Domestic Education* (Cincinnati, 1885); David Wills, "Womanhood and Domesticity in the A.M.E. Tradition: The Influence of Daniel Alexander Payne," in Wills and Richard Newman, eds., *Black Apostles at Home and Abroad: Afro-Americans and the Christian Mission from the Revolution to Reconstruction* (Boston, 1982); and Chapter 2, above.

35. *Annual Catalogue of Wilberforce University, 1897–98* (Wilberforce, 1898). See also Payne's inaugural address, in *Catalogue of the . . . Payne Theological Seminary, 1893–94,* pp. 11–14. Ironically, Wilberforce clung to this nineteenth-century educational ideal at the very time that white universities had begun to deemphasize moral training and to replace their structured classical curricula with the elective system. See Laurence R. Vescey, *The Emergence of the American University* (Chicago, 1965).

36. The Carnegie Library still stands on the old campus at Wilberforce.

37. David Gerber, "Segregation, Separatism, and Sectarianism: Ohio Blacks and Wilberforce University's Effort to Obtain Federal Funds, 1891," *Journal of Negro Education* 45, no. 1

(1976), pp. 1–20; *Annual Catalogue of Wilberforce University, 1897–98*, p. 10. See also "Industrial Department" file in the Wilberforce University Archives, especially the 1891 report by Sarah C. B. Scarborough. The CNI Department eventually cleaved off from Wilberforce to become Central State University.

38. Xenia *Daily Gazette*, January 28, 1895; *Voice of Missions*, July 1895, September 1898, July 1899. Kakaza's recollection, from a 1929 article in *Imvo Zabantsundu*, is quoted in Alexander Ball, "American Negro Influence on Black Nationalist and Proto-nationalist Movements in South Africa, 1898–1930" (B.A. (Hons.) thesis, University of the Witwatersrand, 1979), p. 42.

39. Carrie Lee Bell, "The Future of Africa," reprinted in *Voice of Missions*, July 1899; "Synopsis of Address by Charlotte Manye, Our African Daughter," in *Minutes of the Fifth Annual Convention of the Ohio Conference Branch Woman's Mite Missionary Society of the AME Church, Held July 18–21, 1901, Portsmouth, Ohio*, pp. 34–38, copy in Benjamin Arnett Papers, Wilberforce University Archives, vol. 64; McGinnis, *History and Interpretation of Wilberforce University*, p. 168; Hallie Q. Brown, *Pen Pictures of Pioneers of Wilberforce* (Xenia, Ohio, 1937), p. 12.

40. *Voice of Missions*, March 1895, April 1898, September 1898, August 1899; *Journal* of the 1900 General Conference, pp. 294–95.

41. For an evocation of Wilberforce life, see Reverdy C. Ransom, *School Days at Wilberforce* (Springfield, Ohio, 1894). See also *Annual Catalogue of Wilberforce University, 1897–98*, p. 14; and McGinnis, *History and Interpretation of Wilberforce University*, pp. 159–74.

42. Wilberforce University Archives, Box 15, Committee on Discipline; Payne, *Treatise on Domestic Education*, p. 101; McGinnis, *History and Interpretation of Wilberforce University*, pp. 159–74.

43. *Annual Catalogue of Wilberforce University, 1897–98*, pp. 29–36, 42–48; *Wilberforce Bulletin and Catalogue, 1909–10*, pp. 137–41; *Bulletin and Annual Catalogue, 1912–13*, pp. 151–53. Unfortunately, no other volumes from the period survive in the Wilberforce Archives.

44. *Annual Catalogue of Wilberforce University, 1897–98*, p. 76; TAD 843 G4091/144; *Journal* of the 1900 General Conference, p. 342; *Journal of Proceedings of the Fifteenth Session of the Transvaal and Natal Annual Conferences of the African Methodist Episcopal Church* (n.p., 1913), p. 10, copy in AME Church Archives, Wilberforce University, Box 13.

45. *Voice of Missions*, July 1895; *Annual Catalogue of Wilberforce University, 1897–98*, p. 15; Moses, *Golden Age of Black Nationalism*, pp. 132–33. Du Bois's forgotten eulogy of Douglass is reprinted in *Journal of Negro History* 49, no. 4 (1964), pp. 264–68.

46. W. E. B. Du Bois, "The Conservation of Races," in *The American Negro Academy Occasional Papers* (New York, 1969), p. 15; Moses, *Golden Age of Black Nationalism*, pp. 132–45, 156–69. See also K. Anthony Appiah, "The Uncompleted Argument: DuBois and the Illusion of Race," in Henry L. Gates, ed., *'Race,' Writing and Difference* (Chicago, 1985). For Du Bois's own recollection of his Wilberforce years, see "The Future of Wilberforce University," pp. 553–56; and *Autobiography*, pp. 183–93.

47. Quoted in Gerber, *Black Ohio*, p. 161.

48. Simmons, *Men of Mark;* H. F. Kletzing and W. H. Crogman, *Progress of a Race . . . or . . . the Remarkable Advancement of the Afro-American* (1897; reprint ed., New York, 1969). See also Moss, *The American Negro Academy*, pp. 296–97.

49. Quoted in Gerber, *Black Ohio*, pp. 173, 249–59.

50. L. J. Coppin, *Observations of Persons and Things in South Africa, 1900–1904*, 2 vols. (Philadelphia, 1905), vol. 2, p. 178; *South African Spectator*, September 7, 1901, September 21, 1901.

51. Testimony of Enoch Mamba to *SANAC*, vol. 2, p. 1043. On Mamba, see Colin Bundy, "A Voice in the Big House: The Career of Headman Enoch Mamba," in William Beinart and Bundy, *Hidden Struggles in Rural South Africa: Politics and Popular Movements in the Transkei and Eastern Cape, 1890–1930* (Johannesburg, 1987); and Chapter 6, above.

52. On Wilberforce Institute, see J. Campbell, "Our Fathers, Our Children: The African Methodist Episcopal Church in the United States and South Africa" (Ph.D. diss., Stanford University, 1989), pp. 319–78.

53. GG 886 28/16; GG 886 28/18; SNA 473 2468/10. Some of Molema's letters are preserved in the Plaatje-Molema Papers.

54. Skota, *African Yearly Register*, pp. 282–83. On Crogman Clinic, including the abortive attempt to recruit Banda, see Campbell, "Our Fathers, Our Children," pp. 369–74. Among the AME-sponsored students, at least two others pursued medical training. Wilberforce graduate Theodore Kakaza attended medical school in Toronto and opened a practice in Indianapolis. Marcus Gabashane's son Henry returned to Africa in 1908 with a degree from Meherry Medical College, settling not in South Africa but in Swaziland, where he planned to open a medical mission. His fate thereafter remains obscure. For the continuing debate over African doctors, see Karin A. Shapiro, "Doctors or Medical Aids: the Debate over the Training of Black Medical Personnel for the Rural Black Population in South Africa in the 1920s and 1930s," *Journal of Southern African Studies* 13, no. 2 (1987), pp. 233–55.

55. *Journal* of the 1900 General Conference, pp. 192–94; Ransom, *Preface to History of the A.M.E. Church* (Nashville, 1950), pp. 184–85.

56. *Negro World*, April 21, 1923; *Christian Recorder*, July 14, 1927; *Wilberforce Bulletin and Annual Catalogue, 1909–10*, p. 138; *Wilberforce Bulletin and Annual Catalogue, 1912–13*, p. 151.

57. NTS 2719 394/301. On Tantsi, see *AME Church Review* 41, no. 3 (1925); *African Leader*, September 17, 1932; and A. B. Xuma Papers, University of the Witwatersrand Archives [hereafter ABX], 230216b. On Sishuba, see NTS 2692 4/301/1 vol. 1; on the African Student Union, see King, *Pan-Africanism and Education*, pp. 215–22.

58. Skota, *African Yearly Register*, pp. 282–83; Thomas Karis and Gwendolen M. Carter, eds., *From Protest to Challenge: A Documentary History of African Politics in South Africa, 1882–1964* (Stanford, 1977), vol. 4, pp. 164–66.

59. ABX 361230; ABX 370319. For similar comments, see ABX 370122; ABX 370305; ABX 370310; ABX 400122a/b; ABX 400210; and ABX 400414. For Xuma's service at Wilberforce Institute, see, *inter alia*, ABX Box O, File 22; ABX 340525; ABX 340731; and ABX 360408. On Amanda Mason Xuma, see L. L. Berry, *A Century of Missions of the African Methodist Episcopal Church, 1840–1940*, pp. 137, 155; and the obituary in *Umteteli wa Bantu*, May 6, 1934.

60. The correspondence between Xuma and his emissary, Eva Mahuma Morake, and, later, between Xuma and Madie Hall is scattered through the Xuma papers; see particularly ABX 250636 and ABX 110139. On Hall's career in South Africa, see Karis and Carter, *From Protest to Challenge*, vol. 4, pp. 166–67. For a wrenching tale of an American-educated South African and his African American bride, based loosely on Xuma and Hall, see Mbulelo Mzamane's "Soweto Bride," in *Mzala: The Stories of Mbulelo Mzamane* (Johannesburg, 1981).

61. See footnote 3, above.

62. Quoted in Ellen Kuzwayo, *Call Me Woman* (London, 1985), pp. 102–103. On Dube, see Marks, "John Dube and the Ambiguities of Nationalism."

63. *Umteteli wa Bantu*, September 7, 1929.

64. Alfred B. Xuma, *Charlotte Manye: What an Educated African Girl Can Do* (n.p., 1930), copy in ABX Box S, File 38.

65. See rosters and minutes, ca. 1927–28, Papers of the Johannesburg Joint Council, University of the Witwatersrand Archives; C. M. Maxeke, "The Progress of Native Womanhood," in J. Dexter Taylor, ed., *Christianity and the Natives of South Africa* (Lovedale, 1928); and Maxeke's address in *The Evangelization of South Africa: Being the Report of the Sixth General Missionary Conference of South Africa . . .* (Cape Town, 1925), pp. 127–34. On interwar liberalism and the American connection, see Tim Couzens, "'Moralizing Leisure Time': The Transatlantic Connection and Black Johannesburg," in Shula Marks and Richard Rathbone, eds., *Industrialisation and Social Change in South Africa: African Class Formation, Culture and Consciousness, 1870–1930* (London, 1982); Baruch Hirson, "Tuskegee, the Joint Councils, and the All-Africa Convention," *Collected Seminar Papers of the Societies of Southern Africa in the 19th and 20th Centuries*, vol. 10 (London, 1980); Paul Rich, *White Power and the Liberal Conscience* (Dover, N.H., 1984); and Chapter 9, below.

66. On Gow, see R. R. Wright, Jr., *The Bishops of the A.M.E. Church* (Nashville, 1963), pp. 188–90; Gavin Lewis, *Between the Wire and the Wall: A History of South African 'Coloured' Politics* (Cape Town, 1987), pp. 203–204; R. E. van der Ross, *The Rise and Decline of Apartheid: A Study of Political Movements Among the Coloured People of South Africa* (Cape Town, 1986), pp. 169–85; and the Gow file in the R. Langham Carter Papers, Cape Archives Depot, Accession A1691. For Gow's career at Tuskegee, see "Annual Catalogue Editions" of the *Tuskegee Institute Bulletin*, vol. 15 (1920), pp. 10, 130–35; vol. 16 (1921), p. 11; vol. 17 (1922), p. 9; vol. 18 (1923), pp. 10, 112–18. Among Gow's musical achievements was a musical production of Booker T. Washington's *Up From Slavery;* see NTS 1423 12/214.

67. Adam Ashforth, *The Politics of Official Discourse in Twentieth-Century South Africa* (Oxford, 1990); Saul Dubow, "Holding 'A Just Balance Between Black and White': The Native Affairs Department in South Africa c. 1920–33," *Journal of Southern African Studies* 12, no. 2 (1986), pp. 217–39. See also Rodney Davenport, "African Townsmen? South African Natives (Urban Areas) Legislation Through the Years," *African Affairs* 68, no. 1 (1969), pp. 95–109; and Davenport, "The Triumph of Colonel Stallard: The Transformation of the Natives (Urban Areas) Act between 1923 and 1937," *South African Historical Journal* 2, no. 1 (1970), pp. 77–96.

68. Skota, *African Yearly Register*, pp. 144–45, 253, 423–25; *Report of the Natives Land Commission* (Cape Town, 1916), vol. 2, p. 458; GNLB 368 112/26/72; Johannesburg Joint Council, *General Hertzog's Solution to the Native Question, No. 1* (Johannesburg, 1928), copy in Skota Papers, University of the Witwatersrand Archives. On the foreclosure of opportunities for elite accumulation, see J. Campbell, "T. D. Mweli Skota and the Making and Unmaking of a Black Elite," paper delivered to the History Workshop, University of the Witwatersrand, February, 1987.

69. NTS 4/301/1 vol. 1; NTS 1681 2/276 vol. 1; MSCE 793/1947. The question, posed in *The Black Man*, a Cape Town newspaper, was reprinted in *Umteteli wa Bantu*, July 30, 1921. We shall return to these issues in Chapter 9, below.

70. NTS 2708 60/301; Skota, *African Yearly Register*, p. 193; Marable, "African Nationalist: The Life of John Langalibalele Dube," pp. 325–29.

71. Skota, *African Yearly Register*, pp. xiii, 194–95.

72. On Maxeke's role in the travails of the choir, see *Imvo Zabantsundu*, January 14, 1892, March 17, 1892. See also *Christian Express*, March 1, 1892, August 1, 1892. For Maxeke's endurance in the memory of those who encountered her, see Hallie Quinn Brown's unpublished memoir, copy in Hallie Quinn Brown Library, Central State University.

73. *South African Spectator*, September 21, 1901, December 7, 1901, LTG 144 120/05; SNA 207 533/04.

74. TOD 122 E2041; SNA 325 1722/06; SNA 347 3795/06; SNA 350 4170/06; *Voice of the People*, November 1903; *Voice of Missions*, April 1904, July 1904.

75. TOD 122 E2041. See also Chapter 5, above.

76. Xuma, *What an Educated African Girl Can Do*, pp. 14–16. On Mamba, see Bundy, "A Voice in the Big House"; and above.

77. See Maxeke, "The Progress of Native Womanhood"; and her comments in *The Evangelisation of South Africa*, pp. 127–34. See also Charlotte Crogman Wright, *Beneath the Southern Cross: The Story of an American Bishop's Wife in South Africa* (New York, 1955), pp. 111–15; and Cherryl Walker, *Women and Resistance in South Africa* (London, 1982), p. 39.

78. Miriam Basner, *Am I An African? The Political Memoirs of H. M. Basner* (Johannesburg, 1993), pp. 28–29.

79. NTS 2692 4/301/1 vol. 1. On the formation of the Congress, see Peter Walshe, *The Rise of African Nationalism in South Africa: The African National Congress 1912–1952* (Berkeley, Calif., 1971), pp. 30–42.

80. On the Black Peril, see Charles van Onselen, "The Witches of Suburbia: Domestic Service on the Witwatersrand, 1890–1914," in *Studies in the Social and Economic History of the Witwatersrand, 1886–1914*, vol. 2, *New Nineveh*. On racist stereotypes of African women, see K. A. Eales, "Gender Politics and the Administration of African Women in Johannesburg, 1903–1939" (M.A. thesis, University of the Witwatersrand, 1991). On differential patterns of proletarianization, and their implications for men and women, see Belinda Bozzoli, "Marxism, Feminism and South African Studies," *Journal of Southern African Studies* 7, no. 1 (1983), pp. 139–71; Cherryl Walker, "Gender and the Development of the Migrant Labour System c. 1850–1930," in Cherryl Walker, ed., *Women and Gender in Southern African to 1945* (Cape Town, 1990); and Andrea van Niekerk, "The Use of White Female Labour by the Zebediela Citrus Estate, 1926–1953" (M.A. thesis, University of the Witwatersrand, 1988).

81. van Onselen, "Witches of Suburbia," pp. 45–54, ff. On the labor crisis during the reconstruction period, see Peter Richardson and Jean Jacques Van-Helten, "Labour in the South African Gold Mining Industry, 1886–1914," in Marks and Rathbone, *Industrialisation and Social Change*. On the gender politics of imperialism, see A. Davin, "Imperialism and Motherhood," *History Workshop* 5, no. 1 (1978), pp. 9–57.

82. *Report of the Commission appointed to Enquire into Assaults on Women 1913* (Pretoria, 1913). See also Eales, "Gender Politics and the Administration of African Women," pp. 42–96; Deborah Gaitskell, "'Christian Compounds for Girls': Church Hostels for African Women in Johannesburg, 1907–1970," *Journal of Southern African Studies* 6, no. 1 (1979), pp. 44–69; and Linda Chisholm, "Gender and Deviance in South African Industrial Schools and Reformatories for Girls, 1911–1934," in Walker, *Women and Gender in Southern Africa*.

83. GNLB 281 458/17/D72; Julia Christine Wells, "The History of Black Women's Struggle Against the Pass Laws in South Africa, 1900–1960" (Ph.D. diss., Columbia University, 1982), pp. 100–101, 118–19, 172; Walker, *Women and Resistance*, pp. 32–37; Walshe, *The Rise of African Nationalism*, pp. 80–85.

84. GNLB 281 458/17/D72; Wells, "Black Women's Struggle Against the Pass Laws," pp. 183–84; Bloemfontein *Friend* July 14, 1920; Basner, *Am I An African*, p. 23. On the postwar upheaval of the Witwatersrand and its political ramifications, see Philip Bonner, "The Transvaal Congress, 1917–1920: The Radicalisation of the Black Petty Bourgeoisie on the Rand," in Marks and Rathbone, eds., *Industrialisation and Social Change*. For white liberal responses, see Couzens, "Moralizing Leisure Time"; and Chapter 9, below.

85. GNLB 281 446/17/D48; GNLB 281 458/17/D72; NTS 1423 12/214; NTS 7601 9/328; Johannesburg *Star*, August 24, 1923; *Rand Daily Mail*, July 14, 1924.

86. Unidentified clipping in Papers of the Native Pass Laws Commission, Transvaal Archives Depot, K 357, Box 1; Basner, *Am I An African*, p. 23.

87. GNLB 323 52/20/30; NTS 7601 9/328; Johannesburg *Star*, July 23, 1921, August 24, 1923; *Rand Daily Mail*, July 14, 1924; Bloemfontein *Friend*, February 24, 1928; Bonner, "The Transvaal Native Congress," p. 278. Special thanks to P. Bonner for sharing his notes on Maxeke's testimony to the Moffat Commission. Unfortunately, the minutes of evidence from this commission appear to have been misplaced in the Pretoria Archives Depot. When last seen, they were located in the Johannesburg Municipal Council Archives, Box 823 18/37. Maxeke's testimony is on pp. 149–57. For African testimony to the Local Government Commission, see GNLB 323 84/243 and K 5.

88. Maxeke testimony to Moffat Commission, K 357, Box 1, pp. 154–56.

89. NTS 7601 9/328; Basner, *Am I An African*, pp. 17–19 ff; *Cape Times*, May 4, 1921.

90. NTS 7601 9/328; Basner, *Am I An African*, pp. 18, 22–26.

91. Johannesburg *Star*, August 24, 1923, October 17, 1923; *Rand Daily Mail*, July 24, 1924; NTS 7601 9/328. See also Fanny Jackson Coppin, *Reminiscences of School Life, and Hints on Teaching* (Philadelphia, 1913); and Chapter 7, above.

92. Johannesburg *Star*, October 17, 1923, August 24, 1923.

93. NTS 7601 7/328; Papers of the Joint Council of Johannesburg, University of the Witwatersrand Archives, AD1433 Cj 2.4.1; Maxeke, "The Progress of Native Womanhood," pp. 178–81; Eales, "Gender Politics and the Administration of African Women in Johannesburg," pp. 133–42; Philip Bonner, "'Desirable or Undesirable Basotho Women?' Liquor, Prostitution and the Migration of Basotho Women to the Rand, 1920–1945," in Walker, *Women and Gender in Southern Africa*. On the origins of the 1930 legislation, see Marks, "Patriotism, Patriarchy and Purity."

94. NTS 7601 9/328; NTS 7601 7/328 pt. II; Basner, *Am I An African*, p. 23; Skota, *African Yearly Register*, p. 70. For an obituary of Marshall Maxeke, see *Umteteli wa Bantu*, January 12, 1929.

95. NTS 7601 9/328; Bloemfontein *Friend*, February 24, 1928.

96. NTS 7601 9/328; Wright, *Beneath the Southern Cross*, pp. 111–15. On Wilberforce Institute in the Depression, see Campbell, "Our Fathers, Our Children," pp. 359–64.

97. Quoted in Kuzwayo, *Call Me Woman*, pp. 102–103. On the formation of the N.C.A.W., see Walker, *Women and Resistance*, pp. 35–37; and Wells, "The History of Black Women's Struggle Against the Pass Laws," p. 275.

98. NTS 7601 7/328 pt. II; NTS 7601 9/328.

99. NTS 7601 9/328.

100. W. E. B. Du Bois, *Dusk of Dawn: An Essay Toward an Autobiography of a Race Concept* (New York, 1940), p. viii.

Chapter 9. Middle Passages

1. Magistrates' reports to the Native Churches Commission, 1924, in NTS 1434 28/214 vol. 1.

2. BNS 1/2/48 A1842.

3. This paragraph and the several that follow rely heavily on recent work by Milton C. Sernett and Robert S. Gregg. See Sernett, "If Not Moses, Then Joshua: African Methodists and the Great Migration of 1916–1918," unpublished paper; and Gregg, "Sparks from the Anvil of Oppression: Philadelphia's African Methodists and the Great Migration, 1890–1930" (Ph.D. diss., University of Pennsylvania, 1989). On the migration, see Joe William Trotter, Jr., ed.,

The Great Migration in Historical Perspective: New Dimensions of Race, Class and Gender (Bloomington, Ind., 1991).

4. Sernett, "If Not Moses, Then Joshua," pp. 11–22; Gregg, "Sparks from the Anvil of Oppression," pp. 310–18. (Lee and Ransom are quoted on p. 15 and p. 315, respectively.)

5. Sernett, "If Not Moses, Then Joshua," pp. 10, 20–28, 32–35; Gregg, "Sparks from the Anvil of Oppression," pp. 338–40.

6. See David Wills, "Reverdy C. Ransom: The Making of an A.M.E. Bishop," in Randall K. Burkett and Richard Newman, eds., *Black Apostles: The Afro-American Clergy Confront the Twentieth Century* (Boston, 1978); R. C. Ransom, *The Pilgrimage of Harriet Ransom's Son* (Nashville, n.d.); Ransom, *School Days at Wilberforce* (Springfield, Ohio, 1894); R. R. Wright, Jr., *The Bishops of the African Methodist Episcopal Church* (Nashville, 1963), pp. 287–92; and August Meier, *Negro Thought in America, 1880–1915: Racial Ideologies in the Age of Booker T. Washington* (Ann Arbor, Mich., 1963), pp. 180–85, 220–33 ff.

7. Sernett, "If Not Moses, Then Joshua," pp. 12–14; Gregg, "Sparks from the Anvil of Oppression," pp. 87–89, 311–12, 324–26. See also R. R. Wright, Jr., *Eighty-Seven Years Behind the Black Curtain: An Autobiography* (Philadelphia, 1965), and Wright, *Bishops of the A.M.E. Church*, pp. 371–77. For samples of his sociology, see Wright, *The Negro in Pennsylvania: A Study in Economic History* (Philadelphia, 1912); Wright, "The Northern Negro Population," *Southern Workman*, June 1912; Wright, "Migration of Negroes to the North," *Annals of the American Academy of Political and Social Science* 27, no. 1 (1906), pp. 559–78; and Wright's chapter on Xenia, Ohio, in W. E. B. Du Bois, ed., *The Negro Church: Report of a Social Study made under the Direction of Atlanta University* (Atlanta, 1903). On R. R. Wright, Sr., see Elizabeth Ross Haynes, *The Black Boy of Atlanta* (Boston, 1953); and H. F. Kletzing and W. H. Crogman, *Progress of a Race, or the Remarkable Advancement of the Afro-American* (1897; reprint ed., New York, 1969), pp. 477–79.

8. Wright, *Eighty-Seven Years Behind the Black Curtain*, p. 11; Wright, *Mission Study Course No. 2: Compiled as a Practical Aid for Those Studying for Missionary Work* (n.p., 1944). (While published only in 1944, the mission course was compiled in the early 1910s.) On the years in South Africa, see Charlotte Crogman Wright, *Beneath the Southern Cross: The Story of an American Bishop's Wife in South Africa* (New York, 1955); and J. Campbell, "Our Fathers, Our Children: the African Methodist Episcopal Church in the United States and South Africa" (Ph.D. diss., Stanford University, 1989), pp. 364–75.

9. Imanuel Geiss, *The Pan-African Movement: A History of Pan-Africanism in America, Europe and Africa* (New York, 1974), pp. 229–82; Alain Locke, ed., *The New Negro* (1925, reprint ed., New York, 1969). On links between Garveyism and developments in African American arts and letters, see Tony Martin, *Literary Garveyism: Garvey, Black Arts and the Harlem Renaissance* (Dover, Mass., 1983).

10. Smith's and Franklin's comments were reprinted in *Umteteli wa Bantu*, July 30, 1921, September 24, 1921, December 18, 1926. On the role of black churchmen in the first Congress, see Geiss, *The Pan-African Movement*, pp. 163–98.

11. See Randall K. Burkett, *Garveyism as a Religious Movement: The Institutionalization of a Black Civil Religion* (Metuchen, N.J., 1978), pp. 135–49 ff; Burkett, "The Religious Ethos of the Universal Negro Improvement Association," in Gayraud S. Wilmore, ed., *African American Religious History: An Interdisciplinary Anthology* (Durham, N.C., 1989); and Burkett, ed., *Black Redemption: Churchmen Speak for the Garvey Movement* (Philadelphia, 1978), pp. 4–18, 43–49, 65–84. The most prominent AME laypeople to identify publicly with U.N.I.A. were Ida B. Wells and T. Thomas Fortune. At least one minister, R. H. Tobitt, was suspended for supporting the movement.

12. On the 1914 Rebellion, see *The Report of the Judicial Commission of Inquiry into the Causes and Circumstances Relating to the Recent Rebellion in South Africa* (Pretoria, 1916); on the Rand Revolt of 1922, see Robert H. Davies, *Capital, State and White Labour in South Africa, 1900–1960: An Historical Materialist Analysis of Class Formation and Class Relations* (Atlantic Highlands, 1979), pp. 146–75; on postwar discontent among Africans, see Philip Bonner, "The Transvaal Congress, 1917–1920: The Radicalisation of the Black Petty Bourgeoisie on the Rand," in Shula Marks and Richard Rathbone, eds., *Industrialisation and Social Change in South Africa: African Class Formation, Culture and Consciousness, 1870–1930* (London, 1982); on white liberals' attempts to harness the American model, see Tim Couzens, "'Moralizing Leisure Time': The Transatlantic Connection and Black Johannesburg," in Marks and Rathbone, *Industrialisation and Social Change*.

13. This paragraph and much of what follows relies on Robert A. Hill and Gregory A. Pirio, "'Africa for the Africans': The Garvey Movement in South Africa, 1920–1940," in Shula Marks and Stanley Trapido, eds., *The Politics of Race, Class and Nationalism in Twentieth-Century South Africa* (London, 1987). Unfortunately, these pages were written before the publication of Garvey's Africa papers, an event that promises to transform our understanding of these connections.

14. *Negro World*, October 23, 1920, January 25, 1930, December 27, 1930; Hill and Pirio, "Africa for the Africans," pp. 210–14 ff.

15. See Helen Bradford, *A Taste of Freedom: The ICU in Rural South Africa, 1924–30* (Johannesburg, 1987), which traces the Union's career in a series of different rural contexts.

16. NTS 1434 29/214 vol. 1; Hill and Pirio, "Africa for the Africans," pp. 215–16. (The comments by Coka and Kadalie are both quoted on p. 215.) Kadalie noted the inspiration of Washington's autobiography in a letter to his son Alexander dated March 22, 1943, one of a collection of letters from father to son deposited at the African Studies Institute, University of the Witwatersrand. For Kadalie's career as correspondent, see *The Messenger*, September 1923, August 1924, November 1924, August 1925, September 1927. See also Kadalie, *My Life and the I.C.U.: The Autobiography of a Black Trade Unionist*, edited, with an introduction by Stanley Trapido (London, 1970).

17. *Negro World*, April 14, 1923, November 17, 1923; Hill and Pirio, "Africa for the Africans," pp. 215–27, 231–34. For police reports on Ncwana and Thaele, respectively, see JUS 915 1/18/26 vol. 3; and JUS 918 1/18/26 vol. 1. On Thaele, and on popular interest in black America in general, see Peter Walshe, *The Rise of African Nationalism in South Africa: The African National Congress, 1912–1952* (Berkeley, Calif., 1971), pp. 163–203.

18. NTS 1434 28/214 vol. 1; NTS 7604 26/328; NTS 7605 26/328. On Wellington, see Robert Edgar, "African Educational Protest in South Africa: The American School Movement in the Transkei in the 1920s," in Peter Kallaway, ed., *Education and Apartheid: the Education of Black South Africans* (Johannesburg, 1984); Edgar, "Dr. Wellington and the American Movement in South Africa, 1920–1940," unpublished paper; and Hill and Pirio, "Africa for the Africans," pp. 238–41. (The phrase "mimetic American Negroes" is from p. 239.)

19. Bradford, *A Taste of Freedom*, pp. 213–45. The "impression that I.C.U. leaders were deputising for Marcus Garvey" was not confined to Pondoland; see *Umteteli wa Bantu*, November 15, 1924, November 29, 1924.

20. NTS 1681 2/276 vol. 1; NTS 2692 4/301/1; GNLB 289 3/127/20 vol. 2; BNS 1/2/48 A1842; *Christian Express*, July 1, 1921; Hill and Pirio, "Africa for the Africans," p. 230.

21. R. Hunt Davis, "Nineteenth-Century African Education in the Cape Colony: A Historical Analysis" (Ph.D. diss., University of Wisconsin, 1969), pp. 220–27.

22. For representative concerns, see testimony of G. A. Wilder to *SANAC*, vol. 4, p. 17;

testimony of J. M. Springer to *SANAC,* vol. 4, pp. 128–29; and testimony of J. Kerr to *SANAC,* vol. 4, p. 213. See also Chapter 4, above.

23. Testimony of J. Stewart to *SANAC,* vol. 4, pp. 896–913. See also James Stewart, *Lovedale: Past and Present. A Register of Two Thousand Names* (Lovedale, 1887); and James Wells, *Stewart of Lovedale: The Life of James Stewart* (New York, 1909).

24. Louis R. Harlan, "Booker T. Washington and the White Man's Burden," *American Historical Review* 71, no. 2 (1966), pp. 441–67; Harlan, *Booker T. Washington: The Wizard of Tuskegee, 1901–1915* (New York, 1983), pp. 274–77. Washington's influence is also discussed in R. Hunt Davis, "The Black American Educational Component in African Responses to Colonialism in South Africa (ca. 1890–1914)," *Journal of Southern African Affairs* 3, no. 1 (1978), pp. 65–83.

25. Segregation remains one of the most frequently debated problems in South African historiography. This paragraph follows the increasingly unfashionable materialist interpretation associated with Harold Wolpe; see Wolpe, "Capitalism and Cheap Labour Power in South Africa: From Segregation to Apartheid," *Economy and Society* 1, no. 4 (1972), pp. 425–56. Saul Dubow advances a more broadly political interpretation, portraying segregation as a "generalised response on the part of the state to the problems wrought by industrialisation." Segregationist ideology's cachet, he suggests, rested precisely in its capacity to mean different things to different people. See Dubow, *Racial Segregation and the Origins of Apartheid in South Africa, 1919–1936* (London, 1989). Stanley Greenberg's *Race and State in Capitalist Development: Comparative Perspectives* (New Haven, 1980) inclines to the former position, while John Cell's *The Highest Stage of White Supremacy: The Origins of Segregation in South Africa and the American South* (New York, 1982) hews more to the latter, though within a broadly materialist framework. George Fredrickson's approach is *sui generis.* Interpreting segregation as a mechanism for establishing whites' distance from those nearest to them socially and culturally, he argues that African American experience can most usefully be compared to the experience of South African Coloured people; see *White Supremacy: A Comparative Study in American and South African History* (New York, 1981), pp. 255–82. See also Fredrickson, "The South and South Africa: Political Foundations of Segregation," in *The Arrogance of Race: Historical Perspectives on Slavery, Racism, and Social Inequality* (Middletown, Conn., 1988).

26. Cell, *The Highest Stage of White Supremacy,* pp. 21–45; Dubow, *Racial Segregation and the Origins of Apartheid,* pp. 21–52.

27. Maurice Evans, *Black and White in South East Africa: A Study in Sociology* (London, 1911); and Evans, *Black and White in the Southern States: A Study of the Race Problem in the United States from a South African Point of View* (London, 1915). See also Cell, *The Highest Stage of White Supremacy,* pp. 27–33 ff; Harlan, *The Wizard of Tuskegee,* p. 278; and C. Vann Woodward, *The Strange Career of Jim Crow,* 3rd ed. (New York, 1974), pp. 111–12.

28. Loram's *The Education of the South African Native* (London, 1917) begins with a tribute to Evans. See also R. Hunt Davis, "C. T. Loram and the American Model for African Education in South Africa," in Kallaway, *Education and Apartheid.* On "Stallardism," see Rodney Davenport, "African Townsmen: South African Natives (Urban Areas) Legislation Through the Years," *African Affairs* 68, no. 1 (1969), pp. 95–109; and Davenport, "The Triumph of Colonel Stallard: The Transformation of the Natives (Urban Areas) Act Between 1923 and 1937," *South African Historical Journal* 2, no. 1 (1970), pp. 77–96. My thanks to my friend Tim Couzens for a truly unique gift: Col. Stallard's copy of Evans's first book.

29. Quoted in Thomas Jesse Jones, *Education in Africa: A Study of West, South, and Equitorial Africa by the African Education Commission, under the Auspices of the Phelps-Stokes Fund* (New York, 1922), p. 193. See also W. G. Bennie, Chief Inspector of Native Education, Cape

Province, "The Education of the Native," in ABX 241007; and Davis, "Charles T. Loram and the American Model."

30. See, for example, F. B. Bridgman, "Social Conditions in Johannesburg," *International Review of Missions* 15, no. 8 (1926), pp. 569–83; J. Dexter Taylor, ed., *Christianity and the Natives of South Africa* (Lovedale, 1928). On liberal initiatives, see Couzens, "Moralizing Leisure Time"; Baruch Hirson, "Tuskegee, the Joint Councils, and the All-Africa Convention," in *Collected Seminar Papers of the Societies of Southern Africa in the Nineteenth and Twentieth Centuries*, vol. 10 (London, 1980); Martin Legassick, "The Rise of Modern South African Liberalism: Its Assumptions and Its Social Base," unpublished paper; Paul Rich, *White Power and the Liberal Conscience* (Manchester, 1984), pp. 10–32; and Chapter 8, above. See also B. J. Schulman, "The Institute of Human Relations at Yale, 1929–1945" (B.A. thesis, Yale College, 1981).

31. Ray Phillips, *The Bantu Are Coming* (London, 1930); and Phillips, *The Bantu in the City* (Lovedale, 1936); Couzens, "Moralizing Leisure Time." For samples of Phillips's journalism, see the sketches of Banneker and Carver in *Umteteli wa Bantu*, March 10, 1926, August 21, 1926.

32. Thomas Jesse Jones, *Negro Education: A Study of the Private and Higher Schools for Colored People in the United States* (Washington, D.C., 1917). On Jones, see Kenneth J. King, *Education and Pan-Africanism: A Study of Race Philanthropy and Education in the Southern States of America and East Africa* (Oxford, 1971), pp. 21–43.

33. Jones, *Education in Africa*, introduction by Anson Phelps Stokes; King, *Education and Pan-Africanism*, pp. 52–57. The standard work on Aggrey remains Edwin Smith, *Aggrey of Africa: A Study in Black and White* (London, 1929).

34. Jones's *Education in Africa* recounts the commission's itinerary. On worries about Aggrey, see NTS 7602 15/328.

35. Jones, *Education in Africa*, pp. xviii–xxii, 179–223; the quotation is from p. 191. Anson Phelps Stokes shared Jones's beliefs about the centrality of South Africa and later traveled there himself as a Carnegie lecturer. He published his findings in *Report on Education, Native Welfare, and Race Relations in East and South Africa* (New York, 1934). The report of the second Phelps-Stokes Commission, which spent considerably less time in South Africa, was again written by Jones; see *Education in East Africa: A Study of East, Central and South Africa by the Second African Education Commission Under the Auspices of the Phelps-Stokes Fund* (New York, 1925). See also Loram's contribution to the *Twenty Year Report of the Phelps-Stokes Fund, 1911–1931* (New York, 1931).

36. Smith, *Aggrey of Africa*, pp. 164–84; Loram's letter is quoted on p. 171. Loram's later reflections on Aggrey's lecturing style were revealing: "He adapted himself to his audience in a most remarkable way. To children he was inspiring; to Europeans humorous, conciliatory and deeply earnest; to Natives graphic, eloquent and vividly emotional." See Smith, *Aggrey of Africa*, p. 173.

37. Loram recollected the event in a 1935 speech at the Bantu Men's Social Centre; see *Umteteli wa Bantu*, May 25, 1935. Aggrey himself told an audience at Lovedale that he was constantly approached by Africans inquiring about the arrival of Garvey's fleet; see *Aggrey of Africa*, p. 122. On the Chilembwe rising, see George Shepperson and Thomas Price, *Independent African: John Chilembwe and the Nyasaland Rising of 1915* (Edinburgh, 1958).

38. The quotation is from Phillips's column in *Umteteli wa Bantu*, June 22, 1926.

39. *Journal of the Twenty-Sixth Quadrennial Session of the General Conference of the African Methodist Episcopal Church. Held in St. Louis, Missouri, May 3–18, 1920* (Nashville, 1920); NTS 1423 12/214; Wright, *Beneath the Southern Cross*, p. 39.

40. W. T. Vernon, *The Upbuilding of a Race—or—The Rise of a Great People: A Compilation of Sermons, Addresses and Writings on Education, the Race Question and Public Affairs* (Quindaro, Kan., 1904), pp. 30–36, 72–73 ff. Vernon's career is described in a campaign pamphlet for the

1920 episcopal elections, titled *William Tecumseh Vernon: A Sketch of the Life and Works of the Most Faithful Servant of the Church of Allen* (n.p., 1920). (Copy in Levi Coppin papers, Wilberforce University Archives.) See also Wright, *The Bishops of the A.M.E. Church*, pp. 344–46.

41. NTS 1423 12/214; BNS 1/2/48 A1842; GG 1899 61/293; GG 1899 61/305; GG 1899 61/313; Hill and Pirio, "Africa for the Africans," pp. 223–24. Documents from the episode are reprinted in C. S. Smith, *A History of the African Methodist Episcopal Church* (Philadelphia, 1922), pp. 331–36.

42. BNS 1/2/48 A1842; NTS 1423 12/214; GG 1899 61/313; Johannesburg *Star*, October 11, 1921, October 12, 1921; *Ilanga lase Natal*, July 7, 1922.

43. NTS 1423 12/214; Johannesburg *Star*, October 12, 1921. The veiled reference to Garveyism was reprinted in *Umteteli wa Bantu*, July 30, 1921.

44. Hill and Pirio, "Africa for the Africans," pp. 224–25. See also "A.M.E. Church and Negro Movement," *The Black Man*, October 1920; and NTS 1681 2/276 vol. 1. My thanks to Tim Couzens for the reference to Tantsi, included in a November 9, 1920, letter from the Bloemfontein Town Clerk to the Secretary for Native Affairs in Pretoria.

45. NTS 1423 12/214; NTS 1423 12/214 (III); NTS 1434 28/214 vol. 1; *Annual Report of the South African Native Affairs Commission* (Pretoria, 1921), p. 12; *Report of the Native Churches Commission* (Cape Town, 1925), p. 35; Allen Lea, *The Native Separatist Church Movement in South Africa* (Cape Town, 1926), pp. 59, 69–71.

46. George Champion Papers, University of South Africa Archives, Box 1 2.2.2. For Champion's career, see Shula Marks, "George Champion and the Ambiguities of Class and Class Consciousness," in *The Ambiguities of Dependence in South Africa: Class, Nationalism and the State in Twentieth-Century Natal* (Johannesburg, 1986).

47. Interview with Selloane Legobathe by M. T. Nkadimeng, March 27–28, 1986, African Studies Institute, Oral History Project, ref. 543–44. See also interview with Kas Maine by C. van Onselen and J. Campbell, August 22, 1985 (notes in author's possession); NTS 1424 12/214; and Bradford, *A Taste of Freedom*, pp. 145–85, 334 n. 21. The case for continuity between the AME Church and the I.C.U. in the southwestern Transvaal is made in Charles van Onselen *Chameleon Among the Boers: The Life Story of Kas Maine* (New York, 1995).

48. Quoted in Hill and Pirio, "Africa for the Africans," pp. 224–25; *Cape Argus*, January 29, 1923; *Negro World*, August 22, 1925, October 16, 1926. (The second quotation is from an undated clipping, ca. April, 1927, given me by Tim Couzens.)

49. GNLB 281 446/17/D48; JUS 920 1/18/26 vol. 18. The C.I.D. records are deposited in the Papers of the Minister of Justice, Pretoria Archives Depot; see especially JUS 915–29.

50. NTS 1424 12/214; JUS 923 1/18/26 vol. 25; Jack and Ray Simons, *Class and Colour in South Africa, 1850–1950* (London, 1983), pp. 376, 417–26; Thomas Karis, Gwendolen Carter, and Gail M. Gerhart, eds., *From Protest to Challenge: A Documentary History of African Politics in South Africa 1882–1964* (Stanford, 1977), vol. 4, p. 153. Tantsi ultimately served as an AME elder for more than three decades, remaining politically active throughout. He served on the Transvaal executive of the A.N.C. through the 1930s and '40s, acceding to the office of acting president in the Transvaal in 1952 while Nelson Mandela was occupied in the Defiance Campaign. He received a government banning order for his efforts. A staunch advocate of African unity, he helped found the Interdenominational African Ministers Federation and worked to broker an agreement between the A.N.C. and the Pan-African Congress in 1960–1961. To top it all, he published a short history of the AME Church; see N. B. Tantsi, *Historical Sketch of the AME Church in South Africa* (n.p., 1940).

51. NTS 2692 4/301/1 vol. 1; JUS 921 1/18/26 vol. 19; NTS 1424 12/214.

52. JUS 916 1/18/26 vol. 5; JUS 916 1/18/26 vol. 6; Walshe, *The Rise of African Nationalism*,

pp. 169–87; Simons and Simons, *Class and Colour,* pp. 343–60, 388–93; Karis, Carter, and Gerhart, *From Protest to Challenge,* vol. 1; *Political Profiles,* p. 50.

53. The list is reproduced in JUS 921 1/18/26 vol. 21.

54. JUS 916 1/18/26 vol. 4. Khaile's fate remains obscure. Several informants suggested that he was killed during a township robbery in the 1930s or '40s, but I have been unable to confirm the account.

55. On Sontaga and the elder Mngqibisa, see Chapter 4.

56. NSNA 1/1/323 1767/05; NSNA 1/1/388 3801/07; NSNA 1/1/428 1909/1068.

57. JUS 919 1/18/26 vol. 15; JUS 921 1/18/26 vol. 20; GNLB 313 125/19/48 vol. 3; NTS 7602 23/328; NTS 7664 32/332 vol. 1.

58. JUS 917 1/18/26 vol. 8; JUS 918 1/18/26 vol. 9; NTS 7602 23/328. On Herschel, see William Macmillan, *Complex South Africa* (London, 1930); and Colin Bundy, *The Rise and Fall of the South African Peasantry* (London, 1979).

59. See Chapter 6, above.

60. NTS 7664 32/332 vol. 1; NTS 7664 32/332 vol. 2; 2/SPT 16 N1/9/2 (Native agitator: Mngqibisa). See also William Beinart, "*Amafelandawonye* (the Die-hards): Popular Protest and Women's Movements in Herschel District in the 1920s," in Beinart and Colin Bundy, *Hidden Struggles in Rural South Africa: Politics and Popular Movements in the Transkei and Eastern Cape, 1890–1930* (Johannesburg, 1987); and Beinart, "Women in Rural Politics: Herschel District in the 1920s and 1930s," in Belinda Bozzoli, ed., *Class, Community and Conflict: South African Perspectives* (Johannesburg, 1987).

61. NTS 483 6/64; NTS 7602 23/328; NTS 7664 32/332 vol. 1; 2/SPT 16 N1/9/2; *Umteteli wa Bantu,* May 8, 1926.

62. NTS 7602 23/328; NTS 7664 32/332 vol. 1.

63. NTS 1423 12/214; NTS 2796 29/302 vol. 1; NTS 7602 23/328; NTS 7664 32/332 vol. 1. For Gregg's prior career in South Africa, see Dennis C. Dickerson, ed., *The Land of the Southern Cross: John A. Gregg and South Africa* (n.p., 1900); and Chapter 7, above. For a sample of Gregg's accommodationist approach, see reports of his speech to Johannesburg's Gamma Sigma Club, *Umteteli wa Bantu,* March 20, 1926.

64. Toba's reports are scattered through the Papers of the Minister of Justice, mostly between JUS 915 and 922.

65. JUS 917 1/18/26 vol. 8.

66. JUS 918 1/18/26 vol. 9; JUS 918 1/18/26 vol. 12.

67. JUS 918 1/18/26 vol. 9; JUS 918 1/18/26 vol. 10; JUS 918 1/18/26 vol. 11; JUS 921 1/18/26 vol. 20.

68. JUS 918 1/18/26 vol. 9; JUS 918 1/18/26 vol. 11.

69. JUS 918 1/18/26 vol. 9.

Epilogue

1. See, for example, NTS 1423 12/214 vol. 3; NTS 1425 12/214 vol. 4; NTS 2719 394/301; and *Umteteli wa Bantu,* October 20, 1934, December 1, 1934, February 16, 1935, February 23, 1935.

2. ABX Box 5 file 38; JUS 923 1/18/26 vol. 27; JUS 925 1/18/26 vol. 34; NTS 1681 2/276 vol. 1; *Umteteli wa Bantu,* April 4, 1934, June 16, 1934.

3. Robert R. Edgar, ed., *An African American in South Africa: The Travel Notes of Ralph J. Bunche, 28 September 1937–1 January 1938* (Johannesburg, 1992).

4. Edgar, *An African American in South Africa,* pp. 55–56, 133–36, 211–12, 265–69 ff. (Jabavu's comment is on p. 135.)

5. Edgar, *An African American in South Africa*, pp. 66, 70–71, 75–81, 89–90. (The quotation is from p. 66.)

6. Edgar, *An African American in South Africa*, pp. 130–37 ff. (The quotation is from p. 137.)

7. "A Hero's Welcome," *Time*, July 2, 1990, pp. 17–19.

8. "Mandela Mania Grips America," *Newsweek*, July 2, 1990, p. 19.

9. "Nelson Mandela: A Special Message to Black Americans," *Ebony*, May 1990, pp. 180–82; "Nelson Mandela Live! A Super Welcome for a Super Hero," *Ebony*, September 1990, pp. 136–38; "Hero's Welcome," *Time*, July 2, 1990, p. 18; "Mandela Mania," *Newsweek*, July 2, 1990, p. 16.

10. "Hero's Welcome," *Time*, July 2, 1990, pp. 19–20.

11. "A Summit of Concern," *Ebony*, January 1992, pp. 28–32.

12. Johannesburg *Star*, February 18, 1993.

INDEX

AME Church: and American Revolution, 13–20; antebellum expansion, 32–35; Board of Church Extension, 234, 297; Book Concern, 39, 49, 81; camp meetings, 33–34, 40–41, 48, 56; dependence on local contributions, 37, 43; early educational initiatives, 26, 34, 38; episcopal elections, 13, 58, 95, 221, 227, 241, 246, 298–99, 313–14; and Great Migration, 296–99; institutionalization, 32, 36–38, 43, 56–57, 142; itinerant ministry, 33–35, 56; lay exhorters, 39, 48–50, 52; ministerial education, 38–39, 43, 48, 58, 62–63; music, 41–43, 57, 62; origins, 10–13; and Reconstruction, 53–63, 348 n.53; struggle over worship, ix, 37, 39–44, 47–48, 61–63; white opposition, 34–35, 57–58; women, xi, 43–53, 93–95

GENERAL CONFERENCES: 1816, 33; 1820, 35; 1844, 38, 74; 1848, 49; 1852, 50; 1864, 50; 1868, 58; 1872, 60; 1880, 58; 1884, 52; 1900, 93, 137, 227, 254–55, 266, 270, 274; 1904, 239, 241–43, 255; 1908, 246; 1920, 297, 313, 315, 318

MISSIONS: Easter Day collection, 90, 95, 217–18, 228, 234, 240, 247; emerging consensus on, 90–96; and emigration, 69–70, 80–81, 84–85, 88–89; to freedmen, 53–63; in Haiti, 71, 95; Home and Foreign Mission Society, 74; hymnody, 97; ideology of, 94–99, 221–22, 332–33; in Liberia, 80, 84, 88–89, 236; Missionary Department, 53, 81, 91, 234, 297; natural fitness argument, 92, 96–98;

in Sierra Leone, 89–92; shortages of funds, 90, 217, 234, 240–43; Woman's Home and Foreign Missionary Society, 93–95, 292; Woman's Missionary Society, 275, 285, 293; Woman's Mite Missionary Society, 93–95, 228, 265, 292, 295, as women's task, 93–95. *See also* AME Church, South Africa

POLITICS AND IDEOLOGY: accommodation, 34–35, 86, 263, 268, 297; defense of autonomy, 20–22, 54–55, 342 n.44; electoral politics, 58–60; elitism, 28, 60, 270; gender ideology, 50–53, 93–95; racial vindication, 22, 25–28, 55, 64, 68, 269–70. *See also* Nationalism, African American; Antislavery; Pan-Africanism

AME Church, South Africa: absorbs mission congregations, 164, 205–7, 232–33, 247; and chiefly authority, 185–93, 197–203; denounced by whites, 138–42, 146, 185, 249; dependence on local contributions, 142, 152, 172, 187, 323; educational initiatives, 148, 152, 154–58, 164, 168, 173; ethnic tensions, 226, 244–45; hailed for stability and moderation, 216, 247, 295–96, 314–16; harassment of mission loyalists, 202–6, 212, 232, 321, 325; institutionalization, 136–38, 142–43, 215–17, 230, 233–34, 246–48; itinerant ministry, 209, 230, 254; lay preachers, 163, 168, 209, ordinations, 138, 230, 363 n.79; in refugee camps, 166, 207; schisms in, 218–22, 240, 244–46; tensions between Africans and African Ameri-

ACME Church, South Africa (*Cont.*)
cans, 231–46; as an urban movement,
153–59, 166–70, 172–74

EXPANSION, 139, 364 n.2; in Barotseland, 191–93; in Bechuanaland,
160, 187–91; in eastern Cape and
Transkei, 159–60, 194–98, 202–6; in
Orange Free State, 160, 163–64,
166–69, 178; in western Transvaal,
160, 179; on Witwatersrand, 145–48,
154–55

GOVERNMENT POLICY: in Boer republics, 137, 150, 171, 222; in
Cape, 189, 204–5, 218, 223–26,
229–30, 233–34, 244, 247; during
imperial reconstruction, 150–52,
154–58, 171–72, 223, 244–46; following retrocession, 156, 176–77,
226; municipal restrictions, 171–75,
179; in Natal, 223, 226, 247; transatlantic connection encouraged, 224–
26, 230–34, 244, 247–48, 295–96,
314–16; in Union, 244, 247–48

POLITICS AND IDEOLOGY: centrality
of land, 152–54, 184–85, 188, 195–
97, 211; denunciations of British hypocrisy, 150–53, 157; eclecticism,
182, 204–12, 319–21; emphasis on
autonomy, 163, 170–73, 178–79,
184, 201, 108–9; and Garveyism,
317–19; and Industrial and Commercial Workers' Union, 317–21, 324–
26; localism, 141–43, 152, 157,
206–7, 212; neotraditionalism, 182,
184, 188, 192–93, 203, 206, 322–
24; proto-nationalism, 141, 151, 158;
racial populism, 151–52, 155–57,
169, 211–12; recourse to courts, 153–
54, 173–74; urban campaigns, 153–
59, 170–76. *See also* Nationalism, African

SOCIAL COMPOSITION: chiefs, 141,
180–82, 185–92, 199–203; Coloured
people, 141, 160; defies generalization, 139–43, 182, 196–97, 206–8,
212; disaffected Christians, 196, 204–
8; domestic servants, 148; mineworkers, 148; railway workers, 148,
169; refugees, 165–66; sharecroppers,

163–64, 177–79, 317–18; tradesmen,
147, 170, 173; traditionalists, 196;
urban Africans, 147–48, 152, 154–
56, 159, 167–73; women, 147, 168

AME Church Magazine, 38

AME Church Review, 87, 95, 97, 227–28,
297–98

AME Zion Church, 13, 45, 81, 252

Abantu Batho, 151

Abolition: in District of Columbia, 53;
Emancipation Proclamation, 77; in
North, 8, 16. *See also* Antislavery

Abyssinia. *See* Ethiopia

Adams, John Hurst, 333

Addams, Jane, 298

Address to the Public and People of Color, 28

Africa, African American images of: as benighted land, 66, 68–70, 74, 80, 84–
87, 96–98; as Christian empire, 81–
83, 85, 89; as cradle of civilization,
75, 82–83, 221–22; as fatherland,
93, 97, 228; as field for heroism, 95–
98, 227; as field of opportunity, 236;
as motherland, 93–94, 228; as promised land, 78–79, 82, 98; self-
referential quality, xii–xiii, 97–99,
222, 231, 300; slumbering continent,
83–84, 266; travellers' accounts, 76–
77, 83–86, 89, 91, 228–29; as white
man's graveyard, 92. *See also* Nationalism, African American; Pan-
Africanism

Africa and African Methodism, 84

African: as designation for African Americans, viii, 73

African Americans

IN SOUTH AFRICA: barred from entry, 257, 305, 314; and chiefly authority, 195–201, 228–29, 241–42;
entrepreneurial activities, 193, 236–
37; in nineteenth century, 120, 125–
27; in 1930s, 328; in 1990s, 333; restrictions on travel, 142, 150, 171,
215, 223–25, 238, 242, 245–47;
sailors, 301, 305

AFRICAN IMAGES OF: as educated,
131–34, 198, 209–11; as free, 132,
135, 210, 232, 304; as liberators,
140, 152–53, 197, 211, 301–4; as

model, 127, 129–33, 136–38, 142,
163, 199, 212, 261, 302, 315; as
powerful, 157–58, 330; self-referential
quality, xii–xiii, 139, 158; as unified,
140–41, 326; as wealthy, 184–85,
198, 222. *See also* Ethiopian Church
African Church, Philadelphia, 10, 20–21
African Church, Pretoria, 115, 121, 144,
181
African Communities League. *See* Universal
Negro Improvement Association
African Farmers' Association, 154, 279
African Jubilee Choir, 133–34, 252, 266,
282
African National Congress: and AME
Church, 117, 319–20; deputations to
Britain, 279, 285; exclusion of
women, 288; and Natives Land Act,
279; and pass laws, 286–87; South
African Native National Congress,
129, 147, 151, 159, 250, 285, 295;
U.S.-educated leadership, 256, 275–
76, 281; Western Cape branch, 303;
Youth League, 275, 281. *See also* Na-
tionalism, African
African Native Church, 115, 123, 194,
323
African Political Union, 151, 157
African Presbyterian Church, 114–15, 130,
194, 256, 306, 321
African redemption (by African Americans):
foretold in Bible, ix, 66, 68, 70,
135, 216; natural fitness argument,
75–77, 81–83, 92; rejected, 92, 220;
slavery as a providential school, 88,
96, 221–22, 315, 322–23
African students: educated in U.S. *See*
Wilberforce University, African Students
African Student Union, 274–75
African Yearly Register, 282
Africans, African American images of: as
ancestors, 82–84, 99; as brethren, 89,
96–97; as children, 70, 85, 93–95,
98–99, 241, 266; as heathens, 83–89,
98, 216, 241; as noble, 135–36; as
savages, 251; as slaves, 97–98, 216
Afrocentrism, xii–xiii. *See also* Ethiopianism; Nationalism, African; National-

ism, African American; Pan-
Africanism
Aggrey, James E. Kwegyir, 250, 252,
311–13, 317, 392 nn.36–37
Agitators: African American, 170, 200,
215, 257, 305; American-educated,
249; C.I.D. 'Native agitator' list,
319–20, 328; theory, 139–40, 177,
215, 324
Akron, Ohio, 270
Alabama, 35, 56
All-Africa Convention, 293
Allen, John, 71
Allen, Richard, 32–33, 35, 38, 43, 63–
65, 67, 74, 103, 116, 119, 269,
275, 321, 333; countenances emigra-
tion, 71; defends black equality, 20,
25, 31, 37, 55, 59, 86, 97, 232;
early life, 5–8, 339 n.10; establishes
AME Church, viii, 11–13; openness
to emotion, 40–41; opposes coloniza-
tion, 68–70, 72–73; opposition to
slavery, 7, 20–28; relationship with
Methodist authorities, 7–14; and
women preachers, 45, 48–49. *See also*
AME Church
Allen, Sarah, 43, 53
Amagqunukhwebe, 123
Amahlubi, 206, 323
Amakolwa, 123, 147, 254–55
Amanzimtoti Institute, 254
American Board of Missions, 107, 252,
254; in Johannesburg, 278, 309–13;
secessions from, 115, 147, 208
American Colonization Society, 14, 19,
30–31, 65, 68–79, 87, 90, 92, 251.
See also Colonization
American Negro Academy, 262, 269
American Revolution: libertarian impetus,
13–16, 24–25, 65; post-revolutionary
reaction, 29–30; and racism, 16–20
American School Movement, 303
American Zulu Mission. *See* American
Board of Missions
Anglicanism: in Philadelphia, 9–10; Episcopal Church, 74, 93; Order of Ethiopia, 218–21; secessions from, 115,
120, 188, 190, 208; South African
missions, 104, 108–9

Angola, 311–12
Antioch College, 259
Antislavery: and American Revolution, 15–17; black contribution to, 20–31; and colonization, 65–69. *See also* Abolition
Apartheid, 122, 195, 293, 334
Apology for African Methodism, 51
Apostolic Faith Mission, 245
Apostolic succession: in AME Church, 219, 375–76, n.9
Appeal to the Coloured Citizens of the World, 22
Arkansas, 79
Armstrong, Samuel Chapman, 306
Arnett, Benjamin, 94, 98, 134, 261–63, 268, 270
Asbury, Francis, 6, 8, 10–11
Ashforth, Adam, 279
Ashmun Institute. *See* Lincoln University
Atkins, Keletso, 126
Atlanta Compromise, 86
Atlanta Cotton States and International Exposition, 86, 92
Atlanta University, 298
Attaway, A. Henry, 193, 235–37, 239, 373 n.30
Augusta, Geo., 56
Autobiography of an Unknown South African, 160
Autobiography of W. E. B. DuBois, 269
Ayliff, James, 325
Azikiwe, Nnamdi, 250, 276
Azor, 79–80, 88–89, 300

Back-to-Africa Movement. *See* Emigration
Bafokeng, 160
Bakhatla, 143, 180; ba Mocha, 185
Bakwena, 143, 160–61
Baltimore, Md., 12, 35, 42, 67–68, 148
Baltimore Annual Conference, 38, 39
Bambatha rebellion, 226, 249
Banda, Hastings K., 250, 257, 273
Bangcolo, Transkei, 203
Bangwaketse, 190
Bangwato, 160–61, 190
Banneker, Benjamin, 29, 310
Bantu are Coming, The, 310
Bantu in the City, The, 310

Bantu Men's Social Centre, 310
Bantu Purity League, 257
Bantu Women's League, 286, 288, 291, 293
Bapedi, 116, 143, 183
Baptist Churches, 6, 62–63, 93; African missions, 70, 93, 351 n.13, 356 n.71
Baraka, Imamu Amiri, 332
Barolong: Ratlou, 188; Seleka, 122, 160, 181, 187–88; Tshidi, 187, 190
Barotseland, 182, 191–93, 236
Basotho, 160
Basotho-Boer Wars, 160, 188
Basutoland: AME Church in, 129, 200, 242; European missions in, 104, 114; migration from, 160–61, 165
Bathoen, Chief, 190–91
Beanes, Scipio, 71–72
Beaumont Commission, 279
Bechuanaland, 160, 186–91, 200–201, 242
Bechuanaland Methodist Church, 169, 244
Benevolent societies. *See* Voluntary associations
Benezet, Anthony, 9, 17
Benoni, Tvl., 322, 324, 326
Bensonvale Institute, 122, 170, 178
Berlin Mission Society, 104, 115, 144, 183, 208
Bethany, O. F. S., 167
Bethel Church, Atlanta, 78, 353 n.33
Bethel Church, Baltimore, 12
Bethel Church, Cape Town, 245
Bethel Church, Charleston, 56
Bethel Church, Philadelphia, 10–11, 21–22, 26, 30, 39–45, 48–49, 68, 71–73, 95, 104, 119, 135, 227
Bethel Institute, 234–35, 238, 243, 247, 282
Bethlehem, O. F. S., 165, 168, 177, 287
Bethulie, O. F. S., 170, 174–76, 211–12
Bible: and African American history, 68; equalitarian implications, 24; and slavery, 4, 6, 23, 132. *See also* Ethiopia; Israelites
  BOOKS: Acts, 44, 47, 119; Corinthians, 47, 94; Deuteronomy, 7; Exodus, iv, ix, 4, 66, 68, 97, 135; Ezekiel, 325–26; Genesis, 1, 55, 119;

Isaiah, vii, 7, 46, 68, 70; Kings, 68; Leviticus, 128; Nehemiah, 12, 68, 101, 135, 325; Peter, 13, 23; Psalms, vii, 41–42, 66, 75, 103, 119, 135, 139, 158, 213; Romans, 231
CHARACTERS: Jacob and Esau, 197, 326; Joseph, 66; Moses, 97, 135, 331; Noah, 50; Paul, 6, 54; Philip, 119; Simon of Cyrene, 119; Solomon and Sheba, 119, 152, 211
Birmingham, Ala., 331
Bizana, Transkei, 185
Black Church: African survivals in, viii–ix, 3, 28, 41–42, 61–64, 338 n.1, 343 n.59; origins of, 3–5; politics and ideology, ix, xi, 13–15. *See also specific denominations*
Black and White in South East Africa, 308
Black and White in the Southern States, 308
Black Man, The, 301, 303, 305, 318
Black Star Line, 80, 300
Bloemfontein, O. F. S., 137, 163, 167, 176, 302, 322; AME Church in, 164, 169–74
Bloemhof, Tvl., 160, 179
Blyden, Edward, 20, 74–76, 78, 81–82, 90
Bokleni, Chief, 203
Boksburg, Tvl., 155, 158–59, 283–84, 289
Boksburg Native Vigilance Association, 158
Bokwe, John Knox, 129–30, 133
Boshof, O. F. S., 168
Boston, Mass., 9, 67
Botha, Louis, 308
Bowen, Thomas, 76
Boweni, Michael, 107
Boycotts: of white institutions, 195, 303–4, 323–25
Boyer, Jean Pierre, 71–72. *See* Haiti
Brander, Samuel, 120, 125, 226, 239–40
Brazil, 3
Brethren Mission Church of South Africa, 245
Bridgman, Clara, 309
Bridgman, Francis, 287, 309
British South Africa Company, 127, 190–93, 307

Broadbent, Samuel, 360 n.34
Brotherhood of Sleeping Car Porters, 303
Brown, Francis, 262
Brown, Hallie Quinn, 93, 262
Brown, Jere, 262
Brown, J. M., 79
Brown, Morris, 35, 39, 49, 74
Brown, Morris, Jr., 42
Brown, Thomas, 262
Bulawayo, Rhodesia, 228
Bulhoek massacre, 248, 316
Bunche, Ralph, 329–30
Bureau of Refugees, Freedmen and Abandoned Lands, 56, 60, 78, 80, 298
Burghersdorp, Cape, 129
Burkett, Randall, 300
Bush, George, 330–32
Buthelezi, Wellington, 303–4, 319
Butterworth, Transkei, 202

Cain, R. H., 56, 58–59, 79, 95, 298
Caluza, Reuben, 257
Campbell, Mary A., 94
Campbell, Robert, 76
Campbell, S. J., 88
Campbell, Tunis, 59
Camphor, Alexander, 97
Canada: AME Church in, 33, 351 n.18; African American expatriate community, 33, 67, 71–74, 76, 89, 262
Cape African Teachers Association, 329
Cape Argus, 318
Cape Colony: annexation of Transkei, 183, 194–95, 197–98; decline of reserves, 194–96, 205; early mission activity, 104; Native Affairs Department, 184, 234; Native Education Commission, 309, 312; reliance on state headmen, 184, 201–4. *See also* AME Church, South Africa, GOVERNMENT POLICY
Cape franchise. *See* Franchise
Cape liberalism, 112, 123, 151
Cape Native Congress, 141
Cape-to-Cairo railroad, 191, 218
Cape Town: AME Church in, 137, 141, 160, 181, 190, 192–93, 221, 226, 231, 234, 236, 243–45, 271, 329;

Cape Town (*Cont.*)
  Coloured elite, 127, 201, 330; dias-
    pora community, 126, 301; dock-
    workers' strike, 302; plague scare,
    141, 155
Carey, Lott, 70, 351 n.13
Carey, Matthew, 27
Carnegie Foundation, 264–65, 309, 328–
  29
Carver, George Washington, 310, 331
Catholic Church, 3, 104
Cecilton, Md., 56–57, 62, 227
Cele, Q. M., 257
*Central Africa: Adventures and Missionary
  Labours in the Interior of Africa*, 76
Central Tennessee College, 251
Chamber of Mines, 278, 310, 321
Champion, George, 316–17. *See also* In-
  dustrial and Commercial Workers'
  Union
Charleston, S. C., 35, 37, 54–56, 80
Chatsworth Normal, Mechanical and Indus-
  trial Institute, 236–37
Chauncey, Charles, 5
Chicago, Ill., 298–99, 332
Chiefly authority: and African Methodism,
  180–82, 187–93, 196, 198–204,
  228–29, 323–24; and colonial state,
  123, 182–84, 189, 191–93, 197–98;
  and European missions, 182–86, 203.
  See also specific chiefs
Chilembwe, John: African uprising led by,
  250, 313
Chillicothe, Ohio, 33, 260
Chinese indentured laborers, 149
Chou, Joseph, 175
Christian Express, 133, 224, 380 n.78
Christian Recorder, 50, 61, 87, 93, 217,
  299
Christiana, Tvl., 160, 179
Christy Minstrels, 127. *See also* Minstrelsy;
  Music, African American
Church of the Province of South Africa. *See*
  Anglicanism
Cincinnati, Ohio, 33, 72, 259–60
Cincinnati Gazette, 260
Citizen and Southern Bank, Phil., 299
Civil Rights Act (1875): overturned by Su-
  preme Court, 78, 81

Civil Rights Act (1990), 332
Civil War, U.S., 53–54, 77, 80, 126–27,
  211, 260
Clarke, Edward, 262
Clay, Edward, 29
Clay, Henry, 68
Claypool, David, 29
Cleveland, Ohio, 133–34, 260, 262
Cofimvaba, Transkei, 194
Coillard, Francois, 191–93
Coker, Daniel, 20, 29, 38, 59, 90, 98; an-
  tislavery career, 23–25, 31, 232; early
  life and career, 12–13; travels to Af-
  rica, 12, 67, 69–70, 72, 74
*Collection of Hymns and Spiritual Songs from
  Various Authors*, 41
Colonization: debate within black commu-
  nity, ix, 31, 68–75, 95; Lincoln on,
  77–78, 353 n.32; origins, 64–65, 68
Coka, Gilbert, 302
Colored Methodist Episcopal Church, 58,
  63
Coloured Advisory Committee, 278
Coloured population: and AME Church,
  141, 160; and African American mu-
  sic, 127–28; in Pretoria, 144; schools,
  154–55, 157
Columbia University, 258; Teachers Col-
  lege, 281, 308
Columbian Exposition: Congress on Africa,
  92, 98
Columbus, Ohio, 270
Commerce: vehicle of African redemption,
  65, 67, 81. *See also* African redemp-
  tion; Emigration
*Commission Appointed to Enquire into As-
  saults on Women*, 286
Committee for the Suppression of Vice and
  Immorality, 28
Communist Party of S. A., 179, 319–21,
  328–29
Complex South Africa, 322
Compound system, 105, 145, 148, 310,
  365 n.17, 366 n.23
Compromise of 1850, 74
Concentration camps, 165
*Condition, Elevation, Emigration and Des-
  tiny of the Colored People of the United
  States, The*, 76

Congo, 97
Congregationalism, 93, 107–8, 142. *See also* American Board of Missions
Congress, U.S., 24–25, 29, 59, 330
Congress on Africa. *See* Columbian Exposition
Conservation of Races, The, 269
Constitution, U.S., 14, 25, 81, 87; Fourteenth and Fifteenth Amendments, 78
Coon Carnival, 128
Cooper, Anna Julia, 44, 94, 262
Coplan, David, 127, 129
Coppin, Fanny Jackson, 44, 93, 227–28, 238, 290
Coppin, Levi: career in South Africa, 200–201, 212, 215, 228–36, 240–43, 282; early life, 56, 227; interest in Africa, 95–97, 227–28, 298; memories of Reconstruction, 56–58, 61–62; respect for African culture, 228–29, 377 n.30
Corporal punishment (of Africans), 167, 289
Coryndon, R. T., 192, 372 n.27
Coryndon Concession, 192
Cotton: in U.S., 16, 78; in South Africa, 126
Countess of Huntingdon Connexion, 89
Couzens, Tim, 310
Cox, Joseph, 45
Cradock, Cape, 252
Crogman, W. H., 270
Crogman Clinic, 275
Crummell, Alexander, 74–76, 78, 81, 83, 228, 268–70, 293
Cuffe, Paul, 67–69, 80–81, 201
Cullen, Countee, 299

Daley, Richard, 332
Dalindyebo, Chief, 184, 284
Dana, Gordon, 256
Dark Continent. *See* Africa, images of
Daughters of Conference, 43–44, 49
Daughters of Zion, 49, 52
Davis, R. Hunt, 305
De Niro, Robert, 332
Dean, Harry, 201, 236
Declaration of Independence, 17, 24–25. *See also* American Revolution

Delany, Martin, 75–79, 91–82, 228, 262, 352 n.29
Delaware, 5, 13, 16
Derrick, William, 245–46, 313, 349 n.62
Detroit, Mich., 331
Dialogue Between a Virginian and an African Minister, 23
Dickson, J. Q., 173
Dinkins, David, 331
Disfranchisement. *See* Franchise
Doctrines and Discipline of the AME Church, 13, 56, 70, 134–35, 137, 142, 219, 230, 243, 321
Domestic ideology, 44, 46, 50, 52–53, 94–95, 228, 288. *See also* AME Church, POLITICS AND IDEOLOGY; Women
Domestic service, 148, 228, 285–90
Don, J. D., 114
Douglas, Aaron, 299
Douglass, Frederick, 5, 51, 57, 75–76, 263, 268–69, 331
Dress Reform Society, 90
Drought, 163, 167, 195, 208
Dube, Adelaide Tantsi, 155, 255, 265–68, 272, 281
Dube, Charles, 254, 267–68, 271–72, 279–81
Dube, Frederick, 281
Dube, John, 250, 252, 254, 272, 276–79, 281, 381 n.8
Du Bois, W. E. B., 20, 26, 75, 259, 294, 298; and Africa, 293, 300; on black church, viii, 32, 338 nn.1,4; invoked by Mandela, 331; at Wilberforce University, 134, 262, 264, 268–71, 277
Dubow, Saul, 279
Dunbar, Paul Lawrence, 262
Duncan, Sara J., 93
Dundee, Natal, 322
Durban, Natal, 116, 126
Dutch Reformed Church, 168, 208, 318, 330
Dwaars River, Tvl., 282–83
Dwane, James: appointed vicar bishop, 135; early life, 123–24; secedes from AME Church, 216–22, 226, 228–29; in the United States, 125, 134–36, 216–17

Early, Jordan, 33–34
East St. Louis, Ill.: race riot, 295, 297
Eastern Branch Native Vigilance Association, 177
Ebony, 331
Edenburg, O. F. S., 167
Edendale, Natal, 121, 123, 125, 163
Edinburgh University, 273
Education. *See* AME Church; AME Church, South Africa; European missions, EDUCATION; Industrial Education; Wilberforce University
Education in Africa, 312. *See* Phelps-Stokes Fund
Education of the South African Native, The, 308–9
Edward, Jonathan, 65
Elaw, Zilpha, 45–49, 52, 94
Elizabeth, 69
Ellison, Ralph, xi
Emancipation. *See* Abolition
Emigration, African: antebellum, 66–68, 74–77; distinct from colonization, 69; opposition to, 85–88, 90, 96; outside Africa, 71–73, 76; postbellum, 77–86; to South Africa, 126. *See also* Colonization; Turner, Henry
Engcobo, Transkei, 194
England. *See* Great Britain
Environmentalism, 17–18, 23, 26, 111
Episcopal Church. *See* Anglicanism
Equiano, Olaudah, ix, 5, 66
Erlmann, Viet, 127
Essay Concerning Human Understanding, 17
Ethiopia: Abyssinia, 218, 361 n.38; as Biblical Africa, vii, 103, 151, 157, 300; as charter for religious independence, 119; Christian past, 66, 70, 184, 222, 246
Ethiopian Catholic Church in Zion, 240
Ethiopian Church, 129, 255, 324; amalgamation with AME Church, 103, 115, 125, 127, 132–39, 363 n.72; leadership, 119–25; origins, 103, 115–19, 142–46. *See also* AME Church, South Africa; Ethiopianism
Ethiopian Church of South Africa, 246, 255, 324

Ethiopianism, 103–4, 114–16, 140–41, 146–48, 152, 194, 357 n.1; and African nationalism, compared, 150–52, 159, 212, 364 n.5; blamed on black Americans, 139–41, 170, 215; denounced as seditious, 139–40, 156; echoes in Garveyism, 301–4; shared African identity, 119–20, 125. *See also* AME Church, South Africa; Ethiopian Church; Nationalism, African; Pan-Africanism
Ethnicity: and AME Church, 146, 168–70, 226; in O. F. S., 160–61; on Witwatersrand, 145–46, 155–56
European missions: African assistants, 107–11, 114–18, 120–22, 207; African ordinees, 108–10, 113–15, 118, 188–89, 191; and antislavery, 111; antiurban bias, 105–6, 120–21, 144–45, 208; assumptions and goals, 104–8; and chiefly authority, 105–7, 182–84, 186; and colonial state, 183–84, 186; lack of evangelical commitment, 109–10, 125; neglect of converts, 144, 166, 188, 204–5, 208, 232; obsession with standards, 110–11, 138, 141, 185–87, 208–10; old and new contrasted, 110–13, 202–6, 212, 359 n.19; and race, 111–15, 118, 185, 208, 249; segregation in, 109–11, 118, 124. *See also specific societies*
EDUCATION, 105–8, 122–25; African frustration with, 115, 249–50, 253–56, 272, 309; alleged to spoil Africans, 113, 146; limitations of, 112–14, 116–18, 173, 210, 283; state grants-in-aid, 150, 152, 155–58, 173, 283–84; use of vernacular languages, 122, 192, 210; value to chiefs, 182–84, 191–93; value to urban Africans, 154–56
CONVERTS: and chiefly authority, 104–6, 161, 195–98; deteriorating economic position of, 195–96, 205–8; disillusionment of, 115, 166, 208; faith in progress, 104–7, 115–16, 125, 134; participation in colonial economy, 106–7, 112–13, 120–21, 123, 147–48, 161, 195, 205; social

origins, 106, 182; urbanization of, 120–21, 144–48. *See also* Ethiopianism

Evans, Maurice, 308

Evaton, Tvl., 177–78, 275, 293, 318, 320, 334. *See also* Wilberforce Institute

Faduma, Orishatukeh, 251

Fauresmith, O. F. S., 122

Ficksburg, O. F. S., 296

Finley, Robert, 65, 68–69

First AME Church, Los Angeles, 333

Fischer, Abram, 177

Fisk University, 128, 251

Fitzpatrick, I. N., 221–223, 225, 227, 230, 236, 333

Flagstaff, Transkei, 202

Flegler, Samuel, 80, 88

Fliegelman, Jay, 17

Florida, 53, 59

Foner, Eric, 31

Foote, Julia, 45–47, 53

Forced removals, 141, 154–56, 158–59

Fore Hare (Inter-State Native College), 249, 307

Fort Sumter, 53

Forten, James, 67–69

Franchise: in South Africa, 150, 195, 279; in U.S., 31, 71, 78, 210, 258–59

Fraternal orders. *See* Masonry; Odd Fellows; Voluntary associations

Frazier, E. Franklin, 53, 300, 338 n.1

Frederick, J. R., 89–91

Free African Society, 9–10, 14; committee of monitors, 9, 28; and emigration, 67

Free blacks. *See* Free people of color

Free Church of Scotland, 306, 311, 313; African adherents, 108, 112, 130, 194, 197, 252–53, 313; secessions from, 114–15, 194, 208

Free people of color: anomalous position of, 14, 19–21; harassment of, 19–21, 24–25, 29–30, 71–74, 259; increase in wake of Revolutions, 15–16, 65; in Philadelphia, 8–10; pressure to lead exemplary lives, 25–27; in South, 34–

35, 37. *See also* AME Church, POLITICS AND IDEOLOGY; Allen, Richard

Free Soil Party, 259

Freedmen, southern: alleged idleness, 55, 60; alleged promiscuity, 55, 61; conceptions of religious authority, 58–60; concern for autonomy, 54, 56–57; and franchise, 31; modes of worship, 54, 61–62. *See also* Reconstruction, U.S.

Freedmen's Banks, 59

Freedmen's Bureau. *See* Bureau of Refugees, Freedmen and Abandoned Lands

Freehling, William, 338 n.4

Freeman, Moses, 33

Freetown, Sierra Leone, 67, 70, 84, 89

French Revolution, 16, 29

Friends of Africa clubs, 92

Fugitive slaves, 21, 30, 74–76, 126

Gabashane, Abel, 122, 152, 160, 188

Gabashane, Henry B., 122–23, 189, 255, 273, 385 n.54

Gabashane, Marcus: early life, 122, 163; educates children, 122–23, 189, 256; frustration with European missionaries, 188–89; joins Ethiopian Church, 123–24; political activities, 154, 372 n.18; spreads AME Church, 160, 179, 187–90, 209

Gabashane, Martin Luther, 187

Gabashane, Salathiel, 122

Gaines, Wesley, 51, 60–61, 86–87, 217–18, 222, 225

Garnet, Henry Highland, 57, 81, 352 n.29

Garrettson, Freeborn, 6

Garrison, William Lloyd, 69

Garvey, Marcus, 82, 274, 296, 300; invoked by Africans, 302–3, 316–17, 331; rumored arrival, 305, 313–15. *See also* Garveyism; Universal Negro Improvement Association

Garveyism, 88, 278, 301, 304; and African Methodism, 300–302, 315–19; feared by South African government, 257, 305, 314

Gaye, Marvin, 331

Geertz, Clifford, 132

General Conference. *See* AME Church,
    General Conference
Georgia, 59, 78, 296
Georgia Annual Conference, 56
Georgia State Industrial College, 298
Germany, 84, 197
Germiston, Tvl., 289
Germiston Native Vigilance Association,
    150–51
Gettysburg, Penn., 37
Ghana, xiii, 65, 231, 250–52, 311–12
Gibbon, Edward, 224
Glass, Fannie, 328
Glen Grey Act, 195–96, 211, 323
Glimpses of Africa, 85, 241
Goduka, Jonas, 115, 123, 194, 323
Gold Coast. *See* Ghana
Gomas, John, 320
Gorham, Sarah, 90, 94
Gow, Francis Herman, xiii, 255, 272,
    274, 278, 318, 330
Gow, Francis, M., 127, 129, 221, 245,
    255, 315, 318
Gow, Hannah, 255, 274
Gow, Levi Coppin, 255
Gow, Sarah, 127
Gqamana, J., 123
Grahamstown, Cape, 321
Grant, Abraham, 52, 217
Great Awakening, 4–5, 104
Great Britain: black population, 67, 108,
    124, 131, 133, 190–91
Great Migration: AME Church, 295–99
Great Trek, 160
Greeley, Horace, 77
Gregg, Celia, 237
Gregg, John A., 237–38, 322, 324–27
Grey, Sir George, 306
Griqua, 160
Groutville, Natal, 147
Gumede, Stephen, 255, 268, 272, 274

Haiti: AME missions in, 93, 95; African
    American emigration to, 71–72, 74,
    77; revolution, 16–17, 24; students in
    U.S., 251
Haley, Alex, 332
Hall, J. D. S., 54
Hall, Prince, 67

Hanna, Marc, 263
Hampton Institute, 128, 258, 264, 306;
    as model, 308, 311, 314; South Afri-
    can students at, 131, 133, 257
Harlem, 331–32
Harrismith, O. F. S., 166
Haytien Emigration Society, 71
Headmen, African: and AME Church,
    201–6, 323; appointed by state, 184,
    195–96, 198
Healdtown Institute, 109, 116, 121, 124,
    254
Heard, William H., 88, 298
Heilbron, O. F. S., 121–22, 164, 171,
    317
Herschel, Cape, 194, 205–7, 237, 322–26
Herskovits, Melville, 338 n.1
Hertzog, J. B. M., 279, 321
History of the Negro Race in America, 127
Hlati, D. H., 153–54
Holiness. *See* Sanctification
Hollenbeck, Henry, 311–12
Holly, James Theodore, 81
Hoopstad, O. F. S., 178–79
Hopkins, Samuel, 65–66, 251
Houseboys. *See* Domestic service
Howard, O. O., 298
Howard University, 258, 264, 329
Hughes, Langston, 299
Huntsville (Alabama) A. & M., 251

Idutywa, Transkei, 203, 284, 319
Illinois, 33–34
Imperial reconstruction: betrayal of African
    hopes, 149–50, 153–54, 293; and
    chiefly authority, 165, 180–81, 184,
    189; repatriation policy, 168, 176. *See
    also* AME Church, South Africa,
    GOVERNMENT POLICY
Imperialism, European, 91–92; African
    American attitude toward, 84–85
Inboekselings, 116, 160, 274
Indiana, 33
Indianapolis Freeman, 85
Indians: in South Africa, 126, 157
Industrial and Commercial Workers Union,
    132, 178–79, 302–5; and AME
    Church 162, 212, 278, 280, 287,
    315–22, 324–26

Industrial education: origins, 305–6, 383
n.31, sought by Africans, 174, 192–
93, 197–201, 283; in South Africa,
306–13; at Wilberforce Institute,
278; at Wilberforce University, 264–
65, 268. *See also* Hampton Institute;
Tuskegee Institute; Washington,
Booker T.
Indwe, Cape, 194
Institute for Colored Youth (Philadelphia),
227–28, 238
Institutional Church and Settlement House,
298
International Conference of Negro Peoples
of the World, 301, 305, 315. *See also*
Garveyism
Inter-State Native College. *See* Fort Hare
Irons, Clement, 88
Islam: African American missionaries and,
75, 90, 355 n.59
Israelites: lesson for Africans, 326; parallels
with African American experience, ix,
12, 66, 75, 157, 211

Jabavu, D. D. T., 277, 301, 303, 329
Jabavu, J. T., 152, 204, 329
Jackson, Andrew, 68, 73
Jackson, Jesse, 332
Jackson, Rebecca Cox, 45–46, 49
Jackson, W. O. *See* Ncwana, S. M. Ben-
nett
Jacottet, Edward, 114
Jeanes teaching system, 257
Jefferson, Thomas: and colonization, 65; on
race, 18–19, 22, 29, 77
Jewison, Norman, 332
Jim Crow. *See* Segregation
Joe Brown's Band of Brothers, 127
Johannesburg, Tvl., 163, 174, 181, 302;
AME Church in, 147–48, 153–55;
African settlement, 117, 120–21,
144–46. *See also* Mineral revolution;
Urbanization; Witwatersrand
Johannesburg Joint Council, 278–79, 287,
291–92
Johannesburg Star, 287, 315
Johnson, John Albert, 246, 295, 313
Joint Conferences of Europeans and Bantu,
278

Jones, Absalom, 9–10, 20–25, 27–28, 31,
66, 68
Jones, J. D. Rheinhallt, 278, 293, 329
Jones, Thomas Jesse, 311–13. *See* Phelps-
Stokes Fund
Jordan, Winthrop, 16
Jubilee Music, 128–29, 131–33. *See also*
Music, African American

Kadalie, Alexander, 303
Kadalie, Clements, 302, 303, 316, 319–
20
Kaffir Express, 127
Kakaza, Theodore, 254, 265, 267–68,
271, 273–74, 385 n.54
Kalane, Thomas, 268
Kama, Chief, 123–24, 190–91, 194, 200–
201
Kama, William Shaw, 124
Kanyane Napo, Joseph, 115, 121, 136,
144, 181, 365 n.13
Kansas-Nebraska Act, 74
Kansas University, 237
Kayne, Bechuanaland, 188, 190
Katiya, Thomas, 252–53, 267
Keegan, Tim, 161–62, 177
Kekana, Chief, 181
Khaile, Edward, 319–21, 327
Khaile, Joseph, 320
Khunwana, Tvl., 188–90, 193, 372 n.22
Kidd, Dudley, 219
Kilner, James, 109, 117, 121
Kilnerton Institute, 117–18, 144, 146,
283
Kimberley, 112, 120, 125, 365 n.17;
AME Church in, 160, 231, 243; Afri-
can Americans in, 127, 201; African
elite in, 132–33, 252–54, 282;
McAdoo Singers in, 128–31. *See also*
Mineral revolution
King, Martin Luther, Jr., 25, 331–32
Kingwilliamstown, Cape, 194, 196, 204
Klerksdorp, Tvl., 160, 187, 283
Kletzing, H. F., 270
Klipspruit, Tvl., 154–59, 272
Kokstad, Transkei, 126
Kolombe, James N., 252–53
Koranta ea Beacona, 180
Kotane, Moses, 319

Krikler, Jeremy, 165
Kroonstad, O. F. S., 164, 317
Kruger, Paul, 128, 137, 150, 222
Krugersdorp, Tvl., 289
Ku Klux Klan, 57
Kubedi, John, 166
Kumalo, Benjamin, 123–24, 163, 174,
    239, 242, 244, 246
Kuruman, Cape, 182
Kuzwayo, Mbulaleni, 255

Labor migration, 116, 120, 191, 201,
    203–5, 252, 373 n.35; in Eastern
    Cape, 322; from Mozambique, 144,
    148, 366 n.23; in O. F. S., 162,
    167; spreads diseases, 195; and urban
    segregation, 308
Lagden, Godfrey, 155–59, 226, 283
LaGuma, James, 320
Land: and chiefly authority, 165, 201–2; as
    focus of African discontent, 152–53,
    195–96, 211–12, 319, 323–24; re-
    strictions on African tenure, 149,
    153–54, 177–78; shortages of, 195–
    96. *See also* AME Church, South Af-
    rica, POLITICS AND IDEOLOGY
Lawrence, Abraham, 272
Lee, Benjamin F., 297
Lee, Jarena, 45–49, 52, 94
Lee, Spike, 332
Lerotholi, Chief, 200, 242
Lesseyton, Tvl., 136
Leverenz, David, 50–51
Levine, Lawrence, 346 n.24
Lewanika, Chief, 191–93, 236
Liberia, 37, 59, 74–76, 275, 312, 355
    n.55; AME Church in, 79–80, 83–
    84, 87–90
Liberian Annual Conference, 89
Liberian Exodus Joint Stock Steamship
    Company, 79–80
Liberia's Offering, 75
Liberty Party, 259
Libode, Transkei, 203
Lichtenburg, Tvl., 190
Lincoln, Abraham, 53, 77–78, 80, 353
    n.32
Lincoln University, 92, 251, 253, 256,
    258, 268, 303

Lindley, O. F. S., 166
Liquor: "beer drinks," 183, 185; illicit
    trade, 154, 285, 321–22; restrictions
    on Africans, 127, 189
Little Rock, Ark., 58
Livingstone, David, 76, 91, 228, 266
Livingstone College, 311
Livingstonia, 313
Lobengula, Chief, 183
Lobola. *See* Marriage
Local Government Commission, 288
Locke, Alain, 299
Locke, John, 17, 19
London Missionary Society, 104, 106,
    108, 110, 115, 182–84, 186, 188–
    91, 208
Loram, C. T., 257, 308–14
Los Angeles riot, 333
Louis, Joe, 331
Lovedale Institute, 112, 114–15, 122–23,
    133, 147, 178, 194, 209, 253–55,
    306. *See also* European missions,
    EDUCATION; Free Church of
    Scotland
Lusikisiki, 199, 202
Lutheran Bapedi Church, 115
Lynch, James, 54, 348 n.55
Lynching, 78, 210, 270

Mabote, Samuel, 166, 244
Mabuze, Lindiwe, 333
Macmillan, William, 322
Macon, Geo., 56, 59
Madison, James, 29
Mafeking, British Bechuanaland, 190, 255,
    372 n.24
Magaba, Pearse, 203–4
Magaya, Edward, 252–53, 267, 272
Magbele, 90
Magdalene Society, 26
Mahuma, Eva, 257
Makapan, Chief Hans, 181
Makapanstad, Tvl., 117, 120
Makgatho, S. M., 117
Makhanya, Sibusisiwe, 257
Makiwane, Elijah, 108, 197
Makone, Nicholas, 166
Makwassie, Tvl., 179
Malawi, 250, 257, 273, 313

Malcolm X, 331
Mamba, Enoch, 203, 272, 284
Mandela, Nelson, 330–32
Mangena, Alfred, 151
Mann, Horace, 259
Manumission: in era of American Revolution, 8, 15–17; and Great Awakening, 4; legal restrictions, 19, 25, 71. *See also* Free people of color
Manye, Charlotte. *See* Maxeke, Charlotte Manye
Manye, Jan, 252
Manye, John, 255, 274
Manye, Kate, 133–34, 252
Marabastad, Tvl., vii, 117, 119, 139, 141, 143–47, 155–57, 181, 230
Marabi, 145
March on Washington, 25
Mareka, A. A., 170, 174–75
Mareka, Theophilus, 170
Marelane, Chief, 200, 374 n.46
Marion, Geo., 56
Marks, Sammy, 161
Marks, Shula, 149
Marrant, John, 23–24
Marriage: among freed people, 61; legal restrictions on AME Church, 84, 185, 187, 228–29, 325; lobola system, 183; polygamy, 84, 185–87, 228–29, 284, 325
Maryland, 3, 5, 12–13, 32, 34
Mashonaland, 107
Mason, George, 19
Mason, M. C. B., 96
Masonry, 26, 29, 34, 67, 236, 269
Massachusetts, 4, 66
Matatiele, Transkei, 194
Mathabathe, Samuel, 107
Maud, Dorothy, 293
Maxeke, Edward Clarke, 281, 292
Maxeke, Charlotte Manye: and African Choir, 129, 133–34; career as social worker, 289–92; early life, 252, 282; final years, 281, 292–93; political career, 277–80, 284–89, 291–93; remembered, 334; returns to South Africa, 235, 271; teaching career, 158, 272, 282–84, 319; at Wilberforce University, 253, 262–68

Maxeke, Marshall, 147–48, 151, 153, 158, 254, 262, 267, 272, 278–85, 290, 292, 319
Maxwell, Campbell, 262
Mayibuye iAfrika, 319, 327
Mbeki, Thomas, 320
Mbongwe, Titus, 131, 133
McAdoo, Orpheus, 128, 131–32, *See also* Orpheus McAdoo's Jubilee Singers
McKinley, William, 136, 263
Mehlomakulu, Joel, 206, 323
Mehlomakulu, Makobeni, 206, 323–24
Mehlomakulu, Ngesman, 206
Mehlomakulu, Read, 323
Men of Mark: Eminent, Progressive and Rising, 270
Messenger, The, 303
Methodism, 5–6, 36–37; in Britain, 36; Free Methodists, 45; lay participation, 107; morphology of conversion, 6, 11, 40–43; and sanctification, 45; structure, 5, 11, 36; suited for African Americans, 9–11
Methodist Episcopal Church, 6, 11–12, 33; and slavery, 13, 37, 340–41 n.27
Methodist Episcopal Church, North, 57, 63, 92, 93, 263
Methodist Episcopal Church, South, 56–58, 63, 349 n.62
Mfecane, 116, 121, 125, 160, 187, 206, 323, 360 n.31
Mfengu, 106, 160, 194–95, 325
Mgijima, Enoch, 248
Mhlangaso, Chief, 197–98
Middelburg, Tvl., 321
Middledrift, Cape, 123, 194
Milner, Alfred, 149, 235, 286. *See also* Imperial reconstruction
Mineral revolution, 126, 143–44, 149, 160, 284; prompts reassessment of Africans' place, 112–13, 208, 286, 306. *See also* Johannesburg; Kimberley; Imperial reconstruction; Witwatersrand
Minstrelsy, 29, 127–28. *See also* Music, African American
Missions. *See* European missions
Missionary Record, The, 79
Missionary Searchlight, 93
Mississippi, 35

Mitchell, John G., 262
Mitchell, Samuel T., 262
Mngqibisa, Abraham, 121, 125, 130, 136,
    321–22
Mngqibisa, Joubert, 324
Mngqibisa, Timothy, 321–27
Moepi, Robert, 185
Moffat, J. S., 189
Moffat, Robert, 111, 189, 228
Moffat Commission, 288–89
Mokalapa, Willie, 192–93
Mokgatle, Naboth, 160
Mokone, Jonathan, 255, 272, 274–75,
    360 n.31
Mokone, Mangena: early life, 109, 116–
    17; faith in U.S. education, 252,
    254, 257, 274; corresponds with
    Bishop Turner, 134, 136, 199, 216–
    18, 221; founds Ethiopian Church,
    vii, 115, 118–19, 246; frustration
    with European missionaries, 117–18;
    perspectives on black America, 129–
    31, 135, 139; recruits ministers,
    119–24, 194–95; work in urban
    Transvaal, 144–47, 150–51, 154,
    157, 181. *See also* Ethiopian Church
Molema, Sebopioa, 255, 268, 272–73
Molema, Silas, 255
Molotsi, Solomon, 244
Montgomery, Ala., 331
Montsioa, 190, 372 n.24
Morant Bay uprising, 112
Moravian Church, 104
Morehead State University, 281
Moroka, Chief, 122, 160, 181, 187
Moroka, Samuel, 187–88, 372 n.18
Morris Brown College, 61, 281
Morrison, A. A., 160
Mosebi, Chief, 181
Moses, Wilson J., 74, 341 n.30, 383 n.31
Moshette, Aaron, 189–90
Moshette, Chief, 188–89
Moss, Chalmers, 253–54
Moss, Joseph S., 253
Mothers' Associations, 43–44
Mothibi, Petrus, 170, 172–73
Motown, 331
Moynihan Report, 61
Mpela, Edward, 174–75

Mpondo, 197–98, 201–3
Mpondomise, 203
Mpumlwana, S. J., 121
Msikinya, Charles, 158
Msikinya, David, 254
Msikinya, Henry, 129, 235, 253–54, 266–
    67, 271–72, 282
Msikinya, John, 254
Msikinya, Jonas, 253
Mtimka, William, 323
Mtintso, Samson, 198–99, 202
Mtshula, John, 153–54
Murphy, Eddie, 332
Music, African American: in AME Church,
    41–43, 57, 61–62, 164, 169, 346
    n.26; African Hymnology, 129–30;
    African roots, 41–42, 130, 346 n.24;
    jubilee, 128; mission hymns, 97;
    popularity in South Africa, 127–31,
    278, 330
Mzilikazi, Chief, 122
Mzimba, P. J., 108, 114–15, 127, 130,
    194, 256, 306, 321

Napo, Joseph Kanyane. *See* Kanyane Napo,
    Joseph
Nash, Gary, 5
Nasson, Bill, 165
Natal: African elite, 121, 123, 147, 322;
    Indian indentured labor, 126; labor
    migration to, 116–17; Native Affairs
    Commission, 308. *See also* AME
    Church, South Africa, GOVERN-
    MENT POLICY
Nation of Islam, 332
National Association of Colored Women,
    262, 269
National Council of African Women, 293,
    334
National Emigration Convention, 76, 126.
    See also Delany, Martin; Emigration
National Negro Convention Movement,
    73, 76
National Party, 195, 310
Nationalism, African: and AME Church,
    140–41, 146, 150–52, 159, 182,
    207, 212; and American education,
    250, 269, 276–77, 303; and Ethio-
    pianism, compared, 150–52, 159,

212, 364 n.5; material preconditions, 145–46. *See also* AME Church, South Africa, POLITICS AND IDEOLOGY; African National Congress; Ethiopianism; Pan-Africanism

Nationalism, African American, xi, 13–15, 54, 63, 73–74, 83; and Africa, 74–77, 81–84, 299–300; civilizationism, 74; manhood, 50, 52; self help, 21, 73, 306, 342 n.44; shared black identity, 20–22, 55. *See also* AME Church, POLITICS AND IDEOLOGY; Emigration; Garveyism; Pan-Africanism

Native Administration Act, 328

Native Affairs Commission, 309–10, 316

Native Baptist Church, 245

Native Churches Commission, 316, 359 n.19

Native Economic Commission, 279

Native Pass Laws Commission, 288–89

Native Republic campaign, 319

Natives Land Act, South African, 152–53, 177, 279, 285

Ncwana, S. M. Bennett, 301, 303–4

Ndebele, 122, 181

Negro: replaces African as designation, viii, 72–73

Negro Education: A Study of the Private and Higher Schools for Colored People in the United States, 310. *See also* Industrial education; Phelps-Stokes Fund

Negro World, The, 301–2, 305, 318. *See also* Garveyism

New Jersey, 13, 32

New Negro movement, 299

New Orleans, La., 34

New York, 32, 71, 75

New York, N.Y., 9, 12–13, 15, 87, 231

New York Colonization Society, 310

New York Herald, 91

Newcastle, Natal, 322

Newport, R. I., 9, 65, 67

Ngcayiya, Henry Reid, 129, 133, 151, 226; conflicts with African American church leaders, 233–34, 239; joins Ethiopian Church, 123–24; leaves AME Church, 246; spreads church in

eastern Cape, 159–60, 205, 209, 244; writes Marcus Garvey, 274

Ngcayiya, Patrick, 255, 268, 274

Nhlapo, Jacob, 178

Niagara Movement, 134, 298

Niebuhr, H. Richard, 36

Nigeria, 250, 312; Yorubaland, 76

Njongwana, Amelia, 257

Nkosi Sikelel' iAfrika, 130, 318, 321, 325, 327

Nkrumah, Kwame, 250, 269, 276, 380 n.4. *See also* Nationalism, African

Nongqawuse, 136. *See also* Xhosa cattle killing

North Georgia Annual Conference, 135

North Star, The, 75

Northwestern University, 273

Notes on the State of Virginia, 18, 22, 65

Ntsikana, 130, 133

Ntsiko, Pearl, 257

Nyasaland. *See* Malawi

Nyokana, Booker T. Washington, 147

Nyokana, Luke, 147–48

Nyombolo, Chalmers, 257, 364 n.6

Nyombolo, Eli, 257

Oberlin College, 227, 258–59

Observations of Persons and Things in South Africa, 228

Odd Fellows, Grand Order of, 263, 269–70

Ohio: AME Church in, 33–34, 93; antilynching bill, 270; Black Codes, 34, 72–73, 259, 261; black settlement, 259–60; southwestern, 258; Western Reserve, 259–60. *See also* Wilberforce University

Ohlange Institute, 254, 268, 272, 281. *See also* Industrial education

Oklahoma, 79, 87

Oorlams, 143, 145–47, 160

Orange Free State: African education in, 168, 173–74; impact of South African War in, 164–68; missions in, 122–23, 161; in nineteenth century, 160–63; restrictions on African accumulation, 170–73, 176–78; return of responsible government, 174, 176–77,

Orange Free State (*Cont.*)
226. *See also* AME Church, South Africa, GOVERNMENT POLICY
Orange River Colony. *See* Orange Free State
Orange River Native Congress, 141, 174
Orange River Native Vigilance Association, 174, 242
Order of Ethiopia, 194, 203–4, 218–221
Orpheus McAdoo's Jubilee Singers, 128–33, 137, 282
Oudtshoorn, Cape, 211
Oxford History of South Africa, 146

Pamla, Charles, 109
Pan-African Congress. *See* Pan-Africanism
Pan-Africanism: consanguinity, 74–77, 96–98; and African American mission movement, 96–98; and nationalism, 81–83; origins, 66–68; Pan-African Congress, 179, 251, 296, 299–300, 305. *See also* Ethiopianism; Nationalism, African; Nationalism, African American
Paris Evangelical Mission, 104, 114, 191–92, 200, 208
Parks, H. B., 95, 97, 217, 298
Parys, O. F. S., 164, 317
Pass laws: exemptions, 150, 152, 172–73, 177; in Orange Free State, 122, 167, 169; in Transvaal, 147, 149, 189; and women, 285–91, 370 n.76
Payne, Daniel Alexander, 82, 224, 275, 293, 327; and African missions, 37, 74, 90–93; campaigns to reform African Methodism, ix, 38–43; early life and career, 37–39; gender ideology, 43–44, 49–51, 346 n.28, 383 n.34; rejects colonization, 78; and Wilberforce University, 263–70; work among freedpeople, 54–60, 62. *See also* AME Church, POLITICS AND IDEOLOGY
Payne Theological Seminary (Wilberforce), 263–64, 267, 273
Pearce, J. J., 245
Peddie, Cape, 194, 244
Penn School, South Carolina, 257
Pennsylvania, 8, 12–13, 19, 32–33, 75

Pennsylvania Abolition Society, 8
Pennsylvania Augustine Society, 26
Pennsylvania Gradual Abolition Act, 8, 16
Pennsylvania Supreme Court: establishes independence of Bethel Church, 12
Peregrino, F. Z. S., xiii, 231, 257
Phakane, John, 166
Phalapye, Bechuanaland, 190
Phelps Hall Bible Training School, 274. *See also* Tuskegee
Phelps Stokes, Anson, 311, 392 n.35
Phelps-Stokes Commissions on African Education, 310–13, 392 n.35. *See also* Industrial education
Phelps-Stokes Fund, 257, 309–11, 328, 392 n.35
Philadelphia, Pa., 5, 14, 32, 63, 148, 201; anticolonization meetings, 68–69; black community, 8–9, 37, 49, 67, 227, 297, 299; racial violence in, 30; slavery in, 8, 15; yellow fever epidemic, 27–28
Philadelphia Annual Conference, 38
Philip, John, 111
Phillips, Ray, 278, 287, 309–10, 313, 329
Phoukoutsi, John, 174
Pilane, Segale, 180–81
Pim, Howard, 278, 292
Pittsburgh Annual Conference, 33
Plaatje, Solomon, 133, 152, 177, 180–81, 370 n.2
Polygamy. *See* Marriage
Pondoland: AME Church in, 194, 197–203, 317; annexation of, 183, 195, 198; millenarian movements in, 304
Pondoland Methodist Church, 114, 198
Populist Movement, 314
Port Elizabeth, Cape, 120, 126, 155, 201, 252, 254, 282, 320, 322, 324–28
Port Royal, South Carolina, 54
Port St. Johns, Transkei, 185, 201
Porter, B. F., 79–80
Portuguese: as imperialists, 85; and slave trade, 3
Potchefstroom, Tvl., 117, 160
Powell, Adam Clayton Jr., 331
Presbyterianism (South Africa). *See* Free Church of Scotland

Presbyterianism (U.S.), 62, 65; African missions, 75, 92–93, 97
Pretoria, Tvl., 115, 117, 144, 148, 181, 187, 226, 243
Primitive Methodist Church, 254
Princeton (College of New Jersey), 251
Progress of a Race, 270
Prosser, Gabriel: slave rebellion led by, 17, 19
Providence: apparent hand in human affairs, 5, 12–13, 24, 70, 77, 103–4

Qaukeni, Transkei, 198–200
Quakerism, 9, 33–34, 48, 67
Quamine, John, 65–66, 251
Queenstown, Cape, 109, 136, 159, 194, 204, 233, 252
Quinn, William Paul, 33–34, 49, 74, 138
Qumbu, Transkei, 183, 194–95

Raboteau, Albert, 338 n.4
Racism: intractability of, 28–29; in South Africa, 111–13; in wake of American Revolution, 16–19. *See also* Social Darwinism; AME Church, POLITICS AND IDEOLOGY; Environmentalism
Radasi, John B., 252–53
Ramoghopa, Chief, 181, 282–83
Randloph, A. Philip, 303
Randolph, John, 259
Ransom, Emma, 298
Ransom, Reverdy, 134, 297–99
Reconstruction, South Africa. *See* Imperial Reconstruction
Reconstruction, U.S., 31, 53–63, 349 n.69; observed in South Africa, 112, 127; retreat from, 78–81
Refugee camps, 165–66, 207. *See also* South African War
Reitz, O. F. S., 178
Repository of Religion and Literature, 50. *See also* Payne, Daniel A.
Republican Party, 259, 261, 263
Revels, Hiram, 34, 59
Rhodes, Cecil, 190, 195, 198, 333
Rhodesia, 126–27, 242, 274, 307, 312
Rideout, Conrad, 199–201
Ridgel, Edward, 84–85, 90

Rinderpest, 163, 166, 188–89, 198; allegedly introduced by whites, 195, 373 n.36
Ring shout, 61–62
Ripley, Dorothy, 48
Rodney, Caesar, 19
Rodney, Thomas, 19
Roosevelt, Theodore, 263, 314
Rotary Clubs, 328
Rouxville, O. F. S., 172
Roy, Leo, 311–12
Rush, Benjamin, 10, 17–18, 27

St. Catherine's Island, Geo., 59
St. George's Methodist Church, Philadelphia, 9–11, 38, 103, 333, 340 n.19
St. Louis, Mo., 34, 297
Sakie, Magazo, 252–53, 265
Salvation Army, 145
San Domingo. *See* Haiti
Sanctification, 39, 44–46, 52–53; challenge to motherhood, 46; critique of formalism, 47–48; opposition to, 49–50; subverts political project of African Methodism, 47–48. *See also* Women
Sargent, E. B., 307
Savannah, Geo., 54
Scarborough, William S., 262
Schreiner, W. P., 224–25
Schwarz, Harry, 333
Schweizer-Reneke, Tvl., 179
Scott, Dred. *See* Supreme Court
Seganoe, Michael, 268
Segregation, 78, 210; and education, 308–9; in European missions, 109–11, 118, 124; Group Areas Act, 334; Hertzog bills, 279; in post-revolutionary America, 19, 193; spreads North, 270; U.S. and S.A. compared, 307–8, 351 n.20, 391 n.25
Sekukuni (younger), 181
Sekukuni (older), 183–84
Sekukuniland, 116, 183, 252
Selborne, Earl of, 245
Seme, Pixley, 151, 154, 256, 279, 285
Sernett, Milton C., 340 n.19

Serowe, Bechuanaland, 190

Seventeen Years' Explorations and Adventures in the Wilds of Africa, 76

Seymour, Cape, 252

Shabazz, Betty, 332

Shadow and Act, xi

Shakers, 45

Sharecroppers: campaign against, 176–79; consciousness of, 161–63, 170, 176–78; historiography, 368 n.49; in S.A., 161–64, 167; in U.S., 78–79, 81

Shawbury Institute, 198

Sheep stealing. *See* Proselytism

Shepperson, George, 151

Sherbro Island, West Africa, 69–70

Sierra Leone, 66–67, 83, 89–91, 201, 275, 312

Sigcau, Chief, 198–202, 206, 211, 244, 304

Simmons, W. J., 270

Sims, D. H., 328

Sinamela, Paul, 133

Sinamela, Simon, 129, 133, 152, 154, 164, 226, 252

Singing and praying bands. *See* Sanctification

Sishuba, Isaiah, 123, 204, 246

Sishuba, Melrose, 256, 274

Skota, T. D. Mweli, 282

Slave trade: end of Atlantic, 16, 66; horrors of interstate, 25, 35; recaptives, 67, 89; trauma of, 66; within Africa, 70, 84

Slaveowners: and Great Awakening, 4; skepticism of Christianity, 3–7

Slavery: African invocations, 132, 134–35, 138, 332–33; and American Revolution, 15–18, 24–25, 65; and black Christianity, 3–5; blighting effect on slaves, 17–18, 22–23; economic fortunes, 5, 8, 15, 35; in Latin America, 3, 338 n.2. *See also* AME Church, POLITICS AND IDEOLOGY; Abolition; Antislavery; Free people of color; Nationalism, African American

Smith, Amanda, 46–47, 49, 53, 94

Smith, Charles Spencer, 85–86, 241–46, 298, 313, 356 n.73

Smith, David, 33–34

Smith, Samuel Stanhope, 17–18

Smithfield, O. F. S., 164, 170, 173–75

Smuts, Jan, 156, 308–9, 316, 321

Social Darwinism, 81, 83, 112, 235

Social Gospel: and AME Church, 297–99

Society for the Propagation of the Gospel, 4

Soga, Tiyo, 108

Sondezi, Albert, 255

Sondezi, David, 255

Sonjica, John, 256

Sontaga, Enoch, 130, 321

Souls of Black Folk, The, 32. *See also* Du Bois, W. E. B.

South African Compounds and Interior Mission, 105, 110

South African Annual Conference, 221, 228, 234, 243–44, 315

South African Christian Recorder, 96, 238

South African College: pledges to build, 136, 189, 217–18, 222, 229, 234; sites offered by chiefs, 190–91, 199–201. *See also* Bethel Institute; Chatsworth Normal, Mechanical and Industrial Institute

South African General Missionary Conference, 113

South African Institute of Race Relations, 278, 293, 329

South African Native Affairs Commission, 113–14, 140–41, 155, 173–74, 180, 191, 203, 212, 225–26, 235, 240, 242, 249. *See also* AME Church, South Africa, GOVERNMENT POLICY

South African Native National Congress. *See* African National Congress

South African Spectator, 231

South African War, 139, 141, 145, 148–49, 153, 159, 164–67, 180–81, 208, 218, 229, 242, 306

South Carolina, 4, 54, 59, 79, 296

South Carolina Annual Conference, 35, 56

Southern Workman, 299

Soweto, 154, 284, 334

Spiritual narratives, 5–7, 46–48, 116–19; contrasted with slave narratives, 342 n.46, 347 n.35. *See also* Sanctification

Springfield, Ohio, 260, 270
Springfontein, O. F. S., 172
Stallard, F. W., 308
Stanford, Walter, 224–26, 247–48
Stanley, Henry Morton, 85, 91, 228
Steward, Theophilus G., 57, 59, 62, 81, 262
Stewart, James, 112, 114, 209, 256, 306–7
Stewart Missionary Foundation, 92, 96–97
Stiles, Ezra, 65, 251
Stringer, T. W., 59
Student Volunteer Movement, 266
Sturgis, Stokely, 5–7
Suffrage. *See* Franchise
Sundkler, Bengt, 357 n.1
Supreme Court: Dred Scott decision, 74; repeals Civil Rights Act, 81–82
Svin'in, Pavel, 40–42
Swedenborg, Emmanuel, 81

Taft, William H., 314
Taney, Roger, 74
Tanner, Benjamin, 51, 86–87, 90–91, 95–96, 228, 238, 268, 295; death, 295; disavows politics, 228
Tanner, Carleton, 96, 238–40
Tantsi, Adelaide. *See* Dube, Adelaide Tantsi
Tantsi, Harsant, 255, 268, 272, 274
Tantsi, J. Z., 129, 147, 159, 216–17, 221, 239, 319; early life, 121, 125; political leadership, 153, 155–56; sends children to U.S., 254–55
Tantsi, James Yapi: attends Wilberforce University, 141, 254–55, 268, 272; political activities, 151, 153–54, 278–80
Tantsi, Nimrod, 319–21, 393 n.50
Taung, Cape, 115
Tawawa Springs, Ohio. *See* Wilberforce University
Taylor, J. Dexter, 278, 287, 309
Taxes: on Africans, 149–50, 152, 155, 157, 173, 183–84, 198, 201, 203, 304, 323–25
Terrell, Mary Church, 262
Texas, 53, 71

Thaba 'Nchu, O. F. S., 122, 160, 163, 165, 172, 181, 187–88, 244
Thaele, James, 303–4
Thembuland, 183, 284, 319
Thompson. Will, 132–3
Tile, Nehemiah, 115
Tile Thembu Church, 114–15, 123, 184, 194
Tlokoa, 160
To the People of Color, 21, 26. *See also* Allen, Richard; Jones, Absalom
Toba, A. A., 325
Tobacco, 5, 8
Tradesmen, African, 162, 170–74
Transkeian Territories, 184, 194–96, 303–4
Transvaal: African education in, 150–51, 306–7; Native Affairs Department, 154–56, 189; restrictions on African landholding, 153, 189; return of responsible self-government, 149, 156, 226; South African War in, 148–49; urban growth, 143–45; Zuid Afrikaansche Republiek, 104, 117, 120, 137, 144–45, 150. *See also* AME Church, South Africa, GOVERNMENT POLICY
Transvaal Annual Conference, 136–37, 238
Transvaal Education Department, 156, 226
Transvaal Native Congress, 141, 151, 157, 159, 285, 322
Transvaal Native Vigilance Association, 151
Trapido, Stanley, 112, 149
Truth, Sojourner, 331
Tsewu, Edward, 108, 137, 145, 151–54, 159, 211; *ex parte Tsewu,* 153–54, 174
Tshipinare, Chief, 187
Tsime, Chief, 191
Tsomo, Transkei, 195
Turner, Henry M.: advocates emigration, 80–85, 265, 300; death, 295; opposed by co-religionists, 85–88, 91, 327; and Reconstruction, 56–59, 61–62; and South African AME Church, 103, 134–38, 142, 145, 160, 163, 166, 171, 180–81, 187, 189, 198–99, 215–18, 221, 226–27, 230, 254–

Turner, Henry M. (*Cont.*)
   56, 268, 315; visits West Africa, 92–
   93, 95–96. *See also* Emigration; Nationalism, African American
Turner, Nat: slave rebellion led by, 17, 73
Tuskegee Institute: African students at,
   256–57, 273–74, 278, 318, 330;
   praised by AME leaders, 235, 237,
   314; white South African interest,
   306–8; and Wilberforce, compared,
   264. *See also* Industrial education;
   Washington, Booker T.

U.S. Army, 53–54, 78, 80, 262, 311
U.S. Congress. *See* Congress
U.S. Constitution. *See* Constitution
U.S. Supreme Court. *See* Supreme Court
Uitenhage, Cape, 252, 282
Umteteli wa Bantu, 278, 280, 292, 310
Union of South Africa: creation of, vii–viii,
   139, 225; Criminal Investigation De-
   partment, 318–320, 327–28; Native
   Affairs Department, 226, 247, 289;
   restricts entry by African Americans,
   305, 314. *See also* AME Church,
   South Africa, GOVERNMENT
   POLICY
Universal Negro Improvement Association
   and African Communities League,
   296, 299–303, 315–18, 328. *See also*
   Garveyism
Up from Slavery, 302
University of Chicago, 298
University of Minnesota, 273
University of Pennsylvania, 299
Urban Areas Act (1923), 308; amended
   (1930), 291. *See also* Segregation
Urbanization, African: of African women,
   285–86; and class formation, 147–48,
   169–70; demand for schools, 154–57;
   generates new forms of consciousness,
   145–46, 365 n.17; in Orange Free
   State, 164–68, 175; and shortage of
   rural labor, 167–68, 170–71; spurred
   by mineral revolution, 120–21, 143–
   45. *See also* Witwatersrand

Van Onselen, Charles, 161
Van Riebeek, Jan, 104

Vereeniging, Tvl., 164
Vereeniging Estates, 161, 164, 166
Vernon, William T., 313–17, 322, 324,
   327
Versailles Peace Conference, 299, 305;
   African mandates, 305, 311
Vesey, Denmark: slave conspiracy led by,
   35, 37, 54
Vicksburg, Miss., 59
Victoria East, Cape, 194
Victoria, Queen, 133, 287, 303
Viljoensdrift, O. F. S., 164, 368 n.55
Virginia, 3–5, 15, 19, 34, 55
Virginia Declaration of Rights, 19
Voice from the South, A, 94, 262
Voice of Missions, The, 82, 93, 135–36,
   188–90, 199, 216, 221, 226, 253,
   283
Voice of the People, The, 82, 180, 354 n.42
Voluntary associations, African American,
   9–10, 26, 34, 54, 261–63, 269. *See
   also* Masonry; Odd Fellows
Voortrekkers, 122
Vredefort, O. F. S., 164
Vryburg, Cape, 160

Walker, Clarence, 54
Walker, David, 7, 22
War of 1812, 67
Warwick, Peter, 165
Washington, Booker T.: and African edu-
   cation, 250, 256, 302, 305–10; and
   AME Church, 82, 199, 237, 268;
   Atlanta Compromise, 86, 92; in-
   voked by Africans, 302, 331. *See also*
   Industrial education; Tuskegee Insti-
   tute
Washington, D. C., 34, 53, 68
Washington, Bushrod, 68
Washington, George, 68
Waterberg, 117–18, 125, 139
Watson, John, 39–40
Watt, Isaac, 41
Wauchope, Isaac, 282
Wayman, Alexander, 55–56, 349 n.62
Wellington, Dr. Butler Hansford. *See*
   Buthelezi, Wellington
Wepener, O. F. S., 172
Wesleyan Methodist Church of South

Africa. *See* Wesleyan Methodist Missionary Society
Wesleyan Methodist Missionary Society, 104, 252, 358 n.10; and colonial state, 183–84; loses adherents, 119–25, 164, 168, 170, 194; in Orange Free State, 161, 187, 360 n.34; reliance on African assistants, 107, 109–10, 223
Wesley, Charles, 6, 41, 54
Wesley, John, 13, 45, 47, 54
Western University (Kansas), 314
West Indians: in North America, 4; in South Africa, 125–27, 160, 245, 301; transition from slavery in, 112, 305–6
Wheatley, Phillis, 29, 66
Whitefield, George, 4
Whittier, James Greenleaf, 298
Wilberforce Institute, 178, 247, 255, 272, 275, 278, 281–83, 292–93, 318, 320, 334
Wilberforce Singers, 278
Wilberforce University: Commercial, Normal and Industrial Department, 265, 267, 383–84 n.37; curriculum, 264–65; daily life, 266–67; faculty, 262–63; founding, 39, 258–60, 263–64; Haitian students, 274; Payne Theological Seminary, 262; political culture, 268–71; surrounding community, 261–62
AFRICAN STUDENTS: 147, 155, 158, 178, 215, 235, 293, 314, 320; adopted by churchwomen, 265, 282; and African nationalism, 250, 276–77, 303; courses of study, 267–68; identification with black America, 273–76; inflated expectations, 203, 256, 271–72, 293; political careers, 151, 275–81; professional careers, 272–80; scale of traffic, 254–55, 257–58; sense of exceptionalism, 253–56, 266, 270–71, 273, 276–79; social origins, 252–57; trained as missionaries, 255, 272–74; from West Africa, 251–52; white anxieties about, 249, 257. *See also specific students*
Wilkie, Arthur, 311

Willan, Brian, 132
Williams, George Washington, 127
Willoughby, W. C., 190
Willowvale, Transkei, 194, 203–4
Witbooi, Hendrik, 211
Witwatersrand, 105, 126–27, 160, 167–70; AME Church on, 145, 153–59; crucible of Ethiopianism, 112, 120–21, 125, 141, 143–44; postwar upheaval on, 285–88, 301, 319, 322. *See also* Johannesburg; Mineral revolution; Urbanization
Wolmaransstad, Tvl., 179
Women: and African missions, 93–95, 356 n.71; in antebellum AME Church, 44–53; and European missions, 106, 182–83; excluded from A.N.C., 288; excluded from revolutionary compact, 341 n.33; moral reform efforts, 26, 44, 52, 55, 61; in Orange Free State, 164, 168; and pass laws, 169, 173, 285–91. *See also* AME Church, South Africa, SOCIAL COMPOSITION; Domestic Ideology; Maxeke, Charlotte Manye; Sanctification
Women's Light and Love for Heathen Africa, 93, 298
Wood, Yankee, 126
Wool, 160, 237; dipping ordinances, 201, 203
World War I, 257, 287, 295, 301, 309–11. *See also* Witwatersrand
Wright, Richard R. Jr., 262, 298–99, 328

X, Malcolm. *See* Malcolm X
Xaba, Jacobus G.: death, 361 n.44; early life, 121–25, 163; enthusiasm for African Methodism, 134–35, 139, 160, 164, 209; identifies with black America, 129, 135, 216
Xaba, Jonathan, 121
Xaba, Thomas, 121
Xalanga, Transkei, 194
Xenia, Ohio, 33, 258–61. *See also* Wilberforce University
Xhosa cattle killing, 106, 136, 197
Xiniwe, Paul, 282
Xuma, A. B., 256, 273, 275–78, 280–81,

Xuma, A. B. (*Cont.*)
    284, 293. *See also* African National
    Congress; Nationalism, African
Xuma, Amanda Mason, 275–76
Xuma, Madie Hall, 276

Yale University, 251; Institute of Human
    Relations, 310
Yamma, Bristol, 65–66, 251
Yellow Springs, Ohio, 33, 259–60

Young, Charles, 262, 267
Young, G. B., 328
Y.W.C.A., 276

Zion Apostolic Church, 245
Zionist churches, 142, 245, 357 n.1. *See
    also specific denominations*
Zonnebloem College, 254
Zuid Afrikaansche Republiek. *See* Transvaal
Zululand, 104

Printed in the United States
54749LVS00002B/113

9 780195 078923